1 MONTH OF
FREE
READING

at

www.ForgottenBooks.com

By purchasing this book you are eligible for one month membership to ForgottenBooks.com, giving you unlimited access to our entire collection of over 1,000,000 titles via our web site and mobile apps.

To claim your free month visit:

www.forgottenbooks.com/free152043

ISBN 978-1-5280-8594-6
PIBN 10152043

This book is a reproduction of an important historical work. Forgotten Books uses
state-of-the-art technology to digitally reconstruct the work, preserving the original format
whilst repairing imperfections present in the aged copy. In rare cases, an imperfection in
the original, such as a blemish or missing page, may be replicated in our edition. We do,
however, repair the vast majority of imperfections successfully; any imperfections that
remain are intentionally left to preserve the state of such historical works.

REPORTS OF CASES

DECIDED IN THE

COURT OF APPEALS

OF THE

STATE OF NEW YORK

FROM AND INCLUDING DECISIONS OF OCTOBER 3, 1911, TO
DECISIONS OF JANUARY 9, 1912,

WITH

NOTES, REFERENCES AND INDEX.

J. NEWTON FIERO,
STATE REPORTER.

VOLUME 203.

ALBANY
J. B. LYON COMPANY.
1912.

JUDGES OF THE COURT OF APPEALS.

EDGAR M. CULLEN, Chief Judge.

JOHN C. GRAY,

ALBERT HAIGHT,

IRVING G. VANN,

WILLIAM E. WERNER,

WILLARD BARTLETT,

FREDERICK COLLIN,

Associate Judges.

FRANK H. HISCOCK,

EMORY A. CHASE,

Justices of the Supreme Court Serving as Associate Judges.*

---

* Designated by the Governor January 8, 1906, under section 7 of article VI of the Constitution, as amended in 1899.

TABLE OF CASES

REPORTED IN THIS VOLUME.

TABLE OF CASES

CITED IN THE OPINIONS REPORTED IN THIS VOLUME.

B   xvii

C.

D.

TABLE OF CASES CITED. xxvii

PAGE.

Weed v. Paine.................... 31 Hun, 10............ 257, 258
Weet v. Trustees, Village of
  Brockport.................... 16 N. Y. 161, note............ 117
Welch v. Mandeville........... 1 Wheat. 233 515
Wells v. Lachenmeyer........... 2 How. Pr. (N. S.) 252 463
Wells v. Town of Salina......... 119 N. Y. 280................. 205
Weyler v. Rothschild & Bros.... 53 Neb. 566.................. 376
Wheeler v. Ruckman............ 51 N. Y. 391................. 186
White v. Howard...... .... 46 N. Y. 144, 162.... 481
Wilt v. Welsh.................. 6 Watts, 9................... 468
Windsor v. Brown.............. 15 R. I. 182................. 496
Wisner v. Ocumpaugh........... 71 N. Y. 113................. 458
Wood v. Leadbitter............. 13 Mees. & W. 838........... 358
Woods v. Wiman.............. 122 N. Y. 445................. 82
Woolsey v. Crawford........... 2 Camp. 445................. 104
Worthington v. London G. & A.
  Co.......................... 164 N. Y. 81................. 165
Wright v. Cabot............... 89 N. Y. 570................. 190

Y.

Young Women's C. Home v.
  French...................... 187 U. S. 401.. 388

TABLE OF CASES

AFFECTED BY DECISIONS REPORTED IN THIS VOLUME.

C

MODIFIED.

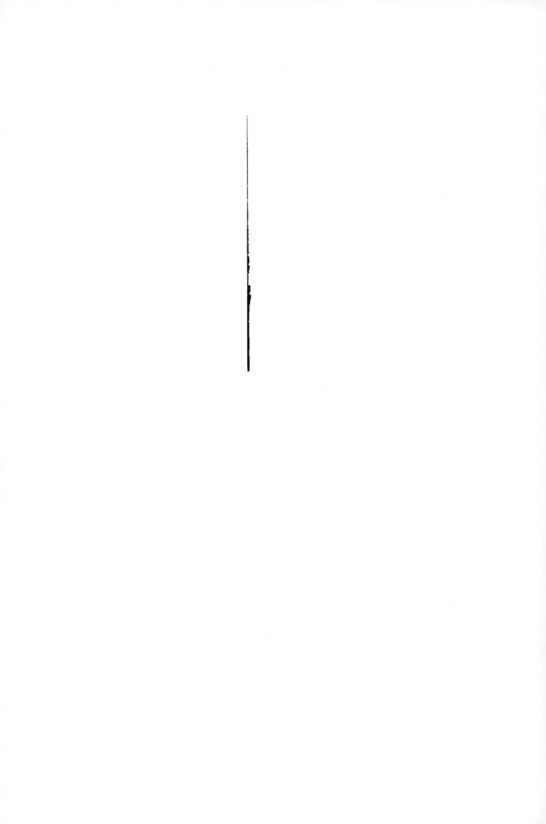

TABLE OF CASES

DISTINGUISHED, ETC., IN, OPINIONS REPORTED IN THIS VOLUME.

Cases Decided

IN THE

COURT OF APPEALS

OF THE

State of New York,

COMMENCING OCTOBER 8, 1911.

·

THE PEOPLE OF THE STATE OF NEW YORK ex rel. MICHAEL J. DADY, Respondent, *v.* WILLIAM A. PRENDERGAST, as Comptroller of the City of New York, Appellant.

Mandamus — when writ will be issued directing comptroller of New York city to examine claim, illegal in form, against city and certify his opinion whether it should be paid.

Where the board of estimate and apportionment of the city of New York refers an application made by a person having an illegal or invalid claim against the city to the comptroller for investigation and opinion as to whether it should be paid or compromised under section 246 of the charter (L. 1907, ch. 601), it is his duty to consider the claim, and if in his judgment it is equitable and proper for the city to pay the same in whole or in part to so certify to the board, and this duty may be enforced by mandamus.

People ex rel. Dady v. *Prendergast*, 144 App. Div. 808, modified.

(Submitted June 9, 1911; decided October 3, 1911.)

APPEAL from an order of the Appellate Division of the Supreme Court in the second judicial department, entered April 21, 1911, which affirmed an order of Special Term granting a motion for a peremptory writ of mandamus to compel the defendant to take action under section 246 of the charter of the city of New York concerning a claim made by the relator against said municipality.

The facts, so far as material, are stated in the opinion.

Archibald R. Watson, Corporation Counsel (*R. Percy Chittenden, Terence Farley* and *John Lehman* of counsel), for appellant. Section 246 of the charter confers upon the board of estimate and apportionment and the comptroller of the city of New York uncontrollable authority to pay claims repugnant to section 10 of article 8 of the Constitution, and is, therefore, unconstitutional. (*People ex rel. Wood* v. *Lacombe,* 99 N. Y. 43; *Matter of M. H. Bank,* 153 N. Y. 199; *People ex rel. Balcom* v. *Mosher,* 163 N. Y. 32; *Stewart* v. *Palmer,* 183 N. Y. 188; *Colon* v. *Lisk,* 153 N. Y. 188; *Smith* v. *People,* 47 N. Y. 331; *Williams* v. *City of New York,* 118 App. Div. 756; 192 N. Y. 541; *Stemmler* v. *Mayor, etc.,* 179 N. Y. 473.) To uphold the constitutionality of this law of 1907, which will be done if possible, the statute may be interpreted to exclude claims which are void, and not merely illegal or invalid. The relator's claim is void. (*City of Los Angeles* v. *City Bank,* 100 Cal. 18; *C. Nat. Bank* v. *Rich,* 81 Me. 164; *M. B. L. Ins. Co.* v. *Winne,* 20 Mont. 20; *Smith* v. *City of Buffalo,* 159 N. Y. 429; *McDonald* v. *Mayor, etc.,* 68 N. Y. 23; *Vil. of Fort Edward* v. *Fish,* 156 N. Y. 363; *Marie* v. *Garrison,* 13 Abb. [N. C.] 210; *People ex rel. Ritterman* v. *Kelly,* 1 Abb. [N. C.] 437; *Miller* v. *Ammon,* 145 U. S. 421; *Anderson* v. *Roberts,* 18 Johns. 515.) The judgment in *Dady* v. *City of New York* is a judicial determination upon the merits that the claim in controversy is null and void. Giving section 246 a construction which would empower the comptroller and board of estimate to again determine the validity of the claim and pay the same would render it obnoxious to the constitutional provisions. (*Matter of Greene,* 166 N. Y. 485.)

George K. Jack and *Jerry A. Wernberg* for respondent. The claim presented to the board of estimate and apportionment is a proper one for the consideration of the said board under the statute. (L. 1907, ch. 601,

§ 246; L. 1910, ch. 683, § 14.) The contention of the appellant, that the judgment in *Dady* v. *City of New York* is a judicial determination that the claim in controversy is null and void and that to give section 246 a construction which would empower the comptroller to determine the validity of this claim would render it obnoxious to the Federal and State Constitutions, is without merit. (*W. I. B. Co.* v. *Town of Attica*, 119 N. Y. 204; *Matter of Green*, 166 N. Y. 494.)

Chase Mellen for the T. A. Gillespie Company et al., intervening. The intention of the legislature in enacting section 246 of the Greater New York charter was to confer upon the board of estimate and apportionment, the responsible governing body of the city, substantially the same power to do justice to an honest claimant who has given value to the city as that possessed by a private individual or private corporation in a like matter. (Dillon on Mun. Corp. [4th ed.] § 477; *O'Brien* v. *Mayor, etc.*, 40 App. Div. 331; 160 N. Y. 691; *B. G. L. Co.* v. *Claffy*, 151 N. Y. 24; *Keane* v. *City of New York*, 88 App. Div. 542; *Hunter* v. *Pittsburgh*, 207 U. S. 161; *State* v. *Richmond*, 26 N. H. 232; *C., B. & Q. R. R. Co.* v. *McGuire*, 219 U. S. 549; *Hills* v. *Peekskill Bank*, 101 N. Y. 490; *Matter of Borup*, 182 N. Y. 222; *New Orleans* v. *Clark*, 95 U. S. 644; *McCord* v. *Lauterbach*, 91 App. Div. 315.) The argument that it is dangerous to intrust to the board of estimate and apportionment power to pay the city's money on so-called void or illegal claims is not tenable. (*Bertholf* v. *O'Reilly*, 74 N. Y. 509; *People ex rel. Eckerson* v. *Bd. of Education*, 126 App. Div. 414.)

Hiscock, J. The relator entered into two valid and binding contracts with the city of New York to perform work and furnish materials for the purpose of perfecting or extending its water supply. In connection with the

performance of these contracts he was ordered by an
official of the engineering department to do certain other
work and furnish other materials, which he did, but
owing to the failure to comply with statutory provisions
governing such matters no valid and binding contract
arose between the relator and the municipality for the
last-mentioned work and materials. It has been conceded that they were of the value of upwards of $2,000
and were honestly and actually a benefit to the city.
Refusal having been made to pay the claim therefor
because of said invalidity, relator brought an action at
law to recover the value thereof. As sufficiently appears
herein he was defeated in said action because he could
not establish a valid claim at law, and the court had no
power to excuse the failure to comply with the statutory
provisions with reference to contracts and give judgment
on any merits which the claim might possess.

Thereafter he sought to procure action on and payment
of his claim under section 246 of the charter of New York,
which provided in part as follows:

"§ 246. Claims against the city. The board of estimate
and apportionment may, in its discretion, inquire into,
hear and determine any claim against the city of New
York which has been certified to said board in writing by
the comptroller as an illegal or invalid claim against the
city, but which, notwithstanding, in his judgment it is
equitable and proper for the city to pay in whole or in
part, and if upon such inquiry the board by an unanimous
vote determines that the city has received a benefit and
is justly and equitably obligated to pay such claim and
that the interests of the city will be best subserved by the
payment or compromise thereof, it may authorize the
comptroller to pay the claim and the comptroller shall
thereupon pay the claim in such amount as the board of
estimate and apportionment shall so determine to be just,
in full satisfaction of such claim, provided that the claimant shall fully release the city, upon any such payment,

in such form as shall be approved by the corporation counsel. The provisions of this section shall not authorize the audit or payment of any claim barred by the statute of limitations, nor any claim for services performed under an appointment in violation of any provision of the civil service law." (L. 1907, ch. 601.)

In accordance with the provisions of said section the board of estimate and apportionment referred the relator's application to the comptroller for investigation and opinion, but he declined to give the claim any official consideration whatever solely because he was advised that he had no power to consider the same. The courts below have disapproved this attitude and required him to make certificate in accordance with said section "whether or not in his judgment it is equitable and proper for the city to pay " said claim.

Two reasons are urged why this action and order should be reversed and the action of the comptroller be upheld. It is said that the legislature has no right by provisions such as those which have been quoted to deprive the city of the benefit of the judgment heretofore rendered in the action at law dismissing plaintiff's claim. It is further urged in substance that relator's claim is absolutely void because of failure to comply with the statutory provisions with reference to letting and making municipal contracts, and that, therefore, the legislature has no right to authorize the city and its officials to disregard these defects in the claim and pay it even if found to be equitable.

In a most excellent and well-considered opinion in the Appellate Division Mr. Justice CARR has given the reasons why these views should not prevail. So far as the first one is concerned he has pointed out that the rule invoked by appellant does not apply to an adjudication dismissing a claim against a municipality for failure to comply with some statutory provisions as distinguished from an adjudication dismissing a claim because of its inherent and substantial invalidity. He has shown with reference to the second argument that the attempt to distinguish relator's claim as one which is utterly void rather than merely invalid under the statute is not well founded; that the legislature has ample power in the case of a truly meritorious claim to authorize a municipality or its officers to overlook the failure to comply with statutory provisions relating to the letting of a contract which the legislature might have refrained from enacting in the first instance; that relator's claim is not unconstitutional and inherently bad, but is affected only by the failure to comply with rules which the legislature need not have prescribed in the first instance.

There is nothing to be added to the opinion which has thus been summarized, and we should have been quite content to rest our disposition of the appeal thereon, except for one error which probably through inadvertence has crept into the order appealed from.

The statute as has been shown permits the board of estimate and apportionment to consider and order payment of any claim which has been certified to it by the comptroller as an "illegal or invalid claim, but which notwithstanding in his judgment it is equitable and proper for the city to pay in whole or part." Under this provision the board can only consider a claim in the event that the comptroller has certified that it is an equitable one which it is proper to pay notwithstanding it is in law illegal or invalid. Therefore, there is no object in or authority for requiring the comptroller to certify any claims except those which he thus regards as equitable and proper to be paid. He should not be required under the statute to certify his opinion on all manner of illegal claims where he reaches an adverse opinion and conclusion concerning the equitable nature thereof. The present order is faulty in this respect. It requires him to certify "whether or not in his judgment it is equitable and proper for the city to pay the claim" in question.

That is, it requires a certificate even though adverse to the payment of the claim.

It should be modified so as to direct that the mandamus to be issued to the appellant as comptroller shall direct and command him to consider the claim in question, and if in his judgment it is equitable and proper for the city to pay the same in whole or part, notwithstanding it is an illegal or invalid claim, to so certify to the board of estimate and apportionment, and as so modified the order should be affirmed, without costs.

CULLEN, Ch. J., GRAY, HAIGHT, VANN, WERNER and COLLIN, JJ., concur.

Ordered accordingly.

THE PEOPLE OF THE STATE OF NEW YORK ex rel. BINGHAMTON LIGHT, HEAT AND POWER COMPANY, Appellant, *v.* FRANK W. STEVENS et al., Constituting the PUBLIC SERVICE COMMISSION OF THE STATE OF NEW YORK FOR THE SECOND DISTRICT, Respondents.

Public service commissions — when discretion of commission cannot override the discretion of the officers of a corporation — duty and powers of commission to determine under section 69 of the Public Service Commissions Law whether a proposed bond issue is necessary for purposes of corporation and authorized by law — evidence — procedure.

1. One of the paramount purposes of the legislature in establishing the public service commissions was to protect and enforce the rights of the public, and the statute should be construed with that in view.

2. The discretion of a public service commission cannot override the discretion of the officers of a corporation in the management of its affairs, or the provisions of the statute which prescribes the cases in which securities are permitted to be issued. Its duty upon an application under section 69 of the Public Service Commissions Law (Cons. Laws, ch. 48) is to determine whether a proposed issue of bonds is necessary for the proper purposes of the company, is authorized by law and is to by used in a proper manner. If such are the

facts it cannot withhold its certificate; otherwise it cannot grant it. (*People ex rel. Delaware & Hudson Company* v. *Stevens*, 197 N. Y. 1, 10, approved and followed.)

3. It is beyond the power of the commission to permit the issue of improper securities upon condition that the company reduce its capital stock and such a condition is wholly unauthorized.

4. A reasonable consideration of the interests of a corporation and the ultimate good of its stock and bondholders, and a regard for the investing public and that fair dealing which should be observed in all business transactions, require that machines and tools paid for and charged to capital account but which necessarily become obsolete or wholly worn out within a period of years after the same are purchased or installed, should be renewed or replaced by setting aside from time to time an adequate amount in the nature of a sinking fund or that by some other system of financing the corporation put upon the purchaser from the corporation the expense not alone of the daily maintenance of the plant but a just proportion of the expense of renewing and replacing that part of the plant which although not daily consumed must necessarily be practically consumed within a given time.

5. The question as to what expenditures are a proper basis for permanent capitalization is always a proper and necessary object for consideration, not alone by the directors of a corporation, but by any commission that has authority to grant or withhold its consent to the issue of new stock or bonds which are to become a part of the corporation's permanent capitalization, and it is the duty of the public service commission to determine whether the stock and bonds proposed by a corporation are to secure money to pay floating indebtedness incurred in the ordinary running expenses of the corporation. Such determination by the commission would not be substituting the judgment of the commission for the judgment of the directors of the company in the management of its affairs.

6. A statement of a petitioner's financial transactions in proceedings of this kind should be made in sufficient detail and with sufficient classification to show with reasonable certainty the exact question to be determined.

7. While the commission may not be bound by technical rules of evidence, still it is plainly intended that the whole proceeding for leave to issue bonds should assume a quasi-judicial aspect.

8. The commission being empowered to subpœna witnesses and take testimony, its inspectors or agents can be required to appear and verify any reports made by them, or if such reports could be received in the first instance without verification, the inspectors or

agents can be compelled to attend at the instance of either party and be examined as to the truth of the statements in their reports and their knowledge of the facts therein contained.

People ex rel. Binghamton L., H. & P. Co. v. *Stevens*, 143 App. Div. 789, reversed.

(Argued May 29, 1911; decided October 3, 1911.)

APPEAL from an order of the Appellate Division of the Supreme Court in the third judicial department, entered March 11, 1911, which confirmed an order of the public service commission for the second district requiring that the relator credit its fixed capital with the sum of $100,000 as a condition precedent to its execution and delivery of a mortgage and the issue of corporate bonds thereunder.

The facts, so far as material, are stated in the opinion.

Adrian H. Joline for appellant. The issue of securities petitioned for by the relator is necessary for the discharge of its obligations and should have been permitted under the provisions of section 69 of the Public Service Commissions Law (L. 1907, ch. 429). (*People ex rel. D. & H. Co.* v. *Stevens*, 197 N. Y. 1; *Gamble* v. *Q. C. W. Co.*, 123 N. Y. 91; *Matter of W. G. L. Co.*, 127 App. Div. 462.) The amendment of the Public Service Commissions Law, which went into effect after the application of this relator to the commission had been decided, was not retroactive and is not to be considered in the determination of this case. (*People ex rel. P. S. L. A. Society* v. *Miller*, 179 N. Y. 227; *G. & W. Ry. Co.* v. *N. Y. C. & H. R. R. R. Co.*, 163 N. Y. 228.) The fact that the property acquired and the improvements made by the relator may have consisted partly of replacements of its existing plant and property is wholly immaterial. (*Matter of W. G. L. Co.*, 127 App. Div. 462; *Willcox* v. *C. G. Co.*, 212 U. S. 19; *Lough* v. *Outerbridge*, 143 N. Y. 271; *M. & St. L. R. R. Co.* v.

Minnesota, 186 U. S. 257; *A. C. L. R. R. Co.* v. *Florida,* 203 U. S. 256; *C., etc., Ry. Co.* v. *Becker,* 35 Fed. Rep. 883; *Matter of Freight Rates,* 9 I. C. R. 382; Beale & Wyman on Railroad Rate Regulation, §§ 319, 411, 412; Watkins on Shippers & Carriers of Interstate Freight, § 52.) The provision contained in the order of the commission of January 31, 1910, making it a condition of the proposed issue of bonds that·the relator should credit its fixed capital with the sum of $100,000, is erroneous. (*Matter of W. G. L. Co.,* 127 App. Div. 462.) The commission erred in basing its determination in any degree upon alleged information not adduced as evidence upon the hearing. (*People ex rel. Joline* v. *Willcox,* 134 App. Div. 503; 198 N. Y. 433; *Village of Saratoga Springs* v. *Saratoga,* 191 N. Y. 123; *People ex rel. Clark* v. *Roosevelt,* 168 N. Y. 488; *People ex rel. McAleer* v. *French,* 119 N. Y. 502; *People ex rel. Joline* v. *Willcox,* 194 N. Y. 388.)

Ledyard P. Hale and *Henry C. Hazzard* for respondents. Relator has no statutory or common-law right to capitalize expenditures made for replacements where the cost of the property replaced was originally charged to fixed capital and has not been credited thereto concurrently with its consumption in use. (*People ex rel. J. W. S. Co.* v. *Tax Comrs.,* 196 N. Y. 39, 57; 128 App. Div. 13; *People ex rel. Third Ave. R. R. Co.* v. *Tax Comrs.,* 136 App. Div. 155; *Knoxville* v. *Water Co.,* 212 U. S. 1; *Reagan* v. *Farmers' Loan & Trust Co.,* 154 U. S. 362; *Davison* v. *Gillies,* [L. R.] 16 Ch. D. 347, n.; *Kennebec Water District* v. *Waterville,* 97 Maine, 185; *Long Branch Commission* v. *Tintern Manor Water Co.,* 70 N. J. Eq. 71.)

CHASE, J.   Public service commissions were established in this state by chapter 429 of the Laws of 1907, to take effect July 1 of that year. The act was amended and revised by chapter 480 of the Laws of 1910, which took effect June 14, 1910. Section 69 of the act of 1907 as amended by the act of 1910 (Cons. Laws, ch. 48), so far as now material, is as follows: "A gas corporation or electrical corporation organized or existing, or hereafter incorporated, under or by virtue of the laws of the state of New York, may issue stocks, bonds, notes or other evidence of indebtedness payable at periods of more than twelve months after the date thereof, when necessary for the acquisition of property, the construction, completion, extension or improvement of its plant or distributing system, or for the improvement or maintenance of its service or for the discharge or lawful refunding of its obligations *or for the reimbursement of moneys actually expended from income or from any other moneys in the treasury of the corporation not secured or obtained from the issue of stocks, bonds, notes or other evidence of indebtedness of such corporation, within five years next prior to the filing of an application with the proper commission for the required authorization, for any of the aforesaid purposes except maintenance of service and except replacements in cases where the applicant shall have kept its accounts and vouchers of such expenditure in such manner as to enable the commission to ascertain the amount of moneys so expended and the purposes for which such expenditure was made;* provided and not otherwise that there shall have been secured from the proper commission an order authorizing such issue, and the amount thereof, and stating *the purposes to which the issue or proceeds thereof are to be applied,* and that, in the opinion of the commission, *the money, property or labor to be procured or paid for by the issue of such stock, bonds, notes or other evidence of indebtedness is or has been reasonably required for the purposes specified in the order, and that except as otherwise permitted in the order in the case of bonds, notes and other evidence of indebtedness, such purposes are not in whole or in*

12 People ex rel. B. L., H. & P. Co. *v.* Stevens.

[203 N. Y.]   Opinion, per Chase, J.   [Oct.,

part reasonably chargeable to operating expenses or to income. Nothing herein contained shall prohibit the commission from giving its consent to the issue of bonds, notes or other evidence of indebtedness for the reimbursement of moneys heretofore actually expended from income for any of the aforesaid purposes, except maintenance of service and replacements, prior to five years next preceding the filing of an application therefor, if in the judgment of the commission such consent should be granted; provided application for such consent shall be made prior to January first, nineteen hundred and twelve. For the purpose of enabling it to determine whether it should issue such an order, the commission shall make such inquiry or investigation, hold such hearings and examine such witnesses, books, papers, documents or contracts as it may deem of importance in enabling it to reach a determination. *Such corpordtion shall not without the consent of the commission apply said issue or any proceeds thereof to any purpose not specified in such order.* Such gas corporation or electrical corporation may issue notes, for proper corporate purposes and not in violation of any provision of this or of any other act, payable at periods of not more than twelve months without such consent; but no such notes shall, in whole or in part, directly or indirectly be refunded by any issue of stock or bonds or by any evidence of indebtedness running for more than twelve months without the consent of the proper commission. Provided, however, that the commission shall have no power to authorize the capitalization of any franchise to be a corporation or to authorize the capitalization of any franchise or the right to own, operate or enjoy any franchise whatsoever in excess of the amount (exclusive of any tax or annual charge) actually paid to the state or to any political subdivision thereof as the consideration for the grant of such franchise or right. * * * "

That part of the section quoted which is in italics was

added by the amendment of 1910, and in place of the paragraph beginning with the words "the money" and ending with the words "hundred and twelve" there was in the act of 1907 a clause as follows: "The use of the capital to be secured by the issue of such stock, bonds, notes or other evidence of indebtedness is reasonably required for the said purposes of the corporation."

The relator is a domestic corporation organized in 1902 for the purpose of generating and selling electricity for light, heat and power. On the last day of February, 1902, it acquired the property and franchises of the Binghamton General Electric Company, which company had on and prior to that day supplied electric light and power in the city of Binghamton. At the close of business on that day the balance sheet of the Binghamton General Electric Company showed so far as now material as follows:

Total fixed capital including franchises..... $585,954 92
Total floating capital..................... 21,204 66
                                           ——————————
                                            $607,159 58

Liabilities.
Capital stock................. $280,000 00
Funded debt.................. 266,500 00
Bills payable................. 20,000 00
Accrued interest............. 6,687 50
Surplus.. .... 33,972 08
                            ——————————— $607,159 58

It is asserted by the petition hereinafter mentioned that the relator issued for the assets of said company its common stock to the amount of $500,000 and its refunding mortgage bonds presumably upon the property purchased to the amount of $325,000. It does not appear just how the sale was consummated, who were the stock and bondholders of the Binghamton General Electric Company or of the relator, how or upon what terms the bonds and stock of the old company were taken up or retired and the assets of the old company transferred to the new company. It does appear, however, that on the next day (March 1, 1902), the books of the relator were opened with a statement of assets as follows: " Plant, real estate, personal and other property, franchise rights, etc., not noted below and heretofore owned by Binghamton Gen. Elec. Co., $759,231.19." The other items of assets referred to as noted below are principally taken from the items comprising the floating capital as stated on the balance sheet of the Binghamton General Electric Company. The book value of the plant, etc., increased to the extent of $173,276.27 in one day. Such increase is unexplained in the record but it does appear that the increase did not arise from charging organization expenses to the capital account prior to the entry of March 1, 1902, because subsequently there was charged to capital account the organization expenses aggregating $79,795.83, the details of which it is unnecessary to enumerate at this time. From March 1, 1902, until the filing of the petition hereinafter mentioned the relator spent for what it terms new plant and property improvements and betterments or became liable therefor pursuant to contract obligations the sum of $441,792.90. In the meantime and prior to July 1, 1907, it had issued and sold $175,000 more of its first refunding mortgage bonds and $150,000 of six per cent cumulative preferred capital stock. During the same time it had sold property for $15,618.88 which it had credited to capital account.

On February 17, 1909, the relator filed with the public service commission in the second district its petition alleging facts from which the most of those above were taken, and asked for an order under section 69 of the Public Service Commissions Law authorizing,

1. A mortgage to be dated April 1, 1909, to secure $1,000,000 of five per cent bonds with the right to issue forthwith, a, $500,000 of said bonds to enable the peti-

tioner to acquire an equal amount of its bonds then outstanding; b, $180,000 additional of said proposed bonds.

2. $50,000 of its six per cent cumulative preferred stock.

It was stated in the petition that the petitioner proposed to use the proceeds of the $180,000 of bonds and of said proposed stock to pay and discharge its promissory notes outstanding, amounting to $158,000, and the balance in paying, to the extent thereof, its floating indebtedness.

It is alleged in a schedule attached to the petition that the petitioner was indebted to the extent of $244,315.76, not including the funded debt of $500,000, and such indebtedness is made up of notes payable not exceeding twelve months from date, amounting to $158,000, and open accounts amounting to $86,315.76.

A hearing was had before the commission, and on August 4, 1909, it made an order denying the application but continuing the proceeding to enable the petitioner to proceed therein upon the lines suggested in the written opinion filed by the commission, if it should so desire. A reference to the record shows that the commission was of the opinion that the indebtedness represented by the $158,000 of notes was incurred for construction purposes, but that it was further of the opinion that the construction was in whole or in part mere renewal or replacement of old and obsolete plant and it accompanied its order denying the application not only with a provision continuing the proceeding for the purposes stated but it stated in its opinion that "A mere denial of this part of the application does not fully meet the situation. The notes in question are lawful obligations and must be paid. The case should be continued for the purpose of ascertaining by full and detailed proof the sum at which the old plant is now carried in fixed capital. As above stated, the exact amount the commission has been unable to

16 People ex rel. B. L., H. & P. Co. v. Stevens.

[203 N. Y.]   Opinion, per Chase, J.   [Oct.,

ascertain. When such amount is ascertained then various courses are open."

Referring to the application of the relator and its indebtedness other than the $158,000 represented by said notes the commission further say: "Of the proceeds only $158,000 would be required to pay the notes in question. What does it propose to do with the remainder of the proceeds? It points out nothing which comes within any of the purposes enumerated in section 69 of the Public Service Commissions Law, for which it may be allowed to issue stock or bonds. It desires to acquire no property. It does not ask to extend or improve its plant or distributing system. It suggests nothing for the improvement or maintenance of its service. It names no obligation and no creditor to be paid.

"Its floating indebtedness as shown by balance sheet submitted is as follows:

Bills payable..............................	$158,000 00
Accounts payable..........................	19,109 96
Dividends payable Jan. 15, 1909..........	6,000 00
Consumers' deposits......................	345 76
Accrued interest on bonds.................	6,250 00
Accrued taxes.............................	869 00
Total current liabilities...............	$190,574 72

"Bills payable have been fully considered. Accounts payable are not proper subjects of capitalization, being in general mere operating expense and in this case are offset by accounts receivable to the amount of $25,127.87. Dividends, consumers' deposits, accrued interest on bonds and accrued taxes should be paid out of income."

After conferences with the representatives of the petitioner a further order was made January 31, 1910, which recited among other things: "The applicant is understood to have assented, so far as it is able to do so without a meeting of its stockholders, to a reduction of its capital stock to the amount of $100,000 to the end that thereby its fixed capital may be credited with said sum of $100,000."

The order provided for the issue of bonds to the extent of $197,500 to be sold and disposed of at not less than 80% of their par value and the avails thereof used for the sole and only purpose of paying and discharging the indebtedness aggregating $158,000 represented by said notes and the order was accompanied with a condition as follows: "Provided that this authorization is upon condition to be assented to by said Binghamton Light, Heat and Power Company that contemporaneously with issuing said bonds to said amount of $197,500 or any part thereof, it shall credit its fixed capital with the sum of $100,000 which may be accomplished by a reduction of the common capital stock of said company to a like amount, and this authorization to issue bonds to said amount of $197,500 shall not become effective until said company shall have filed with this commission its written acceptance of said condition."

Thereafter a further application was made to the commission by the relator for a rehearing of said application so far as the commission had denied the original request of the petitioner. On August 25, 1910, the application for a rehearing was denied. The relator on September 19, 1910, filed its petition with the Supreme Court asking for a writ of certiorari to the end that the three orders made by the commission be reviewed and reversed or so modified that the prayer of the original petition be granted. The writ was allowed and the matter was heard in the Appellate Division, third department, where the orders of the commission were confirmed by a divided court. (*People ex rel. Binghamton L., H. & P. Co.* v. *Stevens,* 143 App. Div. 789.)

By the report of the relator to the public service commission as of December 31, 1908, it appears that the fixed capital account as carried on the books of the company

2

amounted to $1,302,725.72.   It appears to have been made up of three items as follows:

Organization expenses......	$79,795 83	
Franchise, land, old plant and property account.........	781,136 99	
Other fixed capital.........	441,792 90	
		$1,302,725 72

As against this item the company showed that they had outstanding bonds to the extent of $500,000; preferred stock, $150,000; common stock, $500,000; making a total of stock and funded debt, $152,725.72, less than the amount of its fixed capital as shown by the report.

The item of $441,792.90 in fixed capital represents the expenditures on the plant after the purchase of the Binghamton General Electric Company.   It further appears from the record that substantially all of the physical property purchased of the Binghamton General Electric Company has passed out of existence by the complete rebuilding of the plant.   Nevertheless, it is all carried on the books of the company as capital without any part of the cost being charged off in any way because of the renewal or replacement of the generating station, equipment and tools constituting the relator's plant.

It is noticeable that the $100,000 which the commission directed should be taken from the capital account of the relator by a reduction of its capital stock as a condition of granting its consent to the issue of $195,000 of the bonds of the relator is not based upon findings of the commission relating to its expenditures.   There is nothing before us to show that the difference between such two amounts constitutes a legitimate increase of the capital account of the relator.   A careful examination of the record satisfies us that the order of January 31, 1910, was an arbitrary one not based upon any determination in detail of the facts relating to the application, but a compromise based upon an assumption that the relator and its stockholders would assent thereto. No such assent has ever been given and the assumption of the commission was based upon a statement made by certain representatives of the relator, with whom the matter was orally discussed.

The several owners of the capital stock of the relator as *bona fide* holders thereof had vested interests therein which the officers of the relator and the relator itself were powerless to take from them without compensation or in pursuance of a voluntary surrender.

The relator is not bound by the assumption of the commission even if the order was made in good faith relying upon it. On any determination of the reason that induced the commission to make the order of January 31, 1910, we agree with Justice KELLOGG wherein he says in his dissenting opinion in the Appellate Division as follows: "It is beyond the power of the Commission to permit the issue of improper securities upon the condition that the company cancel stock of about half the amount. Read together, the two orders permit the company to issue unauthorized securities, but attempt to lessen the harm to the public which may result therefrom. The Commission has no power to thus barter away the public interests, or on its own terms to permit the issue of securities which the law prohibits. Its discretion cannot override the discretion of the officers of the company in the management of its affairs, or the provisions of the statute which prescribe the cases in which securities are permitted. Its duty in the premises is to determine whether the proposed issue is necessary for the proper purposes of the company, is authorized by law and is to be used in a proper manner. If such are the facts it cannot withhold its certificate; otherwise it cannot grant it." (p. 801.)

The condition imposed by the commission, unless perhaps to adjust the financial affairs of the corporation with the consent of the stockholders or stockholders and bondholders, was wholly unauthorized.

If when an order is granted a condition is imposed by consent it should be based upon facts justifying the order with the imposition of the condition. The record before us does not permit this court if it had the authority to determine what if any order should be made by the commission. That the views of the court may not be misunderstood on a rehearing we repeat what was said by this court in *People ex rel. Delaware & Hudson Company* v. *Stevens* (197 N. Y. 1, 10): "We do not think the legislation alluded to was designed to make the commissioners the financial managers of the corporation, or that it empowered them to substitute their judgment for that of the board of directors or stockholders of the corporation as to the wisdom of a transaction, but that it was designed to make the commissioners the guardians of the public by enabling them to prevent the issue of stock and bonds for other than the statutory purposes; these purposes we have already enumerated in quoting the statute, the last being for the discharge or lawful refunding of its obligations."

The language quoted was used in considering the action of the board of directors of the relator in that case in the purchase of the stock of another corporation and of certain real property.

There was not in that case before the commission or the court for consideration the question as to whether an outstanding indebtedness for which stocks and bonds were sought to be issued was incurred in purchasing property for or in making betterments and enlargements of the plant of the relator, or for renewals and replacements of the plant or any part of it as it had theretofore existed. The court in that case, in referring to the intent of the legislature, said that by its enactment the commissioners should have supervision over the issuing of long time bonds to the extent of determining whether they were issued under and in conformity with the provisions of the statute for the purposes mentioned therein, or whether they were issued for the discharge of the actual and not the fictitious debts of the company, or whether they were issued for the refunding of its actual obligations and not for the inflation of its stocks or bonds; and continuing the court further say: "Beyond this it appears to us that the power of the commissioners does not extend, unless it may pertain to the power to determine whether an obligation should be classified as operating expenses and as to whether such expenses should be paid by obligations running beyond a year." (p. 13.) The question as to whether the commission has authority to classify the expenditures of a corporation and ascertain what part thereof should be charged to capital account and what part to operating expenses was thus expressly reserved for further consideration.

The amendment of the statute in 1910 gives to the commission authority to authorize the issue of stocks, bonds, notes or other evidences of indebtedness of a corporation payable at periods of more than twelve months after the date thereof for the discharge or lawful refunding of its obligations or for the reimbursement of moneys actually expended from income or from any other moneys in the treasury of the corporation not secured or obtained from the issue of stocks, bonds or other evidence of indebtedness of such corporation within five years next prior to the filing of the application, but it expressly excepts from such authority of the commission the right to authorize the issue of such stocks, bonds or other evidence of indebtedness for maintenance of service and for replacements. It also provides that the applicant for such permission must have kept accounts and vouchers in such manner as to enable the commission to ascertain the amount of money so expended and for the purposes for which the expenditure was made. The question as to what expenditures are a proper basis for permanent capitalization is an important one, always a proper and necessary subject for consideration, not alone by the

22 People ex rel. B. L., H. & P. Co. *v.* Stevens.

[203 N. Y.]   Opinion, per Chase, J.   [Oct.,

directors of a corporation, but by any commission that has authority to grant or withhold its consent to the issue of new stock or bonds which are to become a part of the corporation's permanent capitalization.

Wholly apart from the claim of the commission that this case must be determined upon the statute as it now exists, and assuming for the purpose of what we are here saying that the relator is right in claiming that this appeal must be determined upon the statute as it existed on the day when the original petition herein was filed, we are nevertheless of the opinion that it was the duty of the commission to determine whether the stock and bonds proposed by the relator were to secure money to pay floating indebtedness incurred in the ordinary running expenses of the corporation. Such determination by the commission would not be substituting the judgment of the commission for the judgment of the directors of the company in the management of its affairs at least if the directors of the company had wholly and intentionally ignored the self-evident proposition that except for special and extraordinary circumstances some part of the expenses of renewing machines and plant originally charged to capital account must be paid as a part of the operating expenses of a corporation from year to year. We refer to the necessity of a corporation providing for some part of the expenses of renewing machinery and plant from year to year as self evident, because it has been so considered and expressed by the courts in many cases. (*People ex rel. Jamaica Water Supply Company* v. *Tax Commissioners*, 196 N. Y. 39, 57, 58; *S. C.*, 128 App. Div. 13, 17, 18; *People ex rel. Third Avenue R. R. Co.* v. *Tax Commissioners*, 136 App. Div. 155, 159; affd., 198 N. Y. 608; *City of Knoxville* v. *Knoxville Water Company*, 212 U. S. 1.)

In the *Jamaica Water Supply Company* case this court said : " We suppose that judicial notice may be taken of the fact that in the conduct of many industrial enterprises there is a constant deterioration of the plant which is not made good by ordinary repairs, which, of course, operates continually to lessen the value of the tangible property which it affects. The amount of this depreciation differs in different enterprises, but the annual rate is usually capable of estimate and proof by skilled witnesses. No corporation would be regarded as well conducted which did not make some provision for the necessity of ultimately replacing the property thus suffering deterioration." (P. 57.)

In that case in the Appellate Division it was said: "The net income of a corporation for dividend purposes cannot be determined until all taxes, depreciation, maintenance and up-keep expenditures have been deducted. Otherwise the dividend is not paid from the earnings but by a depreciation of the capital account. To earn a dividend and be honest with itself, its stockholders, its creditors and the public it has to serve, a corporation cannot distribute earnings at the expense of its capital." (p. 17.)

In the *Third Avenue Railroad* case it was said: "The annual ordinary expenditures for repairs, replacements and renewals upon such a property cannot be assumed to make it unnecessary to provide a fund which will replace its engines, electrical equipment and other physical property which at some time must be replaced." (p. 159.)

In the *City of Knoxville* v. *Knoxville Water Co.* case it was said: "It is entitled to see that from earnings the value of the property invested is kept unimpaired, so that, at the end of any given term of years the original investment remains as it was at the beginning. It is not only the right of the company to make such a provision, but it is its duty to its bond and stockholders, and, in the case of a public service corporation at least, its plain duty to the public. If a different course were pursued the only method of providing for replacement of property which has ceased to be useful would be the investment of new capital and the issue of new bonds or stocks. This course would lead to a constantly increasing variance between present value and bond and stock capitalization — a tendency which would inevitably lead to disaster either to the stockholders or to the public, or both. If, however, a company fails to perform this plain duty and to exact sufficient returns to keep the investment unimpaired, whether this is the result of unwarranted dividends upon over issues of securities, or of omission to exact proper prices for the output, the fault is its own." (p. 13.)

It is said by the relator that the Public Service Commissions Law as it existed in 1909 did not make any distinction between expenditures for operating purposes and expenditures for permanent improvements, but provided generally for the issue of stocks, bonds, notes or other evidence of indebtedness payable at periods of more than twelve months after the date thereof " when necessary for *the acquisition of property*, the construction, completion, extension or improvement of its plant or distributing system, or for the improvement *or maintenance* of its service *or for the discharge or lawful refunding of its obligations*."

Omitting from that part of the statute just quoted the words in italics it would then clearly refer to the permanent improvement of the plant or distributing system, and not to mere renewals or replacements. The words in italics, although of broader meaning than those not in italics, should be construed in connection with them, and in view of one of the paramount purposes of the legislature in establishing the commissions, which was to protect and enforce the rights of the public. The contention of the relator would enable any corporation to pay for labor, fuel and other supplies constituting the most ordinary of all operating expenses by obligations extending less than twelve months and then apply from time to time to the commission for authority to issue stock or bonds for the payment of such obligations and insist upon the same as a matter of right, without limit.

It will not be denied that fuel and such other materials as are consumed from day to day and the labor incurred in daily maintenance should be paid for from the earnings of the corporation as a part of its running expenses prior to the payment of interest upon bonds or dividends upon capital stock. A reasonable consideration of the interests of a corporation and the ultimate good of its stock and bondholders, and a regard for the investing public and that fair dealing which should be observed in all business transactions, require that machines and tools paid for and charged to capital account but which necessarily become obsolete or wholly worn out within a period of years after the same are purchased or installed, should be renewed or replaced by setting aside from time to time an adequate amount in the nature of a sinking fund or that by some other system of financing the corporation put upon the purchaser from the corporation the expense not alone of the daily maintenance of the plant but a just proportion of the expense of renewing and replacing that part of the plant which although not daily consumed must necessarily be practically consumed within a given time. If that is not done and renewals and replacements are continually added to the capital account the capital account must necessarily become more and more out of proportion to the real value of the property of the corporation.

The amendment of the statute made in 1910 was, so far as it affects the determination of this appeal, a statement in clearer terms of the intention of the statute of 1907, and it did not in the respect now considered give to the commission new and theretofore non-existing power. There is a wide difference in the claim of the parties as to the amount of the relator's floating debt, and some of the statements of fact in this opinion relating thereto may not meet with the approval of both parties. Such difference chiefly arises from the fact that the evidence and schedules before the commission and the record before us are quite unsatisfactory. A statement of a petitioner's financial transactions should be made in proceedings of this kind in sufficient detail and with sufficient classification to show with reasonable certainty the exact question to be determined.

The commission, with the assent of the relator, sent an accountant to examine its books and an engineer to examine and appraise its plant, but the details of the report of each need not be stated.

This court, in *Village of Saratoga Springs* v. *Saratoga Gas, Electric Light & Power Company* (191 N. Y. 123, 148), referring to the power of the state commission of gas and electricity under chapter 737 of the Laws of 1905 and the *ex parte* reports of inspectors and agents, say: "It is plain that no corporation could make its defense until it was clearly notified of what was charged against it and the proof to support such charge was given. While the commission might not be bound by technical rules of evidence, still it was plainly intended that the whole proceeding should assume a quasi-judicial aspect. This is necessarily so, for the Appellate Division is empowered to review the order of the commission, a review which requires something in the shape of a record of the proceedings of the commission. The commission being empowered to subpœna witnesses and take testimony, its inspectors or agents could be required to appear and verify any reports made by them, or if we assume that such reports could be received in the first instance without verification, the inspectors or agents could be compelled to attend at the instance of either party and be examined as to the truth of the statements in their reports and their knowledge of the facts therein contained." The language used in that case is applicable to this case so far as the reports of the engineer and accountant are concerned. It is not necessary to consider whether the relator is estopped

from asserting that the commission in this case should
not have considered the reports of the accountant and
engineer in view of the disposition about to be made of
this appeal.

The order of the Appellate Division and the three orders
made by the commission should be reversed, without
costs, and in the discretion of the relator the proceeding
should be held open for a further hearing herein or a new
application and a new hearing may be had unprejudiced
by the orders that have already been made.

CULLEN, Ch. J., GRAY, HAIGHT, WERNER, WILLARD
BARTLETT and COLLIN, JJ., concur.

Order reversed, etc.

THEODORE A. BINGHAM, Respondent, *v.* WILLIAM J.
GAYNOR, Appellant.

Libel — privileged communications — qualified privilege —
pleading — general allegation charging a person with something libelous per se cannot be defended under general allegation that charge is true — facts must be stated.

1. On an occasion that rebuts any presumption of express malice
one may publish statements, although defamatory of the person
referred to, if he does so in the performance of a legal or moral duty
and in good faith believing that such statements so made by him
are true, without being liable for damages arising from such publication. Such privilege is known as a qualified privilege.

2. A person having an interest as a citizen or otherwise in a public official may, in good faith, make a statement to the superior of
the person to whom the communication refers. In a communication so privileged it is not necessary in defense of an action for an
alleged libel by reason thereof to show that the statements contained therein are true, except, perhaps, as the truth of the allegations bear upon the question of express malice.

3. This qualified privilege does not extend to communications to
newspapers and to the public generally. The publication of a letter
containing libelous matter in a newspaper in advance of its delivery
to the officer to whom it is addressed destroys the qualified privilege in the writer to send such communication solely for the pur-

pose of presenting facts to such officer in order that he may determine whether the plaintiff should be continued in such office or removed therefrom.

4. A well-established rule of law, also commonly called a qualified privilege, protects a person in making any fair and honest criticism of the conduct of a public officer. In such a communication the writer makes statements of fact at his peril, and if the statements made therein are libelous and untrue the fact that they are about a public officer does not exempt the writer on the ground of privilege.

5. A general allegation charging a person with something that is libelous *per se* cannot be successfully answered by a general allegation in the answer that the charge is true. The answer in such a case should set forth the *facts* upon which it is alleged that the allegations of the complaint are true.

6. Upon examination of the allegations of plaintiff's complaint, of two separate defenses interposed thereto and of a demurrer to the defenses and on application thereto of the principles stated, *held*, that such defenses are insufficient either as pleas of privilege or in justification.

Bingham v. *Gaynor*, 141 App. Div. 301, affirmed.

(Submitted June 13, 1911; decided October 3, 1911.)

APPEAL, by permission, from an order of the Appellate Division of the Supreme Court in the first judicial department, entered December 30, 1910, which reversed an interlocutory judgment of Special Term overruling a demurrer to the separate defenses contained in the answer and sustained such demurrer.

The following questions were certified:

" 1. Is that portion of the defendant's amended answer contained in paragraph numbered ' I ' thereof, and designated as a 'defense,' insufficient in law upon the face thereof?

" 2. Is that portion of defendant's amended answer designated as ' a further defense to the alleged libelous statements, matters and things set out in paragraphs XIII and XVI of the complaint ' insufficient in law upon the face thereof? "

This action was brought to recover damages for libel. The gravamen of the complaint is the sending of an

alleged libelous letter concerning plaintiff in his office of
police commissioner of the city of New York, to the
mayor of said city, the giving of copies of said letter to
the public press and the subsequent publication to the
press of a defamatory statement concerning plaintiff in
his said office.   The answer contained a general denial
of the allegations of the complaint and defenses of privilege and justification.   Plaintiff demurred to the separate
defenses of privilege and justification.

Further facts are stated in the opinion.

Stephen C. Baldwin and *Charles H. Hyde* for appellant.   The first defense pleaded is sufficient in law upon
the face thereof. (*Woods* v. *Wiman*, 122 N. Y. 445; *Ashcroft* v. *Hammond*, 197 N. Y. 488; *Wright* v. *Lothrop*,
149 Mass. 300; *Hoey* v. *N. Y. Times Co.*, 138 N. Y. 149;
Mattice v. *Wilcox*, 147 N. Y. 624; *Littlejohn* v. *Greely*,
13 Abb. Pr. 41; *Triggs* v. *Sun P. & P. Co.*, 179 N. Y.
144; *U. P. R. R. Co.* v. *Bottsford*, 141 U. S. 250;
McQuigan v. *D., L. & W. R. R. Co.*, 129 N. Y. 50;
Lapstina v. *Santangelo*, 124 App. Div. 519.) Plaintiff
asserts that defendant's letter to the mayor is libelous in
its entirety.   He pleads no innuendo.   He does not
attempt to separate the statements contained in the letter, and he must, therefore, stand or fall in his objection
to our pleading upon the letter as a whole. (*Wallace*
v. *Bennett*, 1 Abb. [N. C.] 478; *Schoonoven* v. *Beach*, 23
Wkly. Dig. 348; *Randell* v. *Butler*, 7 Barb, 260; *Berg-
man* v. *Jones*, 94 N. Y. 51; *Soper* v. *Asso. Press*, 57
Misc. Rep. 445; *Sanderson* v. *Caldwell*, 45 N. Y. 398;
Church v. *N. Y. Tribune*, 63 Misc. Rep. 578.) The
defense of justification as pleaded is good.   The plaintiff
having set forth several alleged libelous charges as the
gravamen of his action, it was not necessary for the
defendant to plead a justification of all the charges. (*Hol-
lingsworth* v. *Spectator Co.*, 53 App. Div. 291; *Lan-
pher* v. *Clark*, 149 N. Y. 472; *Brush* v. *Blot*, 16 App. Div.

80; *Baldwin* v. *Gennung*, 70 App. Div. 271; *Saunders* v. *Post-Standard Co.*, 107 App. Div. 84; *Holmes* v. *Jones*, 121 N. Y. 461.)

E. C. Crowley for respondent. The articles complained of are not privileged as communications to plaintiff's superior officer. (*Hunt* v. *Bennett*, 19 N. Y. 173; *Woods* v. *Wiman*, 122 N. Y. 445; *Sunderlin* v. *Bradstreet*, 46 N. Y. 188; *Mattice* v. *Wilcox*, 147 N. Y. 624; *Lovell Co.* v. *Houghton*, 116 N. Y. 525; *Hoey* v. *N. Y. Times Co.*, 138 App. Div. 149; *Ashcroft* v. *Hammond*, 197 N. Y. 488; *Hamilton* v. *Eno*, 81 N. Y. 116.) The articles complained of are not privileged as fair comment on plaintiff's official acts. (*Hamilton* v. *Eno*, 81 N. Y. 116; *Hoey* v. *N. Y. Times Co.*, 138 App. Div. 149; *Mattice* v. *Wilcox*, 147 N. Y. 624; *Littlejohn* v. *Greely*, 13 Abb. Pr. 41; *Triggs* v. *Sun P. & P. Assn.*, 179 N. Y. 144; *Moore* v. *M. N. Bank*, 123 N. Y. 426; *Rose* v. *I. E. Co.*, 110 App. Div. 437; *Byam* v. *Collins*, 111 N. Y. 143; *Lewis & Herrick* v. *Chapman*, 16 N. Y. 369; *Klinck* v. *Colby*, 46 N. Y. 427.) The defense of justification is defective because it is not as broad as the charges. (*Wachter* v. *Quenzer*, 29 N. Y. 547; *Brush* v. *Blot*, 16 App. Div. 80; *Nunnally* v. *M. & E. Co.*, 113 App. Div. 831; *Southwick* v. *Spencer*, 11 Johns. 573; *Nunnally* v. *N. Y. Z. P. Co.*, 117 App. Div. 1; *Stilwell* v. *Barter*, 19 Wend. 487; *Skinner* v. *Powers*, 1 Wend. 451; *Price* v. *D. C. Co.*, 128 App. Div. 472.)

CHASE, J. I concur in the result reached by the Appellate Division. I also concur in the opinion of that court as written by McLAUGHLIN, J., except as it is qualified by what I shall say in this opinion.

A person on an occasion that rebuts any presumption of express malice may publish statements, although defamatory of the person referred to in the communication, if he does so in the performance of a legal or moral duty and in good faith believing that such statements so made by him are true, without being liable for damages arising from such publication. The rule of law that permits such publications grew out of the desirability in the public interest of encouraging a full and fair statement by persons having a legal or moral duty to communicate their knowledge and information about a person in whom they have an interest to another who also has an interest in such person. Such privilege is known as a qualified privilege. It is qualified because it does not extend beyond such statements as the writer makes in the performance of such duty and in good faith believing them to be true.

A person having an interest as a citizen or otherwise in a public official may, in good faith, make a statement to the superior of the person about whom the communication refers. He is not liable by reason of an erroneous and untrue statement so made if it is found that it was made in good faith and in the performance of such duty. It was said in this court, in *Byam* v. *Collins* (111 N. Y. 143), quoting in part from *Harrison* v. *Bush* (5 Ellis & Black. [Q. B.] 344): "The general rule is that in the case of a libelous publication the law implies malice and infers some damage. What are called privileged communications are exceptions to this rule. Such communications are divided into several classes, with one only of which we are concerned in this case, and that is generally formulated thus: 'A communication made *bona fide* upon any subject-matter in which the party communicating has an *interest*, or in reference to which he has a *duty*, is privileged if made to a person having a corresponding *interest* or *duty*, although it contained criminating matter which, without this privilege, would be slanderous and actionable; and this though the duty be not a legal one, but only a moral or social duty of imperfect obligation.'" (p. 150.)

In a communication so privileged it is not necessary in defense of an action for an alleged libel by reason of such communication to show that the statements contained therein are true, except, perhaps, as the truth of the allegations bear upon the question of express malice. The test in such a case, assuming that the party making the communication has an interest in the subject-matter and the party to whom the communication is delivered also has an interest as the superior of the person referred to therein, or particularly, as in this case, where the person to whom it was delivered had power to redress the wrong complained of, is whether the communication was made in good faith believing the statements are true and for the purpose of performing the legal or moral duty resting upon the person making the communication to make the same.

As has already been said by the Appellate Division, the publication of the letter in the newspapers of the city in advance of its delivery to the mayor personally takes away and destroys the qualified privilege in the writer to send such communication to the mayor solely for the purpose of presenting facts to him that he might determine whether the plaintiff should be continued in office or removed therefrom. (*Woods* v. *Wiman,* 122 N. Y. 445; *Hunt* v. *Bennett,* 19 N. Y. 173; *Sunderlin* v. *Bradstreet,* 46 N. Y. 188.)

The qualified privilege that we have considered does not extend to communications to newspapers and to the public generally. There is, however another well-established rule of law, also commonly called a qualified privilege, that protects a person in making any fair and honest criticism of the conduct of a public officer. This rule is quite independent of the one first stated, but it is also based upon the desirability of allowing such fair and honest criticism because it tends to the good of the public service. It is qualified because it does not extend beyond fair and honest comment and criticism. It is no protection to the writer if he therein makes false statements or unjustifiable inferences. In such a communication the writer makes statements of fact at his peril, and if the statements made therein are libelous and untrue the fact that they are made about a public officer does not exempt the writer on the ground of privilege. The privilege in such a case extends to a fair and honest statement of actual facts relating to public acts and to reasonable and justifiable comment thereon and criticism thereof. It does not extend to attacks upon private character or to publishing defamatory things about an official even if the writer in good faith makes the publication believing his statements are true, neither does it permit a person to draw conclusions that are or that the jury may find are improper and unjustifiable.

It is not clear whether the defendant in his first defense intends to allege a qualified privilege by reason of the letter having been written as a matter of duty to the person who had power to redress the wrong complained of, or whether he intends therein to allege that the letter and interview were fair and reasonable criticisms of the acts of the plaintiff as a public official or whether he intends that the defense shall be considered as a plea of qualified privilege for both reasons. The defendant does not in the first defense deny that the letter was given to the newspapers and published before it was received by the mayor, nor does he therein admit the allegation of fact in the complaint except as to the delivery of the letter to the newspapers in advance of delivering the same to the mayor. Assuming that the defendant could by proper allegations have raised the question of qualified privilege in sending the letter to the mayor, if it should appear on the trial that it was never given to the newspapers by him, he wholly failed to do so by the allegations of the first defense. In the first defense he alleges '' that the matters of fact stated in the letter referred to in Paragraph XIII and in the statement referred to at Paragraph XVI are true and the opinions therein fair comments on the said acts of the plaintiff, and only such as to bring properly before said mayor the official misconduct of the plaintiff." It is quite clear that the alleged first defense is not intended as a plea in justification, but it is intended as expressly stated therein to be a plea of privilege. In my opinion the defense cannot now be considered as one of justification simply because it alleges generally the truth of the statements of fact alleged in the complaint. The allegations therein are not made as a justification but as a part of the plea of privilege. I agree with the Appellate Division that it is insufficient as such, and that the demurrer thereto was properly sustained by the Appellate Division.

It is asserted that in the second defense there is a general statement that the allegations contained in the letter and in the interview are true, and that the defense may be sufficient as a justification by reason of such general allegation. A general allegation charging a person with something that is libelous *per se* cannot be successfully answered by a general allegation in the answer that the charge is true. In *Wachter* v. *Quenzer* (29 N. Y. 547) this court referring to this subject say: "Take, for instance, a charge that one is a thief or a murderer, or that he has committed perjury. A statement in the answer that the words are true would not be a justification, and it would fall just as far short of being a statement of facts to be proved by way of mitigation. It is a statement of nothing. It is simply a repetition of the libel." (p. 552.)

The reason for this rule is that it does not give to the plaintiff any clue of what the defendant intends to prove upon the trial. The answer in such a case should set forth the facts upon which it is alleged that the allegations of the complaint are true. A mere general statement of the truth of the allegations of the complaint is a conclusion and does not constitute a sufficient answer when considered upon demurrer. There is an exception, however, to the rule that an answer must be specific in its denial and that is where the charge is specific. Take for instance a charge that the defendant on a day and at a place named took specified articles of personal property under such specified circumstances as to justify the conclusion that the taking was willful and a larceny. In such a case an answer can be interposed alleging generally the truth of the specific statements of fact alleged in the complaint by the publication of which it is charged that the plaintiff has been libelled.

The plaintiff in this case alleges generally that the letter and the further statement were each made and published concerning him, and while they must each be considered as a whole, we refer now to some of the general statements therein, and confining ourselves to such statements as are particularly mentioned in the opinion of McLAUGHLIN, J., we find that the defendant in connection with all the other statements in said letter and said interview has charged of some one generally, "scoundrelism," "the police commissioner is doing all he can to make it impossible for him (Duffy) to lead an honest life and make an honest living and to force him (Duffy) instead to a life of crime," "incompetents, corruptionists and sometimes buffoons who are put in rulership over," * * * "It is an ordinary thing for the police commissioner to refuse to obey the decisions of the courts and compel the police force to disobey them," "The despotism and lawlessness of the police commissioner is shocking."

These allegations are general in terms and in my opinion they each refer unmistakably to the plaintiff. The avowed purpose of the letter was to secure through the mayor the removal of the plaintiff from office. It was the only redress advocated or suggested. The general charges in the letter and statement require a specific and not a general answer. The answer is in part specific, but it is not as broad as the charge, although the charge is considered as composed of the letter and of the interview as a whole, and it does not, therefore, constitute a complete defense of the causes of action set forth in the complaint.

The order of the Appellate Division should be affirmed, with costs, and the questions certified answered in the affirmative.

CULLEN, Ch. J., GRAY, VANN, WERNER and HISCOCK, JJ., concur; WILLARD BARTLETT, J., dissents.

Order affirmed.

MARY E. COLEMAN, Appellant, *v.* FRANK C. CLARK, Respondent.

Contract — "tourist parties" — when person engaged in managing "tourist parties," who engaged to look after baggage of tourist, not liable for baggage lost while in custody of steamship company upon whose ship the tourist was a passenger.

Plaintiff was a passenger on board a steamship under a contract with defendant who was engaged in managing tourist parties, by which "every detail, baggage, carriages, hotel rates, fees, everything pertaining to the tour from New York back to New York would be attended to." On arrival at plaintiff's destination a steamer steward took plaintiff's trunk from her stateroom and thereafter it could not be found. In this action, brought to recover damages for its loss, the court charged: "I leave to the jury the question of whether a substantial compliance with that contract required the service of a representative of the defendant upon the steamer." *Held*, error.

Coleman v. *Clark*, 135 App. Div. 55, affirmed.

(Argued June 13, 1911; decided October 8, 1911.)

APPEAL from an order of the Appellate Division of the Supreme Court in the first judicial department, entered December 13, 1909, reversing a judgment in favor of plaintiff entered upon a verdict and granting a new trial.

The nature of the action and the facts, so far as material, are stated in the opinion of GRAY, J.

Samuel H. Evins and *J. O. Venino* for appellant.

Alexander S. Bacon for respondent.

HISCOCK, J. I find myself compelled to concur with Judge GRAY in an affirmance of the order appealed from but on grounds other than those stated by him.

I agree with him that actually the contract between the parties was a written one contained in the receipt or certificate issued by defendant to plaintiff and the prospectus or programme therein referred to as part thereof. Nevertheless, the court without any objection on the part of defendant's counsel allowed the jury, if it so desired, to find that the contract was an oral one made by the conversation between plaintiff and defendant's agent in New York before the written one was executed, and, therefore, plaintiff would be entitled, if she could, to sustain her recovery under either alleged contract. The so-called oral one did not materially differ from the written one in respect to the question here under discussion. Plaintiff testifies that "He (defendant's agent) told me every detail, baggage, carriages, hotel rates, fees, everything pertaining to the tour from New York back to New York would be attended to. I had nothing whatever to do with the details."

On the theory that it might find an oral contract, the jury were instructed that "then it was the duty of the defendant to substantially perform his contract, including the provision to look after and take care of the transportation of plaintiff's baggage, and it would be for the jury to say whether a substantial compliance with defendant's contract in that regard required the presence on the steamer *Romanic* of a representative of the defendant to look after and take charge of the plaintiff's baggage on the trip from New York to Naples, and whether the defendant did substantially comply with his contract in providing that the baggage should be handled

and looked after by the representatives of the steamship
company, without any accompanying conductor between
New York and Naples." I think the defendant's counsel intended to take exception to this portion of the
charge, but through carelessness either in taking the
exception or the printing of the record his exception,
which is applicable only to this portion of the charge,
is stated to be taken to the charge in connection with the
written contract, where no such instructions as to the
obligations of the defendant had thus far been given.
However, in response to this exception, the court did
then charge: "I leave to the jury the question of
whether a substantial compliance with *that* contract
required the services of a representative of the defendant upon the steamer. I grant you an exception to that."
Therefore, when this was all over, there was an exception
which was understood to refer to what had already been
said with reference to the obligations of the defendant
under the alleged oral contract or there were some new
instructions subject to exception which referred to the
written contract.

The defendant did not assume any such obligations
as were defined by the court under either contract. Of
course it could not have been the expectation of the
parties either under the written contract or under the
conversation between plaintiff and defendant's agent
in New York that the defendant would send a representative to retain the custody of or maintain personal
guard over baggage while it was in the possession of a
public carrier under a regular passage ticket which had
been issued to and accepted by the owner of the baggage.
That would be absurd. What the contract meant, so far
as applicable to the facts of this case, was that the defendant would furnish a representative who would discharge
those duties and exercise that care concerning the baggage of plaintiff and those like her which an ordinary
traveler would exercise concerning his own baggage. This

at most required him to see to it that baggage belonging to members of the party was correctly checked or labeled and delivered to the proper carrier and that it was carefully looked after on delivery by the carrier at the end of the route, or, in case of a failure to deliver at the proper time and place, that it was promptly hunted up and delivery secured. Certainly this obligation did not require the defendant to maintain a representative on the steamer for the entire voyage. · I do not think that it even required him to furnish a representative on board at Naples to stand by the baggage as it was being transferred from the steamer to the tender for delivery at the pier. It was still in the custody of the carrier and defendant had a right to assume in the first instance that the steamship company would properly discharge its obligations and so deliver the baggage. If this view is correct it was error for the court to charge as it did.

I do think, however, that the defendant by an agent was bound under the circumstances to attend at the pier and look after plaintiff's trunk if it was delivered there, or in case it was not delivered at the proper time with the other baggage to take prompt measures to look it up and see that it came off the steamer before the latter sailed away. And I further believe that certain aspects of the evidence would have justified the jury in finding that the defendant did not properly discharge this duty and in holding him responsible for the loss of plaintiff's trunk. It is not profitable to consider this question at length, for I concede that the court committed error in permitting the defendant to be charged with too great a responsibility in the respects mentioned. If the plaintiff's counsel had seen fit to go back and take a new trial under the decision of the Appellate Division this error might have been eliminated on a new trial, but as the case stands now, it is available to the defendant and must lead us to grant judgment absolute against the plaintiff on the stipulation of her attorney.

In accordance with these views I vote for an affirmance of the order of reversal, with costs in all courts.

GRAY, J. By this action, the plaintiff has sought to hold the defendant responsible in damages for the loss of a trunk and its contents. The defendant was engaged in the business of organizing and managing " tourist parties from New York and other places to Europe, Africa, Asia and other countries." In June, 1905, the plaintiff applied to him for information about a trip to Europe and was advised to become a member of a party, which was to sail in July upon a tour, satisfactory to her in its route. She was going alone and was assured that every detail would be attended to, "baggage, carriages, hotel rates, fees, everything pertaining to the tour." At this time, she paid a deposit of $25 on account of the cost of membership in the party. Some days later, she returned to the defendant's office and paid the sum of $385, as the balance due for the proposed tour. She, then, was handed a paper signed by the defendant; which acknowledged the receipt of her money and expressed the terms and conditions upon which she became a member of the party. At the same time, she was given a ticket of the White Star Line, entitling her to a first class passage from New York to Naples on the steamship *Romanic*. The party sailed the next month for southern Europe and landed at Naples, by means of a tender. The plaintiff's trunk, which had been in her stateroom, was taken out of it by a steamer steward and was never seen again by her.

Inasmuch as the plaintiff elected to proceed as for a breach of contract, it is necessary to refer to the written receipt, which the plaintiff obtained upon paying her money and which contained the defendant's undertaking in consideration of its payment. Whatever the prior oral negotiations, they were merged in this writing and, so far as material, it reads that the defendant had received from the plaintiff " the sum of $410, being full payment for Membership in Fourth Vacation Party sailing per steamer *Romanic* on July 6, 1905. This amount includes transportation, hotel accommodation and other items, as set forth in the printed programme, from New York 1905 to New York 1905. This certificate is issued subject to the conditions mentioned in the programme and to the provisions applying to the transportation of passengers, as set forth in the regulations of each of the transportation companies employed in the conveyance of passengers.". The printed programme, which is referred to and which must, of course, be considered in determining the legal relations entered into, after giving the date of the proposed sailing of a "select private party" in the *Romanic* to Naples, describes the territorial extent of the proposed tour; states its cost and the route, with a daily and descriptive itinerary, and what the sum paid will include, as to the nature and class of conveyances and accommodations and in the way of traveling expenses. It was stated in the programme that "a first class conductor, supplied by Clark's Tours, will accompany the party through Europe to look after the baggage and all details of the trip." Nothing else in the paper need be quoted as pertinent to the issue. The ticket, with which the plaintiff embarked upon the *Romanic,* was expressed in the usual form and with the regular conditions of steamship tickets. It embodied a valid contract between the White Star Line, or Oceanic Steam Navigation Company of Great Britain, and the plaintiff for the transportation of herself and of her personal effects from New York to Naples. When she embarked, she brought and delivered her trunk to the steamship and had it placed in her stateroom. It is not pretended that the defendant could have assumed any care of it as yet. According to the defendant's agreement, the plaintiff became subject to the regulations of the steamship company, which was to transport her. When she arrived at Naples, the steward of the steamship helped the plaintiff to

[208 N. Y.]   Opinion, per GRAY. J.   [Oct.,

pack her trunk and took it from the statereom.   The defendant's authorized representative, or "conductor," Hillier, met the party upon the steamship's arrival, and accompanied the members from the steamship upon the tender to the wharf.   The hand baggage and the trunks were not sent ashore with the passengers, but came on separate tenders.   On landing, Hillier informed the plaintiff that she might "go up with the party," and that he would "attend to the trunks," meaning at the custom house.   After passing the customs, the passengers were sent on to a hotel and afterwards visited various objects of interest in the city.   Upon returning to the hotel the plaintiff found her hand luggage; but her trunk was not there.   Upon inquiry Hillier stated to her that he would send to the custom house and subsequently reported that he could not find it.   It had not come ashore and the steamship had sailed for Genoa.   Subsequent inquiries, and a correspondence with the White Star Line officials, failed to discover what had become of the trunk.   The plaintiff continued on with the party upon the tour under Hillier's guidance.

It is difficult to understand the theory upon which the defendant can be made liable for the loss of the plaintiff's baggage.   That the steamship company might be liable is fairly intelligible; as both passenger and baggage were in its care and by its contract were to be delivered at the place of destination.   When and where did the defendant come under any responsibility for the safe transportation of the baggage?   Certainly not until it came actually, or at least constructively, into his agent's care, and that could only be upon its delivery at Naples by the steamship company.   There is no charge of any wrongful conduct on the part of the defendant, or of his agent; the claim is for an alleged breach of his contract.   That contract, as we have seen, covers a receipt for the money and an agreement that it shall pay all the expenses as specified, and that a "first-class conductor will accompany the party *through Europe to look after the baggage and all details of the trip.*" It is true that the plaintiff testified that, in a prior interview, the defendant's clerk had said that the members of the party would be "under the direct charge of a director" and that the plaintiff "would have no care whatever of herself in any personal way, or baggage, everything would be looked after * * * on the voyage, on the trip." That was a representation; but what the defendant became bound to do was, subsequently, expressed in the writing given her. Then it was that she received the ticket, which entitled her to transportation to Europe on a vessel of the White Star Line, and with respect to that transportation the defendant neither assumed, nor could he assume, any responsibility beyond delivering a valid first-class ticket. At the end of the voyage, he, for the first, undertook and, indeed, became able to assume the care of plaintiff's baggage. Then this "personally conducted" party was to be taken through Europe by the defendant's representative and then he assumed all the obligations legally attendant upon the undertaking, as expressed in the receipt and "programme" he had delivered to the plaintiff. The basis of a liability to respond in damages for this plaintiff's loss must be found in some agreement, which the defendant failed to perform; or it does not exist at all. Such an agreement may, or may not, be in writing; but if it is, then, it becomes the best evidence of the final intentions of the parties and resort must be had to it to ascertain what the engagement is, which is in question. The defendant was not a common carrier and he could not come under a common carrier's liabilities. He had not insured the safe delivery of plaintiff's baggage in Europe. The trunk was never delivered to him; it was delivered to the steamship by the plaintiff and placed in her stateroom, upon embarking, and, prior to disembarking, the steamship company took possession of it through a steward of the vessel. When Hillier said to the plaintiff that he would "attend to the trunks," it was a promise, which carried as yet no liability, and none could commence, until the trunks, by delivery upon the dock at Naples, might be said to have come into his custody. For any loss, through theft or other cause, before such delivery, whatever liability existed for it, was that of the company.

There was no question of fact and the case should not have been submitted to the jury. Would a jury have the right to find the undertaking of the defendant to have been anything other than, for the sum named, to procure for the plaintiff a first-class steamship passage to the port named in Europe and to conduct her through Europe by a first-class conductor, who should assume the care of her baggage, when and as received, and should attend to all details of the tour? I think that was the extent of it, clearly, and, in my opinion, to hold that a jury might legally find that more was, actually and finally, contracted for, would be unreasonable.

The order should be affirmed and judgment absolute ordered against the appellant under her stipulation; with costs in all the courts to the respondent.

CULLEN, Ch. J., VANN, WERNER, WILLARD BARTLETT and CHASE, JJ., concur with HISCOCK, J.; GRAY, J., also reads for affirmance, etc.

Order affirmed, etc.

THE PEOPLE OF THE STATE OF NEW YORK, Respondent, *v.* BERT L. BROWN, Appellant.

Murder — evidence examined and held sufficient to sustain judgment of conviction — when verdict of murder in the first degree eliminates any question arising from failure of court to charge as to the various degrees of manslaughter.

1. The defendant was convicted of murder in the first degree. The conviction was clearly warranted by the evidence, and none of the exceptions are of sufficient importance to justify a reversal of the judgment.

2. The defendant, in exercising his right to become a voluntary witness on this trial, subjected himself to all the rules under which the testimony of witnesses may be probed by cross-examination. The People had the right to test the truth and accuracy of his statements, made as a witness upon the trial, by eliciting any other statements previously made either as a witness in some prior proceeding or otherwise.

3. The trial justice charged "that William Brown, the deceased, bullied and beat the defendant prior to May 21st, and that they (the jury) may take that into consideration on the question as to whether or not it furnished a motive for the crime." *Held,* that although this charge is technically open to criticism, the evidence as to the homicide was so unequivocal that the question of motive was not one of controlling importance.

4. When a jury excludes from the case the alternative of murder in the second degree by a finding of murder in the first degree, all lower degrees are necessarily eliminated. In such case failure to charge fully as to the degrees of manslaughter is not error.

(Argued June 13, 1911; decided October 3, 1911.)

APPEAL from a judgment of the Supreme Court, rendered June 24, 1910, at a Trial Term for the county of Westchester, upon a verdict convicting the defendant of the crime of murder in the first degree.

The facts, so far as material, are stated in the opinion.

George C. Andrews for appellant. The court committed error upon the trial in stating that the defendant voluntarily testified before the coroner. (*People* v. *Mondon,* 103 N. Y. 211.) The court erred in permitting the district attorney to read, in the form of questions, under objection and exception, a large portion of the defendant's testimony taken while he was under arrest accused with the crime, before the coroner. (*People* v. *Mondon,* 103 N. Y. 211; *People* v. *McMahon,* 15 N. Y. 384.) The court erred in charging the jury that the deceased bullied and beat the defendant prior to May twenty-first, and that the jury may take that into consideration on the question as to whether or not it furnished a motive for this crime. (*People* v. *Walker,* 198 N. Y. 334.) The court committed error in not defining and applying the facts in the case to manslaughter. (*People v. Fiorentino*, 197 N. Y. 560.) The court erred in charging the jury that the law presumes that a man intends the natural and necessary consequences of his acts, (*People v. Fish*, 125 N. Y. 138; *People v. Stokes*, 53 N. Y. 179; *People v. Baker*, 96 N. Y. 340; *People v. Conroy*, 97 N. Y. 76; *People v. Barone*, 161 N. Y. 451; *People v. Martin*, 33 App. Div. 282; Code Crim Pro. § 528.) ·

Francis A. Winslow, District Attorney (*Lee Parson Davis* of counsel), for respondent. Having assumed the character of a witness the defendant exposed himself to the legitimate attacks which may be made upon any witness. (*People v. Hinksman*, 192 N. Y. 421.) No error was committed in the reception of evidence on cross-examination of the defendant relative to a sworn statement made by him before the coroner. (*People v. Hinksman*, 192 N. Y. 421.) No error calling for reversal was committed by the court in charging upon the question of deceased having bullied and beaten defendant. (*People v. Walker*, 198 N. Y. 329.) The verdict being that of murder in the first degree it was not material whether the court applied the facts to manslaughter. (*People v. Granger*, 187 N. Y. 67; *People v. Serimarco*, 202 N. Y. 225.) No error was committed by the court in charging the jury that the law presumes that a man intends the natural and necessary consequences of his acts. (*People v. Fish*, 125 N. Y. 136 ; *People v. Conroy*, 97 N. Y. 62.)

WERNER, J. On the 24th day of June, 1910, the defendant was convicted of the crime of murder in the first degree. From the judgment of death entered upon that conviction the defendant has appealed to this court. Very little need be said in disposing of the appeal, since the defendant's conviction was clearly warranted by the evidence, and none of the exceptions are of sufficient importance to justify a reversal of the judgment.

The story of the homicide, as told by the witnesses for the prosecution, is short and simple. The defendant and the deceased were half-brothers, both living under the same roof, but not in one family, in the village of Rye, in Westchester county. William Brown, the deceased, lived on the first floor with his mother and a woman called Minnie Brown. The defendant occupied the upper part of the house with a woman known as Martha Lewis. The homicide occurred in the evening of May 21st, 1910. Earlier in the evening the defendant and some of his associates met at the saloon of one Flood. The deceased was in the party. At first they played pool, but later they engaged in a game called "craps." Meanwhile they all drank more or less beer or liquor, and the game ended when the deceased had won all the money of the other members of the party. At that juncture the deceased left for his home, and soon thereafter the proprietor of the saloon requested the others of the party to leave. The defendant and two of his companions named Goff and Nichols went to the home of Nichols, where Flood had some laundry waiting for him. While there the defendant arranged to borrow a revolver from Nichols and then this trio went to the house of the deceased. The defendant rapped at the entrance door and asked for his mother. Minnie Brown answered that they had all retired for the night. The defendant was insistent, however, and the deceased came to the door and opened it, when the defendant at once fired two shots in quick succession, both of which lodged in the body of the deceased. One of these shots penetrated the abdominal aorta, causing internal hemorrhage, which resulted in death within a few minutes. As to these facts there is no controversy, and they are established by direct testimony which clearly proves that the deceased met his death at the hands of the defendant. There was other evidence on the part of the prosecution tending to show that the shooting was done with premeditation and deliberation.

The defendant, although admitting that he fired the fatal shot, claims to have done so in self-defense. He testified that when the deceased opened the door the latter gave utterance to an obscene and threatening remark and took the defendant by the throat, making an attempt to get at the revolver, which was held by the defendant, and cutting the defendant about the neck and chest. The defendant also insisted that he shot not to kill his brother, but to scare Nichols and Goff so as to keep them from hurting the deceased. This testimony was offset by various statements made by the defendant at different times indicating that he had been bullied and beaten by the deceased, and that the homicide was not justifiable, but was committed with deliberate and murderous intent. It would serve no useful purpose to recite in detail the evidence which characterizes the defendant's act. It is enough to say that the evidence presented an issue of fact, and that the finding of the jury is fully sustained by the record. Without further discussion of the main issue we, therefore, proceed at once to a consideration of the exceptions upon which this appeal is founded.

The learned counsel for the defendant urges that the trial court committed error in stating to the jury that the defendant had voluntarily appeared as a witness at the coroner's inquest, when he was in fact then under arrest; and in permitting the district attorney to elicit upon the trial a substantial part of the testimony given by the defendant before the coroner. The exceptions taken to these features of the trial seem to be based upon the sections of the Code of Criminal Procedure (188, 196, 198), which relate to the safeguarding of the rights of a person accused of crime pending a magistrate's preliminary investigation of the same, and the authority relied upon is the case of *People* v. *Mondon* (103 N. Y. 211), in which it was held that a person under arrest is entitled to the same rights when being examined at a coroner's inquest as he has before a committing magistrate. The difficulty with the rule invoked by counsel for the defendant is that it has no application to the case at bar. The defendant, in exercising his right to become a voluntary witness on this trial, subjected himself to all the rules under which the testimony of witnesses may be probed by cross-examination. (*People* v. *Hinksman,* 192 N. Y. 421, 432.) The district attorney had the right to test the truth and accuracy of his statements, made as a witness upon the trial, by eliciting any other statements previously made either as a witness in some prior proceeding or otherwise. There are two reasons why the exception of defendant's counsel to the statement of the trial justice that the defendant had voluntarily appeared as a witness is not well taken. There is nothing in this record to show that the statement was not true, even if we assume it to have referred to the defendant's appearance before the coroner. Beyond that, however, there is the conclusive answer that the remark obviously referred to the defendant's appearance as a witness upon this trial. The learned justice said: "The defendant voluntarily going upon the stand, *he is subject to the same rule of cross-examination that any witness is subject to.*" These considerations also dispose of the exception to that portion of the charge to the jury in which the trial justice characterized as voluntary the statement of the defendant made before the coroner. There is nothing before us to indicate that this remark of the trial justice was not literally true; and in any event it was clearly harmless.

At the request of the district attorney the trial justice charged "that William Brown, the deceased, bullied and beat the defendant prior to May 21st, and that they (the jury) may take that into consideration on the question as to whether or not it furnished a motive for the crime," and this charge was excepted to by defendant's counsel.

There was testimony from which the jury were at liberty
to find that the defendant had stated that the deceased
had bullied and beaten him, and the defendant also testified that there had been no quarrel or rupture between
him and the deceased. It would, therefore, have been
better for the trial justice to have stated the proposition
in the alternative instead of assuming it to be true that
the deceased had bullied and beaten the defendant. We
are not convinced, however, that this charge, although
technically open to criticism, did any harm to the defendant's cause. The evidence as to the homicide was so
unequivocal that the question of motive was not one of
controlling importance.

In the main charge the trial justice defined accurately
and fully the law relating to murder in the first and sec-
ond-degrees, but made no reference to the statutes defining the two degrees of manslaughter. Thereupon the
defendant's counsel asked the court to charge as to the
various degrees of manslaughter. This request was only
partially complied with, for the trial justice simply paraphrased very briefly that section of the statute which
defines manslaughter in the first degree. No exception
was taken to this part of the charge and no request was
made for any further charge in that respect. This
feature of the trial may also be summarily disposed of.
The court had correctly and fully charged as to the two
degrees of murder. Had the jury found the defendant
guilty of murder in the second degree, there might be
some ground for the assumption that the defendant's
cause was prejudiced by the action of the court. Such a
situation would have lent support to the claim that the
jury might have declared the defendant guilty of a still
lower degree of homicide had they received proper instructions from the court. All such speculations are dissipated, however, by the fact the defendant was found
guilty of murder in the first degree. When the jury
excluded from the case the alternative of murder in the

second degree, all lower degrees were necessarily eliminated by the same rule. (*People* v. *Granger*, 187 N. Y. 67, 72.)

The counsel for the defendant also criticises the charge in so far as it referred to the legal presumption that a man intends the natural and necessary consequences of his acts. There is no exception to this part of the charge, but, even if there were, we find no error in what the trial justice said upon this subject. It was made perfectly plain to the jury that the court, in referring to this presumption, was simply quoting from the argument of the district attorney to the effect that the defendant's use of a deadly weapon, in the conditions disclosed by the evidence, naturally gave rise to the inference that it was used with the intent to kill. At the end of this reference to the district attorney's argument the trial justice said: "Do not understand, gentlemen, that I make that statement; that is the claim made by the district attorney and I simply state to you the law, which is, that a man is presumed to intend the natural consequences of his act." This was a perfectly accurate statement of an abstract legal rule, and that it could not have misled the jury to the defendant's prejudice is rendered evident by a subsequent charge made at the request of the defendant's counsel to the effect that "even though death might have been the natural consequence of the defendant's act, it does not establish premeditation or deliberation."

There are other exceptions to which we shall not refer, since we do not regard them as of sufficient importance to justify discussion. After a careful study of the record we conclude that the defendant has had a fair trial and that the judgment of conviction must be affirmed.

CULLEN, Ch. J., GRAY, VANN, WILLARD BARTLETT, HISCOCK and CHASE, JJ., concur.

Judgment of conviction affirmed.

LELIA A. MORGAN, Respondent, *v.* WILLIAM H. WOOL-
VERTON, as President of the NEW YORK TRANSFER
COMPANY, Appellant.

**Baggage — meaning of term "baggage" as used in section 38 of
Public Service Commissions Law — liability of express company
for baggage lost in transit not limited by provisions of that
section.**

The term "baggage," used in section 38 of the Public Service
Commissions Law (Consol. Laws, ch. 48), does not include property
which is being moved by express or otherwise apart from and
disconnected with the transportation of the owner; hence, a company, which enters into a contract with a passenger on a railroad
train to deliver a trunk at his home or other designated point,
cannot avail itself of the limitation in that section upon the amount
of the recovery against a common carrier, where the value of the
baggage is not stated.

Morgan v. *Woolverton*, 136 App. Div. 351, affirmed.

(Argued June 13, 1911; decided October 3, 1911.)

APPEAL from a judgment of the Appellate Division of the
Supreme Court in the second judicial department, entered
January 14, 1910, affirming a judgment in favor of
plaintiff entered upon a verdict directed by the court.

The nature of the action and the facts, so far as
material, are stated in the opinion.

Morgan J. O'Brien, Robert L. Redfield and *John L.
Hill* for appellant. The provision of the Public Service
Commissions Law, taken as an entirety, clearly shows the
legislative intention to be that the entire section 38 should
apply to "every common carrier." (L. 1907, ch. 429.)

Herman Aaron and *John Hill Morgan* for respondent.
Section 38 of the Public Service Commissions Law does
not apply. (L. 1907, ch. 429.)

HISCOCK, J. The respondent was a passenger on a
train coming into New York city. The appellant was

engaged in the business of taking up from the railroad
company the baggage of a passenger and delivering it
at his home or other designated point in the city of New
York. While the train was still in the state of New
Jersey appellant's agent received from respondent her
railroad check for a trunk to be delivered in New York
city and gave her a receipt or check therefor which contained a clause limiting its liability to $100. The trunk
was received from the railroad company but somehow
was lost or miscarried, and subsequently a judgment
was recovered for the full value thereof, which exceeded
$1,200.

Originally appellant seems to have relied mainly on
the clause in its receipt limiting its liability. Without
summarizing the evidence on this point, however, it is
clear that it was a question of fact whether the acceptance by respondent of appellant's check or receipt took
place under such circumstances as to bind her by this
limitation, and appellant's trial counsel by his course at
the close of the trial permitted this question to be disposed of by the court rather than by the jury, and is
now concluded by the adverse disposition thereof. In
fact, to some extent on the trial and still more on this
appeal the appellant has ceased to rely on its original
defense, as above stated, and has come to rest its claim
of limitation of liability on the provisions of the Public
Service Commissions Law.

Section 38 of that law reads as follows:

"Liability for damage to property in transit. * * *
Every common carrier and railroad corporation shall be liable for loss, damage and injury to property carried as baggage up to the full value and regardless of the character
thereof, but the value in excess of one hundred and fifty
dollars shall be stated upon delivery to the carrier, and a
written receipt stating the value shall be issued by the
carrier, who may make a reasonable charge for the
assumption of such liability in excess of one hundred

and fifty dollars and for the carriage of baggage exceeding one hundred and fifty pounds in weight upon a single ticket."

The appellant urges that under its · contract with respondent for the delivery of her trunk it was a carrier of "baggage" within the meaning of said section; that inasmuch as the first clause enlarges the responsibility of a carrier of baggage, the second clause providing that "the value in excess of one hundred and fifty dollars shall be stated upon delivery to the carrier," is in the nature of a condition precedent to be performed by the passenger before he can get the benefit of the enlarged liability prescribed by the first clause, and that, therefore, the burden rests upon him to disclose the value of his baggage in excess of the sum stated rather than upon the carrier to ascertain such value by inquiry; that inasmuch as the respondent did not disclose the value of her trunk in excess of $150 she cannot recover for such value beyond said sum. Of course the appellant, in order to secure the reversal of the judgment appealed from, must maintain both claims in regard to this section — that it applies to this case, and that the interpretation outlined is correct. Without discussing the last one I do not think that it can succeed on the first one.

Assuming for the purposes of this appeal that respondent's contract to deliver appellant's trunk, although entered into in the state of New Jersey, is to be governed by the laws of New York state because there to be performed, I do not believe that it was covered or controlled by the section which is relied on. That section relates to property "carried as baggage." Its language as a whole has a well-established meaning. Baggage has been defined in the dictionary as "trunks * * * etc., which a traveler carries with him on a journey," and a great volume of decisions and text law has fixed the status of baggage or articles "carried as baggage" as that of property which is transported under or as an incident to the contract of transportation of the owner as a passenger. Under the principles which have been thus abundantly established we do not define as "baggage" in a proper sense property which is being moved by express or otherwise apart from and disconnected with the transportation of the person who owns the same, even though it be a trunk. The origin and purpose of the section in question almost conclusively indicates that its application is to property carried in connection with the owner. The earlier rule of liability had been built up that the carrier generally speaking was only liable for such property, as baggage, as was appropriate to the journey being taken by its owner, indicating clearly an essential relation of baggage to the transportation of the the person who owned it. The section now before us did not in the least impair this fundamental idea. It did not change the conditions under which property might become baggage, but, in full recognition of them, simply enlarged conditionally the limitations upon the value and kind of property which might be brought within this classification.

Thus it seems very clear that the terms of this statute take into account the conditions under which property is carried quite as much as the primary character of the property and that these conditions must establish a certain transportation relationship between it and its owner to make it baggage.

If this interpretation is correct it is equally clear that the provisions do not apply to this case. Appellant did not undertake to transport respondent and incidentally her trunk. Its contract for the delivery of the latter did not take effect until that for the transportation of the owner even on the railroad had come to an end. It related exclusively to the movement of property presumably in consideration of a sum paid solely and specifically for that purpose. In this case it related to the carriage of a trunk from the railroad station to some other point, but so far as this question is concerned it might as well have related to the carriage of a box between two houses, and there is entirely wanting that character and those conditions of transportation which enter as essential elements into the definition of baggage and of property carried as such.

I think that a further sentence in the section emphasizes the idea that it applies only to property which is being carried under the circumstances and in the relationship to a passenger which I have indicated. This sentence provides that the carrier "may make a reasonable charge for the assumption of such (increased) liability in excess of one hundred and fifty dollars and for the carriage of baggage exceeding one hundred and fifty pounds in weight upon a single ticket." While appellant's counsel has sought to escape from it I think the fair interpretation of this sentence indicates that it relates to property being carried as baggage on the ticket of a passenger.

By way of general argument it is said that the interpretation which we are giving is in opposition to certain other provisions of the statute. Our attention is called in turn to section 25 (L. 1907, ch. 429), which says: "The provisions of this article shall apply to the transportation of passengers, freight or property, from one point to another within the state of New York, and to any common carrier performing such service;" and to section 2 of the same chapter, which provides: "The term 'common carrier,' when used in this act, includes all railroad corporations, * * * express companies, * * * and all persons and associations of persons * * * operating such agencies for public use in the conveyance of persons or property within this state;" and to the sentence in the section in question, "Every common carrier and railroad corporation shall be liable for loss, damage and injury to property," etc.

Undoubtedly the various provisions of the act are to be

applied generally where it is justifiable so to do, and I assume that the appellant comes within the definition of a "common carrier," and is not to be deprived of any benefits which may go with that occupation.   But the section in question is applicable only to common carriers when engaged in certain transactions, namely, in transportation of property "carried as baggage," and if I am right the appellant was not engaged in that kind of a transaction and, therefore, is not entitled to the benefit of the section.

In accordance with these views I think the judgment appealed from must be affirmed, with costs.

CULLEN, Ch. J., GRAY, VANN, WERNER, WILLARD BARTLETT and CHASE, JJ., concur.

Judgment affirmed.

THE PEOPLE OF THE STATE OF NEW YORK, Respondent, *v.* FRANK SCHERMERHORN, Appellant.

Murder — sufficiency of indictment in common-law form — evidence examined, and held that case was properly submitted to jury to determine if murder was committed while defendant was engaged in commission of felonies of rape and burglary — confessions — possession of stolen property as evidence that defendant committed burglary.

1. An indictment in the common-law form is sufficient to sustain a conviction of murder in the first degree, even though there is no evidence of premeditation and deliberation, where the proof clearly brings the case within the statutory definition that a homicide committed by a person while engaged in the commission of a felony constitutes the crime of murder in the first degree.

2. On examination of the evidence against defendant who was convicted of murder in the first degree, *held*, that the case was properly submitted to the jury to find whether it was committed while the perpetrator was engaged in the commission of the two distinct felonies of rape and burglary, since the evidence connects him with both, and discloses facts which tend to unite the two felonies as parts of one general scheme and to identify the defendant as its author and perpetrator.

3. Several separate statements in the nature of confessions were made by defendant. The question whether the last of these confessions was made under the influence of fear and hope of leniency was submitted to the jury on conflicting evidence; and the verdict necessarily implies that the confessions were fairly obtained. *Held,* that the facts disclosed by the record show that the confessions were properly admitted in evidence.

4. The district attorney was clearly within his rights in arguing to the jury that the defendant's unexplained possession of the stolen property was evidence which should be considered upon the question whether the defendant committed the burglary, and in the commission thereof perpetrated the murder.

(Submitted June 14, 1911; decided October 3, 1911.)

APPEAL from a judgment of the Supreme Court, rendered June 22, 1910, at a Trial Term for the county of Dutchess, upon a verdict convicting the defendant of the crime of murder in the first degree.

The facts, so far as material, are stated in the opinion.

George Wood and *John F. Ringwood* for appellant. The alleged confession of defendant was obtained under threats and through promises of immunity and should have been excluded. (*People* v. *McMahon*, 15 N. Y. 384; *People* v. *Mondon*, 103 N. Y. 211; *People* v. *Kennedy*, 159 N. Y. 355; *People* v. *O'Brien*, 48 Barb. 274.) The reference made by the district attorney to the failure of the defendant to take the stand in his own behalf was clearly wrong, unfair, and against the letter and spirit of section 393 of the Code of Criminal Procedure and clearly against the established practice and constituted reversible error. (*People* v. *McMahon*, 15 N. Y. 384; *People* v. *O'Brien*, 48 Barb. 274; *People* v. *Kennedy*, 159 N. Y. 355; *People* v. *Mondon*, 103 N. Y. 211.)

John E. Mack, District Attorney (*Edward A. Conger* and *William A. Mulrey* of counsel), for respondent. The confessions were properly admitted in evidence.

(*People* v. *Rogers,* 192 N. Y. 331; *People* v. *Brasch,* 193 N. Y. 46.) The comments of the district attorney in summing up were proper. (*People* v. *Jackson,* 182 N. Y. 66; *Knickerbocker* v. *People,* 43 N. Y. 177.)

WERNER, J. The homicide for the commission of which the defendant has been convicted was one of peculiar atrocity. The victim had been a nurse in the family of the Comptons, who lived at Milbrook, near Poughkeepsie. She was found dead in her bed on the night of January 13, 1910, under circumstances which indicated that she had been strangled. The autopsy which was performed upon her body confirmed these indications and also revealed the fact that she had been car-- nally outraged. Other circumstances pointed to a burglary and larceny in the Compton residence, and still other incidents tended to identify the defendant as the perpetrator of all of these crimes. The defendant was arrested and later indicted under a presentment in the common-law form. His trial and conviction followed in June, 1910. The evidence against him was largely circumstantial, but was strongly supplemented by the defendant's confessions which, if accepted as true, leave not a shadow of a doubt as to the defendant's guilt. Upon this appeal the defendant asserts that these confessions, received in evidence against him at the trial, were wrung from him under circumstances which rendered them inadmissible, and that without them the evidence is not strong enough to support the conviction; that, although the indictment against him was in the common-law form, there was no evidence tending to show that the homicide was committed with premeditation and deliberation, and that the case was not submitted to the jury upon that theory; that it was error to submit the case as one of murder in the first degree upon the assumption that it was committed while the perpetrator was engaged in the commission of the two distinct felonies of rape and

burglary, because there was no evidence to connect the
burglary with the murder. These contentions are obviously important, for if they are well founded it must
logically follow that the defendant's conviction cannot be
upheld. It becomes our duty, therefore, to examine with
critical minuteness the circumstances surrounding the
homicide.

At the time of the homicide the Compton family consisted of the husband and his wife and a child about four
years of age. They employed a number of servants,
among whom were the defendant, who served as coachman, the deceased, who was nurse to the child, Ohashi, a
Japanese butler, and two maids named Alice Dutcher and
Mary Farrell. The defendant, a married man, lived in the
coachman's house, which was something more than six
hundred feet westerly of the Compton residence and on the
opposite side of the highway. His wife had for some time
been absent at a hospital for treatment, and he was temporarily the sole occupant of this dwelling. The deceased
and the Compton child slept in an open-air apartment or
porch at the westerly end of the Compton residence, and
the other servants, Ohashi, Dutcher and Farrell, occupied rooms on the same floor but at the easterly end of
the house, so that there was an intervening distance of
about forty feet between the two places. On the night
of January 12, 1910, Mr. Compton and his wife were
in the city of New York. In the early evening the
defendant took the maids, Alice and Mary, out for a
drive and returned at about nine-thirty. The two maids
entered the house, had some refreshments with the
deceased and then retired. Ohashi, the butler, was then
in his room. At about half-past three o'clock the next
morning the maid Alice was awakened by sounds indicating that some one was trying to gain entrance to her
room, and in the same instant the maid Mary screamed
and said she had been awakened by a flash of light which
caused her to bound out of bed into the middle of the

room, where she found herself quite close to a man, who at once ran out of her door and down the stairs to the kitchen. The screams of the two maids, Alice and Mary, brought Ohashi, the butler, from his room across the hall, and together the three went downstairs. There they discovered that the silver chest had been rifled, and that Mrs. Compton's room was in such disorder as to indicate that a burglary had been committed. The maid Alice then called the defendant on a telephone connected with the stable, and from thence with the coachman's house by means of an electric bell, which the defendant had been instructed to answer directly in person whenever it rang at night or at any unusual hour. Contrary to these instructions the defendant, instead of answering the bell directly, first answered the telephone, which could only be done from the stable, and then made his appearance at the Compton house. As he came in each of the other servants, Ohashi, Alice and Mary, noticed that his face was blackened over the eyebrows, under the eyes, on each side of the nose and across the lips. He explained to Alice that he had been putting coal on the fire and must have daubed some of the soot on his face. His next remark was, "we must go up and see if Miss Polly (the child) is safe; that is what we are here for." Together the·four servants, Ohashi, Mary, Alice and the defendant, went upstairs. The defendant went directly to the bed where the body of the deceased lay and shouted: "This girl is dead, Alice, this girl is dead." Meanwhile Alice had looked into Polly's cot and 'at first thought she was gone, but the defendant raised the bedclothing and disclosed her sleeping safe and sound. Efforts were made to resuscitate the deceased with ammonia and whisky, and when these failed Alice directed the defendant to telephone for Dr. McKenzie. He called Dr. Knott, a veterinary, and when Alice remonstrated with him he told her to go to hell. The prosecution refers to this circumstance as indicating that the defendant was so confused that he did not know the difference between Dr. Knott, the veterinary, and Dr. McKenzie, the physician, but this point is greatly weakened, if not destroyed, by the testimony of the maid Mary, who said she suggested telephoning Dr. Knott as well as Dr. McKenzie, for they wanted Mrs. Knott more than her husband. Having finished telephoning, the defendant said something about going back to his house as he was not dressed and wanted to wash the black from his face. Alice begged him to remain and told him to wash in Mrs. Compton's room. Meanwhile Alice procured a pair of trousers, which she offered to the defendant, but he declined them with the remark that he had trousers on. At twenty minutes past four o'clock in the morning Dr. McKenzie arrived. He at once made such observations as would naturally suggest themselves to the experienced physician. He found the body of the deceased in the bed slightly turned to the right side. The face was dark, discolored, distorted and swollen; the eyes somewhat protruding and partially open, and the tongue swollen. There were bruises on the neck which might have been made by the grip of a human hand. Dr. McKenzie noticed dark, black dirt on her breast and some on her underwear. There were marks on both wrists as if a cord had been wound twice around the wrists, and subsequently the strings, belonging to the pajamas worn by the deceased, were found beneath the bed; and there was testimony to the effect that the marks on the wrists might have been produced by these strings. Later in the day an autopsy was performed by Doctors Jacobus and McKenzie under the direction of Dr. Andrews, one of the coroners of Dutchess county. These three doctors were all agreed that the death of the deceased was due to asphyxiation from strangulation. The earlier observations made by Dr. McKenzie were supplemented by others indicating that the deceased had been the victim of a carnal assault. Black sooty spots, of the same character as those noticed on the breast of deceased, were found at the

1911.] Opinion, per WERNER, J. [203 N. Y.]

crotch of the underclothing worn by her. There were abrasions and black dirt on the vulva. In the vagina there was a fluid which was withdrawn with a syringe and subjected to a microscopical examination. It was found to be human semen. There were also injuries to the lower limbs. Without going further into these nauseating physical details, it suffices to say that the facts disclosed by the autopsy and the trial warranted the conclusion that the deceased came to her death by strangulation at the hands of a man who was at the time engaged in the commission of a criminal assault upon her person. The next step in the logical development of this gruesome story will be to ascertain in what manner the defendant is connected with this foul deed.

The defendant was a young man twenty-two years of age. His wife had for some time been absent from home. On the evening preceding the homicide he had been out driving with the maids, Alice and Mary, and had been drinking at least enough to thoroughly fire his blood. There was evidence to the effect that in November he stated to a man engaged in clipping a pony for Mr. Compton that the deceased was a nice girl, and he would have sexual intercourse with her if he had to do it when the Comptons were in New York; that, about a week before the tragedy he had made a remark to a man employed on the place, indicating that he had lascivious designs on the person of the deceased; that a day or two later he made a similar statement to another in language too vulgar to print; and on the day of the homicide he confided his lust to still another employee. Upon the body and clothing of the deceased were found black spots apparently of the same color and substance as the marks upon his face. When he returned from the drive with Alice and Mary he asked the former what she was going to give him for the ride. When he, with Ohashi, Alice and Mary, went upon the sleeping porch, he at once exclaimed: "This girl is dead, Alice, this girl is dead," although he had done no more than to place his hand upon her person. After the arrival of Dr. McKenzie Alice and the defendant again went up to the place where the deceased lay, and the defendant then said the husband of the deceased must have done the deed. He was the only one of the Compton servants who manifested any interest or anxiety as to the movements of the officers. This is indicated by his going out to meet them on the road, and suggesting that they could not get through with their automobile, and again in his inquiries of other servants or employees designed to elicit information as to the suspicions expressed by the officers. He was the person who suggested that Ohashi had gone westerly, in the direction of the ice house, at an hour when Ohashi must have been in the Compton house; and the ice house is the place where the Compton revolver was found by Duncan on the morning of January 13th. These were the circumstances which the jury might have found to have been established by the testimony, and we think that, standing alone, they would have justified the conclusion beyond a reasonable doubt that the rape and the murder were the work of the defendant.

But we must go farther. The case was submitted to the jury upon the theory that the homicide was committed by the defendant while engaged in the commission of the two distinct felonies of rape and burglary, and it is important to determine whether the evidence connects him with both. As regards the burglary, the evidence leads us through a sequence of circumstances quite as incriminating against the defendant and no less convincing to the impartial mind. There is in this branch of the case, moreover, a disclosure of facts which tend to unite the two distinct felonies of rape and burglary as parts of one general criminal scheme, and to identify the defendant as its author and perpetrator.

Early on the morning of the homicide the chief of police of the city of Poughkeepsie, with an under sheriff and several assistants, went to the Compton residence. They made the journey in an automobile which became stalled in the deep snow about a quarter of a mile from the Compton residence. They were met by the defendant who told them that they could not get through. Despite this information, the officers proceeded on their way, accompanied by the defendant. After arriving at the house the servants were interviewed, the defendant with the others, and thus the day wore on into the afternoon. During the afternoon the defendant asked Maroney, one of the Compton employees, who it was whom the officers suspected, and Maroney replied that he did not know. Soon after this McCabe, the chief of police, went over to the defendant's house in the pursuit of his investigations. Entering the house and exploring two or three rooms he called, "Frank," and received no answer. Just then McCabe heard a sound, as of something dripping on the floor, and he went into a bedroom, drew a curtain and saw a bloody razor on the bed and a pool of blood on the floor. He looked under the bed and there he saw the defendant with his throat cut. McCabe directed him to come out and as he did so he said, "I didn't do it, chief, I don't want to go to jail, but I didn't kill Sarah." A doctor was sent for and the defendant was taken to the Vassar Hospital where he recovered. After the defendant had been sent to the hospital, McCabe searched the defendant's house. Lying upon a bureau there was a note in the handwriting of the defendant and evidently intended for his wife. It read, "Oh, sweetheart, I am not guilty of this crime, believe me. Your loving husband but no more. Frank." In the cellar, in the bottom of a barrel partially filled with potatoes, he found a silk dress, a silk corset and some stockings. These were later identified as belonging to Mrs. Compton. Meanwhile the silverware and some other articles which had been stolen from the Compton house were still missing. On Sunday, January 16th, there

5

was a further search of the coachman's house by Chief of
Police McCabe and Under Sheriff Hornbeck, assisted by a
number of others.   On the second floor it was seen that a
metal collar, which had covered the stovepipe hole in
the chimney, had been removed and had been partially
replaced.   A man named Burch thrust his arm into this
hole and down the flue but felt nothing.   He then took a
stick and reached farther down the flue, this time producing sounds which indicated that the silverware was in
the chimney.   Another man went to a lower opening in
the chimney and there was the Compton family silver to
the number of more than a hundred pieces.   This silver
bore marks of having been subjected to great heat, and
the soot by which it was more or less discolored tended to
explain the place and the manner in which the defendant
had covered his face and hands with a black substance.
A further search revealed, in the parlor stove of the coachman's house, the charred or partially consumed remains
of various articles of wearing apparel which had belonged
to Mrs. Compton.   In these circumstances there is evidence which points very directly to the defendant as the
perpetrator of the burglary.

The purpose of the burglary and theft is not so
obvious.   Neither can the exact sequence of the events
of that night be demonstrated.   It is evident, of course,
that if the defendant committed either the rape or the
burglary it must have been done before the servants,
Ohashi, Alice and Mary, were aroused from their sleep;
and it is practically certain that the man who committed
either of these crimes was also guilty of the others.   It
is quite within the bounds of reasonable probability that
the defendant, intent upon the crime of rape, first committed the burglary and afterwards the murder for the
purpose of diverting suspicion from himself.   This theory,
and every other that may be suggested by the circumstances, excludes the possibility of so segregating the
burglary from the other events of this tragedy as to

render it a distinct and separate crime which had no relation to the homicide. The burglary was no less a part of the offense than the rape, and it was not error to charge that if the homicide was perpetrated by the defendant while engaged in the commission of either of these felonies, it was murder in the first degree. The language of the statute defining murder in the first degree includes in that category a homicide committed without a design to effect death by a person engaged in the commission of, or in an attempt to commit, a felony, and it would be absurd to hold that it applies to a person engaged in the commision of a single felony, but not to one who is engaged in the commission of two or more felonies.

We now turn to the confessions of the defendant. That they were made is not disputed, but it is said that they were extorted from him under circumstances which render them inadmissible as evidence. The defendant made his first statement at the hospital on January 14th, the day succeeding the homicide. There is no pretense that it was not made voluntarily. Neither is it now claimed that it was true, and it is in fact at variance with his later statements. It is to the effect that he had been out with Alice and Mary and had been drinking quite freely; that after they returned and he had taken care of his horse he went to his house and retired; that at about one o'clock in the morning he heard Polly cry; that he lay down again until she cried a second time, when he arose and walked carefully to the west side of the Compton house; that as he stood there he heard a conversation between Ohashi, the butler, and Sarah, the deceased; that Ohashi said, "You know, Sarah," and then he heard Sarah gurgle, and a little later he heard Polly again; that he also saw Ohashi flash a light across Mary's bed and saw him with a light coat on; that in a few minutes Ohashi came out of the south end of the house with a bundle under his arm and walked down to Samuel Thorne's place; that he, the defendant, then went back to his own house, where he remained in bed until he was called by telephone at about three o'clock in the morning; that he answered the call and went quickly to the Compton house, where he was met by Ohashi, Alice and Mary, who told him there were burglars in the house; that they' searched the house and could not find anybody, and so he, the defendant, suggested that they go upstairs to see about Sarah; that they went up and found her dead; that he then went to the sink and washed his face, which had become blackened, as he thought, when he was putting coal in the stove. This statement was signed by the defendant in the presence of witnesses, and apparently without any solicitation or coercion. It cannot be seriously contended that the officers were over-zealous in trying to get a further statement from the defendant. The one just referred to was so manifestly incredible that the officers would have laid themselves open to the charge of stupidity or inefficiency if they had halted there. The story that the defendant had heard the deceased gurgle and had seen the butler emerging from the house with a bundle in the stillness of the night, without so much as a suggestion that the defendant had concerned himself about this unusual proceeding, is too fantastic for belief, and his failure to mention the matter when Sarah was found dead plainly stamps the tale as a clumsy fabrication. The defendant's second statement was made to Under Sheriff Hornbeck at the hospital on the next day, January 15th, and is substantially the same as the first one made to McCabe, although it goes into greater detail in suggestive insinuations that Ohashi was the murderer.

The defendant's third statement was made at the hospital on Sunday, January 16th, after McCabe, the chief of police, had been at the Compton house, and the hidden silverware had been discovered. If anything beyond its inherent improbability had been needed to refute defendant's first story, the discovery of these chattels clearly demanded further investigation. With that in view McCabe went to the defendant, told him of having found the silver, and taxed him with having been untruthful. Thereupon, according to McCabe, the defendant said, " Now I will tell you the truth." The statement which he then made and signed is, in substance, as follows: That on the night of the sleigh ride after the defendant returned, Ohashi came up to the stable and said, " Frank, you help me and I will help you. I want you to come down at midnight to the house; " that Ohashi then gave the defendant a drink of whisky; that at midnight the defendant went to the Compton house and Ohashi brought him out a bundle of dresses and silverware; that the defendant took the articles to his house where he burned them in the parlor stove and then he tried to burn the silverware but without success and so he dropped it into the chimney flue where it was found; that Ohashi wanted to give him some money which he refused to take. At this point in the progress of the defendant's third statement, the chief of police said to him, " Now I don't think you are telling the truth yet," and the defendant replied, " I won't tell you any more, chief, but when my mother comes here, and I see my mother, you come back here and I will tell you the whole truth." Here again is a statement in which the defendant refers to some clearly established facts, such as the burning of the dresses, the attempts to burn the silver, and the place in which it was hidden, but his story as to the manner in which they came into his possession was such a transparent invention as to emphasize his practical admission that he had not yet told the whole truth.

In the defendant's fourth and final statement he at last admitted the commission of the murder, although disclaiming any intention to kill the deceased, and this is the only statement which is said to have been improperly obtained from him. We have referred at some length to the defendant's prior statements, partly to disclose the contradictions which they contained, but more for the purpose of showing how natural and proper it was for the officers to work for still further statements under such conditions. This last confession, which is printed in full in the record, is to the effect that the defendant killed the deceased but that he did it only for a scare and not for murder; that he had been drinking while out driving with the maids, and had another big drink of whisky from Ohashi when he returned; that he had a very faint recollection of getting home; that when he had taken care of the horse, he changed his clothes and went over to the kitchen in the Compton house; that he went upstairs and into the nursery or open-air sleeping porch; that he remembered something about Sarah but he was just crazy drunk and did not know what he was doing; that he faintly remembered being on the porch where Sarah and Polly were asleep, and that he intended to scare Sarah; that he did the deed; that no one else had any thing to do with this crime, and that nothing was locked when he entered the house.

As bearing upon the manner in which this last confession was obtained, the defendant's mother and sister testified that the former had been sent for by Under Sheriff Hornbeck, who told her that the only thing that would save the defendant from the electric chair would be for him to make a confession; that under the influence of the fear and the hope of leniency produced by this statement, she pleaded with her son to confess that he had committed the murder; that for some time he was obdurate and continued to repeat his denials, but he finally yielded to her tearful entreaties and thus made the confession. Hornbeck was very positive and explicit in his denial that he had made any such statement to the defendant's mother and insisted that the confession was voluntary. The issue of fact raised by this conflict of testimony was fairly and fully submitted to the jury, and the verdict necessarily implies that the jury accepted the testimony of Hornbeck as true. Our first reading of the record left upon our minds the impression that the police officers had united in a systematic and persistent attempt to wring a confession from the defendant. The number and variety of defendant's confessions, supplemented by the able argument of his counsel, were well calculated to raise the suspicion that the defendant had been subjected to what, in criminal parlance, is known as the third degree; but the facts as disclosed by the record, when carefully studied, absolve the police officers from any such imputation.

A short and compact *resumé* of the facts and circumstances will be helpful in determining the question whether the evidence was sufficient to warrant the verdict of the jury. The defendant had expressed lecherous designs upon the person of the deceased. He had been drinking on the night of January 12th, and his wife had been absent from home for some weeks. The deceased was found strangled to death under circumstances which leave no doubt that she was killed by the man who raped her. Her body and her clothing bore marks which can be explained only upon the theory that a part of the soot upon the defendant's face and hands had been transferred to her body by personal contact. A burglary had been committed in the Compton house and the property stolen was found hidden in the defendant's house, charred, partially consumed by fire, and covered with soot. The defendant made statements which, at first, were intended to throw suspicion upon Ohashi, but finally admitted the commission of the murder by the defendant. The question whether these statements were voluntarily made was fairly submitted to the jury and the verdict implies that these confessions were regarded as freely made. Upon this record there is no escape from the conclusion that the cause of the death of Sarah Brymer was conclusively established as an independent fact, and that the defendant's guilt of the homicide, committed while engaged in the two felonies of rape and burglary, was proven beyond a reasonable doubt.

The confessions were properly admitted in evidence (*People* v. *Rogers*, 192 N. Y. 331; *People* v. *Brasch*, 193 N. Y. 46), and the indictment in the common-law form was sufficient to sustain a conviction of murder in the first degree, even though there was no evidence of premeditation and deliberation, for the proof clearly brought the case within the statutory definition that a homicide committed by a person while engaged in the commission of a felony constitutes the crime of murder in the first degree. (*People* v. *Giblin*, 115 N. Y. 196; *People* v. *Meyer*, 162 N. Y. 357, 370; *People* v. *Sullivan*, 173 N. Y. 122.) The exceptions taken by defendant's counsel to the remarks made by the district attorney in the course of his summary were not well taken. The district attorney made it perfectly plain that the defendant was not to be prejudiced by his failure to testify, and he was clearly within his rights in arguing to the jury that the defendant's unexplained possession of the stolen property was evidence which should be considered upon the question whether the defendant committed the burglary, and in the commission thereof perpetrated the murder.

We have carefully examined this record with a constant appreciation of the responsibility which comes with the power to order a new trial in any capital case when justice requires it, even when no exceptions have been taken, but we can find nothing which would justify a reversal and the judgment of conviction must, therefore, be affirmed.

CULLEN, Ch. J., GRAY, VANN, WILLARD BARTLETT, HISCOCK and CHASE, JJ., concur.

Judgment of conviction affirmed.

THE PEOPLE OF THE STATE OF NEW YORK, Respondent, *v.*
ALBERT BRIGHT, Appellant.

**Gambling — a person who takes part in a game, or games, of
poker for amusement is not a "common gambler" within the
meaning of the statute (Penal Law, § 970) — when person playing
poker is not an accomplice of dealer or gamekeeper with whom
he was playing.**

1. A person who merely takes part in a game or series of games of
poker on precisely the same terms as the other participants in the
game, for mere amusement or recreation and not as a professional
gamester, does not thereby become a common gambler under our
statute.

2. Defendant was indicted for and convicted of being a common
gambler under section 970 of the Penal Law. He was convicted
on the testimony of a single witness who participated with him in a
game of draw poker. The defendant was indicted not for engaging as a player in a game of poker but for engaging therein as a
dealer and gamekeeper. *Held,* that the witness was not an accomplice in the sense of being a gamekeeper within the meaning of the
statute requiring the testimony of an accomplice to be corroborated
(Code Crim. Pro. § 399); hence, the evidence was sufficient to warrant the conviction and the court was not called upon to charge
that "if the jury find that the People's witness was an accomplice
their verdict must be a verdict of acquittal."

People v. *Bright,* 140 App. Div. 945, affirmed.

(Argued June 14, 1911; decided October 3, 1911.)

APPEAL from a judgment of the Appellate Division of
the Supreme Court in the third judicial department,
entered December 7, 1910, unanimously affirming a judgment of the Albany County Court rendered upon a verdict
convicting the defendant of the crime of being a common
gambler.

The facts, so far as material, are stated in the opinion.

John H. Gleason for appellant. The prosecuting witness, Brown, was an accomplice, and the trial judge
committed reversible error in ruling to the contrary.

(1 Abb. Law Dict. 10; Penal Law, art. 1, § 2; Foster Crim. Cases, 341; 1 Russell on Crimes, 21; 4 Black. Comm. 331; 1 Phillips on Ev. 28; *State* v. *Light,* 17 Oreg. 358; *Davidson* v. *State,* 33 Ala. 350; *English* v. *State,* 35 Ala. 428; *Bird* v. *State,* 36 Ala. 279; *State* v. *Quarles,* 13 Ark. 307; *People* v. *McGuire,* 135 N. Y. 639; *People* v. *Dunn,* 53 Hun, 381; *People* v. *McGonegal,* 136 N. Y. 62.) The trial judge committed reversible error in withholding from the jury the question of the sufficiency of the evidence relied upon by the prosecution to corroborate the accomplice. (*People* v. *Mayhew,* 150 N. Y. 346; *People* v. *Elliott,* 106 N. Y. 292; *People* v. *Everhardt,* 104 N. Y. 591; *People* v. *O'Farrell,* 175 N. Y. 323; *People* v. *Patrick,* 182 N. Y. 157.)

Rollin B. Sanford for respondent. The witness Brown was not an accomplice. (*People* v. *Stedeker,* 175 N. Y. 57; *People ex rel. Lichtenstein* v. *Langan,* 196 N. Y. 266; *People* v. *Vedder,* 98 N. Y. 630; *People* v. *Zucker,* 20 App. Div. 363; 154 N. Y. 770; *People* v. *Smith,* 1 N. Y. Cr. Rep. 72; *People* v. *Winant,* 25 Misc. Rep. 361; *People* v. *Cook,* 5 Park. Cr. Rep. 351.)

WILLARD BARTLETT, J.   Section 970 of the Penal Law provides that a person "who engages as dealer, game-keeper, or player in any gambling or banking game, where money or property is dependent upon the result" is a common gambler and punishable by imprisonment for not more than two years or by a fine not exceeding one thousand dollars or both.

The indictment charged that Albert Bright, on the 2d day of March, 1910, at the city of Albany, was a common gambler, and in a certain room in a certain building, known as No. 426 Broadway, unlawfully and feloniously did engage as dealer and gamekeeper in a certain gambling game where money was dependent upon the result, to wit, a certain gambling game commonly called draw poker, consisting of certain gambling tables, cards, chips, devices and apparatus for gambling, a more particular description of which was to the grand jury unknown and could not then be given.

Upon the issue joined by his plea of not guilty, the defendant went to trial and was convicted, and the judgment upon the conviction has been unanimously affirmed by the Appellate Division. Under the Constitution the unanimous affirmance requires us to assume that the proof sufficed to establish every element of the crime charged in the indictment.

Only one witness was called in behalf of the People. He testified to having participated with the defendant in playing a game of draw poker for money on the 2d day of March, 1910, at No. 426 Broadway in the city of Albany. When the People rested, and also at the close of the defendant's case, counsel for the defendant moved for a dismissal of the indictment on the ground, among others, that the jury could not be permitted to convict upon the testimony of an accomplice alone. (Code Crim. Proc. § 399.) The motion was denied in each instance and the defendant duly excepted. These exceptions do not survive the unanimous affirmance. There is one exception in the record, however, which suffices to raise the question whether the sole witness against the defendant was an accomplice. This is an exception to the refusal of the learned county judge to charge "that if the jury find that the People's witness was an accomplice their verdict must be a verdict of acquittal." There is no suggestion that this witness was in any manner corroborated, and if there was any evidence from which the jury could have found that he was an accomplice the defendant was entitled to have this instruction given.

"A conviction cannot be had upon the testimony of an accomplice, unless he be corroborated by such other evidence as tends to connect the defendant with the commission of the crime." (Code Crim. Proc. § 399.)

The statute under which the defendant was indicted condemns as a common gambler any person "who engages as dealer, game-keeper or player in any gambling or banking game where money or property is dependent upon the result." The indictment is directed against the defendant not for engaging as player in a game of draw poker, but for engaging therein as dealer and game-keeper. The evidence indicates that it was not merely as a player that he participated. The game was played with colored chips, each chip representing a certain sum of money determined by the color. These chips or checks were "edged up" by the players toward the center of the table, and then "before the hand was opened," sometimes the defendant and sometimes another party took off one or two checks and placed them in front of him in a separate pile from the checks he was playing with. The inference sought to be drawn from this evidence was that the defendant thus reserved to himself a percentage over and above any of his winnings as a player, upon the amount at stake in each game where he so withdrew one or two chips. This action on the defendant's part distinguished his conduct from that of the People's witness and all the other players except the other party, who is described as having likewise withdrawn checks "at the time the pot was made up," to quote the language of the witness. The jury was justified in finding that such a proceeding brought the defendant within the purview of the statute as one who was thus engaging as gamekeeper in a gambling game, provided the sole witness whose uncorroborated testimony was relied on to establish the charge was not an accomplice.

It is plain that he was not an accomplice in the sense of being also a gamekeeper within the meaning of the statute. According to the evidence the only such gamekeepers present were the defendant and the other party who has been mentioned. Each participant in every game of poker that was played, however, on the occasion in question, acted as dealer when it became his turn to deal. The charge in the indictment is that the defendant "did engage as *dealer* and gamekeeper" therein; and, hence, it is argued that the defendant and the People's sole witness must be deemed to have been accomplices as dealers in a gambling game, whatever view may be entertained of the case in any other aspect.

It is to be observed that there were no particular persons who can be said to have been engaged as dealers in these games of poker as distinguished from the players in general, each of whom acted as dealer in turn.

The entire phraseology of the statute must be considered in order to ascertain its purview and determine what degree of participation in the games which it denounces is necessary to constitute a player an accomplice. It reads as follows:

"§ 970. Common gambler. A person who is the owner, agent, or superintendent of a place, or of any device, or apparatus, for gambling; or who hires, or allows to be used a room, table, establishment or apparatus for such a purpose; or who engages as dealer, game-keeper, or player in any gambling or banking game, where money or property is dependent upon the result; or who sells or offers to sell what are commonly called lottery policies, or any writing, paper, or document in the nature of a bet, wager, or insurance upon the drawing or drawn numbers of any public or private lottery; or who indorses or uses a book, or other document, for the purpose of enabling others to sell, or offer to sell, lottery policies, or other such writings, papers, or documents, is a common gambler, and punishable by imprisonment for not more than two years, or by a fine not exceeding one thousand dollars, or both."

This section of the Penal Law is a re-enactment of section 344 of the Penal Code. In *Lyman* v. *Shenandoah Social Club* (39 App. Div. 462) Mr. Justice BARRETT pointed out that that section did not by any means prohibit every indulgence in gambling. In *People* v. *Stede-*

ker (175 N. Y. 57, 62) this court said: "There has always been observed a distinction between betting or gambling and maintaining a gambling house or a place to which people resorted to gamble. While at common law wagers on indifferent subjects were legal and might be enforced, a gambling house or a resort for gamblers was a public nuisance for which its keeper might be indicted. (Wharton Crim. Law, sec. 2446.) The same distinction has obtained in this state where ordinary betting has never been made a crime, though in some cases subject to small pecuniary mulcts, while the keeping of a gambling house, selling lottery tickets and the profession of a common gambler have been subjected to severe punishment." (See, also, *People ex rel. Lichtenstein* v. *Langan*, 196 N. Y. 260.)

The context makes it unreasonable to suppose that the legislature in enacting the clause under which this indictment was found intended to include every game in which money is at stake in the phrase "gambling or banking game," or that every occasional participant in a money hazard at cards, who deals in turn, was designed to be comprehended in the term "common gambler." The phrase "who engages" is significant. It means something more than occasional participation. It imports some continuity of practice, just as the epithet "common" implies that a common gambler is a person who customarily or habitually or frequently carries on the gambling practices which are denounced by the statute. The underlying idea is the habitual participation in gaming as a money-making pursuit.

The proof sufficed to establish such participation on the part of the defendant. It warranted the inference that he was conducting a gambling establishment which yielded him a profit on each game played therein. Nothing of the kind was proved in reference to the People's witness. "To constitute an accomplice one must be so connected with a crime that at common law he might himself have been convicted either as the principal or as an accessory before the fact." (*People* v. *Zucker*, 20 App. Div. 363, 365; affd. on opinion below, 154 N. Y. 770.) There is no view of the evidence which would have justified the jury in convicting the witness of the crime of which they found the defendant guilty.

Whatever may eventually be determined to be the extent of the participation in gambling or banking games which is necessary to make a person liable under this provision of the Penal Law for engaging therein *as player*, we are quite clear that a person who merely takes part in a game or series of games of poker on precisely the same terms as the other participants in the game, for mere amusement or recreation and not as a professional gamester, does not thereby become a common gambler under our statute.

This was all that the People's witness appears to have done in the case at bar. It follows that he was not an accomplice of the defendant.

The judgment at the Appellate Division should, therefore, be affirmed.

CULLEN, Ch. J., GRAY, VANN, WERNER, HISCOCK and CHASE, JJ., concur.

Judgment of conviction affirmed.

RICHARD V. MATTISON, JR., Respondent, *v.* AGNES C. MATTISON, Appellant.

Evidence — action for divorce — erroneous admissions of entries in hotel register as evidence against defendant in divorce action — judgment of divorce against alleged paramour not admissible evidence against defendant in action for divorce.

1. Where a witness has refreshed his recollection by reference to an entry or memorandum and testified to the fact therein set forth, such entry is not thereafter properly received in evidence.

2. Entries on a hotel register made by an alleged paramour and conversations between him and a hotel clerk not made or had in defendant's presence are not proper evidence against her.

3. A judgment for divorce against a paramour not a defendant in the action is erroneously received in evidence, although the court states that it was not admitted as against the actual defendant.

4. Entries claimed to be in the handwriting of the alleged paramour upon the register of a hotel other than that where the adultery is claimed to have been committed, were admitted upon the statement of counsel that they were offered as standards of handwriting and as bearing on the question whether the writer may have registered elsewhere under an assumed name. *Held*, error.

Mattison v. *Mattison*, 137 App. Div. 918, reversed.

(Argued June 15, 1911; decided October 8, 1911.)

APPEAL from a final judgment in favor of plaintiff, entered March 31, 1910, and from an order of the Appellate Division of the Supreme Court in the first judicial department, entered March 11, 1910, affirming an interlocutory judgment in favor of plaintiff entered upon a decision of the court on trial at Special Term.

The nature of the action and the facts, so far as material, are stated in the opinion.

Edward Hymes and *Michael Schaap* for appellant. The admission in evidence of an interlocutory and final judgment of divorce against Dr. Wainright, the corespondent in an action in which he had been defendant and of questions as to his acts upon which that divorce was predicated was error. (*Stevens* v. *Stevens*, 54 Hun, 490; *Beadleston* v. *Beadleston*, 20 N. Y. S. R. 21; *Davis* v. *Davis*, 4 Misc. Rep. 454; 150 N. Y. 571; *Goldie* v. *Goldie*, 39 Misc. Rep. 389; *Hulish* v. *Boller*, 72 App. Div. 559; *People* v. *Molineux*, 168 N. Y. 328.) The admission of the entries in the register of the Hotel Minot was error. (*Berkowsky* v. *N. Y. C. Ry. Co.*, 127 App. Div. 544; *People* v. *McLaughlin*, 150 N. Y. 392.)

Edmund L. Mooney for respondent. The rulings of the trial justice on the evidence do not warrant a reversal of the judgment. (*Townsend* v. *Bell*, 167 N. Y. 462; *New York Water Co.* v. *Crow*, 110 App. Div. 32; *Matter of Bernsee*, 141 N. Y. 389; *Post* v. *Brooklyn Heights R. R. Co.*, 195 N. Y. 62; *Forrest* v. *Forrest*, 25 N. Y. 501.) The trial court did not err in admitting a judgment roll in an action of divorce obtained against the corespondent by his wife prior to the commencement of this action, and the questions regarding the acts upon which the divorce was based. (*People* v. *Irving*, 95 N. Y. 541; *People* v. *Dorthy*, 156 N. Y. 237; *Shepard* v. *Parker*, 36 N. Y. 517; *People* v. *Smith*, 37 App. Div. 281; *People* v. *Webster*, 139 N. Y. 73; *People* v. *Gluck*, 117 App. Div. 432; *People* v. *Casey*, 72 N. Y. 393; *Bronner* v. *Frauenthal*, 9 Bosw. 350, 356; 37 N. Y. 166; *Hine* v. *N. Y. El. R. R. Co.*, 149 N. Y. 154; *Hoag* v. *Wright*, 174 N. Y. 36.)

CHASE, J. The plaintiff is a young man, a native of Philadelphia, and the son of wealthy parents. The defendant is the daughter of respectable and refined parents who lived in London and in Glasgow. In 1904 the plaintiff was traveling abroad. In that year the defendant, then being an orphan, lived temporarily with her two sisters in London and was filling an engagement on the English stage. The parties met in October and soon became engaged to be married. They were married in the Church of St. Clement Danes, in London, on November 26, 1904, without the presence or knowledge of the relatives of either. It was a hasty marriage. Like the outcome of many another such a marriage it has proven most unfortunate for both. The plaintiff stated to the defendant in substance that if his father knew of the marriage he would disinherit him and that it must be kept a secret until he had an opportunity to return to his parents to get their consent and approval and then they would have another church wedding. Three days after the marriage he left London for his home and reported to his parents that he had become engaged to a girl in London. The history of the parties from the date of the marriage until August 5, 1905, is in part, at least, discreditable to both, although it is not claimed that either violated their marriage vows so far as chastity is concerned. In 1905 the defendant came to New York, arriving here May 21, to see her husband. Thereafter the plaintiff's parents were, for the time being, reconciled to the plaintiff's marrying the defendant, and arrangements were made for the marriage of the parties at the summer home of the plaintiff's parents at Newport, R. I., on a day named, and the proposed marriage was formally announced. Circumstances occurred that brought about an entire change of purpose at least on the part of the plaintiff's parents, and on August 5, 1905, the plaintiff came with his wife to New York city and took rooms at a prominent hotel. He left the rooms in the evening on the pretense of going downstairs to write some letters and did not return to his wife. In the morning she received a note from him written the night before, as follows:

"MY DEAR NANCY: It is best that we should not be together to night so I have gone to investigate as I said. When my bag comes in the morning please keep it until I come for it tomorrow.   DICK."

He never returned to her, neither was his bag ever delivered at the hotel. He not only left her never to return, but he asked her if she had any money and she gave him two one-hundred-dollar bills and also about twenty dollars in gold which she had in her purse, and he took it away with him. She was left in a strange land, without friends, and except ten dollars which she found in the bottom of her trunk on the following day, wholly penniless. During much of the time thereafter until this action was commenced she was watched by private detectives. This action was commenced August 13, 1907, and she is charged in the complaint with many acts of adultery with a physician whom she first met when she called him to treat her during an illness in January, 1906.

An answer was interposed and the court before whom
the action was tried found against the defendant as
alleged in the complaint upon various times between
February 18, 1906, and August 14, 1907, at five places
mentioned in the findings, including Hotel Minot in the
city of New York. The court also found that said adulteries were committed without the consent, connivance,
privity or procurement of the plaintiff. It also found
that the plaintiff left the defendant August 5, 1905, and
has since been voluntarily and continuously absent from
her, but refused to find that he abandoned her or that he
has sought to lead or entrap her into such conduct as
might furnish him apparent ground for a divorce.

The Appellate Division has unanimously affirmed the
judgment entered upon said findings and this court cannot look at the record except for the purpose of ascertaining whether, as claimed by the appellant, certain errors
were committed upon the trial which entitle the defendant to a new trial.

None of the findings relating to the charges alleged
against the defendant are based upon direct evidence.
The evidence was wholly circumstantial and the findings
of adultery are the conclusions of fact found by the court
from such circumstantial evidence. The findings relating to the occurrences at Hotel Minot are based solely
upon the testimony of a young man who was a night
clerk at the hotel and upon the registers of the said hotel.
Said young man testified that he saw the defendant with
Charles F. Wainwright, said physician, at the hotel four
times and upon the following dates, viz., February 19,
April 1, 8 and 24, all in 1906. The witness was allowed
to examine the hotel register to refresh his memory as to
the dates. He testified that after one o'clock on the
morning of February 19 the defendant, whom he had
never seen before, and Wainwright, whom he knew by
sight, came to the hotel, both in a state of intoxication,
and that the man walked up to the desk and started to

register, but that he told him he could not register. He further testified that the man declared himself to be Dr. Wainwright and said he would make it hot for the witness and insisted upon registering, but that he put him out of the house. He further testified: "I mean by putting them out of the house, he threatened me and I had to lay hold of a club to frighten him a little bit, and finally pushed them out of the door and bolted the door." He says that the elevatorman was there at the time of such occurrence and that he must have assisted in ejecting them and he also says that one bell boy was on duty and that two or three persons were there. The witness also testified that he remembers seeing the defendant and said physician leave the hotel on April 1, and also on April 8, and that he also recalls their coming to the hotel on April 24. He had testified to the dates from memory after looking at the register. Subsequently the witness was asked to refer to the register again and fix the date of the first occasion in April. The defendant's counsel stated his objections. The record then continues as follows: "The Court: That is right; you must lay proper foundation before he can refresh his memory by reference to a memorandum.

"Mr. Mooney: It is not for that purpose I intended to ask the question. The witness having testified he has a recollection of the incident without the date I am now preparing to offer the book itself on that point."

The witness looked at the book and stated that apart from the book he could state that the date was April 1st. The record then further continues as follows:

"Mr. Mooney: I offer in evidence the fourth line and in connection with that, the date of Sunday, April 1st, indicated by the witness.

".Objected to as immaterial and incompetent.

"The Court: The witness' memory having been refreshed he may testify from his recollection as refreshed but the writing itself is not evidence.

" Objection overruled. Exception taken. Same marked Plffs. Exhibit No. 2.

" Mr. Mooney: The entry is 'Sunday April 1, 1906,' and the line as near as I can read it is ' E. L. Stern & Wife, Phil.' "

The witness did not see the writing put on the register but he says that it was called to his attention by a fellow-clerk when he came on duty and that subsequently the physician and the defendant came down the stairs and the physician, not in the presence of the defendant, gave up a key but he did not notice whether it corresponded with the number opposite the entry which was read in evidence.

Similar evidence was offered relating to an entry on the register of April 8, except that the witness stated that the key that the physician returned to the office when he left on April 8 corresponded with the number opposite the entry that was afterward received in evidence. The objection, ruling and entry are as follows:

" Q. Will you please refer to the entry in the book which refreshes your recollection?

" Objected to as immaterial. Objection overruled. Exception taken. A. On the second line (pointing to entry).

" Mr. Mooney: The second line is offered in evidence together with the date.

" Objected to as immaterial, irrelevant and incompetent and that no proper foundation has been laid. Objection overruled. Exception taken. Said entry and date marked Plaintiff's Exhibit No. 3.

" Mr. Mooney: I do not offer in evidence the entry as proof of the substantive fact, but only in connection with the oral testimony of the witness and only to the extent of the oral testimony.

" Mr. Hymes: Do I understand it is in evidence now. The Court: I overruled your objection."

The entry is E. J. Jinney and wife, New York city.

He also testified that he was present at the hotel April 24, when the defendant and the physician entered the hotel. He testified that the physician came to the desk but that the defendant was not present at the desk but remained in the front of the hotel. The testimony as to the transaction was objected to as incompetent as against the defendant. The record is as follows:

" Q. Proceed.

" Objected to as incompetent as against the defendant. Objection overruled. Exception taken.

" A. I handed the book to him to register and said you better register in your own name, and he did. "

The record immediately connected with the receipt of the entry is as follows :

" Q. I ask you to refer to the book which you have spoken of and tell us what you find in the entry therein relating to this last occasion.

" Objected to as incompetent and also involving a conclusion. Objection overruled. Exception taken. Witness examines the book.

" A. All the handwriting on that line is in Dr. Wainwright's hand. * * *

" Mr. Mooney: I offer in evidence the date and line referred to. Objected to as incompetent as against the defendant. Objection overruled. Exception taken. Same marked Plaintiff's Exhibit No. 1. The entry is as follows: ' Mr. & Mrs. J. E. Wainright, City.' "

It is not shown or claimed that the defendant ever saw the register at said hotel or its contents or that she heard anything that was said at the hotel desk. It is beyond dispute that the clerk testified to the dates without the book, and there was not the slightest excuse for putting the register in evidence. (*People* v. *McLaughlin*, 150 N. Y. 365, 392.) The defendant and the physician each testify positively that they were never at the hotel. The elevatorman on duty at the time when it is claimed that the defendant and the physician came to the hotel in a state of intoxication on February 19 testified that no such occurrence ever took place. Neither the bell boy then on duty, the others present at that time, nor the person in charge of the desk when it is alleged that the physician registered on April 1 and 8, and when it is alleged that they left the hotel following the entry in the register of April 24, have been produced as witnesses. The findings as to the occurrence at Hotel Minot depend upon the truth of the testimony of the night clerk who left the hotel shortly after the occurrence of April 24. The alleged fact of the defendant's going to the hotel with the physician on February 19 and April 24, and of her leaving there with him on April 1 and 8, was fully stated by him with all of the circumstances occurring in the defendant's presence. Such testimony was properly received, but the entries on the register and the conversation at the desk, not made or had in her presence, were not proper evidence as against her. The entries on the register were no more admissible than would have been oral statements made to the clerk by the person registering relating to his purposes and derogatory of the defendant.

Notwithstanding the various statements of the court and of the plaintiff's counsel relating to the receipt in evidence of the entries in the register, they were actually received when there was no valid reason for admitting them. The persistent effort to make such entries a part of the record was to obtain through such evidence an influence in favor of the plaintiff in the determination of very material facts. It was unjustifiable and their admission error.

Dr. Wainwright had been married and his wife obtained a final judgment of divorce against him in April, 1905, in an action brought by her against him, and which he did not defend. Both the interlocutory and final judgment of divorce were obtained against him on his default. On his cross-examination in this action the interlocutory and final judgment in the action against him were offered in evidence and received subject to an objection by the defendant that such judgments are immaterial and inadmissible against her. After they were so received in evidence the court said: "I will admit it. It is not admitted as against the defendant. There is nothing here admitted so far as the Supreme Court record is concerned between this witness and the former wife as against the defendant. It is admitted as against him." Dr. Wainwright was not a defendant in this action. He appeared in the action by attorney soon after it was commenced, but he did not appear on the trial by attorney or take any part therein. He was present at the trial and was called as a witness by the defendant. The statement that the evidence was received against the witness was volunteered by the court. It was made when he was being cross-examined as a witness called by the defendant. He not only did not appear at the trial in his own behalf, but he had not made any personal statement, nor had he asked to be heard. Following the statement by the court the record is as follows:

"Q. Were not the adulteries for which you were convicted based upon your having registered under an assumed name on two occasions in a hotel known as the Garden Hotel?

"The Court: The word 'convicted' might carry with it under the new Code some criminal punishment. I think you should change the language.

"Q. Was that judgment of divorce against you based upon adulteries committed by you at the time when you registered under an assumed name at a hotel in this city?

"Mr. Hymes: I object on the ground that it is immaterial in any event and incompetent as against this defendant in any event, and that the question itself is incompetent in any event, even as to this witness, as to what the judgment is based upon and not the best evidence.

"The Court: The same ruling. The proof in the case is the best evidence. Exception taken.

"A. According to my personal knowledge, and what I heard of the proceedings, in regard to which I saw, I know nothing about it, it must have been."

His answer is somewhat confused but it is in substance that he knows nothing about it personally, only what he heard of the proceedings. It may be assumed that the summons and complaint were served upon him and from it he would know of the charges made against him. Evidence had to be given in the action against him even upon his default. Therefore, from what he knew of the proceedings he answered the question, "It must have been." The plaintiff then asked the witness whether he made the entry referred to on the Garden Hotel register and he declined to answer. Plaintiff was not content but called a witness who was a waiter at the Garden Hotel, who testified that he had seen Wainwright and he was then shown a register and asked who made certain entries called to his attention and he answered, "Dr. Wainwright," subject to an objection that the evidence was immaterial and not within the issues and to an exception. The entries were then offered in evidence and received subject to an objection that they are immaterial and not within the issues and as being in reference to a collateral matter brought out on cross-examination and an exception was taken. Subsequently plaintiff's counsel stated "That the entries are offered on a two-fold theory, *first,* as standards of handwriting — the handwriting in the other register having been disputed by Dr. Wainwright, and, *secondly,* on the ground that it bears on the question as to whether the doctor may have registered elsewhere under an assumed name." The entries in the Garden Hotel register should not have been received for the purpose of comparing the handwriting with the handwriting on the register of the Hotel Minot, as, if otherwise proper, the entries on the Hotel Minot register were not properly in evidence. The entries were not properly received to affect the credibility of the witness, as the witness' admissions, if they were otherwise material and proper, did not show the actual commission of adultery by Wainwright. The answers to the questions on the cross-examination of Wainwright simply show that he had been informed and that he assumed that the decree of divorce against him had been based on evidence, whatever it was, which had been received in such uncontested divorce action. The entries on the register of the Garden Hotel constitute but one step among many others that were necessary to be shown before the commission of adultery at that hotel could be inferred. The evidence as to the testimony upon which the decree of divorce against Wainwright was obtained and the entries in the register of the Garden Hotel were clearly erroneous and improper and it tended to influence the court against the defendant in the determination of all the issues presented in this action and it should not have been received.

The defendant insists that the plaintiff deliberately and willfully abandoned the defendant and that if adultery was committed by her it was with the plaintiff's consent, procurement and connivance and that for both reasons the plaintiff is not entitled to a judgment of divorce. Those questions, which have been elaborately argued by the appellant and an intervenor, are not under the findings unanimously affirmed by the Appellate Division, presented upon this appeal.

For the errors pointed out, the interlocutory and final judgment of divorce should be reversed and a new trial granted.

CULLEN, Ch. J., GRAY, VANN, WERNER, WILLARD BARTLETT and HISCOCK, JJ., concur.

Judgment reversed, etc.

ADOLPH PAVENSTEDT, Appellant, *v.* NEW YORK LIFE
    INSURANCE COMPANY, Respondent.

**Bills, notes and checks — foreign bills of exchange — what
damages recoverable by payee upon foreign bill of exchange
protested for non-payment.**

1. The damages recoverable by the payee of a negotiable foreign
bill of exchange protested for non-payment against the drawer may
be deemed to be made up as follows: (1) The face of the bill;
(2) interest thereon; (3) protest fees; (4) re-exchange, *i. e.*, the additional expense of procuring a new bill for the same amount payable
in the same place on the day of dishonor; or a percentage in lieu of
such re-exchange in jurisdictions where it is prescribed by statute.

2. Where a bill of exchange was drawn in South America by a
New York corporation directed to itself in New York, and requiring
itself to pay a certain sum in New York in our currency, the measure
of damages to the payee upon its refusal to pay is the amount of
the draft, with interest and protest fees. This is true although the
currency of the country in which the bill was drawn depreciated
after the date of the bill and its dishonor, so that the holder was
required to pay a larger number of dollars in such depreciated currency for the amount of American money for which the bill was
drawn than he was able to realize upon the draft in the country
where it was drawn in the first instance.

Pavenstedt v. *N. Y. Life Ins. Co.*, 113 App. Div. 866, affirmed.

(Argued May 30, 1911; decided October 3, 1911.)

APPEAL, by permission, from an order of the Appellate
Division of the Supreme Court in the first judicial department, entered June 15, 1906, which reversed an interlocutory judgment of Special Term overruling a demurrer to
the complaint and sustained such demurrer, with leave to
plaintiff to amend the complaint.

The nature of the action, the facts, so far as material,
and the question certified are stated in the opinion.

Robert E. L. Lewis and *William D. Lewis* for appellant. The question raised by the demurrer is one to be
decided in accordance with the Law Merchant or the law
of commerce. (*Faulkner* v. *Hart,* 82 N. Y. 413; *Mead*

v. *Beale*, Taney, 339; Norton on Bills & Notes, 22, 24; 1 Randolph on Com. Paper, § 5; 3 Kent's Comm. 79, 80, 94; 2 Greenl. on Ev. 253, 278, §§ 253, 265.) Plaintiff is entitled to recover from defendant the special damages claimed in the complaint. (2 Daniel on Neg. Inst. § 1438; *Birdsall* v. *Russell*, 29 N. Y. 220; *Evertson Bank* v. *Nat. Bank*, 66 N. Y. 14; *Spooner* v. *Holmes*, 102 Mass. 503.) The holder of the foreign negotiable bill of exchange upon its non-payment is entitled to recover as damages in an action against the drawer or indorser, not only the principal sum and interest, but protest fees and whatever damages he may be able to show he has sustained by reason of exchange and re-exchange. (*D'Tostet* v. *Baring*, 11 East, 265; 2 Daniel on Neg. Inst. § 1445; Byles on Bills, 588; Randolph on Com. Paper, § 1714; Tiedeman on Com. Paper, § 407; *Bank of United States* v. *United States*, 2 How. [U. S.] 737; *O. L. & Co.'s Bank* v. *Walbridge*, 19 N. Y. 135; *Pollard* v. *Herries*, 3 Bos. & Pull. 355; *Mellish* v. *Simeon*, 2 H. Black. 378.) The bill, having been drawn by defendant, by its agents, upon itself, the payee was at liberty to treat it either as a bill of exchange or a promissory note. (1 Daniel on Neg. Inst. § 398; *Bank of Genesee* v. *Patchin*, 19 N. Y. 312; *First Nat. Bank* v. *Wallis*, 150 N. Y. 455; *Mechanics' Bank* v. *Bank of Columbia*, 5 Wheat. 356; *Jackson* v. *Claw*, 18 Johns. 348; *Shaw* v. *Stone*, 1 Cush. 256; *Sally* v. *Terrill*, 55 L. R. A. 730; *Clarke* v. *L. A. P. S. & L. Assn.*, 48 N. Y. S. R. 189; 20 N. Y. Supp. 363; Tiedeman on Com. Paper, 211, § 128; *Cunningham* v. *Wardwell*, 12 Me. 466; 4 Am. & Eng. Ency. of Law [2d ed.], 119; *McCann* v. *Randell*, 147 Mass. 91; *Fairchild* v. *Ogdensburgh R. R. Co.*, 15 N. Y. 337; *Bull* v. *Sims*, 23 N. Y. 370.)

James H. McIntosh for respondent. Defendant has already discharged its entire obligation on account of the draft. (*Loudon* v. *Taxing District*, 104 U. S. 771; *City of Memphis* v. *Brown*, 20 Wall. 289; *Arnott* v. *Spokane*, 6 Wash. 442; *Mason* v. *Callender*, 2 Minn. 350; *Thayer* v. *Hedges*, 23 Ind. 141; *Guy* v. *Franklin*, 5 Cal. 416; *Ferris* v. *Barlow*, 2 Aiken [Vt.], 106.) Plaintiff is not entitled to recover damages by reason of exchange and re-exchange. (*Williams* v. *Ayres*, L. R. [3 App. Cas.] 133; *Chrysler* v. *Renois*, 43 N. Y. 209; *Hendricks* v. *Franklin*, 4 Johns. 119.)   •

WILLARD BARTLETT, J.   This action is brought by the assignees of the payee of a foreign bill of exchange to recover damages from the drawer for the failure of the drawee to accept or pay the bill when duly presented for acceptance and payment.

The demurrer attacks the sufficiency of the complaint, the material allegations of which may be summarized as follows:

The defendant is a New York corporation. On May 22, 1902, in the United States of Colombia the defendant by its agent made and delivered to one Gonzalez its negotiable bill of exchange directed to itself in New York, requiring itself to pay in New York to the order of the said Gonzalez three days after sight the sum of $4,181.60. The next day Gonzalez sold and indorsed the bill in Colombia to Bruer, Moller & Co., receiving therefor $234,169.60 in Colombian money, one dollar in American money being then worth fifty-six dollars in the money of Colombia. Bruer, Moller & Co. thereafter indorsed said draft to their agent in New York, G. Amsinck & Co., who duly presented the same to defendant for acceptance and payment, but acceptance and payment were refused, whereupon the draft was duly protested therefor. Subsequently G. Amsinck & Co. returned the draft to Bruer, Moller & Co., who in turn returned the same to Gonzalez and demanded of him $4,181.60, together with $20.96 interest and $2.90 expenses of protest, in American money which said several sums Gonzalez thereupon paid to

Bruer, Moller & Co. At the time when the defendant refused to pay said draft or bill of exchange and at the time of its return to Gonzalez and the payments made by him to Bruer, Moller & Co. one dollar of American money was worth ninety dollars of Colombian money. By reason of the refusal of the defendant to pay the draft presented Gonzalez was compelled to procure and did procure at the city of Bucaramanga $4,204.86 and was compelled to pay and did pay therefor $376,344 of Colombian money whereby Gonzalez has been damaged in addition to the face value of the draft and interest and protest fees in the sum of $1,579.72 in American money, and on April 21, 1904, there was due from defendant to Gonzalez the sum of $5,785.18 in American money with interest thereon. Upon that day Gonzalez assigned his claim to the plaintiff. No part thereof has been paid except $4,859.31, which has been paid to the plaintiff by the defendant since the commencement of this action and which was received by the plaintiff in payment and satisfaction of the face of said draft, interest thereon and protest fees under a written stipulation that the acceptance of the amount paid would in no way affect, limit or prejudice the plaintiff's right to recover from the defendant the balance of $1,579.72 with interest from the 25th day of August, 1902, for which amount the plaintiff demands judgment.

To this complaint the defendant demurred on the ground that it did not state facts sufficient to constitute a cause of action. The demurrer was overruled at Special Term and the defendant appealed to the Appellate Division where the interlocutory judgment entered upon the demurrer was reversed and the demurrer was sustained, with leave to the plaintiff to serve an amended complaint. Nearly a year after the order of reversal the Appellate Division granted the defendant leave to appeal to the Court of Appeals, and pursuant to such leave the case now comes here. The question certified to this court by the Appellate Division is: "Does the complaint state facts sufficient to constitute a cause of action ?"

The question presented by the appeal is a question of the measure of damages. What damages are recoverable in a suit brought in the state of New York by the holder of a dishonored bill of exchange drawn in the United States of Colombia and payable in the state of New York?

The damages recoverable by the payee of a negotiable foreign bill of exchange protested for non-payment against the drawer may be deemed to be made up as follows: (1) The face of the bill; (2) interest thereon; (3) protest fees; (4) re-exchange, *i. e.*, the additional expense of procuring a new bill for the same amount payable in the same place on the day of dishonor; or a percentage in lieu of such re-exchange in jurisdictions where it is prescribed by statute. (2 Sedgwick on Damages [8th ed.], § 700; Wood's Byles on Bills, p. 418; 2 Daniel on Negotiable Instruments [4th ed.], § 1444; 3 Kent's Com. [14th ed.] p. 115; *Bank of United States* v. *United States,* 2 How. [U. S.] 745, 764; *Oliver Lee & Co.'s Bank* v. *Walbridge,* 19 N. Y. 134; 2 Halsbury's Laws of England, pp. 524, 525.)

By some judges and text writers the term re-exchange is employed in a broader sense to signify all these elements taken together; that is, the *whole* amount for which the payee is entitled to draw a new bill by reason of the dishonor of the original instrument. (4 English Ruling Cases, p. 574, note to *In re General South American Co.)*

The appellant is clearly right in contending that the instrument in controversy must be treated as a foreign bill of exchange and not as a simple order for the payment of money. It is expressly alleged in the complaint to have been "a negotiable bill of exchange in writing dated at Curacao, 10th August, 1901," and directed to the defendant in New York. Where a bill of exchange is drawn by a corporation upon itself the instrument may be treated as an accepted bill or as a promissory note at the election of the holder. (1 Daniel on Negotiable Instruments, § 424; Negotiable Instruments Law, § 214.)

There is no express mention of re-exchange in the complaint nor are any facts alleged from which it can be inferred that a new draft would have cost the payee any more than the old one.

It seems to have been the intent of the pleader to construct a claim for special damages out of the transactions between Gonzalez and Bruer, Moller & Co., with which the defendant had nothing to do; and such a claim might be established if it appeared that the repayment which Gonzalez had to make to that firm upon the return of the dishonored bill was in excess of what the defendant has paid or avowed its willingness to pay to Gonzalez (or the plaintiff as his assignee).

Taking the facts just as they are stated in the complaint and bearing in mind that the payee of the bill (or his representative) is suing here, what amount of money will afford him complete redress? He sold the bill to parties in Colombia. If he is enabled to retain the sum they paid him for it and is provided with a sufficient additional amount of funds to pay them whatever they may lawfully demand of him on account of the dishonor of the bill by the drawee, he will have suffered no loss.

It is to be observed that the doctrine of re-exchange has generally been applied to bills drawn in the *locus fori* upon foreign places and not to bills drawn in foreign places and payable in the jurisdiction where the suit is brought — as in the case here. In reference to bills drawn outside the state of New York on parties here, it was said in *Guiteman* v. *Davis* (45 Barb. 576 n.) that the principle of re-exchange does not apply; and all the holder is entitled to recover is the amount named in the bill without exchange. To the same effect is *Chrysler* v. *Renois* (43 N. Y. 209).

But let us assume that the damages recoverable on behalf of the payee or other holder of a protested bill drawn elsewhere and payable here are to be measured upon the principle of re-exchange and proceed to inquire whether that leaves the plaintiff in any better position.

The subject of re-exchange as an element in measuring damages has been discussed by almost all the leading text writers who consider the Law Merchant and by a comparatively small number of judges in adjudicated cases. The judicial observations on the subject have rarely been necessary to the point decided and are usually *obiter dicta.*

Re-exchange under the Law Merchant is the price which the holder of a dishonored bill would have to pay in the currency of the country where the original bill was drawn for a good bill payable where the original bill was payable for the same amount of money and the expenses of protest.

Formerly the damages recoverable in an action upon bills of exchange drawn or negotiated within this state and upon parties in other states or foreign countries were regulated by statute, but not the damages recoverable upon foreign bills of exchange payable here. Since the enactment of the Negotiable Instruments Law, however, the whole subject has been relegated to the Law Merchant. (Laws of 1897, chap. 612, § 7.) In the case of inland bills, where there is no difference between the currency or rates of exchange at the time and place where it is payable, the measure of damages is the same as that in the case of promissory notes; "but in regard to foreign bills of exchange," says Mr. Sedgwick in his well-known treatise on the Measure of Damages, "the question becomes more complicated by the introduction of the element of re-exchange;" and he states the general rule to be "that the holder of a bill protested for non-payment is entitled to the amount of the bill, re-exchange and charges." (2 Sedgwick on Damages

[8th ed.], § 700.) As has already been intimated, some difficulty arises in ascertaining the precise meaning and application of the authorities relating to re-exchange on account of the different senses in which that term is used by different judges and text writers, the expression being sometimes employed to signify the whole amount of the damages recoverable upon a protested foreign bill of exchange and sometimes to signify merely the excess of such damages above the face of the bill and protest fees. The definition of re-exchange most frequently quoted is that given and illustrated by Mr. Justice BYLES as follows: "Re-exchange is the difference in the value of a bill, occasioned by its being dishonored in a foreign country in which it was payable. The existence and amount of it depend on the rate of exchange between the two countries. The theory of the transaction is this: A merchant in London indorses a bill for a certain number of Austrian florins, payable at a future date in Vienna. The holder is entitled to receive in Vienna, on the day of the maturity of the bill, a certain number of Austrian florins. Suppose the bill to be dishonored. The holder is now, by the custom of merchants, entitled to immediate and specific redress, by his own act, in this way. He is entitled, being in Vienna, then and there to raise the exact number of Austrian florins, by drawing and negotiating a cross-bill, payable at sight, on his indorser in London, for as much English money as will purchase in Vienna the exact number of Austrian florins, at the rate of exchange on the day of dishonor; and to include in the amount of that bill the interest and necessary expenses of the transaction. This cross-bill is called in French the *retraite.* The amount for which it is drawn is called in low Latin *ricambium,* in Italian *ricambio,* and in French and English re-exchange. If the indorser pay the cross or re-exchange bill, he has fulfilled his engagement of indemnity. If not, the holder of the original bill may sue him on it, and will be entitled to recover in that action the amount of the *retraite* or cross-bill, with the interest and expenses thereon. The amount of the verdict will thus be an exact indemnity for the non-payment of the Austrian florins in Vienna the day of the maturity of the original bill." (Wood's Byles on Bills, 418.) According to Mr. Justice STORY re-exchange means "the amount for which a bill can be purchased in the country where the acceptance is made, drawn upon the drawer or indorser in the country where he resides, which will give the holder of the original bill a sum exactly equal to the amount of that bill at the time when it ought to be paid, or, when he is able to draw the re-exchange bill, together with his necessary expenses, and interest." (Story on Bills, § 400.) "In point of fact, the re-exchange bill is seldom, if ever, drawn in England or in the United States, but the right of the holder to draw it is recognized by the law merchant of all nations, and it is by reference to this supposed re-draft upon the drawer that the re-exchange is computed." (2 Daniel on Negotiable Instruments, § 1445.) Senator Daniel in the same section defines re-exchange as "the amount for which a bill may be purchased in the country where the original bill is payable, drawn upon the drawer in the country where he resides, which will give the holder a sum exactly equal to the amount of the original bill at the time when it ought to be paid, or when he is able to draw the re-exchange bill, together with the expenses and interest; for that is precisely the sum which the holder is entitled to receive, and which will indemnify him for its non-payment." Chancellor KENT, with characteristic clearness, explains how the element of re-exchange enters into the calculation of the damages sustained by the holder of a foreign bill protested for non-payment, as follows: "The general law merchant of Europe authorizes the holder of a protested bill, immediately to redraw from the place where the bill was payable, on the drawer or indorser, in order to reimburse himself for the principal of the bill protested, the contingent expenses attending it, and the new exchange which he pays. His indemnity requires him to draw for such an amount as will make good the face of the bill, together with interest from the time it ought to have been paid, and the necessary charges of protest, postage, and broker's commission, and the current rate of exchange at the place where the bill was to be demanded or payable, on the place where it was drawn or negotiated. The law does not insist upon an actual redrawing, but it enables the holder to recover what would be the price of another new bill at the place where the bill was dishonored, or the loss on the re-exchange; and this it does by giving him the face of the protested bill, with interest, and the necessary expenses, including the amount or price of the re-exchange." (3 Kent's Com. 115.)

"As conclusive proof that the holder of a foreign bill of exchange which has not been paid when presented is entitled to damages in addition to the principal sum and interest thereon," the learned counsel for the appellant says that it is only necessary to refer to the statutes of the various states of the United States which prescribe an arbitrary sum that the holder of a dishonored bill of exchange is to receive in addition to the principal sum with interest. An examination of the provisions of the New York Revised Statutes on this subject which were repealed by the Negotiable Instruments Law shows that they prescribed damages in lieu of re-exchange only in the case of bills drawn in this state and payable in other jurisdictions but had no reference to a case like this where the bill was drawn in another jurisdiction and payable here. Before the enactment of any New York statute on the subject immemorial usage in this state allowed twenty per cent damages on the protest of a bill drawn in New York on Great Britain. (*Hendricks* v. *Franklin*, 4 Johns. 119.) This was reduced to ten per cent by the Revised Laws (1 Revised Laws, 770, 771), and remained the same under the Revised Statutes.

It will aid us in applying the rule of re-exchange to the circumstances of the present case to paraphrase the illustration above quoted from Byles on Bills by substituting Colombia and New York for London and Vienna and the drawer of the bill for the indorser. It will then read as follows : A merchant in Colombia draws a bill for a certain number of American dollars payable at a future date in New York. The holder is entitled to receive in New York, on the day of the maturity of the bill, a certain number of American dollars. Suppose the bill to be dishonored. The holder is now by the custom of merchants entitled to immediate and specific redress, by his own act, in this way. He is entitled, being in New York, then and there to raise the exact number of American dollars by drawing and negotiating a cross bill, payable at sight, on his drawer in Colombia for as much Colombian money as will purchase in New York the exact number of American dollars, at the rate of exchange on the day of dishonor; and to include in the amount of the bill the interest and necessary expenses of the transaction. In the case at bar under the allegations of the complaint the cross bill would have had to be for $376,344 in Colombian money. If the payee has received from the defendant enough American money to equal that amount in Colombian money he has received all that he needed to make good his obligations to Bruer, Moller & Co. upon the return of the dishonored bill. The equivalent of $376,344 in Colombian money was $4,264.86 in American money at the time when the payee or holder was entitled to draw the new bill. The defendant has paid the plaintiff that amount in American money, being the face of the original bill together with interest and protest fees. Therefore, nothing more is needed to make good the loss consequent upon the non-payment of the original bill at the time when and place where it ought to have been paid. Even if the defendant had not actually paid this amount representing the face of the original bill with interest and protest fees, that sum would have been the limit of the plaintiff's recovery; because it would have sufficed to pay the new draft which he was entitled to draw under the doctrine of re-exchange.

In the case of a contract made in one country for the payment of money in another the place where the money is payable as well as the currency in which the payment is to be made are material ingredients to be considered. (Story on Conflict of Laws [8th ed.], § 308.)   In *Cash* v. *Kennion* (11 Vesey, 314) it was held by Lord ELDON that if a man in a foreign country agreed to pay one hundred pounds in London upon a specified day he ought to have that sum in London on that day, and if he failed so to do wherever the creditor may sue him the law of the forum ought to give him just as much money as he would have received if the contract had been fully performed. According to the theory of re-exchange, as soon as the bill in the present case was dishonored in New York it was the privilege of the holder to draw a new bill in New York upon the defendant in Colombia for such an amount as would afford perfect indemnity.   (*Oliver Lee & Co.'s Bank* v. *Walbridge*, 19 N. Y. 134.)

According to the complaint the defendant has paid to the plaintiff and the plaintiff has received in payment and satisfaction of the face of the draft, interest thereon and protest fees the sum of $4,859.31.   This must be made up of $4,181.60, the face of the draft, the balance of $677.71 representing interest and protest fees.   While it is stipulated that the receipt of this amount is not to affect the plaintiff's right to recover the balance which he claims on account of re-exchange, the payment, nevertheless, is a recognition by the defendant of its liability to that extent.   It is an acknowledgment that on the day when the bill was protested for non-payment the holder was entitled to receive from the defendant the face of the bill, $4,181.60, with the expenses of protest and interest if any had then accrued.   The contention of the plaintiff on this appeal is that inasmuch as Gonzalez paid Bruer, Moller & Co. $376,344 in Colombian money when the original bill was returned by that firm to him he is entitled to have recourse against the defendant for indemnity. I have endeavored to show, however, that he would have received full indemnity at that time by the payment to him of the face of the bill in American money, together with the protest fees and interest, for that amount would have enabled him to purchase the precise sum in Colombian currency which he was obliged to pay Bruer, Moller & Co. upon the return of the dishonored paper. The damages recoverable now are to be measured by the rights and obligations of the parties as they existed then; and it follows that the defendant is not liable for any more than it has paid.

My conclusion is that the theory of measuring his damages upon which the plaintiff insists when applied to the facts set out in his complaint does not entitle him to demand any more from the defendant than he has already received. Hence the Appellate Division was right in sustaining the demurrer, although I am not able fully to concur in the reasoning which led the learned judges of that court to this result. The order appealed from should, therefore, be affirmed, with costs, and the question certified answered in the negative.

CULLEN, Ch. J. I concur in the opinion of WILLARD BARTLETT, J., for the affirmance of the judgment. If the old statutes of this state were still in force they would have no relevancy to this controversy. They applied only to bills of exchange drawn or negotiated in this state and payable elsewhere, not to bills drawn elsewhere payable here. This is necessarily the case, for unless the drawee accepted the draft no action would lie against him in favor of the holder, while if he did accept the draft, on failure to pay, he was liable to a holder only for its face, interest and protest fees and not for re-exchange (2 Sedg-

wick on Damages [8th ed.], § 700; *Bowen* v. *Stoddard,*
10 Metc. 375; *Manning* v. *Cohen,* 44 Ala. 343; Byles on
Bills [7th ed.], 420; *Napier* v. *Shneider,* 12 East, 420;
Woolsey v. *Crawford,* 2 Camp. 445), though his liability
might be greater to the drawer of the bill. (*Riggs* v.
Lindsay, 7 Cranch, 500; *In re General South American
Company,* L. R. [7 Ch. Div.] 637.) Being practically
a bill of exchange drawn on itself, the defendant might
be sued either as a drawer or acceptor, though in form
the bill had not been accepted. But as acceptor its liability was, under the authorities cited, limited to the
face of the bill, which it has since paid. Therefore, if
the plaintiff is entitled to recover any greater sum it
must be by treating the action as brought against the
defendant as drawer. We may assume for the argument that in that view of the case the plaintiff is entitled
to recover any damage of whatever character he suffered
by the defendant's failure to pay the bill. The plaintiff
believes that he has been damaged by the depreciation in
the Colombian currency, as a result of which he had to
pay the person to whom he sold the bill of exchange
$376,344 of the money of that state, while on the sale
of the bill he had received only $234,169.60 of the same
kind of money. This belief is a pure delusion. Not
merely in law but in fact this depreciation was no more
an element or factor in the plaintiff's damage than any
fluctuation in the price of cotton or sugar that may have
occurred in the period elapsing between the sale of the
bill by the plaintiff and his taking it up after it was protested as unpaid. A moment's reflection will show this
to be the case. When the plaintiff was compelled to take
up the bill he either had the money, realized no matter how, or was obliged to borrow it. If when the defendant subsequently paid the draft there had been no change
in the value of Colombian money it is plain that he lost
nothing (other than interest and exchange), for he could
sell the American money and realize on the sale the exact

sum he had been compelled to pay in Colombian money. On the other hand, if Colombian money had still further depreciated, it would inure to the plaintiff's advantage, for on the sale of the American money he would be able to repay his debt in Colombian money and have a surplus.   But if Colombian money appreciated during this interval the plaintiff would, on the sale of the American money, be unable to realize the amount in Colombian money which he had paid on taking up the bill, and might be considered the loser in Colombian money of the amount of the difference, as occurred in many instances with us when, during the war, men entered into obligations for the payment of money with gold at a premium of over one hundred per cent, which they had to pay when the premium on gold had fallen to a small fraction of that amount.   Thus it may be seen how, to a man living and doing business in Colombia, fluctuations in the value of Colombian money during the time a party is in default in the payment of his obligation in American money may cause damage.   The price at which the holder of the obligation originally sold it has nothing whatever to do with the existence or amount of such damage. In this case there is no complaint of any loss by appreciation in Colombian money after defendant's failure to pay the draft, the only way in which damage by fluctuations in value could occur.   It is doubtful whether such a claim if made could be sustained, as there are decisions to the effect that where default is made in the payment of foreign money, recovery in our money is to be computed on the basis of the relative values of the two currencies at the time of default.   (*Bissell* v. *Heywood*, 96 U. S. 580, 587; *Comstock* v. *Smith*, 20 Mich. 338; *Sheehan* v. *Dalrymple*, 19 Mich. 239.)

GRAY, HAIGHT, WERNER, CHASE and COLLIN, JJ., concur with WILLARD BARTLETT, J., and CULLEN, Ch. J.

Order affirmed.

LOUIS SMYTH et al., as Administrators with the Will Annexed of·HUGH SMITH, Deceased, Appellants, *v.* THE CITY OF NEW YORK et al., Respondents.

Municipal corporations — construction of subway by contractors — when city not liable for negligence of contractor — contractor's liability to abutting owner for damages caused by explosion of dynamite due to sub-contractor's negligence.

Through the negligence of a sub-contractor engaged in the construction of the rapid transit subway in New York city, plaintiff's abutting property was injured by an explosion of dynamite. The contract between the contractor and the city provided: "The contractor shall be responsible for all damage which may be done to abutting property or buildings or structures thereon by the method in which the construction hereunder shall be done, but not including in such damage any damage necessarily arising from proper construction pursuant to this contract or the reasonable use, occupation or obstruction of the streets thereby." *Held, First,* that the city is not liable for the negligence of the contractor to whom the work had been let, nor is it liable on the ground that it suffered a nuisance to be maintained in the street. *Second,* the contractor is liable for the damages sustained by reason of the negligence of the sub-contractor. *Third,* as this was not an agreement of indemnity to the city, but an agreement to be responsible to abutting owners for damages arising from improper construction or unreasonable use and occupation of the streets, an abutting owner can maintain an action under this provision of the contract, although he was not a party thereto.

Murphy v. *City of New York*, 128 App. Div. 463, modified.

(Argued May 8, 1911; decided October 3, 1911.)

APPEAL from a judgment of the Appellate Division of the Supreme Court in the first judicial department, entered November 20, 1908, affirming a judgment in favor of defendants entered upon a dismissal of the complaint by the court at a Trial Term.

The nature of the action and the facts, so far as material, are stated in the opinion.

Henry de Forest Baldwin for appellants. The city is bound to exercise due care to keep the streets in a safe condition and is liable for permitting dangerous nuisances therein. (*Landau* v. *City of New York*, 180 N. Y. 48; *Vogel* v. *Mayor, etc.*, 92 N. Y. 10; *Storrs* v. *City of Utica*, 17 N. Y. 104; *Requa* v. *City of Rochester*, 45 N. Y. 129; *Wilson* v. *City of Watertown*, 3 Hun, 508; *Carpenter* v. *City of New York*, 115 App. Div. 552.) The city and the contractor were guilty of a breach of duty in not seeing to it that the quantities of dynamite necessary for the prosecution of the work were handled carefully and in such a way as not to create a nuisance. (*Matter of Rapid Transit Comrs.*, 197 N. Y. 81; *Deming* v. *Terminal Railway*, 169 N. Y. 1; *Johnston* v. *Phœnix Bridge Co.*, 44 App. Div. 581; 169 N. Y. 581; *Mullins* v. *Siegel-Cooper Co.*, 183 N. Y. 129; *Downey* v. *Low*, 22 App. Div. 460; *Woodman* v. *Met. R. R. Co.*, 149 Mass. 335; *Flynn* v. *N. Y. E. R. Co.*, 17 J. & S. 60; *Morris* v. *Salt Lake City*, 101 Pac. Rep. 373; *Brusso* v. *City of Buffalo*, 90 N. Y. 679; *Turner* v. *City of Newburgh*, 109 N. Y. 301; *Cameron* v. *Oberlin*, 19 Ind. App. 142; *Bower* v. *Peate*, L. R. [1 Q. B. D.] 321; *Chicago* v. *Robbins*, 2 Black, 418.) McDonald contracted that he would be responsible for all damage which might be done to abutting property by the method by which the construction was done. This provision prevents him from shifting the responsibility thus assumed to a sub-contractor. (*Johnston* v. *Phœnix Bridge Co.*, 44 App. Div. 581; *Matter of T. F. St. R. R. Co.*, 102 N. Y. 343; *Smith* v. *Mayor, etc.*, 68 N. Y. 552; *People* v. *O'Brien*, 111 N. Y. 1; *Thompson* v. *People*, 23 Wend. 537; *McGregor* v. *Erie Ry. Co.*, 35 N. J. L. 89, 97; *Police Jury* v. *Bridge Co.*, 44 La. Ann. 137.)

Archibald R. Watson, Corporation Counsel (*Terence Farley* and *Theodore Connoly* of counsel), for city of New York, respondent. In order to entitle the plaintiffs to recover against the city of New York it was essential that they prove either that the city was guilty of negligence or of authorizing or maintaining a public nuisance. (*Froelich* v. *City of New York*, 199 N. Y. 466; *Turner* v. *D. M. Cont. Co.*, 99 App. Div. 135; 184 N. Y. 525; *Mahoney* v. *City of Boston*, 171 Mass. 427; *Haefelin* v. *McDonald*, 96 App. Div. 219; *Sander* v. *State*, 182 N. Y. 400; *Carpenter* v. *City of New York*, 115 App. Div. 562.) The same rule applies when the independent contractor, over whom the employer has no control, creates a nuisance which is not the consequential result of the work which he is constructing. (*A. & F. R. Co.* v. *Kimberly*, 87 Ga. 161; *Vogel* v. *Mayor, etc.*, 92 N. Y. 10; *Cuff* v. *N. & N. Y. R. R. Co.*, 35 N. J. L. 17; *Berg* v. *Parsons*, 156 N. Y. 120.) The exceptions to the rule of non-liability for the acts of an independent contractor have no application to the case at bar. (*Booth* v. *R., W. & O. R. R. Co.*, 140 N. Y. 267; *Pack* v. *New York*, 8 N. Y. 222; *Kelly* v. *New York*, 11 N. Y. 432; *French* v. *Vix*, 143 N. Y. 90; *McCafferty* v. *S. D. & P. M. R. Co.*, 61 N. Y. 178; *Berg* v. *Parsons*, 156 N. Y. 109; *Herrington* v. *Lansingburgh*, 110 N. Y. 145; *Hunt* v. *Vanderbilt*, 115 N. C. 559; *Schnurr* v. *Huntington Co.*, 22 Ind. App. 188; *Blumb* v. *Kansas*, 84 Mo. 112.) The city, through its bureau of combustibles of the fire department, having granted a permit to Shaler to store dynamite, had the right to assume and were justified in believing that he would comply with its terms and conditions, and it is not responsible for his failure to do so. (*Vil. of Port Jervis* v. *F. Nat. Bank*, 96 N. Y. 556; *Susquehanna Depot* v. *Simmons*, 112 Penn. St. 384.) The city is not responsible because of its neglect to enforce its ordinances and by-laws regulating the storage of dynamite. (*Leonard* v. *Hornellsville*, 41 App. Div. 106; *Griffin* v. *Mayor, etc.*, 9 N. Y. 456; *Lorillard* v. *Munroe*, 11 N. Y. 392; *Coonley* v. *City of Albany*, 132 N. Y. 145; *Stillwell* v. *Mayor, etc.*, 17 J. & S. 360; 96 N. Y. 649; *Levy* v. *Mayor, etc.*, 1

Sandf. 465.) The city is not responsible for the omission of the employees of the fire department in failing to enforce the regulations of that department. (*O'Meara* v. *Mayor, etc.*, 1 Daly, 425; *Woolbridge* v. *Mayor, etc.*, 49 How. Pr. 67; *Thompson* v. *Mayor, etc.*, 20 J. & S. 427; *Smith* v. *City of Rochester*, 76 N. Y. 506; *Terhune* v. *Mayor, etc.*, 88 N. Y. 247.)

De Lancey Nicoll, Courtland V. Anable and *Raymond D. Thurber* for John B. McDonald et al., respondents. The plaintiffs' damages were, as matter of law, caused solely by Shaler and his servants, for whose acts or omissions none of the defendants is responsible. (*Uppington* v. *City of New York*, 165 N. Y. 222; *Pack* v. *Mayor, etc.*, 8 N. Y. 222, *Kelly* v. *Mayor, etc.*, 11 N. Y. 432; *Slater* v. *Mersereau*, 64 N. Y. 138; *King* v. *Livermore*, 9 Hun, 298, 71 N. Y. 605; *City of Buffalo* v. *Clement*, 46 N. Y. S. R. 676, 679; *Overton* v. *Freeman*, 11 C. B. 867; Moll on Independent Contractors, § 57.) McDonald did not assume, in his contract with the city, an obligation to pay to abutting owners the damage caused them by the torts of sub-contractors. (*Haefelin* v. *McDonald*, 96 App. Div. 213, *Rooney* v. *Brogan Const. Co.*, 194 N. Y. 32; *Hoffman* v. *Æ. L. Ins. Co.*, 32 N. Y. 405; *Gillet* v. *Bank of America*, 160 N. Y. 549; *Marshall* v. *C. T. M. Assn.*, 170 N. Y. 434.) On no possible theory is the defendant Rapid Transit Subway Construction Company liable in this action. (*Miller* v. *N. Y., L. & W. R. R. Co.*, 125 N. Y. 118; *Pack* v. *Mayor, etc.*, 8 N. Y. 222; *Kelly* v. *Mayor, etc.*, 11 N. Y. 432; *Uppington* v. *City of New York*, 165 N. Y. 222.)

CULLEN, Ch. J. This action is brought by the owners of the Murray Hill Hotel, which abutted on Park avenue, borough of Manhattan, city of New York, to recover damages to such hotel caused by the explosion of a dynamite magazine located on said avenue during the construction of the rapid transit subway. The construction of the subway at this point was being carried on by one Shaler, a sub-contractor. The excavation was being made through rock which had to be removed by blasting. For this purpose dynamite was employed — the central part of the carriageway of the avenue being fenced against use by the public, and a small wooden building was placed there in which the dynamite for use was kept. Of the details of the explosion, it is enough to say that in our opinion the evidence was sufficient to authorize the jury to find that an excessive amount of dynamite was stored in the magazine and that proper precautions had not been taken for guarding it against the danger of explosion. The action, however, is not brought against the sub-contractor, but against the city of New York, McDonald, who contracted with the city for the construction and subsequent operation of the subway, and the Rapid Transit Subway Construction Company, which rendered financial aid to McDonald in the execution of his contract. The question presented on this appeal is whether any of these defendants is liable for the negligence of the sub-contractor.

On February 21, 1900, under the provisions of the Rapid Transit Act (L. 1892, ch. 556; L. 1896, ch. 729; L. 1900, ch. 16; L. 1901, ch. 4; L. 1904, ch. 752), the rapid transit commissioners were authorized to enter into a contract on behalf of the city for the construction and equipment of a railroad upon the route and in accordance with the general plans adopted by the commissioners. Subdivision 5, section 24 of the Rapid Transit Act authorized the contractor to enter upon and underneath the several streets of the city for the prosecution of the work and the use of such streets was declared to be a public use. In September, 1900, Shaler entered into a sub-contract with McDonald to do the work along the line of which the explosion occurred.

We think it clear that under previous decisions of this

court the city was not liable for the negligence of the contractor to whom the work had been let. (*Froelich* v. *City of New York*, 199 N. Y. 466; *Uppington* v. *City of New York*, 165 N. Y. 222.) Nor do we think the city can be held liable on the ground that it suffered a nuisance to be maintained in the street, the street having been withdrawn from its possession and control. It was not liable for the default of the fire department or of the bureau of combustibles. (*Maxmilian* v. *Mayor, etc., of N. Y.*, 62 N. Y. 160; *Ham* v. *Mayor, etc., of N. Y.*, 70 N. Y. 459; *Smith* v. *City of Rochester*, 76 N. Y. 506, 513; *Terhune* v. *Mayor, etc., of N. Y.*, 88 N. Y. 247.) Nor was there evidence to show that the city authorities were aware that any excessive quantity of dynamite was being stored. The complaint was, therefore, properly dismissed as against the city, and it may be that the same doctrine that gives immunity to the city would also give immunity to the defendant McDonald, the principal contractor, for the negligence of his independent sub-contractor. Whether this is so, it is unnecessary to determine, as we are of opinion that McDonald was liable in this case by the express terms of his contract with the rapid transit commissioners. The contract contained the following provisions :

"Traffic to be Maintained. Indemnification for accidents.— The contractor shall during the performance of the work safely maintain the traffic on all the streets, avenues, highways, parks and other public places in connection with the work, and take all necessary precautions to place proper guards for the prevention of accidents, and put up and keep at night suitable and sufficient lights and indemnify and save harmless the city against and from all damages and costs to which it may be put by reason of injury to the person or property of another or others, resulting from negligence or carelessness in the performance of the work or from guarding the same, or from any improper materials used in its construction, or by or on account of any act or omission of the contractor or the agents thereof.

"Contractor's Liability for Damage to abutting property.— *The contractor shall be responsible for all damage which may be done to abutting property or buildings or structures thereon by the method in which the construction hereunder shall be done, but not including in such damage any damage necessarily arising from proper construction pursuant to this contract or the reasonable use, occupation or obstruction of the streets thereby.*"

An analysis of this portion of the contract shows that it contained three independent and different covenants or agreements on the part of the contractor. The first is one to safely maintain traffic on the public streets and to take necessary precautions and erect proper guards for the prevention of accidents; the second, to indemnify the city against any or all damage to which it might be put by reason of negligence in the performance of the work; the third, to be responsible for damages to abutting property, buildings or structures arising from other than the proper construction of the work and the reasonable use and occupation of the streets. As we construe this last clause — a construction supported by the marginal notes — it was not an agreement of indemnity to the city, for that was sufficiently covered by the preceding provisions, but an agreement to be responsible to abutting owners for damages arising from improper construction or unreasonable use and occupation of the streets. Therefore, the question before us is further narrowed to this: Can an abutting owner maintain an action under this provision of the contract to which contract he is not a party? To sustain a negative answer the respondent relies upon the decision of this court in *French* v. *Vix* (143 N. Y. 90). In that case the owner of a lot of land entered into a contract with the defendants for the construction of a house, under which the latter agreed to become answerable "and accountable for any damages that may be done to the property or person of any neighbor" during the performance of the work. The defendants made a sub-contract for the excavation, the sub-contractor agreeing to assume all responsibility for damage to persons or property. The plaintiff owned an adjoining house which was injured by the blasting carried on by the sub-contractor. She sought to maintain the action on the provision of the defendant's contract with the owner of the adjacent land. She was defeated in this court on two grounds: 1. That the contract was simply one of indemnity and was not intended for the plaintiff's benefit. That ground has no application to the present case under the construction we have given to the defendant's contract. 2. That even if the contract was intended for her benefit she could not recover because she was not a party to it, nor in privity with the parties, and as to her it was without consideration. The second ground is but a reiteration of the general rule of law that a stranger to a contract cannot maintain an action upon it, and if the defendant's contract were with private persons that rule of law would be applicable. But even between private parties the rule is not universal, and a third party may maintain an action on a contract against the promisor where the contract is made for his benefit and some obligation or duty to the third party rests on the promisee. Thus, where the promisee is indebted to a stranger to the contract, a promise made on sufficient consideration may be enforced by the latter. (*Lawrence* v. *Fox*, 20 N. Y. 268; *Burr* v. *Beers*, 24 N. Y. 178.) In *Todd* v. *Weber* (95 N. Y. 181) it was held that the relation of parent and child was sufficient consideration for a contract made by the parent with others for the support of the child, and that the latter might enforce it by action. In *Buchanan* v. *Tilden* (158 N. Y. 109) the same doctrine was held in regard to a contract made by a husband for the benefit of his wife. A

8

still broader doctrine is held in the case of what may be termed public contracts. In *Little* v. *Banks* (85 N. Y. 258) it was said: "Contractors with the State, who assume, for a consideration received from the sovereign power, by covenant, express or implied, to do certain things, are liable, in case of neglect to perform such covenant, to a private action at the suit of the party injured by such neglect, and such contract inures to the benefit of the individual who is interested in its performance." (p. 263.) In that case the defendant had a contract with the state officers to sell and deliver to the public volumes of the law reports, which he was about to publish, at certain specified prices, and upon failure to comply with that agreement he agreed to pay to any persons aggrieved the sum of $100. It was held that the plaintiff, a person to whom the defendant had refused to deliver such reports, might maintain his action to recover the stipulated damages. In *Robinson* v. *Chamberlain* (34 N. Y. 389) a contractor for keeping the state canal in repair was held liable for injuries sustained by the canal boat of a private individual by the failure of the defendant to perform his contract. In *Cook* v. *Dean* (11 App. Div. 123; affd. on opinion below, 160 N. Y. 660) a contractor who entered into a contract with the supervisors of two counties for the construction of a bridge over a creek dividing the two counties, and also for the construction and maintenance of a temporary bridge during the progress of the main work, was held liable for defects in the temporary structure through which the plaintiff was injured, though neither of the counties would have been liable for such neglect. (*Markey* v. *County of Queens*, 154 N. Y. 675, 684.) The most recent case in this court is that of *Pond* v. *New Rochelle Water Co.* (183 N. Y. 330). There the predecessor of the defendant had made a contract with the village of Pelham Manor for supplying not only the village itself, but also all its inhabitants with a supply of water at certain specified rates. The plaintiff, who was a resident and householder of said village, brought the action to restrain the defendant from exacting from him a higher water rate than that specified in the agreement with the village. The objection that the plaintiff was a stranger to the contract was overruled. Judge EDWARD T. BARTLETT, writing for the court, said: " In the case before us we have a municipality entering into a contract for the benefit of its inhabitants, the object being to supply them with pure and wholesome water at reasonable rates. While there is not presented a domestic relation like that of father and child or husband and wife, yet it cannot be said that this contract was made for the benefit of a stranger. In the case before us the municipality sought to protect its inhabitants, who were at the time of the execution of the contract consumers of water, and those who might thereafter become so, from extortion by a corporation having granted to it a valuable franchise extending over a long period of time." (See, also, *Rochester Telephone Co.* v. *Ross,* 195 N. Y. 429.)

In principle the case cited and the one before us seem to be almost identical. There, as here, the first object of the contract was for the supply of a corporate, as distinguished from a governmental want; there it was supplying water for the hydrants, street and fire purposes; here the construction of a railroad. In the first case it was held that the village in its governmental character had sufficient interest in the welfare of its citizens and inhabitants to secure to each of them a supply of water at reasonable rates. In the case before us it was well known and generally appreciated that for at least some very substantial part of the discomfort, damage and injury occasioned to the abutters by even the most careful and proper prosecution of the work, the abutter could not recover indemnity or compensation. It was also appreciated that in the prosecution of all great works, at times negligence and fault will occur, and that such fault will often be on the part of irresponsible parties from whom there would be small chance of recovering pecuniary redress. Therefore, though the city might not be liable for injuries occasioned by such negligence, it was entirely proper, if not morally obligatory upon the part of the rapid transit commissioners to secure the abutting owners from loss or damage occasioned by negligence and improper conduct of the work. This could only be accomplished by placing liability for the negligence upon a responsible contractor to whom they might give out the work, for the commissioners could not dictate the sub-contractors with whom he might contract. We are of opinion, therefore, that the defendant McDonald was, under his contract, liable for the damages sustained by the plaintiffs, and as to him the judgment below should be reversed, and a new trial granted, with costs to abide the event. It should be affirmed, with costs, as to the city of New York and the Rapid Transit Subway Construction Company, as to which last defendant we see no possible theory for imposing liability on it.

HAIGHT, J. (dissenting in part). I concur in the opinion of the chief judge, in so far as he holds that the judg-. ment of nonsuit should be reversed as to McDonald; but I am also of the opinion that there should be a reversal as to the city of New York.

Assuming that the fire department and the bureau of combustibles exercised a governmental function and that such bureau was charged with the duty of regulating the use of dynamite, yet I think the city is not relieved from liability in this case by reason of such facts. The care and maintenance of highways in a safe condition was also the exercise of governmental functions. But it was long since held in this court that municipalities which exist under charters issued by the state, vesting in them the care and maintenance of the highways, were by reason of the acceptance of such charters impliedly deemed to have contracted to keep and maintain the high-ways in a safe condition; and that for a failure so to do, the municipalities became liable in damage to the persons injured. (*Conrad* v. *Trustees of Village of Ithaca*, 16 N. Y. 158. See, also, *Weet* v. *Trustees of Village of Brockport*, reported in note, 16 N. Y. 161.) If placing the public ways under the care of the police or fire departments will relieve the municipalities from liability for injuries resulting from unsafe highways, then an easy way has been discovered by which they can annul their contractual relation to the people of the state. I am unwilling to assent to such a doctrine. I am of the opinion that the city of New York in accepting its charter from the state has undertaken to keep the streets and highways in a safe condition, and this duty being contractual it becomes a municipal duty and remains such even though they may employ policemen or firemen to assist in the discharge of that duty.

It appears from the evidence that the contractor in constructing a subway underneath Park avenue was permitted to sink two shafts in the avenue at the corner of Forty-first street, one on the west side in front of the Murray Hill Hotel and the other on the east side of the avenue. These shafts were inclosed by a fence, but between the westerly curb and the inclosure there was retained a passageway for vehicles. Inside of the fence, on the highway, was constructed a platform upon upright posts about twelve feet high, on which was placed an engine and boiler and hoisting apparatus. Underneath the platform, which supported the engine and boiler, was maintained a magazine for dynamite. The magazine was a wooden shanty, entrance to which was had through a door which was frequently left open. In cleaning out the fire under the boiler they dumped the fire on the floor of the platform above the magazine or else threw it on to the pavement below. Inside the shanty was erected a cupboard with sliding shelves made of wire netting for holding the dynamite, and underneath this cupboard was a coil of steam pipes which were heated by live steam from the boiler above and used for the purpose of thawing the dynamite when frozen. The shanty, having no windows, was dark and consequently a light was necessary. This was furnished by a candle on the south wall which was held in place by two nails crossing each other and driven into the woodwork. The candle was left burning nearly all the time. Occasionally paper used in tamping was left under the candle and only two feet away from it. The fixing of the explosive caps to the dynamite sticks and making up the tamping paper into cartridges for blasting purposes was done inside of the shanty, and the magazine was frequently left with no one in charge, with the candle burning and with the door unlocked. The evidence further tends to show that in the magazine there was usually stored from one hundred and fifty to six hundred pounds of dynamite, and on the day of the explosion, the 27th day of January, 1902, there was at least three hundred and fifty pounds, and perhaps six hundred and fifty pounds, therein. This structure had been maintained for such a length of time that the city must be deemed to have had notice of its existence.

I am of the opinion that the evidence was sufficient to justify a finding that the city had suffered a dangerous nuisance to be maintained in Park avenue, a public highway, in violation of its agreement with the people of the state, and that consequently it was responsible for the damages caused by the explosion.

WERNER, WILLARD BARTLETT, CHASE and COLLIN, JJ., concur with CULLEN, Ch. J.; HAIGHT, J., reads opinion dissenting from affirmance of judgment in favor of the city of New York; HISCOCK, J., absent.

Judgment accordingly.

THE PEOPLE OF THE STATE OF NEW YORK ex rel. HUDSON AND MANHATTAN RAILROAD COMPANY, Appellant, *v.* THE STATE BOARD OF TAX COMMISSIONERS, Respondent.

THE CITY OF NEW YORK, Intervening, Appellant.
(Two Proceedings.)

Tax — special franchise tax upon railroad corporation's right to construct, maintain and operate its railroad in, under, above or through streets, highways or public places — when right of way for tunnel under Hudson river not subject to franchise tax — when subject thereto — duty and powers of state board of tax commissioners in making assessments on special franchises.

1. A special franchise, so far as railroads are concerned, is the right or permission to construct, maintain and operate the same in, under, above, on or through streets, highways or public places. The Hudson river is a highway in the broad sense of that term, and its waters being subject to the ebb and flow of the tide, the title to the bed of the river is in the state, but navigable streams do not fall within the ordinary nomenclature of highways, unless the intent to include them is apparent.

2. Where relator's predecessor in title acquired land from the state by grant for the purpose of building a railroad under the Hudson river, its tunnels and railroads constructed in this part of its route are constructed on its own right of way and are not to be deemed the exercise of a special franchise.

3. This principle does not apply to tunnels, the relator's right to construct and maintain which proceeds entirely from the grant of the rapid transit commission as a part of a continuous subway road under the streets of the city of New York and the waters of the Hudson to the state line, and hence such property is taxable as a special franchise.

4. No one has a right to use the streets of the city of New York for the purpose of a railroad except by virtue of a franchise proceeding from the state. The right to enter the streets is unquestionably a special franchise and the state board is expressly directed to include as part of the special franchise the value of the tangible property. Relator may be taxed on such property the same as any other property situated within the state.

5. Where a railroad under construction under the Hudson was uncompleted and it was uncertain whether it would be a profitable

venture or otherwise, the structure was properly assessable under the Special Franchise Act at the cost of reproduction, but under the circumstances no assessment should have been placed upon the franchise.

6. There is no authority in the state board to assess special franchises at less than their full value, or to consider the general rate of taxation in any particular taxing district. In the absence of a finding to the contrary, it must be assumed that the state board assessed the relator's property at its full value, and the court should equalize such assessment with that of other property when such other property is not assessed at full value.

People ex rel. H. & M. R. R. Co. v. *Tax Comrs.*, 142 App. Div. 220, reversed.

People ex rel. H. & M. R. R. Co. v. *Tax Comrs.*, 143 App. Div. 26, reversed.

(Argued June 2, 1911; decided October 3, 1911.)

CROSS-APPEALS by the relator and the intervenor from an order of the Appellate Division of the Supreme Court in the third judicial department, entered January 4, 1911, which reversed an order of Special Term reducing the special franchise tax of the relator, for the year 1908, from $6,900,000, as fixed by the state board of tax commissioners, to $3,596,326.35, but modified the determination of said tax board by reducing the valuation to $6,141,000.

Cross-appeals by the relator and the intervenor from an order of the Appellate Division of the Supreme Court in the first judicial department, entered March 22, 1911, which modified and affirmed as modified an order of Special Term confirming the assessment of a special franchise tax against the relator for the year 1909.

The facts, so far as material, are stated in the opinion.

Frederic B. Jennings and *Edward R. Greene* for relator, appellant. Until the work under these special franchises was so far progressed as to constitute a railroad, either in operation or at least ready for operation, it was not assessable under the special franchise tax provisions of the act. (Cons. Laws, ch. 60, § 2, subd. 3.) Until some part of the railroad authorized by such franchise is completed and ready for operation, so as to realize a value in earning capacity, the intangible part of the franchise has no assessable value. (*People ex rel. Met. St. Ry. Co. v. Tax Comrs.*, 174 N. Y. 417, 440; *People ex rel. J. W. S. Co. v. Tax Comrs.*, 128 App. Div. 17; *People ex rel. Bryan v. Tax Comrs.*, 67 Misc. Rep. 479; *People ex rel. B. H. R. R. Co. v. Tax Comrs.*, 69 Misc. Rep. 646.) The assessment upon the tangible property at what was assumed to be the cost of reproduction was clearly made upon an erroneous basis and is greatly in excess of any fair value of such tangible property. (*People ex rel. C. S. Co. v. Barker*, 7 App. Div. 27; 151 N. Y. 639; *People ex rel. D., L. & W. R. R. Co. v. Clapp*, 152 N. Y. 490; *People ex rel. Edison E. L. Co. v. Barker*, 139 N. Y. 61; *People ex rel. N. Y. & W. Ry. Co. v. Tax Comrs.*, 132 App. Div. 608.) The inclusion in the assessment of the portions of the uptown tunnels between the bulkhead and the center of the river and also of the bridge across Dey street connecting the terminal buildings on either side was illegal, erroneous and improper. (*People ex rel. Met. St. Ry. Co. v. Tax Comrs.*, 174 N. Y. 417, 435; *Saunders v. N. Y. C. & H. R. R. R. Co.*, 144 N. Y. 87; *People ex rel. Retsof Co. v. Priest*, 75 App. Div. 131.) The assessment of the special franchise is illegal because any attempt of the legislature to assess or tax the right to carry on interstate commerce is unconstitutional. (*People ex rel. P. R. R. Co. v. Wemple*, 138 N. Y. 1; *Ratterman v. W. U. Tel. Co.*, 127 U. S. 411; *Leloup v. Port of Mobile*, 127 U. S. 640; *G. H., etc., Ry. Co. v. Texas*, 210 U.S. 217; *People ex rel. P. R. R. Co. v. Tax Comrs.*, 104 N. Y. 240; *Fargo v. Michigan*, 121 U. S. 230; *P. S. S. Co. v. Pennsylvania*, 122 U. S. 326.) The assessment was unequal because the property was assessed at what the state board considered its full value, while real estate generally in the city of New York was assessed at only eighty-nine per cent of its

value, as shown by the equalization table, and as found
by the court below. Any valuation made must accordingly be reduced to eighty-nine per cent to equalize with
real estate generally. (*Jamaica Water Supply Co.* v.
Tax Comrs., 196 N. Y. 63.)

Archibald R. Watson, Corporation Counsel (*Curtis
A. Peters* and *Addison B. Scoville* of counsel), for city
of New York, appellant. The intangible special franchises possessed by the relator constitute property. (*People* v. *O'Brien*, 111 N. Y. 1.) As the intangible special
franchises in question constitute property they are taxable. (*Saunders* v. *N. Y. C. & H. R. R. R. Co.*, 144
N. Y. 75; *Coxe* v. *State*, 144 N. Y. 396; *Matter of City
of New York*, 168 N. Y. 134.) The relator failed to
prove either to the tax commissioners or to the court that
the assessment was erroneous by reason of overvaluation.
(*People ex rel. D., L. & W. R. R. Co.* v. *Clapp*,
152 N. Y. 490; *People ex rel. J. W. S. Co.* v. *Tax
Comrs.*, 196 N. Y. 59; *People ex rel. N. Y. & N. J. Tel.
Co.* v. *Neff*, 15 App. Div. 8; 156 N. Y. 701; *Brown* v.
Otis, 98 App. Div. 554; *People ex rel. Greenwood* v.
Feitner, 77 App. Div. 428; *People ex rel. German Look-
ing Glass Plate Co.* v. *Barker*, 75 Hun, 6; *Matter of
Winegard*, 78 Hun, 58.) The Appellate Division erred
in reducing the assessment for purposes of equalization.
(*People ex rel. Fiske* v. *Feitner*, 95 App. Div. 217; 180
N. Y. 536; *People ex rel. Stewart* v. *Feitner*, 95 App.
Div. 481; *People ex rel. Warren* v. *Carter*, 109 N. Y.
576; *People ex rel. W. F. Ins. Co.* v. *Davenport*, 91
N. Y. 574; *People ex rel. Osgood* v. *Commissioners*, 99
N. Y. 154; *People ex rel. Burke* v. *Wells*, 184 N. Y. 275,
279.) The tax in question does not constitute an inter-
ference by the state with interstate commerce. (*P. T. C.
Co.* v. *Adams*, 155 U. S. 688.)

Thomas Carmody, Attorney-General (*C. R. McSpar-
ren* of counsel), for respondent.

CULLEN, Ch. J.   The appeals in these two proceedings present, with a single exception, the same questions for review, and, therefore, in this opinion may be considered together — the exception, which occurs in the 1909 assessment, being treated separately.   The assessment for the year 1908 was reviewed by the Special Term of the Supreme Court in the county of Albany, which court reduced the valuation as fixed by the state board of tax commissioners almost one-half.   On appeal the Appellate Division of the third department reversed the decision of the Special Term both on the facts and the law, and confirmed the action of the state board, except that it reduced said valuation by the amount of 11%, it appearing by stipulation of the parties that the average assessed valuation of real estate in the city of New York for the year in question was 89%.

On a certiorari to review the assessed valuation for the year 1909 the Special Term in the county of New York wholly confirmed the action of the state board.   The Appellate Division, first department, modified this determination in one respect, reducing the assessed value by the amount of 11% on the same principle on which the action of the Appellate Division in the other proceeding was based, and from these final orders the relator and the intervenor, the city of New York, have taken appeals to this court.

The controversy in these cases presents chiefly questions of fact which this court cannot review, provided there is any evidence to sustain the findings of the courts below, and unless the relator is right in certain propositions of law which it contends should govern assessments of this class.   That there is evidence to sustain the determinations of the state board is reasonably clear.   The expert evidence shows that the assessed valuation of the tangible property does not exceed the cost of reproduction.   The relator, however, contends that the cost of reproduction does not necessarily determine the value of the property. That proposition may be conceded, but nevertheless it is some evidence of value. In 1908 no part of the relator's tunnel, structures and roadway was so far completed as to enable it to put any part of its railroad in operation. It may possibly happen that when the work is completed and the railroad operated, the enterprise will turn out to be so unremunerative as to make the tangible property worth less than the cost of reproduction. On the other hand, it may be that the expectations of the promoters of the enterprise will be realized or exceeded and the road prove highly profitable. The promoters evidently had faith in it, for they continued its prosecution. There is no claim that there has been any mistake in the plans or construction of the work which necessitates the abandonment or replacing of any part of the structure and the substitution of a new structure. Under these circumstances, we think until it is shown by actual experience that the structure is worth less than the cost of reproduction, such cost is the best evidence of value.

It is contended by the relator that until the work under the special franchise had progressed so far as to constitute a railroad, it was not assessable under the Special Franchise Act. To this we can only answer, why? A house partly constructed but not completed is taxed at the value of the structure as it exists at the time of the assessment, and the same is true of a partially completed railroad running through the country. If under the general laws existing before the enactment of the Special Franchise Tax Act, the uncompleted structure of the relator would be taxable, it certainly was not the intent of the special franchise statute to relieve it from taxation.

It is next urged that as the intangible property of the relator, to wit, the right to use the streets, was found in the assessment of 1908 to be of no value, the state board had no jurisdiction to assess the tangible property of the relator. Again, we can only answer, why? The right to enter the streets is, under the statute, unquestionably a special franchise and the state board is expressly directed by the statute to include as part of the special franchise the value of the tangible property. It is entirely possible that in some cases the intangible right may be of no value, nevertheless this cannot operate (except in the manner hereinbefore suggested) to reduce the value of the tangible property or to relieve the state board from the duty of ascertaining and determining its value.

Again, it is contended that the taxation of the relator's property is illegal because it imposes a burden upon interstate commerce. This claim hardly needs refutation. The streets and public places belong to the public. In the old city of New York the fee is in the city in trust for the public. No one has a right to use such streets for the purpose of a railroad except by virtue of a franchise proceeding from the state. That franchise is property which cannot be revoked except for cause, unless the right of revocation is reserved in the grant. (*People* v. *O'Brien*, 111 N. Y. 1.) It is difficult to see why the relator may not be taxed on such property the same as any other property situated within the state.

In one claim, however, we agree that the relator is right. As to what are termed the upper tunnels under the Hudson river, the relator had the right to construct and maintain those apart from the certificate granted by the rapid transit railroad commissioners of New York city. Such certificate does include the upper tunnels, but there is an express provision in it that the payment of $100 a year required by said certificate should not be considered a waiver of the rights which the grantee had to the bed of the Hudson river by deed from the state of New York. The Hudson Tunnel Railroad Company was incorporated under the laws of the states of New York and New Jersey for the purpose of building a railroad from the state of New Jersey under the Hudson river to and in the city of New York. By L. 1890, ch. 164, it

126   People ex rel. R. R. Co. v. Tax Comrs.

[203 N. Y.]   Opinion, per Cullen, Ch. J.   [Oct.,

was allowed four years from the passage of the act to complete its tunnel and railroad. In June, 1890, it presented its petition to the commissioners of the land office for a right of way 160 feet in width and 40 feet in height beneath the lands under the waters of the Hudson river for the construction of its tunnels and the use of the company's railroad. Thereafter, and on February 24th, 1891, under the provisions of the General Railroad Act (L. 1850, ch. 140), and in pursuance of a resolution of the commissioners of the land office, the state of New York by letters patent granted to the said company the right of way asked for. The relator has succeeded to the rights and property of the said tunnel company. Therefore the tunnels and railroad of the relator on this part of its route, being constructed on its own right of way, are not to be deemed the exercise of a special franchise under the statute. A different view of this question seems to have been taken by the Appellate Division of the first department in a decision by a divided court (*People ex rel. Bryan* v. *State Board of Tax Comrs.*, 142 App. Div. Div. 796) where it was held that the tunnels of the New York & Long Island R..R. Co. under the East river between the boroughs of Manhattan and Queens in the city of New York were properly assessed by the state board of tax commissioners instead of the local authorities. The definition of a special franchise is found in subdivision 3 of section 2 of the Tax Law (Cons. Laws, ch. 60), which reads as follows:

·   "The terms 'land,' 'real estate,' and 'real property,' as used in this chapter, include the land itself above and under water, all buildings and other articles and structures, substructures and superstructures, erected upon, under or above, or affixed to the same; all wharves and piers, including the value of the right to collect wharfage, cranage or dockage thereon; all bridges, all telegraph lines, wires, poles and appurtenances; all supports and inclosures for electrical conductors and other appurtenances upon, above and under ground; all surface, underground or elevated railroads, including the value of all franchises, rights or permission to construct, maintain or operate the same in, under, above, on or through, streets, highways or public places; all railroad structures, substructures and superstructures, tracks and iron thereon; branches, switches and other fixtures permitted or authorized to be made, laid or placed in, upon, above or under any public or private road, street or ground; all mains, pipes and tanks laid or placed in, upon, above or under any public or private street or place for conducting steam, heat, water, oil, electricity or any property, substance or product capable of transportation or conveyance therein or that is protected thereby, including the value of all franchises, rights, authority or permission to construct, maintain or operate, in, under, above, upon, or through, any streets, highways or public places, any mains, pipes, tanks, conduits or wires, with their appurtenances, for conducting water, steam, heat, light, power, gas, oil or other substance, or electricity for telegraphic, telephonic or other purposes; all trees and underwood growing upon land, and all mines, minerals, quarries and fossils in and under the same, except mines belonging to the state. A franchise, right, authority or permission specified in this subdivision shall for the purpose of taxation be known as a 'special franchise.' A special franchise shall be deemed to include the value of the tangible property of a person, copartnership, association or corporation situated in, upon, under or above any street, highway, public place or public waters in connection with the special franchise. The tangible property so included shall be taxed as a part of the special franchise. No property of a municipal corporation shall be subject to a special franchise tax."

An analysis of this section shows that a special franchise, so far as railroads are concerned, is the " rights or permission to construct, maintain and operate the same (railroads) in, under, above, on or through streets, highways or public places." Of course, the Hudson river is a highway in the broad sense of that term, and its waters being subject to the ebb and flow of the tide, the title to the bed of the river was in the state. But navigable streams do not fall within the ordinary nomenclature of highways, unless the intent to include them is apparent. None such appears in this statute. Wharves and piers constructed in the navigable waters of the state, including the value of the right to collect wharfage, cranage or dockage, are to be assessed in the same manner as real estate, and are not enumerated as special franchises. The statute assessing for the purpose of taxation special franchises was undoubtedly intended, at least in the first instance, to reach the right to use the public streets by public service corporations, such as street railroad, lighting, telegraph and telephone companies — a valuable property right which had hitherto escaped taxation. Were it not for the amendments to the statute which have been from time to time enacted, I should doubt whether it was intended to include the mere crossing of public streets or highways by the ordinary general railroads constructed and operated upon their own rights of way. Such roads and structures had always been subject to taxation as other real estate. The amendments to that statute, however, have set that question at rest, and it cannot now be denied that the right of such railroad companies to cross intersecting streets and highways in existence at the time of their construction is, in certain cases, a special franchise within the statute. Outside of the limits of villages and cities such crossings are not special franchises, unless they exceed 250 feet in length.

In the present case the Hudson Tunnel Company was incorporated under the former General Railroad Act. By its incorporation it received from the state the franchise to build a railroad. To do that it was necessary that it should acquire title to the right of way on which the road was to be built. The land to be acquired belonged to the state. The General Railroad Act (L. 1850, ch. 140, sec. 25) authorized the commissioners of the land office to grant to any railroad company formed under the act any land belonging to the state and required for the purpose of its road upon terms that might be agreed upon, or the company was authorized to acquire the same by appraisal in the same manner as the lands of individuals. The action of the land commissioners was not a grant to the company of any franchise. It was simply a grant of a title to land. Whether the letters patent conveyed a fee or an easement is immaterial. The company acquired by it such an interest in the land as authorized it to construct thereon its tunnels and railroad, not under any special franchise, but by virtue of its ownership of either land or an easement therein. As was pointed out by Judge EARL in *Langdon* v. *Mayor, etc., of N. Y.* (93 N. Y. 129), there are two distinct rights in navigable waters — ownership of the soil under water analogous to the ownership of dry land, regarded as a *jus privatum* vested in the crown, and the right to use and control both land and water, regarded as a *jus publicum* and vested in Parliament — both of which rights in this country are vested in the state. It was said by that judge: "The crown could convey the soil under water so as to give private rights therein, but the dominion and control over the waters, in the interest of commerce and navigation, for the benefit of all the subjects of the kingdom, could be exercised only by Parliament." (p. 155.) The right here granted was the private right or title to the soil, which in no way conflicted with or affected the rights of the public in the river. It is some privilege that has been given a party either in derogation of the public right, or as sharing in or by virtue of the public right that is a special franchise, not where all that has been done is done by virtue of the ownership of the soil or some interest therein. Thus, we are holding in a case decided at this time (*People ex rel. N. Y. Central & H. R. R. R. Co.* v. *Woodbury,* 203 N. Y. 167) that

9

where highways have been laid out across the rights of way of railroads subsequent to their construction, there exists no special franchise. I do not see how it is possible to differentiate this case from great portions of the New York Central railroad which, between New York and Albany, have for long distances been constructed within the bounds of the Hudson river under authority given that company's predecessor by the act of 1846 to so construct its road, and the title to the land acquired from grant of the land commissioners. (*N. Y. Central & H. R. R. R. Co.* v. *Aldridge*, 135 N. Y. 83.) Surely nobody has ever thought that that company was exercising any special franchise within the meaning of the statute, where the road runs in the bed of the river from point to point.

The principle which we have stated does not apply to the lower tunnels, the relator's right to construct and maintain which proceeds entirely from the grant of the rapid transit commission as a part of a continuous subway road under the streets of the city of New York and the waters of the Hudson to the state line. It follows that the upper tunnels should be assessed by the local officers of the city of New York as other property is assessed, and the assessment made by the state board should be reduced proportionately.

Accepting the cost of reproduction as proved in opposition to the relator's application for reduction as the fair value of the tangible property of the relator, it falls short of the assessment fixed by the state board for the year 1909 by something over $350,000. To support the assessment this discrepancy must be charged to the relator as the value of the intangible part of the special franchise. Personally I am of opinion that at this time no assessed value should be attributed to such privilege. It is true that no statute prescribes the net earnings rule as the method by which the value of a special franchise is to be computed, nor is there any decision of the courts that this method is to be exclusively adopted. It is also true that

that method of computation is not universally applicable. Nevertheless, in ordinary cases it is the best practical method that the taxing officers and the courts have as yet been able to evolve. I have said that in some cases it would be inapplicable; for instance: We all know that a franchise to maintain a street railroad on Fifth avenue in New York city would be worth a fortune and could be easily disposed of by the holder though not a rail had been laid or bought. If in that case the owner of the franchise were hawking it for sale, the mere privilege or franchise might probably be assessed at a large sum, its value being so great in proportion to the cost of the plant necessary for the exercise of the franchise. In this case, however, the amount which it is necessary to invest in the construction of the relator's tunnels and railroads is very large and the return that it will ultimately derive therefrom uncertain. If the expectations of the promoters are realized the franchise will prove very valuable and will then be so assessed. If these expectations are disappointed — promoters' expectations are often disappointed — the value of the privilege or franchise may be very small. It appears that so far as the road was completed for operation in the year 1909, the net earnings over operating expenses were only the sum of $35,000, with which to pay taxes and interest upon millions of bonds outstanding. I think under such circumstances no present value should have been attributed to the franchise.

The city appeals from the reduction made by the Appellate Division of 11% from the valuation made by the state board to equalize such valuation with the assessment of other property in the borough. This is in accordance with the rule laid down by this court in *People ex rel. Jamaica Water Supply Co. v. State Board of Tax Commrs.* (196 N. Y. 39). There is no authority in the state board to assess special franchises at less than their full value, or to consider the general rate of taxation in any particular taxing district. In a recent

case (*People ex rel. Manhattan Ry. Co. v. Woodbury,*
143 App. Div. 905; 203 N. Y. 231) the Supreme Court
refused to reduce an assessment made on the relator's
property in the borough of the Bronx so as to conform
with the general rate of assessment on real property
in that borough, but this was by reason of an express
finding made by the court that the assessed value of the
relator's property was less than its true value, even when
reduced so as to accord with the prevailing rate of assessment. In the absence of such a finding, it must be
assumed that the state board assessed the relator's property at its full value — a presumption which the evidence
in this case fully supports, and the relator was entitled to
the reduction.

The orders of the Special Term and Appellate Division
must be reversed, without costs in this court to either
party, and the proceedings remitted to the Special Term
for further hearing and disposition in accordance with
this opinion.

GRAY, J. I think I can quite concur with the chief
judge's opinion upon the question of special franchise, as
upon the merits. A special franchise granted to a railroad corporation is a right accorded to it to maintain its
road, where, without such authority, to do so would be
unlawful. What public places, or highways, are within
the legislative intent, when defining special franchises
can be determined, only, by the language of the statute.
While the river is a public highway, that such a highway
was not in contemplation, when speaking of the operation
of railroads, is sufficiently evident from the context; or,
if not, it is left in such doubt as to demand more explicit
legislation.

HAIGHT, WERNER, WILLARD BARTLETT, CHASE and
COLLIN, JJ., concur with CULLEN, Ch. J.; GRAY, J.,
concurs, in memorandum, with CULLEN, Ch. J.

Orders reversed, etc.

ATLANTIC BUILDING SUPPLY COMPANY, Respondent, *v.*
VULCANITE PORTLAND CEMENT COMPANY, Appellant.

**Bailment — contracts — person in possession of property of
another, as bailee, cannot appropriate it under, and for the purpose of carrying out, another contract between the same parties.**

A party having in his possession property of another as bailee has
no right to appropriate it contrary to the direction of the owner for
the purpose of carrying out the terms of another and independent
contract between them, by which the owner was to sell and deliver
to such bailee property of like character. Such action on the part
of the bailee justifies the owner in canceling the contract of
bailment.

Atlantic Building Supply Co. v. *V. P. Cement Co.*, 187 **App. Div.**
907, reversed.

(Argued June 18, 1911; decided October 8, 1911.)

APPEAL from a judgment of the Appellate Division of
the Supreme Court in the first judicial department, entered
April 4, 1910, affirming a judgment in favor of plaintiff
entered upon a verdict.

The nature of the action and the facts, so far as material, are stated in the opinion.

W. F. Upson and *William Forse Scott* for appellant.
Plaintiff was guilty of conversion of the cement it held
for defendant, and thus invited and justified a rescission
of the contract. (Greenl. on Ev. § 642; *Murray* v. *Bur-
ling,* 10 Johns. 172; *Bristol* v. *Burt,* 7 Johns. 254; *Frish-
berg* v. *Wissner,* 125 App. Div. 627; *Buchanan* v. *Smith,*
10 Hun, 474; *Collins* v. *Bennett,* 46 N. Y. 490; *Ross* v.
Southern C. O. Co., 41 Fed. Rep. 152; *Homer* v. *Thwing,*
3 Pick. 492; *Kowing* v. *Manly,* 49 N. Y. 192; *Ouderkirk*
v. *Central Bank,* 119 N. Y. 263; *Clark* v. *Whitaker,* 19
Conn. 319; *Osgood* v. *Nichols,* 5 Gray, 420: *Bursley* v.
Hamilton, 15 Pick. 40; *Simpson* v. *Wrenn,* 50 Ill. 222.)

Edward D. O'Brien for respondent. Taking cement
from the defendant's stock at Jersey City afforded no

ground for rescission of the trucking contracts, inasmuch as plaintiff had an express contract with the defendant entitling it to a quantity of cement in excess of the quantity taken; and the trucking contracts and the contract relating to the sale of cement to the plaintiff as a dealer were separate and distinct, having no relation to each other, and, therefore, a breach of the cement contract on the part of the plaintiff, if breach there was, does not affect plaintiff's right to recover under the trucking contract. (*Milage* v. *Woodward*, 186 N. Y. 252; *Joost* v. *B. H. R. R. Co.*, 113 App. Div. 499; *People* v. *Waters*, 114 App. 669; *Wyse* v. *Wyse*, 155 N. Y. 367, 372; *Sternaman* v. *Met. Life Ins. Co.*, 94 App. Div. 610; *Kenyon* v. *Knights Templars Assn.*, 122 N. Y. 247; *Nichols* v. *Mase*, 94 N. Y. 160; *West Shore R. R. Co.* v. *Hart*, 35 Hun, 576; *Pordage* v. *Cole*, 1 Saund. 320; *Jones* v. *Barkley*, 2 Doug. 689.)

CULLEN, Ch. J. The plaintiff dealt in the supply of building materials and transportation of the same. The defendant was engaged in the manufacture and sale of cement. The plaintiff made a contract with the defendant for the purchase of five thousand barrels of cement to be delivered from time to time. Subsequent to the execution of this contract the parties entered into another contract by which the plaintiff agreed to receive and store all the cement that the defendant might ship to Jersey City and deliver it from time to time to the various parties the defendant might direct, at specified rates. The contract was to last for one year or until ninety days' after notice of its termination. The parties entered upon the discharge of this last contract and during its prosecution the plaintiff, against the direction and command of the defendant, took from time to time such quantities of the cement as it wished, claiming the right to do so under the executory contract of purchase. For this reason, among others, the defendant refused to further employ the plaintiff in the storage or transportation of its cement and for that breach of the contract the plaintiff brought this action.   Against defendant's motion for the direction of a verdict and its exception to the denial thereof the court submitted it to the jury to determine as a question of fact whether the defendant had legal justification for canceling the contract.   It denied the defendant's request to charge that "If the plaintiff took the cement for its own purpose without authority the discharge was justified."

It is conceded that the two contracts between the parties, the one for the purchase of the cement and the other for the storage and transportation of that article, were entirely independent.   It requires no argument to show that whether the first contract be considered one for the purchase of an article to be manufactured or for the purchase of an existing article, the plaintiff acquired no title to any cement until it was delivered to it by the defendant or the particular articles to be delivered were designated and identified. (*Andrews* v. *Durant*, 11 N. Y. 35; *Kein* v. *Tupper*, 52 N. Y. 550; *Foot* v. *Marsh*, 51 N. Y. 288.)   The contracts being independent the the rights and obligations of the plaintiff under each contract were no greater nor different from what they would have been had there been no other.   Under the trucking contract, for the breach of which this suit is brought, the plaintiff was the mere bailee of the defendant, and it engaged to follow its directions in the delivery of the cement.   The fact that the plaintiff had also the contract for purchase, already mentioned, gave it no more right, against the defendant's direction, to appropriate, under that contract of purchase, the cement in its possession as bailee than it would have had to take the property from any other bailee of the defendant.   Nor had the plaintiff as bailee any greater right to take the property than it would have had to deliver it over to some other party who had or claimed to have a contract with the defendant for the purchase of cement. It is true that the defendant was under an obligation to sell the plaintiff cement. For a failure to comply with that obligation it was doubtless liable for damages; but it may have been under similar obligations to many other parties, all of which obligations it was unable to keep. This failure may not have been the result of any moral fault, but of accident or misfortune. However that may be, the · cement was the defendant's property, and it had the right to deliver it to whom it saw fit, remaining liable to the plaintiff for damages for the breach of its contract to sell, and the plaintiff, as bailee under the trucking contract, had no greater right to dispose of it, contrary to the defendant's instructions, than a shipping clerk in the latter's employ would have had. The defendant's cancellation of the contract was, therefore, justified as a matter of law, and the complaint should have been dismissed.

The judgment should be reversed and a new trial granted, costs to abide the event.

GRAY, VANN, WERNER, WILLARD BARTLETT, HISCOCK and CHASE, JJ., concur.

Judgment reversed, etc.

In the Matter of the Application of PETER W. FRASER et al., Appellants, for a Peremptory Writ of Mandamus against WILLIAM E. BROWN et al., Constituting the Board of Inspectors of Election for the Second Election District of the Town of Rutland, Respondents.

Election Law — registration of electors — unconstitutionality of the statute (L. 1911, ch. 649, § 6) requiring personal registration of electors residing outside of cities or villages with a population of five thousand or more.

1. Whatever is necessary to render effective any provision of a Constitution, whether it is a grant, restriction or prohibition, must be deemed implied and intended in the provision itself. Hence,

when the Constitution provides that certain voters "shall not be required to apply in person for registration at the first meeting of the" inspectors, it is implied that the legislature is prohibited from passing any statute to the contrary, because that implication is necessary to render the provision effective.

2. The legislature exceeded its power in providing that all voters residing outside of cities or villages with a population of five thousand or more whose names do not appear on the poll book of the last general election shall apply in person in order to be registered, and the attempt to impose this requirement, as made by section 6 of chapter 649 of the Laws of 1911, is unconstitutional and void.

Matter of Fraser v. *Brown,* 146 App. Div. 898, reversed.

(Argued October 2, 1911; decided October 10, 1911.)

APPEAL from an order of the Appellate Division of the Supreme Court in the fourth judicial department, entered September 28, 1911, which affirmed an order of Special Term denying as matter of law, and not in the exercise of discretion, a motion for a peremptory writ of mandamus requiring the registration of the appellants without their personal appearance before the board of election inspectors.

The facts, so far as material, are stated in the opinion.

Elon R. Brown and *Henry H. Babcock* for appellants. Section 159 of the Election Law, as amended by chapter 649 of the Laws of 1911, is unconstitutional, because it requires personal registration by large numbers of voters not residing in cities or villages. (Const. of N. Y. art. 2, § 4.)

D-Cady Herrick, Abram I. Elkus and *George R. Van Namee* for respondents. Section 159, as amended by chapter 649 of the Laws of 1911, is in conformity with the Constitution. (*People ex rel. Kemmler* v. *Durston,* 119 N. Y. 569; *People ex rel. Bolton* v. *Albertson,* 55 N. Y. 50; *People ex rel.* v. *Briggs,* 50 N. Y. 554; *People* v. *Gillson,* 109 N. Y. 389; *People ex rel.* v. *Rice,* 135 N. Y. 484; *Matter of Ahern* v. *Elder,* 195 N. Y. 493; *Rathbone* v.

Wirth, 150 N. Y. 475; *Matter of Albany Street*, 11 Wend. 148.) The statute will not be declared unconstitutional by reason of any alleged violations of the spirit of the Constitution or of the implications to be derived therefrom. (*People ex rel. Sinkler* v. *Terry*, 108 N. Y, 1; *People ex rel.* v. *Tax Comrs.*, 174 N. Y. 417; *People ex rel.* v. *Lochner*, 177 N. Y. 145.)

VANN, J. The counsel for the respondents waive all irregularities and unite with the counsel for the appellants in urging a decision of this appeal as soon as possible, so that the result may be known in time to govern inspectors of election in preparing the registry lists for the annual election now near at hand. The limited time at our disposal while the court is in session renders extended discussion impossible, but as the single question involved is within a narrow compass and does not require elaborate treatment, the interest of the public leads us to a brief expression of our views at the earliest moment practicable after they were matured in consultation.

The question presented for decision is whether the amendment of section 159 of the Election Law, as made by section six of chapter 649 of the Laws of 1911, is a violation of section four of article two of the Constitution of our state. Stated in another form the question is whether the legislature has the constitutional power to prohibit the registration of a duly qualified elector, who did not vote at the last general election and who does not reside in a city or village with a population of five thousand or more, without his personal appearance before the board of inspectors.

The Constitution provides that "Laws shall be made for ascertaining, by proper proofs, the citizens who shall be entitled to the right of suffrage hereby established, and for the registration of voters; which registration shall be completed at least ten days before each election. Such registration shall not be required for town and village elections except by express provision of law. In cities and villages having five thousand inhabitants or more, according to the last preceding state enumeration of inhabitants, voters shall be registered upon personal application only; but voters not residing in such cities or villages shall not be required to apply in person for registration at the first meeting of the officers having charge of the registry of voters." (Article 2, § 4.)

The Election Law prior to the amendment in question provided as follows:

"§ 150. Meetings for registration. Before every general election, the board of inspectors for each election district in every city, and in villages having five thousand inhabitants or more, shall hold four meetings for the registration of the voters thereof, at the place designated therefor, to be known respectively as the first, second, third and fourth meetings for registration. * * * In all election districts other than in cities or villages having five thousand inhabitants or more, the board of inspectors of election for each such election district shall hold two meetings for the registration of voters thereof, at the places designated therefor, before each general election, namely, on the fourth and third Saturdays before the election, to be known respectively as the first and second meetings for registration, * * *."

"§ 159. At the first meeting for registration in any election district where only two meetings for the registration of voters are held for any general election, as provided in section one hundred and fifty of this article, the inspectors shall place upon the register the names of all persons who voted at the last preceding general election, as shown by the register or poll book of such election, except the names of such voters as are proven to the satisfaction of such inspectors to have ceased to be voters in such district since such general election, and also at said first meeting and at the second meeting, they shall place on the register the names of all persons known or proven to the satisfaction of the inspectors to be then or thereafter entitled to vote at the election for which such registration is made." (L. 1909, ch. 22.)

Section 159 of the Election Law, as amended by section six of chapter 649 of the Laws of 1911, is as follows: "At the first meeting for registration in any election district wholly outside of a city or a village · having five thousand inhabitants or more, the inspectors shall place upon the register the names of all persons who voted at the last preceding general election, as shown by the register or poll-book of such election and also those presenting themselves in person, except the names of such electors as are proven to the satisfaction of such inspectors to have ceased to be electors in such district since such general election, and upon all days of registration the names of all other persons who may appear in person before the said board and apply for registration and who are or who will be at the election for which the registration is made qualified electors."

The effect of the amendment is to require all voters residing in the country who did not vote at the last general election to apply in person in order to be registered at the first meeting of the inspectors, for obviously no voter can be registered except as authorized by the amendment.

We think that the Constitution, in providing that voters residing in rural districts shall not be required to apply in person at the first meeting of the officers having charge of the registry of voters, necessarily implies that such voters may be registered at that meeting without applying in person. We quote again the last sentence of the constitutional provision: "In cities and villages having five thousand inhabitants or more, * * * voters shall be registered upon personal application only; *but voters not residing in such cities or villages shall not be required to apply in person for registration at the first meeting of the officers having charge of the registry of voters.*"

This is a single sentence consisting of two clauses, which must be read together in order to discover the meaning of the sentence as a whole. The entire sentence divides voters into two classes, depending on the political division in which they reside. The first clause applies exclusively to voters who reside in cities or villages with the population named, and expressly restricts the registration of that class to such as apply in person. The second clause applies exclusively to voters who do not reside in such cities or villages and impliedly permits the registration of that class at the first meeting of the officers in charge without personal application. The second clause commences with the word "but," which, as thus used, indicates transition of thought or a change in the nature of the rule, and reading on we find the change to be that voters residing in country districts need not apply in person at the first meeting. While the legislature may provide that an application must be made by a voter of either class, it cannot provide that those belonging to the second, or such as reside in rural sections, shall apply in person on the first day, although it may require them to apply by letter, or through an agent, or in any reasonable way that it sees fit, other than by personal application. The obvious reason for the distinction is that personal appearance before the board is much less convenient in those localities where many of the electors live far from the place of registration, than in cities and villages where they live comparatively near. In some towns certain voters would have to travel many miles over poor roads and it may be in bad weather, in order to appear in person to be registered. This would be a hardship tending to hinder registration in many cases, and in the case of some aged or infirm electors, a hardship so severe as to prevent their registration altogether. The discussion in the constitutional convention tends strongly to show not only that this was the reason for making the discrimination, but that the provision was understood to mean that voters from farming communities could be registered on the first day without attending in person, even if they did not vote the year before. (Revised Records Cons. Conv. of 1894, vol. 4, pp. 111, 112 and 716 to 723; Lincoln's Cons. History, vol. 3, pp. 102 to 107.)

If the Constitution does not mean this, what does it mean? What was the object of the last clause of the sentence in question? It has some important function to perform or it would not appear in a solemn and dignified instrument enacted by the people themselves as the structural law of the state. If it was intended, as the respondents claim, to permit registration by copying the last poll list, it does not say so. No such idea would be suggested to the minds of the "plain people" for whom the Constitution was written. Moreover, no such permission was needed, for independent of the last clause, the legislature may make reasonable regulations to govern registration, provided they do not conflict with any constitutional requirement. If by the last clause it was intended simply to require more than one day for registration in country districts, as the respondents also claim, why was it not required expressly, instead of in a roundabout way, resting wholly on an implication for which we find no warrant in the language of the Constitution?

"Proper proofs" may be required by the legislature and, within the limits of reason, the nature of the proof is under its control, except that proof involving personal appearance cannot be required on the first day. Proof by affidavit, or by the testimony of a third person may be required by statute, but if the proof so required is furnished at the first meeting, to the satisfaction of the inspectors, the legislature can neither authorize nor require those officers to refuse to register without the personal appearance of the applicant. That is one thing that it is prohibited from doing.

It is true that the prohibition rests on implication, but

so do many commands of the Constitution, including the construction contended for by the respondents. No Constitution was ever drawn so as to be an effective foundation for the government of a state without applying thereto the doctrine of implication. It is well established that whatever is necessary to render effective any provision of a Constitution, whether it is a grant, restriction or prohibition, " must be deemed implied and intended in the provision itself." (Black's Constitutional Law, 78; Endlich on Interpretation of Statutes, § 535; Story on the Constitution, § 428, and cases cited.) Hence, when the Constitution provides that certain voters "shall not be required to apply in person for registration at the first meeting of the " inspectors, it is implied that the legislature is prohibited from passing any statute to the contrary, because that implication is necessary to render the provision effective.

After considering the question with the serious concern which its importance demands, we are compelled to adjudge that the legislature exceeded its power in providing that all voters residing outside of cities or villages with a population of five thousand or more whose names do not appear on the poll book of the last general election, shall apply in person in order to be registered and that the attempt to impose this requirement, as made by section six of chapter 649 of the Laws of 1911, is unconstitutional and void. As this is a test case and the respondents not only acted in good faith but co-operated with the appellants in the effort to settle the law for the benefit of the public at large, no costs are allowed to either party.

The orders should be reversed and the motion for a peremptory writ of mandamus granted, without costs.

CULLEN, Ch. J., HAIGHT, WERNER, WILLARD BARTLETT, HISCOCK and CHASE, JJ., concur.

Orders reversed, etc.

In the Matter of the Application of JOHN J. HOPPER, Appellant, *v.* J. GABRIEL BRITT et al., Constituting the Board of Elections of the City of New York, Respondents.

Constitutional law — legislation contravening the spirit of the Constitution is void as well as legislation which violates its express commands — Election Law — unconstitutionality of the statute (L. 1911, ch. 649, § 12) providing that the name of a person, nominated by more than one party, shall be printed but once upon the ballot.

1. Not only is legislation contravening the express commands of the Constitution void, but legislation contravening what the Constitution necessarily implies is also void.

2. The power granted to the legislature to prescribe the method of conducting elections cannot be so exercised as to disfranchise constitutionally qualified electors, and any system that unnecessarily prevents the elector from voting or from voting for the candidate of his choice violates the Constitution.

8. The provision of section 12 of chapter 649 of the Laws of 1911, that the name of a person nominated by more than one political party shall be printed but once upon the ballot, and regulating in detail the method of carrying out such provision, is unconstitutional as unjustly discriminating between electors in the facility afforded them for casting their votes for the candidates of their choice.

Matter of Hopper v. *Britt*, 146 App. Div. 363, reversed.

(Argued October 8, 1911; decided October 10, 1911.)

APPEAL from an order of the Appellate Division of the Supreme Court in the first judicial department, entered September 28, 1911, which reversed, as matter of law, an order of Special Term granting a motion for a peremptory writ of mandamus to compel the board of elections of the city of New York to print sample and official ballots for the ensuing general election in accordance with the provisions of section 331 of the Election Law as they stood prior to the passage of chapter 649 of the Laws of 1911.

The facts, so far as material, are stated in the opinion.

Herbert R. Limburg and *Clarence J. Shearn* for appellant. The portions of chapter 946 of the Laws of 1911 which amend sections 331, 368 and 134 of the Election Law are clearly unconstitutional and void. (*Matter of Halpin,* 108 App. Div. 271; *Matter of Callahan,* 200 N. Y. 60; *Matter of McCloskey,* 21 Misc. Rep. 365; *Matter of Bolger,* 48 Misc. Rep. 584; *Matter of Independent Nominations,* 186 N. Y. 278; *Wynehamer v. People,* 13 N. Y. 393; *People ex rel. Devery v. Coler,* 173 N. Y. 103; *People ex rel. Goring v. President, etc.,* 144 N. Y. 616; *Matter of Madden,* 148 N. Y. 136; *Fernbacher v. Roosevelt,* 90 Hun, 441.)

A. S. Gilbert and *Julius M. Mayer* for appellant. The law under discussion violates the provisions of section 1 of article 1 and of article 2 of the Constitution of the state. (*Wynehamer v. People,* 13 N. Y. 393; *Taylor v. Porter,* 4 Hill, 140; *White v. White,* 5 Barb. 474; *People v. Toynbee,* 20 Barb. 198; *Burby v. Howland,* 155 N. Y. 270; *People ex rel. Bolton v. Albertson,* 55 N. Y. 50; *Matter of Callahan,* 200 N. Y. 60.)

Albert S. Bard for Citizens' Union, intervening. The ballot provisions of the statute are unconstitutional because of the arbitrary discrimination between different political organizations with respect to the granting or withholding of a place on the ballot. Among other discriminations " political parties " are given a place on the ballot, but " independent bodies " are denied a place under precisely similar circumstances. (*Matter of Callahan,* 200 N. Y. 59; *Murphy v. Curry,* 137 Cal. 479.) The obvious purpose of the act is to put artificial and arbitrary barriers in the way of fusion of parties and independent voting. These are violations of equal rights of suffrage and render the act unconstitutional. The right to nominate is an empty right unless a political organiza-

10

tion may compete with other organizations at the polls upon equal terms. (*Matter of Callahan*, 200 N. Y. 59.)

Archibald R. Watson, Corporation Counsel (Abram I. Elkus, Terence Farley and *George P. Nicholson* of counsel), for respondents. The act is a reasonable regulation, and is within the legislative discretion. (*Matter of Madden*, 148 N. Y. 136.) The only rights which the Constitution safeguards are the rights of electors. No such rights are violated by the act of 1911. (*Matter of Madden*, 148 N. Y. 136; *Todd v. Election Comrs.*, 104 Mich. 474; *State v. Bode*, 55 Ohio St. 224.) The Constitution does not guarantee to a party a column on the ballot. (*State ex rel. Runge v. Anderson*, 100 Wis. 525.)

D-Cady Herrick, R. Burnham Moffat, John B. Stanchfield, Bartow S. Weeks, Ellwood M. Rabenold and *Frank M. Patterson* for Democratic State Committee, intervening.

CULLEN, Ch. J. This appeal presents a single issue, the constitutionality and validity of certain provisions of an act of the legislature of this year (Chap. 649, Laws 1911) entitled "An act to amend the election law generally." In this state for some years in the conduct of elections we have had the official ballot. Under the various statutes prescribing the form and character of that ballot, every political party that cast at the preceding election 10,000 votes for governor is entitled to a column on the ballot in which are placed the names of its nominees for the various offices to be filled by election. In the caption of the column is the name of the party and also any emblem that it may select to designate it. Further provision is made for independent nominations; that is to say, any body of electors may by certificate place in nomination for offices any persons they choose and select a party name and party emblem. Such independent nominations are given a column or part of a column as may be requisite, together with a caption giving the name and emblem adopted by the body, the same as in the case of nominations by political parties. For such independent nominations, if the nominees are candidates for state offices, six thousand or more voters are required to execute the certificate; if for municipal offices, two thousand in cities of the first class, one thousand in those of the second class, and five hundred in those of the third. Finally, there is a blank column containing no names of candidates, in which the elector may write the name of any person whom he chooses. Prior to the legislation under review a voter might by a cross mark in the circle at the head of any column vote for all of the nominees contained in such column, and if he chose to vote for some other person for any particular office he might make a similar mark opposite the name of that person, if such name was printed on the ballot; or, if not, write the name in the blank column. Physically disabled or illiterate voters, unable to read the ballot, are entitled to assistance in preparing their votes. A narration of further details is unnecessary for the disposition of this case.

It will be seen by this statement that the names of various candidates if placed in nomination by more than one political party or independent body would appear on the ballot in more than one place. By the statute of this year it has been enacted that " If any person shall have been nominated by more than one political party or independent body for the same office, his name shall be printed but once upon the ballot, and shall appear in the party column of the party nominating him which appears first upon said ballot, unless the said candidate shall by a certificate in writing duly signed and acknowledged by him request the custodian of primary records to print his name in the column of some other party or independent body which shall have nominated him, in which event

his name shall be printed in such other column only.
* * * When the same person has been nominated for
the same office to be filled at the election, by more than
one party or independent body, the title of such office
shall be printed in the columns where his name is not
printed, and underneath such title shall be printed in
brevier capital type the words 'See column,' the blank
space to contain the name of the party column in which
his name is printed, excepting that if any independent
body shall have nominated only the candidates of the
other party or independent body, no separate column for
the independent body in which the candidates' names do
not appear shall be printed upon the ballot." (Section
12.) The relator contends that the statute is unconstitutional as unjustly discriminating between electors
in the facilities afforded them for casting their respective
votes, because where candidates are nominated by two or
more organizations they can receive the "straight vote"
of the electors of but one organization, while those
affiliated with the other organizations which have placed
them in nomination are compelled to seek other columns
on the ballot referred to only by name, and there make the
necessary additional marks, thus tending to confuse the
electors and defeat their intention to vote for all the
nominees of their organization. The Special Term of the
Supreme Court held these provisions of the statute bad
and granted a writ of mandamus to the election
officers commanding the preparation and issue of the
ballots in accordance with the old form. The Appellate
Division has, by a divided court, reversed this order and
denied the application as a matter of law and not in the
exercise of discretion.

In the consideration of the question before us we are
not unmindful of the principle that before a court should
declare a statute of the legislature invalid it must be
clearly shown that the statute is irreconcilable with the
Constitution; nor do we fail to appreciate the hesita-

tion with which courts should hold enactments of the legislature void. It may be true, as urged by the learned counsel for the respondents, that at the present day some courts are disposed to invade the constitutional prerogatives of a co-ordinate branch of the government by regarding what they believe to be the spirit of the Constitution, rather than its express mandates. But necessarily in all Constitutions or other instruments there are certain propositions which the instruments import, as well as those they expressly and in terms assert. Therefore, it is well settled that legislation contravening what the Constitution necessarily implies is void equally with the legislation contravening its express commands. A notable instance of this is the right to condemn private property. Our Constitution has never expressly forbidden taking private property for private use, but only prescribes that "Nor shall private property be taken for public use without just compensation." (Article 1, section 6.) Yet the courts early held that this necessarily excluded the right to take such property for private use, with or without compensation (*Matter of Albany Street*, 11 Wend. 149), a doctrine which has been steadily adhered to. (*Taylor* v. *Porter*, 4 Hill, 140; *Matter of Ryers*, 72 N. Y. 1.) The only provision of the Federal Constitution on the subject which affects the power of the states is that contained in the fourteenth amendment, that no state shall deprive any person of property without due process of law. It was said by the Supreme Court of the United States in *Madisonville Traction Company* v. *Saint Bernard Mining Company* (196 U. S. 239, 251): "There ought not to be any dispute, at this day, in reference to the principles which must control in all cases of the condemnation of private property for public purposes. It is fundamental in American jurisprudence that private property cannot be taken by the Government, National or state, except for purposes which are of a public character, although such taking be accompanied by compensation to the owner. That principle, this court has said, grows out of the essential nature of all free governments."

The qualifications of voters are prescribed by section 1 of article 2 of the Constitution and those qualifications are exclusive. By section 5 of the same article it is provided that "All elections by the citizens, except for such town officers as may by law be directed to be otherwise chosen, shall be by ballot, or by such other method as may be prescribed by law, provided that secrecy in voting be preserved." By section 1 of article 1 it is enacted that no member of this state shall be disfranchised unless by the law of the land or the judgment of his peers. It is, therefore, clear that the otherwise plenary power granted to the legislature to prescribe the method of conducting elections cannot be so exercised as to disfranchise constitutionally qualified electors, and any system of election that unnecessarily prevents the elector from voting or from voting for the candidate of his choice violates the Constitution. We have said "unnecessarily," for there is no practicable system of conducting elections at which some electors by sickness or other misfortune may not be able to vote. Under our law the blanket ballot affords a voter who may be unable to read the ballot from illiteracy or physical defect, an opportuity to vote by securing assistance, and to every elector the right to vote for whom he chooses by writing the name in the blank column if the name of his candidate is not on the ballot. If these rights were not accorded, the present Election Law would be unconstitutional. In *People ex rel. Goring* v. *President, etc., of Wappingers Falls* (144 N. Y. 616) a vacancy occurred in the office of the police justice of the village. At the next election the official ballot did not contain the name of that office or of any candidate to be voted therefor. The relator received votes at the election, the voters writing his name and the office on the ballot. It was contended that under the language of the Election

Law, the votes were invalid. This court held the election good, saying: "The legislature may prescribe regulations for ascertaining the citizens who shall be entitled to exercise the right of suffrage, for that power is given to it by the Constitution. In prescribing regulations for that purpose, or in respect to voting by ballot, it does so subject to and, presumably, in furtherance of the constitutional right and its enactments are to be construed in the broadest spirit of securing to all citizens, possessing the necessary qualifications, the right freely to cast their ballots for offices to be filled by election and the right to have those ballots, when cast in compliance with the law, received and fairly counted. Legislation which fails in such respects and prevents the full exercise of the right as secured by the Constitution is invalid." (p. 229.) Indeed, there has been serious criticism on the constitutionality of the system because so many votes have been declared void by reason of the irregularity in the form of the marks made by the voters.

We think the constitutional provisions recited and the provision that certain officers shall be chosen by the electors necessarily further imply that every elector shall have the right to cast his vote with equal facility to that afforded to other voters, or, to speak more accurately, without unnecessary discrimination against him as to the manner of casting his vote. The learned counsel for the respondents have cited the decisions of the courts of several states upholding election laws with provisions similar to that under discussion. The clearest expression of the ground on which the decisions of those courts proceed is found in the opinion of the Supreme Court of Michigan in *Todd* v. *Election Commrs.* (104 Mich. 474): "The Constitution does not guarantee that each voter shall have the same facilities with every other voter in expressing his will at the ballot-box, or, to apply the rule to the present case, it does not guarantee to each voter the right to express his will by a single mark. * * * It follows then that every voter has a reasonable opportunity to vote for him (the candidate). This is the sole constitutional right guaranteed him."

Doubtless the Constitution of this State does not guarantee to each voter the right to express his will by a single mark or in any other particular manner, but with great deference to the learned court from which we have quoted, in our opinion the Constitution, by providing that certain officers shall be chosen by the electors, does guarantee that each voter shall have the same facilities as any other voter in expressing his will at the ballot-box, so far as practicable. Any other principle, in our judgment, would be destructive of fair elections. Some impediments to the exercise of the right to vote are, as already stated, under any practicable system of conducting elections unavoidable, and when these impediments are dependent on circumstances and conditions not connected with the status of the candidates, for whom the vote is to be cast, they rarely affect the result of an election — the losses of one candidate being offset by those of the others. Not so with the impediments of the kind prescribed by this statute, which are directed solely at the status of the particular nominee for whom the vote is to be cast. The change from the old system does not diminish the size of the ballot, nor does it decrease the printing on it; it does not tend to make voting easier for the elector, or to avoid confusion on his part, but has the contrary effect. Surely the name of a candidate printed in the appropriate column is less confusing to the elector than a reference to some other column denoted only by its party name. While the Constitution does not guarantee that the elector shall be allowed to express his vote by a single mark, our position is that he is guaranteed the right to express his will by a single mark if other voters are given the right to express theirs by a single mark and there is no difficulty in according the right to all. It is said by the Supreme Court of Ohio in *State* v. *Bode* (55

Ohio St. 224), in upholding a law of this kind: "There is no discrimination against or in favor of any one; and if any inequality arises, it arises not from any inequality caused by the statute, but by reason of inequalities in the persons of the voters, and such inequalities are unavoidable. It is always much more difficult for some electors to cast their ballots than others. Distance, bad roads, means of transportation, bad health, and many other considerations, may and do render it much more difficult for some men to cast their ballots than others. But these difficulties inhere in the men themselves, and not in the law. * * * The inconvenience is only that experienced by every one who votes other than a straight ticket." This argument ignores the distinction between difficulties or inconveniences occurring by nature or accident and inconvenience created by statute. Inequality in the facilities afforded the electors in casting their votes may defeat the will of the people as thoroughly as restrictions which the courts would hold to operate as a disfranchisement of voters. In 1884 the control of the government of the whole country was transferred from one political party to another through the vote of this state by an average plurality of less than 1,150 votes. The vote for the electors of the successful party was over 560,000. Therefore, if an inconvenience in the method of casting his vote applicable to one candidate only had affected the vote of but one man in 470, the result would have been changed. If it were provided that voting on the blanket ballot should be done by either writing or pasting thereon under the names of the offices to be filled, the names of the candidates, it is not certain that this plan could be condemned as creating such obstacles to the exercise of the rights of the electors as to render the scheme unconstitutional; but if the plan went further and provided that the candidates of the party polling the highest vote at the last election should be printed in one column and the electors allowed to vote therefor by a cross-mark, while all the other candidates were required to be voted for by writing or pasting their names on the ballots, I think no one would hesitate to condemn the scheme as unconstitutional. Certainly under that plan there would be great difficulty in turning out the party in power. The condemnation of such a statute would proceed, at least primarily, not on the ground that it disfranchised the voters, but on account of the unequal opportunities to vote afforded the electors. That we are right in the position that equality of opportunity should be afforded electors is a fundamental principle of the constitutional law of this state, we need only refer to the first Constitution adopted by us. Previous to the Revolution elections in the colony were held *viva voce.* The Constitution of 1777 recited: "Whereas, an opinion has long prevailed among divers of the good people of this State, that voting at elections by ballot would tend more to preserve the liberty and *equal* freedom of the people than voting *viva voce:* to the end, therefore, that a fair experiment be made, which of these two methods of voting is to be preferred:" and it directed that after the termination of the war then existing between the colonies and Great Britain the legislature should enact that elections for senators and representatives should be by ballot, and should direct the manner in which the same should be conducted. We, therefore, hold the statutory provisions challenged to be unconstitutional because they unnecessarily and substantially discriminate between electors in the opportunities and facilities afforded for voting for the candidates of their choice. If the discrimination were trivial our decision would be different, but we know from the election litigations that have come before us that the discrimination here is of a very substantial character, and where voting machines are used the difficulty of voting a split ticket is still greater than where voting is by ballot.

At this point we may call attention to a later decision

made by the Supreme Court of Michigan. In *Dapper v. Smith* (138 Mich. 104) the validity of a provision which required that before the name of any candidate should be placed on the ballot such candidate should on oath declare his purpose to become such, was challenged and held unconstitutional. It was said by the learned court: "The man who may be willing to consent to serve his State or his community in answer to the call of duty when chosen by his fellow-citizens to do so is excluded, and the electorate has no opportunity to cast their votes for him. It is not an answer to this reasoning to say that the electors may still vote for such a man by using 'pasters.' We cannot ignore the fact that parties have become an important and well-recognized factor in government. Certain it is that this law fully recognizes the potency of parties, and provides for party action as a step towards the choice of an officer at the election. The authority of the legislature to enact laws for the purpose of securing purity in elections does not include the right to impose any conditions which will destroy or seriously impede the enjoyment of the elective franchise." As already said, we think it doubtful whether a form of official ballot by which all voting should be done by pasters which are easily attached to the ballot, could be held such an obstacle as to destroy or defeat the enjoyment of the elective franchise. But the decision could very properly have proceeded on the ground that an unnecessary and substantial discrimination against any body of electors was unconstitutional.

It is urged that there are inequalities under the old form of ballot, but, at least, the most of those inequalities are unavoidable. The party that polled at the last election the greatest number of votes is given the first column on the ballot. As long as the face of the ballot is a plane surface, which has always been the case with us, and there is a party column, some party must have the first place. Every candidate is not given the right to have his name printed on the official ballot.   Such a provision would render an official ballot impossible.   But not only are all parties or bodies polling 10,000 votes, which is less than one per cent of the whole vote of the state, given the right to a separate column, but independent bodies, on the petition of but a small fraction of the electorate, have the same right.   Thus, the rights of the electors of all organizations which have the most remote or shadowy chance of electing their nominees are given equal rights with those of the great parties, while the inviolable right of every elector is secured by the blank column.   But if the character of the ballot necessarily involves discrimination against certain classes or bodies of electors, it is a reason that the statute should not increase the discrimination.

It has been urged in justification of the statutory provisions before us that independent bodies are often organized for the sake of trading or combining with the regular parties or other organizations on corrupt considerations. It is not pretended, however, that the statute tends to prevent that evil, save in one way, by making it more difficult to vote fusion or coalition tickets.   The same argument was advanced in *Matter of Callahan* (200 N. Y. 59), where it was held that the legislature could not constitutionally prevent the nomination of fusion or combination candidates.   We there said: " The liberty of the electors in the exercise of the right vested in them by the Constitution to choose public officers on whatever principle or dictated by whatever motive they see fit, unless those motives contravene common morality and are, therefore, criminal, such as bribery, violence, intimidation or fraud, cannot be denied." (p. 62.)   The legislature might make combinations effected by bribery or illegal considerations criminal and punish the actors.   On proof that an organization was effected and nominations made in pursuance of such criminal bargain the courts might be authorized to strike such nominations from the ballot.

1911.] Opinion, per CULLEN, Ch. J. [Vol. 203.]

But because many coalitions between various bodies of electors are corrupt and criminal it cannot forbid coalition nominations or indirectly effect the same thing by rendering it more difficult to vote for a coalition nominee. One great object of the present ballot was to prevent bribery by rendering it difficult to determine how any elector voted. There is, however, an opportunity for identification left. The elector may, in the blank column, write the name of some particular candidate and thus identify his vote. Undoubtedly the voter may be punished for so doing on proof of the unlawful purpose for which he wrote the name of the particular person. Fortunately the evil does not seem at all common. But even if it were prevalent, to correct the evil the inviolable right of the elector to vote for whom he chose could not be invaded.

The method of voting on an official ballot which has prevailed with us now for a number of years probably has corrected evils that formerly were prevalent. But, personally, I fear that, in some respects, it has undermined public morality on the question of the right of the elector to vote for whom he will, provided it is dictated by no criminal consideration. Ever since the adoption of the present scheme there has been an attempt to provide a ballot in such form as to prevent the elector from voting in the way he wishes to vote. In this constant effort it must be conceded that persons desirous of so-called ballot reform, and not political partisans, have been the most active, though by the present legislation the latter seem to have been more successful. All labors by a citizen to induce his fellow-citizens to change the principle on which they cast their votes, when he believes that principle is injurious to the welfare of the community, are praiseworthy and patriotic. But however gross may be the error of his fellows he has no moral right to correct that error by making it difficult for them to exercise their constitutional rights.

The order of the Appellate Division should be reversed and that of the Special Term in substance affirmed, without costs.   There are some errors, however, in the form of the Special Term order, for which reason it must be modified, and the order may be settled on two days' notice before the judge writing the opinion.

HAIGHT, VANN, WERNER, WILLARD BARTLETT, HISCOCK and CHASE, JJ., concur.

Ordered accordingly.

In the Matter of the Application of WILLIAM H. MARK-LAND, Respondent, for a Peremptory Writ of Mandamus against PATRICK J. SCULLY, City Clerk of the City of New York, et al., Appellants.

Constitutional law — New York (city of) — justices of the Municipal Court — unconstitutionality of statute (L. 1907, ch. 603, § 3) amending section 1357 of New York city charter relative to vacancies in office of justices.

1. The statute of 1907 (Ch. 603, § 3), amending section 1357 of the charter of the city of New York, relating to vacancies in office of justices of the Municipal Court, violates the Constitution. *First,* in prohibiting an election unless the vacancy occurs three months before the general election. *Second,* in requiring the mayor to appoint a person to fill the vacancy in the interim, which in this case would be for two years and about five months. *Third,* in requiring the election to fill vacancies to be for a full term, which might occur in an even numbered year. Hence the section of the charter as it existed before the amendment must be deemed to remain in force.

2. Where a justice of the Municipal Court of the city of New York died on the eighth day of August, and the annual election occurs on the seventh day of November thereafter, an election to fill the vacancy should be had at such annual election, and no appointment to fill a vacancy can continue longer than to the first day of January after such annual election.

3. The city clerk of the city of New York being required by the statute to give notices of an election and of the offices to be filled, it is his duty to do so upon the happening of a vacancy which is required to be filled at the ensuing election, notwithstanding that

such vacancy occurred after said clerk had issued notices of election in accordance with conditions then existing, and such duty may be enforced by mandamus.

Matter of Markland, 146 App. Div. 350, affirmed.

(Argued October 2, 1911; decided October 10, 1911.)

APPEAL from an order of the Appellate Division of the Supreme Court in the second judicial department, entered September 25, 1911, which affirmed an order of Special Term granting a motion for a peremptory writ of mandamus to compel the city clerk · of the city of New York to issue a notice for an election of justice of the Municipal Court, sixth district, in the borough of Brooklyn.

· The facts, so far as material, are stated in the opinion.

Archibald R. Watson, Corporation Counsel (James D. Bell of counsel), for appellants.   Whether a justice of the Municipal Court of the city of New York can or cannot be elected at the coming general election in the sixth district of the borough of Brooklyn, the present proceeding is unauthorized in law, without precedent and entirely unnecessary. (*People ex rel. Davis* v. *Cowles*, 13 N. Y. 350; *People ex rel. Meagher* v. *Voorhis*, 115 App. Div. 891; *People* v. *O'Brien*, 38 N. Y. 193; *People ex rel. Goring* v. *President*, 144 N. Y. 616.) Conceding for the purposes of the argument the relator's claims as adopted by the courts below, that the Municipal Court of the city of New York is a district court created by the legislature under article 6, section 17, of the Constitution, and that section 5 of article 10 of the Constitution applies to vacancies therein, there can be no election to fill any such vacancies at the coming general election, because there is no provision of law authorizing such election. (*People ex rel. Fowler* v. *Bull*, 46 N. Y. 57; *Matter of Schultes*, 33 App. Div. 524; *People ex rel. Lyon* v. *Wallin*, 141 App. Div. 34; *People ex rel. Woods* v. *Crissey*, 91 N. Y. 616.)   The Municipal Court of. the city of New York is fully provided for in the judiciary article of the Constitution, and section 5 of article 10 of the Constitution does not apply to it. (*People ex rel. Hatfield* v. *Comstock,* 78 N. Y. 356; *People ex rel. Furman* v. *Clute,* 50 N. Y. 451; *Koch* v. *Mayor, etc.,* 152 N. Y. 72.) A Municipal Court justice is not an elective officer within the meaning of article 10, section 5, of the Constitution. (*People* v. *Keeler,* 17 N. Y. 370; *People ex rel. Hatfield* v. *Comstock,* 78 N. Y. 356; *People ex rel. Ward* v. *Scheu,* 167 N. Y. 292; *People ex rel. Howard* v. *Supervisors,* 42 App. Div. 510; 160 N. Y. 688; *Worthington* v. *L. G. & A. Co.,* 164 N. Y. 81.)

Arnon L. Squiers and *Charles B. Law* for respondent. The office of justice of the Municipal Court of the city of New York is created and made elective by the provisions of the Constitution of the state of New York, section 17, article 6. (*Worthington* v. *L. G. & A. Co.,* 164 N. Y. 86; *Routenberg* v. *Schweitzer,* 165 N. Y. 175; *People* v. *Dooley,* 69 App. Div. 523; *People* v. *Unger,* 123 App. Div. 312.) An election to fill the vacancy created by the death of Judge Fielder must be held at the coming annual election in November, 1911, within the provisions of the Constitution of the state of New York, section 5 of article 10. (*People ex rel. Howard* v. *Supervisors,* 42 App. Div. 510; *People ex rel. Ward* v. *Scheu,* 167 N. Y. 292; *People* v. *Green,* 2 Wend. 268; *People* v. *Keeler,* 17 N. Y. 370; *Weller* v. *Townsend,* 102 N. Y. 430.) Section 5, article 10 of the Constitution applies to judicial officers as well as other elective officers. (*People* v. *Keeler,* 17 N. Y. 375; *People ex rel. Davies* v. *Cowles,* 13 N. Y. 350; *People ex rel. Ward* v. *Scheu,* 167 N. Y. 296.) It is the duty of the city clerk, as provided by section 293, chapter 649 of the Laws of 1911, to make and transmit to the custodian of primary records a notice under his hand and seal, stating each city officer to be voted for at the coming election, and it is also the duty of the board of elections, as custodian of primary records, to publish a notice which will contain a list of all city officers who may lawfully be voted for at the coming election by the electors of the city or any part thereof. (*Ziegler* v. *Corwin*, 12 App. Div. 67.)

HAIGHT, J. On the 8th day of August, 1911, George Fielder, of the sixth district Municipal Court of the city of New York, died, and a question has arisen as to whether the vacancy caused by his death can be filled by an election at the next ensuing election which occurs on the 7th day of November. For the purpose of determining that question the relator made an application for a peremptory writ of mandamus and, by the orders appealed from, the courts below have determined that such election should be had.

Upon the argument of this appeal a preliminary question was raised by the appellant as to whether mandamus would issue against the clerk of the city, the contention being that the death of the justice occurred after he had issued his notices of election, and that he was not required to issue any second notice, having once performed the duty placed upon him by the statute. It may be that the validity of an election does not depend upon the issuing of the notice for the filling of the vacancy, and it is quite true that the clerk had already issued his notice of election, specifying the positions to be filled before the death of Justice Fielder. But the purpose of the statute requiring notice to be given of the election and of the places to be filled at such election is to inform the electors of the positions to be filled so that they may have the requisite time to select the persons who should be nominated and voted for at the election. It would seem, therefore, that the clerk being required by the statute to give such notices, it became his duty to do so upon the happening of a vacancy which was required to be filled at the ensuing election. In the apportionment cases this court has recently held that the question as to the validity of the act apportioning the state into senatorial districts could be reviewed upon a mandamus requiring state officers charged with the duty to give notices of the election to be had in the senatorial districts. We, therefore, are of the opinion that the question presented should be determined upon the merits.

The death of Justice Fielder having occurred on the 8th day of August, the vacancy occurred less than three months prior to the next general election, and it consequently becomes necessary to determine the validity of the provisions of the statute of 1907 (ch. 603, section 3), amending section 1357 of the charter of the city of New York. It provides as follows: "Vacancies occurring in the office of justice of said court otherwise than by expiration of term shall be filled at the next general election, in an odd numbered year happening not less than three months after such vacancy occurs, for a full term commencing on the first day of January next after said election; and the mayor of the city shall appoint some proper person to fill such vacancy in the interim within twenty days after the same occurs." Under the provisions of the statute it will be readily seen that inasmuch as three months will not intervene after the vacancy before the ensuing election, the vacancy cannot be filled at the next election. It cannot be filled at next year's election, for that will be an even numbered year and consequently the election will be postponed until November, 1913. It consequently would follow that the vacancy cannot be filled by election until the first day of January thereafter, which would be two years and five months after the happening of the vacancy. In determining the validity of this statute it becomes necessary to examine three provisions of the Constitution. The first is section 17, article 6, which provides that "The electors of the several towns shall, at their annual town meetings, or at such other time and in such manner as the Legislature may direct, elect Justices of the Peace, whose term of office shall be four years. *In case of an election to fill a vacancy occurring before the expiration of a full term, they shall hold for the residue of the unexpired term.* * * * Justices of the Peace and District Court Justices may be elected in the different cities of this State in such manner and with such powers, and for such terms, respectively, as are or shall be prescribed by law; all other judicial officers in cities, whose election or appointment is not otherwise provided for in this article, shall be chosen by the electors of such cities, or appointed by some local authorities thereof."

Section 5, article 10, of the Constitution provides: "The Legislature shall provide for filling vacancies in office, and in case of elective officers, no person appointed to fill a vacancy shall hold his office by virtue of such appointment longer than the commencement of the political year next succeeding the first annual election after the happening of the vacancy."

Section 3, article 12, provides: "All elections of city officers, including supervisors and judicial officers of inferior local courts, elected in any city or part of a city, and of county officers elected in the counties of New York and Kings, and in all counties whose boundaries are the same as those of a city, *except to fill vacancies*, shall be held on the Tuesday succeeding the first Monday in November in an odd numbered year, and the term of every such officer shall expire at the end of an odd numbered year."

The purpose of the last section of the Constitution was to separate the election of city officers from that of state officers, so that they would not occur in the same year; and inasmuch as the state officers were elected on an even numbered year, it was arranged that the city officers should be elected on an odd numbered year. Under the provisions of the Greater New York charter elections were arranged in accordance with this provision of the Constitution. The terms of the district judges or the judges of the Municipal Court were fixed at an even num-

ber of years; their elections to be had at an odd numbered year, which would make their terms expire at the
end of an odd numbered year; and consequently the
election of their successors would occur at the annual election of an odd numbered year. It will be observed, however, that this provision of the Constitution expressly
excepts therefrom an election to fill a vacancy. But if an
election were to be held to fill a vacancy on an even numbered year, and it was for a full term, then the term
would expire in an even numbered year and thus require
the successor to be elected in an even numbered year, which
would be in violation of the terms of the Constitution.

Returning to a consideration of section 17, article 6,
we find that justices of the peace and District Court justices may be elected in the different cities and in such manner and with such powers and for such terms, respectively,
as are or shall be prescribed by law. Independent of this
and following the provision with reference to the election
of justices of the peace in towns is the provision that in case
of election to fill a vacancy occurring before the expiration
of a full term they shall hold for the residue of the unexpired term. It is claimed that this clause has reference
to filling vacancies of justices of the peace in towns, and
not to justices of the peace and District Court justices in
cities. But it will at once be seen, on referring to the
election of judicial officers in section 3, article 12, that if
the vacancy is filled for a full term, it will in every case,
where the vacancy occurs in an odd numbered year, violate the provisions of that section. It consequently
appears to me that the provision with reference to filling
vacancies for the unexpired term must also apply to the
election of judicial officers to fill vacancies in cities, at
least in so far as the cities embraced in that section are
concerned, which are those of the first and second class,
excluding those of the third class. As to the justices of
the peace and District Court justices elected in cities
under the provisions of section 17, article 6, we fully con-

cur in the opinions below that such officers, under the Constitution, are elected officers; and that the district justices in the city of New York forming the Municipal Courts must be elected by the electors thereof for their respective districts. We do not deem it necessary to further discuss this question, for it has already received the attention of this court on different occasions, and at least four of our members have written upon this subject. (*Worthington* v. *London G. & A. Co.*, 164 N. Y. 81; *People* v. *Dooley*, 69 App. Div. 512; affirmed, 171 N. Y. 74.)

Justice Fielder's office, therefore, being elective, it is brought under the provisions of section 5, article 10, in which the legislature *shall* provide for filling the vacancies, and no person appointed to fill a vacancy shall hold his office by virtue of such appointment longer than the commencement of the political year next succeeding the first annual election after the happening of the vacancy. It consequently appears from this provision that inasmuch as Fielder died on the 8th day of August, and the annual election occurred on the 7th day of November thereafter, an election to fill his vacancy should be had at the annual election, and no appointment to fill a vacancy can continue longer than to the 1st day of January after such annual election. It follows that, if I am correct with reference to the construction that should be given this provision of the Constitution, the statute of 1907, amending section 1357 of the charter, violates the provision of the Constitution. *First*, in prohibiting an election unless the vacancy occurs three months before the general election. *Second*, in requiring the mayor to appoint a person to fill the vacancy in the interim, which in this case would be for two years and about five months. *Third*, in requiring the election to fill vacancies to be for a full term, which might occur in an even numbered year.

It is now contended that there is no statute under

which an election could be had.   Prior to the amendment
of 1907 section 1357 of the charter (L. 1901, ch. 466) provided: "Vacancies occurring in the office of justice of
said court shall be filled at the next ensuing general election for the unexpired term commencing on the first day
ot January next after said election; and the mayor of the
city shall appoint some proper person to fill such vacancy
in the interim within twenty days after the same occurs."
This provision of the charter was carefully drawn and is
in accord with the three sections of the Constitution to
which allusion has been made.   This provision of the
charter, as we have seen, was amended in 1907; but in
every clause in which it was amended, some one of the
three articles of the Constitution to which I have referred
has been violated.   It consequently follows that this
amendment was void; and the section of the charter as it
existed before the amendment must be deemed to remain
in force.   (*People ex rel. Farrington* v. *Mensching*, 187
N. Y. 8.)

In view of the fact that the city officers were proceeding in good faith under a provision of the statute which
they had no power to adjudge invalid, I think they should
not be charged with costs.   The order should, therefore,
be affirmed, without costs.

CULLEN, Ch. J. (dissenting).   While I concur with
Judge HAIGHT in the view that the appointee of the mayor
cannot hold office under his appointment beyond the end
of this year, I think that no duty is cast by statute upon
the defendants to give notice of vacancies that may occur
within three months prior to the election.   They discharged their duty when they gave the notice required
by law in accordance with the conditions then existing.

For this reason I dissent.

VANN, WERNER, WILLARD BARTLETT, HISCOCK and
CHASE, JJ., concur with HAIGHT, J.; CULLEN, Ch. J.,
reads dissenting memorandum.

Order affirmed.

THE PEOPLE OF THE STATE OF NEW YORK ex rel. THE
NEW YORK CENTRAL AND HUDSON RIVER RAILROAD
COMPANY, Appellant, *v.* EGBURT E. WOODBURY et al.,
Constituting the State Board of Tax Commissioners,
et al., Respondents.

**Tax — special franchise tax upon steam railroad crossings over
public streets and highways — when highway is opened across
right of way owned and occupied by railroad, such crossing is
not subject to the tax.**

1. On review and examination of the statutory provisions on the
subject, *held,* that the term " surface " as applied to railroads in the
statute (Laws of 1899, ch. 712, § 1; Tax Law, Cons. Laws, ch. 60, § 2,
subd. 3) defining special franchises for the purpose of taxation, does
not refer exclusively to street railroads, and hence a special franchise includes railroads operated by steam, running across the state
from one terminal point to another, and the crossings made by constructing such railroads across streets already in existence.

2. The object of the Special Franchise Tax Act is to tax railroad
corporations for privileges granted them in the streets which they
occupy on their lines of railway, and if, after they have their rights
of way secured over private land, a public highway is laid across
the tracks, while there is a crossing, it is not a crossing made by the
railroad, or through public favor so far as the railroad is concerned,
and hence is not liable to taxation as a special franchise.

People ex rel. N. Y. C. & H. R. R. R. Co. v. *Woodbury,* 145 App.
Div. 900, modified.

(Argued June 5, 1911; decided October 17, 1911.)

APPEAL from an order of the Appellate Division of the
Supreme Court in the third judicial department, entered
May 4, 1911, which affirmed an order of Special Term
in a certiorari proceeding instituted for the purpose of
reviewing assessments of relator's special franchises in the
city of Buffalo.

The facts, so far as material, are stated in the opinion.

Alfred L. Becker, Alex. S. Lyman and *Lester F.
Stearns* for appellant. The sections of the Tax Law

authorizing the valuation of special frachises by the state board of tax commissioners have no relation to the relator's occupations of streets, highways and public places in the city of Buffalo, for the reason that the legislature did not intend, and could not constitutionally intend, to give them any such application. The state board of tax commissioners in assuming to make the valuations acted without jurisdiction, and the assessments in pursuance of said valuations are void. (*Tyrrell* v. *Mayor, etc.*, 159 N. Y. 239; *People ex rel. M. T. Co.* v. *Miller*, 177 N. Y. 51; *People* v. *Kerr*, 27 N. Y. 188; *N. Y. C. & H. R. R. R. Co.* v. *City of New York*, 202 N. Y. 212.) In the phrase all "surface, underground or elevated railroads," the meaning of the word "surface" is controlled by the rule of *ejusdem generis.* It is also controlled by the rule *expressio unius est exclusio alterius.* (*Matter of N. Y. D. Ry. Co.*, 107 N. Y. 52; *People ex rel. N. Y. E. R. R. Co.* v. *Comrs.*, 19 Hun, 460; 82 N. Y. 459; *People* v. *Manhattan Beach Ry. Co.*, 84 N. Y. 568; *People* v. *Rogers*, 108 N. Y. 148; *McGaffin* v. *Cohoes* 74 N. Y. 389; *Mangam* v. *City of Brooklyn*, 98 N. Y. 585; *Danziger* v. *Simpson*, 116 N. Y. 333; *Burks* v. *Bosso*, 180 N. Y. 341; *Matter of Reynolds*, 124 N. Y. 388.) The seventh clause of the act of 1881, which next follows the clause "All surface, underground or elevated railroads," is a part of the context of the entire subdivision 3, section 2, of the act of 1881, and shows clearly and conclusively that the word "surface," as well as the words "underground," "elevated," in clause 6, means street railroads only. (Potter's Dwarris on Statutes, 183, 189; *Manhattan Co.* v. *Kaldenberg*, 165 N. Y. 1; *Palmer* v. *Van Santvoord*, 153 N. Y. 616; *U. S.* v. *U. P. R. R. Co.*, 91 U. S. 72; *Standard Radiator Co.* v. *Fox*, 85 Ill. App. 398; *People* v. *B. R. R. Co.*, 126 N. Y. 29; *Matter of N. Y. & Brooklyn Bridge*, 72 N. Y. 530; *Tonnele* v. *Hall*, 4 N. Y. 140; *People ex rel. Gilmour* v. *Hyde*, 89 N. Y. 18; *Matter of Ward*, 154 N. Y. 344; *Benton* v.

Wickwire, 54 N. Y. 226; *Moore* v. *Mausert,* 49 N. Y. 332.)   In many streets the railroad company acquired its right of way in fee by purchase or condemnation prior to the extension of the street across such right of way, and never received any grant of a franchise from any public authority, so that such street crossings are still occupied by the relator under its original purchase, and are assessable only by the local assessors. (*People ex rel. Ins. Co.* v. *Coleman,* 121 N. Y. 542; *Bank of Augusta* v. *Earl,* 13 Pet. 519; *Jersey City Gas Light Co.* v. *United Gas Imp. Co.,* 46 Fed. Rep. 265; *Feitsam* v. *Hay,* 122 Ill. 293; *Bridgeport* v. *New York, etc., Co.,* 36 Conn. 251; *Curtis* v. *Leavitt,* 15 N. Y. 170; 3 Kent's Comm. 458; *Spring Valley Water Works* v. *Schettler,* 62 Cal. 69; *People ex rel. M. S. Ry. Co.* v. *Tax Comrs.,* 174 N. Y. 417; *People ex rel. R. M. Co.* v. *Priest,* 175 N. Y. 511; *People ex rel. Abraham* v. *Perley,* 67 Misc. Rep. 471.)

Alfred A. Gardner, Edgar J. Kohler and *Joseph F. Keany* for Long Island Railroad Company et al., intervening.   There is no special franchise at the intersection of a prior steam railroad right of way and a subsequent highway. (*New Mexico* v. *U. S. Trust Co.,* 172 U. S. 181; *W. U. Tel. Co.* v. *Penn. R. R. Co.,* 195 U. S. 570; *Donovan* v. *Penn. R. R. Co.,* 199 U. S. 294; *Vandermulen* v. *Vandermulen,* 108 N. Y. 202; *Roby* v. *N. Y. C. & H. R. R. R. Co.,* 142 N. Y. 180; *People ex rel. Erie R. R. Co.* v. *Beardsley,* 52 Barb. 105; *People ex rel.* v. *Barker,* 48 N. Y. 70; *People ex rel. D., L. & W. R. R. Co.* v. *Clapp,* 152 N. Y. 490.)

Thomas Carmody, Attorney-General, and *Clark H. Hammond, Corporation Counsel* (*Philip A. Laing* and *George E. Pierce* of counsel), for respondents.   In construing the words " all surface, underground, or elevated railroads," the referee has given an erroneous interpreta-

170 People ex rel. N. Y. C. R. R. Co. *v.* Woodbury.

[203 N. Y.]   Opinion, per Vann, J.   [Oct.,

tion of the word "surface," and one not warranted by the subdivision of the Tax Law and one shown to be erroneous by the language used in the many acts of the legislature and in many decisions of the court. (*P. H. T. Co.* v. *Dash*, 125 N. Y. 93; *People ex rel. N. Y. & H. R. Co.* v. *Miller*, 94 App. Div. 587; *Fobes* v. *R., W. & O. R. R. Co.*, 121 N. Y. 505; *Renning* v. *N. Y., L. & W. R. R. Co.*, 128 N. Y. 157; *Mearns* v. *C. R. R. Co.*, 163 N. Y. 108; *City of Yonkers* v. *N. Y. C. & H. R. R. R. Co.*, 165 N. Y. 142; *Matter of Ludlow St.*, 172 N. Y. 542; *Bennett* v. *L. I. R. R. Co.*, 89 App. Div. 379.) The amendments to the Special Franchise Law made subsequent to 1899 show that the act was intended to apply to steam railroads. (*Smith* v. *People*, 47 N. Y. 330; *People* v. *Wemple*, 115 N. Y. 302.) The courts have held that the act in question does apply to the relator. (*People ex rel. N. Y. C. & H. R. R. R. Co.* v. *Woodbury*, 140 App. Div. 848; *N. Y. C. & H. R. R. R. Co.* v. *Gourley*, 198 N. Y. 486; *People ex rel. E. R. R. Co.* v. *Woodbury*, 70 Misc. Rep. 261.) The assessments for the crossing of streets opened after the relator's road was built should be sustained. (*People ex rel. N. Y. C. & H. R. R. R. Co.* v. *Gourley*, 198 N. Y. 486; *D., L. & W. R. R. Co.* v. *City of Buffalo*, 158 N. Y. 480; *Craig* v. *R. C. & B. R. R. Co.*, 39 N. Y. 404; *People* v. *Cassity*, 46 N. Y. 46; *City of Yonkers* v. *N. Y. C. & H. R. R. R. Co.*, 165 N. Y. 142.)

Vann, J. By this proceeding the appellant, as relator, sought to review by certiorari certain special franchise taxes assessed upon its occupation of streets and crossings in the city of Buffalo for the year 1908. One hundred and thirty-nine separate assessments were involved, but seventeen of them have dropped out of sight so far as this review is concerned, owing to the stipulations of the parties by which they were canceled and annulled.

A return was filed by the board of tax commissioners

and, under an order of the court at Special Term, an amended return. The city of Buffalo having been allowed to intervene, also filed a return, and upon the argument of this appeal, certain intervenors, who had not been made parties of record, were permitted to file briefs. The issues were referred to a referee to report the facts with his opinion, a trial was had, much documentary and some oral evidence received, findings made, an elaborate opinion written and the conclusion reached that the assessments should be annulled, because the Tax Law does not authorize the taxation of steam railroad crossings. A multitude of findings of fact were regarded as necessary, because each assessment stood by itself, but most of the findings are typical, involving the ordinary street crossing at grade, the overhead crossing made pursuant to the action of grade crossing commissioners and the occupation of a street lengthwise for a certain distance.

Upon the motion to confirm the report a different view was taken both of the law and the facts by the Supreme Court at Special Term. Mr. Justice CHESTER did not adopt the facts as found by the referee, but making findings for himself, overruled all the contentions of the relator, except that he adjusted the tax on the basis of seventy-six per cent, according to the actual valuation of other property in the city of Buffalo, the valuation made by the tax commissioners having been based on the actual value. His able opinion leaves comparatively little to be said upon the main questions involved.

Upon appeal to the Appellate Division the order of the Special Term was affirmed, all the justices concurring except two who dissented only in part, as the record states, "being of the opinion that the relator is not assessable for street occupation where the street was opened and extended across the right of way, the fee of which had been purchased and conveyed to the relator before the street was opened."

The main contention of the appellant is that the statute authorizing the taxation of special franchises does not apply to steam surface railroads, because their crossings are not land according to the provisions of the Tax Law. The history of legislation relating to land as the subject of taxation shows many changes made to conform to the progress of invention resulting in new structures on, over and under land, which were not regarded as land until made such by statute. The original definition of land as made in 1827 included the land itself, buildings erected and trees growing thereon and all mines, minerals, etc., except mines belonging to the state. (1 R. S. 388, § 3.) Under this statute it was held that iron mains laid beneath the surface of streets to conduct illuminating gas to consumers, not being erected upon or affixed to land owned by the gas company, could not be regarded as real estate for the purpose of taxation. (*People ex rel. Citizens' Gaslight Company of Brooklyn* v. *Board of Assessors of the City of Brooklyn*, 39 N. Y. 81, 87.)

This decision doubtless led to the change made in 1881 whereby the definition of land was expanded in several particulars and among others so as to include "all surface, underground or elevated railroads; all railroad structures, sub-structures and superstructures, tracks and the iron thereon; branches, switches and other fixtures permitted or authorized to be made, laid or placed in, upon, above or under any public or private road, street or grounds; all mains, pipes and tanks laid or placed in, upon, above or under any public or private street or place;" etc. (L. 1881, ch. 293, § 2.) In 1896 the definition was further extended so as to include all supports and inclosures for electrical conductors and other appurtenances, and to agencies for conducting steam, heat, water, oil, electricity, etc. (L. 1896, ch. 908, § 3.)

In 1899 the Tax Law was so amended as to include special franchises in the definition of land. The essential change was made by adding to the words "all surface, underground or elevated railroads," the following: ".including the value of all franchises, rights or permission to construct, maintain or operate the same in, under, above, on or through, streets, highways or public places." (L. 1899, ch. 712, § 1.)

It is claimed by the appellant, and the referee so held, that the word "surface," as used in the statute of 1899, refers exclusively to street railroads operated by horses or electricity and running from point to point within a city or village, and that it does not include railroads operated by steam and running across the state from one terminal point to another. It must be conceded that the statute in this form was open to such construction, which under the rule of *ejusdem generis* would not be unreasonable; still steam railroads are operated upon the surface the same as street railroads and the definition includes all surface roads. If the object of the legislature was to describe railroads with reference to their location, no more appropriate word could have been used than the word "surface" to describe all railroads located on the surface of the ground. Every railroad with reference to its location must fall within one of three classes, those constructed on the surface, those underground and those elevated above the ground. A road with its tracks depressed somewhat in an excavation, or elevated on an embankment so as to make a good grade, is a surface road, because it is on the surface as changed for gradient purposes. If the intention was to confine the statute to street surface roads why was the word "street" not used as it had been in the Constitution as amended in 1874 and in several acts of the legislature, including the act of 1884 relating to "street surface railroads," and the General Railroad Act of 1890? (Const. art. 3, § 17; L. 1884, ch. 252; L. 1890, ch. 565, art. 4; L. 1897, ch. 415, § 5.) It may be observed that in addition to the description thus adopted in the statutes cited, the phrases "surface railroads not operated by

174 People ex rel. N. Y. C. R. R. Co. *v.* Woodbury.

[203 N. Y.] Opinion, per Vann, J. [Oct.,

steam" and "steam surface railroads" were also in general use. (L. 1896, ch. 908, §§ 184, 185 and 194; L. 1897, ch. 754, § 1; L. 1898, ch. 80, § 1; L. 1898, ch. 520, § 1.)

Under the statute as amended in 1899 the state board of tax commissioners at once assumed jurisdiction and assessed steam railroad crossings by the thousand. In 1900 a case arose where a steam railroad had been assessed for the privilege of crossing six public highways at grade, and it was contended that such highway crossings did not constitute special franchises within the meaning of the statute and were not taxable as such. The question was argued by distinguished counsel before Justice KENEFICK, who wrote an elaborate and well-considered opinion, which was promptly published, sustaining the tax and holding that the language of the Franchise Tax Law included the crossings made by steam railroads over public streets. (*New York, Lackawanna & Western Ry. Co. v. Roll*, 32 Misc. Rep. 321.) That decision was not appealed from but stood unchallenged for six or seven years. Similar assessments were made year after year in a vast number of cases affecting all the steam railroads in the state, and as a rule they acquiesced and paid the taxes, although some attacked the statute on other grounds. In 1900 the state board of tax commissioners when reporting to the legislature recommended that special franchises should not include the crossing of a street unless it was of a certain length, "because the taxes resulting from purely highway crossing valuations are not adequate to the cost to the state of making the same" and because the "identification of many highway crossings is impracticable." The governor called the attention of the legislature to this recommendation in his annual message. The legislature responded promptly by adding a new subdivision which provided that "the term special franchise shall not be deemed to include the crossing of a street, highway or public place where such crossing is not at the intersection of another street or highway, unless such crossing shall be at other than right angles for a distance of not less than two hundred and fifty feet, in which case the whole of such crossing shall be deemed a special franchise." (L. 1901, ch. 490, § 1.) This amendment, especially when read in connection with the recommendation, indicates that the crossings referred to were in the country and, hence, belonged mainly to steam railroads. The tax commissioners, thereupon, assessed on this basis by including all crossings not thus excluded and the steam railroads paid the taxes without attempting to review the legality of the assessments in this respect, and acquiesced in the construction of the tax commissioners that "surface" railroads meant steam railroads as well as street railroads. Although the statute was frequently attacked in other respects, the question now under consideration does not appear to have been brought before the courts.

In 1907 upon the statement of the state tax commissioners that a great deal of property was escaping taxation and their recommendation that a further change was desirable, the statute was so amended as to provide that "the term 'special franchise' shall not be deemed to include the crossing of a street, highway or public place *outside* the limits of a city or incorporated village where such crossing is less than two hundred and fifty feet in length * * *." (L. 1907, ch. 720, § 1.) It is expressly provided by the amendments of 1901 and 1907 that they shall not apply to any elevated railroad.

I see no escape from the position that any doubt existing in the statute of 1899 was removed by the amendments of 1901 and 1907. The legislature knew from the reports of the state tax commissioners that they were assessing steam surface railroads the same as street surface railroads. It is presumed to have known of the decision of Justice KENEFICK made in 1900, yet they enacted these amendments, not only without expressly excluding steam railroads from the operation of the act, but even including them by necessary implication. The exclusion of certain crossings outside the limits of a city or incorporated village shows an intent to include all other crossings, including those in the country which were largely those of steam railroads, and the provision that the amendments should not apply to elevated railroads raises the implication that it does apply to all other railroads. Even if the legislature in 1881 and 1899 used the word "surface" with the meaning claimed by the appellant, it obviously changed that meaning by subsequent amendments, impliedly but necessarily extending it to steam roads. We think that the statute as it stood when the assessments in question were laid, included the crossings made by constructing steam surface railroads across streets already in existence.

Only one other question requires discussion, and that is whether the statute applies to a crossing made by the construction of a new street across a railroad after it had acquired its right of way, built its road and was in full enjoyment of every privilege needed for effective operation. The trial court found that as to thirty-two of the crossings affected the railroad was built first and the street extended across it afterward. In other words, it was not a case of the railroad crossing the street but of the street crossing the railroad, because the existence of the railroad antedated the existence of the street. A street crossing franchise consists of the right to lay tracks across a street and use them, when but for a grant of the right to do so from competent public authority it would be a trespass. (*People ex rel. Metropolitan Street Ry. Co.* v. *State Board of Tax Comrs.*, 174 N. Y. 417, 435.) The franchise is created by grant and cannot be acquired by purchase or condemnation. The appellant contends that in the instances now under consideration there was no grant, because it already owned the right of way and needed no further privilege. It had all that it could have and when the street came to it a burden was added but no right granted.

The argument of the respondent is that when the predecessor of the relator was incorporated, the state said to it in substance: "You may construct your railroad along the line laid down on your map and cross any existing street, and as the state extends new streets across your road you may operate your road across them." To support the position that this was tantamount to a grant to take effect in the future, reliance is placed upon a case decided in 1862 in which Chief Judge DENIO held that a highway might be extended across the track of an existing railroad without compensation and that this was not taking private property for public use in violation of the Constitution. (*Albany Northern R. R. Co.* v. *Brownell*, 24 N. Y. 345.) The argument of the court was that ".railroad companies under the general act do not acquire the same unqualified title and right of disposition, to the real estate taken for the road and paid for according to the act, which individuals have in their lands. The statute declares the effect of the proceedings which it authorizes to be, that the company 'shall be entitled to enter upon, take possession of, and use the said land *for the purposes of its incorporation* during the continuance of its corporate existence;' and it further declares that the land which it thus appropriates shall be deemed to be acquired for public use. The title to the land being thus limited to its use for the purposes of the railroad enterprise, it is necessarily subject to the exercise of all those powers reserved to the legislature to which the franchises of the corporation are subject. If the latter can be restricted or modified by subsequent legislation, the uses to which the land which the corporation has acquired may be changed by the same authority. * * * A railroad laid out upon or near the natural surface of the earth may be crossed, without material inconvenience, by a common highway, on the same grade with the railroad track. The property of the railroad is not taken away from the proprietors, who are still allowed to use it for all the purposes for which it was acquired from the original owner." (p. 349.)

The actual decision was that chapter 62 of the Laws of 1853, now repealed but re-enacted with some safeguards by the Grade Crossing Act, in authorizing the construction of highways across railroad tracks without compensation, does not violate the constitutional provision against taking private property for public use or impair the obligation of contracts. This is far from holding that the charter of a railroad company involves the grant of a franchise by anticipation whenever a new street is laid out across its tracks. When the relator or its predecessor acquired its right of way, whether in fee or not is unimportant, it had the right to use it without the grant of any further privilege from the state. It was its own property, acquired by the condemnation or purchase of land or an interest therein from private owners, with no grant from the state. Years afterward, when a highway was extended over its right of way, no grant was made to it of a franchise or anything else, but something was taken away from it without compensation, which could be justified only upon the ground that Judge Denio placed it. In other states compensation has been held under such circumstances essential to the validity of the statute. (*Illinois Central R. R. Co.* v. *City of Bloomington,* 76 Ill. 447; *Chicago & Grand Trunk R. Co.* v. *Hough,* 61 Mich. 507; *Old Colony & Fall River R. R. Co.* v. *County of Plymouth,* 14 Gray, 155.) As the relator owned its right of way it had all it could get and all that it needed. No grant of a special franchise was necessary and never became necessary, for it built its road on its own private right of way. It did not cross an existing street, but a new street came to it and crossed its tracks, thereby adding a burden but conferring no benefit. Instead of the railroad having an easement to cross the street the street has an easement to cross the railroad. (*N. Y. C. & H. R. R. R. Co.* v. *City of Buffalo,* 200 N. Y. 113, 119.)

The relator accepted its charter to be a railroad corporation, and the charter was subject to amendment under the power reserved by the legislature and hence was subject to the prospective burden of streets being extended across the tracks; still the statute subsequently imposing that burden did not make a grant or create a special franchise. In other words, the general franchise or charter of the relator or its predecessor authorized the construction of a railroad from the city of Buffalo to some other terminal point. Afterward, the fee of the land necessary to construct the road, or a right of way over the same, was acquired and after the railroad had been in operation for years the street came along and crossed it, but the right of the railroad to keep its tracks where they were continued the same as before. It remained in possession by virtue of its original property right only. When the legislature under its reserved power so amended the charter of all railroad corporations as to authorize new streets to be extended over their tracks already laid on private rights of way, it did not intend to grant and did not in fact grant a special franchise. Nothing in the statute or in the history of legislation upon the subject warrants such an inference. The question is not what the legislature may do but what it has done.

The object of the Special Franchise Tax Act is to tax railroad corporations for privileges granted them in the streets which they occupy on their lines of railway and if, after they have their rights of way secured over private land, a public highway is laid across the tracks, while there is a crossing it is not a crossing made by the railroad or through public favor so far as the railroad is concerned. The relator, or one of its predecessors, was given the right to be a corporation, to acquire land and to build its road between certain terminal points. It bought its right of way and built its road accordingly. It needed no special franchise in order to use and enjoy its right of way to the utmost extent possible for railroad purposes. Years afterward a street was run across its tracks and a crossing thus created. Such a crossing, made under such circumstances, is not a special franchise within the meaning of the statute, because the railroad was built on its own right of way before the street came into existence and no additional right was granted to the railroad company by the extension of a highway across its tracks.

All the other contentions of the relator, after due consideration, are overruled without discussion.

The order appealed from should be so modified as to exclude from taxation such crossings as were made after the relator or its predecessor in title had acquired its right of way and laid its tracks thereon, and as thus modified affirmed, without costs in this court to either party, and the proceeding remitted to the Supreme Court at Special Term to enter judgment accordingly.

HAIGHT, J. (dissenting in part). I concur in the opinion of Judge VANN in so far as he holds that steam railroad companies can be assessed a special franchise tax for crossing public highways, but I dissent from so much of his opinion as limits the assessing of such franchise tax to highways that existed at the time the railroad was constructed.

In this case the opinion proposes to relieve the company from taxation as to thirty-two highway crossings, upon the theory that the railroad being an old road, built many years ago, it cannot be assessed for the new streets and highways that have been constructed across its right of way since the construction of the road. Such a construction of the statute operates most unjustly to railroads that have been constructed into the city of Buffalo in recent years over these identical thirty-two streets, and makes the act discriminate in favor of the old roads and against the new. This I think was never intended by the legislature. I, therefore, favor an affirmance of the determination of the courts below.

Cullen, Ch. J., Gray, Werner, Hiscock and Collin, JJ., concur with Vann, J; Haight, J., reads dissenting memorandum.

Ordered accordingly.

Julia W. Porges, Appellant, *v.* United States Mortgage and Trust Company, Respondent.

Practice — appeal — when defendant, by introducing evidence, waives exception to refusal of trial court to dismiss complaint — on appeal from judgment, without motion for new trial, appellate courts are limited to review of questions of law raised by exceptions taken at the trial — principal and agent — construction of power of attorney — when indorsement of check by agent constitutes forgery.

1. A defendant, by introducing evidence on the defense, waives an exception to the refusal of the court to dismiss the complaint at the close of plaintiff's evidence in chief.

2. Where the defendant did not move for a new trial, but appealed from the judgment rendered upon a verdict, both the Appellate Division and the Court of Appeals are limited to an examination of errors of law raised and pointed out by exceptions taken by the defendant during the trial.

3. A motion by defendant to dismiss the complaint at the close of the entire evidence upon the grounds "that no cause of action has been proven" may be treated as a motion for a nonsuit, and exception taken by defendant to a denial of the motion raises the question whether, admitting all the facts presented and giving to the plaintiff the advantage of every inference that could properly be drawn from them, there is any evidence to support the plaintiff's cause of action.

4. The extent to which a principal shall authorize his agent is completely within his determination, and a party dealing with the agent must ascertain the scope and reach of the powers delegated to him and must abide by the consequences if he transcends them. A power of attorney, like any other contract, is to be construed according to the natural meaning of the words in view of the pur-

pose of the agency and the needs to its fulfillment. The authority within it under such construction is not to be broadened or extended.

5. The holder of a power of attorney from plaintiff indorsed a check payable to her order and converted the proceeds to his own use by depositing it with the defendant which collected the check and placed the amount thereof to his credit. *Held,* upon examination of the power of attorney, that it did not authorize the holder to indorse the check for his own benefit and that plaintiff is entitled to recover from defendant the amount of the check and interest, less a sum found by the jury as damages to defendant by reason of the failure of plaintiff to exercise due diligence in notifying defendant of the alleged forgery.

Porges v. *U. S. Mortgage & Trust Co.,* 135 App. Div. 484, reversed.

(Argued May 15, 1911; decided October 17, 1911.)

APPEAL from an order of the Appellate Division of the Supreme Court in the first judicial department, entered December 30, 1909, reversing a judgment in favor of plaintiff entered upon a verdict directed by the court and granting a new trial.

The nature of the action and the facts, so far as material, are stated in the opinion.

Henry Amerman and *Thomas H. McKee* for appellant. Hoyt had no express or implied power to indorse checks. The power of attorney conferred broad authority in disposing of Mrs. Porges' property, but nowhere is authority to indorse commercial paper hinted. (1 Clark & Skyles on Agency, § 268; *Jackson Paper Mfg. Co. v. Com. Nat. Bank,* 199 Ill. 151; 1 Parsons on Cont. [6th ed.] 82; Meachem on Agency, § 398; 1 Daniels on Neg. Inst. [4th ed.] § 292; *Doubleday v. Kress,* 50 N. Y. 410; *Smith v. Association,* 12 Daly, 304; *Atkinson v. Manufacturing Co.,* 24 Me. 176; *Smith v. Gibson,* 6 Blackf. 370; *R. E. & P. Co. v. Lincoln Nat. Bank,* 82 Hun, 8; *New York Iron Mine v. First Nat. Bank,* 39 Mich. 644; *Vanbibber v. Bank,* 14 La. Ann. 486; *Graham v. Institution,* 46 Mo. 186; *Jackson v. Bank,* 92 Tenn. 154; *Lawrence v. Gebhardt,* 41 Barb. 575.) The defendant can rely only

upon express and implied power as distinguished from
apparent power, because the agency was undisclosed.
Defendant dealt with Hoyt as a principal and did not rely
upon his authority as agent. (*Blass* v. *Perry*, 156 N. Y.
122.) The power of attorney given to Hoyt was a broad,
special power, and must be strictly construed. (*Rossiter*
v. *Rossiter*, 8 Wend. 494; *Henry* v. *Lane*, 128 Fed. Rep.
243; *Hall* v. *Hartford*. 50 Misc. Rep. 133; *Martin* v.
Farnsworth, 49 N. Y. 555.)

Charles H. Tuttle and *Harold Harper* for respondent.
If Hoyt had the power to convert the check into cash,
this action for its conversion must fail. The bank cannot be held responsible in this action for any use, wrongful or otherwise, which he may have made of its proceeds.
(*G. C. B. & L. Assn.* v. *Nat. Bank*, 126 Mo. 82; *Oddie*
v. *Nat. City Bank*, 45 N. Y. 735; *Con. Nat. Bank* v.
First Nat. Bank, 129 App. Div. 538; *Nat. Bank* v. *Burk-
hardt*, 100 U. S. 686; *St. Louis, etc., Ry. Co.* v. *Johnston*, 133 U. S. 566.) The power of attorney, both
expressly and impliedly, authorized Hoyt to procure cash
for any check received as an incident of the exchange,
and for this purpose to transfer the check by appropriate
indorsement. (*Carson* v. *Smith*, 5 Minn. 58; *G. C. B.
& L. Assn.* v. *Nat. Bank*, 126 Mo. 82; *Gould* v. *Bowen*,
26 Iowa, 77; *Nat. Bank* v. *O. T. Bank*, 112 Fed. Rep.
726; *Dollfus* v. *Frosch*, 1 Denio, 367; *Comm.* v. *Walker*,
6 How. [Miss.] 143; *Morris* v. *Hofferberth*, 81 App. Div.
512.) Even if the power to sell the check or indorse it
for transfer had not been expressly given or included in
broader powers expressly given, such power would have
been implied as a necessary incident of powers expressly
conferred. Where an entire business is placed under the
management of an agent, the power to make or indorse
negotiable paper is implied whenever proper for the
effectuation of the agency. (*C. S. C. Co.* v. *Brinson*,
128 Ga. 487; *Nelson* v. *H. R. R. R. Co.*, 48 N. Y. 498;

Morris v. *Hofferberth,* 81 App. Div. 512; 180 N. Y. 545; *B. & L. Assn.* v. *Nat. Bank,* 126 Mo. 82; *Auldjo* v. *McDougall,* 3 U. C. [Q. B.] 199; *Whitten* v. *Bank of Fincastle,* 100 Va. 546; *Gould* v. *Bowen,* 26 Iowa, 77; *Charles* v. *Blackwell,* 46 L. J. [N. S.] 368; *Graton* v. *K. Mfg. Co.,* 28 Wash. 370.)

COLLIN, J. On May 14, 1907, Adelbert E. Hoyt had in his possession a certified check, dated May 10, 1907, drawn on the Chatham National Bank by J. L. Van Sant to the order of himself and by him indorsed: "Pay to the order of Julia W. Porges. J. L. Van Sant." Hoyt on that date indorsed it thus: "Pay to the order of A. E. Hoyt. Julia W. Porges," and thereunder: "A. E. Hoyt," and deposited it to his account with the defendant, which placed the amount thereof to his credit and collected the check from the Chatham National Bank. This plaintiff, alleging that she was the owner and entitled to the possession of the check, and that defendant converted it to its own use, seeks in this action to recover the resulting damages.

At the close of plaintiff's evidence in chief the defendant's counsel moved upon specified grounds to dismiss the complaint and excepted to the denial of the motion. At the close of the entire evidence he renewed the motion with the grounds, stating in reply to the inquiry of the trial judge that the motion was not for a direction of a verdict and took an exception to its denial. He then asked to go to the jury on the question of the laches of the plaintiff in notifying the defendant of the alleged forgery of her indorsement of the check, which request the court granted. He asked the court to submit to the jury the question as to whether a power of attorney from the plaintiff to Hoyt, which was in evidence, gave him power to make the indorsement. This the court refused and the defendant excepted to the ruling. The plaintiff's counsel asked the court to direct a verdict for the plaintiff for the amount demanded in the complaint, to wit, $4,000 and interest thereon from May 14, 1907. The court denied such request. Two questions were submitted to the jury. "*First.* Did the plaintiff, or her representative, Mr. Amerman, after she or her said representative had discovered the alleged forgery, exercise due diligence in notifying the defendant of the fact that she claimed that the indorsement of her name on the check in suit had been forged. *Second.* If, in answer to the preceding question, the jury finds that the plaintiff or her representative failed to exercise due diligence in notifying the defendant of the alleged forgery, then, did such delay damage the defendant in any amount, and, if so, in what amount?" The jury answered the first question "No;" the second question "$500," and the court thereupon said: "Now, gentlemen of the jury, by direction of the court, you will find a verdict in favor of the plaintiff for the sum of $3,860." To this direction the defendant did not take an exception. In accordance therewith the jury rendered the verdict, which was for the principal of the check and interest, minus the $500 the damage to the defendant, as found by the jury, because of the plaintiff's delay in notifying defendant of the alleged forgery. The defendant did not move for a new trial, but appealed to the Appellate Division from the judgment rendered upon the verdict. The Appellate Division, in reaching its determination, was limited to an examination of errors of law raised and pointed out by exceptions taken by the defendant during the trial of the action, and upon them the new trial was granted (*Allen v. Corn Exchange Bank,* 181 N. Y. 278), and to them our review is limited. (*Wangner v. Grimm,* 169 N. Y. 421.)

The defendant waived by introducing evidence in the defense the exception taken by it to the refusal of the court to dismiss the complaint at the close of plaintiff's evidence in chief. (*Bopp v. New York Electric Vehicle Transportation Co.,* 177 N. Y. 33.)

The motion of defendant at the close of the entire evidence to dismiss the complaint was upon the grounds "that no cause of action has been proven against this defendant, the particular defect in the proof being that the plaintiff has failed to prove title to the entire proceeds of the check, and the immediate right to the possession to the check and the entire proceeds on May 14, 1907." Such being its grounds it was equivalent to and may be treated as a motion for a nonsuit. In an action at law, after the parties have had the opportunity of exhausting their evidence and have rested, the motion to dismiss the complaint is improper, and when used by a defendant must be deemed, as its form and grounds indicate the intention of counsel, a motion for a nonsuit or a direction of a verdict. (*Wheeler* v. *Ruckman*, 51 N. Y. 391; *Dillon* v. *Cockcroft*, 90 N. Y. 649.) The exception of the defendant to the denial of the motion that the plaintiff be nonsuited raised the question whether, admitting all the facts presented and giving to the plaintiff the advantage of every inference that could properly be drawn from them, there was any evidence to support the plaintiff's cause of action, and its consideration necessitates the statement of the following facts: In April, 1907, the plaintiff, a resident of New York city, owned the properties known as numbers 218 and 220 West Twenty-first street in New York city. A mortgage thereon was in process of foreclosure, and it came to pass that Hoyt, who through the fifteen years last prior had been a friend of the plaintiff and was a clerk in the office of a dealer in real estate, undertook to aid her. To that end he obtained from her on April 25, 1907, an instrument in writing reading as follows:

"*Apr.* 25, 1907.

"For and in consideration of one dollar, to me in hand paid, the receipt whereof is hereby acknowledged, I, Julia W. Porges, individually and as Executrix of the late John H. Porges, do hereby authorize Adelbert E.

Hoyt to dispose of my property No. 218 and 220 West
21st Street, Borough of Manhattan, City of New York, at
such price and under such conditions as he may see fit
and to accept either cash or other property, or both, and
take any property subject to existing encumbrances (if
any) on said property so taken in exchange, and I hereby
give to said Hoyt my full power of attorney to sign contracts and to execute any and all papers in connection
therewith and also full authority to sign, sell and manage
any property so accepted in exchange and to pay out any
necessary money in settlement of interest, taxes, water,
salaries or other bills or court costs and commissions for
the sale of any of the said properties, the same as if I did so
myself, it being understood that the said 21st Street
property is now under foreclosure, and money must be
paid in settlement in order to deliver deed of same, and
that I shall lose my entire equity in same unless said
Hoyt can effect some sale or exchange whereby some
benefit may accrue, and therefore I give unconditional
and unlimited authority to him to do anything he deems
advisable with said property, and any money that must
be paid in excess of what may or may not be received in
said transaction I will pay to him in case when called
upon without accounting or defense of any character.

"JULIA W. PORGES."

On May 10, 1907, Hoyt, acting in behalf of the plaintiff
under this power of attorney, and Alexander D. Duff and
J. L. Van Sant executed an exchange of properties and
as a part of that transaction there was delivered to Hoyt
in payment of the excess value of the plaintiff's properties two checks, the one for $2,772.83 payable to the order
of the plaintiff or Hoyt; the other, the check already
described. The record contains other facts proving spoli-
ations of plaintiff by Hoyt through deceit and dishonesty,
but none opposing or inconsistent with the decision we are
about to make.

The title to and ownership of the check passed to the plaintiff by the indorsement of Van Sant and his delivery of it to Hoyt. Hoyt received and held it as her agent under the provisions of the power of attorney which has been set forth at length. The acceptance, control and collection of the check by the defendant was a wrongful conversion of it, unless directed or authorized by the plaintiff, or in more direct words, unless the power of attorney empowered Hoyt to place upon it the indorsement of the plaintiff and deposit it to his credit with the defendant. It is a general rule that every species of personal property subject to private ownership is susceptible of conversion. (*Davis* v. *Funk,* 39 Penn. St. 243.) Equally clear it is that the defendant did, by receiving the check for the credit of Hoyt and collecting and receiving its proceeds, convert the check, unless the acts of Hoyt in relation to it were within his agency. (*Robinson* v. *Chemical National Bank,* 86 N. Y. 404; *Graves* v. *American Exchange Bank,* 17 N. Y. 205; *Colson* v. *Arnot,* 57 N. Y. 253.) His rightful dominion over it was created and defined by the contents of the power of attorney. No fact or condition modifying or changing any effect of it arose or existed between the plaintiff and the defendant or between Hoyt and the defendant, and the defendant, in order to legalize and justify its treatment of the check, must establish that Hoyt kept within the authority it contained.

The power of attorney, like any other contract, is to be construed according to the natural meaning of the words in view of the purpose of the agency and the needs to its fulfillment. The authority within it under such construction is not to be broadened or extended and the sole right of a court is to ascertain, through the rule stated, and apply the authority. The extent to which a principal shall authorize his agent is completely within his determination, and a party dealing with the agent must ascertain the scope and reach of the powers delegated to him and must abide by the consequences if he transcends them. (*Craighead* v. *Peterson*, 72 N. Y. 279.)

The power of attorney in question, put forward by the defendant as the source of adequate authority to Hoyt and the defendant to make the disposition of the check which was in fact made, lacks · substantially that vigor or effect. The record presents conspicuously two reasons for this conclusion. *First.* The evidence is barren of any proof that the sale or exchange of the plaintiff's property, 218 and 220 West 21st street, or the payment by Hoyt of any money in settlement of any of the charges or liabilities named in the power of attorney, or the accomplishment of any act authorized by it necessitated the indorsement and transfer of the check; or yielding to the defendant the uttermost vantage ground claimable by it under the record, whether the indorsement and transfer were necessitated by the acts authorized to Hoyt was a question of fact. Express authority to Hoyt to make the plaintiff an indorser of this check the power of attorney did not give. If he possessed it, it inhered in the authority expressly given to do other acts, and this it did not do unless it was reasonably necessary to effectuate the objects of the agency, and, therefore, within the intent of the plaintiff; and it must appear clearly that the accomplishment of the acts expressly authorized required the exercise of the authority to indorse. The express authority to receive negotiable paper does not imply the power to indorse it. (*Holtsinger* v. *National Corn Exchange Bank*, 1 Sweeny, 64; affirmed by the Court of Appeals, 3 Alb. L. J. 305; *National City Bank of Brooklyn* v. *Westcott*, 118 N. Y. 468; *Rossiter* v. *Rossiter*, 8 Wend. 494; *Filley* v. *Gilman*, 2 J. & S. 339; *Jackson Paper Mfg. Co.* v. *Commercial Nat. Bank*, 199 Ill. 151.) In *Robinson* v. *Chemical National Bank* (86 N. Y. 404), EARL, J., after citing authorities, said: "The rule as derived from these authorities is well expressed by Prof. Parsons, as follows: 'An agent's acts in making or transferring negotiable paper (especially if by indorsement) are much restrained. It seems that they can be authorized only by express and direct authority, or by some express power which necessarily implies these acts, because the power cannot be executed without them.'" (p. 407.) As already stated, proof that the indorsement of the check was essential to the execution of the power of attorney in any of its purposes is wholly lacking. *Second.* Hoyt and the defendant applied and appropriated the check to the use of Hoyt. Conceding to Hoyt the power, under the instrument, to indorse the check in the name and behalf of plaintiff, his indorsement thereof for his personal use and gain was not within that power. If the power of attorney, invoked by defendant, did establish the power and right of Hoyt to effect plaintiff's indorsement of the check, it established at the same time that the depositing of it in and the receipt of it by the defendant for the credit and account of Hoyt exceeded his agency and authority. A power to act for another, however general its terms, or wide its scope, presupposes integrity and faithfulness in its exercise and cannot be enlarged by implication or construction to the justification of a diversion to the use of the agent of moneys or property subject to the agency. Manifestly this instrument did not transfer to Hoyt the ownership of the property to which it related. By virtue of it Hoyt was the plaintiff's attorney or agent with the powers it contained and for the purposes it prescribed. The law will not permit an attorney or agent under color of the authority bestowed by his principal to apply the property of that principal to his own use. That is a breach of trust which a court will not sanction or tolerate. (*Robinson* v. *Chemical National Bank,* 86 N. Y. 404; *Wright* v. *Cabot,* 89 N. Y. 570; *Kern's Estate, Gilpin's Appeal,* 176 Penn. St. 373.)

The defendant contends that it was a mere agency or conduit through which Van Sant paid Hoyt the cash which Hoyt might rightfully receive. Without considering to any extent the effect of such assertion were it true, it is a sufficient answer that the fact is otherwise. The defendant was not the drawee named in or did not pay the check. It received payment of it from the Chatham National Bank. The transaction was the transfer, in form, to the defendant of the check as an instrument for the payment of money, through and by virtue of the indorsement of the plaintiff, imposing upon her the liabilities and obligations inherent in that contract, not in behalf of the plaintiff or for her benefit or advantage, but for that of Hoyt.

The question of the ratification by the plaintiff of the transaction between Hoyt and the defendant is not considered by us because, if involved, it was under the evidence one of fact. The trial court did not err in denying the motion for the dismissal of the complaint. We think, after examination, that none other of the exceptions of defendant merits discussion.

The order of the Appellate Division and judgment entered thereon should be reversed and the judgment of the Trial Term affirmed, with costs in both courts.

CULLEN, Ch. J., GRAY, VANN, HISCOCK and CHASE, JJ., concur; WILLARD BARTLETT, J., dissents.

Order reversed, etc.

GEORGE A. KELLOGG, Respondent, *v.* THE CHURCH CHARITY FOUNDATION OF LONG ISLAND, Appellant.

Negligence — charitable corporations not exempt from liability for tort — when not liable for injuries due to negligence of ambulance driver furnished by livery stable — ambulance not a dangerous instrumentality as a matter of law.

1. A charitable corporation is not exempt from liability for a tort against a stranger because of the fact that it holds its property in trust to be applied to purposes of charity.

2. Where an ambulance owned by the defendant and bearing the name of its hospital was kept at a livery stable, the proprietor of which furnished a horse to draw the ambulance and a man to drive

it on such occasions as the defendant might indicate, the driver having been hired and paid by the livery stable keeper, who alone had the power to discharge him, the relation of master and servant is not established between the defendant and such ambulance driver as might be furnished from the livery stable. Such a contract does not make the driver the servant of the hirer or render his negligence imputable to the latter.

8. The fact that a city ordinance gives the right of way to ambulances in the public streets in no manner authorizes the driving of such vehicles at a dangerous rate of speed. There is no foundation, therefore, for the doctrine that an ambulance is necessarily a dangerous instrumentality. (*Baldwin* v. *Abraham*, 57 App. Div. 67; affd., 171 N. Y. 677; and *Howard* v. *Ludwig*, 171 N. Y. 507, distinguished.)

Kellogg v. *Church Charity Foundation*, 135 App. Div. 839, reversed.

(Argued May 17, 1911; decided October 17, 1911.)

APPEAL from a judgment of the Appellate Division of the Supreme Court in the second judicial department, entered January 7, 1910, affirming, by a divided court, a judgment in favor of plaintiff entered upon a verdict.

The nature of the action and the facts, so far as material, are stated in the opinion.

Edward M. Shepard, Omri F. Hibbard, Hiram Thomas and *Edward T. Horwill* for appellant. The testimony was undisputed that the driver was not in defendant's employ. (*Lomer* v. *Meeker*, 25 N. Y. 361; *Hull* v. *Littauer*, 162 N. Y. 569; *Heinemann* v. *Heard*, 62 N. Y. 448; *King* v. *N. Y. C. & H. R. R. R. Co.*, 66 N. Y. 181; *Hexamer* v. *Webb*, 101 N. Y. 377; *Kueckel* v. *Ryder*, 54 App. Div. 252; 170 N. Y. 562; *Dutton* v. *Amesbury Nat. Bank*, 181 Mass. 154; *McInerney* v. *Delaware & Hudson Canal Co.*, 151 N. Y. 411; *Reedie* v. *L. & N. W. Ry. Co.*, 4 Exch. 244; *Quarman* v. *Burnett*, 6 M. & W. 499.) The fact that defendant owned and was using an ambulance which, under the ordinance, had the right of way, did not make the driver the defendant's servant, or make the defendant responsible for his acts. (*Engel* v. *Eureka Club*, 137 N. Y. 100;

McCafferty v. *S. D., etc., R. R. Co.*, 61 N. Y. 178; *Farley* v. *Mayor, etc.*, 152 N. Y. 222.)

John J. Kuhn and *Owen N. Brown* for respondent. There is evidence from which the jury could find that the driver of the ambulance which collided with plaintiff was the servant or agent of defendant, and the trial court properly denied defendant's motion for a dismissal of the complaint. (*Wyllie* v. *Palmer*, 137 N. Y. 248; *Baldwin* v. *Abraham*, 57 App. Div. 67; 171 N. Y. 677; *Jones* v. *Scullard*, L. R. [2 Q. B. 1898] 565; *Seaman* v. *Kohler*, 122 N. Y. 646; *Howard* v. *Ludwig*, 171 N. Y. 507; *Diel* v. *Zeltner Brewing Co.*, 30 App. Div. 291; *Mullins* v. *Siegel-Cooper Co.*, 95 App. Div. 234; *Schubert* v. *Cowles*, 31 App. Div. 218; *Gulliver* v. *Blauvelt*, 14 App. Div. 523.) Even if it should be held that the evidence in this case shows that the driver of the ambulance was at the time of the accident under the direction and control of his general employer, Williamson, defendant's liability is still a question for the jury because this case presents an exception to the general rule exempting a contractee from liability for the negligence of the servants and agents of an independent contractor. (*Railroad Co.* v. *Morey*, 47 Ohio St. 107; *Davie* v. *Levy*, 39 La. Ann. 551; *Wertheimer* v. *Saunders*, 95 Wis. 576; *Covington Bridge Co.* v. *Steinbrock*, 61 Ohio St. 215; *St. L. & San F. R. R. Co.* v. *Madden*, 93 Pac. Rep. 586; *Dalton* v. *Angus*, L. R. [6 A. C.] 740; *Hardeker* v. *Idle District Council*, L. R. [1 Q. B. Div.] 335; *Boucher* v. *N. Y., N. H. & H. R. R. Co.*, 196 Mass. 355; *P. B. & W. R. R. Co.* v. *Mitchell*, 107 Md. 600; *Loth* v. *C. T. Co.*, 197 Mo. 328.)

WILLARD BARTLETT, J.   The defendant is a charitable corporation, maintaining St. John's Hospital in the borough of Brooklyn.   On May 21, 1904, a collision occurred at the corner of Lewis avenue and Decatur street in that borough between the hospital ambulance and a bicycle upon which the plaintiff was riding.   The plaintiff was so severely injured thereby that he suffered the loss of an eye; and he brought this suit to charge the hospital corporation with liability for the negligence of the driver of the ambulauce in causing the accident. The defendant contended originally that even if the driver were in its employ his negligence could not be imputed to a purely charitable corporation, and it prevailed on this ground on the first trial. This view, however, was rejected by the Appellate Division (*Kellogg* v. *Church Charity Foundation*, 128 App. Div. 214); and it must now be regarded as settled that a charitable corporation is not exempt from liability for a tort against a stranger because of the fact that it holds its property in trust to be applied to purposes of charity. (*Hordern* v. *Salvation Army*, 199 N. Y. 233.) As the case now comes before us on appeal from the affirmance of a judgment in favor of the plaintiff on the second trial, the first question which it is necessary to consider is whether there was any evidence to go to the jury tending to show that the relation of master and servant existed between the defendant and the driver of the ambulance at the time of the accident. If that question is resolved in the negative, there will be no need of discussing any other. If it is answered in the affirmative, we shall still have to inquire whether the jury could be permitted to find negligence on the part of the driver of the ambulance and the absence of contributory negligence on the part of the plaintiff.

The negligent conduct attributed to the driver (who could not be called as a witness, as he died before the case was tried) was his failure to comply with a municipal ordinance requiring a vehicle, which is about to turn to the left into another street, to pass to the right of and beyond the center of the street intersecting before turning. The plaintiff contended that the collision occurred solely by reason of the driver's omission to conform to this requirement. The evidence in his behalf showed that the words "St. John's Hospital" appeared on the cap of the driver and also on the body of the ambulance; and the answer admitted that the defendant "owned, controlled and managed a certain hospital known as St. John's Hospital * * * and that in connection with said hospital the defendant owned and used an ambulance." After the accident the plaintiff was placed in the ambulance which, by direction of the ambulance surgeon who was in the vehicle, was thereupon driven to St. John's Hospital.

These facts were sufficient to warrant the inference, *prima facie*, that the ambulance and the horse by which it was drawn were the property of the managers of St. John's Hospital and that the driver was in their employ. But, as Mr. Justice RICH points out in the able dissenting opinion below, when the case was closed a very different state of facts was presented. "The *prima facie* case had been met and overcome by undisputed evidence, which the court was not at liberty to disregard, conclusively establishing that the defendant did not own the horse drawing its ambulance, did not employ or pay the driver, and did not possess the power or right to discharge him." (135 App. Div. 839, 847.)

The relations between the defendant and the driver of the ambulance were disclosed by the testimony of Steve Williamson, the livery stable man at whose establishment the ambulance was kept. He said he furnished a horse and driver for the hospital on the day of the accident. "The name of the driver was Flood. He is dead now. I also furnished the horse; sometimes used their harness. I could not say on this occasion; sometimes they used my harness, sometimes the ambulance harness. * * * On that day when the call came in for the ambulance, I selected this Flood to go; he was out there often before. I employed him as a driver. I paid him by the week. He was not sent out on any livery call which might be made; he worked around the stable and driving the ambulance, that is all. * * * The defendant did not ask me to send Flood on that day. They never asked for any driver, only telephoned down for a horse and man.   *   *   *   On the 21st of May, 1904, we had three or four drivers in our employ whom we sometimes sent on these ambulance calls and we would select whichever one would be in to go.   *   *   *   There was no different, no other arrangement with the Church Charity Foundation in regard to hiring out this driver than there was with any livery call I received."

When asked whether the defendant corporation had any right to discharge Flood the witness answered, "Well, they could have sent him back.   He was in my employ," and went on to explain that the hospital people could have sent the driver home, and that he could not send him up if he did not suit them.   "Would you have discharged him then?" inquired counsel.   "Well, if I could not work him there I would have to discharge him," said Mr. Williamson.   "He had some other duties besides driving the ambulance."

When the evidence on both sides is considered all together and as a whole it really presents no contradiction of fact nor any condition of facts from which contradictory inferences can be drawn.   An ambulance owned by the defendant and bearing the name of its hospital was kept at a livery stable, the proprietor of which furnished a horse to draw the ambulance and a man to drive it on such occasions as the defendant might indicate.   The driver was hired and paid by the livery stable keeper who, it is evident, alone had the power to discharge him.   This is the fair import of Mr. Williamson's testimony.   It is apparent that if Flood, or any other driver whom he furnished to go with the amubulance, had proved unsatisfactory to the hospital authorities, Mr. Williamson would have substituted another driver, and would have discharged the objectionable individual unless he had enough other work for him to do.   There is nothing in this fact which tends to establish the relation of master and servant between the defendant and such ambulance driver as might be furnished from the livery stable. On the contrary, the case is analogous to the hiring of a team with a driver from a liveryman, in which the liveryman remains liable for any injury to third persons due to the negligence of the driver, notwithstanding the fact that the person hiring the team may direct the driver where to go and at what speed. Such a contract does not make the driver the servant of the hirer or render his negligence imputable to the latter. (*Quarman* v. *Burnett*, 6 Mees. & W. 497; *Laugher* v. *Pointer*, 5 Barn. & Cress. 547; *Jones* v. *Corporation of Liverpool*, L. R. [14 Q. B. D.] 890; *Little* v. *Hackett*, 116 U. S. 366; *Lewis* v. *L. I. R. R. Co.*, 162 N. Y. 52; *Driscoll* v. *Towle*, 181 Mass. 416; *N. Y., L. E. & W. R. R. Co.* v. *Steinbrenner*, 47 N. J. L. 161, and see *Murray* v. *Dwight*, 161 N. Y. 301.)

While it is thus clear that when one lets out a vehicle and driver on hire to another, he does not place the coachman under the control of the hirer except so far as the destination and stopping places are concerned, and generally the rate of speed at which the vehicle is to be driven, it is equally plain that cases may arise in which there is such active interference by the hirer with the management of the team as to render him responsible for any negligent injury which may be inflicted upon a stranger by reason of such mismanagement. (*Donovan* v. *Laing, etc., Construction Syndicate*, L. R. [1 Q. B. D. 1893] 629.) In that event, however, as was pointed out by Lord Justice BOWEN in the case cited, the hirer becomes liable "not as a master but as the procurer and cause of the wrongful act complained of." The defendant in the present case could not be charged with negligence on this theory. Its ambulance surgeon in no wise participated in any negligent act of the driver, assuming the driver to have been negligent. He had merely directed the driver where to go and had told him "to make time" or to go fast. He was seated at the rear of the ambulance where he could not and did not see the accident. There is nothing in the evidence to warrant an inference that he directed the driver to take the wrong side of the street in turning the corner or that he sanctioned the conduct of the driver in so doing.

The driver of the ambulance being at the time of the accident the servant of his general employer, Mr. Williamson, and subject primarily to his control, no liability for the driver's negligence toward the plaintiff can be imputed to the defendant in the absence of proof that the ambulance surgeon participated in such negligence. The learned counsel for the respondent, however, insists that even if this be true the hospital corporation may be held liable on another ground. He asserts that ordinances are passed permitting ambulances and fire trucks to travel along the streets at a rate of speed which is prohibited in respect to other vehicles as being dangerous and perilous to life and property; and he contends in substance that those who introduce such a dangerous agency in the public streets assume a duty to exercise reasonable care in its operation which duty cannot be delegated to any one else so as to avoid liability. This argument is based upon a misapprehension as to the legal effect of the ordinances. The ordinance specially relied upon which gives ambulances the right of way in no manner authorizes the driving of such vehicles at a dangerous rate of speed. It does not prescribe a high rate of speed or any rate whatever, but is merely equivalent to a command or direction that other vehicles shall give way to ambulances in the public streets. There is no foundation, therefore, for the doctrine that an ambulance is necessarily a dangerous instrumentality. Furthermore, it does not appear that the accident in the present case was in any manner due to the speed at which the ambulance was driven.

I do not deem it necessary to say anything further in support of the conclusion that it is our duty to reverse this judgment, except to point out briefly certain essential differences which seem to me to exist between the facts in two cases largely relied upon by the respondent and the facts in the case at bar.

In *Baldwin* v. *Abraham* (57 App. Div. 67; affd., 171 N. Y. 677) the plaintiff had been injured by collision with a van bearing the defendants' name.   The evidence did not point to any person other than the defendants as responsible for the driver's negligence except, possibly, a firm from which the defendants hired a large number of trucks to make Christmas deliveries of merchandise.   As to these hired wagons the testimony indicated that the defendants exercised some control over the delivery of their goods by these hired wagons; and the Appellate Division was of the opinion that the unknown owner of the truck in question could not be said as matter of law to have contracted independently for the delivery of the defendants' goods even if the driver had been hired with the truck.   The case differs radically from the present case in the actual absence of any real evidence tending to disprove the inference of ownership and control properly deducible from the fact that the van bore the name of the defendants.

In *Howard* v. *Ludwig* (171 N. Y. 507) a firm of truckmen furnished to the defendants a truck, horses and driver for the purpose of delivering goods sold by them to their customers on Staten Island.   The driver reported every morning with the truck and horses at the defendants' place of business, received a list of deliveries from the defendants' shipping clerk, loaded the goods upon the wagon, delivered them to the various customers and after his work was done returned to the stable of the contracting truckman.   At the time when the accident occurred which injured the plaintiff the driver was fulfilling the defendants' contracts by delivering their goods on Staten Island.   It was held by a closely divided court that the arrangement whereby the driver thus took charge of the delivery of the goods created the relation of master and servant between him and the defendants so that they became liable for his negligent acts. There, however, the original master had entirely abandoned all control of the driver to the new master who for the time being appropriated and controlled his service in carrying on their business. The distinction is plain between such an arrangement and one whereby a driver in the employ of a liveryman is sent out upon special occasion or whenever required to drive an ambulance. There is nothing in either of these decisions which can fairly be regarded as sustaining the position of the respondent.

The distinction between such cases and one like the present is well pointed out by Mr. Justice MOODY in *Standard Oil Co.* v. *Anderson* (212 U. S. 215). Where one furnishes another with men to do work for him and places them under his exclusive control in its performance those men become *pro hac vice* the servants of him to whom they are furnished and he is responsible for their negligence because the work is his work and they are his workmen for the time being. On the other hand, where work is undertaken to be performed by the person who furnishes the workmen through servants of his selection and he retains direction and control he remains responsible for any negligence on their part in the conduct of the work. "The simplest case, and that which was earliest decided, was where horses and a driver were furnished by a liveryman. In such cases the hirer, though he suggests the course of the journey and in a certain sense directs it, still does not become the master of the driver and responsible for his negligence, unless he specifically directs or brings about the negligent act." (p. 222.)

The judgment should be reversed and a new trial granted, costs to abide the event.

CULLEN, Ch. J., GRAY, VANN, HISCOCK, CHASE and COLLIN, JJ., concur.

Judgment reversed, etc.

People ex rel. Hon Yost *v.* Becker.   201

1911.]   Statement of case.   [203 N. Y.]

The People of the State of New York ex rel. Nicholas Hon Yost, Appellant, *v.* Daniel P. Becker, as
Sheriff of Oneida County, Respondent.

**Constitutional law — unconstitutionality of statutes (L. 1896,
ch. 812 and L. 1901, ch. 361) creating a municipal corporation
which is not a county, city, town or village — invalidity of commitment issued by a justice of the peace of the "area or territory known as Sylvan Beach."**

1. The Constitution constitutes the counties, cities, towns and
villages of the state the civil divisions for political purposes and
indispensable to the continuation of the government organized by
it, and this is equivalent to a direct prohibition against the creation
of any other civil divisions vested with similar powers.

2. The legislative acts, chapter 812 of the Laws of 1896 and chapter
361 of the Laws of 1901, purporting to revise and consolidate previous acts creating the "area or territory known as Sylvan Beach,"
are without constitutional warrant, and a commitment issued by a
police justice claiming to hold his office under such acts is void.

People ex rel. Hon Yost v. *Becker*, 142 App. Div. 929, reversed.

(Argued June 1, 1911; decided October 17, 1911.)

Appeal from an order of the Appellate Division of the
Supreme Court in the fourth judicial department, entered
January 27, 1911, which affirmed an order of Special
Term dismissing a writ of certiorari directing the defend-
ant to certify to the court the cause of the imprisonment
of the relator.

The facts, so far as material, are stated in the opinion.

J. T. Durham for appellant. The area or territory of
Sylvan Beach was incorporated and now exists in violation of the Constitution of the state of New York and
the office of police justice created thereunder is a nullity
and Thomas P. Bryant had no right or jurisdiction to
commit the relator. (Const. of N. Y. art. 3, § 18; *Read*

v. *Schmit.* 39 Hun, 223; *People ex rel. Townsend* v. *Porter*, 90 N. Y. 68.)

Edwin J. Brown for respondent. The area or territory of Sylvan Beach is not a village within the inhibition of section 18 of the Constitution, but is a municipal corporation according to the definition of section 3 of the General Corporation Law. (*Yellow Pine Lumber Co.* v. *Board of Education*, 15 Misc. Rep. 58; *Bassett* v. *Fish,* 75 N. Y. 311; *People ex rel. Wood* v. *Draper*, 15 N. Y. 532; *People* v. *Shepard*, 36 N. Y. 285; *Bank of Chenango* v. *Brown*, 26 N. Y. 467; *People* v. *Wilber*, 39 N. Y. S. R. 743.)

COLLIN, J. In July, 1910, the relator was imprisoned in the jail of Oneida county under a commitment issued by "Thomas P. Bryant, Police Justice of the Area or Territory of Sylvan Beach, N. Y.," as a Court of Special Sessions of the town of Vienna, Oneida county. The respondent, by his return to the writ and arguments, contends that the commitment defends the imprisonment. The relator argues that the area or territory of Sylvan Beach was incorporated as a village in violation of the section of the Constitution of the state which prohibits the legislature from passing private or local bills incorporating villages, and, as a corollary, that the Court of Special Sessions or Police Court and the office of police justice within the area or territory of Sylvan Beach, N. Y., were non-existent and the commitment was void.

The character of the area or territory of Sylvan Beach in July, 1910, was fixed by chapter 812 of the Laws of 1896 and chapter 361 of the Laws of 1901. The first act named was entitled "An act to revise, amend and consolidate the several acts relating to the area or territory known as Sylvan Beach, in the town of Vienna, county of Oneida, and to repeal certain acts and parts of acts." The second act named was entitled "An act to amend, revise and consolidate chapter eight hundred and twelve of the laws of eighteen hundred and ninety-six, entitled ' An act to revise, amend and consolidate the several acts relating to the area or territory known as Sylvan Beach, in the town of Vienna, county of Oneida, and to repeal certain acts and parts of acts.' " In aid of clearness and brevity we will here speak of them as a single act. The act provides: It shall affect all that part of the town of Vienna known as Sylvan Beach, which it particularly describes. (Section 1.) On the Tuesday succeeding the first Monday in August in each year, the owners of real property within the said area or territory particularly described, as appearing upon the assessment rolls of said territory for the then current year and who are qualified to vote at town meetings or city elections in the town or city in which they respectively reside, and all persons who actually reside within such area or territory and are qualified to vote at town meetings in the town of Vienna, shall hold a meeting for the election of officers of said territory, who shall have the powers conferred by the act. (Section 2.) The officers of said territory of Sylvan Beach shall be a president, four trustees, a clerk, a treasurer, an assessor, a collector, a street commissioner, a chief of the fire department, a police justice, a chief of police and the necessary patrolmen and special police, whose respective qualifications and terms of office and official duties and powers are prescribed. The president and trustees shall constitute the board of trustees for said area or territory. (Section 3.) Section 4 enumerates in eighteen subdivisions the powers of the trustees. They may, for said area or territory, construct a drainage and sewage system, establish sanitary, police and fire regulations, prevent vice and immorality, preserve order and control public entertainments, build station houses and lockups, organize and maintain a fire department, exercise the same power as village boards of health, enact such regulations as they may deem proper from time to time and enforce them with penalties, violations of which shall be misdemeanors, and appoint officers other than those named in the act, or committees, deemed necessary or useful in carrying out the act or for the good government and maintenance of the government of the area or territory. Policemen for such territory shall have the powers and duties of constables in towns and peace officers. (Section 16.) It provides for the assessment of the persons and property within the said territory and the voting, levying and collection of the taxes to defray the expenses authorized by the act. (Sections 8, 9, 10, 17, 19, 20.) The territory is constituted a separate highway district, wherein the trustees have all the powers and shall perform all the duties of commissioners of highways in towns. (Section 11.) Public parks and a park commissioner (Section 14) and an officered and equipped fire department are authorized. (Section 15.) It enacts that there shall be elected within and for said territory a police justice who shall have the power and jurisdiction in all cases of the violation of the regulations and ordinances of said territory of Sylvan Beach, and in all criminal cases of police justices under the village laws of the state, or which may be thereafter conferred by said laws on police justices, and shall be subject to the same duties and liabilities as police justices in villages and in all other respects be governed by said village laws conferring the powers and rights and defining the duties and liabilities of justices in villages. In case of the absence or inability of said police justice to act in his official capacity, any justice of the peace of the towns of Vienna or Verona shall have authority to act in his place. (Section 13.) The said territory is subject to actions to enforce any claim or demand against it and process therein shall be served on the president of the board of trustees or clerk. (Section 22.) The foregoing statement, although imperfect, sets forth the salient and characterizing effects of the legislation. The antecedent legislative acts relating to this area or territory are chapter 308 of the Laws of 1887 and chapter 194 of the

Laws of 1888. Those subsequent are chapter 292 of the Laws of 1906 and chapter 80 of the Laws of 1910. Thomas P. Bryant was elected, in accordance with the provisions of the statute, the police justice of the area or territory of Sylvan Beach, N. Y., and his term had not in July, 1910, expired.

The statutes were inhibited by the Constitution of the state. The powers they purported to confer upon the area or territory related to health, order, good government, police and fire protection, highways, public grounds, the expending of money for public purposes and the levying and collecting of taxes within it. It was invested with perpetuity of existence and the right to acquire, hold and dispose of property. It was given a governing body with the power of appointing officers and agents, the power to enact regulations and ordinances, enforce them and punish for their infractions. It held its powers and rights for public purposes and for the peculiar benefit of its inhabitants and the owners of real property within it. It was a body politic and corporate and, as such, the local recipient of administrative and judicial functions to be used as a part of the state government for the public good, by the exercise of which it become a participant in the government of the state. (*MacMullen* v. *City of Middletown,* 187 N. Y. 37; *Barnes* v. *District of Columbia,* 91 U. S. 540; *People ex rel. Devery* v. *Coler,* 173 N. Y. 103; *Wells* v. *Town of Salina,* 119 N. Y. 280.) It was a legal municipal corporation unless the people of the state had by their supreme and paramount law restrained the legislature from instituting it. The legislature may exercise the whole legislative power of the people except as the Constitution expressly or by implication forbids. The people of the state, in and by means of the Constitution of 1777, constructed in broad and general language the framework of the system or the machinery through the operation of which they would be governed. They would neither found nor tolerate a government which did not include and guard the principle that all local concerns and affairs should be regulated by the voice and action of the local community, subject only to the control and supervision of the general state government. Essential for the existence and sway of that principle were separate territorial subdivisions of the state, possessing respectively the chartered or delegated powers and rights in which were its authorization and opportunity. Neither in theory nor in operation was the principle new and through centuries in England, and in the existence of the colony of New York, it had been vital. In the colony the territorial subdivisions which were its domain were counties, towns and cities, each of which had in England its prototype or model, the first and last in its counties or shires and its cities, the second in its hundreds. The Duke's Laws, promulgated in 1665, required the election "by the plurality of voices of the freeholders in each town" of eight overseers for the town, "men of good fame and life," and provided "all votes in the private affairs of Particular Townes shall be given and Determined by the inhabitants, freeholders, householders," and justices of the peace were commissioned for the various towns. (1 Lincoln's Const. Hist. of New York, pages 423, 424, 458.) The colonial territory had not then been divided into counties; it was divided into twelve counties by an act of November 1, 1683, passed by the first representative assembly of the colony. (3 Lincoln's Const. Hist. of New York, pages 137, 138, 139.) The first English charter of New York city (the first city of the colony), known as the Dongan charter, was granted April 27, 1686, and the first charter of the city of Albany (the second city of the colony), the Dongan charter, was granted July 22, 1686. The Constitution of 1777 was in large measure the adaptation of established civil rules and institutions to the new conditions wrought by the complete dissolution of the allegiance of the colonies to the British crown. It adopted counties, towns and

cities as the civil units of the state and the local
auxiliaries of its government. (Articles 4, 5, 7, 12, 29.)
During the first half century succeeding the birth of the
state, the growth of urban communities was slow and
it was not until 1785 that the third city of the state, the
city of Hudson, was incorporated, and in 1790 the first
incorporated village, the village of Lansingburg, received
existence. (Laws of 1790, chap. 49; Laws of 1795,
chap. 4.) The Constitution of 1821 recognized and
adopted the village as an additional civil subdivision of
the state (Article 2, section 1), and thenceforth counties,
towns, cities and villages are the subordinate governmental units recognized by the Constitution of the state.
The third Constitution, that of 1846, reaffirmed the substance of the provisions of those of 1777 and 1821 relating
to counties, towns, cities and villages, and added others,
making more firm their places in the political system
and more clear the intendment of those who framed it
that they were and should remain the only territorial
divisions for the purpose of local government. It
empowered the legislature to enlarge the powers of boards
of supervisors to legislate locally (Article 3, section 17);
made it the duty of the legislature to provide for the
organization of cities and incorporated villages and to
restrict their power of taxation, assessment, borrowing
money, contracting debt and loaning their credit (Article 8,
section 9); promulgated the familiar home rule provision
(Article 9, section 2); enjoined, by an amendment adopted
in 1874, the legislature from passing a private or local bill
incorporating villages (Article 3, section 18), and by an
amendment of 1884 provided: "No county, city, town or
village shall hereafter give any money or property, or loan
its money or credit to or in aid of any individual, association
or corporation, or become directly or indirectly the owner
of stock in, or bonds of, any association or corporation; nor
shall any such county, city, town or village be allowed
to incur any indebtedness except for county, city, town or

village purposes." (Article 8, section 10.) All of these provisions are continued and others relevant to the discussion are contained in the Constitution of 1894. From this brief review of the parts of the Constitution which relate to the instrumentalities and methods of local government, it is apparent that it constitutes the counties, cities, towns and villages of the state the civil divisions for political purposes and indispensable to the continuation of the government organized by it. Their distinctive character and attributes cannot be conferred upon municipal corporations differently denominated without subverting the form of government which it framed. The constitutional provisions to which we have referred, and legislative acts, such as, for instance, the Election Law, the Public Health Law or the Liquor Tax Law, would be foreign and inoperative as to a shire, parish, manor or area or territory although given the powers conferred upon counties, towns, cities and villages, and therefrom would result uncertainty and disorder superseding government. We hold that the adoption by the Constitution of counties, towns, cities and villages as the civil divisions exercising general powers of local government and the local auxiliaries of the state government is equivalent to a direct prohibition against the creation of other civil divisions vested with similar powers. This conclusion is supported by the opinion of this court in *People ex rel. Bolton* v. *Albertson* (55 N. Y. 50) and *People ex rel. Townsend* v. *Porter* (90 N. Y. 68). There is nothing inconsistent with this view in the organization of boroughs in the city of New York, under its charter, as these are merely subordinate subdivisions of a city.

The appellant argues that the territory was incorporated a village in violation of the constitutional provision that a private or local bill incorporating villages shall not be passed, and calls our attention to various parts of the incorporating statutes which in substance are in the Village Law. The respondent, citing from the General

Corporation Law (Cons. Laws, chap. 23) "A 'municipal corporation' includes a county, town, school district, village and city and any other territorial division of the state established by law with powers of local government" (General Corporation Law, section 3), argues that it was not incorporated a village but a " territorial division of the state established by law with powers of local government." This contention we are not required to consider. It is an element essential in the incorporation of a county, town, city or village that it be incorporated by expressed classification a county, or a town, or a city, or a village. The legislature must, in order that our political system have orderly and intended operation, give to a body corporate having general powers of local government a classification or denomination and thereby fix its proper place in the governmental machinery. The body at the bar it denominated "area or territory," and in case we amended it to village or city, or deemed it thus amended, we would perform a legislative and not a judicial act.

The statutes purporting to incorporate the area or territory of Sylvan Beach, N. Y., are, for the reasons stated, unconstitutional and void. It follows that an incorporated area or territory of Sylvan Beach, N. Y., or the office of police justice of the area or territory of Sylvan Beach, N. Y., did not exist and the commitment was void.

The orders appealed from should be reversed and the relator discharged from imprisonment.

CULLEN, Ch. J., GRAY, HAIGHT, WERNER, WILLARD BARTLETT and CHASE, JJ., concur.

Orders reversed, etc.

14

AUGUST HECKSCHER, Appellant, *v.* WILLIAM EDENBORN, Respondent.

Principal and agent — syndicate contract by which subscribers agree to take stock in corporation organized to take business and property of existing corporations — when person acting as agent and organizer for subscribers sells property of his own to new corporation without knowledge of his principals, the syndicate agreement is voidable.

1. A person occupying a position of agent to purchase may not sell his own property to his principal. If one by misrepresentation or suppression of facts, when he ought to speak, induces another ignorantly to make a contract appointing the first his agent to buy and conferring upon him discretionary power to purchase his own property, the contract is voidable; and even if executed may be rescinded and the money recovered back upon restoration of what has been received.

2. In this action, brought to recover amounts subscribed and paid by plaintiff and his assignors to defendant under a syndicate agreement on the ground that they were induced so to do by fraud of defendant, the jury was entitled to find that the defendant was the chief promoter and organizer of an enterprise which contemplated as its basis the purchase of a million dollars par value of the stock of a corporation of which he was the majority owner; that the syndicate agreement made defendant and his two associate managers agents of the various subscribers and gave them discretionary power to purchase this stock; that defendant in effect invited or solicited plaintiff's assignors to become subscribers to the agreement; that at the time they were ignorant of his interest in the property to be acquired, and that he did not inform them of such interest, but on the contrary his apparent subscription on the paper showed to them, and various statements which he made, tended to exclude the idea that defendant was the owner of a large amount of property to be acquired, and which would in effect offset or pay his large subscription, when, as a matter of fact, he always intended to transfer his stock to the syndicate as he did. *Held*, that if these facts should be found a court would be entitled to find fraud as a matter of fact, for which the agreement could be rescinded and moneys paid thereunder recovered back.

3. Defendant and his associates acquired not only his stock in the corporation but also other property, and all of this was

transferred to a reorganized corporation and represented by new stock issued to the syndicate subscribers. Plaintiff and his assignors tendered to defendant the stock so issued to them and demanded the return of the money subscribed. *Held,* that such tender was a sufficient offer to restore defendant to his original position, so as to entitle plaintiff and his assignors to recover the moneys which had been paid to him; that the agreement cannot be subdivided and a rescission allowed as to part and not as to the rest; that on a rescission of the agreement and on restoration of what they received plaintiff and his assignors would be entitled to recover the entire amounts paid to defendant, even though part of such moneys were applied to the purchase of other property than that owned by defendant.

Heckscher v. *Edenborn,* 137 App. Div. 899, reversed.

(Argued June 14, 1911; decided October 17, 1911.)

APPEAL from a judgment of the Appellate Division of the Supreme Court in the second judicial department, entered March 31, 1910, affirming a judgment in favor of defendant entered upon a verdict directed by the court.

The action was brought by plaintiff in behalf of himself individually and also as assignee of several others to recover the amounts which they severally subscribed and paid under a syndicate agreement, on the ground that they were induced so to subscribe and pay by the fraud of the defendant. On the first trial of the action plaintiff secured a verdict and judgment for the full amount of these claims, but this was reversed by the Appellate Division, and on the second trial, in accordance with the views of the latter court, a verdict was directed in behalf of defendant.

The defendant was the principal promoter and organizer of a syndicate which had for its purpose the raising of $2,500,000 to be expended in the acquisition, improvement and development of certain iron properties. The basic property in the enterprise and the one which indirectly has furnished the occasion for this litigation was the United States Iron Company of New Jersey, with a capital of $1,000,000, of which defendant owned more than one-half.

The syndicate agreement which was formulated by or under the supervision of the defendant in its opening paragraph is stated to be " by and between William Edenborn, August Mann and J. C. Walker (hereinafter called the ' Syndicate Managers '), parties of the first part, and the subscribers hereto, severally, parties of the second part * * * and all of whom, together with the said parties of the first part, constitute the Syndicate." It sets forth the advantageous opportunities for acquiring the ownership and control of the various properties involved, specifically mentioning the "ownership, control and possession of the United States Iron Company of New Jersey at par," and the location of blast furnaces thereon; the necessity for raising $2,500,000 and the desirability that "a syndicate be formed which shall furnish and supply said sums * * * for the purposes above mentioned." It then recites: "This agreement witnesseth, that in consideration of the premises and the mutual promises herein contained, the parties hereto agree and the subscribers, severally, agree with each other and with the Syndicate Managers as follows:

"*First.* The parties hereto hereby form a Syndicate to purchase, acquire, use, develop and dispose of the lands and properties above mentioned or so much or such part thereof as, in the judgment and opinion of the said Syndicate Managers, is deemed advisable and proper.

"*Second.* Each subscriber shall set opposite his name the amount of his subscription to the said Syndicate."

Said agreement then in substance amongst other things provides that calls on subscribers shall be made by the syndicate managers who "shall issue, or cause to be issued to the subscribers, receipts in respect of payments made hereunder or certificates of interest in said Syndicate, of such tenor and form as they deem suitable;" that the syndicate managers "shall have the direction and management of the subject-matter of said Syndicate, and each subscriber nominates and appoints the Syndicate Managers, his agents and attorneys, * * * to exercise all the rights of the subscribers in and to the properties proposed to be acquired, and to enter into and execute any and all arrangements or agreements deemed by the Syndicate Managers expedient or necessary to carry out and perform the object and purpose of this Syndicate;" that said syndicate managers "shall take the title to any of the lands and properties to be acquired by the Syndicate in such form and in the names of such persons, firms or corporations as in their judgment and opinion shall be deemed proper and advisable;" that in case said syndicate managers "in the exercise of their absolute power and discretion hereunder, sell, convey or transfer any of the money or properties acquired by the Syndicate, for either cash, bonds, stocks or securities, each of the subscribers hereto shall be entitled to receive, on the termination of this agreement and the dissolution of the Syndicate, his *pro rata* share thereof. And, if the money and property acquired by the Syndicate, or any part thereof, is caused to be sold and conveyed to any corporation which may be formed for the purpose of acquiring the same from the Syndicate, and issuing in payment therefor its stocks, bonds or other forms of securities, then and in that event the Syndicate Managers shall have and retain the exclusive right and power to supervise and superintend each and all of the steps and proceedings in respect to the organization of any such corporation." In addition to the enumeration of specific powers said agreement confers " all other general and specific powers which, from time to time they (the managers) may deem necessary in order fully and effectively to carry out the purposes of this agreement and of this Syndicate." The assent of two of the three syndicate managers was necessary to any act to be performed by them.

The defendant was in terms the largest subscriber to this agreement, and the plaintiff and his assignors severally subscribed and paid in substantial sums.

The defendant did not in any manner solicit or invite the plaintiff himself to subscribe, but the latter so subscribed of his own volition and at his own suggestion. In answer to his inquiries the defendant did say, and this is claimed to be material in view of what subsequently took place, that "every one (of the subscribers) was to pay cash, and it was exactly on the same basis; that there would be no commissions nor any profit to any one."

The defendant did in effect solicit the subscriptions of plaintiff's assignors, in general terms characterizing the enterprise as a promising one, and in connection with the agreement, which showed his own subscription of $500,000, did state in substance in varying terms to some of the assignors that every subscriber was to pay his subscription in cash.

The syndicate agreement having been executed by a sufficient number of persons, the parties thereto proceeded to carry the same out.

The syndicate managers seem to have effected an organization by making the respondent chairman. From time to time calls were made by and in behalf of the managers for payments by the various subscribers on account of their syndicate subscriptions, and payments were made by the plaintiff and his assignors. The checks by which these payments were made were in most cases payable to the order of the respondent as chairman, but in some cases seem to have been payable to him individually. But however this may be, it is apparent that the payments were all in legal effect made to the syndicate managers, and that the moneys paid in were legally and constructively in their possession, and were expended by their joint action as such managers.

The moneys which were collected were expended in purchasing properties in accordance with and within the terms of the agreement. Of the $2,500,000 subscribed $647,500 in effect was expended for purchasing the entire capital stock of the United States Iron Company at $70 per share instead of par. The balance of the aggregate subscriptions, with the exception of something over $900,000, which was reserved for future use, was expended in purchasing other properties. As has already been indicated, respondent purported to pay his subscription of $500,000 to a large extent by turning in his holdings of the capital stock of the iron company at $70 per share.

Thereafter, and in purported compliance with the terms of the syndicate agreement, the managers, instead of organizing a new corporation to take over the properties which had been acquired and the balance of the subscriptions remaining in cash assets, caused the United States Iron Company to be reorganized under the name of the Sheffield Coal & Iron Company, and caused its capital stock to be increased from $1,000,000 to $2,500,000 par value, and thereafter said managers transferred the properties which they had acquired and the cash assets above mentioned, all aggregating a face value of $2,500,000, to said Sheffield Coal & Iron Company, which thereupon issued certificates of its capital stock made out to and in the name of the various syndicate subscribers for an amount representing at par their respective subscriptions, and these certificates of stock through the syndicate managers were delivered to the various subscribers, including the plaintiff and his assignors.

For some reason the enterprise did not prove successful, and plaintiff and his assignors then first discovered, as they claim, that respondent owned a majority of the capital stock of the United States Iron Company which had been purchased by him and his associate managers in behalf of the syndicate, as above stated. After making this alleged discovery, claiming that respondent had been guilty of fraud in procuring them to become subscribers to the syndicate agreement which authorized him and his associate managers in their discretion to buy property from himself without disclosing this ownership and interest, plaintiff and his assignors tendered back to respondent the stock which had been issued and delivered to them respectively as above stated, and demanded from him payment back of the moneys subscribed and paid by them respectively under the agreement.

Henry Wollman, Timothy M. Griffing, Edward S. Seidman and *Henry M. Blackmar* for appellant. Edenborn's failure to disclose his interest in the property which he had himself appointed agent to purchase, was a fraud upon his principals. This rendered the entire transaction voidable *ab initio* as to each person who did not know the facts. (*Britton* v. *Ferrin,* 171 N. Y. 235; *Munson* v. *S. G. & C. R. R. Co.,* 103 N. Y. 58; *Munson* v. *Magee,* 161 N. Y. 182; *Clark* v. *Bird,* 66 App. Div. 284; *Porter* v. *Woodruff,* 36 N. J. Eq. 174; *Ex parte James,* 8 Vesey, 337; *Smith* v. *S. L. S. & E. Ry. Co.,* 72 Hun, 202; *M. E. Ry. Co.* v. *M. Ry. Co.,* 14 Abb. [N. C.] 103; *McDonald* v. *Lord,* 26 How. Pr. 404; *Morganstern* v. *Hill,* 8 Misc. Rep. 365.) If Edenborn had been merely a "constructive" trustee instead of an "express" trustee, and even if he had not come into personal contact with the plaintiff and his assignors he would nevertheless have been liable to them. (*Brewster* v. *Hatch,* 122 N. Y. 349; *Mack* v. *Latta,* 178 N. Y. 525; *Schwenk* v. *Naylor,* 102 N. Y. 683; *Hedden* v. *Griffin,* 136 Mass. 229; *Nash* v. *M. T. Ins. & T. Co.,* 163 Mass. 574.) The burden was upon Edenborn to show that before he got the plaintiff and his assignors to appoint him their agent to purchase the United States Iron Company, he made a full, fair and thorough disclosure to the plaintiff and each of his assignors of his interest in the property to be bought and of everything connected with the entire matter, and that each of them understood everything thoroughly. (*Barnard* v. *Gantz,* 140 N. Y. 249; *C. C. Co.* v. *Sherman,* 30 Barb. 553; *Clark* v. *Bird,* 66 App. Div. 284; *Kissam* v. *Squires,* 102 App. Div. 536; *Ten Eyck* v. *Whitbeck,* 156 N. Y. 341;

Bauchle v. *Smylie*, 104 App. Div. 513; *Matter of L. I. L. & T. Co.* [*In re Garretson*], 92 App. Div. 1; 179 N. Y. 520; *Rose* v. *M. T. Co.*, 130 N. Y. S. R. 946.)

Frederic B. Jennings and *Allen Wardwell* for respondent. Even if there were proof of actual fraud inducing the subscriptions the plaintiff would not be entitled to recover in this suit upon any theory of rescission of the syndicate agreement, because that agreement.was not made with the defendant, and the money, which plaintiff seeks to recover, was not paid to the defendant or received by him. (*Sim* v. *Edenborn*, 163 Fed. Rep. 655; Kerr on Fraud & Mistake, 331; *Upton* v. *Tribilcock*, 91 U. S. 45; 1 Bigelow on Fraud, 123, 135; Smith on Frauds, § 267; *Southern Development Co.* v. *Silva*, 125 U. S. 247; *Hubbell* v. *Meigs*, 50 N. Y. 480; *Tyrrell* v. *Bank of London*, 10 H. L. Cas. 26.) The only contract which could have been rescinded in this case as against Edenborn was not the syndicate agreement, but the contract under which the syndicate purchased Edenborn's interest in the United States Iron Company. A rescission of that contract by the plaintiff alone, as one of the members of the syndicate, would be impossible because he was not a party to it and also because the *statu quo* could not be restored; but, even if possible, the plaintiff would not be entitled upon such rescission to recover the amount of his subscription to the syndicate agreement. (*New Sombrero Phosphate Co.* v. *Erlanger*, L. R. [5 Ch. Div.] 73; *Bagnall* v. *Carlton*, L. R. [6 Ch. Div.] 371; *Twycross* v. *Grant*, L. R. [2 C. P. Div.] 469; *W. B. C. P. Co.* v. *Green & Smith*, L. R. [5 Q. B. Div.] 109; *Emma Silver Mining Co.* v. *Grant*, L. R. [11 Ch. Div.] 918; *Lydney & Wigpool Iron Co.* v. *Bird*, L. R. [33 Ch. Div.] 85; *Joplin Land Co.* v. *Case*, 104 Mo. 572; *Cortes Co.* v. *Thannhauser*, 45 Fed. Rep. 730; *Simons* v. *Vulcan Oil, etc., Co.*, 61 Penn. St. 202; *Pittsburg Mining Co.* v. *Spooner*, 74 Wis. 307; *Parker* v. *Michigan*, 112 Mass. 195; *Yale Gas Stove Co.* v. *Wilcox*, 64 Conn. 101;

Chandler v. *Bacon*, 30 Fed. Rep. 538; *Ex-Mission Land Co.* v. *Flash*, 97 Cal. 610.) The plaintiff's tender to and demand upon the defendant Edenborn did not place him in *statu quo.* (*Cobb* v. *Hatfield*, 46 N. Y. 537; *Francis* v. *N. Y. & B. E. R. R. Co.*, 108 N. Y. 97; *Hammond* v. *Pennock*, 61 N. Y. 145; *Pullman* v. *Alley*, 53 N. Y. 637; *Gould* v. *Cayuga Nat. Bank*, 86 N. Y. 75; *Hogan* v. *Weyer*, 5 Hill, 389; *Bedell* v. *Bedell*, 3 Hun, 580; *Matter of Cape Breton Co.*; L. R. [29 Ch. Div.] 795; *Ladywell Mining Co.* v. *Brookes*, L. R. [35 Ch. Div.] 400; *Bentinck* v. *Fenn*, L. R. [12 App. Cas.] 652.) The defendant Edenborn and his associate syndicate managers, by the syndicate agreement, were expressly authorized to purchase the interest of any member of the syndicate or of the syndicate managers in the United States Iron Company and expressly relieved from liability so long as they acted in good faith. (*White* v. *Wood*, 129 N. Y. 527.) The action of the syndicate managers in purchasing the stock of the United States Iron Company held by Edenborn was duly ratified, and the plaintiffs are bound by such ratification. (*May* v. *Chapman*, 16 M. & W. 361; *Gale* v. *Morris*, 30 N. J. Eq. 289; *Haslett* v. *Stephany*, 55 N. J. Eq. 68; *Durfee* v. *O. C. R. Co.*, 5 Allen, 242; *San Diego* v. *P. B. Co.*, 112 Cal. 53; *Stetson* v. *N. I. Co.*, 104 Iowa, 393.)

HISCOCK, J. Plaintiff in his own behalf and as assignee of several others asks that he and they be relieved and released from the contract which they respectively made as subscribers to the syndicate agreement hereinbefore summarized and that they be repaid by defendant, who was one of the three syndicate managers, the amounts which they paid in as subscribers to said agreement. They demand this relief on the ground that the latter induced them respectively to become parties to said agreement and that while doing so he was guilty of such fraud as to make the contract voidable at their election, and to entitle them to recover their moneys. While plaintiff's counsel on the argument has charged the defendant with many misdeeds, there is only one charge of fraud which finds any basis in the most favorable evidence. This is in substance that defendant procured plaintiff and his assignors to sign the agreement whereby the former and two others were appointed syndicate managers and were in their discretion authorized to purchase certain properties in behalf of plaintiff and the other subscribers, and that at the time when he and his associates were thus authorized to and at the time when they did in fact purchase, defendant was a large owner in one of the properties in question and that he concealed or failed to impart information of this fact and adverse interest of which plaintiff and his assignors were ignorant. I do not find any evidence that the defendant was guilty of that active fraud disclosed in many cases where conscienceless promoters have accumulated property at a low price under a well-devised scheme to unload it upon others at a high price. There is nothing to indicate that defendant acquired his stock in the United States Iron Company for any such purpose or that the stock purchased by him and his associate managers in that company was not fairly worth the price paid for it which was $30 per share less than the price fixed in the syndicate agreement. But broadly speaking, the complainants must rest their claim to relief on the basic principle that defendant induced them ignorantly to execute an agreement which violated the rule that an agent to buy may not purchase of himself.

Since that question is somewhat debated, it will be best in the first place to determine the exact character of the action which appellant is seeking to maintain and then decide whether on the facts he can successfully maintain it.

It seems clear that the action must succeed if at all as one based on an attempted and purported rescission of a

contract rendered voidable by reason of fraud wherein the
defrauded party having tendered back what he received
under the voidable contract attempts to recover that
with which he has parted. It must stand as one
directed against the syndicate agreement itself. If
that was valid plaintiff cannot succeed because under
it and subsequently defendant did some illegal act in
violation of it.

Assuming that the complainants were induced by
fraud to enter into the syndicate agreement three lines
of relief were open to them. ' They might retain
that which they received and bring an action at law
against the guilty party to recover damages sustained
by reason of his fraud; they might bring an action for
rescission of the contract in which it would be sufficient
to tender back anything which they might have received
under the contract; they might bring an action based on
a prior rescission wherein, having previously tendered
back what they had received, they would recover that
which had been taken from them. (*Vail* v. *Reynolds,*
118 N. Y. 297.)

This action is not one for damages or one to secure
the rescission of a contract, but is one based on a prior
rescission. In each cause of action plaintiff alleges in
substance that he or his assignor, as the case might be,
after learning of the interest of respondent in the properties to be purchased "and the falsity of his representations hereinbefore set forth," tendered back to him all of
the stock received under said syndicate agreement on
account of his payment of the amount subscribed "and
demanded of said Edenborn the return to him of said
sum * * * so paid by him as aforesaid." Said complaint also in like manner alleges that the plaintiff and
his respective assignors have respectively "rescinded said
Syndicate agreement and his subscription thereto, and is
entitled to receive from said defendant said sum " subscribed and paid as aforesaid, and in conclusion the com-

plaint demands judgment for the aggregate amount of the sums paid in by said parties.

Therefore, both by the process of exclusion and by reason of its allegations the action must be treated as one based on rescission.

Such being the nature of the action, the next question is whether plaintiff or his assignors on any aspect of the evidence were entitled for fraud, actual or constructive, to rescind their syndicate contract and recover moneys paid thereunder on restoration of what they had received. I think that the latter were, yielding some doubts in the case of the assignor Moen to the judgment of my associates, and that the former was not, for, as I shall attempt to show, there is a difference in their respective positions.

The jury were entitled to find, amongst other facts, that the defendant was the chief promoter and organizer of an enterprise which, however reputable and legitimate, contemplated as its very basis the purchase of a million dollars par value of the stock of a certain corporation of which he was the majority owner; that the syndicate agreement made defendant and his two associate managers agents of the various subscribers and gave them discretionary power to purchase this stock; that defendant, who had held rather intimate and influential relations with some at least of plaintiff's assignors, in effect invited or solicited them to become parties to the project and subscribers to the agreement; that at the time they were ignorant of his interest in the property to be acquired and that he did not inform them of such interest, but on the contrary his apparent subscription of $500,000 on the paper showed to them, and various statements which he made, as that he was "putting in cash the same as" one of the subscribers, and that "any man in joining (the syndicate) puts in a dollar against the other man's dollar," and that there were no "inside profits," at least tended to exclude the idea that defendant was the owner of a large amount of property to be acquired and which would in effect offset or pay his large subscription, when as a matter of fact he always intended to transfer his stock to the syndicate as he did. It seems to me that if these facts should be found a court would be entitled to find fraud as a matter of fact for which the agreement could be rescinded and moneys paid thereunder recovered back.

The principle that a person occupying a position of agent to purchase may not sell his own property to his principal is so elementary that it need only be stated. It must be quite as elementary and true that if one by misrepresentation or suppression of facts when he ought to speak induces another ignorantly to make a contract appointing the first his agent to buy and conferring upon him discretionary power to purchase his own property, the contract is voidable and even if executed may be rescinded and the money recovered back on restoration of what has been received.

The defendant comes within these principles. When he solicited plaintiff's assignors to become parties to the syndicate and appoint him one of their agents under the circumstances referred to, he must be held to have represented that he was legally qualified to discharge the powers which were being conferred upon him, and the obligation affirmatively rested upon him to inform them of his interest in the property which he was securing authority to buy if he would hold them to their contract and avoid that imputation of legal misconduct which the law fastens on an agent who attempts to serve the interests of both the principal and himself.

He did not occupy the position of an ordinary vendor but he was inviting others to confer upon him a fiduciary relationship. If he knew and they were ignorant of some fact which touched the very substance of that relationship and legally destroyed his ability to meet its full requirements, it was his duty to advise them of it, and for his failure so to do they were entitled to repudiate the agreement and avoid what had been done under it. (*Virginia Land Co.* v. *Haupt*, 90 Va. 533, 537; *Brewster* v. *Hatch*, 122 N. Y. 349; *Bentinck* v. *Fenn*, L. R. [12 App. Cases] 652, 658, 661.)

It is urged that these principles do not apply to this case because the defendant was not an agent to buy generally in the market but was appointed to buy specific property at a specific price and, therefore, vested with no discretion which he could abuse because of opposing personal motives. This is hardly the fact. The syndicate agreement makes it plain by specific clauses as well as by general construction that defendant and his associate managers were intrusted with a discretion which they were called on to exercise in the interest of the various subscribers and which the law holds might be warped by conflicting interests.

While it is debated somewhat by him in the briefs, there is no real question but that subsequent transactions did amount to a purchase by defendant in behalf of his principals of property which belonged to him. It is said that he but exchanged stock in the original company for stock in the reorganized company, and that this did not amount to a purchase of his property at the expense of plaintiff and his assignors, but this does not seem to me to be the fact. Having subscribed a large amount in the syndicate, he turned in to himself and his associate managers his stock largely in payment of his subscription. This was the same as, and on the very theory that it amounted to paying his subscription to the managers in cash and then the purchase by the managers of his stock out of the cash which had been subscribed. Subsequently the stock acquired from him and others in part with the money subscribed by plaintiff and his assignors was turned over to the reorganized steel company, which became the depositary of the syndicate subscribers' rights, and new stock issued to defendant and all other subscribers in proportion to their subscriptions. Treated as a whole and in its entirety, it is clear that the transaction amounted to a purchase with the syndicate subscriptions of defendant's stock as well as of the other properties involved. This was his own theory, for the minutes of the syndicate managers show that at a given meeting "the Chairman (defendant) reported that he had purchased all the outstanding stock of the United States Iron Company." Even if this were technically otherwise, it is clear that the defendant, as its largest stockholder, had a personal, adverse interest because of benefits expected to accrue in the application of the syndicate subscriptions to the acquisition, reorganization and development of the iron company.

As I have indicated, I think the plaintiff himself stands in a less advantageous position than his assignors. He sought participation in the agreement. He was never urged or invited by respondent or by any one else to invest his money in the enterprise. The only affirmative statement or representation of alleged importance made by respondent to him when he subscribed to the agreement was to the effect that the former's subscription of $500,000 then appearing on the agreement would be paid in cash. I do not think that this statement would amount to a fraudulent misrepresentation entitling appellant to rescind the agreement if the subscription was paid by turning in stock instead of cash, provided the purchase by the syndicate managers of respondent's stock was proper. Therefore, the question in plaintiff's case becomes whether respondent was guilty of a fraudulent suppression of material facts because he did not voluntarily inform him that he had an interest in some of the property which was to be purchased by himself and the other syndicate managers. It does not seem to me that this was the case. There was no fiduciary or confidential relationship between appellant and respondent when the former sought permission to become a subscriber. They dealt as entire strangers. There was no solicitation by the defendant that the appellant should make him his agent, and, therefore, no implied representation that he was legally qualified to be one. Under these circumstances the burden rested on appellant to ascertain by proper investigation whether the scheme to which he was about to subscribe was a good one and whether respondent was a proper person to be intrusted as his agent with power to carry out the same, and respondent had the right to assume that he had made such investigation and understood the facts involved, and, therefore, was not guilty of fraud because he did not inform him of the facts which form the basis of the present complaint.

But, further, the respondent argues that plaintiff's theory presupposes a contract between his assignors and defendant which the former have been induced by the latter's fraud to make for the payment or delivery to him of money or property and the actual payment or delivery in accordance with the contract rescinded of such money or property to the latter for his individual account, and that neither of these conditions exist. And in amplification of this contention it is insisted that the syndicate subscriptions were received by respondent under the syndicate agreement simply as agent for the subscribers; that said agreement was made by plaintiff's assignors with the other syndicate subscribers to it and not with respondent at all, and that, therefore, it would not be rendered voidable even if respondent was guilty of fraud, he not being a party to it; that any relief must lie in an action in behalf of all the syndicate subscribers or their successors simply to rescind the purchase by defendant of his own property. In support of this argument the principle is cited, "If the party by whose representation a transaction has been induced, is not a party to the transaction, the transaction stands good and cannot be avoided, unless one of the parties to the transaction was implicated in the fraud." (Kerr on Fraud and Mistake

[3d ed.], p. 361. See, also, *Sim* v. *Edenborn*, 163 Fed. Rep. 655.)

I do not think that the principle invoked is applicable to the facts which may be found in this case.

It is, of course, true that in an action between two parties to a contract, one cannot avoid it as against the other who is entirely innocent, on the ground that he was induced to make it by the fraud of a third party wholly disconnected with the transaction. So far as I can find, however, this principle has never been applied in an action by the injured party against a person claiming protection as agent under a contract which he had fraudulently induced. But beyond this I do not think that it can be said that the moneys of plaintiff's assignors were not paid to defendant under a contract for his benefit and to which he was a party. He was the promoter of the enterprise and procured the execution of the syndicate agreement. By its express terms it was made by each subscriber not only with the other subscribers but also with him as a syndicate manager, and it was for his benefit not only in authorizing him to purchase the property in question but also in conferring upon him general powers as a manager. If the contract be regarded as a single one between each subscriber on one side and his fellow-subscribers and the managers on the other, it must follow that the fraud of either of the latter in inducing it would be a ground of rescinding it against all parties. If the agreement should be regarded as embracing two contracts, one made by each subscriber with his fellow-subscribers, and a second one made by him with defendant as agent and manager, it may be that in an action between the subscribers the contract could not be avoided because of the latter's fraud, although I have doubts about that.

In *Metropolitan Coal Consumers Case* (66 Law Times [N. S.], 700) it was held, after consideration of the principle now being urged by defendant, that a subscriber could be relieved from a subscription for corporation shares because of false statements made by promoters in a prospectus issued before the corporation was organized, "although not made by the company or its agents."

But however this may be, this is an action between the subscriber and the agent, between whom in terms there existed a contract authorizing the transactions here involved, and in view of this and of the surrounding circumstances I do not think it possible for the latter to say that he was not a party to the contract and to the transactions which occurred under it within the rule now being discussed.

The claim that no moneys were paid to or received by the defendant under the contract thus made with him must be based on an interpretation of the legal effect of what was done rather than on the exact facts themselves, for there is no question that all of the subscriptions of plaintiff's assignors and other subscribers were paid to the defendant and his associate managers. I suppose the real meaning of this part of the argument is that because they received them as managers or agents under the agreement, the payment is to be regarded as having been made to the syndicate rather than to the managers. This argument, however, cannot be sustained. When the agreement under which the moneys were paid to the managers was rescinded it was destroyed *ab initio* and can no longer be utilized as an authority either for the payment by the agent to his principal or for the longer retention of the moneys by himself. (*Nash* v. *Minn. T. Ins. & Trust Co.*, 163 Mass. 574, 581. See, also, *Mack* v. *Latta*, 178 N. Y. 525, and cases cited.)

The only benefit which the defendant would secure from the agreement thus rescinded would be that before recovery of the moneys paid to him he should be restored to his original condition as against the acts which he had performed under the agreement before rescission. Even this general rule is not enforced with unvarying strictness and amongst the exceptions to it is the case where the wrongdoer has so complicated matters as between him and the party seeking relief that complete restoration is impossible. (*Masson* v. *Bovet,* 1 Denio, 69; *Hammond* v. *Pennock,* 61 N. Y. 145.)

Therefore, defendant's claims bring us to the final question whether plaintiff's assignors did so properly and sufficiently offer to restore him to his original position as to entitle them to recover the moneys which had been paid to him.

It will be recalled in this connection that defendant and his associate managers transferred the property acquired with the syndicate subscriptions and any unexpended balance of said subscriptions to a reorganized corporation as permitted by the syndicate agreement and that for this property this reorganized corporation issued capital stock at par which was delivered to the defendant and his associates and by them distributed to the various subscribers in proportion to their subscriptions, and that plaintiff and his assignors tendered to defendant the stock so issued to them on demanding the return of the money.

If the only transaction involved had been the purchase of defendant's stock and this stock after purchase had been transferred to the corporation which had issued receipts or stock as against it to the various subscribers in proportion to their subscription and the assignors had tendered to defendant this stock on demand of their money, I think that there is no doubt but that this would have been a sufficient offer to restore defendant to his original position. This not only would seem to be so on principle but to be settled by authority.

In *Getty* v. *Devlin* (54 N. Y. 403) it appeared that plaintiffs had been induced by fraud to sign a subscription paper for the purchase of certain property owned by promoters of the scheme and subsequently they paid in their subscriptions which were received and divided by the associated schemers. A company was thereupon organized, the property transferred to it, stock being issued in payment therefor to the various subscribers. On discovery of the fraud the plaintiffs offered to return to the fraudulent promoters the stock which had thus been received by them and sought to be relieved from the fraud which had been perpetrated upon them. It appeared, however, that in the meantime the real estate which had been thus conveyed to the corporation had been sold on claims held by the plaintiffs themselves against the corporation. Their complaint was dismissed at the Trial Term and on the appeal to this court Judge EARL wrote as follows: " I am, therefore, clearly of the opinion that the plaintiffs were entitled to relief in some form. They could not, on account of the fraud, recover back all the money paid by them, because they could not restore the four defendants to the position they were in before the transfer of the real estate to the company. The real consideration for the money subscribed and paid was the real estate which was conveyed to the company at the request of the subscribers. The company took the title to the real estate, and then their interest in the company and through it in the real estate was represented by shares of stock. The plaintiffs did not place the four defendants in the position they were before the real estate was conveyed, by returning their stock, because what the defendants parted with was the real estate, and that had passed beyond their control. The plaintiffs caused it to be seized and sold for their debts against the company, after the discovery by them of the fraud of which they complain. It is a rule, quite uniform, that a party who seeks to recover back money which he has been induced to pay for property by fraud, must restore the property before he can rescind the contract of purchase and recover the money paid." (p. 414.)

By what was thus said I think it was fairly implied that if the corporation had still been in possession of the real estate which formed the subject of the fraudulent contract, plaintiffs, by tendering the stock which represented their interest in the real estate to the defendant, would have offered a sufficient restoration.

In this case, however, defendant and his associates acquired not only his stock in the corporation but also various other property, and all of this was transferred to the corporation and represented by the new stock, of which plaintiff's assignors received and tendered back their share. It is urged that even assuming an illegal purchase of defendant's stock, plaintiff's assignors should not be allowed to tender him certificates which represented not only their interest in that stock but also in the other property transferred to the corporation, and compel him to refund their entire syndicate payments, and thus take up their interest in all of the property acquired; that such a proceeding would not only be inequitable in this case but that the principle might lead to almost absurd results where the property improperly purchased was smaller in proportion to the entire property acquired than here. I am not unprepared to admit that there may be some equity in this argument in this case, for it sometimes does occur that at the end of an unsuccessful enterprise those who have lost their money are not averse to transferring their losses to some one else because of alleged faults which as a matter of fact never exercised any substantial influence on the enterprise. I do not, however, see how this result can be avoided. The agreement authorizing the purchase and organization of various properties was an entire one. The conclusion has been reached that so far as it authorized the purchase of or related to defendant's property it was constructively fraudulent even though there was no actual fraudulent motive on his part. I see no way in which the agreement can be subdivided and a rescission allowed as to part and not as to the rest, and of course it follows that if the entire agreement is vitiated and rescinded the plaintiff's assignors are entitled to recover all that was paid under it on restoration of what they received.

I recommend that the judgment appealed from should be affirmed as to the appellant personally, and should be reversed and a new trial granted, with costs to abide event, as to the causes of action assigned to him by Daniels, Moen, Lott, Miller and Frank Baackes.

Judgment reversed and new trial granted, costs to abide event. All concur, except HISCOCK, J., who writes for reversal as to claims assigned to the plaintiff, but for affirmance as to his individual claim, with whom GRAY, J., concurs. All others concur in opinion of HISCOCK, J., except as to such individual claim.

THE PEOPLE OF THE STATE OF NEW YORK ex rel. MANHATTAN RAILWAY COMPANY, Appellant, *v.* EGBURT E. WOODBURY et al., Constituting the State Board of Tax Commissioners, Respondents.

THE CITY OF NEW YORK, Respondent.

Tax — assessments upon special franchises — rule for ascertaining value of tangible property — method of ascertaining net earnings in assessment of special franchises — rate by which capitalization should be fixed.

1. In fixing the value of the relator's special franchises the court applied the net earnings rule to the evidence. *Held*, that in ascertaining the value of the relator's tangible property, upon which a return should be allowed, there should have been included the value of the relator's interest in the subway, or subservice conduits, through which its power and light cables pass, the cash and cash items on hand, and the cost of relator's easements.

2. The rule as to net earnings is to ascertain the gross earnings of the corporation and then deduct the operating expenses, together with the annual taxes paid. From the remainder there should also be deducted a fair and reasonable return on that portion of the capital of the corporation which is invested in tangible property, the result becoming the net earnings contributable to the special franchise; which, when capitalized at a certain fixed rate, becomes the

232 People ex rel. Manhattan Ry. Co. *v.* Woodbury.

[203 N. Y.]   Statement of case.   [Oct.,

value of the tangible property of the special franchise. The question of the fair and reasonable return is one of fact under the control of the courts below and one which this court should not review.

3. To provide against unforeseen contingencies that may arise in the prosecution of the business of a corporation, which may result in the impairment of the net earnings, a gross sum should be deducted annually for the purposes of reconstruction, and the rate of capitalization to meet depreciation should be at least one per cent higher than the rate of income allowed. (*People ex rel. Jamaica Water Supply Co.* v. *State Board of Tax Commissioners,* 196 N. Y. 89, followed.)

People ex rel. Manhattan Ry. Co. v. *Woodbury,* 143 App. Div. 905, modified.

(Argued June 5, 1911; decided October 17, 1911.)

APPEAL from an order of the Appellate Division of the Supreme Court in the first judicial department, entered February 10, 1911, which affirmed an order of Special Term reducing an assessment for purposes of taxation against special franchises of the relator.

The facts, so far as material, are stated in the opinion.

Richard Reid Rogers, Charles F. Kingsley, Ralph Norton and *James L. Quackenbush* for appellant. The amounts paid for rights to maintain an elevated structure, acquired by the relator and its predecessors from the abutting property owners, are not a part of the value of the special franchise. (*People ex rel. Panama R. R. Co.* v. *Comrs.,* 104 N. Y. 240; *People ex rel. Manhattan Ry. Co.* v. *Barker,* 146 N. Y. 304; *People ex rel. D., L. & W. R. R. Co.* v. *Clapp,* 152 N. Y. 490; *People ex rel. Manhattan Ry. Co.* v. *Barker,* 152 N. Y. 417; *People ex rel. M. S. Ry. Co.* v. *Tax Comrs.,* 174 N. Y. 417; *People ex rel. N. Y. C. & H. R. R. R. Co.* v. *Gourley,* 198 N. Y. 486; *People ex rel. Retsof Mining Co.* v. *Priest,* 75 App. Div. 131; affd., 175 N. Y. 511; *People ex rel. Abraham* v. *Perley,* 67 Misc. Rep. 471; *People ex rel. N. Y. El. R. R. Co.* v. *Comrs. of Taxes,* 82 N. Y. 459.) The percentages of return proved on behalf of the relator are properly applicable. (*People ex rel. T. A. R. R. Co.* v. *Tax Comrs.*, 136 App. Div. 155; *Mayor, etc.*, v. *M. Ry. Co.*, 143 N. Y. 1.) Relator is entitled to a return upon "subways" and "cash" and " cash items." (*C. G. Co.* v. *City of New York*, 157 Fed. Rep. 849.) A sum equal to the average actual annual depreciation of the plant and property proved should be deducted. (Beale & Wyman on R. R. Rates, § 430; *People ex rel. B. H. R. R. Co.* v. *State*, 69 Misc. Rep. 646.) The assessments reviewed are erroneous by reason of inequality. (*People ex rel. J. W. S. Co.* v. *Tax Comrs.*, 196 N. Y. 39.)

Archibald R. Watson, Corporation Counsel (*Curtis A. Peters* and *Addison B. Scoville* of counsel), for respondents. The value of the easements owned by the relator were properly included in the valuation of the tangible property forming part of its special franchise. (*People ex rel. M. R. Co.* v. *Barker*, 165 N. Y. 305; *People ex rel. Poor* v. *O'Donnell*, 139 App. Div. 83; 200 N. Y. 519; *People ex rel. Topping* v. *Purdy*, 128 N. Y. Supp. 569.) No allowance should be made from annual earnings to provide for a fund to substitute modern for obsolete property. (*S. V. W. Works* v. *City of San Francisco*, 124 Fed. Rep. 574; *Cotting* v. *K. C. S. Y. Co.*, 82 Fed. Rep. 839.) The trial court was justified in refusing to equalize the assessment against the relator's special franchises in the borough of the Bronx. (*People ex rel. Dexter* v. *Palmer*, 86 Hun, 513.)

GRAY, J. In this proceeding the relator, the Manhattan Railway Company, in the city of New York, has sought to review a determination of the state board of tax commissioners assessing its special franchises in the borough of Manhattan at $75,000,000, and in the borough of the Bronx at $3,500,000. The trial court has reduced the assessment in the borough of Manhattan to $66,661,930.05 and has confirmed the assessment in the borough of the Bronx. In fixing the values of the relator's special franchises, the court applied the net earnings rule to the evidence, as it was laid down in the case of *People ex rel. Jamaica Water Supply Company* v. *State Board of Tax Commissioners* (196 N. Y. 39). The Appellate Division has affirmed the order of the Special Term.

With respect to all the items, except those which will be referred to, I am of the opinion that the determination below was right. I think, in ascertaining the value of the relator's tangible property, upon which a return of six per cent. should be allowed, that there should have been included the value of the relator's interest in the subway, or subservice conduits, through which its power and light cables pass. While it is true that this subway property, or structure, was owned by another corporation, the Consolidated Telegraph and Electrical Subway Company, nevertheless, the relator had invested in it the sum of $936,879. This investment was essential to the operation of the relator's road and there is no good reason why it should not be entitled to a return upon it.

I think, also, that there should have been included in the tangible property the sum of $537,139, consisting in cash and other cash items on hand. This item may, properly, be considered as a part of the relator's working capital, which it was entitled, in the prudent management of its business, to keep on hand. Whether or not it was, in fact, essential to the operation of the railroad is not material; but it was, nevertheless, an item of its property, which it may fairly claim to have considered with the rest of its tangible property, upon which the return should be estimated.

The inclusion of these two items in the relator's tangible property, of subways and of cash, would result, by the methods of computation adopted, in reducing the value of the special franchises in the borough of Manhattan from $66,661,930.05 to the sum of $65,350,060.26. In

PEOPLE EX REL. MANHATTAN RY. CO. *v.* WOODBURY. 235

1911.]   Opinion, per GRAY, J.   [208 N. Y.]

the borough of the Bronx the reduction would be from $4,907,652 to $4,805,399. This difference, however, in the case of the borough of the Bronx, is not material and does not affect the determination; inasmuch as it was, very properly, held, as the sum fixed by the tax commissioners at $3,500,000 was less than the full value of the special franchise, that the relator was not aggrieved and that no allowance should be made for equalization.

Whether the rate of return to be allowed to the relator upon its tangible property, or whether the rate at which the net income should be capitalized, should be six per cent., as determined below, was a question of fact decided upon, concededly, conflicting evidence and is one with which, therefore, this court should not interfere. In the *Jamaica Water Supply Company's Case*, (196 N. Y. 39), the character of the plaintiff's business affected the question of the rate of capitalization of net income; a consideration which, I think, does not obtain in this case.

I think that the cost of the easements was properly included in ascertaining the value of the relator's tangible property. The structures in the street, upon the acquisition of those easements, became lawful as to the abutting property owners. They, then, became appurtenant to the railroad property and, necessarily, enhanced its value.

The courts below determined that the relator was entitled to make annual depreciation charges, amounting in the case of the borough of Manhattan to the sum of $360,613.65 and in the case of the borough of the Bronx to the sum of $37,435.67, for the purpose of creating a fund to provide for the depreciation of its various properties; upon which interest at four per cent., compounded, would produce a sum, at the termination of the ascertained physical life of the several classes of property, equal to the cost of the particular property. While I am, personally, of the opinion that the creation of such an amortization fund furnishes the best rule for adoption in such a case as this, in working out the value of special franchises, the majority of my brethren entertain a different view. They think that the annual allowance for depreciation should be computed by dividing the values of the various kinds of tangible property by the number of years of their respective estimated physical lives and that will be the opinion of the court.

The orders of the Special Term and Appellate Division must, therefore, be modified and the proceeding is remitted to the Special Term for further action in accordance with this opinion; without costs as against either party.

HAIGHT, J. I concur in the opinion of GRAY, J., except as to the questions hereinafter discussed.

In this case the courts below adopted the net earnings rule, so called, in determining the value of the relator's special franchise. No question has been raised upon this review as to the propriety of adopting that rule in this case. The rule has been approved by this court in cases in which the business of the corporation has been conducted honestly and economically and where the net earnings have not been dissipated by extravagance and mismanagement. Therefore, in reviewing the case it becomes our duty to see whether the rule has been properly followed and the result reached is just and fair both to the public and the relator. The rule, in brief, is to ascertain the gross earnings of the corporation and then deduct the operating expenses, together with the annual taxes paid. From the remainder there should also be deducted a fair and reasonable return on that portion of the capital of the corporation which is invested in tangible property, the result becoming the net earnings contributable to the special franchise, which, when capitalized at a rate which I shall hereafter consider, becomes the value of the intangible property of the special franchise.

The courts below have allowed the relator six per cent on the value of its tangible property as a fair and reasonable return for the investment. The relator claims that the rate should have been higher; that the business engaged in, of constructing and operating an elevated road, involved a great hazard, but has resulted in a great public benefit, and that investors in such an enterprise ought to be allowed a greater income therefrom than the ordinary rate of interest allowed by statute upon the loan of money. It may be, as claimed, that the confining of the income to the statutory rate of interest will operate to prevent persons having money to loan from investing in new and dangerous enterprises. But the question of the fair and reasonable return, we regard as one of fact under the control of the courts below and one which this court should not review. We, therefore, cannot interfere with the determination made upon this branch of the case.

The courts below have also held that the net earnings should be capitalized upon the basis of six per cent, the same percentage that was allowed for income on the tangible property. In this determination I think the court failed to follow the net earnings rule. That rule is not a question of fact but a plan devised for the purpose of ascertaining the value of intangible property, which has met the approval of this court in cases of this character, for the reason that it seemed just and fair, and perhaps as furnishing as safe a rule as any that has thus far been devised. Prominent authorities in discussing this method of valuing special franchises have suggested that the rate of capitalization should be at least one per cent higher than the rate of income allowed. The purpose of this is to provide against unforeseen contingencies that may arise in the prosecution of the business of the corporation, such as unusual storms, floods, fires, explosions and accidents, which may result in the impairment of net earnings, and cannot be foreseen and estimated in advance. This question was considered by this court in the case of *People ex rel. Jamaica Water Supply Co.* v. *State Board of Tax Commissioners* (196

N. Y. 39), and we then reached the conclusion that such a rule was reasonable and fair to the parties and should be followed, and we consequently reversed the determination of the Appellate Division, which fixed the rate of capitalization at the same percentage allowed for income and affirmed the rate adopted by the referee. This was done, not upon the ground that it involved any question of fact, but because it was part of the plan or rule which we approved for the determination of a just result between the parties. It, therefore, seems to me that the rule should not be departed from in this case, and that the capitalization should be based upon a seven per cent rate.

In the *Jamaica Water Supply Case* (*supra*) we held that there should be an annual deduction made out of gross earnings in order to meet the general deterioration of the property and provide for its replacement. WILLARD BARTLETT, J., in delivering the opinion of the court, says: "We suppose that judicial notice may be taken of the fact that in the conduct of many industrial enterprises there is a constant deterioration of the plant which is not made good by ordinary repairs which, of course, operates continually to lessen the value of the tangible property which it affects. The amount of this depreciation differs in different enterprises, but the annual rate is usually capable of estimate and proof by skilled witnesses. No corporation would be regarded as well conducted which did not make some provision for the necessity of ultimately replacing the property thus suffering deterioration; and we cannot see why an allowance for this purpose should not be made out of the gross earnings in order to ascertain the true earning capacity." (p. 57.)

In the case of *People ex rel. Third Avenue Railroad Co.* v. *State Board of Tax Commissioners* (136 App. Div. 155), KELLOGG, J., in delivering the opinion of the Appellate Division, after referring to our decision in the *Jamaica* case, says that "a public service corporation, with reference to its property which will become worthless by use and must be replaced, is entitled to set aside each year from its earnings a reasonable sum to provide for its replacement. This is outside of the ordinary annual expenses for maintenance, renewals and repairs." (p. 158.) This case was affirmed in this court without opinion in 198 N. Y. 608. The Special Term in this case, however, adopted a plan of amortization upon which an annual sum was authorized to be set apart as a sinking fund, which, by compounding the interest thereon for a period equal to the life of the structure, tracks, engines, machinery and rolling stock, would at the end of that period create a fund sufficient to replace the property. The difficulty with such holding is that railroad corporations do not reconstruct their railroads and rolling stock in that way. In order to afford proper protection to the public they are required to maintain a high state of efficiency both in roadbed and rolling stock. The relator's railroad has been in existence already for about thirty years and some portion of its property has already suffered from decay and use to such an extent that portions thereof have to be reconstructed and made new each year. Old ties have to be removed and replaced with new ones; old rails that have become worn and battered have to be removed and their places supplied with new rails and so the work of reconstruction progresses from year to year. It is not the waiting forty or sixty years to reconstruct, during which time the amount set apart as a sinking fund may be doubled many times over by compounding the interest, but it is the annual expenditure for reconstruction which is to be paid for at the time that the construction is made. To illustrate: Suppose the average life of the tangible property of a railroad, outside of the land itself, to be sixty years and the cost of reconstruction to be sixty million dollars, it would follow that one million dollars would have to be used each year in reconstruction and that amount would have to be annually used for that purpose, but under the plan adopted in this case, instead of deducting from the gross earnings the amount necessarily expended for that purpose a small fraction of that sum, viz., $4,200, only is allowed to be deducted, a sum which, with the interest compounded for the next sixty years would amount to a million dollars. Under such a plan the company would be practically prohibited from annually constructing a portion of its road and thus prevented from keeping it in that state of efficiency which the public demands. Of course the necessities of reconstruction vary from year to year; some years it may be greater than others, but the assessors each year can easily ascertain the sum required for that purpose. I think, therefore, that we should adhere to the rule sanctioned in the *Jamaica* case, and that a gross sum should be deducted annually for the purposes of reconstruction.

I am aware that some corporations have in the past met with heavy losses by reason of their machinery becoming obsolete. This is especially true with reference to those corporations using electricity for power and other purposes. Such use is the result of modern inventions which have been improved from year to year, thus rendering obsolete and practically useless expensive dynamos and machinery, but there is a difficulty in making any estimate as to the amount of depreciation in the assessable value of tangible property which may result from future invention, and, therefore, this species of property should be left to be considered when such depreciation actually occurs.

CULLEN, Ch. J., VANN, WERNER, HISCOCK and COLLIN, JJ., concur with GRAY, J., except as to rate of interest at which the net income should be capitalized to ascertain value of special franchise. All agree with HAIGHT, J., on that question, except GRAY and COLLIN, JJ.: COLLIN, J., concurring in opinion of GRAY, J.

Orders modified, etc.

In the Matter of the Application of J. EDWARD SIMMONS et al., Constituting the Board of Water Supply of the City of New York, Respondents, to Acquire Real Estate Required for Purposes of Water Supply of the City of New York.

WILLIAM R. WARE et al., as Trustees under the Will of ENOCH R. WARE, Appellants.

Appeal — practice — condemnation of property for water supply for city of New York — Special Term order, vacating an award by commissioners of appraisal, appealable to Appellate Division.

An appeal lies to the Appellate Division from an order of the Special Term which vacated an award made by the commissioners of appraisal to ascertain the compensation to be made for land taken for water supply for the city of New York, by virtue of chapter 724 of the Laws of 1905, and the acts amendatory thereof.

Matter of Simmons, 144 App. Div. 255, reversed.

(Argued October 4, 1911; decided October 24, 1911.)

APPEAL, by permission, from an order of the Appellate Division of the Supreme Court in the second judicial department, entered April 21, 1911, which dismissed an appeal from an order of Special Term setting aside a report of commissioners of appraisal in condemnation proceedings and remitting the matter to new commissioners.

The facts, so far as material, and the question certified are stated in the opinion.

Benjamin Trapnell and *Joseph A. Flannery* for appellants. By force of the express terms of section 22 of chapter 724 of the Laws of 1905 an appeal will lie to the Appellate Division from an order of the Special Term which sets aside a report and appoints new commissioners. (*Manhattan Ry. Co.* v. *O'Sullivan*, 6 App. Div. 571; *Matter of Simmons*, 139 App. Div. 273; 141 App. Div. 120; 202 N. Y. 92; *Matter of City of New York*, 129 App. Div. 707.) The Special Term had inherent power to set aside the report, and the Appellate Division which, under the Constitution, succeeded to the jurisdiction of the General Term, can review the exercise of that power. (*Manhattan Ry. Co.* v. *O'Sullivan,* 6 App. Div. 571; 150 N. Y. 569; *Matter of N. Y. C. & H. R. R. R. Co.,* 65 N. Y. 60; *Matter of Daly,* 189 N. Y. 34.)

Archibald R. Watson, Corporation Counsel (*H. T. Dykman* of counsel), for respondents. Under the statute in question no appeal lies to the Appellate Division from an order at Special Term refusing to confirm the report of the commissioners of appraisal and sending the matter back to the same or new commissioners. (L. 1905, ch. 724, § 16; *Matter of Daly,* 189 N. Y. 34; *Matter of Comr. of Public Works,* 185 N. Y. 391; *Real Estate Corp.* v. *Harper,* 174 N. Y. 123; *Matter of City of New York,* 182 N. Y. 281; 192 N. Y. 295.)

HAIGHT, J. This proceeding was instituted under chapter 724 of the Laws of 1905 for the purpose of acquiring land for water supply purposes. Commissioners were appointed and a report was made valuing the parcel in question at the sum of $76,200. Upon an application for a confirmation of the report at Special Term the petitioners objected, and the court set aside the report and directed a new appraisal before new commissioners. Thereupon the claimants appealed from an order of the Special Term to the Appellate Division, second department, and upon the hearing of that appeal the Appellate Division dismissed the appeal upon the ground that the statute did not provide for an appeal from an order refusing to confirm the award of the commissioners. The Appellate Division then allowed an appeal to this court, certifying the following question: "Was the order of the Special Term herein, which vacated the award made by the commissioners of appraisal for damage parcel No. 5 in this proceeding, and appointing new

Commissioners of Appraisal to ascertain and determine the compensation to be made therefor, an order from which an appeal would lie to the Appellate Division under the provisions of chapter 724 of the Laws of 1905 and the acts amendatory thereof?"

It must be conceded that the question presented is not free from difficulty, owing to apparently conflicting decisions made upon the subject, although they were made in construing different statutes from that which we now have under consideration. In this case we are called upon to review the revision of the statute for acquiring land for water purposes in the city of New York, made by chapter 724 of the Laws of 1905, which, so far as is material upon the consideration of the question, is as follows:

"Section 16. The application for the confirmation of the report shall be made to the Supreme Court at a special term thereof held in the judicial district in which the land or some part thereof is situated. Upon the hearing of the application for the confirmation thereof, the said court *may* confirm such report *or may in its discretion order that the report or any portion thereof affecting one or more parcels be referred to the same commission, or a new commission, for a new hearing,* and make an order containing a recital of the substance of the proceedings in the matter of the appraisal with a general description of the real estate appraised and for which compensation is to be made; and shall also direct to whom the money is to be paid or in what bank or trust company and in what manner it shall be deposited by the comptroller of the city of New York. Such report when so confirmed shall (except in case of an appeal, as provided in this act) be final and conclusive as well upon the city of New York as upon owners and all persons interested in or entitled to, said real estate; and also upon all other persons whomsoever."

"Section 22. Within twenty days after notice of the

confirmation of the report of the commissioners, as provided for in the sixteenth section of this act, which notice
may, as to parties who have not appeared before the commissioners, be given in the manner provided in the fif-
teenth section of this act, either party may appeal, by
notice in writing to the other party, to the supreme
court, from the appraisal and report of the commissioners. Such appeal shall be heard on due notice thereof
being given, according to the rules and practice of said
court, either at a special term or appellate division
thereof as the appellant may desire. On the hearing of
such appeal, the court may direct a new appraisal and
determination of any question passed upon, by the same
or new commissioners, in its discretion, but from any
determination of the special term an appeal may be taken
to the appellate division and from any determination of
the appellate division, either party, if aggrieved, may
take an appeal which shall be heard and determined by
the court of appeals. In the case of a new appraisal, the
second report shall be final and conclusive on all parties
and persons interested."

This revision of the statute was taken from chapter 189
of the Laws of 1893, and is the same except as to the
word " may " which in the former statute was "shall."
And the other provision, "or may in its discretion order
that the report or any portion thereof affecting one or
more parcels be referred to the same commission, or a
new commission, for a new hearing " is inserted as a new
provision not appearing in the old statute.

In *Matter of Daly* (189 N. Y. 34) we had occasion to
review the former statute, for the purpose of determining
whether a similar order in which the Special Term had
set aside the first report of the commissioners, for the
purpose of determining whether the new report would be
final and conclusive upon the parties. We then reached
the conclusion, following the case *Matter of N. Y. C. &
H. R. R. R. Co.* (64 N. Y. 60), that the Special Term

had the power, in its discretion, to vacate and set aside the report of the commissioners, even though the statute gave it no authority to do so in the first instance, and that the party aggrieved could, by appeal to the General Term, review the order of the Special Term, but, it being discretionary, it could not be reviewed in this court. An application to condemn lands for public use is a special proceeding under the statute, and under the provision of section 1356 of the Code of Civil Procedure an appeal may be taken to the General Term, now the Appellate Division, of the Supreme Court from an order affecting a substantial right, made in a special proceeding at a Special Term. It follows, says Judge FOLGER, in delivering the opinion of the court in that case, "That at Special Term the court has all its powers in dealing with those cases, among which is the power to control all the proceedings had before it and to set them aside on sufficient cause shown. * * * It was exercising its inherent power over the proceedings of the court to annul, vacate and set them aside, which power stands by the side of the statute and goes with it." (p. 62.) But now, under the new revision, the Special Term is given express power, in its discretion, to send the report back to the same commission, or a new commission, for a new hearing. May that order be reviewed by an appeal therefrom?

In *Matter of Application of the Commissioner of Public Works of the City of New York, to Acquire Lands for the Construction of a Bridge over the Harlem River* (185 N. Y. 391) it was held, notwithstanding the opinion of Judge FOLGER, above alluded to, that an order of the Special Term denying a motion to confirm the report of commissioners of estimate was not appealable to the Appellate Division. That determination, however, was made under chapter 147 of the Laws of 1894, in which the provisions of the law relating to the taking of private property for public streets and places in the city of New York was made applicable to

the proceedings taken under the act, and are found in
the Greater New York charter. Those provisions authorize the Special Term to confirm the report in whole, or in
part, or to refer the same, or a part thereof, back to the
commissioners, or to new commissioners, for revision or
correction, or for reconsideration; and it was held that
the provision giving the party aggrieved by the report,
when confirmed, the right to appeal to the Appellate
Division of the Supreme Court, in effect, excluded the
right to appeal from the order of the Special Term which
refused confirmation, and that it was not affected by the
provisions of the Code of Civil Procedure applicable to
appeals.

In *Matter of Manhattan Railway* v. *O'Sullivan* (6 App.
Div. 571) it was held that where the award of commissioners is set aside by the Special Term as excessive, the Appellate Division has an inherent power to
review the order. BARRETT, J., in delivering the opinion
of the court, says: "There is nothing in the Condemnation Law which revokes or modifies the rule that discretion is vested in the appellate branch of the court equally
with the Special Term. Nor is there any provision which
directly, or by necessary implication, takes away the fundamental and inherent power to review any exercise of
discretion by the Special Term. Under the law as it
existed prior to this Condemnation Act, the court was, in
the first instance, required to make a final order confirming the commissioners' report. Within twenty days
thereafter either party might appeal. The appeal was
to 'the Supreme Court,' and the direction was that such
appeals should be heard by 'the Supreme Court at any
General or Special Term thereof.' Under the present
law the old practice was varied in form because of the
manifest inconvenience of permitting an appellant to
choose his tribunal in the first instance, and because the
old practice on that head was exceptional. But the substance remained the same. The confirmation *pro forma*

is not now permitted. Nor can the appellant choose, in the first instance, the branch of the tribunal which he prefers. But his appeal is still to the Supreme Court. Now he must proceed in the first instance at Special Term. He cannot, as formerly, go directly, if he pleases, to the appellate branch. But clearly it was only intended to prevent his going there in the first instance — not to prevent his going there in the usual way, and in accordance with the established practice." (p. 574.) It is true that Justice BARRETT had under consideration the condemnation law now embodied in the Code of Civil Procedure, but his remarks are quite pertinent upon the question which we have under consideration. That case was affirmed in this court on his opinion. (150 N. Y. 569.)

Our attention has been called to numerous cases in which the General Terms and the Appellate Divisions have entertained appeals of this character, but no question appears to have been made with reference to the jurisdiction of the court to review. I have thus called attention to the chief cases upon the subject, and to the apparent conflict that exists.

In the case under review, the Special Term vacated the report of the commission, upon the ground that it adopted a wrong basis in determining the value of the property sought to be taken, thus raising the old question as to whether it should be valued as city lots or farm property. The Appellate Division in its opinion expresses the view that the Special Term erred in setting aside the report, but concludes by holding that it has no power to review. We thus have a record covering upwards of eighteen hundred pages of testimony sent back for a new trial before new commissioners with instructions to determine the value of the property upon a basis which the Appellate Division insists is erroneous; and yet that court is powerless to correct the error until a new report is made and confirmed. The learned Appellate Division, speaking with reference to the duties of the new commissioners, says: "We may not assume that commissioners will fail to observe their obligations under the Constitution and laws of this State because of an error of law on the part of the Court at Special Term." It must be remembered that under the statute the Special Term had the power to refuse confirmation of the report of the commissioners and to send it back for correction, either to the same commission or to new commissioners. That court had the power to specify what the correction should be, and its determination became the law of the case until its order had been reversed by some court having the power to do so. It, therefore, became the duty of the commissioners to take the law from the Special Term and determine the value of the property upon the basis specified by that court.

In view of what was said in *Matter of Commissioner of Public Works* (*supra*) we shall not consider the question as to whether an appeal could be taken under the Code, but confine our determination to the statute under which the proceedings were instituted. Under section 16 of that statute, as we have seen, the report of the commissioners, when confirmed, becomes final and conclusive, except in case of an appeal, as provided in section 22 of the act. Referring, then, to the provisions of that section we find that under the first provision an appeal may be taken within twenty days by either party "after notice of the confirmation of the report of the commissioners." The appeal, however, provided for is not from the order of confirmation, but is from "the appraisal and report of the commissioners." The statute further provides that such an appeal shall be heard either at a Special Term or Appellate Division, as the appellant may desire. We thus have a peculiar statute, which seemingly enables a successful party at Special Term to take an appeal from an appraisal in his favor, and then upon the appeal he may select the same Special Term to hear the appeal that confirmed his appraisal in the first instance. If this was the only appeal provided for by the statute, it may be that we should be compelled to hold that an appeal only lay from a confirmation of a report. But we find that upon proceeding further with the provisions of this statute it concludes as follows; "But from *any determination* of the Special Term an appeal may be taken to the Appellate Division and from any determination of the Appellate Division, either party, if aggrieved, may take an appeal which shall be heard and determined by the Court of Appeals. In the case of a new appraisal, the second report shall be final and conclusive on all parties and persons interested." Under this provision it appears to us that "any determination of the Special Term" means any or every order of the Special Term; and that "any determination of the Appellate Division" means any order of the Appellate Division. If this be the correct construction of the provisions of the act, it follows that an appeal from an order of the Special Term vacating the report of the commissioners is authorized by this statute, and that the Appellate Division has the power to determine the same. We conclude, therefore, that the Appellate Division had the power to review the order appealed from in this case, and that its order dismissing the appeal should be reversed and the case remitted to that court for hearing upon the merits, with costs to the appellant to abide the final award of costs, and that the question certified should be answered in the affirmative.

CULLEN, Ch. J., VANN, WERNER, WILLARD BARTLETT, HISCOCK and CHASE, JJ., concur.

Order reversed, etc.

JOSHUA J. WARREN, Appellant, v. WILLIAM WARREN, Defendant, and MARY RUPORT et al., Respondents, Impleaded with Others.

KECK & ROGERS et al., Appellants.

Partition — costs — practice — extra allowances of costs — total amount allowed to all parties cannot exceed five per cent of value of property — allowance to plaintiff based on value of the whole property — allowance to any defendant based on value of that defendant's interest in the property —construction of provision limiting allowance to $2,000 to each side of action.

1. In no event can the total allowance in actions for partition exceed five per centum upon the value of the subject-matter involved.

2. For the purpose of fixing the allowance which may be made to the plaintiff, the value of the subject-matter involved is the value of the whole property, and for the purpose of fixing the allowance to any defendant, the value of that particular defendant's interest is the value of the subject-matter involved.

3. The limitation that in no event shall the allowances to a plaintiff, or to a party or two or more parties on the same side exceed $2,000, means that the allowance to a plaintiff cannot exceed $2,000, and the allowance to all the defendants, considered as a class or " side," shall not exceed another $2,000.

Warren v. *Warren*, 142 App. Div. 923, affirmed.

(Argued October 5, 1911; decided October 24, 1911.)

APPEAL, by permission, from an order of the Appellate Division of the Supreme Court in the third judicial department, entered January 21, 1911, which affirmed an order of Special Term striking out provisions for extra allowances of costs from a judgment in partition.

The facts, so far as material, and the questions certified are stated in the opinion.

H. D. Wright, William C. Mills, W. W. Smith and *A. C. Houghton* for appellants. The court may not, on motion, review its own judgment, or re-exercise its discretionary powers. (Code Civ. Pro. § 3253; *Kiernan* v. *A. Ins. Co.*, 3 App. Div. 26; *Gennert* v. *Butterick*, 133 App. Div. 86.) The allowance made by the court was right and within its power. (Code Civ. Pro. § 3253; *Van Meter* v. *Kelly*, 137 App. Div. 455; *Crossman* v. *Wyckoff*, 64 App. Div. 554; *Chittenden* v. *Gates*, 25 App. Div. 623; *Defendorf* v. *Defendorf*, 42 App. Div. 167; *Bryant* v. *Allen*, 54 App. Div. 500; *L. I. L. & T. Co.* v. *L. I. C. & N. R. R. Co.* 85 App. Div. 36; *Waterbury* v. *Cordage Co.*, 152 N. Y. 610.)

Alfred D. Dennison for respondents. Extra allowances to all the parties may not exceed in the aggregate five per cent. (Code Civ. Pro. §§ 3253, 3254; *Doremus* v. *Crosby*, 66 Hun, 125; *Fraser* v. *McNaughton*, 58 Hun, 30; *MacFarlane* v. *Brower*, 63 Misc. Rep. 183; *Van Meter* v. *Kelly*, 137 App. Div. 455.) The court has no power to grant extra allowances to parties who are not entitled to tax costs. (*Couch* v. *Millard*, 41 Hun, 212; *Jordan* v. *Hess*, 54 N. Y. S. R. 326; *Kahn* v. *Schmidt*, 83 Hun, 541; *Frost* v. *Reinach*, 40 Misc. Rep. 412.) Excessive and unauthorized allowances may be stricken out on motion. (Code Civ. Pro. § 724; *Cooper* v. *Cooper*, 51 App. Div. 595; 164 N. Y. 576; *Schulte* v. *Lestershire B. & S. Co.*, 88 Hun, 226; *Bockes* v. *Hathorn*, 17 Hun, 87; *Clapp* v. *McCabe*, 155 N. Y. 525; *Cooper* v. *Cooper*, 51 App. Div. 595; *Corn Exchange Bank* v. *Blye*, 119 N. Y. 414; *Ladd* v. *Stevenson*, 112 N. Y. 325; *Clark* v. *Scovill*, 198 N. Y. 279; *Supervisors* v. *Briggs*, 3 Den. 173; *Stephens* v. *Central Nat. Bank*, 168 N. Y. 560; *Conaughty* v. *Saratoga County Bank*, 92 N. Y. 401; *Kraushaar* v. *Meyer*, 72 N. Y. 602; *Leonard* v. *Columbia*, 84 N. Y. 48.) The court may open and amend its judgment at the instance of defaulting defendants. (Code Civ. Pro. § 724; *Cooper* v. *Cooper*, 51 App. Div. 595; 164 N. Y. 576; *Corn Ex. Bank* v. *Blye*, 119 N. Y. 414; *Ladd* v.

Stevenson, 112 N. Y. 325; *Clark* v. *Scovill,* 198 N. Y. 279.)

WERNER, J. This is an action for partition of real property, in which the court at Special Term fell into the error of granting extra allowances of costs which were so obviously unauthorized that the same court, upon motion of certain defendants who had not answered and had been awarded no costs, vacated its first order and then refused to allow any costs beyond those which were regularly taxable. From the order embodying this latter decision, the attorneys for the plaintiff took an appeal to the Appellate Division where there was an unanimous affirmance, with permission to appeal to this court upon two questions which have been certified to us. These questions are as follows:

" 1. In a partition suit where several different attorneys appear for several different defendants and file answers creating issues, can the trial court, in the exercise of its discretion under section 3253 of the Code of Civil Procedure grant an extra allowance of five per cent to the plaintiff and any further sums not exceeding five per cent to the attorneys for the defendants?

" 2. The trial court having exercised its discretion and having granted five per cent extra allowance to a plaintiff, and five per cent to each of four different sets of defendants appearing by separate attorneys, can such court, on motion, after the entry of judgment, at the instance of a defendant who has defaulted without showing excuse for his default, amend the judgment by striking out all extra allowances so granted?"

These questions, although evidently framed with a view to minimizing rather than emphasizing the malpractice which is the proper ground for criticism in the case at bar, are comprehensive enough to permit of answers which will lay down a general rule of practice under the sections of the Code of Civil Procedure relating to extra allowances of costs, and to that end a short discussion may be of some value.

First of all it is to be noted that extra allowances of costs, pursuant to sections 3253 and 3254 of the Code of Civil Procedure are in no case a matter of right, but may be granted or withheld in the discretion of the court. The proper exercise of that judicial discretion necessarily includes the power to correct mistakes or abuses in the granting or withholding of extra allowances, and that is palpably true where the amount limited by the statute has been either inadvertently or consciously exceeded. The statute (section 3253) provides that the allowance shall not exceed five per centum upon the sum recovered or claimed, or the value of the subject-matter involved, and that is subject to the further limitation that in no case shall the sum awarded to a plaintiff, or to a party or two or more parties on the same side, exceed in the aggregate, two thousand dollars. In the case at bar the allowances granted to the attorneys for the plaintiff and for several defendants amount in the aggregate to more than twenty-eight per centum of the price for which the property was sold. When this error was brought to the attention of the court, it was at once corrected by striking from the order all provisions for extra allowances. That was an exercise of discretion as clearly within the power of the court as the granting of the excessive allowances was beyond its power. The mistake made by the court, in assuming to exercise a power and discretion which it did not have, was properly subject to correction under the broad provisions of sections 723 and 724 of the Code of Civil Procedure, and we may, therefore, end the discussion as to the second question certified to us by answering it in the affirmative. The court clearly had the power to correct its mistake, even to the extent of refusing to grant any extra allowance.

The first certified question cannot be disposed of so summarily for it involves an analysis and interpretation of sections 3253 and 3254 above referred to. The question, fairly paraphrased, is whether the court has power in a partition suit, where several different attorneys appear for different defendants and file answers creating issues, to grant an extra allowance of five per cent to the plaintiff, and any further sums not exceeding five per cent to the attorneys for the defendants. It will be noted that this question as certified is much too broad to permit of a categorical answer, for it omits any reference to either of the limitations of sections 3253 and 3254 fixing the point beyond which the court may not go in awarding extra allowances, and it mentions one limitation which is not to be found in these sections as they now exist. The framer of the question apparently assumed that the power of the court to award extra allowances to defendants, in suits for partition, was confined to defendants who file answers creating issues. No such restriction is to be found in section 3253, for it distinctly provides that the power may be exercised in " any action, or special proceeding, specified in this section, where a defense has been interposed, *or in an action for the partition of real property.*" In the italicized part of this sentence extracted from the statute, we find a clear negation of the assumption that the power of the court to award extra allowances in partition suits is limited, so far as defendants are concerned, to those who have filed answers creating issues. No such restriction is to be found in the statute.

Passing to the limitations of the statute which, as we have pointed out, are ignored by the first certified question, it is to be noticed that the language of sections 3253 and 3254, as applied to partition suits, is so general as to be open to divergent interpretations except in one particular, and that is that the total allowance must not exceed five per centum. When we look further to ascertain the subject-matter upon which this percentage is to be based, we are confronted by the very comprehensive phrase

1911.] Opinion, per WERNER, J. [203 N. Y.]

"upon the sum recovered or claimed, or the value of the subject matter involved." (Section 3253, subd. 2.) Does this mean the value of the whole subject-matter as to each party who may ask for an extra allowance? Obviously not, for that view would sanction an allowance in excess of five per cent of the value of the subject-matter involved. Does it mean that a plaintiff with a small interest in the property to be partitioned or sold is to be limited to an allowance of five per cent upon the value of his interest? That view is open to the practical objection that many partition suits involve a vast amount of labor, the burden of which falls principally upon the plaintiff's attorney. Almost of necessity we are driven to the conclusion that so narrow an interpretation of the statute would tend to defeat the very purpose for which the provisions for extra allowances were enacted. But if we adopt the reasonable view that as to a plaintiff in partition the value of the subject-matter involved is the value of the whole property, we are met by the impossibility of fixing the allowances to defendants upon the same basis without exceeding the limitation that the aggregate allowances shall not exceed the sum of five per centum upon the value of the subject-matter involved. Therefore, the only workable rule that can be evolved out of this situation is to hold that as to a plaintiff the value of the subject-matter is the value of the whole property, and as to each defendant it is the value of his interest in the property. Upon first consideration this seems to result in unfair discrimination in favor of a plaintiff with a small interest, as against defendants who have larger interests, but it is a discrimination which is proper and necessary in the nature of the case. Upon the plaintiff falls the burden of conducting the litigation and of attending to the numerous technical details which are essential to the validity of judgments involving the transmission of titles to real property by judicial process. Defendants in partition suits are, as a rule, mere passengers in the litigation who are simply interested in seeing that their interests are not overlooked or misstated. These are the practical reasons which justify the adoption of one standard as to plaintiffs and another as to defendants.

In connection with the limitation of section 3253, that the total of the allowances shall not exceed the sum of five per centum upon the value of the subject-matter involved, we must consider the further limitation of section 3254, that all sums "awarded to the plaintiff, * * * or to a party or two or more parties on the same side * * * cannot exceed, in the aggregate, two thousand dollars." Here again the phraseology of the statute is very general and somewhat ambiguous. Does it mean that not more than two thousand dollars shall be allowed to all the parties? Or does it mean that a sum not in excess of two thousand dollars may be allowed to each of the parties? Or does it mean that not more than two thousand dollars shall be allowed to a plaintiff on one side and another sum not to exceed two thousand dollars to all the defendants on the other side? The latter seems to be the only practicable view of the statute. If we should construe it to mean that the total allowances to all the parties cannot exceed the sum of two thousand dollars, it would work great injustice to many plaintiffs' attorneys who have fairly earned that sum and much more. If we should hold that it means an allowance not to exceed two thousand dollars to each defendant, it would in many cases render it impossible to keep within the limit of five per cent of the value of the subject-matter involved, and in many other cases it would result in annihilating estates for the enrichment of lawyers. The view which we are inclined to favor as reasonable is the one which avoids both of these extremes and permits the allowance to a plaintiff of a sum not to exceed two thousand dollars, and to the defendants, as a class or side, another sum not in excess of two thousand dollars.

Although this court has apparently not before been called upon to interpret these two sections of the Code of Civil Procedure the foregoing views are not original, for they were first advanced in 1892 by the late Mr. Justice Barrett in the General Term of the first department in the case of *Doremus* v. *Crosby* (66 Hun, 125), and they were expressed with characteristic precision and clarity. "We agree," said he, "with the appellants in their second contention, namely, that the court cannot allow the parties in the aggregate more than five per centum upon the whole value of the property sought to be partitioned. Section 3253, as it bears upon this question, reads as follows : 'In an action * * * for the partition of real property * * * the court may also, in its discretion, award to *any* party * * * a sum not exceeding five per centum upon * * * the value of the subject-matter involved.' Clearly, the words 'any party,' as here used, do not mean 'each party.' Otherwise, the court might, if there were twenty parties, allow 100 per centum. The object was to give the court discretion as to the proper distribution of whatever allowance should be granted within the limit fixed. But such limit was to be five per centum upon the value of the property. It was so held in *Fraser* v. *McNaughton* (58 Hun, 34), and we concur in the conclusion there arrived at. Our construction is not in conflict with the views expressed in *Weed* v. *Paine* (31 Hun, 10). It was there held that the restriction in amount contained in section 3254, applied only to each side of the litigation, and that, consequently, the court had power, in a proper case, to award $4,000 in the aggregate. This is entirely consistent with the primary limitation of five per centum upon the subject-matter involved in the action. Undoubtedly, what the court meant was that where the value of the subject-matter equalled or exceeded $80,000, the court had power to award $2,000 to each side." (p. 127.)

For nearly twenty years the rule thus laid down in

17

The order of the Appellate Division should be affirmed, with costs.

CULLEN, Ch. J., HAIGHT, VANN, WILLARD BARTLETT, HISCOCK and CHASE, JJ., concur.

Order affirmed.

SECONDO GUASTI et al., Respondents, *v.* TOBIAS MILLER, Appellant.

Special proceedings—judgment against bankrupt will not be canceled under statute (Debtor and Creditor Law, Cons. Laws, ch. 12, § 150) when schedule states residence of creditor was "unknown," although bankrupt had notice thereof.

1. An application by a bankrupt for an order canceling a judgment under section 1268 of the Code of Civil Procedure, now section 150 of the Debtor and Creditor Law (Cons. Laws, ch. 12) is a special proceeding and an order made therein is appealable to the Court of Appeals.

2. On examination of defendant's schedules in bankruptcy, it sufficiently appears that the claim from which he seeks to be discharged was not scheduled in accordance with the requirement of section 7 of the Bankruptcy Act, in that it stated that the residence of the claimant was "unknown," when defendant had actual notice thereof, and hence his application to have the judgment canceled was properly denied.

Guasti v. *Miller*, 144 App. Div. 898, affirmed.

(Submitted October 6, 1911; decided October 24, 1911.)

APPEAL from an order of the Appellate Division of the Supreme Court in the first judicial department, entered April 28, 1911, which affirmed an order of Special Term denying a motion made on behalf of defendant, after his discharge in bankruptcy, to cancel a judgment theretofore obtained by the plaintiffs against him.

The facts, so far as material, are stated in the opinion.

Doremus v. *Crosby*, and the other cases therein referred to apparently stood unchallenged. In 1910 it was disregarded or violated by the Special Term in the case of *Van Meter* v. *Kelly*, an action for partition, in which the allowances exceeded the sum of five per centum upon the amount for which the property was sold. Upon appeal by a defendant who felt aggrieved, the Appellate Division in the fourth department, speaking through Mr. Justice KRUSE (137 App. Div. 455), reaffirmed the rule of *Doremus* v. *Crosby* and *Weed* v. *Paine* (*supra*). Thus this rule has the support of authority, of long-continued usage and, we believe, of reason based upon controlling practical considerations. For the sake of emphasis we, therefore, restate in compact sequence the views which are more or less scattered through this opinion.

1. In no event can the total allowances in actions for partition exceed five per centum upon the value of the subject-matter involved.

2. For the purpose of fixing the allowance which may be made to the plaintiff, the value of the subject-matter involved is the value of the whole property, and for the purpose of fixing the allowance to any defendant, the value of that particular defendant's interest is the value of the subject-matter involved.

3. The limitation that in no event shall the allowances to a plaintiff, or to a party or two or more parties on the same side exceed $2,000, means that the allowance to a plaintiff cannot exceed $2,000, and the allowances to all the defendants, considered as a class or " side," shall not exceed another $2,000.

If the certified question No. 1 were to be construed as recognizing these limitations, it would have to be answered in the affirmative; if it is not so construed it will have to be answered in the negative, for it is literally much too broad for the rule. We regard it as not fairly susceptible of an interpretation which is consonant with the rule, and we, therefore, answer it in the negative.

The order of the Appellate Division should be affirmed, with costs.

CULLEN, Ch. J., HAIGHT, VANN, WILLARD BARTLETT, HISCOCK and CHASE, JJ., concur.

Order affirmed.

SECONDO GUASTI et al., Respondents, *v.* TOBIAS MILLER, Appellant.

Special proceedings — judgment against bankrupt will not be canceled under statute (Debtor and Creditor Law, Cons. Laws, ch. 12, § 150) when schedule states residence of creditor was "unknown," although bankrupt had notice thereof.

1. An application by a bankrupt for an order canceling a judgment under section 1268 of the Code of Civil Procedure, now section 150 of the Debtor and Creditor Law (Cons. Laws, ch. 12) is a special proceeding and an order made therein is appealable to the Court of Appeals.

2. On examination of defendant's schedules in bankruptcy, it sufficiently appears that the claim from which he seeks to be discharged was not scheduled in accordance with the requirement of section 7 of the Bankruptcy Act, in that it stated that the residence of the claimant was "unknown," when defendant had actual notice thereof, and hence his application to have the judgment canceled was properly denied.

Guasti v. *Miller*, 144 App. Div. 808, affirmed.

(Submitted October 6, 1911; decided October 24, 1911.)

APPEAL from an order of the Appellate Division of the Supreme Court in the first judicial department, entered April 28, 1911, which affirmed an order of Special Term denying a motion made on behalf of defendant, after his discharge in bankruptcy, to cancel a judgment theretofore obtained by the plaintiffs against him.

The facts, so far as material, are stated in the opinion.

William C. Rosenberg and *Jesse S. Epstein* for appellant. Plaintiffs' claim against the defendant was duly and properly scheduled according to the provisions of the United States Bankruptcy Law, and the decree discharging the defendant released him from the plaintiffs' judgment. (*Lent* v. *Farnsworth*, 94 App. Div. 99; 180 N. Y. 503; *Lutz* v. *Kalmus*, 115 N. Y. Supp. 230; *Matter of Mollner*, 75 App. Div. 441; *People ex rel. Kenyon* v. *Sutherland*, 81 N. Y. 1.) Unless the debt of the respondents is within one of the exceptions contained in section 17 of the Bankruptcy Act, the discharge of the appellant is effective to release the same. (*Matter of Petersen*, 137 App. Div. 435; *New York Inst.* v. *Crockett*, 117 App. Div. 269; *Sherwood* v. *Mitchell*, 4 Den. 435; *Brereton* v. *Hull*, 1 Den. 75; *Harrison* v. *Lourie*, 49 How. Pr. 124; *Stevens* v. *King*, 16 App. Div. 377; *Chapman* v. *Forsythe*, 2 How. [U. S.] 202; *Matter of Herring*, 133 App. Div. 295; 196 N. Y. 218.)

Albert M. Yuzzolino for respondents. The judgment cannot be canceled unless it was so scheduled as to be covered by the discharge in bankruptcy. (*Feldmark* v. *Weinstein*, 45 Misc. Rep. 329.) Plaintiffs' judgment was not duly scheduled pursuant to the provisions of the Bankruptcy Act. (*Feldmark* v. *Weinstein*, 45 Misc. Rep. 329; *Columbia Bank* v. *Birkett*, 195 U. S. 345; 174 N. Y. 112; *Hitchings* v. *Simmons*, 53 Misc. Rep. 399; *Sutherland* v. *Lasher*, 41 Misc. Rep. 249; *Haack* v. *Theise*, 51 Misc. Rep. 3; *Weidenfeld* v. *Tillinghast*, 54 Misc. Rep. 90; *Westheimer* v. *Howard*, 47 Misc. Rep. 145; *Matter of Boom*, 48 Misc. Rep. 632.)

HAIGHT, J. The judgment sought to be canceled was docketed in the office of the clerk of the county of New York on April 16, 1895, and the discharge in bankruptcy was obtained May 9th, 1903. The defendant's schedule, with his petition in bankruptcy, was filed September

26th, 1902, and set forth the plaintiffs' judgment in the following words:

"Name of Creditor	Residence and Occupation.	Nature and Consideration of Debt, etc.
Guasti & Bernard	Unknown, California.	Goods sold and delivered. * * * Judgment was rendered in the City Court of The City of New York, April 16, 1895."

The defendant applied to the Special Term for an order canceling the judgment under section 1268 of the Code of Civil Procedure, which has been repealed and is now embraced in section 150 of the Debtor and Creditor Law (Consol. Laws, ch. 12), and provides as follows: "At any time after one year has elapsed, since a bankrupt was discharged from his debts, pursuant to the acts of congress relating to bankruptcy, he may apply, upon proof of his discharge, to the court in which a judgment was rendered against him, or if rendered in a court not of record, to the court of which it has become a judgment by docketing it, or filing a transcript thereof, for an order, directing the judgment to be canceled and discharged of record. If it appears upon the hearing that he has been discharged from the payment of that judgment or the debt upon which such judgment was recovered, an order must be made directing said judgment to be canceled and discharged of record," etc. The Bankruptcy Act, section 7, among other things, provides that the bankrupt shall file a schedule of his property, and also give "a list of creditors showing their residences if known, if unknown, that fact to be stated." The Special Term denied the defendant's application upon the ground, as stated by the judge in his memoranda filed, that the affidavits clearly show that the plaintiffs' judgment was not duly scheduled, as required by the Bankruptcy Act, basing his decision upon *Columbia Bank* v. *Birkett* (174 N. Y. 112) and *Graber* v. *Gault* (103 App. Div. 511). That order has been affirmed in the Appellate Division.

A preliminary objection has now been raised, to the effect that the application was for an order in the action, and for that reason it is not appealable to this court. The application is based upon the result of a proceeding in bankruptcy that has been conducted in the Federal court, and the application may be made not only by the bankrupt himself, but by any person who has succeeded to the rights of the bankrupt in the property affected thereby. (*Graber* v. *Gault*, 103 App. Div. 511.) We are of opinion that it is a special proceeding. (*Peri* v. *N. Y. C. & H. R. R. R. Co.* 152 N. Y. 521; *Conlon* v. *Kelly*, 199 N. Y. 43.)

In considering the case upon the merits, we find that the schedule states the residence and occupation of the plaintiffs as Unknown, California; and stating the nature and consideration of the debt, it is said in the schedule to be for goods sold and delivered. The affidavits read upon the motion show that the plaintiffs were wine merchants and producers, doing business at Los Angeles, California, and had been engaged in that business for upwards of twenty-five years past; and that the claim on which the judgment was entered against the defendant was based on the acceptance of a draft drawn on the defendant by the plaintiffs, containing their post office address as Los Angeles, California, which was accepted by him and was given in payment of a carload of wine purchased by said Miller from the plaintiffs in Los Angeles, California. There were additional facts made to appear by the affidavits, which we do not deem it necessary to here refer to, for we deem them sufficient to sustain the finding of the Special Term that the defendant had actual notice of the plaintiffs' residence and post office address. It also is made to appear that the plaintiffs knew nothing of the proceedings in bankruptcy, or that the defendant had instituted such proceedings, until August 23, 1910, long after the discharge had been granted by the Bankruptcy Court. We are, therefore, of the opinion that the claim of the plaintiffs was not properly scheduled by the defendant, and .that consequently the Special Term properly denied the defendant's application. (*Columbia Bank* v. *Birkett*, 174 N. Y. 112; affirmed, 195 U. S. 345.)

The order should be affirmed, with costs.

CULLEN, Ch. J., WERNER, WILLARD BARTLETT, HISCOCK and CHASE, JJ., concur; VANN, J., absent.

Order affirmed.

EARL A. CASE, Respondent, *v.* BERT L. CASE, Appellant.

Contract — agreements under seal — contract under seal, by which one brother agrees to support his mother, cannot be enforced by another brother not a party to it, although the latter joined in the consideration for the contract.

1. As a general rule an instrument under seal cannot be enforced by or against one who is not a party to it, although a different rule exists as to simple contracts on which an action may be brought by or against the real principal, although he is not named in the instrument.

2. This action is brought by the plaintiff against his brother, upon a contract under seal, made by the latter with his mother for her support and maintenance. The contract recites that it was entered into by the defendant upon the consideration that the mother, who is the other party thereto, had united with the plaintiff in a deed of a farm to the defendant, and that by the contract, based upon that consideration, the defendant bound himself to support the mother during her life. The complaint alleges that the defendant failed to keep this covenant, and that by reason of such failure the plaintiff has been compelled to support and maintain the mother, for the expense of which he asks judgment. *Held*, that the action cannot be maintained as the mother alone has the right to enforce the contract.

Case v. *Case.* 137 App. Div. 393. reversed.

(Argued October 10, 1911; decided October 24, 1911.)

APPEAL from a judgment of the Appellate Division of the Supreme Court in the fourth judicial department, entered March 12, 1910, unanimously affirming a judgment in favor of plaintiff entered upon a verdict.

The nature of the action and the facts, so far as material, are stated in the opinion.

D. P. Morehouse for appellant. No cause of action in favor of the plaintiff was proven upon the trial. (*Buchanan* v. *Tilden*, 158 N. Y. 109; *Van Cleave* v. *Clark*, 3 L. R. A. 519; *Durnherr* v. *Rau*, 135 N. Y. 219; *Garnsey* v. *Rogers*, 47 N. Y. 233; *Vrooman* v. *Turner*, 69 N. Y. 280; *Lorillard* v. *Clyde*, 122 N. Y. 498; *Lawrence* v. *Fox*, 20 N. Y. 268.)

F. T. Cahill for respondent. If one person makes a promise to another for the benefit of a third person, the third person may maintain an action on the promise. (*Todd* v. *Weber*, 95 N. Y. 181; *Sullivan* v. *Sullivan*, 161 N. Y. 554; *Lawrence* v. *Fox*, 20 N. Y. 268; *Shepard* v. *Shepard*, 7 Johns. Ch. 56; *Barker* v. *Bucklin*, 2 Den. 45; *Judson* v. *Gray*, 17 How. Pr. 289; *Hendrick* v. *Lindsay*, 93 U. S. 143; *Schemerhorn* v. *Vanderheyden*, 1 Johns. 139; *Turk* v. *Ridge*, 44 N. Y. 201; *Thorp* v. *Keokuk Coal Co.*, 48 N. Y. 254.)

WERNER, J. The controlling question in this case is whether an action can be maintained upon a contract under seal by one who is not a party to the instrument. The action is brought by the plaintiff against his brother, upon a contract under seal, made by the latter with his mother for her support and maintenance. The contract recites that it was entered into by the defendant upon the consideration that the mother, who is the other party thereto, had united with the plaintiff in a deed of a farm to the defendant, and that by the contract, based upon the consideration, the defendant bound himself to support the mother in health and in sickness during her life.

The complaint alleges that the defendant failed to keep the covenant thus entered into by him, and that by reason of such failure the plaintiff has been compelled to support and maintain the mother at an expense to him in the sum of five hundred dollars, for which amount, with interest, he asks judgment. The case was tried and submitted to a jury with the result that the plaintiff was given a verdict for three hundred and ninety-two dollars. From the judgment entered upon that verdict an appeal was taken to the Appellate Division where there was a unanimous affirmance.

Before any evidence had been taken, counsel for the defendant moved to dismiss the complaint upon the ground that it does not state a cause of action in favor of the plaintiff against the defendant, and on the argument in support of the motion he directed the attention of the trial court to the specific objection that the contract, being a sealed instrument, was not between the plaintiff and the defendant, but between the defendant and his mother, and that the latter was not a party to the action. The motion to dismiss the complaint, thus made at the opening of the case, was denied, and to this ruling of the court the defendant's counsel duly excepted. Upon appeal to this court, such an exception survives the unanimous affirmance at the Appellate Division, and it is, therefore, our duty to determine whether the exception was well taken.

Nothing is more definitely settled in our law than that an instrument under seal cannot be enforced by or against one who is not a party to it. This is so elementary as to be axiomatic and needs no support in the citation of authorities. A different rule exists as to simple contracts upon which, for reasons adverted to in *Briggs* v. *Partridge* (64 N. Y. 357, 362), actions may be brought by or against the real principal although he is not named in the instrument. There are exceptions to the rigid rule that only the parties to a contract under seal can be parties to a litigation for its enforcement, such, for instance, as a suit to enforce an ante-nuptial agreement for a marriage settlement by the person for whose benefit it was made (*Phalen* v. *U. S. Trust Co.*, 186 N. Y. 178, 187), but even in such cases it is the rule, both in law and equity, that mere volunteers or strangers to the consideration have no standing in court. (*Borland* v. *Welch*, 162 N. Y. 104.) The case at bar is not within this or any other exception to the general rule, for the plaintiff is a mere volunteer who is not a party to the contract and who is an utter stranger to the consideration.

The learned justice who wrote for the Appellate Division was impressed with the view that the contract was made for the benefit of the plaintiff, since he was under the legal and moral obligation to support his mother, and that the effect of the contract was to relieve him from that obligation. It was also deemed a circumstance of controlling weight that the conveyance to the defendant of the farm, the title to which appeared to have been in the plaintiff, furnished a consideration which invested the latter with the right to enforce the contract. We are unable to subscribe to that view and we find direct authority against it in one of the cases cited to support the judgment below. In *Durnherr* v. *Rau* (135 N. Y. 219) the plaintiff sought to enforce a covenant in a deed made by her husband to the defendant, to the effect that the grantee would pay certain mortgages upon the premises conveyed. The wife had joined her husband in the execution of these mortgages, but had expressly reserved her dower right from the operation of the deed. In that case this court held that the wife's joinder in the mortgages was a voluntary surrender of her right for the benefit of her husband, and bound her interests to the extent necessary to protect the mortgagees. There, in short, the whole doctrine was summed up in one pregnant paragraph. "It is not sufficient," said Judge Andrews, "that the performance of the covenant may benefit a third person. It must have been entered into for his benefit, or at least such benefit must be the direct result of performance and so within the contemplation of the parties, and in addition the grantor must also have a legal interest that the covenant be performed in favor of the party claiming performance." (p. 222.) In the case at bar the covenants of the agreement were made for the benefit of the mother, and she alone had a legal interest in their enforcement. Without going further into the by-paths of distinctions and refinements, it is enough to repeat that this is an action upon an agreement under seal to which the plaintiff is not a party. It can only be enforced by the mother, who is a party thereto, and for whose benefit it was made.

The judgment should be reversed and a new trial granted, with costs to abide event.

CULLEN, Ch. J., WILLARD BARTLETT, HISCOCK, CHASE and COLLIN, JJ., concur; VANN, J., absent.

Judgment reversed, etc.

THE PEOPLE OF THE STATE OF NEW YORK, Respondent, *v.* WALTER K. FREEMAN, Appellant.

Crimes — evidence — district attorney may not attempt to create false impressions by questions concerning matters foreign to the issues.

A district attorney may not, by questions actually containing no element of misconduct and by calling witnesses as a challenge to the defendant to go into the details of transactions foreign to the issues, create false impressions that defendant has been guilty of misdeeds similar to those charged against him, when the evidence does not sustain such a conclusion.

People v. *Freeman,* 133 App. Div. 630, reversed.

(Argued June 16, 1911; decided November 3, 1911.)

APPEAL from an order of the Appellate Division of the Supreme Court in the first judicial department, entered July 13, 1909, which unanimously affirmed a judgment of the Court of General Sessions of the Peace in the county of New York rendered upon a verdict convicting the defendant of the crime of grand larceny in the first degree, the specific charge being that on November 30, 1904, he obtained the sum of $2,250 from a corporation called Park, Davis & Company by false representations. The indictment contained two counts. The first one alleged the details of grand larceny by means of false representations. The false representations charged were that here presented that he had expended the sum of money in question in the purchase of platinum for the benefit of complainant when he had not, and it was alleged that both the false representations and receipt of the money occurred in the city of New York. The second count simply charged common-law larceny, but the consideration of this was withdrawn on the trial.

There is quite a history behind the alleged offense, which, however, for all needful purposes of this discussion may be very briefly summarized. The appellant was a chemist. The complainant was a large dealer in drugs, etc., having its principal place of business in the state of Michigan and a branch in the city of New York under the management of one Turrell. Appellant claimed to be able, amongst other things, to produce synthetically camphor from spirits of turpentine. In some way he and the complainant through various representatives became engaged in negotiations on this subject, resulting in a contract by which the complainant was to furnish certain moneys towards developing the aforesaid process and was to have a certain interest in the results. Amongst the other moneys to be advanced by it where those required by appellant for supplies and labor in connection with the project. It was under this arrangement and under these circumstances that the appellant, as claimed, falsely represented to the complainant's representative Turrell that he had spent money for necessary platinum when he had not and thereby secured the money in question.

Alexander Rosenthal, David Steckler and *Clark L. Jordan* for appellant. Incompetent testimony was improperly admitted, whereby an atmosphere was created on the trial unfair to the defendant and so prejudicial to him as to call for a reversal of the judgment, and such incompetency and unfairness must have been clearly known to the district attorney. (*People* v. *Crapo,* 76 N. Y. 292; *Langley* v. *Wadsworth,* 99 N. Y. 63; *Van Boppelin* v. *Bendell,* 130 N. Y. 145; *People* v. *Genung,* 11 Wend. 19; *People* v. *Brown,* 72 N. Y. 571; *People* v. *Kohler,* 93 Mich. 625; *People* v. *Un Dung,* 39 Pac. Rep. 12; *State* v. *Gleim,* 17 Mont. 31; *Bates* v. *State,* 60 Ark. 450; *People* v. *Wolf,* 183 N. Y. 472.)

Charles S. Whitman, District Attorney (*Robert S. Johnstone* of counsel), for respondent. The questions concerning the McKinley, Jarvis and Lockhurst transactions tended to show criminal fraud and misconduct on the defendant's part and were properly allowed for the purpose of affecting his credibility, (*People* v. *Irving,* 95 N. Y. 541; *People* v. *Noelke,* 94 N. Y. 137; *People* v. *McCormick,* 135 N. Y. 663; *People* v. *Webster,* 139 N. Y. 73; *People* v. *De Garmo,* 179 N. Y. 131; *People* v. *Hinksman,* 192 N. Y. 421; *La Beau* v. *People,* 34 N. Y. 223; *Gt. West. T. Co.* v. *Loomis,* 32 N. Y. 127; *Langley* v. *Wadsworth,* 99 N. Y. 61; *People* v. *Clark,* 102 N. Y. 735; *People* v. *Tice,* 131 N. Y. 651; *People* v. *Dorthy,* 156 N. Y. 237.)

HISCOCK, J. Many allegations of error are made by the appellant. Some of these are not well founded, and others do not have as a necessary basis any proper exception taken at the trial. The result is that we should be able to affirm the judgment appealed from except for the unjustifiable methods, savoring too much of pettifoggery, employed by the assistant district attorney who tried the case, for the purpose of producing on the minds of the jury the impression that defendant had been guilty of various misdeeds when as a matter of fact the evidence did not justify any such inference.

As has been stated, the charge against the appellant is that he procured money from the complainant by false representations in connection with his claim that he could synthetically produce camphor from spirits of turpentine. The case was very closely contested on the facts, and if the People could convince the jury that the appellant was in the habit of obtaining money from people by virtue of dishonest schemes of this nature, it can readily be seen that this would substantially influence the jury in their final conclusion. The attempt was made to produce this impression by improper methods.

While he was being cross-examined the appellant was asked whether he had not entered into an arrangement with one Weir to manufacture rubber synthetically, and he answered that he had. Then he was asked whether he had not represented that he could produce rubber synthetically for him, and pursuant to that representation had secured several thousand dollars. This question he answered in the negative, but being asked further did admit that on such a representation he had procured money from Weir to the amount of about eight hundred dollars, and then being asked whether he had ever returned that money to him, he responded in the negative.

Next he was asked whether he did not represent to one McKinley that he could manufacture rubber synthetically and under that representation procure from him an amount in the neighborhood of twenty thousand dollars. He answered this in the negative, but did admit that upon such representation he had procured some money from Mr. McKinley.

He was then asked whether he had not represented to one Lockhurst falsely that he had a plant equipped for the manufacture of a patented device by virtue of which representation he procured several thousand dollars and he answered in the negative.

Finally he was asked whether he had not procured money from one Jarvis by representation of ability to manufacture rubber synthetically and responded in the negative.

Subsequently Jarvis and Lockhurst were called to the stand by the prosecution and after being asked trivial questions allowed to depart. Weir had been called to the stand before this cross-examination and asked questions of a similar character and each of the witnesses stated that he knew the defendant and two of them that they had met him during the period covered by the questions making up the cross-examination heretofore referred to.

It is perfectly apparent that the only object of this cross-examination and the only purpose of parading these witnesses before the jury was to create the impression that the defendant had been engaged in fraudulent schemes similar to the one charged against him in this case and to challenge him before the jury either by his own testimony or by a cross-examination of the witnesses referred to, to go into the details of those transactions. As it was conducted, it was an entirely unjustifiable proceeding. The evidence as it was actually produced did not show that the appellant had been guilty of any dishonest conduct and there was nothing in the answers which he did give which properly called for further testimony or explanation by him. On this theory the evidence at best would be utterly immaterial and inadmissible, and under the circumstances I have no doubt that it was worse than immaterial. The entire series of questions as they were framed, his admissions that he had received certain sums of money, and the presence of the individuals from whom it was insinuated by the district attorney's questions he had improperly collected money, inevitably must have combined to produce in the minds of the jury the conclusion that appellant had been guilty of misconduct. He was forced to submit his case to the jury either under this false impression thus improperly created, or else enter on the trial of issues involving foreign transactions which had no part

in the trial.   Either burden was one which the court had
no right to impose upon him.   While of course the court
has the power to allow much latitude in the cross-examination of a witness, and while the district attorney many
times may be led in good faith and legitimately to enter
upon a cross-examination of a witness which proves fruit-
less and discloses no circumstances impeaching his credibility, there must be a limit to these practices.   One of
these limits should be that a district attorney shall not
deliberately, by questions really containing no element of
misconduct and by parading witnesses as a challenge to
the defendant, create false impressions that he has been
guilty of misdeeds when the evidence does not sustain
any such conclusion.

The judgment of conviction should be reversed and a
new trial granted.

GRAY, J. (dissenting).   I dissent, for the reason that a
reversal of the judgment of conviction upon the errors
alleged is not justified.   They were neither serious, nor
prejudicial.   The course of the district attorney, in asking the unnecessary questions alluded to in the opinion,
may well have been open to censure; but that the evidence could prejudice the defendant's case is incredible.
As to three of the four cases where these questions were
asked, they contained no suggestion of false representations
by the defendant in obtaining the money for his chemical
productions.   As to the other case, where they did enter
into the question, the defendant denied the offense.

The verdict of the jury was abundantly sustained by
the proofs and the Appellate Division justices have unanimously affirmed the judgment, upon their review of the
trial.   I think it is going too far for this court to hold
that it should be now reversed for the reasons assigned.

CULLEN, Ch. J., VANN, WERNER, WILLARD BARTLETT
and CHASE, JJ., concur with HISCOCK, J.; GRAY, J.,
reads dissenting opinion.

Judgment of conviction reversed, etc.

Jardine, Matheson & Company, Limited, Respondent,
v. Huguet Silk Company, Appellant.

Sale — construction of contract for purchase and sale of foreign goods — when buyer may not repudiate contract and refuse to accept goods, because invoices were mutilated and because goods were not imported expressly for buyer — rejection of evidence.

1. Defendant contracted to purchase from plaintiff certain bales of silk as specified. The defendant refused to receive the silk when tendered upon the ground that the documents attached to the invoice had been mutilated and that the silk was not imported by plaintiff but bought by it on the market expressly for the defendant. *Held*, that as the alleged mutilation consisted only of cutting out the name of the person to whom certain certificates were issued as to qualities of the silk, and as it was no part of the contract that the silk should be imported by plaintiff, defendant had no right to reject it on either ground.

2. As to some of the silk offered by plaintiff to meet the requirements of the contract, defendant offered evidence tending to show that it did not comply with its terms. Objection was taken that the silk was not rejected upon the question of quality, and upon inquiry by the court as to the object of the evidence, which was not disclosed, the objection was sustained. *Held*, that it is apparent from the record that the evidence was offered as matter of defense rather than in reduction of damages, and if the plaintiff wished to introduce the evidence in order to reduce damages it should under the circumstances have so stated so that the court could have understood its position.

Jardine, Matheson & Co. v. *Huguet Silk Co.*, 138 App. Div. 903, affirmed.

(Argued October 13, 1911; decided November 8, 1911.)

Appeal from a judgment of the Appellate Division of the Supreme Court in the first judicial department, entered May 20, 1910, affirming a judgment in favor of plaintiff entered upon a verdict.

The plaintiff is a corporation organized under the laws of the colony of Hong Kong, and the defendant is a corporation organized under the laws of the state of New York.

The action was brought to recover damages for an alleged breach of contract for the purchase of raw silk sold by plaintiff to defendant. On the trial it appeared that on the sixth of September, 1907, the parties entered into a contract, in writing, whereby the plaintiff sold to the defendant and the defendant purchased from the plaintiff fifteen bales of silk described as " To arrive, 15 bales Italian Extra Classical 10/12 (Reeled from White Bagdad Cocoons) $6.05 per pound. Silk to be delivered here 1 B during the first week of January, 1908, and 1 B weekly thereafter. Weights, Conditioned weight. Terms, 90 days from delivery." The silk thus contracted for was a specialty used in this country chiefly by the defendant.

On the 30th of December, 1907, the defendant wrote the plaintiff as follows: " Please take note to ship on Friday next, January 3rd, one bale silk 10/12 out of our last contract No. 10,575 we have with you. As we are badly in need of this silk, we request you to see that this bale is shipped exactly as directed." Beneath the signature of the defendant there was written a request to ship to " Canisteo Silk Co., Canisteo, N. Y.," which company at the time "carried on manufacturing for the defendant." This letter was received by the plaintiff on Thursday, January 2d, 1908, and the next day it wrote to the defendant stating that "Your silk under contract No. 10,575 has not yet arrived; but we shall be able to make delivery the first of next week. Our reason for delaying response has been that we wished to ascertain just what is our position regarding deliveries, and we now take pleasure in advising that the first bale can be delivered early next week." On Saturday, January 4th, the defendant wrote to the plaintiff, and after acknowledging receipt of its letter of the third instant, said: " Your not being ready to deliver this week one bale of silk 10/12 is not in accordance with our contract No. 10,575 of Sept. 6th past, which calls that one bale out of this contract is to be delivered here during the first week of Jan. 1908 and in reference to this fact you have not yet executed above contract and we consider same as canceled." The plaintiff answered this letter on the 6th of January, 1908, and stated: "You are quite correct that under this contract we are obligated to ship you one bale Italian Extra Classical 10/12 White Bagdad Cocoons during the first week of January. You are, however, under a misapprehension as to when the 'first week of January' ends. The first week of January ends with the first seven days, that is, a shipment made on or before the afternoon of Jan. 7th would be a proper delivery."

The plaintiff alleged in its complaint that on the 6th of January it shipped to the Canisteo Silk Company one bale of silk of the description and at the price mentioned in the contract and sent to the defendant sizing and conditioning certificates and a bill amounting to $1,153.19. The defendant in its answer denied the shipment but admitted the sending of the bill.

On the seventh of January the defendant wrote the plaintiff acknowledging receipt of its letter of the sixth, and after expressing surprise at its contents, said: "Instructions have been given to our mills to refuse any bale from the railroad company and we return to you enclosed your invoice dated Jan. 6th, which we cannot accept. The documents attached to your invoice are not correct, having part of them cut out and show that for some particular reason something is wrong. It is the unquestionable proof that this bale was not imported by yourselves, but bought on the market expressly for us."

The plaintiff replying on the same date, after reciting its obligation under the contract, said: "We shipped you a bale of this quality and size yesterday, thus complying with the first delivery of our contract. The succeeding deliveries will be made literally on time and you must accept your obligations under this contract. The documents attached to our invoice for bale 9,150 are correct. We cut out the name of the firm for whom the silks had been conditioned in Europe and their mark. This is quite customary and permissible in silk transactions. Our contract does not obligate us to state to our buyer from whom the silk has been purchased. We simply must deliver a certain article at a specified time and this we are doing. It is not within your province to question whether we bought the silk expressly for you or not; in other words, where or how we secured the silk, is irrelevant and immaterial under the terms of our contract.   *   *   *   Regarding bale 9,150, we beg to suggest that you instruct your mill to accept this bale without prejudice to the rights of either party in the premises. We on our part are quite willing to agree that this should not be used against you in any arbitration or legal action. It will avoid the risk and inconvenience of returning it to our warehouse. Your prompt decision as to which course you wish to pursue in settling this question would be much appreciated as we must, under our contract, bill and ship you the second bale not later than Monday the 13th, inst., which bale is now awaiting your shipping instructions."

To this letter the defendant replied on the next day as follows: "All our contracts with you, were made to have the silks bought and delivered through Messrs. Chabrieres, Morel & Co., Lyons, France, for whom you are agents. The documents attached to every invoice must not bear any cut out, as official paper should be. They show, as we wrote you, that this silk was not imported as above mentioned — but simply bought here, on the market, the latter part of the past week. We confirm you again that we will refuse any bale from the Railroad Company and we return to you enclosed, your invoice dated Jan. 6th, which we do not accept."

Between the date of the contract in September and the commencement of this correspondence there had been a decided fall in the price of raw silk and the decline continued for some time after the correspondence ceased. In due time and upon due notice the plaintiff sold the silk in question on the defendant's account for the net price of $12,883.06 and brought this action to recover the sum of $7,313.76, the difference between the contract price and the price for which the silk was sold.

The plaintiff alleged in its complaint the foregoing facts in substance, among others, and the defendant by its answer, after admitting some of the allegations and denying others, alleged as a separate and distinct defense " that the plaintiff herein failed to deliver to the defendant one bale silk 10 '12 of the description and at the price referred to in the contract set forth in the complaint during the first week of January, 1908, as therein provided and that thereupon and because of such failure so to deliver the said defendant canceled said contract and notified the plaintiff of such cancellation."

The jury found a verdict in favor of the plaintiff for the amount claimed and interest, and the judgment entered accordingly was affirmed by the Appellate Division, one of the justices dissenting.

James F. Lynch and *D. E. Lynch* for appellant. The appellant is not restricted by any causes for rejection stated in the cancellation notice of January 4, 1908, because of respondent's failure to treat such notice as a rescission, and its subsequent tender of performance. (*Richard* v. *Haebler,* 36 App. Div. 94.) The appellant in proving its right to reject was restricted only by the causes for rejection set forth in letter of January 7, 1908, returning invoice and conditioning and sizing certificates. (*Browne* v. *Patterson,* 165 N. Y. 460; *Cunningham* v. *Judson,* 100 N. Y. 179; *Wallace, Muller & Co.* v. *Valentine,* 10 Misc. Rep. 645; *Lake* v. *McElfatrick,* 139 N. Y. 349; *Dauchey* v. *Drake,* 85 N. Y. 407; *Hill* v. *Blake,* 97 N. Y. 216; *Tobias* v. *Lissberger,* 105 N. Y. 404; *Bank of Montreal* v. *Recknagel,* 109 N. Y. 482; *Clark* v. *Fey,* 121 N. Y. 470; *Norrington* v. *Wright,* 115 U. S. 188; *Glaholm* v. *Hays,* 2 M. & G. 265.)

Carlisle Norwood for respondent.   When the refusal to accept purchased goods is based upon particular objections, formulated and deliberately stated, all other objections are deemed waived and the vendor to recover the price need only prove compliance with the contract of sale in the particulars covered by the stated objections.   (*Browne* v. *Patterson,* 165 N. Y. 460; *Hess* v. *Kaufherr,* 128 App. Div. 526; *Littlejohn* v. *Shaw,* 159 N. Y. 188; *Rochevot* v. *Wolf,* 96 App. Div. 506.)

VANN, J.   Both parties agree that the defendant is not restricted by the grounds for rejecting the silk as stated in the cancellation notice of January 4th, 1908, because the plaintiff failed to treat such notice as a rescission and tendered performance after that date.   They further agree that the defendant, in proving its right to reject, was restricted only by the grounds for rejection set forth in its letter of January 7th, 1908, returning the invoice and certificates.   Those grounds were that the documents attached to the invoice had been mutilated and that the silk was not imported by plaintiff but bought by it on the market expressly for the defendant.

The documents in question are known as " conditioning and sizing certificates," which are issued by licensed persons in Milan and Florence, the one to establish the weight of the silk and the other the thickness of the thread.   They are accepted in the silk trade for these purposes.   The certificates furnished showed both weight and thickness and in great detail the special process, through drying and other preliminary preparation, by which each was arrived at.   This is the sole object of such certificates and the name of the person to whom they are issued is incidental merely and immaterial.   The contract between the parties required the silk to be conditioned as to weight,

but not as to size, and the certificates rejected by the
defendant were conditioned as to both. The name of the
person to whom the certificates were issued did not concern the defendant and the plaintiff had the right to cut
out the name in order to keep it secret if it so desired.
The certificates showed on their face that the part removed
was simply the name of the one for whom the work of
conditioning was done, leaving the remainder untouched
and complete in every respect. We think that the first
ground upon which the defendant planted itself did not
warrant its action in attempting to cancel the contract.

The silk was sold " to arrive," which means that it was
to be imported and the words " Italian " and " White
Bagdad " carry the same implication. Such silk is not produced in this country and if used here must be imported.
There is nothing in the contract, however, to indicate
by whom the importation was to be made and any
imported silk which met the terms of the contract in
other respects was a sufficient compliance therewith. It
matters not that the plaintiff at first intended to deliver
silk imported by itself and that the defendant expected
it would, for when its own silk failed to arrive in time it
had the right to purchase and deliver other imported silk
of the kind called for by the contract. It was no part of
the contract or of the description of the silk that it should
or should not be imported by the plaintiff or by any particular person. The substance of the agreement on the
part of the plaintiff was that imported silk of a certain
quality should be delivered at a certain time and the
defendant had no right to reject silk which satisfied these
requirements.

The defendant claims the silk was not only to be
imported but that it was to be imported between the date
of the contract and the date of delivery. Assuming this
to be so, the date of the conditioned certificates, " Milano,
23 Novembre, 1907," indicates that the silk arrived after
the date of the contract and before the attempt to deliver.

This was presumptive evidence of the date of importation, which was within the limitations of the contract even when construed according to the defendant's theory.

The defendant further claims, although it did not take this position until the eighth of January, 1908, when the rights of the parties had become fixed, that under its previous contracts with the plaintiff the latter had delivered only silk purchased by it from a particular firm in France and it attempted to show this fact by offering certain letters which were excluded by the court as immaterial. As the letters are not referred to in the contract, they form no part of it and hence the previous dealings between the parties were of no importance. If the plaintiff did what it agreed to do the defendant cannot lawfully complain if there was a departure from its custom in procuring part of the silk required from a new source. It had the right to get the silk wherever it could and was under no obligation to buy it of any particular concern, even if in past transactions with the defendant this had been its custom. The contract as written measures the rights and obligations of both parties and as the silk offered was the silk sold, the defendant had no right to rescind upon any grounds which it relied on in its letter of January 7th, 1908, refusing to accept any silk for the reasons therein stated. When that letter was written and received there was still time for the plaintiff to ship the first bale. While there is some evidence that the shipment had already been made, even if there were none the plaintiff was not obliged to attempt any delivery after receipt of that letter from the defendant stating that it had instructed its mills " to refuse any bale from the railroad company." A refusal to accept made when there was still time to deliver, relieved the plaintiff from making any further effort to deliver. We hold that the reasons relied upon and stated by the defendant did not warrant rescission and as by its own action it is limited to those reasons it follows that, according to the record now before us, the contract was in force when this suit was commenced.

Shortly after the contract between the parties was made the plaintiff ordered fifteen bales of silk from a firm in Lyons, France, but as they failed to arrive in time for the first delivery it bought two bales of an importing firm in New York in order to meet the requirement to deliver "one bale during the first week of January, 1908, and one bale weekly thereafter." These two bales were all that the plaintiff had in readiness to deliver during that week. By a witness who qualified as an expert, the defendant attempted to show that these bales did not contain silk "Italian Extra Classical 10/12 Reeled from White Bagdad cocoons" but that they contained silk "Italian Extra Classical 10/12 Bagdad." This was objected to as immaterial and the objection was sustained. Many questions upon the subject were asked commencing with this: "From what cocoons is 'silk Bagdad' produced?" This was objected to by the counsel for the plaintiff as immaterial and he added: "These were not rejected for quality. They are trying to introduce quality. There is no question of quality. They were not rejected on the question of quality." The objection was sustained and an exception was taken. To all the questions immediately following relating to quality the objection interposed was simply "immaterial," as before, and no suggestion was made by the defendant's counsel that he had any purpose in offering the evidence except to show that as the quality was inferior there was the right to reject on that ground. Among other questions asked was the following: "Is there any distinction in the silk trade between 'silk Bagdad' and 'silk reeled from white Bagdad cocoons?'" This also was objected to as immaterial and the objection was sustained. The defendant's counsel thereupon remarked: "I think we ought to have (the evidence) that there is a distinction between them. He can testify that there is a difference in the trade in the classification as 'silk Bagdad' and 'silk reeled from white Bagdad cocoons.' I think the witness should be allowed to say that there is a difference." The court: "How does it apply to this case?" Defendant's counsel: "It applies in my conception of the case and in my presentation of the case." The court: "You can take the benefit of an exception to my ruling." Defendant's counsel: "There is nothing to show that those terms have any import unless this witness testifies that there is a difference between the two. I take an exception."

The defendant now claims that as the two bales were sold with the others on account of the defendant for $4.20 per pound, or $1.85 less than the contract price, the difference formed part of the damages assessed by the jury. It further claims that the damages are an independent factor in the cause of action and, hence, even if it had no right to refuse delivery on the ground of quality because it did not take that position in the first place, still it had the right to the evidence offered in order to show that the two bales were worth less than the others, so that it might reduce the damages accordingly.

There would be force in this position if the evidence had been offered for that purpose, but it is apparent from the record that it was offered as matter of defense rather than in reduction of damages. If the plaintiff wished to introduce the evidence in order to reduce damages it should have said so under the circumstances, so that the court could have understood its position. No suggestion of that kind was made even when the court asked how such evidence applied to this case, and it is now too late for the defendant to take a position which it did not take and apparently did not think of on the trial. Its effort was to defeat the contract and justify its attempt to rescind it. The main struggle was not over the amount of damages flowing from the inclusion of the two bales, but over the right to recover at all. The defendant tried to get rid of a bargain which turned out to be a losing one and fought hard to defend its right to reject the goods altogether. The minds of the court and the counsel for the plaintiff were obviously on that subject and not on the subject of damages when the evidence in question was offered, and it was incumbent upon the defendant to state the object of the evidence, when expressly asked, if it was other than to defeat the contract. While the evidence may have been competent for one purpose, it was evidently offered for another and the ruling made on that theory does not involve reversible error.

The judgment should be affirmed, with costs.

CULLEN, Ch. J., WERNER, WILLARD BARTLETT, HISCOCK, CHASE and COLLIN, JJ., concur.

Judgment affirmed.

ALBERT J. WHEELER, Individually and as Executor of MARY J. WHEELER, Deceased, et al., Appellants, *v.* THE PHENIX INSURANCE COMPANY OF BROOKLYN, Respondent.

Insurance (fire) — liability of insurer for loss resulting from explosion preceded and caused by fire.

When a policy of insurance against fire upon a grain elevator provides that the company should not be liable for loss by explosion of any kind unless fire ensues, and in that event for the damage by fire only, a fire preceding and causing the explosion is not embraced in the exception from the provision which insures against all direct loss or damage by fire, and if a negligent or hostile fire exists within the insured premises and an explosion results therefrom under such circumstances as to constitute the fire the proximate cause of the loss and the explosion merely incidental, the company becomes liable upon its policy for the loss resulting therefrom.

Wheeler v. *Phenix Ins. Co.*, 136 App. Div. 909, reversed.

(Argued October 23, 1911; decided November 3, 1911.)

APPEAL from a judgment of the Appellate Division of the Supreme Court in the fourth judicial department, entered December 16, 1909, affirming a judgment in favor of defendant entered upon a dismissal of the complaint by the court at a Trial Term.

The nature of the action and the facts, so far as material, are stated in the opinion.

Charles Diebold, Jr., for appellants. The explosion clause does not relieve an insurance company from liability for loss directly caused by an accidental fire in the insured premises. (Richards on Ins. Law [3d ed.], 370; Kerr on Ins. 370; 2 May on Ins. [4th ed.] § 416a; 3 Joyce on Ins. § 2772; Elliott on Ins. 212; *Washburn v. A. Ins. Co.*, 29 Fed. Cas. 308; *Washburn v. U. F. Ins. Co.*, 29 Fed. Cas. 329; *Washburn v. M. V. Ins. Co.*, 2 Fed. Rep. 633; *La Force v. W. F. Ins. Co.*, 43 Mo. App. 518; *Cohn v. Nat. Ins. Co.*, 96 Mo. App. 315; *T. A. F. Ins. Co. v. Dorsey*, 56 Md. 70; *Mitchell v. P. Ins. Co.*, 183 U. S. 42; *G. A. Ins. Co. v. Hyman*, 42 Col. 156.)

Edgar J. Nathan for respondent. The policy exempts the insurer from liability for loss caused directly or indirectly by explosion of any kind. (*Beakes v. P. Ins. Co.*, 143 N. Y. 402; *Hoffman v. King*, 160 N. Y. 618; *Hustace v. P. Ins. Co.*, 175 N. Y. 302; *St. John v. A. M. F. & M. Ins. Co.*, 11 N. Y. 516; *Briggs v. N. A. Ins. Co.*, 53 N. Y. 446; *Miller v. L. & L. Ins. Co.*, 41 Ill. App. 395; *G. F. Ins. Co. v. Roost*, 55 Ohio St. 581; *Heuer v. N. W. Nat. Ins. Co.*, 144 Ill. 393; *Stanley v. Western Ins. Co.*, L. R. [3 Exch.] 71.) The complaint was properly dismissed for failure of proof. (*Clark v. F. M. F. Ins. Co.*, 111 Wis. 65; *W. A. Co. v. Mohlman Co.*, 83 Fed. Rep. 811; 1 Clement on Ins. 126; *Lamb v. Union R. Co.*, 195 N. Y. 260; *Milbaur v. Richard*, 188 N. Y. 453; *Pinder v. B. H. R. R. Co.*, 173 N. Y. 519; *Cassidy v. Uhlmann*, 170 N. Y. 505; *Fealey v. Bull*, 163 N. Y. 397; *Babcock v. F. R. R. Co.*, 140 N. Y. 308; *Pauley v. S. G. & L. Co.*, 131 N. Y. 90; *Schoepflin v. Coffey*, 162 N. Y. 12; *Ruppert v. B. H. R. R. Co.*, 154 N. Y. 90; *Hudson v. R., etc., R. R. Co.*, 145 N. Y. 408; *People v. Harris*, 136 N. Y. 429; *Clarke v. Koeppel*, 119 App. Div. 458; *Gunther v. L. & L. & G. Ins. Co.*, 134 U. S. 110.)

HAIGHT, J. This action was brought to recover the amount of a policy of insurance issued by the defendant to the plaintiffs, insuring them against direct loss or damage by fire to the Ontario elevator situated on the east side of the Evans ship canal in the city of Buffalo.

The complaint alleges that the property was wholly destroyed by fire on the 30th day of October, 1904, and that the plaintiffs sustained a loss of $103,000, with an aggregate insurance of $94,750, and demands judgment for the amount of the policy. The answer admits the issuance of the policy and denies the other material allegations of the complaint, and alleges as a defense: *First*, that the damage was caused by an explosion for which the defendant, under its policy, is not liable; and, *second*, that the elevator fell, not as a result of fire.

The Ontario elevator was a wooden structure built in the year 1889, the main building being one hundred and nine feet front and eighty-three feet deep, having two marine towers, one on the north and the other on the south end thereof. The bins in the building were constructed of hemlock plank laid flatwise to the height of fifty-two feet, and on top thereof there was a double floor, over which there was a vast open space of irregular shape because of the gables in the roof, about seventy-eight feet in height, in which was located the machinery by which the grain was hoisted to the machinery floor and then distributed by means of spouts to the different bins below. In the northeast corner of the machinery floor was a matched board closet, planed on one side and called a locker or cupboard, in which the workmen kept their clothes, supplies for the machinery, lamps and a quantity of beef suet. The building was used for the elevating and storage of grain that came from vessels down the lakes. On the arrival of a vessel loaded with grain the leg of the marine tower containing an endless belt on which were fastened buckets at regular intervals would be lowered into the hold of the vessel and then by causing the belt to revolve the buckets would fill with grain and elevate the same to the tower above where it would be deposited in large hoppers which would convey it to the machinery floor where it would be distributed by means of spouts as before stated. The engines and boiler which furnished the power by which the elevator was operated were located in a brick building near by but in nowise connected with the elevator building. In withdrawing grain from the elevator for the purpose of loading cars or canal boats or other means of transportation the grain is run through a spout in the bottom of each bin into pits or conveyors on the ground floor and is then taken by an elevator similar to the marine leg, where it is conveyed to the machinery floor near the peak of the roof where it is weighed and then conveyed to its destination by means of spouts, the same as when it was elevated originally from the vessel. In elevating the grain from a vessel for storage, or in elevating it from the bins to be withdrawn from storage, a great amount of dust is created and brought into the machinery room above the top of the bins.

On Friday night preceding the destruction of the elevator the steamer *Penobscot* arrived with a cargo of over one hundred thousand bushels of barley, which was elevated in the manner already disclosed, which contained great quantities of dust which was deposited on the floor and disseminated into the atmosphere of the machinery room. The work ceased about two o'clock Saturday morning, but during Saturday the elevator was in operation transferring grain from different bins and in loading cars. After the work ceased on Saturday night the watchman made his rounds regularly until four o'clock in the morning, and when he left all the windows of the machinery floor were closed and there was then no light or fire in the building. A few minutes after eleven o'clock in the forenoon of Sunday a great explosion occurred, in which the building was wrecked, and at that time it contained 297,000 bushels of grain.

The theory of the plaintiffs is to the effect that spontaneous combustion occurred among the material contained in the locker, so called, which created a fire that burned over and charred the boards out of which the closet was constructed, and that this fire ignited the dust that was contained in the machinery room and caused the explosion which wrecked the building.

Upon the trial the court directed a nonsuit at the close of the plaintiff's evidence upon the ground that the defendant was not liable under its policy even though the explosion was caused by fire, under the authority of *Hustace v. Phenix Ins. Co. of Brooklyn* (175 N. Y. 292) and *Briggs* v. *North American & M. Ins. Co.* (53 N. Y. 446). He, however, held that the evidence tending to show that the explosion was caused by fire was sufficient to make that a question of fact for the jury.

The policy of insurance upon which this action is based undertook to insure the plaintiffs "against all direct loss or damage by fire except as hereinafter provided." Under the provision thereafter provided as the exception is the following: "This company shall not be liable for loss caused directly or indirectly by invasion, insurrection, riot, civil war or commotion, or military or usurped power, or by order of any civil authority; or by theft; or by neglect of the insured to use all reasonable means to save and preserve the property at and after a fire or when the property is endangered by fire in neighboring premises; or (*unless fire ensues*, and, in that event, *for the damage by fire only*) *by explosion of any kind*." Webster defines "ensues" as meaning "to follow or come afterwards; to follow as a consequence or in chronological succession, to result." The provision, therefore, embraced in the exception "unless fire ensues" should be read as meaning "unless fire follows or comes after or as a consequence of the explosion." This being the meaning of the provision it is apparent that a fire, which precedes and causes the explosion, is not embraced in the exception contained in the policy from the provision which insures against all direct loss or damage by fire. Nor do we think that the words "by explosion of any kind" were intended to refer to the agency which produced the explosion but have reference to the different kinds of material that explode, such as powder, dynamite, gas, dust, etc. Had the legislature, in adopting the standard form of policy, intended to have included explosions caused by fire with explosions from which fire ensues among the loses excepted from the provisions of the policy it doubtless would have done so in express terms. That such was not its intention we think is clearly evident from the fact that they were careful to limit the exception to those explosions from which a fire ensues. This form of fire insurance policy and the construction which we have given to it is not new. It has frequently been considered by the courts and text writers upon the subject, who have quite uniformly reached the conclusion that when a negligent or hostile fire exists within the insured premises and an explosion results therefrom under such circumstances as to constitute the fire the proximate cause of the loss and the explosion merely incidental the company becomes liable upon its policy for the loss resulting therefrom.

In the case of *Washburn* v. *Miami Valley Insurance Co.* (2 Fed. Rep. 633) it was held that where a policy of insurance against loss by fire contains the condition that the insurance company shall not be liable for any loss or damage occasioned by explosion of any kind unless fire ensues, and then for the loss or damage by fire only, and when a fire originates in the insured premises which produces an explosion by which that property is destroyed such destruction is a loss by fire within the meaning of the policy. Justice SWAYNE of the Supreme Court of the United States, before whom the case was tried, in his opinion, says: "Explosives are named only in connection with fires which they have produced. There is nothing said about them in connection with fires which have pro-

duced them. The policies on that subject are wholly
silent. Is not this somewhat remarkable, if the construction contended for by the companies be correct? In that
case would not the language of the context have naturally been that the company will not be liable for explosions,
and will not be liable for fires which produce them, or
fires which they have produced? The first may define the
liability of the company, and the sentence I have just read
is certainly important. Would not the policies have read
' that they will not be liable for explosions caused by
fires, or for fires caused by explosions?' I repeat, and it
is a feature of great significance in the case, as it seems
to me, that where explosions are produced by fires —
accidental fires — the policy is wholly silent." He then
proceeds with an elaborate discussion of the question,
reaching the conclusion that the explosion was a part of
the fire and as such was covered by the general language
of the insurance policy. (See, also, Richards on Insurance Law [3d ed.], p. 370; Kerr on Insurance, 370; 2
May on Insurance [4th ed.], § 416a; 3 Joyce on Insurance,
§ 2772; Elliott on Insurance, 212; *Washburn* v. *Artisan
Ins. Co.* and *Washburn* v. *Penn. Ins. Co.*, 29 Fed.
Cases, 308; *La Force* v. *Williamsburg F. Ins. Co.*, 43
Mo. App. 518; *Transatlantic F. Ins. Co.* v. *Dorsey*, 56
Md. 70; *Ger. Am. Ins. Co.* v. *Hyman*, 42 Col. 156, and
Mitchell v. *Potomac Ins. Co.*, 183 U. S. 42.)

We do not regard the case of *Briggs* v. *North American
and Mercantile Insurance Co.* (53 N. Y. 446) or the case of
Hustace v. *Phenix Ins. Co. of Brooklyn* (175 N. Y. 292) as
in conflict with the views hereinabove expressed. In the
Briggs case the explosion was caused by the vapors from
rectifying spirits coming in contact with the flame of a
lamp. It was held that the lamp was not a fire within
the meaning of the policy. It was not a hostile fire
which made the explosion the incident, but itself became
the incident. But in that case Judge PECKHAM, in
delivering the opinion of the court, was careful to distin-

19

guish it by stating "where, however, the explosion is the incident and the fire the principal, a different question would be presented. Had the building been on fire, and in the course of a general conflagration there had been an explosion of a boiler, which injured some machinery that the fire was rapidly consuming, different views and considerations might well obtain" (p. 449), thus recognizing the principle to which we have already alluded.

In the *Hustace* case a large building at the corner of Warren and Greenwich streets, in the city of New York, occupied by dealers in drugs and chemicals, was on fire. The fire had raged for half an hour and then a terrific explosion took place caused by the igniting of the chemicals stored therein, wrecking several buildings, among which was that of the plaintiff's, which was located across a street or alley some fifty-seven feet distant therefrom. The plaintiff's building fell by reason of the concussion caused from the explosion. No hostile fire was in progress upon the plaintiff's premises and no explosion occurred therein. It was held in this court that the loss sustained by the plaintiffs was not a "direct loss or damage by fire" within the meaning of the policy, but the fire was only a remote and indirect cause of the concussion which caused the plaintiff's building to fall. There is nothing in that case which is in conflict with the views that we have expressed in this case. It may be true that in the opinion discussing the various cases upon the subject there may be some expression that has misled the trial court in this case, but the learned chief judge in concluding his opinion in that case was careful to limit the decision to the peculiar facts presented in that case. We, consequently, conclude that the trial court erred in granting a nonsuit upon this branch of the case.

It is now contended on behalf of the respondent that, notwithstanding the ruling of the trial court, the evidence is insufficient to warrant a submission of the question to the jury as to whether a fire existed in the building which caused the explosion. In the first place it appears from the evidence that there were a number of pieces of matched boards, planed on one side and rough on the other, which were found after the explosion, burned and charred to such an extent as to indicate that a blaze must have existed. These boards were found embedded in the grain bin underneath the closet or locker and were positively identified, by the carpenter who constructed the closet and another witness, to be part of the boards which constituted the closet and which were not burned or charred before the day of the explosion. It further appears by the testimony of a large number of witnesses who were in the vicinity at the time of the explosion that their attention was attracted to the building by a loud noise likened by many to the boom of a cannon and that immediately thereafter the roof of the building appeared to raise and split in two, then go off toward Norton street, emitting therefrom a great volume of smoke followed by dust and that this was followed a few seconds afterwards by a crash, a breaking of timbers and the falling of the building. Of course the witnesses speaking upon this subject, occupying different positions in the vicinity of the elevator, did not all see the same things alike; some described the scene as the puffing of smoke and dust together, while others were positive that the puff of smoke preceded the dust; one stating that his attention was attracted by a dull, heavy report more like a cannon shot off in a covered inclosure; that he turned and saw the roof of the elevator as it was going off toward Norton street in the air, and that there was a cloud of black smoke with a reddish tinge, full of sparks all through under the roof, which were flashing and going out, and that several seconds afterwards there was a crash and a breaking and crunching like timbers or woodwork breaking, and that a dense gray cloud of dust came across the street, blotting everything out of sight. There was also evidence tending to show that on Saturday preceding the explosion there was a great quantity of dust in the machinery room suspended in the air, and that dust in a closed room without a current of air circulating through it would remain suspended for many hours. It also appeared from the testimony of experts, one of whom was a professor of chemistry in the George Washington University, who had formerly been a professor of chemistry in Harvard, and who had made a special study, and had written upon the subject of grain dust and had made experiments with reference thereto, that barley dust was not explosive but was combustible when mixed with air, and if ignited the combustion would proceed with such velocity as to produce an explosion; that the dust of barley was composed of organic matter from the barley.

Upon this review it is not our province to determine the credibility of witnesses or to carefully weigh the conflicting evidence produced. We are only called upon to determine whether there is evidence sufficient to require the submission of the question of fact to the jury. If it be true that barley dust is not explosive but is combustible only, then it would be difficult to account for the explosion which wrecked the building and the smoke and dust that followed, unless there was fire in the building which ignited the dust. The testimony, therefore, of the plaintiffs' witnesses with reference to the quantity of dust suspended in the closed room on the machinery floor, with the explosion and the smoke and dust and sparks arising therefrom, together with the fact that charred and burned boards were subsequently found out of which the closet or cupboard was constructed, together with the testimony of the expert, in our judgment was sufficient to carry that question of fact to the jury.

The judgment of the Appellate Division and that of the trial court should be reversed and a new trial ordered, with costs to abide the event.

CULLEN, Ch. J., GRAY, VANN, WERNER, CHASE and COLLIN, J., concur.

Judgment reversed, etc.

In the Matter of the Protest of WILLIAM H. BURKE, Respondent, to the Board of Elections of the City of New York, Respondent, against the Certificate Nominating EDMUND R. TERRY, Appellant, for Member of Assembly in the First Assembly District of Kings County.

Election Law — section 123 (as amended by L. 1911, ch. 649), relating to the signing and filing of certificates of independent nominations, construed and held to be constitutional.

The Election Law (Cons. Laws, ch. 17, as amended by L. 1911, ch. 649) permits an independent certificate of nomination to be made up of several different sheets. Section 123 provides that "The signatures to the certificate of nomination need not all be appended to one paper," and further that "No separate sheet comprising an independent certificate of nomination, where such certificate consists of more than one sheet, shall be received and filed with the custodian of primary records if five per centum of the names appearing on such sheet are fraudulent or forged." *Held*, that the latter provision may be upheld because independent nominators are not constrained to subject themselves to its operation. They may all sign a single sheet or each may sign a sheet by himself. This liberty of action relieves the provision from any constitutional objection.

Matter of Terry, 146 App. Div. 520, affirmed.

(Argued November 2, 1911; decided November 3, 1911.)

APPEAL from an order of the Appellate Division of the Supreme Court in the second judicial department, entered October 31, 1911, which affirmed an order of Special Term declaring the certificate of the independent nomination of Edmund R. Terry as candidate for member of assembly from the first assembly district in the county of Kings to be insufficient and invalid and enjoining and restraining the board of elections of the city of New York from having printed the name of the said Edmund R. Terry as such candidate upon the official ballot.

Edmund R. Terry and *Theodore F. Kuper* for appellant.

William W. Wingate for William H. Burke, respondent.

Archibald R. Watson, Corporation Counsel (James D. Bell of counsel), for Board of Elections, respondent.

WILLARD BARTLETT, J.   Section 1 of article 1 of the Constitution of the state of New York provides as follows: "No member of this State shall be disfranchised, or deprived of any of the rights or privileges secured to any citizen thereof, unless by the law of the land, or the judgment of his peers."

It is contended on the present appeal that this prohibition of the Constitution has been violated by the action of the board of elections of the city of New York in denying to certain citizens the right to participate effectively in nominating Edmund R. Terry as an independent candidate for member of assembly from the first district of Kings county.

The Election Law (Cons. Laws ch. 17, as amended by L. 1911, ch. 649) permits an independent certificate of nomination to be made up of several different sheets. "The signatures to the certificate of nomination need not all be appended to one paper." (Election Law, § 123.) It is conceded that the citizens to whom we refer possess all the qualifications requisite to entitle them to join in executing an independent certificate of nomination; but it has been held by the courts below that the sheets upon which their signatures appear should be rejected and refused consideration by the board of elections under section 123 of the Election Law which provides that "no separate sheet comprising an independent certificate of nomination, where such certificate consists of more than one sheet, shall be received and filed with the custodian of primary records if five per centum of the names appear-

ing on such sheet are fraudulent or forged." The board
of elections is the custodian of primary records in the city
of New York. (Election Law, § 202.)

The objection to the statutory provision invalidating
every separate sheet of an independent certificate of nomination which bears five per cent of forged or fraudulent
signatures is that it deprives the qualified signers thereof
of all right to participate in the independent nomination
which they desire to make, and this without the slightest
element of wrongdoing on their part. They are made to
lose this right simply because others over whom they have
no control have done wrong. They are punished for an
offense which others have committed and their candidate,
who may be equally innocent, may consequently thus be
debarred of the benefit of having his name printed upon
the official ballot. That this is an injury to honest
electors and an honest candidate there can be no doubt;
but the question upon which the determination of this
appeal depends is whether its effect on qualified signers
of the rejected sheets amounts to disfranchisement under
the Constitution.

The franchise of which no " member of this state " may
be deprived is not only the right of citizens who possess the
constitutional qualifications to vote for public officers at
general and special elections, but it also includes the right
to participate in the several methods established by law for
the selection of candidates to be voted for. The legislature
of this state in its wisdom decided some years ago to adopt
an official ballot, to be printed at the public expense,
upon which the voter indicates his preference by cross
marks placed opposite the names of those candidates
whose election he desires. In providing for such a ballot it was not only proper but necessary to prescribe the
conditions which should entitle political parties and independent bodies of citizens to have the names of their
nominees appear upon the ballot in print. It is argued
that these conditions are wholly within the discretion of

the legislature and not subject to judicial review or control; but this proposition is subject to the qualification that no condition can be imposed which conflicts with the constitutional rights of electors, express or implied. We have recently held that one of these implied constitutional rights is equality of opportunity so far as practicable. The chief judge, speaking for a unanimous court in *Matter of Hopper* v. *Britt* (203 N. Y. 144, 151), said: "We think the constitutional provisions recited and the provision that certain officers shall be chosen by the electors necessarily further imply that every elector shall have the right to cast his vote with equal facility to that afforded to other voters, or, to speak more accurately, without unnecessary discrimination against him as to the manner of casting his vote." The same rule applies to the right to participate in making independent nominations. In prescribing reasonable rules regulating that right, the legislature may not unnecessarily discriminate against honest electors who without fault on their own part find that forged or fraudulent signatures have been attached to the certificate. If the Election Law absolutely nullified the honest signatures of qualified nominators in the case of a certificate of independent nomination, by reason of the presence of forged or fraudulent signatures thereon, a majority of the court would deem it unconstitutional to that extent; but it is only where such certificate consists of more than one sheet that the prescribed percentage of forged or fraudulent signatures has the effect of nullifying the honest signatures thereon. If the certificate consist of one sheet only, or if a separate sheet be provided for each signature, no such result could follow. It might be difficult, but it would not be impossible to resort to either of these methods. Hence the provision which is attacked in this proceeding does not necessarily operate to disfranchise electors desiring to participate in an independent nomination, who have done no wrong. By placing all the signa-

tures on one sheet or each signature on a sheet by itself
the effect of the provisions can be wholly avoided.

The Appellate Division was of the opinion that the
provision for the rejection of the sheets bearing. five per.
cent of forged or fraudulent signatures might be regarded
merely as the statutory establishment of a rule of presumptive evidence, leaving the independent candidate or
his friends at liberty to prove that the other signatures
were genuine, in which event it would be the duty of the
board of elections to treat them as effective. The difficulty with this view is that there is no warrant for it in
the language of the statute, which manifestly contem-
plates the absolute rejection of all separate sheets bearing the specified percentage of forged or fraudulent signatures. Nor are we able to concur in the suggestion
that the person who obtains the signatures to a certificate
of independent nomination or the notary who takes the
acknowledgments is the agent of all the signers so as to
make those who are honest chargeable with his knowledge that some of the signatures are forged or fraudulent. There is no presumption that any one knowing of
such wrongdoing would disclose it. The presumption is
just the other way.

Still another suggestion requires notice. It is said that
no regulation which the legislature may see fit to impose
in respect to independent nominations can be subject
to any attack for invalidity under the Constitution,
inasmuch as the legislature need not have permitted
independent nominations to be printed upon the official
ballot at all. To this view we are unable to assent. The
framers of the Election Law which first provided for the
official ballot properly recognized the unquestionable fact
that it is a great practical advantage to political parties
and their candidates to have the names of the nominees
appear upon the ballot in print. They also properly
recognized the possibility, which experience has proved to
be a probability not to say certainty, that large bodies of

citizens not constituting political parties might desire to unite in the effort to elect candidates of their own selection; and that these bodies might justly claim a place for their nominees in print upon the official ballot. This claim is so manifestly just and its recognition so essential to prevent that unconstitutional discrimination against the rights of electors which was condemned in the *Hopper Case* (*supra*) that we should regard any legislation as plainly invalid which allowed only the names of party candidates to be printed upon the official ballot, to the exclusion of candidates named by considerable bodies of citizens acting independently of party. If there were no provision for printing the names of independent candidates nominated by such bodies, the electors would be denied that equality of opportunity in the exercise of the right of suffrage which it is the aim of the Constitution to preserve.

It should be distinctly understood, therefore, that the provision invalidating separate sheets of an independent certificate of nomination by reason of the presence of five per cent of forged or fraudulent signatures thereon is not sustained on any such ground as this. We think it may be upheld because independent nominators are not constrained to subject themselves to its operation. They may all sign a single sheet or each may sign a sheet by himself. This liberty of action, we think, relieves the provision from any constitutional objection and, hence, requires an affirmance of the order under review.

The order should be affirmed, without costs.

CULLEN, Ch. J., GRAY and VANN, JJ., concur; HAIGHT, HISCOCK and COLLIN, JJ., concur in result.

Order affirmed.

THE PEOPLE OF THE STATE OF NEW YORK ex rel. THIRD
AVENUE RAILWAY COMPANY et al., Respondents, *v.*
THE PUBLIC SERVICE COMMISSION FOR THE FIRST DIS-
TRICT OF THE STATE OF NEW YORK et al., Appellants.

**Public Service Commissions Law — provisions not in conflict
with sections 9–12 of Stock Corporation Law — reorganization
of railroad corporation — authority of commission as to issue
of securities.**

1. The enactment of the Public Service Commissions Law (Cons.
Laws, ch. 48) did not repeal the provisions in the Stock Corporation Law (Cons. Laws, ch. 59) for the reorganization of the property
and franchises of corporations sold under foreclosure, and, on the
other hand, the provisions of the Stock Corporation Law do not
withdraw corporations formed on reorganizations from compliance
with section 55 of the Public Service Commissions Law. The two
statutes must be construed together.

2. Sections 53 and 54 of the Public Service Commissions Law,
requiring the approval by a public service commission of the exercise or transfer of franchises by a railroad corporation, do not
apply to a corporation formed on the reorganization of a railroad
corporation after foreclosure.

3. Under the provisions of section 55 of the Public Service Commissions Law, a public service commission is not justified in refusing
to consent to the issue of securities by a railroad corporation under
a plan of reorganization after foreclosure because the value of the
mortgaged property and the amount of new capital to be invested
is less than the amount of securities sought to be issued.

People ex rel. Third Ave. Ry. Co. v. *Public Service Comm.*, 145
App. Div. 318, affirmed.

(Argued October 16, 1911; decided November 21, 1911.)

APPEAL, by permission, from an order of the Appellate
Division of the Supreme Court in the first judicial department, entered June 21, 1911, which annulled and set
aside a determination of the defendant Public Service
Commission denying an application for an order authorizing the Third Avenue Railway Company to issue cer-

tain stocks and bonds and remitted the matter to said commission to proceed as directed by the opinion of the court.

The facts, so far as material, and the questions certified are stated in the opinion.

Charles F. Brown, George S. Coleman and *Oliver C. Semple* for appellants. The Stock Corporation Law and the Public Service Commissions Law may reasonably be construed together; so far as the reorganization of railroads is concerned the effect of the Public Service Commissions Law is to require certain additional steps to be taken and certain additional consents to be secured. (*Vatable* v. *N. Y., L. E. & W. R. R. Co.*, 96 N. Y. 49; *People ex rel. Schurz* v. *Cook*, 110 N. Y. 443; 148 U. S. 397; *Minor* v. *Erie R. R. Co.*, 171 N. Y. 566; *M., etc., R. R. Co.* v. *Commissioners*, 112 U. S. 609.) Under section 55 of the Stock Corporation Law, and under section 55 of the Public Service Commissions Law, prescribing for what security issues of new stock and bonds may be made, the duty of the commission in authorizing the issue and fixing the amount thereof must be to determine whether the issue is for the acquisition of property, or for the construction or improvement of facilities, or for maintenance of service, or for discharge or lawful refunding of the company's obligations, or for reimbursement of money spent out of the treasury for improvements, etc., and whether the amount is such as should be authorized therefor. The duty to fix the amount of the issue and to state the purposes to which the issue is to be applied must require a determination of the identity and the value of the property for which the stock or bonds are to be put out, and if the issue is for money then a determination of the purpose to which that money is to be put, and it is to be noted that under the statute the corporation cannot, without the consent of the commission, apply the issue or any proceeds thereof to any purpose not specified in the order.

The duty of deciding as to whether such issues are reasonably required and whether they are reasonably capital or operating charges is part of what the commission under the statute is called upon to determine. (*People ex rel. D. & H. Co.* v. *Public Service Commission*, 140 App. Div. 839; *People ex rel. B. L., H. & P. Co.* v. *Stevens*, 203 N. Y. 7.)

Ledyard P. Hale for Public Service Commission, Second District, intervening.   Since July 1, 1907, it has been the duty of the courts to construe the several provisions of the Public Service Commissions Law together with all the statutes relating to or including railroad, street railroad, gas and electric corporations (and since September 1, 1910, telegraph and telephone corporations), in harmony if possible, but giving effect to every affirmative provision of the later act.   (*Matter of N. Y., W. & B. R. Co.*, 193 N. Y. 72.)   If sections 55, 69 and 101 of the Public Service Commissions Law cannot be construed with sections 9, 10 and 55 of the Stock Corporation Law the latter and not the former must give way.   (*Pratt* v. *Munson*, 84 N. Y. 582.)

William D. Guthrie, Victor Morawetz, Herbert J. Bickford and *John M. Bowers* for respondents.   The reorganization statute was not repealed by the Public Service Commissions Law.   (*Vil. of Fort Edward* v. *H. V. R. R. Co.*, 192 N. Y. 139; *People ex rel. N. Y., N. H. & H. R. R. Co.* v. *Willcox*, 200 N. Y. 423; *Hawkins* v. *Mayor, etc.*, 64 N. Y. 18; *Davis* v. *Supreme Lodge*, 165 N. Y. 159; *Matter of Tiffany*, 179 N. Y. 455; *Woods* v. *Supervisors*, 136 N. Y. 403; *People ex rel. Brown* v. *Metz*, 119 App. Div. 271; 189 N. Y. 550; *Red Rock* v. *Henry*, 106 U. S. 596; *Cope* v. *Cope*, 137 U. S. 68. Sections 53, 54 and 55 of the Public Service Commission Law do not apply to the reorganization of railroad corporations under sections 9 and 10 of the Stock Corporation

Law. (*People ex rel. D. & H. Co.* v. *Stevens*, 197 N. Y.
1; *People ex rel. N. Y., etc., R. R. Co.* v. *Willcox*, 200
N. Y. 423; *People ex rel. B. L., H. & P. Co.* v. *Stevens*,
203 N. Y. 7; *Vil. of Fort Edward* v. *H. V. Ry. Co.*, 192
N. Y. 139; *People ex rel. S. S. Traction Co.* v. *Willcox*,
196 N. Y. 212.) If section 55 of the Commissions Law
applies to reorganizations, the approval of the commission
should have been granted. (*People ex rel. D. & H. Co.*
v. *Stevens*, 197 N. Y. 1; *Gamble* v. *Q. C. W. Cp.*, 123
N. Y. 91; *State* v. *G. N. Ry. Co.*, 100 Minn. 445; *Shepard* v. *N. P. Ry. Co.*, 184 Fed. Rep. 765; *Ives* v. *S. B.
Ry. Co.*, 201 N. Y. 271; *Biglow* v. *Sanders*, 22 Barb.
147; *Clinton* v. *Rowland*, 24 Barb. 634; *Fitch* v. *Mayor,
etc.*, 88 N. Y. 500; *Dewey* v. *Hotchkiss*, 30 N. Y. 497;
Stokes v. *Stokes*, 91 Hun, 605; *Raymond* v. *Howland*,
17 Wend. 389.)

CULLEN, Ch. J. The road and property of the Third
Avenue Railroad Company (street railroad) was sold
under foreclosure and at the sale was purchased by a committee of the bondholders. This purchase was made
under a plan entered into by the parties in interest, bondholders and stockholders, by which it was agreed that a
new corporation should be formed and the securities of
the new corporation distributed among the bondholders
and stockholders of the old corporation in certain pro-
portions and on the payment of certain amounts in
money. The securities — stocks and bonds — called for
by the plan of reorganization did not exceed the amount
of outstanding securities of the old company and the
additional money to be paid to the corporation. After
the sale the committee caused to be organized the Third
Avenue Railway Company, one of the relators herein.
It applied to the public service commission under section 55 of the Public Service Commissions Law (L. 1910,
ch. 480; Consolidated Laws, ch. 48) for an order authorizing the securities called for by the reorganization plan.

This application was denied by the commission on the ground that the amount of such securities exceeded the value of the property of the corporation. On certiorari this determination was reversed by the Appellate Division and the matter remitted to the public service commission to proceed in accordance with the opinion of the court. From that order the Appellate Division has allowed an appeal to this court and certified the following questions for our determination:

"1. Have the statutory provisions for the reorganization of corporations embodied in sections 9 to 12 of the Stock Corporation Law been repealed by implication as to railroad corporations by the provisions of the Public Service Commissions Law?

"2. The Third Avenue Railway Company being a corporation duly created under sections 9 and 10 of the Stock Corporation Law, pursuant to a plan of reorganization and agreement of readjustment duly entered into, to take and possess the property and franchises of the Third Avenue Railroad Company, a domestic street railroad corporation, sold by virtue of a mortgage or deed of trust duly executed by said railroad company and pursuant to the judgment or decree of a court of competent jurisdiction, may such street railroad corporation lawfully issue its stock and bonds to the amount specified in such plan and agreement without first securing from the Public Service Commission for the First District an order authorizing such issues pursuant to section 55 of the Public Service Commissions Law?

"3. The Third Avenue Railway Company being a street railroad corporation duly organized under sections 9 and 10 of the Stock Corporation Law, and the issues of stock and bonds proposed to be made by said new corporation being in all respects in conformity with the provisions of sections 9 and 10 of said law and of the plan of reorganization and agreement of readjustment duly entered into pursuant thereto, and the amount of stock

and bonds so proposed to be issued by the new corporation being substantially less than the aggregate of the
amount of capital stock of the old corporation issued for
cash at par and of valid bonds issued for full value
received by the corporation and duly adjudged to be
valid obligations by a court of competent jurisdiction,
together with interest on said bonds, and new cash to be
contributed by stockholders for strictly corporate purposes, may the Public Service Commission for the First
District nevertheless lawfully refuse to authorize the said
company to issue such stock and bonds to the amounts
and for the purposes specified in such plan and agreement, including the discharge and refunding of obligations under such plan and agreement, for the reason that
in the opinion of the Commission the present actual value
of the property to be acquired by the new or reorganized
corporation under said plan and agreement is not equal
to the aggregate of the par of the proposed new stock and
the market value of the proposed new bonds?

"4. If section 55 of the Public Service Commissions
Law applies to the reorganization of a street railroad corporation and to the issue of stock and bonds of the successor corporation duly created under sections 9 and 10 of
the Stock Corporation Law in pursuance of a plan of reorganization and agreement of readjustment, were the
relators entitled under the facts shown in the record to
secure from the Public Service Commission for the First
District an order authorizing the issue and the amount
of the proposed securities as provided in the plan and
agreement?

"5. The Third Avenue Railway Company being duly
organized under sections 9 and 10 of the Stock Corporation Law, pursuant to a plan of reorganization and
agreement of readjustment duly entered into, to take and
possess the property and franchises of the Third Avenue
Railroad Company, a domestic street railroad corporation, sold by virtue of a mortgage or deed of trust duly

executed by it and pursuant to the judgment or decree
of a court of competent jurisdiction, must such reorganized or successor corporation first obtain the permission
and approval of the Public Service Commission under
section 53 of the Public Service Commissions Law before
it may exercise and enjoy any of the rights, privileges
and franchises which at the time of such sale belonged to
or were duly vested in the corporation last owning the
property sold or its receiver?

" 6. The Third Avenue Railway Company being duly
organized under sections 9 and 10 of the Stock Corporation
Law, pursuant to a plan of reorganization and agreement
of readjustment duly entered into, to take and possess the
property and franchises of the Third Avenue Railroad
Company, a domestic street railroad corporation, sold by
virtue of a mortgage or deed of trust duly executed by it
and pursuant to the judgment or decree of a court of competent jurisdiction, must such reorganization or successor
corporation first obtain the approval of the Public Service
Commission under section 54 of the Public Service Commissions Law to the transfer or assignment to it of the
franchises and of any right to or under any franchise to
own or operate a railroad or street railroad which at the
time of such sale belonged to or were duly vested in the
corporation last owning the property sold or its receiver,
and must it first obtain the consent of such commission
under said section 54 to the purchase, acquisition, taking
or holding of any part of the capital stock of any street
railroad corporation organized or existing under or by
virtue of the laws of this state which at the time of such
sale belonged to or was duly vested in the corporation last
owing the property sold or its receiver?"

The determination of this appeal depends on the construction and effect of certain provisions of the Stock
Corporation Law (L. 1909, ch. 61; Consolidated Laws,
ch. 59) and of the Public Service Commissions Law.
Section 9 of the Stock Corporation Law authorizes the

purchaser on a foreclosure or execution sale of the franchises and property of any domestic corporation to form a new corporation, and prescribes the steps necessary to effect that purpose. Section 10 authorizes the purchasers at such a sale, or the persons for whom such a purchase is made, to enter into a plan or agreement in anticipation of the readjustment of the respective interests of creditors, mortgagees and stockholders of the corporation " for the representation of such interests in the bonds or stock of the new corporation to be formed." It then authorizes the new corporation when organized to issue its bonds and stock in conformity with the provisions of the plan and agreement, and to settle or assume the payment of any debt, claim or liability of the former corporation upon such terms as may be agreed upon, and to establish preferences in favor of any portion of its capital stock, and to divide its stock into classes, but such stock of the new corporation cannot exceed " in the aggregate the maximum amount of stock mentioned in the certificate of incorporation." A brief history of the legislation on this subject may throw some light on the question before us. The General Railroad Law of 1850 (Ch. 140) authorized railroad companies to mortgage their property and franchises. Necessarily a purchaser on foreclosure would have the right to maintain and operate the railroad, of which he could not be deprived. By chapter 282 of the Laws of 1854 such person was authorized to form a new corporation for that purpose. Meanwhile a statute had been passed (L. 1853, ch. 502) by which, in case of a foreclosure sale of a railroad or plankroad, any stockholder of the company could, at any time within six months, pay to the purchaser a share of the price for which the property sold equal to the proportion his stock in the company bore to the whole capital stock and thereupon become vested with the same interest in such road and property. With unsubstantial changes this remained the law until 1874.

During that period unfortunately railroad foreclosures had been common, not only in this state but throughout the whole country, and the common practice had been that upon reorganization after foreclosure, the stockholders and the holders of junior securities were allowed some interest in the new corporation, the stockholders often being required to make some contribution of fresh capital. This course was doubtless dictated by two objects: 1st. To prevent delay and procrastination in the foreclosure proceedings. 2nd. To get fresh capital from the stockholders who would be induced to advance it in the hope of saving some part of their previous investment and which could not be obtained from third parties having no such inducement. Such being the common practice, by chapter 430 of the Laws of 1874 there was enacted a provision for the reorganization of railroad properties sold under foreclosure substantially in the same form as that now provided in the Stock Corporation Law by which the provision is extended to all corporations. In 1907 the Public Service Commissions Law was enacted and amended in 1910 (Ch. 480; Cons. Laws, ch. 48). By section 55 of that act common carriers and railroad corporations were authorized to issue stock, bonds, notes or other evidences of indebtedness when necessary for the acquisition of property and construction and improvement of its facilities, "provided and not otherwise that there shall have been secured from the proper commission an order authorizing such issue, and the amount thereof and stating the purposes to which the issue or proceeds thereof are to be applied, and that, in the opinion of the commission, the money, property or labor to be procured or paid for by the issue of such stock, bonds, notes or other evidence of indebtedness is or has been reasonably required for the purposes specified in the order."

We think that these statutes are not inconsistent; that on the one hand the enactment of the Public Service Commissions Law did not repeal the provisions in the

Stock Corporation Law for the reorganization of the property and franchises of corporations sold under foreclosure, and on the other hand that the provisions of the Stock Corporation Law do not withdraw corporations formed on reorganizations from compliance with section 55 of the Public Service Commissions Law. In other words, the two statutes must be construed together, though parts of the later statute may be inapplicable to cases arising under the earlier.

The first and second questions must, therefore, be answered in the negative.

As to sections 53 and 54 of the Public Service Commissions Act we entertain this view: Section 53 provides that without first having obtained the permission and approval of the proper commission no railroad corporation or common carrier shall exercise any franchise or right under any provision of the Railroad Law or any other law, unless prior to the creation of the board of railroad commissioners (the predecessor in many respects of the public service commissions) the corporation or carrier was entitled to exercise such franchises. Section 54 of the act forbids the assignment or transfer of any franchise to operate a railroad unless the transfer shall have been approved by the public service commission. These provisions have no application to the relator company. The franchise of the Third Avenue Railroad Company was property and could not be destroyed. (*People v. O'Brien*, 111 N. Y. 1.) The statute empowered that company to mortgage its property and franchises, and under that authority they were mortgaged and sold to the individual relators, who became the purchasers thereof. The right of the bondholders under the mortgage to have the mortgaged property sold in satisfaction of their claims, and the right of the purchasers to the franchises and property bought by them were inviolable. Therefore, no consent could be made a prerequisite to either the transfer or enjoyment of the franchises. It is

People ex rel. T. A. Ry. Co. *v.* P. S. Comm. 309

1911.]   Opinion, per Cullen, Ch. J.   [203 N. Y.]

true that while the state could not impair the rights of the purchasers to maintain and operate the railroad acquired by them, it might refuse to give them the franchise to be a corporation, or grant it only on such conditions as it might see fit to impose. (*Minor* v. *Erie R. R. Co.*, 171 N. Y. 566; *People ex rel. Schurz* v. *Cook*, 148 U. S. 397.) The provisions of the sections referred to, however, are not directed against corporations particularly, but against corporations and individuals alike, and section 53 expressly excepts franchises held prior to the creation of the railroad commission, when the state first required the consent of that commission to the acquisition of the franchise to construct and maintain a railroad. This exception and the inability of the legislature to invade the rights of bondholders or purchasers, manifested in the statute itself, makes it plain that the provisions of these sections were not intended to apply to the case of a corporation formed on the reorganization of a foreclosed railroad.

Questions five and six must, therefore, be answered in the negative.

Holding, as we do, that the relator corporation falls within the provisions of section 55 of the Public Service Commissions Law, we are brought to the question whether under the provisions of that section and those of the Stock Corporation Law, relative to the reorganization of corporations, the commission was justified in refusing the consent applied for because the value of the mortgaged property and the amount of new capital to be invested were less than the amount of securities to be issued by the corporation. We think it was not. The requirement of the Stock Corporation Law is, that the plan or agreement adopted by the parties in interest shall not be inconsistent with the laws of the state, but there is no provision in the Public Service Commissions Law that the securities issued shall in no instance exceed the value of the property. Indeed it contains no express provision to that effect at all, though doubtless it was intended by the law to prevent the issue of fictitious or " watered " securities, and the Stock Corporation Law (§ 55) forbids the issue of stock or bonds except for money or labor or property at their respective values. As was said by Judge HAIGHT in *People ex rel. Delaware & Hudson Co.* v. *Stevens* (197 N. Y. 1, 9): " For a generation or more the public has been frequently imposed upon by the issues of stocks and bonds of public service corporations for improper purposes, without actual consideration therefor, by company officers seeking to enrich themselves at the expense of innocent and confiding investors. One of the legislative purposes in the enactment of this statute was to correct this evil by enabling the commission to prevent the issue of such stock and bonds, if upon an investiga- tion of the facts it is found that they were not for the purposes of the corporation enumerated by the statute and reasonably required therefor." (See, also, *People ex rel. Binghamton Light, Heat & P. Co.* v. *Stevens,* 203 N. Y. 7.) The requirement of the statute is that the issue of the securities shall be necessary for the acquisition of the property, and although as a general rule under this requirement, the securities should not be authorized except where the value of the property is equal to the amount of the securities issued, there may be exceptions to that rule. One is found in the statute itself. In the case of the merger or consolidation of two or more corporations it is provided that the capital stock of the corporation formed by the merger shall not exceed the capital stock of the corporations consolidated and any additional sum paid in in cash. Thus, in the case of merger the limit of the amount of stock of a corporation is dependent, not on the value of its property, but on the stock outstanding of the constituent corporations prior to the merger. We think the same rule is applicable to the case of a corporation formed on the reorganization of a foreclosed railroad.

It is not necessary to consider the issuance of the securities of the new corporation as a refunding of the outstanding obligations of the old.   It is sufficient to say that the statute authorizes the bondholders, stockholders and creditors to agree upon a plan for the readjustment of their respective interests, and authorizes the new corporation to issue its stock and bonds in accordance with the agreement.   A readjustment of the interests of the parties does not contemplate that the new securities shall necessarily be scaled down to the actual value of the property.   If this was the contemplation of the statute, the statute would be of little value.   The property sold rarely realizes the amount due on the mortgage foreclosed.   If the sale price is considered the criterion of value, there could be no plan which would give the holders of stock or of junior securities any interest in the new corporation, while often the bondholders under the mortgage foreclosed might find themselves without the right to obtain any securities of the new corporation in lieu of their bonds.   The intent of the statute was to enable the various persons interested in an insolvent or defaulted railroad to agree upon some plan or scheme to take the road out of insolvency and a receivership and make the enterprise a going concern.   For this purpose additional money is generally requisite, which, as already said, can be obtained only from those interested in the property, and not even from them unless, as an inducement to advance the money, they are given the opportunity of retrieving their prior investment.   In many instances the growth of the community in which the railroad was located and the improvement in business conditions has ultimately justified the advance of new capital, and the benefit and protection of the original investors in the enterprise was also the object of the statute.   We do not say that in the reorganization of a railroad the new corporation is authorized to issue securities in excess of those of the company to whose property and franchises it has

suceeeded and the new money that may be put in the
enterprise.   Such a plan would be plainly inconsistent
with the spirit of the Public Service Commissions Law
against the issue of "watered" stock or bonds, but, up
to the limit we have named, the new corporation has the
right to issue securities.   The determination of the commission to the contrary was, therefore, erroneous.

The third question should, therefore, be answered in
the negative and the fourth in the affirmative.

The order of the Appellate Division should be affirmed,
with costs.

GRAY, WERNER, WILLARD BARTLETT, HISCOCK, CHASE
and COLLIN, JJ., concur.

Order affirmed.

THE PEOPLE OF THE STATE OF NEW YORK ex rel. TROY
GAS COMPANY, Appellant, *v.* BENJAMIN E. HALL et al.,
Constituting the STATE BOARD OF TAX COMMISSIONERS
et al., Respondents.

**Tax — special franchises — when city assessors may apportion
special franchise assessment between different parts of a tax
district.**

1. The intention of the Tax Law is to give the state board of tax
commissioners exclusive power and authority to fix and determine
the valuation of each special franchise subject to assessment in
each city, town and tax district, and to lodge in local boards and
officers the power and authority to apportion the valuation of a
single special franchise for the purposes of assessment among school
districts and where for other special reason it is required.

2. The state board of tax commissioners performs its full duty
when it fixes and determines in one amount the value of a special
franchise to occupy the streets and public places in a single tax
district, with a continuous and unbroken line of pipes and wires.

3. Where certain territory in a city constitutes a separate school
district which is not subject to taxation for general school purposes,
the city assessors are authorized to apportion a special franchise, the

full value of which has been determined by the state board of tax commissioners, between such school district and the territory under the control of the board of education of such city.

People ex rel. Troy Gas Co. v. *Hall*, 143 App. Div. 756, affirmed.

(Argued October 4, 1911; decided November 21, 1911.)

APPEAL from an order of the Appellate Division of the Supreme Court in the third judicial department, entered March 27, 1911, which reversed an order of Special Term declaring invalid an assessment against the relator's special franchises and quashed a writ of certiorari to review the same.

The assessors of the city of Troy placed upon the assessment roll of said city for the year 1907 a special franchise assessment against the relator of $640,500, in two parts or items, as follows, viz.:

"Troy Gas Co., President and Directors of.

"Special Franchise, value as fixed by State Tax Commissioners of State of New York, under Chapter 712, Laws of 1899, $600,000.00."

"Troy Gas Company, President and Directors of.

"Special Franchise, value as fixed by State Tax Commissioners of State of New York, under Chap. 712, Laws of 1899, $40,500.00."

The first of said parts or items was placed in that part of said assessment roll including the assessments of persons and property in the third ward of said city, and the second of said parts or items in the seventeenth ward of said city.

This proceeding was thereafter commenced by certiorari to have it determined that said assessment was illegal by reason of overvaluation and inequality and because the assessors of the city of Troy had unlawfully apportioned and separated the same in placing it upon said roll.

The Special Term after taking testimony before a referee and obtaining his report with findings of fact

314   People ex rel. Troy Gas Co. *v.* Hall.

[203 N. Y.]   Opinion, per Chase, J.   [Nov.,

and conclusions of law in which he found that the assessment was not illegal by reason of overvaluation or inequality, but was unauthorized and void because of its being placed upon the roll in two parts or items instead of one entry or statement, directed that the said assessment as entered upon the roll be stricken therefrom. On appeal to the Appellate Division of the Supreme Court the order of the Special Term was reversed on the facts and law and the proceeding was quashed. (*People ex rel. Troy Gas Co.* v. *Hall*, 143 App. Div. 756.) Further facts are stated in the opinion.

Alton B. Parker for appellant. The assessments as entered on the Troy assessment books were unauthorized and void, because this relator is not one of the corporations whose franchises can, under the law, be apportioned between school districts. (*People ex rel. W. S. R. R. Co.* v. *Adams*, 125 N. Y. 471; *People ex rel. N. Y. C. & H. R. R. R. Co.* v. *Mohawk*, 61 Misc. Rep. 345; *People* v. *Gourley*, 198 N. Y. 486; *People ex rel. Rochester* v. *Priest*, 181 N. Y. 300; *Paige* v. *Willett*, 38 N. Y. 28.)

George B. Wellington for respondents. The franchises of the relator were taxable under section 2, subdivision 3, and section 43 (formerly section 42) of the Tax Law, and hence an apportionment between school districts was required by the latter section. (*People ex rel. W. S. R. R. Co.* v. *Adams*, 125 N. Y. 471.) The city of Troy is a single tax district. (*People ex rel.* v. *O'Donnel*, 183 N. Y. 9; L. 1906, ch. 473, §§ 11, 160.) The apportionment was made between school districts and was authorized by the Tax Law and the " White " charter of cities of the second class. (L. 1898, ch. 182, § 261; L. 1899, ch. 581; L. 1900, ch. 415.)

Chase, J. The state board of tax commissioners fixed and determined the valuation of the relator's special franchise subject to assessment in the city of Troy for the year 1907 at $640,500. Thereafter and on June 10, 1907, the day fixed in the notice therefor, the relator appeared before such commissioners and asked that the assessment be reduced upon the grounds of overvaluation and inequality. After hearing the relator, and on June 26, 1907, said commissioners finally determined the valuation of said franchise at $640,500 and filed a written statement of the same with the clerk of the city of Troy as provided by statute.

The city of Troy constitutes one tax district and has a board of assessors authorized to assess property therein, among other things, for state and county taxes. The relator is a domestic corporation engaged in the manufacture of gas and electricity. The principal office of the relator is in the third ward of said city, but the pipe lines for the distribution of gas and the wires for the distribution of electric current are necessarily continuous, and they extend through the third and into the seventeenth wards of said city, and the special franchise as defined by statute in this case is one franchise requiring a single assessment in the city of Troy.

The duty of the state board of tax commissioners is to "annually fix and determine the valuation of *each* special franchise subject to assessment in *each* city, town or tax district."

It was held by this court in *People ex rel. N. Y. C. & H. R. R. R. Co.* v. *Gourley* (198 N. Y. 486) that the right of a steam railroad to cross streets and highways constitutes at each such crossing an independent and separate special franchise, and referring to the language of the section directing the state board of tax commissioners to fix and determine the valuation of each franchise the court say: "This language indicates that it is the value of each right to occupy the public property, constituting the special franchise, which the state board is required to determine." (p. 490.) It was consequently

decided in that case that the state board of tax commissioners failed to perform its full duty when it fixed and
determined the value of the franchises at nine independent
public crossings at an aggregate amount, instead of by a
valuation upon each franchise, particularly in view of
the fact that in the case then under consideration, within
the township including said nine crossings, were two
incorporated villages, each having a board of assessors
for village purposes.   There is nothing in the *Gourley*
case that holds that the state board of tax commissioners
is required to divide a single special franchise into parts
for valuation, or holding that the franchise of a railroad,
telegraph, telephone, gas, electric light, pipe line or
other similar company, when it is continuous and
unbroken, is to be considered other than as a single
franchise, except as it is required by the statute to be
valued separately in each city, town or tax district.

This court considered the right of the Metropolitan
Street Railway Company to occupy the streets in the city
of New York as a single franchise in *People ex rel.
Metropolitan Street Railway Company* v. *State Board
of Tax Commissioners* (174 N. Y. 417).   In the opinion
in the *Gourley* case (p. 491), referring to the *Metropolitan
Street Railway* case, the court say:

"The facts were such as to make the particular decision inapplicable here; for the railway was within the
streets of the city of New York and all its properties in
rights and privileges were managed as one piece of property.   As it was said by Judge EARL, the referee in that
case, speaking of the relator's special franchises, 'there
was nothing in the streets to distinguish one from the
other.'"

The state board of tax commissioners performed its full
duty, therefore, when it fixed and determined, in one
amount, the value of the relator's special franchise to
occupy the streets and public places of the city of Troy
with a continuous and unbroken line of pipes and wires.

Except for special circumstances the duty of the assessors of the city of Troy was plain and that was to enter the amount of the assessment of the special franchise as fixed and determined by the state board of tax commissioners upon the assessment roll of the city against the relator in the ward in which its principal office and place of business is located.

There were peculiar facts and circumstances affecting the determination of the tax rate in different parts of the city of Troy. In 1900 the city of Troy enlarged its boundaries by adding a large territory which included all of the then existing village of Lansingburg and other territory. Included in the act so increasing the boundaries of the city of Troy (Laws of 1900, chap. 665) is a section as follows: "Union free school district number one of the town of Lansingburg shall not be affected by this act; and no assessment shall be made or tax levied by the city of Troy, for school purposes, upon real property situate, or personal property of persons residing in that portion of the enlarged city of Troy which is situate within the present limits of. said union free school district." (Section 5.) Union Free School District No. 1 of the town of Lansingburg included in its boundaries the same territory then included in the village of Lansingburg, and it now constitutes the seventeenth and other wards of the present city of Troy. The territory comprising the city of Troy, other than the part thereof included in said Union Free School District Number 1 in the town of Lansingburg, is for school purposes under the control of the board of education of the city of Troy and subject to taxation for school purposes in that part of the city of Troy not including the old village of Lansingburg. Provision was also made in said act enlarging the boundaries of the city of Troy that the portion of the enlarged city of Troy which is bounded by the limits of the city at the time when said act took effect should pay the maturing indebtedness of the said old city of Troy. A similar provision was also made in regard to that part of the new city of Troy within the said village of Lansingburg, and a still further provision for that portion of said city of Troy which then constituted parts of the towns of North Greenbush, Brunswick and Lansingburg.

The assessment against the relator bears the same proportion of all state, county and city tax whether it is placed upon the assessment roll of the city in one or several different amounts.   The valuation of the relator's special franchise was divided for the purpose of determining the rate on that part thereof within the old city of Troy and the old village of Lansingburg respectively for school taxes and for the payment of maturing indebtedness arising prior to the enlargement of the city boundaries in 1900.

It is provided by the Tax Law (Cons. Laws, chap. 60, section 40; former Tax Law, Laws 1896, chap. 908, section 39): " The assessors of each town in which a railroad, telegraph, telephone or pipeline company is assessed upon property lying in more than one school district therein, shall, within fifteen days after the final completion of the roll, apportion the assessed valuation of the property of each of such corporations among such school districts.   *   *   *."

It is also provided by the Tax Law (section 43, former section 42) that the state board of tax commissioners shall annually fix and determine the valuation of each special franchise subject to assessment in each city, town or tax district, as in said section expressly provided, and that the valuation of every special franchise as so fixed by the state board shall be entered by the assessors or other officers in the proper column of the assessment roll before the final revision and certification of such roll by them, and become part thereof with the same force and effect as if such assessment had been originally made by such assessor or other officer.   And it is therein further provided: " The town assessors shall make an apportionment

among school districts at the time and in the manner
required by section forty of this chapter." This part of
the section just quoted refers generally to all valuations
of special franchises and includes the special franchise of
the relator. City assessors are given the same power to
apportion special franchises among school districts as
town assessors.

Under the so-called White Charter (Laws of 1898, chap.
182) it was provided that city assessors "shall perform
the duties and possess the powers conferred upon assessors in the towns of the state" (section 261). A similar
provision is now contained in the Second-Class Cities
Law (Laws of 1906, chap. 473, now chap. 53 of the
Consolidated Laws, chap. 55 of the Laws of 1909, sec.
160).

Authority is also given to local boards and officers
to apportion the valuation of a special franchise by said
section 43, as follows: "If a part only of such special
franchise is in a village, or is in a village situated in more
than one tax district, it shall be the duty of the village
assessors to ascertain and determine what portion of the
valuation of such franchise, as the same has been fixed
by the state board, shall be placed upon the tax roll for
village purposes. The valuation apportioned to the town
shall be the assessed valuation for highway purposes, and
in case part of such special franchise shall be assessed in
a village and part thereof in a town outside a village,
the town assessors shall meet on the third Tuesday in
August in each year and apportion the valuation of such
special franchises between such town outside the village
and such village for highway purposes."

There is no provision of the statute requiring or
authorizing the state board of tax commissioners to divide
and apportion the valuation of a single special franchise.
We repeat that its full duty was performed when it fixed
and determined the valuation of the relator's special
franchise and filed it with the clerk of the city.

It is doubtless true that the direction to apportion a special franchise valuation among school districts has in ordinary cases special reference to an apportionment for an independent roll to be used for school purposes. (*People ex rel. West Shore R. R. Co.* v. *Adams,* 125 N. Y. 471.)

The language of the Tax Law does not, it may be assumed, provide specifically just what shall be done by city assessors in the peculiar and unusual situation which presented itself to the assessors of the city of Troy. Express provision is made for an apportionment among school districts and in other cases where an apportionment is required.

The intention of the Tax Law seems to have been to give the state board of tax commissioners exclusive power and authority to fix and determine the valuation of each special franchise subject to assessment in each city, town and tax district and to lodge in local boards and officers the power and authority to apportion the valuation of a single special franchise for the purposes of assessment among school districts, and where for other special reason it is required.

We think the assessors of the city of Troy were authorized, in want of further legislation on the subject, to apportion the special franchise of the relator as between the school districts comprising the territory of the present city of Troy, and so place the same upon the said assessment roll as to carry out the provisions of the statutes that we have enumerated, providing not only for the assessment of school taxes within the several school districts of said city, but for the payment of the maturing indebtedness incurred prior to the statute of 1900. If the relator was in any way aggrieved thereby, it should have appeared before the local assessors and made its complaint on the grievance day appointed pursuant to the statute. The state board of tax commissioners were not " the proper officers to correct such assessment " within the meaning of section 290 of the Tax Law, so far as the form of entering the same on the assessment roll is concerned.

It does not appear from the record that there was at any time in this proceeding any competent evidence to show that the relator's special franchise is illegal for over-valuation or by reason of inequality of valuation in comparison with other assessments in the city of Troy.

The referee appointed by the Special Term so found, and the order of the Appellate Division necessarily includes a determination to that effect by that court.

The order should be affirmed, with costs.

CULLEN, Ch. J., HAIGHT, VANN, WERNER, WILLARD BARTLETT and HISCOCK, JJ., concur.

Order affirmed.

WILLIAM ENGEL, Respondent, *v.* UNITED TRACTION COMPANY, Appellant.

Negligence — evidence of discharge of motorman — when inadmissible.

On trial of an action to recover damages for injuries alleged to have resulted from negligence of a motorman employed by defendant, rulings on cross-examination of the motorman, that he should state whether or not he was discharged subsequent to the accident, and that he should state the cause of his discharge, are erroneous.

Engel v. *United Traction Company*, 188 App. Div. 981, reversed.

(Argued October 27, 1911; decided November 21, 1911.)

APPEAL from a judgment of the Appellate Division of the Supreme Court in the third judicial department, entered May 6, 1910, affirming a judgment in favor of plaintiff entered upon a verdict.

The nature of the action and the facts, so far as material, are stated in the opinion.

P. C. Dugan and *Lewis E. Carr* for appellant. The plaintiff was permitted to show over the objections and exceptions of the appellant that the motorman was discharged by it subsequent to the accident, and for this reason the judgment should be reversed. (*Winters* v. *Naughton,* 91 App. Div. 80; *Schmidt* v. *D. D., etc., R. R. Co.,* 3 N. Y. S. R. 257.)

William E. Woollard and *Michael D. Reilly* for respondent.

COLLIN, J. The plaintiff seeks in this action to recover the damages to which, as he avers, the injuries received by him through a collision between an electric car of defendant and an automobile in which he was riding entitle him. The accident happened November 22, 1908, at an intersection of streets in the city of Albany. At the close of the entire evidence the trial court denied the motion of the defendant that the plaintiff be nonsuited upon the ground that the proof failed to show negligence on the part of the defendant or freedom from contributory negligence on the part of the plaintiff, and submitted the issues to the jury. Thereto the defendant excepted. Inasmuch as the Appellate Division did not unanimously render its judgment, we have, under the exception and argument of the defendant, examined the record of the proceedings at the trial and find therein evidence supporting the verdict and judgment. It contains, however, erroneous rulings, duly excepted to, necessitating the reversal of the judgment.

The person who was the motorman of the defendant's colliding car was a witness for the defendant, and testified upon his direct examination to the circumstances and conditions attending the collision. He stated upon his cross-examination that he was not then and for about five weeks had not been employed by the defendant. The cross-examination proceeded: "Q. Were you discharged or did you resign the position? Defendant objected as incompetent and immaterial, Overruled. Exception. A. Discharged. Q. Tell the jury what you was discharged for. Defendant objected as incompetent, improper; nothing to do with this action. Overruled. Exception. Q. Tell the jury what the reason was. A. Piece of foolishness. Q. Tell the rest of it now to the jury. Objected to by defendant as entirely immaterial, incompetent and improper. Overruled. Exception. Q. If you don't want to answer that question, tell the jury you don't want to tell, and I'll stop. Same objections; same ruling. Exception. Q. Either tell the truth or say you don't care to tell. A. I don't care to tell." The jury were thus informed that the motorman was (a) discharged subsequent to the accident (b) for a piece of foolishness, the nature and details of which he was unwilling to tell.

The ruling that the motorman should state whether or not he was discharged subsequent to the accident was erroneous. The sole issue upon which the testimony could bear was that of defendant's negligence. It could bear upon this issue only as the source of the inference by the jury that the motorman on the occasion of the accident operated the car negligently, or as an admission of the defendant that his operation of the car was negligent. It was not legitimate or competent for either purpose. Motormen are discharged for many different reasons and for causes which do not arise from or involve a careless or negligent act. An inference from the discharge of the motorman that he was at the time of the accident operating the car negligently does not rest upon reasonable certainty or preponderating probability. Other inferences are just as natural and deducible from the fact of his discharge. A fact is admissible as the basis of an inference only when the desired inference is a probable or natural explanation of the fact and a more probable and natural one than the other explanations, if any. (*Manning* v. *Insurance Company*, 100 U. S. 693; *Philadelphia City Passenger Ry. Co.* v. *Henrice*, 92 Penn. St. 431; *O'Gara* v. *Eisenlohr*, 38 N. Y. 296; 1 Wigmore on Evidence, section 32.) The prolonged interval between the accident and the discharge does not remove but rather emphasizes the incompetency of the evidence. The discharge is vacuous as proof that the defendant was negligent or as an admission by defendant of its negligence. This conclusion has the approval of the authorities. (*Corcoran* v. *Village of Peekskill*, 108 N. Y. 151; *Columbia & P. S. R. R. Co.* v. *Hawthorne*, 144 U. S. 202.)

The ruling that the witness should state the cause of his discharge was likewise erroneous. The negligence of the defendant was determinable from the facts causing and accompanying the accident. An act of the motorman subsequent to and dissociated from the accident was wholly incompetent and immaterial. Nor did the foolishness or immorality of the act or conduct which caused his discharge tend to prove to any extent that he negligently caused the accident. It is generally accepted law that the character of a party or witness in a civil cause cannot be proven as evidence that he did or did not do an act charged.

In *Post* v. *Brooklyn Heights R. R. Co.* (195 N. Y. 62, 63) we said: "Under our system of appeals every error does not require a new trial, for the vast judicial work of the state could not be done on that basis. Unless the error is so substantial as to raise a presumption of prejudice, it should be disregarded, for undue delay is a denial of justice." That rule is salutary and is not infrequently applied by us. It has no application, however, to the error of admitting, under objection and exception, evidence which has no legitimate tendency to prove an issue upon trial and is calculated to prejudice and improperly influence the minds of the jury. The errors we have considered impaired the fairness of the trial and obscured the real issues. Therefore, they cannot be disregarded.

The judgment should be reversed and a new trial granted, with costs to abide the event.

CULLEN, Ch. J., GRAY, HAIGHT, WERNER and CHASE, JJ., concur; VANN, J., concurs in result.

Judgment reversed, etc.

JOHN C. EIDT, Respondent, *v.* MARGARET EIDT, Appellant, and KATIE EIDT et al., Respondents.

Will — rule of construction applied.

1. It is an established rule that the courts should give effect to every word and provision of a will, in so far as they may, without violating the intent of the testator or well-established rules of law.

2. A provision in a will, " I leave to my wife the house and all the furnishings at No. 326 E. 43 St. for the rest of her natural life the interest in the real estate held by me and my brother John C. Eidt to be held together for Two years or less in case of death of my wife within two years or date of settlement one third Interest to go to Mrs. Anna Deibel," is to be construed as a devise to the wife of the one-half interest in the real estate owned by the testator in common with his brother.

Eidt v. *Eidt*, 142 App. Div. 733, reversed.

(Argued October 9, 1911; decided November 21, 1911.)

APPEAL, by permission, from an order of the Appellate Division of the Supreme Court in the first judicial department, entered March 28, 1911, reversing an interlocutory judgment in favor of defendant-appellant entered upon a decision of the court on trial at Special Term in an action of partition.

The complaint in the action alleged that the plaintiff owned an undivided one-half of the premises sought to be partitioned and that Jacob Eidt, Jr., died, owning an undivided one-half, which he by his last will, duly probated, devised absolutely to his wife, the defendant Margaret Eidt. Certain of the defendants and the plaintiff are the heirs-at-law of Jacob Eidt, Jr., and those defendants by their answers denied the making and validity of the alleged will and averred that Jacob Eidt, Jr., died intestate. The interlocutory judgment decreed the validity of the will and that it devised the undivided one-half part of the premises to Margaret Eidt. The following question was certified to this court: "Did Jacob Eidt, Jr., by his last will and testament, dated March 23d, 1908, make any valid disposition of his one-half interest in the real estate owned by him in common with his brother, John C. Eidt, or of any part thereof, and if so, what disposition did he make thereof?" A transcription of the will, apart from the clause appointing the executors and the signatures of the testator and the witnesses, is:

"NEW YORK *March* 23 1908

"I hereby make my last Will & Testament leaving Two thirds of my share in the business Hay & Grain situated at 305 E. 45 St N Y. City to John C Eidt and one third of business to my wife Margaret Eidt the business to continue for two years or less before a settlement can be made my wife to draw one third Interest and John C Eidt to draw two thirds from same I leave to my wife the house and all furnishings at No 326 E. 43 St for the rest of her natural life the Interest in the real estate held by me and my brother John C Eidt to be held to gether for Two years or less in case of death of my wife within two years or date of settlement one third Interest to go to Mrs Anna Deibel."

The will was written by John C. Eidt, the testator's brother and partner in the hay and grain business, at the dictation of the testator when prepared for a surgical operation which resulted in his death. Mrs. Anna Deibel, whom the will mentions, is the mother of Margaret Eidt. The testator owned at his death miscellaneous personal.

property, including money in bank, shares of stock and accounts receivable, amounting in value to $6,924.69.

Carl A. Hansmann for appellant. The will of Jacob Eidt, Jr., contains a valid devise of his share of the premises to his widow, both by direct gift and by necessary implication. (*C. T. Co.* v. *Eggleston*, 185 N. Y. 23; *Starr* v. *Starr*, 132 N. Y. 154; *Lewisohn* v. *Henry*, 179 N. Y. 352; *Thurber* v. *Chambers*, 66 N. Y. 42; *Stimson* v. *Vroman*, 99 N. Y. 74; *Moffett* v. *Elmendorff*, 152 N. Y. 475; *Matter of Goetz*, 71 App. Div. 272; *Roseboom* v. *Roseboom*, 81 N. Y. 356; *Matter of Keogh*, 126 App. Div. 285; *Mills* v. *Tompkins*, 110 App. Div. 212; *Masterson* v. *Townshend*, 123 N. Y. 458; *Matter of Vowers*, 113 N. Y. 569; *Matter of Moore*, 152 N. Y. 602; *Close* v. *F. L. & T. Co.*, 195 N. Y. 92.)

Theodore J. Breitwieser for respondents. The intention of the testator, as clearly manifested by the will itself, was to die intestate as to the real estate in question. (*Kinkele* v. *Wilson*, 151 N. Y. 269; *Roberts* v. *Corning*, 89 N. Y. 226; *Du Bois* v. *Ray*, 35 N. Y. 162; *Matter of Disney*, 190 N. Y. 128.) The word "and" cannot properly be interpolated between the second and third clauses of the will at bar. (*Starr* v. *Starr*, 132 N. Y. 154; *Patchen* v. *Patchen*, 121 N. Y. 432; *Wylie* v. *Lockwood*, 86 N. Y. 297; *Wilson* v. *Wilson*, 120 App. Div. 581; *Schmeig* v. *Kochersberger*, 18 Misc. Rep. 617; *Mead* v. *Maben*, 131 N. Y. 261; *Stokes* v. *Weston*, 142 N. Y. 438; *Campbell* v. *Beaumont*, 91 N. Y. 467; *Christie* v. *Phyfe*, 19 N. Y. 348; *Matter of Donohue*, 109 App. Div. 158.)

COLLIN, J. There arises from the language, "I leave to my wife the house and all furnishings at No 326 E. 43 St for the rest of her natural life the interest in the real estate held by me and my brother John C Eidt to be held together for Two years or less in case of death of my wife within two years or date of settlement one third Interest to go to Mrs Anna Deibel," a legitimate doubt as to the will and intention of the testator concerning the devolution of his interest in the real estate owned by him in common with his brother. The prevailing opinion delivered at the Appellate Division held the view that he made no disposition of the interest, but did direct that the real estate should remain unsold for two years or less. Mr. Justice SCOTT in a dissenting opinion expressed the view that he devised absolutely the interest to his wife.

The question certified imposes upon us the duty of declaring, through interpretation, the effect of the will in the particular it specifies. In the judicial interpretation of a will, which is given only when its language under its natural and ordinary meaning is of doubtful and uncertain effect, the intention of the testator may be sought through the entire contents of the will. If, by a careful study of the entire will, the uncertainty is not eliminated or the intention is not perceived, the relevant and competent facts and circumstances surrounding the testator at the time of the execution of the will, and the rules of judicial interpretation should be resorted to as aids in giving the instrument the meaning which it may contain. Whenever the intention is ascertained or is made satisfactorily apparent through the balance of reasons and probabilities, it becomes obligatory to determine whether it is adequately expressed by the language of the will. Courts will not construct a will in order that an inadequately expressed intention may be fulfilled, or thrust into a will a provision which is neither apparent nor necessarily to be implied. But a testamentary intention declared in a lawful manner and having a legal purpose has paramount potency and cannot be thwarted or nullified. It overrides the inadequacy or incorrectness of the language or the punctuation, or any crudity of the will. To effectuate it the courts will transpose or insert or disregard words or phrases. (*Dreyer* v. *Reisman*, 202 N.Y.

476; *DuBois* v. *Ray*, 35 N. Y. 162; *Kinkele* v. *Wilson*, 151 N. Y. 269; *O'Malley* v. *Loftus*, 220 Penn. St. 424.)

A patient consideration of the brief and imperfect will at bar brings us to the conclusions that the intention of the testator may be gathered with reasonable certainty from it, and that it adequately expresses that intention. The testator when dictating its provisions had evidently two desires, the one to preserve to his brother the hay and grain business in which they were partners and protect it and him against the immediate and injurious winding up of it; the other, to make provision for his wife through the remaining years of her life. The will in its abbreviations, omissions and characters and initial letters in the place of words is in the style and method of merchants. It is businesslike rather than lawyerlike. A communication between merchants by which the one informed the other that he had shipped, as ordered, two designated articles or shipments and omitted the conjunctive "and" between the designations, as for illustration: "We forward this day as ordered 100 doz. eggs 400 bush. potatoes," would be construed as a statement that the two articles or shipments had been forwarded. From the form of the will, it is not unnatural or unwarranted to insert, as Mr. Justice SCOTT did, the conjunction "and" so that the clause would read: "I leave to my wife the house and all furnishings at No. 326 East 43rd street for the rest of her natural life and the interest in the real estate" and plainly devise to Margaret Eidt the one-half interest in the real estate owned by the testator in common with his brother.

The determination that the interest in this real estate was devised to Margaret Eidt has further support. The will is conclusive proof that the testator had a purpose or intention concerning that interest. Under the position taken in the prevailing opinion at the Appellate Division and by the respondents that his purpose was to provide that the real estate should be held together for two years or less, the words "the interest in" are useless and unsuitable. While the will in its entirety is informal, the utility and accuracy of the words used are noteworthy and instructive. It is, moreover, an established rule that the courts should give effect to every word and provision of the will, in so far as they may without violating the intent of the testator or well-settled rules of law. The words "the real estate held by me and my brother John C. Eidt to be held together for two years or less" would have accurately expressed the conclusion of the Appellate Division. Under that conclusion the words "the interest in" make the provision incorrectly expressed. Under the conclusion that the provision is a devise of the interest to the wife, those words are precisely fitting and effective. An exposition of the intention expressed by the will, more clear than that in the will, would be: "I leave to my wife the house and all furnishings at No. 326 East 43rd Street, New York City, for the rest of her natural life. I leave to my wife the interest in the real estate held by me and my brother John C. Eidt, which real estate is to be held together for two years or less. In case of the death of my wife within the two years next after my death or prior to a settlement within that period of the said hay and grain business, I give the one-third interest of that business to Mrs. Anna Diebel."

The order of the Appellate Division should be reversed and the judgment of the Special Term affirmed, with costs in both courts to the appellant, and the question certified should be answered: Jacob Eidt, Jr., by his last will and testament dated March 23rd, 1908, devised in fee simple to his widow Margaret Eidt his one-half interest in the real estate owned by him in common with his brother John C. Eidt.

CULLEN, Ch. J., VANN, WERNER, WILLARD BARTLETT, HISCOCK and CHASE, JJ., concur.

Order reversed, etc.

S. RICHARD DAVIDGE, Respondent, *v.* GUARDIAN TRUST
COMPANY OF NEW YORK, Appellant.

**Trust companies — duties and powers — when trust company
not liable for erroneous statements of an officer thereof as to
value and validity of bonds for which it was trustee.**

1. Trust companies should be confined not only within the words,
but also within the spirit, of the statutory provision which declares
that a corporation shall not possess or exercise any corporate powers
not given by law or not necessary to the exercise of the powers so
given. Such authority does not permit a trust company to enter
into speculative and uncertain schemes, or, unless under peculiar
circumstances, become the guarantor of the indebtedness or business
of others.

2. The plaintiff, a real estate improvement company, executed to
the defendant, a domestic trust company, a mortgage covering a
tract of land to secure bonds to be issued by the improvement
company. There were five prior mortgages on the property and a
sale under prior mortgages left a deficiency. This action is brought
to recover plaintiff's loss on bonds purchased by him. Evidence
was given that a vice-president of the defendant stated, in answer
to an inquiry made by plaintiff at the time of his purchase from
a third party, that these were first mortgage bonds. It is not shown
that defendant was in any way interested in the improvement company or the bonds to secure which the trust mortgage was given,
or that it was to receive a commission or pecuniary advantage by
the sale of the bonds. *Held, first,* defendant was not required by
the trust mortgage, nor, so far as appears, was it authorized by
statute or otherwise to make representations to prospective purchasers as to the value of the bonds or to insure the title to the
mortgaged property or the relative priority of the trust mortgage
upon the improvement company's real property. *Second,* there
is no presumption of law that the vice-president of defendant had
authority to make representations on its behalf in regard to the
priority of the trust mortgage as a lien upon the property.

Davidge v. *Guardian Trust Co.*, 136 App. Div. 78, reversed.

(Argued October 20, 1911; decided November 21, 1911.)

APPEAL from a judgment of the Appellate Division of
the Supreme Court in the third judicial department,

entered January 31, 1910, modifying and affirming as modified a judgment in favor of plaintiff entered upon a verdict.

On November 24, 1905, the Metropolitan Real Estate Improvement Company, a domestic corporation, executed to the defendant, Guardian Trust Company of New York, a domestic trust company corporation, a mortgage covering a large tract of land in the city of Yonkers, to secure two thousand bonds of $500.00 each, to be issued by said improvement company. The mortgage instrument includes a form for the proposed bonds and also the covenants and agreements of the parties in detail. The material part of said bond is as follows:

" * * * This is to certify that in consideration of the sum of fifty dollars and the further payment of a like amount on each anniversary of the date hereof for nine years by   hereinafter called the owner, the Metropolitan Real Estate Improvement Company promises to pay to the owner ten years from the date hereof the sum of five hundred dollars in gold. * * * This bond is one of a series of two thousand bonds of the denomination of five hundred dollars ($500) each numbered consecutively from one to two thousand inclusive amounting in the aggregate to one million dollars, all of which are equally secured by an Indenture of Mortgage bearing date the 24th day of November, A. D. 1905, whereby certain property now owned by this Company has been mortgaged to the Guardian Trust Company of New York City as trustee, and pledged for the benefit of the holders of said bonds. For a statement of the property pledged, the nature of the security, the rights of the holders of the said bonds and conditions upon which bonds are secured and issued reference is hereby made to said Indenture of Mortgage. It is further understood that the said Trustee shall have the right to release from the lien of the said Trust Mortgage any lot or lots that may be sold by this company in the course of its business upon payment to the said Trustee of Two Thousand Dollars ($2,000) on each lot as shown on the map referred to in the said Trust Mortgage which payment shall constitute a sinking fund for the retirement of said bonds. This bond shall not be valid until the Guardian Trust Company shall endorse hereon a certificate that this bond is one of the series of bonds described in the said Indenture of Mortgage."

The form for the trustee's certificate to be executed by the defendant herein as trustee is therein set forth as follows:

"TRUSTEE'S CERTIFICATE.

"The Guardian Trust Company, as trustee, hereby certifies that the within bond is one of the series of bonds described in the trust Deed or Mortgage therein described.

"――――――, *Trustee.*"

Said mortgage contained the following provision: "Twentieth: Whereas there are now existing mortgages which are liens upon the property or a portion thereof hereinbefore described and upon which this mortgage is given and intended to become a lien before the maturity of the said existing mortgages which said mortgages are as follows: A Mortgage held by the Metropolitan Life Insurance Company for $120,000. A Mortgage held by the Valley Farms Company for $55,000. A Mortgage held by the Valley Farms Company for $8,400. Two Mortgages held by the Connecticut Building and Loan Association for $30,000 and $50,000 respectively all of which mortgages amount in the aggregate to the sum of $263,400. Whereas it is desired and intended to pay off the said mortgages and each of them out of the proceeds of the sale of the bonds herein described now Therefore it is hereby agreed by the said Company that during the third year of the life of this trust mortgage it will pay to the Guardian Trust Company as trustee the sum of $60,000 and during the fourth year of the life of this mortgage the sum of $100,000 and such further sum or sums as may be necessary to pay the principal and interest due on the said mortgage and to procure the discharge and satisfaction thereof and the said Guardian Trust Company as trustee hereby agrees to apply such payments when so made to the payment and satisfaction of the said mortgages. That it will make such application of such payments pro rata unless the order of such application shall be differently directed by said Company in which case it will make such application of such payments as directed by such Company."

There is no provision in said mortgage or bond relating to or authorizing payment for said bonds to the improvement company other than as provided in the form of bond which we have quoted.

The twenty-fourth paragraph of said mortgage is as follows: "As a condition precedent to the acceptance of the said trust by the trustee herein it is further stipulated and agreed by the parties hereto and all present and future holders of bonds secured by these presents that the trustees shall not be answerable for any act, default, neglect or misconduct of any of its agents or employees by it appointed or employed in connection with the execution of any of the said trusts nor in any other manner answerable or accountable under any circumstances whatever except for bad faith that the recitals contained herein or in the bonds as priority of lien due authorization or any other matters whatsoever are made by and on the part of the Company and the trustee assumes no responsibility for the correctness of the same also that it shall be not a part of the duty of the trustee to file or record this indenture * * * nor shall it be any part of its duty to effect insurance against fire or other damage on any portion of the mortgaged property or to renew any policies of insurance or to keep itself informed as to the payment of taxes or assessments or to require such payment to be made but the trustee may in its discretion do any or all these things. The trustee shall not be compelled to take any action as trustee under this mortgage unless properly indemnified to its full satisfaction. * * *."

Prior to December, 1906, the plaintiff had purchased of one Russell two bonds issued under said mortgage and had paid the first installment thereon. In December, 1906, said Russell solicited the plaintiff to make further purchases of said bonds and pay for them in full and hold them as "paid up bonds." The plaintiff went with said Russell to the city of New York, and on the morning of December 13th called at the office of the defendant and inquired for Mr. Robinson. The further testimony as to what occurred as given by the plaintiff, together with the objections to his answering the questions submitted to him in regard to the interview, appear in the record as follows: "Q. What, if any, conversation with reference to the bonds of the Metropolitan Real Estate Improvement Company did you have then and there with Mr. Robinson, a vice-president of the Guardian Trust Company of New York?

"Objected to on the ground it is incompetent, improper, not binding upon this defendant, hearsay as to this defendant, that it was a transaction not within the scope of the employment or course of the agency of Mr. Robinson, the vice president, and, therefore, anything that he may have said or may have done at that time is not binding upon this defendant. The Court: I will receive the evidence. Exception by defendant's counsel. Q. Give it as near as you can, word for word? A. I inquired for Mr. Robinson and he came to one of the windows; I asked him if—— I told him I came down to New York to get some information regarding those bonds; the Metropolitan Real Estate Improvement Company bonds. He asked me what I wanted to know about them. I asked him if he would tell me if they were first mortgage bonds or if there were any prior liens on the property.

He said: 'They are; they are first mortgage bonds.'
That is all the conversation I had with him.''

Following that conversation the plaintiff delivered to
Russell, who accompanied him, a draft for the amount
agreed to be paid for the bonds and the bonds were delivered to him by Russell.

There were at that time five prior mortgages on said
real property aggregating $263,400. Subsequently the
fourth and fifth of said prior liens were foreclosed and
the property sold in said foreclosure proceeding. The
property did not sell for enough to satisfy the mortgages
foreclosed and deficiency judgments were entered against
the improvement company aggregating $37,228.41, and
the company went into bankruptcy. This action is
brought to recover the plaintiff's loss from the defendant. The jury found in favor of the plaintiff, and the
judgment as modified by reducing the amount of the
recovery has been unanimously affirmed by the Appellate Division. Other facts appear in the opinion.

Henry D. Hotchkiss for appellant. It was error to
admit evidence of what Robinson told plaintiff. (Angell
& Ames on Corp. 288, 301; *Alexander* v. *Cauldwell,* 83
N. Y. 480; *Leary* v. *Albany Brewing Co.,* 77 App. Div.
6; *M. Life Ins. Co.* v. *Railroad Co.,* 139 N. Y. 151;
Nat. Bank v. *Byrnes,* 84, App. Div. 100; 178 N. Y. 561;
Gause v. *C. T. Co.,* 196 N. Y. 134; *Taylor* v. *Commercial Bank,* 174 N. Y. 181; *First Nat. Bank* v. *Tisdale,*
84 N. Y. 655; *First Nat. Bank* v. *Ocean Nat. Bank,*
60 N. Y. 278; *Ryan* v. *Bank,* 9 Daly, 308; *Tschetinian* v.
City Trust Co., 97 App. Div. 380.)

S. Mack Smith for respondent. There was no error
in the admission of the evidence of the transactions
of the defendant's vice-president. (*C. E. S. Co.* v.
A. T. Co., 161 N. Y. 605; *Strauss* v. *U. C. L. Ins. Co.,*
170 N. Y. 349; *McClure* v. *C. T. Co.,* 165 N. Y. 108;

Hadley v. *Clinton Co.*, 13 Ohio St. 507; *Nash* v. *M. T. & T. Co.*, 159 Mass. 437; *F. S. Bank* v. *Nat. Bank*, 80 N. Y. 162; *N. Y. & N. H. R. R. Co.* v. *Schuyler*, 34 N. Y. 49; *Benedict* v. *G. T. Co.*, 58 App. Div. 302; 180 N. Y. 558; *Booth* v. *C. M. Co.*, 74 N. Y. 15; *Oakes* v. *C. W. Co.*, 143 N. Y. 430.)

CHASE, J. The question for our consideration is whether the court properly admitted the testimony of the plaintiff as to the conversation with Robinson, one of the defendant's vice-presidents. In answering that question, two other questions are involved: 1. Does it appear from the facts disclosed that the defendant had power and authority to make representations in regard to the mortgage given by the improvement company and thereby become an insurer that such mortgage was a first lien on the real property described therein? 2. Does it appear from the facts disclosed that Robinson had authority to speak for the defendant and make it responsible for any damages occurring by reason of a false statement made by him in response to the plaintiff's question?

The questions involved in the admission of plaintiff's conversation with Robinson are open to review in this court, notwithstanding the judgment in favor of the plaintiff has been unanimously affirmed by the Appellate Division. They are questions of law in the consideration of which it is necessary to examine the record so far as it relates to them.

The powers of a trust company are expressly defined by statute, and such powers and also the unexpressed and incidental powers possessed by a corporation were considered by this court in *Gause* v. *Commonwealth Trust Company* (196 N. Y 134), and in that case, in speaking of the power of a trust company, the court say: "The legislature intended, and the public interests demand, that trust companies shall be confined not only within the words, but also within the spirit of the statutory pro-

vision which declares that a corporation shall not possess
or exercise any corporate powers not given by law or not
necessary to the exercise of the powers so given. Such
authority does not permit a trust company to enter into
speculative and uncertain schemes or, unless under peculiar circumstances not disclosed in this case, become the
guarantor of the indebtedness or business of others."
(p. 155.)

It is not shown that the defendant was in any way
interested in the improvement company or the bonds to
secure which the trust mortgage was given, or that it
was to receive a commission or pecuniary advantage by
the sale of the bonds. The bonds sold to the plaintiff had
previously been certified and delivered to the improvement company and at the time of the sale were apparently
owned by Russell who was, so far as appears, in no way
connected with either party to the trust mortgage except
as the owner of such bonds secured thereby.

The defendant's duties as trustee are stated in the trust
mortgage and are substantially confined to the following:

1. The authentication of the bonds by a certificate
thereon.

2. The delivery of the bonds to the treasurer of the
improvement company upon its written order.

3. The execution of releases of lots upon payment of
amounts as specified in the mortgage.

4. The registration of bonds.

5. The foreclosure of the mortgage upon default if
properly indemnified.

6. The payment of prior mortgages as provided in the
twentieth paragraph of said mortgage if money for such
payment is paid to it by the improvement company as
provided by said paragraph.

The defendant was not required by the trust mortgage,
nor, so far as appears from the facts disclosed, was it
authorized by statute or otherwise to make representations to prospective purchasers as to the value of the

bonds or to insure the title to the mortgaged property or the relative priority of the trust mortgage upon the improvement company's real property.

There is no presumption of law that Robinson, as a vice-president of the defendant, had authority to make false or other representations to the plaintiff in regard to the priority of the trust mortgage as a lien upon the improvement company's property. The record does not include the charter or by-laws of the defendant. No evidence was given of any action taken by the defendant through its board of directors relating in any way to the matters under consideration.

All that the record discloses of acts by Robinson in connection with the improvement company's transactions is the fact that he executed the trust mortgage on behalf of the defendant; a letter written by him to a third person purporting to be in behalf of the defendant, but for what purpose does not appear, in which he says: " We have accepted the trusteeship after securing the services of a competent real estate appraiser and it is his opinion that the property covered by the mortgage is ample security for the same; " the conversation with the plaintiff and a similar conversation with a third person in no way associated with the plaintiff.

It is quite unnecessary to consider the competency of the letter because the court found that the statement therein was not shown to be false and the conversation with the third person is not competent as will appear, among other reasons, from what we say regarding the conversation with the plaintiff. It is now claimed that Robinson had apparent authority to act in all matters relating to the improvement company and that authority for the defendant to make the representations to the plaintiff is found in the trust mortgage itself. We do not agree with such contention.

Purchasers of bonds are expressly referred therein to the mortgage for a statement of the property pledged, the nature of the security, the rights of the holders of said bonds and the conditions upon which the bonds are secured and issued. The reference in the bonds is to the mortgage and not to the defendant as the trustee for the mortgage bondholders. The trust mortgage was delivered to the defendant and presumably was in its possession and the plaintiff as a bondholder doubtless could have asked the defendant to show him the mortgage for the purpose of ascertaining, so far as it could be ascertained from the mortgage itself, any of the facts for a statement of which the bond referred to said mortgage.

The plaintiff did not ask the defendant to see the mortgage nor did he ask for the contents of the mortgage as such. Indeed, he testified that he did not assume that the mortgage was in the defendant's possession. The question by the plaintiff was an incidental and collateral one, entirely disconnected from any duty imposed upon the defendant as a trustee under the mortage.

It must again be borne in mind that the defendant had no interest in the bonds or in the mortgage, except as such trustee, and it was in no way the agent of the mortgagor in the sale of the bonds. The recital in the trust mortgage of the prior liens was in connection with the defendant's duty in paying the same if the money therefor was subsequently paid to it as in the trust mortgage provided. No duty was imposed upon the defendant by express terms of the mortgage in regard to the proceeds of the bonds unless such proceeds were paid to it by the improvement company. Nothing by which the defendant became liable to pay the prior liens on the property has been shown. If the plaintiff had asked at the regular place of business of the defendant whether any money had been paid to it for use in paying prior liens, or if it had been asked whether the prior liens had been paid by it pursuant to the terms of the trust mortgage, and a false statement had been made in answer to such question, by reason of which the plaintiff was injured, a very different question would have been presented. The plaintiff did not call upon the defendant to perform a duty under the trust mortgage or attempt to ascertain whether a duty imposed upon it had been performed, but he asked a question in answering which Robinson cannot, from anything that appears, be presumed to have had authority to speak for the defendant, even if the defendant had power and authority to make such representations.

The authorities relied upon by the respondent do not sustain his position. They are each based upon facts entirely different from those shown in this case. As an illustration, in *Nash* v. *Minnesota Title Insurance and Trust Company* (159 Mass. 437), a case much relied upon by him, the representations upon which the action is brought were made in the name of the defendant by an officer fully authorized to act for it, and his authority to speak of the title in question is convincingly shown by the following quotation from the opinion: " It (the trust company) was in the business of insuring titles to real estate, and was paid for issuing policies of insurance on this title; making representations in regard to the title was so far incident to the principal undertaking for which it was paid, that it might properly make such representations to those who were about to take bonds."

The judgment should be reversed and a new trial granted, with costs to abide the event.

CULLEN, Ch. J., GRAY, WERNER, HISCOCK and COLLIN, JJ., concur; WILLARD BARTLETT, J., dissents.

Judgment reversed, etc.

MARY A. FINNEGAN, Individually and as Administratrix
of the Estate of SAMUEL L. McGUFFOG, Deceased, and
as Administratrix of the Estate of JOHN McGUFFOG,
Deceased, et al., Appellants, *v.* JESSIE McGUFFOG,
Respondent.

**Equity — action 'to impress a trust — construction of voluntary
trust of leasehold interest in real property for benefit of children
of a deceased brother of trustee — Statute of Limitations.**

Defendant's husband held a leasehold interest with right of renewal
for two terms. He filed an instrument in the office of the register of
the county of New York declaring a trust under which the children
of his deceased brother became entitled to the transfer of his interest therein on the youngest survivor attaining the age of twenty-
one years on compliance with certain conditions therein contained.
Neither plaintiff, who represents the interest of such children, nor
the defendant had actual notice of the existence of the paper.
Defendant after the death of her husband took renewal leases of the
property. *Held, first*, that in the absence of any fraudulent concealment the trust terminated and the Statute of Limitations began
to run when the youngest child arrived at the age of twenty-one.
Second, that when defendant took the lease in her own name and
entered into possession of the premises she held the same in her
own right and the statute began to run from that date.

Finnegan v. *McGuffog*, 139 App. Div. 899, affirmed.

(Submitted November 3, 1911; decided November 21, 1911.)

APPEAL from a judgment of the Appellate Division of
the Supreme Court in the first judicial department, entered
June 10, 1910, affirming a judgment in favor of defendant entered upon a dismissal of the complaint by the
court on trial at Special Term.

The nature of the action and the facts, so far as material, are stated in the opinion.

Henry C. Henderson for appellants. The defendant is
estopped. (*Colden* v. *Cornell*, 3 Johns. Cas. 174; *Jackson* v. *Ireland*, 3 Wend. 99; *Jackson* v. *Thompson*, 6
Cow. 178; *St. Clair* v. *Jackson*, 8 Cow. 543; *Carves* v.
Jackson, 4 Pet. 1; *Cranes* v. *Morris*, 6 Pet. 611; *A. D.*

D. Co. v. *Leavitt*, 54 N. Y. 35; *Mitchell* v. *Reed*, 61 N. Y. 123.) The defendant herein could acquire no right to the lease or to the leased premises superior to that held by James McGuffog, nor escape the obligations of the declaration of trust. (*Swinburne* v. *Swinburne*, 28 N. Y. 568; *Trustees of Union College* v. *Wheeler*, 61 N. Y. 88; *Bush* v. *Lathrop*, 22 N. Y. 535; *Central Trust Co.* v. *W. W. I. Imp. Co.*, 169 N. Y. 314; Hill on Trustees, §§ 162, 163; Story's Eq. Juris. § 1257.) The defendant herein cannot seek refuge in the claim that she is a trustee *ex maleficio*, or trustee of a constructive trust. (*Lannier* v. *Stoddard*, 103 N. Y. 672; *Thorn* v. *de Breteuil*, 86 App. Div. 405; 179 N. Y. 64; *Anderson* v. *Fry*, 116 App. Div. 740; 194 N. Y. 515; *Lightfoot* v. *Davis*, 198 N. Y. 261.)

John M. Stoddard and *Henry B. Hathaway* for respondent. The recitals in leases made by Hamilton Fish to the respondent create no estoppel in favor of the appellants. (*Clark* v. *Post*, 113 N. Y. 17; *C. & S. L. R. R. Co.* v. *Valentine*, 19 Barb. 484; *Reed* v. *McCourt*, 41 N. Y. 435; *Jewell* v. *Harrington*, 19 Wend. 471; *Dempsey* v. *Tylee*, 3 Duer, 73; *Pope* v. *O'Hara*, 48 N. Y. 446; *Walrath* v. *Redfield*, 18 N. Y. 457; *Bell* v. *City of New York*, 77 App. Div. 437; Herman on Estoppel, §§ 210, 213; *Torrey* v. *Bank of Orleans*, 9 Paige, 650; *Carpenter* v. *Butler*, 8 M. & W. 209; *Bank of America* v. *Banks*, 101 U. S. 240.) Even were it conceded that the respondent became a trustee of an express trust, created by the declaration of trust, the cause of action would have long since outlawed. (*Gilmore* v. *Ham*, 142 N. Y. 1; *Higgins* v. *Crouse*, 147 N. Y. 411; *Carr* v. *Thompson*, 87 N. Y. 160; *Price* v. *Mulford*, 107 N. Y. 303; *Chorrmann* v. *Bachmann*, 119 App. Div. 146; *Mills* v. *Mills*, 115 N. Y. 80; *Yeoman* v. *Townshend*, 26 N. Y. Supp. 606; *Bruce* v. *Tillson*, 25 N. Y. 194; *Lammar* v. *Stoddard*, 103 N. Y. 672; *McCotter* v. *Lawrence*, 4 Hun, 110.) At most, the respondent could have been charged as a trustee by implication. (*Lammar* v.: *Stoddard,* 103 N. Y. 672; *Matter of Neilly,* 95 N. Y. 382; *Price* v. *Mulford,* 107 N. Y. 303; *Pierson* v. *McCurdy,* 33 Hun, 531; *Wood* v. *Supervisors,* 50 Hun, 1.) The ten-year Statute of Limitations applies to this case. (*Yeoman* v. *Townshend,* 26 N. Y. Supp. 606; *Lammar* v. *Stoddard,* 103 N. Y. 672; *McCotter* v. *Lawrence,* 4 Hun, 110; *Bruce* v. *Tillson,* 25 N. Y. 194; *Treadwell* v. *Clark,* 190 N. Y. 51; *Miner* v. *Beekman,* 50 N. Y. 337.)

HAIGHT, J. This action was brought by the next of kin and personal representatives of the next of kin, deceased, of John McGuffog, deceased, to impress a trust upon the lease of a parcel of land situate in the city of New York, fronting on Tenth street, two hundred and twenty feet northwesterly from Third avenue, being thirty-eight feet frontage on the avenue and from twenty to thirty feet in depth, and for an accounting of the rents, issues and profits, etc.

The facts as they appear from the findings, so far as material, are substantially as follows: On the 24th day of October, 1843, Peter Gerard Stuyvesant, being the owner of the premises above described, executed a written lease thereof to Tarrant Putnam for a period of twenty-one years, beginning November 1st, 1843, which contained a covenant to the effect that the lessee should construct a dwelling house thereon, of the size and character described in the lease, and that the landlord, upon compliance therewith by the tenant, would execute three renewal leases for a similar period, upon the terms therein specified. The tenant, having entered into possession of the premises under the lease, erected the building upon the premises, and subsequently the lease through several mesne conveyances became the property of John McGuffog and was so owned by him at the time of his death, intestate, on November 28th, 1860. He left him surviving his widow, Jeannette (since deceased), and three children, Ella, Samuel and Mary Ann, aged ten, eight and

five years, respectively, his only children, next of kin and
heirs at law. His son Samuel died intestate, unmarried
and without issue, on January 30th, 1882, leaving his two
sisters as his only next of kin and heirs at law. The
daughter Ella married James Jardine and died on September 24th, 1886, intestate, and letters of administration
were issued to her husband, who is one of the plaintiffs in
this action. The other daughter, Mary Ann, who is the
other plaintiff in this action, married one Finnegan.

On the 9th day of September, 1862, a warrant to dispossess in summary proceedings was issued by Thomas
Stuart, justice of the first judicial district of the city of
New York, against those in possession of the premises
under the lease for the non-payment of rent, in which the
possession of the premises was awarded to Hamilton Fish,
the then owner of the fee of the premises in question.
Thereafter and on the 1st day of May, 1863, Hamilton
Fish leased the premises to one James McGuffog, a
brother of John McGuffog, for a term of twenty-one
years from the 1st day of November, 1863, which contained provisions for two renewals of twenty-one years
each; and on the 8th day of May thereafter James
McGuffog executed the following written instrument,
which was duly recorded in the office of the register of
the county of New York on May 15th, 1863, in liber 875
of Conveyances, at page 559:

"WHEREAS, John McGuffog, late of the City of New
York, died intestate about the   day of November,
A. D. 1860, leaving him surviving Jeannette McGuffog,
his widow, and children, to wit: Ella McGuffog, aged
about 13 years, Samuel L. McGuffog, aged about 10
years, and Mary Ann McGuffog, aged about 8 years, and
no guardian having been appointed or provision made
for the support of the said children; and the said John
McGuffog having at the time of his decease the unexpired term of a lease for the premises No. 154 East Tenth
street, in the City of New York, with a house and shop

erected thereon, with buildings belonging to the said John McGuffog, which said premises are heavily encumbered with taxes and other charges, and a warrant to dispossess the tenant of said premises for non-payment of rent having been duly issued on the 9th day of September, 1862, whereby possession of the same was restored to the landlord and the said lease cancelled; and the said widow having agreed to lease her right and interest in said premises upon the condition hereinafter named, which agreement has been executed by her and bears date the 23rd day of March, 1863; and

"WHEREAS, the owner of said lot of land is about to give a lease of said premises for a term of years to run upon payment of certain taxes, rents and expenses amounting to the sum of $902.05, or thereabouts, and

"WHEREAS, certain repairs are needed on said building which I propose to make;

"*Now, Therefore,* I, James McGuffog, of the City of New York, do hereby declare that I take and hold said premises for the benefit of the said children of said John McGuffog and in part for the support and maintenance and education of said children after I am first reimbursed for the sums and expenses by me incurred and paid out in payment of the said encumbrances and charges upon said property and such taxes and other expenses or charges as may accrue in holding the said premises and keeping the same in repair and until the youngest survivor of said children shall attain the age of twenty-one years, when and in that event I am to transfer and set over all my right, title and interest in the said lease to the said children above named or the survivor of them after being first reimbursed as aforesaid and the allowance to me of a reasonable sum for such maintenance and education of said children.

"*In Witness Whereof,* I have hereunto set my hand and seal May 8th, 1863.

"JAMES McGUFFOG."

Thereupon the three children of John McGuffog, deceased, were taken into the family of James McGuffog and supported and maintained by him, the son until his death, and the daughters until their marriage, each of whom, after they had arrived at sufficient age, contributed towards their respective support a portion of their earnings.

James McGuffog died intestate on the 24th day of November, 1868, leaving the defendant, Jessie, his widow, him surviving and several children. No letters of administration were ever issued upon his estate, and thereupon his widow continued to occupy the leasehold premises and to support the children of John McGuffog until their death or marriage. The youngest child of John McGuffog attained the age of twenty-one years in 1876, and thereupon, under the declaration of trust executed by James McGuffog, the children became entitled to the possession of the leasehold property upon the payment of the amounts specified in that instrument. But neither the children nor the defendant in this action had ever heard of the declaration of trust and had no knowledge of its existence prior to February, 1906. Upon the expiration of the first lease the defendant, the widow of James McGuffog, applied for a renewal, to her individually, and the same was granted by the then owner on the 28th day of October, 1884, for a further term of twenty-one years, from November 1st, 1884. Thereupon she erected upon the premises a three-story brick building in place of a one-story shop and continued to occupy the same throughout the entire period of the lease, and on October 7th, 1905, she obtained another renewal lease for twenty-one years, from the 1st day of November, 1905. This action was commenced in September, 1907, after the discovery of the existence of the declaration of trust, as before stated. The answer interposed as a bar both the ten-year and the twenty-year Statute of Limitations.

While the declaration of trust was recorded in the

office of the register of the county, and the parties interested are chargeable with constructive notice of its existence, still it satisfactorily appears from the evidence and is found as a fact by the trial court that neither the plaintiffs nor the defendant had actual notice of its existence. There is, therefore, no claim that the defendant was guilty of hiding or secreting the instrument or practicing any fraud in reference thereto, and consequently the provisions of section 382, subdivision 5, of the Code of Civil Procedure, which in substance provide that the cause of action is not deemed to have accrued until the discovery of the facts constituting the fraud, has no application to the claim made by the plaintiffs in this case. It would seem to follow that inasmuch as the defendant did not know of the existence of the trust, she never voluntarily assumed to act as trustee of an express trust. But by reason of the fact that she remained in possession of the premises under the lease to her husband after his decease, she, by construction of law, would be required to account as a trustee of a constructive trust and turn over the premises to the *cestui que trust* upon the termination of the trust estate. This, as we have seen, occurred upon the arrival of the *youngest child at the age of twenty-one years, which occurred in 1876. Thereupon the trust terminated, and the children, upon complying with the conditions imposed by the declaration of trust, would become entitled to the possession of the leasehold estate, and the Statute of Limitations commenced to run from that date. There is still another theory of this case, independent of the provisions terminating the trust in 1876. After the death of her husband and the expiration of the term for which he had leased the premises, she applied to the landlord and obtained a lease in her own name, individually, and thereafter entered into the possession of the premises and held the same in her own right and not on behalf of her husband or those claiming under or through him. This we think would also set the Statute of Limitations running. The right of the plaintiffs to recover possession being dependent upon the conditions embraced in the declaration of trust which involves an accounting by a court of equity, the ten-year Statute of Limitations applies, and it consequently follows that the statute becomes a bar to the prosecution of this case. (*Lammer* v. *Stoddard*, 103 N. Y. 672.)

It is now contended that the defendant is estopped from asserting that she is not a trustee of an express trust, the contention being that by taking the lease in her own name in 1884, containing the recital, "whereas, the party hereto of the second part claims to be the lawful owner and holder of said last mentioned lease, and that the terms and conditions thereof have been complied with, whereby she, the party of the second part, claims and represents herself to be entitled to a renewal of said lease for such further term of twenty-one years," etc., coupled with the renewal of that lease at the expiration of its term in 1905, which contained the recital of the granting of the lease to the defendant in 1884, in which the defendant "represented herself to be the assignee of the term and interest therein of the said James McGuffog, and to be entitled to a renewal of said last mentioned lease," has placed herself in the shoes of her husband, so to speak, and, as assignee, is bound to carry out all of his obligations as a trustee of an express trust. In the first place, it appearing that the defendant knew nothing of the existence of the trust on the part of the husband, she could not well have intended to make herself a trustee in his place and stead. He died intestate, leaving children who were his next of kin and heirs at law. The term for which he had leased the premises had expired and the trust had terminated eight years before. The defendant applied for a new lease, representing herself to be the owner; in other words, that she had purchased the interest of the children, the next of kin and heirs at law. Under such circumstances, she takes the new lease in her own name and right and in hostility to all outstanding claims unknown to her. It consequently follows that the recitals mentioned do not constitute an estoppel.

In the second place, even if the recitals were sufficient to constitute an estoppel, the plaintiffs are not in a position to avail themselves of it.' Hamilton Fish was the owner. He executed the first lease to her. Hamilton Fish Corporation, being the owner, executed the last lease. Hamilton Fish and Hamilton Fish Corporation, as owners and lessors, are not shown to have any relation with John McGuffog or his children, the plaintiffs in this action. The John McGuffog lease was terminated by the warrant dispossessing the tenants for the non-payment of rent, · and the premises thereafter were rented to another person, James McGuffog. It does not appear that Hamilton Fish or Hamilton Fish Corporation ever knew or heard of the declaration of trust that was subsequently made by James McGuffog. The plaintiffs, therefore, do not claim from, through or under Hamilton Fish or the Hamilton Fish Corporation. Their sole claim is through the declaration of trust of James McGuffog and not through the defendant. It consequently follows that they, being strangers to the lessors, are not in a position to claim any benefit for estoppel by reason of recitals appearing in the lease. As we understand the rule, estoppel, as applied to recitals in a deed, is not for the benefit of third parties who were not bound by the recitals, nor can they invoke estoppel by reason of the recitals. If there be an estoppel by reason of a recital it extends only to the parties to the instrument and their privies.

In *Torrey* v. *Bank of Orleans* (9 Paige Ch. 649, 659) Chancellor WALWORTH states the rule as follows: "A recital of a fact in a deed is, as against the grantee in such deed and all persons claiming under him through that deed, evidence of the fact recited therein; so as to save the necessity of further proof thereof by the grantor or those who claim under him. The acceptance of the deed operates as an estoppel upon the grantee and those who claim under him as against the grantor and his assigns or representatives."

In the case of *Jewell* v. *Harrington* (19 Wend. 471, 472) NELSON, Ch. J., says: "The first rule laid down by Lord Coke in respect to estoppels is, that they must be reciprocal: that is, bind both parties; and this is the reason, he observes, that regularly, a stranger shall neither take advantage of nor be bound by an estoppel."

In *Walrath* v. *Redfield* (18 N. Y. 457, 460) SELDEN, J., says: "Estoppels must be mutual; and none can avail themselves of them except parties or privies." (See, also, Herman on Estoppel, sections 210, 213, and *Pope* v. *O'Hara*, 48 N. Y. 446-454.)

The judgment should be affirmed, with costs.

CULLEN, Ch. J., GRAY, VANN, WILLARD BARTLETT, HISCOCK and COLLIN, JJ., concur.

Judgment affirmed.

ADA S. AARON, Respondent, *v.* WILLIAM J. WARD, Appellant.

Contract — action for breach of contract — expulsion from bathhouse of person holding ticket entitling her to admission — price of ticket not measure of damages.

The plaintiff purchased a ticket and took her position in a line of the defendant's patrons leading to a window at which the ticket entitled her to receive, upon its surrender, a key admitting her to a bathhouse. When she approached the window a dispute arose between her and the defendant's employees as to the right of another person not in the line to have a key given to him in advance of the plaintiff. As a result of this dispute plaintiff was ejected from the defendant's premises, the agents of the latter refusing to furnish her with the accommodations for which she had contracted. The plaintiff was awarded substantial damages, defendant contending that she was not entitled to any recovery in excess of the sum paid for the ticket. *Held,* that the jury had a right to award damages for the indignity thus inflicted upon her.

Aaron v. *Ward,* 136 App. Div. 818, affirmed.

(Submitted October 18, 1911; decided November 21, 1911.)

APPEAL, by permission, from a judgment of the Appellate Division of the Supreme Court in the second judicial department, entered March 21, 1910, affirming a judgment of the Municipal Court of the city of New York in favor of plaintiff.

The nature of the action and the facts, so far as material, are stated in the opinion.

Alexander Van Wagoner for appellant. In all cases of breach of contract (breach of promise of marriage excepted) the plaintiff's loss is measured by the benefit to him of having the contract performed, and this is, therefore, the true measure of damages. (*Clark* v. *N. Y., N. H. & H. R. R. Co.,* 40 Misc. Rep. 691; *Jacobs* v. *Sire,* 4 Misc. Rep. 398; *Miller* v. *B. & O. R. R. Co.,* 89 App. Div. 457; *Miller* v. *King,* 166 N. Y. 394; *Aplington* v. *Pullman Co.,* 110 App. Div. 250; *People ex rel. Burnham* v. *Flynn,* 189 N. Y. 180; *Benyakar* v. *Scherz,* 103 App. Div. 192; *Todd* v. *Gamble,* 148 N. Y. 382; *Thorn* v. *Knapp,* 42 N. Y. 474; Sedg. on Dam. [8th ed.] §§ 45, 601, 603, 609.) The cases where actions *ex contractu* have been brought against carriers and transportation companies wherein damages have been allowed for humiliation, indignities and mental suffering or anguish are highly exceptional in their character, and arise altogether out of the peculiar nature and character of the particular contract under consideration. (*Gillespie* v. *B. H. R. R. Co.,* 178 N. Y. 347; *Busch* v. *I. R. T. Co.,* 187 N. Y. 388; *Conlon* v. *Met. St. R. R. Co.,* 34 Misc. Rep. 394; *Thomas* v. *Met. St. R. R. Co.,* 44 App. Div. 634; *Burfiendt* v. *N. Y. C. R. R. Co.,* 52 Misc. Rep. 651;

De Wolf v. *Ford,* 193 N. Y. 397.) The business conducted by the defendant was purely private in its nature, and the ticket of admission by the plaintiff was entirely revocable at the pleasure of the defendant, and the latter could, if necessary, expel the plaintiff from the premises with all reasonable force. (*Collister* v. *Hayman,* 183 N. Y. 250; *People ex rel. Burnham* v. *Flynn,* 189 N. Y. 180; *McCrea* v. *Marsh,* 12 Gray, 211; *Burton* v. *Scherpf,* 1 Allen, 133; *Wood* v. *Leadbitter,* 13 M. & W. 838; *Drew* v. *Peer,* 93 Penn. St. 234; *Smith* v. *Leo,* 92 Hun, 242; *Rhodes* v. *S. & H. Co.,* 120 App. Div. 467; *Preiser* v. *Wielandt,* 48 App. Div. 569.)

Joseph Goldstein for respondent. The trial court having found for the plaintiff it had a right to award the plaintiff compensatory damages and was not limited to the actual loss of money sustained which in this case was twenty-five cents, the price of the ticket. (*Smith* v. *Leo,* 92 Hun, 242; *Busch* v. *Interborough R. T. Co.,* 187 N. Y. 388; *De Wolf* v. *Ford,* 193 N. Y. 397; *Gillespie* v. *Brooklyn Heights R. R. Co.,* 178 N. Y. 347; 1 Sedg. on Dam. [8th ed.] 67.) The case at bar is analogous to that of a passenger for wrongful treatment by a common carrier and to that of a guest for injuries to feelings by an innkeeper. (*Busch* v. *Interborough R. T. Co.,* 187 N. Y. 388; *De Wolf* v. *Ford,* 193 N. Y. 397.) The claim that the business of keeping bathing houses for hire is not of the same public nature as that of a common carrier or an innkeeper and may be said to be a private enterprise may be sound without, however, affecting the rule as to the measure of damages. (*People ex rel. Burnham* v. *Flynn,* 189 N. Y. 180; *Burton* v. *Scherpf,* 83 Mass. 133; *Collister* v. *Hayman,* 183 N. Y. 250; *Purcell* v. *Daly,* 19 Abb. [N. C.] 301.)

CULLEN, Ch. J. The defendant was the proprietor of a bathing establishment on the beach at Coney Island. The plaintiff, intending to take a bath in the surf, purchased a ticket from the defendant's employees for the sum of twenty-five cents, and took her position in a line of the defendant's patrons leading to a window at which the ticket entitled her to receive, upon its surrender, a key admitting her to a bathhouse. When she approached the window a dispute arose between her and the defendant's employees as to the right of another person not in the line to have a key given to him in advance of the plaintiff. As a result of this dispute plaintiff was ejected from the defendant's premises, the agents of the latter refusing to furnish her with the accommodations for which she had contracted. It is not necessary to discuss the merits of the dispute or narrate its details as the questions of fact involved in that matter have been decided in plaintiff's favor by the Municipal Court, in which she subsequently brought suit, and that judgment has been unanimously affirmed by the Appellate Division. The plaintiff was awarded $250 damages against the defendant's contention that she was not entitled to any recovery in excess of the sum paid for the ticket, and the correctness of the defendant's contention is the only question presented on this appeal.

The action is for a breach of the defendant's contract and not for a tortious expulsion. It is so denominated in the complaint and was necessarily so brought as the Municipal Court has no jurisdiction over an action for an assault. It is contended for the defendant that as the action was on contract, the plaintiff was not entitled to any damages for the indignty of her expulsion from the defendant's establishment. It may be admitted that, as a general rule, mental suffering resulting from a breach of contract is not a subject of compensation, but the rule is not universal. It is the settled law of this state that a passenger may recover damages for insulting and slanderous words uttered by the conductor of a railway car as a breach of the company's contract of carriage.

(*Gillespie* v. *Brooklyn Heights R. R. Co.*, 178 N. Y. 347.)
The same rule obtains where the servant of an innkeeper
offers insult to his guest. (*de Wolf* v. *Ford*, 193 N. Y.
397.) And it must be borne in mind that a recovery for
indignity and wounded feelings is compensatory and does
not constitute exemplary damages. (*Hamilton* v. *Third
Ave. R. R. Co.*, 53 N. Y. 25.)

It is insisted, however, that there is a distinction
between common carriers and innkeepers, who are obliged
to serve all persons who seek accommodation from
them, and the keepers of public places of amusement or
resort, such as the bathhouse of the defendant, theaters
and the like. That the distinction exists is undeniable, and
in the absence of legislation the keeper of such an establishment may discriminate and serve whom he pleases.
Therefore, in such a case a refusal would give no cause
of action. So, also, it is the general rule of law that a
ticket for admission to a place of public amusement is
but a license and revocable. It was so said by this court
in *People ex rel. Burnham* v. *Flynn* (189 N. Y. 180).
(See, also, *Burton* v. *Scherpf*, 1 Allen, 133; *McCrea* v.
Marsh, 12 Gray, 211; *Horney* v. *Nixon*, 213 Penn. St. 20;
Purcell v. *Daly*, 19 Abb. [N. C.] 301, and *MacGowan*
v. *Duff*, 14 Daly, 315.) But granting both propositions,
that the defendant might have refused the plaintiff a
bath ticket and access to his premises, and that even
after selling her a ticket he might have revoked the
license to use the premises for the purpose of bathing,
which the ticket imported, neither proposition necessarily
determines that the plaintiff was not entitled to recover
damages for the indignity inflicted upon her by the
revocation. We have seen that in the case of a common
carrier or innkeeper, a person aggrieved may recover such
damages as for a breach of contract, while on the other
hand, on the breach of ordinary contracts, a party would
not be so entitled, and the question is, to which class of
cases the case before us most closely approximates. In sev-

eral of the reported cases the keeping of a theater is spoken of as a strictly private undertaking, and it is said that the owner of a theater is under no obligation to give entertainments at all. The latter proposition is true, but the business of maintaining a theater cannot be said to be "strictly" private. In *People* v. *King* (110 N. Y. 418) the question was as to the constitutionality of the Civil Rights Act of this state which made it a misdemeanor to deny equal enjoyment of any accommodation, facilities and privileges of inns, common carriers, theaters or other places of public resort or amusement regardless of race, creed or color, and gave the party aggrieved the right to recover a penalty of from fifty to five hundred dollars for the offense. The statute was upheld on the ground that under the doctrine of *Munn* v. *Illinois* (94 U. S. 113) theaters and places of public amusement (the case before the court was that of a skating rink) were affected with a public interest which justified legislative regulation and interference. (See, also, *Baylies* v. *Curry*, 128 Ill. 287, and *Ferguson* v. *Gies*, 82 Mich. 358.) In *Greenberg* v. *Western Turf Assn.* (140 Cal. 357) a statute making it unlawful to refuse to any person admission to a place of public amusement and giving the person aggrieved the right to recover his damages and a hundred dollar penalty in addition thereto, was upheld on the authority of the cases we have cited — a decision plainly correct, because if the legislature can forbid discrimination by the owners of such resorts on the ground of race, creed or color, it may equally forbid discrimination on any other ground. Our statute has since been amended so as to expressly include keepers of bathhouses. On the other hand, no one will contend that the legislature could forbid discrimination in the private business affairs of life — prevent an employer from refusing to employ colored servants, or a servant from refusing to work for a white or for a colored master. So, it has been held that a bootblack may refuse to black a colored man's shoes without being liable to the penalty prescribed by our statute. (*Burks* v. *Bosso,* 180 N. Y. 341.) Such conduct may be the result of prejudice entirely, but a man's prejudices may be part of his most cherished possessions, which cannot be invaded except when displayed in the conduct of public affairs or quasi public enterprises. That public amusements and resorts are subject to the exercise of this legislative control shows that they are not entirely private. Therefore, though under the present law the plaintiff might have been denied admission altogether to the defendant's bathhouse, provided she were not excluded on account of race, creed or color (*Grannan* v. *Westchester Racing Assn.,* 153 N. Y. 449), the defendant having voluntarily entered into a contract with her admitting her to the premises and agreeing to afford facilities for bathing, her status became similar to that of a passenger of a common carrier or a guest of an innkeeper, and in case of her improper expulsion she should be entitled to the same measure of damages as obtains in actions against carriers or innkeepers when brought for breach of their contracts. The reason why such damages are recoverable in the cases mentioned is not merely because the defendants are bound to give the plaintiffs accommodation, but also because of the indignity suffered by a public expulsion. In a theater or other place of public amusement or resort the indignity and humiliation caused by an expulsion in the presence of a large number of people is as great, if not greater, than in the case of an expulsion by a carrier or innkeeper, as it is the publicity of the thing that causes the humiliation.

Nor can I find that the decision we are making is in conflict with the authorities in this country. We have not been referred to any decision that holds in the case of a wrongful expulsion from a place of public amusement the aggrieved party is not entitled to compensation for humiliation and indignity. In the two Massachusetts cases cited the actions were for assault, which of course could not be sustained if the license were revocable. Indeed the later case (*McCrea* v. *Marsh*) seems to limit the time for the exercise of the right of expulsion. They did not deal with the rule of damages. The same is true of *Horney* v. *Nixon* (*supra*). It dealt simply with the form of the action, which was trespass, and in the opinion it is said that the action should have been brought in assumpsit. In *MacGowan* v. *Duff* (*supra*) by mistake the plaintiff had been sold tickets for the wrong evening and was compelled to surrender the seats he occupied. It was held that the case did not justify an award of exemplary damages, and the learned court expressed a doubt as to the English doctrine declared in *Wood* v. *Leadbitter* (13 Mee. & W. 838) that on a revocation of the license the plaintiff could only recover the amount paid. On the other hand, in *Macgoverning* v. *Staples* (7 Lans. 145) the right to revoke a license and expel from the grounds of an agricultural fair was denied. *Smith* v. *Leo* (92 Hun, 242) is the only authority to which we have been referred on the precise question before us. There the plaintiff having bought an admission to the defendant's dancing school, was admitted thereto but subsequently expelled. It was held that he was entitled to compensation for the indignity and disgrace of his expulsion.

The judgment of the Appellate Division should be affirmed, with costs.

GRAY, WERNER, WILLARD BARTLETT, HISCOCK, CHASE and COLLIN, JJ., concur.

Judgment affirmed.

LESLIE G. LOOMIS et al., as Copartners under the Firm
Name of L. G. LOOMIS & SON, Respondents, *v.* NEW
YORK CENTRAL AND HUDSON RIVER RAILROAD COM-
PANY, Appellant.

**Carriers — evidence — contract to transport goods signed by
carrier and shipper, but silent as to route, cannot be varied by
evidence of previous parol instructions to ship by a particular
route.**

1. A written contract to transport goods from one place to
another, duly signed by both carrier and shipper, but silent as to
the route, cannot be varied by evidence of previous parol instructions to ship by a particular route. No effect can be given to such
evidence, even when received without objection, provided the court
is asked in due form to instruct the jury that it was merged in the
written agreement if they found there was one.

2. Certain blank spaces in the printed form of a railroad shipping order were left unfilled, such as "Route ......, Charges
advanced $ ...." Such a writing when signed by both parties,
is a contract complete upon its face; the unfilled blanks, although
material, were not necessary to make the contract complete upon
its face and the blanks cannot be filled by parol evidence and effect
given thereto in an action at law.

Loomis v. *N. Y. C. & H. R. R. R. Co.*, 136 App. Div. 913, reversed.

(Argued October 23, 1911; decided November 21, 1911.)

APPEAL from a judgment of the Appellate Division of
the Supreme Court in the fourth judicial department,
entered January 21, 1910, affirming a judgment in favor
of plaintiffs entered upon a verdict.

The nature of the action and the facts, so far as material, are stated in the opinion.

W. Frederick Strang and *Edward Harris, Jr.*, for
appellant. The refusal of the court to instruct the jury
that all directions to ship this car over the Lehigh Valley
railroad were merged in the written contract was most
prejudicial to the defendant, and was contrary to the

established law of this state. (4 Am. & Eng. Ency. of
Law [2d ed.], 515, 516; *Thomas* v. *Scutt*, 127 N. Y. 133;
White v. *Ashton*, 51 N. Y. 280; *Huntington* v. *Dinsmore*, 4 Hun, 66; *Long* v. *N. Y. C. & H. R. R. R. Co.*,
50 N. Y. 76; 4 Elliott on Railroads, § 1423; 4 Wigmore
on Evidence, 3408, § 2425; *Snow* v. *Railroad*, 109 Ind. 422;
Bessling & Co. v. *Railroad*, 80 S. W. Rep. 639; *Bishop*
v. *Empire Co.*, 48 How. Pr. 119; *Renard & Bros.* v.
Sampson, 12 N. Y. 561.)

Edward P. White for respondents. There was no
error in the refusal of the trial court to charge as
requested. (*Meyer* v. *Peck*, 28 N. Y. 590; *Ellis* v. *Willard*, 9 N. Y. 529; *Abbe* v. *Eaton*, 51 N. Y. 410; *Komp*
v. *Raymond*, 175 N. Y. 102; *Smith* v. *Dotterweich*, 200
N. Y. 299; *Tilden* v. *Tilden*, 8 App. Div. 99.)

VANN, J.   The plaintiffs are dealers in produce residing
at Victor, but buying and shipping from Lakeside, New
York, where they are represented by the firm of Furber,
Connell & Norton. D. P. Reynolds & Co. are produce
dealers in Jersey City, New Jersey, where their place of
business is in the freight yard of the Lehigh Valley railroad at Grand street. They sell and deliver produce
from the railroad cars as they stand in the yard at that
point.

Early in June, 1907, D. P. Reynolds & Co. ordered a
carload of potatoes from the plaintiffs at 85 cents per
bushel, delivered, payable on presentation of a sight
draft with bill of lading attached. When this order was
received the plaintiffs had a car partly loaded with potatoes at Lakeside, and Mr. Furber, their representative,
testified that he delivered to the defendant's freight
agent at that place a paper on which was written in
lead pencil the following: "L. G. Loomis & Son, Grand
St., Jersey City, N. J., by L. V. rate 15 c." As Mr.
Furber handed this paper to the freight agent he said:
"Here is the instructions for this car of potatoes."

This was denied by Mr. FitzGerald, the agent of the defendant. The freight agent, however, made out and delivered to Furber a bill of lading in the following form: "New York Central & Hudson River Railroad Company. Received subject to the classification in effect on the date of issue of this bill of lading, at Lakeside Station, 6/12, 1907, from L. G. Loomis & Son, the property described below, in apparent good order, except as noted (contents and condition of contents of packages unknown), marked, consigned and destined as indicated below, which said company agrees to carry to said destination, if on its road, otherwise to deliver to another carrier on the route to said destination. It is mutually agreed in consideration of the rate of freight hereinafter named as to each carrier of all or any of said property over all or any portion of said route to destination and as to each party at any time interested in all or any of said property, that every service to be performed hereunder shall be subject to all the conditions, whether printed or written, herein contained (see conditions on back hereof), and which are agreed to by the shipper and accepted for himself and his assigns as just and reasonable. Marks; consignee, L. G. Loomis & Son; destination, Grand St., Jersey City, N. J.; Route...... Charges advanced $...... Description of articles, C. bulk potatoes S. L. & T. O. K. R E L. Weight subject to correction 24000; 5858, Car No. P M; S E P 12/07. (signed) D. H. FitzGerald Agent." Beneath this signature of the freight agent was the following: "The rate of freight from...... to ...... is in cents per hundred pounds * * * fifth class 15 (signed) D. H. FitzGerald, agent." The various conditions printed on the back are not now material.

At the same time the freight agent made out what is called a shipping order, the material part of which is as follows: "New York Central & Hudson River Railroad Company, Lakeside Station, L. G. Loomis & Son, 6/12 1907. Receive, carry and deliver the articles described

below, in accordance with the classification in effect at the
date of this order and subject to the conditions of the bill
of lading of which this shipping order is a part * * *
Marks, Consignee L. G. Loomis & Son, destination
Grand St., Jersey City, N. J., route ......; charges
advanced $......; prepay $......; description of articles,
C bulk potatoes S L & T O. K. Rel Weight subject to
correction, 24000; 5858 Car No. P M Sep. 12,'07. (L.
G. Loomis & Son, shipper)." On the back of this shipping order, the same conditions were printed as on the
back of the bill of lading. The shipping order, as read in
evidence, purports to have been signed, "L. G. Loomis
& Son, shipper," and the freight agent testified that Mr.
Furber thus signed it in his presence, but Mr. Furber
denied it. The alleged order was retained by the defendant's agent, but the bill of lading was delivered to the
agent of the plaintiffs who mailed it to them at Victor.
They wrote on the face thereof the following: " Deliver to
the order of D. P. Reynolds & Co. L. G. Loomis & Son."
The plaintiffs mailed an invoice to D. P. Reynolds & Co.,
attached a sight draft on that firm to the bill of lading
and mailed it to the First National Bank of Jersey City
for collection. At the same time they gave notice of
these facts to the freight agent of the Lehigh Valley
railroad at its Grand street station in Jersey City.

There are two routes for the shipment of freight from
Lakeside to Jersey City, one by the defendant's road and
that of the Lehigh Valley and the other by the defendant's road and that of the Pennsylvania Railroad Company. At the date of the transaction in question there
was "no fifteen cent rate" from Lakeside to Jersey City
according to the Lehigh schedule, although there was one
by the Pennsylvania route. The freight stations of the
Lehigh Valley and Pennsylvania in Jersey City are about
three-fourths of a mile apart, but cars can be transported
from one to the other by a somewhat circuitous route,
taking about twenty-four hours. The car containing the

potatoes in question was forwarded on the 12th of June, 1907, over the defendant's line to the junction of the Pennsylvania railroad and thence over the latter to Jersey City, where it arrived at the Pennsylvania yard on the eighteenth. The time usually required over the Lehigh route was about two or three days. Upon learning that the car was in the yard of the Pennsylvania railroad D. P. Reynolds & Co. telegraphed plaintiffs that they could not handle the potatoes in the yard of that road. On the same day, June 18th, the plaintiffs wrote Mr. Ewings, the defendant's general superintendent of freight transportation at his office in the city of New York, stating the facts and adding, "Will you kindly have car delivered at Grand street at once? Let us hear fully from you at once regarding these shipments." On June 20th Mr. Ewings replied: "We are arranging with our traffic department to have P M 5858 moved to destination via proper junction point and route and will be pleased to advise you later." On the 24th of June the plaintiffs again wrote Mr. Ewings stating that they were advised by their customer by telegram of even date "that car is still in P. R. R. yards. Will you kindly have this car moved to Grand street, its proper destination at once and wire us when done? We feel that a sufficient length of time has already elapsed in which the same could have been done." On June 25th Mr. Ewings answered stating that "Immediately on receipt of your letter the matter was taken up with Mr. R. L. Calkins, our freight claim agent, and on June 22nd he telegraphed the freight claim agent of the P. R. R. I have asked Mr. Calkins to confer with you in the matter." On the 2nd of July the plaintiffs wrote Mr. Ewings, stating that they had heard nothing from Mr. Calkins regarding the car and continued: "We are, however, advised by our customer that the car arrived at Grand street last Saturday and that owing to the long time it was in transit there was now no market for old potatoes it being too late in the season. He has, therefore, refused same and this is to advise you that the car is at disposal of your company as we shall collect for the value of same through your claim department."

The car was not transported to the Grand street station until June 29th, when D. P. Reynolds & Co. refused to accept it. The potatoes in question were old potatoes for which there is no demand after new potatoes reach the market, or, as one witness stated, "the old potato business is over after the 20th." Moreover, old potatoes loaded in a car sprout and deteriorate rapidly in warm weather. The Lehigh Valley Railroad Company sold the potatoes for less than enough to pay the transportation charges by $60.78.

This action was brought to recover damages from the defendant for its alleged negligence in not following the shipping directions of the plaintiffs and in so diverting the car from the route specified thereby as to prevent it from arriving within a reasonable time at the Grand street station, its proper destination.

The defendant alleged in its answer, among other facts, that the bill of lading was a contract and that the potatoes were transported and delivered pursuant thereto.

Upon the trial the facts were proved substantially as stated and the court charged the jury in substance that if they found that directions were given to the defendant's agent at Lakeside to ship over the Lehigh road they should render a verdict in favor of the plaintiffs for $399.65, the value of the potatoes at 85 cents per hundred pounds, with interest on the balance. They were further told that if there were no specific directions given to the freight agent by Furber to ship over the Lehigh route their verdict should be for the defendant.

Counsel for the plaintiffs requested the court to charge that "If the jury find Grand Street there (in the bill of lading) means a freight station, failure on the part of the defendant to deliver or tender delivery at that point was a breach of their duty which renders them liable to the

plaintiffs in damages." The court thereupon remarked,
" I think it depends on whether there was a direction given
to ship by the Lehigh directly. I am going to adhere to
that." Later, in refusing another request of the plaintiffs, the court said: " I am going to send this case to the
jury on the single proposition that if there was a direction
to ship by the Lehigh the defendant is liable, and if there
was no such direction the defendant is not liable." The
court refused to charge at the request of the plaintiffs
" that the insertion in the bill of lading of the words
' Grand Street' if the jury find that it was intended
thereby to designate a freight station, was a direction to
so ship and deliver."

The defendant's counsel asked the court to charge
" That if Furber, acting for Loomis & Son, signed this
shipping order, that thereupon became the direction of
the railroad in regard to the shipment of this car." The
court remarked: " That is true, but I charge you that if
in addition to the memorandum made by the agent, by
FitzGerald, Furber gave the specified direction to ship
over the Lehigh, that it is also a part of the contract."
Thereupon defendant's counsel said: " What I wish to
have charged is that any directions are merged in this
shipping order, if Furber signed it as agent for Loomis."
The court asked: "Any direction to ship over the Lehigh ?"
By defendant's counsel: " Yes, sir." The court: "I
decline to charge as requested." An exception was taken
to this ruling.

The jury found a verdict for the plaintiffs in the sum
of $399.65, and the judgment entered accordingly was
unanimously affirmed by the Appellate Division. The
defendant thereupon appealed to this court.

Both the bill of lading and the shipping order were
made out by a single operation of a typewriter, manifold
paper having been placed between a blank bill and a
blank order so arranged that the typewritten part was
the same in each. The bill of lading does not refer to

the shipping order nor make it a part thereof; but the shipping order expressly states that it is part of the bill of lading. If both papers, although physically detached and separate, had been duly signed they would have made a contract and would have constituted the entire contract between the parties. If there is any doubt as to the effect of a bill of lading signed by the carrier only but delivered to and retained by the shipper, it is clear that when the bill is signed by both parties it is a contract upon which the minds of both parties have met and it becomes the sole contract between them with reference to the particular shipment involved.

We cannot tell from the verdict, however, whether the shipping order was or was not signed, for the court charged in substance that even if Furber signed the order, still the plaintiffs were entitled to recover if the jury found that he gave the defendant's agent prior oral directions to ship by the Lehigh route and that such directions, if given, were not merged in the written contract. Thus the position of the court was that whether the shipping order was signed or not, if Furber orally directed the shipment to be made by the Lehigh Valley the plaintiffs were entitled to recover. Hence, the jury may have found that Furber signed the shipping order, and also that oral instructions had previously been given to ship by the Lehigh. Thus following the charge of the court that the oral instructions were not merged in the written order, their verdict would have been logically rendered for the plaintiffs. While the parol directions, including the unsigned memorandum, were received in evidence without objection, this did not preclude the defendant from the right to ask that the jury be properly instructed as to the effect thereof, provided they found that the shipping order was in fact signed by the agent of the plaintiffs.

Thus the question presented is whether a written contract to transport goods from one place to another, duly signed by both carrier and shipper, but silent as to the route, can be varied by evidence of previous parol instructions to ship by a particular route. The answer to this question is too clear to require extended discussion. No effect can be given to such evidence, even when received without objection, provided the court is asked in due form to instruct the jury that it was merged in the written agreement if they found there was one. In order to prevent fraud, perjury and mistake, one of the primary rules of evidence forbids that a written contract should be varied by evidence of previous conversations or unsigned memoranda, which are all conclusively presumed to be embodied in the written instrument expressing the final meeting of the minds of the parties. Thus we have recently held, as required by previous decisions on the subject for time out of mind, that "where a written contract is without ambiguity, clear and complete on its face, with no doubt as to the meaning of any word, no evidence that any term is technical or local, nothing to open the door to proof of extrinsic facts, no effort at reformation either by the pleadings or proof, and the rulings, admitting statements of what was said between the parties before the contract was signed, are not covered by any exception to the general principle of exclusion, parol evidence cannot be received to vary or contradict its terms." (*Lossing* v. *Cushman*, 195 N. Y. 386.)

The respondents, however, insist that the writing in question does not appear on its face to be a complete contract; that the parol evidence was consistent therewith and not contradictory thereof, and hence, that the rule opens to admit such evidence in order to complete an entire contract of which the writing is only a part. (*Thomas* v. *Scutt*, 127 N. Y. 133.) It is further insisted that as certain blank spaces in the printed form were left unfilled, such as "Route ......, Charges advanced $......," it was competent to fill them by parol.

The writing, however, upon the assumption that it was signed by both parties as the jury may have found, was a contract complete upon its face, for the unfilled blanks were incidental merely and not essential to a perfect agreement for the transportation of merchandise by a carrier. Although material they were not necessary to make the contract complete on its face. There are few written contracts to which some material provision might not be added, yet it would be against the law to hold that they are incomplete on their face. The blank for " Charges advanced " could not be filled, for no charges were advanced, and the effect of leaving the blank space unfilled was the same as if it had been filled by a cipher or by some negative equivalent. The effect of not specifying the route was simply to leave that subject open to the choice of the carrier, which could select any route that it chose. Some shippers do not care what route their goods take, as their object is fully attained by delivery at the place of destination regardless of how they came. Many promissory notes are made out upon printed forms with a blank space for the place of payment, and sometimes with another for the rate of interest, but the contract, even with these spaces unfilled, if complete in other respects, is complete on its face. The provisions suggested by the unfilled blanks are not essential to the validity of the note, because the law takes care of those subjects just as it takes care of the route in a bill of lading when the parties omit to specify it. It would tend to undermine business transactions and render contracts insecure if such blanks could be filled by parol evidence and effect given thereto in an action at law. Such evidence is competent only and should be given effect only in an action in equity brought to reform the writing, because through mutual mistake, or mistake on one side and fraud on the other, something was omitted which the parties had agreed to. It has no place in the trial of an action at law, such as the one before us, and the refusal of the court to charge that it was merged in the writing, if duly signed, was an error calling for a new trial.

Whether the case should have been sent to the jury upon some other theory, such as was suggested by the counsel for the plaintiffs in his requests to charge, already quoted, is not now before us. It was not thus submitted, but on the other hand the theory adopted was such that according to the charge and the refusals to charge the verdict may have no foundation to rest upon except an error of law.

The judgment should be reversed and a new trial granted, with costs to abide the event.

CULLEN, Ch. J., GRAY, WERNER, CHASE and COLLIN, JJ., concur; HAIGHT, J., dissents.

Judgment reversed, etc.

WILLIAM H. HARRISON, Respondent, *v.* ISABELLA SCOTT et al., as Executors of WALTER SCOTT, Deceased, Appellants.

Sale — when acceptance of machine by vendee question for a jury — when execution by vendee of chattel mortgage on machine before test not a waiver of right of inspection.

Defendant's testator sold a machine to plaintiff's assignor under a contract which provided that the price should be $8,000, and that settlement should be "made for same as follows: On the acceptance of this proposition you (the vendee) to pay us the sum of $3,000 cash, which amount will be returned to you if the machine does not prove satisfactory." Thereafter to secure his indorsement of certain notes and before the testing of the machine had been completed, the vendee executed a chattel mortgage on this and other property to plaintiff, who was the president of the vendee and who testified, among other things, that he was acquainted with the terms under which the company held the machine, and was present at a meeting of its board of directors and voted for a resolution authorizing the vice-president to execute the mortgage, that he knew that no test had been made, and subsequently requested the vendor to remove the machine on the ground that it was not satisfactory. At the sale under this mortgage the interest sold was "the interest that the Arto-Litho Company (the vendee) has in this machine to the extent of $3,000. * * * The right, title and interest that was in there," the vendor at that time giving notice of its claim of title. At such sale a claim was made in its behalf that the title remained in the vendor. The machine was subsequently retaken by the vendor because of alleged default by the vendee in the performance of its contract. *Held*, that a jury would have had the right to determine that the mortgage was executed and accepted subject to the terms of the contract of sale and subject to the right of the mortgagor to complete its test and return the machine if it proved unsatisfactory, leaving the mortgagee in that case to recover under his mortgage, as the interest covered thereby, the payment which had been made, and that there was no intention on the part of the vendee to waive its right of inspection and accept the machine irrespective thereof.

Harrison v. *Scott*, 135 App. Div. 546, affirmed.

(Argued October 12, 1911; decided November 21, 1911.)

APPEAL from an order of the Appellate Division of the Supreme Court in the first judicial department, entered December 30, 1909, reversing a judgment in favor of defendants entered upon a dismissal of the complaint by the court at a Trial Term and granting a new trial.

The nature of the action and the facts, so far as material, are stated in the opinion.

Charles D. Ridgway for appellants. The giving by the Arto-Litho Company of the chattel mortgage upon the press and other machinery, and obtaining thereon the sum of $10,000 to use in its business, allowing the mortgagee to take possession under this mortgage and selling the press at public auction to satisfy the indebtedness secured by the mortgage, was a waiver of all right under its contract to claim that the press was unsatisfactory. (*Morton* v. *Tibbett*, L. R. [15 Q. B.] 428; *Blenkinsop* v. *Clayton*, 7 Taunt. 597; Schouler on Pers. Prop. [3d ed.] § 407; *Browne* v. *Forbes*, 108 N. Y. 387; *Levison* v. *Seybold Machine Co.*, 22 Misc. Rep. 327; *Allen* v. *G. S. H. Co.*, 85 Hun, 537; *Kienle* v. *Klingman*, 24 Misc. Rep. 708; *Van Winkle* v. *Crowell*, 146 U. S. 42; *Houston* v. *Clark*, 62 Ill. App. 174;

Wyler v. *Rothschild*, 53 Neb. 566; *Hansen* v. *Bebee*, 111 Iowa, 534; *L. & M. T. Co.* v. *Collier*, 89 Iowa, 144.)

Ross W. Lynn for respondent. The giving of the chattel mortgage upon the press before the test, contemplated to be made, had been made, constituted no acceptance of the machine as a matter of law. (*Gurney* v. *A. & G. W. Ry. Co.*, 58 N. Y. 358; Benjamin on Sales [5th ed.], 752; *Osborne & Co.* v. *McQueen*, 67 Wis. 392; *Tompkins* v. *Lamb*, 121 App. Div. 366; 195 N. Y. 518; *Cassidy* v. *Horton*, 32 Misc. Rep. 148; *Bensler* v. *Locke*, 4 Misc. Rep. 486; *Cooke* v. *U. Mfg. Co.*, 57 Hun, 107; 138 N. Y. 610.)

HISCOCK, J. This action was brought by the respondent as assignee of the Arto-Litho Company, to recover $3,000 paid by the latter on the purchase price of a printing machine bought by it from appellants' testator. The action was based on the allegations that said machine proved unsatisfactory to the vendee and that, therefore, under the contract of sale it could be returned and said money recovered. The only question urged for our consideration on this appeal is the one springing out of the defense that after delivery to it of said machine the vendee executed a chattel mortgage thereon, and that this was such conclusive evidence of its acceptance as to preclude a return thereof and recovery of the moneys paid thereon.

The substantial facts by which the answer to the question thus presented is to be determined are as follows:

The appellants' testator sold the machine to respondent's assignor in January, 1907, under a contract which provided that the price of the machine should be $8,000, and that settlement should be "made for same as follows: On the acceptance of this proposition you (the vendee) to pay us the sum of $3,000 cash, which amount will be returned to you if the machine does not prove

satisfactory. * * * It is understood and agreed that
the title to the above-mentioned property does not pass
out of our possession until fully paid for.   And in case
of any default in any of the conditions herein named, we
shall have the right to take immediate possession of the
property."   There was more or less delay in testing the
machine, and correspondence between the parties relating
thereto was passing as late as August 29, 1907.   No
claim seems to have been made on the trial that the
vendee, as a matter of law, unreasonably delayed making
this test, but on the evidence as now presented to us this
claim, if made, could not have been sustained.

July 25, 1907, the vendee executed to respondent a
chattel mortgage on various property, including this
press, as security for his indorsement of certain notes.
Respondent was the president of the vendee, and, in addition to the presumption which would prevail that he was
acquainted with the terms of the purchase of said machine
and with the fact that a test thereof had not been completed, he testified specifically that he was so acquainted
with the terms under which the company held the
machine; that the vendor had title to it until it was paid
for; that no test of the machine had been made; that he
was present at a meeting of the board of directors, and
voted for a resolution authorizing the vice-president to
execute the mortgage.   On two occasions subsequent to
the execution thereof he wrote a letter requesting the
vendor to remove the press on the ground that it was not
satisfactory and to refund the $3,000.   The notice of sale
under this mortgage which the mortgagee caused to be
given was of "the right, title and interest of the Arto-
Litho Company in and to" the press in question, and at
the sale it was stated that the only interest which would
be sold was "the interest that the Arto-Litho Company
has in this machine to the extent of $3,000. * * *
The right, title and interest that was in there."   In addition, a representative of the vendor was present and

"made a protest against the sale on the ground that the title to the machine still remained in the Walter Scott & Co." The machine was subsequently retaken by the vendor because of alleged default by the vendee in the performance of its contract.

On evidence of these facts and some others of less importance the learned trial justice dismissed plaintiff's complaint on the ground that his assignor had accepted the press, the theory of course being that the execution by the vendee of the chattel mortgage was such an assertion of absolute ownership as to be utterly and conclusively inconsistent with the idea that it still retained the machine on trial with power to return and recover the money paid on it.

In this determination I think he erred, and that the learned Appellate Division was correct in reversing the judgment.

It will be assumed without discussion for the purposes of this case that the execution under ordinary circumstances by the vendee of a mortgage on personal property subject to inspection to a *bona fide* mortgagee for value would be conclusive evidence of an acceptance. This conclusion would not be altered by the fact that it was executed before inspection or testing because a vendee might if he chose waive such rights and elect to take the machine independent thereof. The fact that an examination had not been completed might be one to be considered with others in a proper case as indicating lack of intention on the part of the vendee to make an acceptance of the article in question. In such a case as is suggested between the alternative that the vendee was unlawfully mortgaging property which he did not own, and the other one that he intended to accept the property and become qualified to execute a mortgage, the law certainly ought to adopt the latter one.

But the facts in this case as bearing on the intent of the vendee may be clearly and widely distinguished from those which have been assumed.   The mortgagor had a right to test the machine and return it if not satisfactory and recover the payment made thereon, and until the entire purchase price was paid the title expressly remained in the vendor.   This process of testing was still incomplete at the time the mortgage was executed.   The mortgagee was the president of the mortgagor and knew that at the time the instrument was executed no satisfactory test had been secured and that inspection was still being continued for the purpose of determining whether the machine was satisfactory, and he voted to have the mortgage executed under these circumstances.   As further indicative of the intent with which the instrument was executed and accepted by the respective parties, the tests were continued after its execution, as might be found, by and with the participation and consent of the mortgagee, and he it was who finally notified the vendor that they had proved unsatisfactory and that the machine must be retaken and the money returned.   Still further, as giving character to the acts of the parties in executing the mortgage, the mortgage, only purported to offer on the sale under it the right and interest of the mortgagee, namely, the right to recover the three thousand dollars which had been paid.

From all these facts and possibly some others which have not been stated I think that the jury would have had the right to determine that the mortgage was executed and accepted subject to the terms of the contract and subject to the right of the mortgagor to complete its test and return the machine if it proved unsatisfactory, leaving the mortgagee in that case to recover under his mortgage as the interest covered thereby the payment which had been made; that there was no intention on the part of the vendee to waive its right of inspection and accept the press irrespective thereof.   And this independent of the question whether the vendee under the contract of sale could acquire title until full payment of the purchase price. Certainly, if there had been inserted in the instrument a provision to the effect that the mortgagor had not completed its test of the machine, but reserved the right so to do, and return it and recover back its payment if the same proved unsatisfactory, the mortgage in that case covering the money to be recovered, nobody would say that as a matter of law the execution of the mortgage amounted to an acceptance of the machine. I think that the facts which a jury would have been permitted to find as surrounding the transaction would have justified the conclusion that this was the very understanding which did exist between the parties. It may be possible that as between the mortgagor and the mortgagee, this evidence could not have been introduced as varying the terms of the instrument. But in this case between one of the parties and a third party involving merely the question of intent with which an act was performed the evidence was competent and as I have indicated justified the conclusion in favor of respondent's right to recover. The act of mortgaging, certainly viewed in the light of this evidence, was not as a matter of law inconsistent with an intent to hold the machine on trial and subject to examination and, therefore, it did not come within the rule which makes inconsistent acts of that general character conclusive evidence of acceptance.

These conclusions are not at variance but rather in harmony with the rules laid down by the text writers and established by various decisions.

Mechem on Sales (section 1387) says: "The buyer may also manifest an acceptance by dealing with the goods in a manner inconsistent with an intention to reject them. Selling them as his own, giving a chattel mortgage upon them, * * * and the like, have been held to be acts so far indicative of ownership, and only to be justified by it, as to be inconsistent with the position that the ownership was still in the seller by reason of non-acceptance."

Williston on Sales (Section 77) says: "If he (the buyer) assents to take specific goods as his there seems to be no reason to doubt that he has accepted them within the terms of the statute (of frauds). If, therefore, he does an act in relation to specified goods which necessarily involves the conclusion that he has taken them as owner there is an acceptance. * * * So mortgaging the goods implies acceptance."

In *Leggett & Meyer Tobacco Co.* v. *Collier* (89 Iowa, 144) the question was raised whether the title to goods delivered under an order which had been countermanded had vested in the vendee. This question arose between the vendors and the mortgagee under a trust mortgage for creditors. It was held that the execution by the vendee of the mortgage on the property in connection with other circumstances established an acceptance of the goods as matter of law. The court said: "We think that the evidence shows an acceptance of the tobacco. When the tobacco came to the store the shipping clerk of the firm was aware of the fact and knew that the order for it had been countermanded. The firm with knowledge that the tobacco had been delivered took no steps to return the same but the next day exercised an unequivocal act of ownership over it by mortgaging it to the trustee If the defendant firm did not consider it their property, if they had not accepted it, why did they mortgage it? They undertook to make a disposition of it absolutely inconsistent with any claim that they had not accepted the property."

In like manner it was held that a sale or mortgage of property by a vendee was evidence of acceptance, apparently in some of the instances for the consideration of a jury, in each of the following cases: *Marshall* v. *Ferguson* (23 Cal. 66); *Hill* v. *McDonald* (17 Wis. 97); *Weyler* v. *Rothschild & Bros.* (53 Neb. 566); *Phillips* v. *Ocmulgee Mills* (55 Ga. 633).

An examination of all of these authorities, however,

shows that the facts widely and strongly differed from those now presented to us as indicating a deliberate intention to deal with the property in a manner consistent only with an unqualified ownership which necessarily implied acceptance, and thereby they make it apparent that the facts in this case fall short of warranting the application of the rule which was made the basis for the dismissal of plaintiff's complaint.

On the other hand, it has been written by text writers and held by the courts that various acts by a vendee, quite as indicative of an intent to assume ownership over property as those described here, did not establish acceptance conclusively as matter of law but constituted evidence from which a jury might find such acceptance as matter of fact.

Benjamin on Sales (p. 752, 5th ed.) writes: " The two preceding cases show that a resale by the buyer after he has had an opportunity of exercising an option either of accepting or of rejecting the goods delivered is an acceptance, for by reselling he is presumed to have determined his election. Accordingly a resale will not necessarily be an acceptance, for the facts may show that no such determination of an election can be presumed, as where the buyer resells before he has had an opportunity of examining the goods."

When a person who has contracted for the purchase of goods offers to resell them as his own it is a question for the jury whether this is proof of a delivery to him. (*Blenkinsop* v. *Clayton*, 7 Taunt. 597.)

In *Morton* v. *Tibbett* (15 A. & E. [N. S.] 428) it appeared in an action of debt for goods sold and delivered that the defendant purchased wheat of plaintiff by sample and directed that the bulk should be delivered on the next morning to a carrier named by himself who was to convey it to market, and defendant himself took the sample away with him. On the following morning the wheat was delivered to the carrier and the defendant resold it on that day by the same sample. The carrier conveyed the wheat by order of the defendant who had never seen it to the sub-vendee who rejected it as not corresponding to the sample and the defendant on notice of this repudiated his contract with the plaintiff on the same ground. Under these circumstances it was held that it was for the jury to determine from the evidence whether there had been an acceptance, an actual receipt by the defendant within the Statute of Frauds. Lord CAMPBELL delivered the opinion to this effect after a review of many authorities.

In *Osborne & Co.* v. *McQueen* (67 Wis. 392) a controversy was presented between the vendor and vendee of a harvester and the question of acceptance by the latter arose. It appeared that there was dissatisfaction by the vendee with the machine and attempts by the vendor to remedy the same and that while these were in progress the vendee mortgaged the machine. The mortgage, however, was released about the same time the vendee notified the vendor to take back the machine and some time before the action was commenced, and it was held and written that the mortgage "cut no figure as evidence of the acceptance of the machine in its then condition, or of a waiver of the conditions of the warranty. The defendant was then waiting for the plaintiff to repair the machine, and had notified it to do so or to take it back."

Jones v. *Reynolds* (120 N. Y. 213) was an action to recover on an alleged sale by plaintiff to defendant of a patented device for shoe lasts. One of the questions involved was whether the defendant had made use of the invention and in that connection it appeared that he had received from the plaintiff a model of the device and thereafter had applied for and obtained a patent for a combination of the several elements or parts of a model shoe last which included the device sold him by the plaintiff. It was claimed by the latter that this act amounted to a use of the invention. In discussing this claim and reaching the conclusion that simply a question of fact was presented, Judge PARKER, in behalf of the court, wrote:

"It is insisted that inasmuch as the contract was not 'made in writing' it is void, because the defendant did not 'accept and receive' the thing sold. * * * It will be observed that the plaintiff did not undertake to procure or sell a patent. He sold the device merely. * * * And the plaintiff, at the time, made the only delivery possible of the thing sold. He delivered to defendant a model of the invention. * * * As no part of the purchase money was paid, the question presented is, whether the defendant accepted and received the thing sold so as to take the contract out of the statute. The act of acceptance is something over and beyond the agreement of which it is a part performance and which it assumes as already existing. It is a fact to be proven as are other facts. Acts of ownership constitute strong evidence of acceptance. * * * If a vendee does any act with reference to the thing sold, of wrong if not the owner, or of right if he is the owner, it is evidence that he has accepted it. * * * The rule may be broadly stated, that any act from which it may be inferred that the buyer has taken possession as owner presents a question for the jury to determine whether the act was done with intent to accept." (p. 216.)

In accordance with these views I recommend that the order and judgment appealed from be affirmed and judgment absolute ordered against appellants on their stipulation, with costs in all courts.

VANN, CHASE and COLLIN, JJ., concur; CULLEN, Ch. J., and WERNER, J., concur in result; WILLARD BARTLETT, J., not voting.

Order affirmed, etc.

In the Matter of the Probate of the Will of MARY S.
ROBINSON, Deceased.

BURTON C. MEIGHAN, as Executor and Trustee, et al.,
Appellants; OTHEMAN A. STEVENS et al., Respondents.

Testamentary trusts — trusts for benefit of "religious, educational, charitable or benevolent uses" — rules for construction of testamentary provisions creating such trusts — will examined and held to create a valid trust within the meaning of the statute.

1. A will must sufficiently define the beneficiaries and the purpose of the testator so that a trust can be enforced by the courts, otherwise the will does not come within the provisions of the statutes which permit gifts for religious, educational, charitable or benevolent uses, to indefinite or uncertain beneficiaries. The gifts must also be for a public and not for a private purpose.

2. Where certain things are enumerated and such enumeration is followed or coupled with a more general description, such general description is commonly understood to cover only things *ejusdem generis* with the particular things mentioned. In such case it is presumed that the testator had only things of that class in mind.

8. A construction which is fairly within the rules of law and that sustains a trust and devotes the fund included therein to purposes permitted by law and to the good of humanity should be preferred.

4. Testatrix directed her trustees to disburse the principal or interest of her residuary estate, or both, in their discretion "To provide shelter, necessaries of life, education, general or specific. and such other financial aid as may seem to them fitting and proper to such persons as they shall select as being in need of the same," and authorized her trustees to carry out such provisions or to cause to be created a corporation therefor. *Held*, that the purpose of the testatrix was within the language of the statute which authorizes gifts "to religious, educational, charitable, or benevolent uses." and that the courts can and will, at the suit of the attorney-general of the state, compel the trustees to carry out the will according to such purpose and for such uses.

Matter of Robinson, 145 App. Div. 925, modified.

(Argued October 5, 1911; decided November 28, 1911.)

APPEAL from an order of the Appellate Division of the Supreme Court in the second judicial department, entered

June 16, 1911, so far as it affirms that part of a decree of the Westchester County Surrogate's Court which adjudged a specified trust contained in the will of the testatrix invalid.

Mary S. Robinson, the testatrix, died a resident of Westchester county, October 16, 1909, leaving an estate consisting of personal property only. She left an instrument in writing bearing date January 26, 1904, purporting to be her last will and testament. It was offered for probate in the Surrogate's Court of Westchester county and her next of kin and the attorney-general of the state of New York were duly cited to appear in the proceeding. The next of kin and said attorney-general thereafter duly appeared and one of said next of kin filed an answer to the petition for the probate of said will expressly putting in issue the validity, construction, and effect of the 6th to 11th paragraphs inclusive, of said instrument, and in said answer denied that the said provisions constitute a valid disposition of personal property by will under the laws of this state.

The surrogate found that the will was duly executed in accordance with the laws of the state of New York, and that it is the last will and testament of said deceased, but he found as a conclusion of law that the trusts attempted to be created by the 6th, 7th and 9th paragraphs of said will are invalid and that the 8th, 10th and 11th paragraphs of said will are void and that the testatrix died intestate as to all of her property except that part thereof given and bequeathed by the 2d, 3d and 4th paragraphs of her said will, and that the next of kin of the testatrix are entitled to her residuary estate in equal shares. (*Matter of Robinson*, 71 Misc. Rep. 87.) An appeal was taken by the executor and trustees named in the will from the decree of the Surrogate's Court entered in accordance with said findings to the Appellate Division of the Supreme Court so far as it declares parts of said will invalid or void. The Appellate Division modified said degree by declaring valid the trust set forth in the 6th and 7th paragraphs of the will and as so modified said decree was affirmed. (*Matter of Robinson*, 145 App. Div. 925.)

The 8th paragraph of the will provides in case of the death of certain persons and the survivor of them, or of certain other contingencies, for a gift over of the fund given in trust by the 6th and 7th paragraphs of the will to the fund provided by the 9th paragraph of the will. The 11th paragraph of the will provides that if any person named in the will contests the same, such person shall forfeit any right to participate in the estate.

The 9th and 10th paragraphs of the will are as follows: "*Ninth.* I direct my said executor to pay over the rest, residue and remainder of my estate to the said Burton C. Meighan and Frank B. Upham, in trust, however, for the following uses and purposes: The said trustees are to invest such portion of the fund as shall not be used for the purposes herein specified, in the securities prescribed by law as savings bank investments, and they are to disburse the principal or interest, or both, of said fund in their discretion as follows, to wit:

"To provide shelter, necessaries of life, education, general or specific, and such other financial aid as may seem to them fitting and proper to such persons as they shall select as being in need of the same. Preference is to be given to persons who are elderly or disabled from work, and to persons who are Christians, of good moral character, members of one of the so-called evangelical churches, to wit, the Methodist, Baptist, Presbyterian, Congregational, Moravian or Episcopal, and who are not addicted to the use of intoxicants or tobacco, nor to attendance at theatrical entertainments.

"*Tenth.* I authorize and empower my said trustees, in their discretion, to appoint other persons, not exceeding five, to act with them in the execution of the trusts, or either of them, herein provided for; and I direct that the

1911.] Points of counsel. [Vol. 203.]

execution of said trusts shall thereupon devolve upon all of the said trustees jointly and upon the survivors of them. If the said two trustees, Burton C. Meighan and Frank B. Upham, deem it advisable, they may cause a corporation to be created for the purpose of executing the trusts provided for in this will."

The executor and trustees named in the will appeal from that part of the order of the Appellate Division which affirmed the decree of the surrogate declaring the 9th paragraph of the will invalid and the 10th and 11th paragraphs void.

Lewis E. Carr, Arthur M. Johnson and *Henry Necarsulmer* for appellants. Trusts for religious, charitable, educational or benevolent uses are recognized by the statute law of the state of New York, and such trusts are not invalid by reason of the indefiniteness or uncertainty of the beneficiaries named therein and such trusts are not subject to the statute against perpetuities. (L. 1909, ch. 45, § 12; L. 1909, ch. 52, § 113; *Matter of Shattuck*, 193 N. Y. 446; *Allen* v. *Stevens*, 161 N. Y. 122; *Rothschild* v. *Schiff*, 188 N. Y. 327; *Bowman* v. *D. & F. M. Soc.*, 182 N. Y. 494; *Mount* v. *Tuttle*, 183 N. Y. 358; *St. John* v. *Andrews Institute*, 191 N. Y. 254; *Murray* v. *Miller*, 178 N. Y. 316.) The construction of the provisions of paragraph ninth of the will made by the surrogate and adopted by the Appellate Division was erroneous. (*Roosa* v. *Harrington*, 171 N. Y. 341; *Kahn* v. *Tierney*, 135 App. Div. 897; *Crozier* v. *Bray*, 120 N. Y. 366; *Matter of Hermance*, 71 N. Y. 481; *People ex rel. Huber* v. *Feitner*, 71 App. Div. 479; *Matter of Reynolds*, 124 N. Y. 388; *Donohue* v. *Keeshan*, 91 App. Div. 602; *Du Bois* v. *Ray*, 35 N. Y. 162; *Mee* v. *Gordon*, 187 N. Y. 400; *Lewis* v. *Howe*, 174 N. Y. 340; *Haug* v. *Schumacher*, 166 N. Y. 506.) Properly construed, the provisions of paragraph ninth of the will of Mary S. Robinson constitute a valid gift in trust for educational, charitable and benevolent uses under the provisions of the statutes. (*Kelly* v. *Hoey*, 35 App. Div. 273; *Allen* v. *Stevens*, 161 N. Y. 122; *Matter of Shattuck*, 193 N. Y. 446; *Manley* v. *Fiske*, 139 App. Div. 665; 201 N. Y. 546; *Matter of Griffin*, 167 N. Y. 71; *F. L. & T. Co.* v. *Ferris*, 67 App. Div. 1; *Matter of Durand*, 56 Misc. Rep. 235.) The purpose and intention of the testatrix in making the trust contained in paragraph ninth of the will of Mary S. Robinson are sufficiently defined, and no objection on that ground can properly be urged to the validity of the trust. (*Matter of Shattuck*, 193 N. Y. 446; *Rothschild* v. *Schiff*, 188 N. Y. 327; *St. John* v. *Andrews Inst.*, 191 N. Y. 254; *Fairchild* v. *Edson*, 154 N. Y. 199; *Kelly* v. *Hoey*, 35 App. Div. 273; *Bowman* v. *D. & F. M. Society*, 182 N. Y. 494; *Hull* v. *Pearson*, 36 App. Div. 224; *Matter of Griffin*, 167 N. Y. 71; *Allen* v. *Stevens*, 161 N. Y. 122.)

Edward R. Otheman for respondents. The ninth clause of the will does not constitute a charitable trust, and was, therefore, correctly held by the Appellate Division to be void. (*Matter of Shattuck*, 193 N. Y. 446; *Schettler* v. *Smith*, 41 N. Y. 328; *Morris* v. *Bishop of Durham*, 9 Ves. 399; *Matter of Scott*, 31 Misc. Rep. 85; *Matter of Seymour*, 67 Misc. Rep. 347; *Manley* v. *Fiske*, 139 App. Div. 665.)

CHASE, J. Gifts for religious, educational, charitable or benevolent uses, to indefinite or uncertain beneficiaries, are now permitted in this state by express provision of statute. (Personal Property Law, sec. 12, Laws of 1909, chap. 45; Real Property Law, sec. 113, Laws of 1909, chap. 52.)

The law relating to gifts for charitable uses as it existed prior to chapter 701 of the Laws of 1893, which was substantially re-enacted in said Personal Property Law and said Real Property Law, has been changed. (*Matter of Shattuck*, 193 N. Y. 446; *Bowman* v. *Domestic & For-*

eign Miss. Soc., 182 N. Y. 494; *Allen* v. *Stevens*, 161 N. Y. 122.)

The spirit of love and religion which is the basis of charity should be exercised in construing the provisions of such acts. A will, however, must sufficiently define the beneficiaries and the purpose of the testator so that the trust can be enforced by the courts, otherwise the will does not come within the provisions of the acts. The gifts must be also for a public and not for a private purpose. This court has recently construed the provisions of the act of 1893 in the *Shattuck* case and there say : " It is manifest that it is necessary for a testator to define his purpose and intention in making a trust sufficiently so that the court at the instance of the attorney-general representing the beneficiaries, can by order direct in carrying out the trust duty." And the court further say: " The intention of the legislature in passing the act of 1893, was to save to the public, charitable gifts made in trust to uncertain and indefinite beneficiaries. Gifts for the benefit of private institutions or individuals were not intended to be included within its provisions." (pp. 451, 452.)

It is not seriously contended but that the trust attempted to be created by the 9th paragraph of the testatrix's will is within the provisions of the Personal Property Law and can be carried out, providing the purpose and intention of the testatrix in defining the beneficiaries is lawful and sufficiently clear so that the same can be enforced by the courts.

The important question for determination on this appeal is whether the gift provided by the will is confined to religious, educational, charitable or benevolent uses. The answer to such question involves the purpose of the testatrix.

The Personal Property Law so far as necessary for the present discussion is as follows : " No gift, grant, or bequest to religious, educational, charitable, or benevolent uses, which shall in other respects be valid under the laws of this state, shall be deemed invalid by reason of the indefiniteness or uncertainty of the persons designated as the beneficiaries thereunder in the instrument creating the same * * *." The purpose of the trust must come within the uses specified in the act. In construing the will now under consideration the words "such other financial aid" must be read with the words that precede them, and the expression of preference in selecting persons to receive the fund subsequently stated in the same paragraph, and as so read the preceding words not being exhaustive, such comprehensive words should be held to refer to financial aid of the same general character and purpose as that included in such preceding words. They should be construed to mean other financial aid for similar urgent and necessary purposes. (*Matter of Reynolds*, 124 N. Y. 388; *Matter of Hermance*, 71 N. Y. 481, 487; *Lewis v. Howe*, 174 N. Y. 340, 346; *People ex rel. Huber v. Feitner*, 71 App. Div. 479; *Garvey v. Garvey*, 150 Mass. 185; 1 Jarman on Wills [5th ed.], 417.)

The rule which we are applying is that where certain things are enumerated, and such enumeration is followed or coupled with a more general description, such general description is commonly understood to cover only things *ejusdem generis* with the particular things mentioned. In such case it is presumed that the testator had only things of that class in mind. (*Given v. Hilton*, 95 U. S. 591.)

The word "need" is used in the same paragraph of the will as a noun and as such it is defined to mean "A state requiring supply or relief; pressing occasion for something; urgent want; necessity; exigency." It is also defined to mean "The lack of anything desired or useful, as, 'He felt the need of a better education.'" The latter meaning is by lexicographers said to be its meaning in a milder sense. Its general and more commonly accepted meaning is stated in the first quoted definition, and also as "Want of the means of subsistence; poverty; indigence; destitution."

Reading the statement of preference in the selection of beneficiaries in connection with the words "shelter, necessaries of life, education, general or specific," and also associating with such words the thought of want and necessity which in the connection in which they are used they naturally and commonly imply, it is plain and unmistakable that the testatrix intended the trust for the benefit of those in need who require shelter, necessaries of life and education, and not for those simply desiring something useful, and that the discretion vested in her trustees extends only to selecting such persons as to them shall seem fit and proper among those in want, necessity, exigency, poverty, indigence and destitution.

Construed as stated, the purpose of the testatrix was within the language of the statute which authorizes gifts "To religious, educational, charitable, or benevolent uses" Shelter, necessaries of life, education and other like benefactions to be supplied to those in need to be selected by the trustees is a definite purpose.

It is urged, however, by the respondent that the will authorizes the trustees to expend the fund for special education and that to such extent it is not within the terms of the statute. The language of the statute does not confine educational uses to such as are general. There is nothing in the fact that specific education as distinguished from general or common school education was contemplated by the testatrix that condemns the trust as being one other than for charitable uses. Charity at least includes any department or extent of education primarily and fairly calculated to make the recipient self supporting. A gift is not without the bounds of charity because the training contemplated thereby may include special or specific education. (*St. John* v. *Andrews Institute*, 191 N. Y. 254; *Rothschild* v. *Schiff*, 188 N. Y. 327; *Matter of Shattuck, supra.*)

The respondent refers to the *Shattuck* case as specifically holding that the word "educational" as used in the statute, does not necessarily indicate a public charitable use. In that case this court say : "The word 'educational' does not necessarily describe a public or charitable institution and for that reason as we will show the trust is not saved by the provisions of the act of 1893." (p. 452.) That language was used with reference to an educational *institution* and in connection with a will that gave in general terms the trustee authority to use the income of the trust by paying the same "to religious, educational or eleemosynary *institutions* as in his judgment shall seem advisable."

It was there held that an educational institution includes a private as well as a public institution, and that so far as it included a private institution it was without the terms of the statute.

In the will now under consideration a gift to an institution is not contemplated. It authorizes the use of the money included in the trust to furnish an "education, general or specific." A specific education is no more without the charitable purpose of the testatrix than is a general education, and the construction of the words relating to education are in no way controlled by what was said in the *Shattuck* case.

It is doubtless true that the paragraph of the will by which the trust is attempted to be created is susceptible of more than one construction, but a construction which is fairly within the rules of law and that sustains the trust and devotes the fund included therein to purposes permitted by law and to the good of humanity should be preferred. (*Crozier* v. *Bray*, 120 N. Y. 366, 375; *Mee* v. *Gordon*, 187 N. Y. 400, 410; *Young Women's C. Home* v. *French*, 187 U. S. 401; *Goodwin* v. *Coddington*, 154 N. Y. 283; *Kelly* v. *Hoey*, 35 App. Div. 273; Thomas Law of Estates Created by Wills, 1657.)

In our judgment the construction of the will as we

have indicated is the more reasonable one. It being determined from the will that the trust and the purpose of the testatrix in her attempt to establish it are for the uses enumerated in the statute, the courts can and will, at the suit of the attorney-general of the state, compel the trustees to carry out the same according to such purpose and for such uses.

Trusts otherwise valid under the acts mentioned are sustained, although the beneficiaries are not necessarily or in terms confined to residents of this state. (*St. John* v. *Andrews Institute, supra; Manley* v. *Fiske*, 139 App. Div. 665; affd., 201 N. Y. 546; *Allen* v. *Stevens, supra; Rothschild* v. *Schiff, supra; Bowman* v. *Domestic & Foreign Miss. Soc., supra.*)

A gift for the uses specified in the statute may, under the direction of the will, be administered and enforced by and through a corporation subsequently created for that purpose. (*St. John* v. *Andrews Institute, supra.*)

The validity and effect of the 11th paragraph of the will was not discussed, nor was a decision upon the appeal so far as it relates thereto insisted upon in this court.

The order of the Appellate Division so far as it relates to the 9th and 10th paragraphs of the will should be reversed, and the provisions of the said paragraphs of the will should be declared valid and enforcible, with costs to all parties appearing and filing briefs, payable out of the fund.

CULLEN, Ch. J., HAIGHT, VANN, WERNER, WILLARD BARTLETT and HISCOCK, JJ., concur.

Ordered accordingly.

AIMEE S. GUGGENHEIM, Appellant, *v.* GRACE B. WAHL, Respondent.

Foreign judgment — divorce — courts of this state will not restrain prosecution of action in another state to annul a judgment of divorce previously rendered in that state by a court of competent jurisdiction.

The courts of this state will not restrain a party from prosecuting an action in another state, the object of which is to annul a judgment of divorce obtained by her in that state when such judgment was rendered by a court of competent jurisdiction over the parties and the subject-matter of that action, and it has been held in a previous action in the courts of this state to which this plaintiff was a party that such judgment was binding and conclusive.

Guggenheim v. *Wahl*, 139 App. Div. 931, affirmed.

(Argued October 23, 1911; decided November 28, 1911.)

APPEAL from a judgment of the Appellate Division of the Supreme Court in the first judicial department, entered July 14, 1910, affirming a judgment in favor of defendant entered upon a dismissal of the complaint by the court on trial at Special Term.

The nature of the action and the facts, so far as material, are stated in the opinion.

Samuel Untermyer and *Abraham Benedict* for appellant. The power of a court of equity to restrain the prosecution of the defendant's suit in Illinois is undoubted. (*Cole* v. *Cunningham*, 133 U. S. 107; *Hayes* v. *Ward*, 4 Johns. Ch. 123; *Ward* v. *Arredondo*, Hopk. Ch. 243; *Mitchell* v. *Bunch*, 2 Paige, 606; *N. Y. & N. H. R. R. Co.* v. *Schuyler*, 17 How. Pr. 464; 17 N. Y. 592; *People* v. *Erie Ry. Co.*, 36 How. Pr. 129; *Claflin & Co.* v. *Hamlin*, 62 How. Pr. 284; *Vail* v. *Knapp*, 49 Barb. 299; *Kittle* v. *Kittle*, 8 Daly, 72; *Forrest* v. *Forrest*, 2 Edm. 180; *Erie Ry. Co.* v. *Ramsey*, 45 N. Y. 637; *Williams* v.

Ingersoll, 89 N. Y. 508; *Pond* v. *Harwood,* 139 N. Y. 111; *N. & N. B. Hosiery Co.* v. *Arnold,* 143 N. Y. 265; *Dinsmore* v. *Neresheimer,* 32 Hun, 204; *Gibson* v. *A. L. & T. Co.,* 58 Hun, 443; *White, Stokes & Allen* v. *Caxton B. B. Co.,* 10 Civ. Pro. Rep. 146; *Stevens* v. *Central Natl. Bank,* 52 N. Y. S. R. 894; *A. & K. R. R. Co.* v. *Weidenfeld,* 5 Misc. Rep. 43; *Edgell* v. *Clarke,* 19 App. Div. 199; *Locomobile Co.* v. *American Bridge Co.,* 80 App. Div. 44; *Webster* v. *C. Nat. Life Ins. Co.,* 131 App. Div. 837; 196 N. Y. 523.) The plaintiff has a very direct interest, and one which equity must recognize, in maintaining the integrity of the Illinois decree. (*Heidritter* v. *Elizabeth,* 112 U. S. 294; *Leadville Coal Co.* v. *McCreery,* 141 U. S. 475; *Shields* v. *Coleman,* 157 U. S. 168; *Beardslee* v. *Ingraham,* 183 N. Y. 411; *New York* v. *Connecticut,* 4 Dallas, 1; *Siemen* v. *Austin,* 33 Barb. 9; *Adams* v. *Harris,* 47 Miss. 144; *McDowell Appeal,* 123 Penn. St. 381; *Davidson* v. *Reed,* 111 Ill. 167; *Breeding* v. *Davis,* 77 Va. 639.) The present plaintiff is entitled to the benefit of the estoppel created by the judgment of the courts of this state in *Guggenheim* v. *Guggenheim,* and the defendant should be restrained from acting in disregard thereof. (U. S. Const. art. 4, § 1; *Dobson* v. *Pearce,* 12 N. Y. 156; *Everett* v. *Everett,* 180 N. Y. 452; 215 U. S. 203; *Bidwell* v. *Bidwell,* 139 N. C. 402.) The defendant's bill of review in Illinois having been filed more than eight years after the Illinois decree of divorce procured by her, and more than five years after the present plaintiff innocently married the divorced husband of the defendant, and after the defendant herself had again married, in reliance upon that decree, a court of equity will not permit the original decree of divorce to be interfered with, since the defendant not only is estopped to assail the decree, but has accepted its benefits and has repeatedly confirmed it by her acts, and especially since a vacatur of that decree would prejudice the plaintiff's marital and property rights in Illinois and be made the foundation of new and harassing litigation in New York. (2 Bishop on Mar., Div. & Sep. §§ 1533, 1534, 1553; 2 Nelson on Div. & Sep. §§ 1050, 1053, 1056; *Singer* v. *Singer*, 41 Barb. 139; *Parish* v. *Parish*, 9 Ohio St. 537; *Adams* v. *Adams*, 51 N. H. 388; *Nicholson* v. *Nicholson*, 113 Ind. 131; *Maher* v. *T. G. & T. Co.*, 95 Ill. App. 365; *Nichols* v. *Nichols*, 52 N. J. Eq. 60; *Bidwell* v. *Bidwell*, 139 N. C. 402; *Ruger* v. *Heckel*, 85 N. Y. 483; *Lacey* v. *Lacey*, 38 Misc. Rep. 196; *Dow* v. *Blake*, 148 Ill. 76.)

John J. Lordan for respondent. The appellant is not entitled to injunctive relief. (*Pect* v. *Jennes*, 48 U. S. 621; *C. Nat. Bank* v. *Stevens*, 169 U. S. 432; 144 N. Y. 50; *Matter of Chetwood*, 165 U. S. 443; Joyce on Injunction, § 608A; *Griffith* v. *Dodgsaw*, 103 App. Div. 542; *Butchers' Assoc.* v. *Cutler*, 26 La. Ann. 500; *Chadoin* v. *Megee*, 20 Tex. 476; *Wyeth Mfg. Co.* v. *Lang*, 54 Mo. App. 147; *Edgell* v. *Clarke*, 19 App. Div. 199; *Grant* v. *Moore*, 88 N. C. 77; *Murrell* v. *Murrell*, 84 N. C. 182.)

GRAY, J. The complaint of the plaintiff in this action prays for a judgment, which shall restrain the defendant from prosecuting an action, or proceeding, in the Circuit Court of Cook county, in the state of Illinois, against William Guggenheim, this plaintiff's husband; which action, or proceeding, has for its object the review, impeachment and annulment of a judgment, theretofore rendered by that court at the suit of this defendant against said William Guggenheim, at that time her husband, dissolving their marriage. At the trial, the complaint was dismissed upon the pleadings and the judgment thereupon entered in favor of the defendant has been affirmed by the Appellate Division. In the review of the case, therefore, the sole question presented is whether the complaint, its allegations of facts being deemed to be admitted, states a cause of action, entitling the plaintiff to the relief prayed for. That pleading is very full in its narrative of facts and, with its numerous exhibits, resumes the acts of these three persons, in and out of the courts, for the previous nine or ten years.

In November, 1900, this defendant was married to William Guggenheim, in the state of New Jersey, and in February, 1901, she commenced an action to obtain an absolute divorce from him, in the Circuit Court of Cook county, state of Illinois, a court of competent jurisdiction, upon the allegation of his adultery, committed in the city of Chicago, in that state. In her bill of complaint she alleged her actual residence in Cook county, then and at the time of the commission of the act of adultery. Guggenheim appeared in the action and made answer, denying the allegation of his adulterous act. There was replication to the answer and the case, being at issue, came on in due form to be tried; when a decree was entered which dissolved the bonds of matrimony existing between the parties. The decree recites that the court had heard the testimony in support of the complaint and finds that the complainant was an actual resident of Cook county at the time of the commission of the alleged act of adultery; that for a long time she had been a *bona fide* resident of the state and that the defendant had been guilty of adultery, as charged in the complaint. The Circuit Court was a constitutional court, whose jurisdiction extended to the case presented by the pleadings and proofs, and to the granting of the decree. Subsequently, the alimony of $500 a month, which the decree had ordered to be paid to the plaintiff in that action, and all dower rights, were released by her to Guggenheim upon the payment by him of $150,000 in money. She then resumed her maiden name and, later in the same year, remarried. Some three years afterwards, in 1904, the plaintiff in this action, a resident of this state, went to Chicago and was married there to Guggenheim, and they have, since then, been living here as husband and wife. In 1908, this defendant, whose subsequent marriage, after obtaining her divorce from Guggenheim, had resulted in a separation, for reasons quite immaterial here, commenced an action in the Supreme Court of this state, suing in the name of Grace B. Guggenheim, wherein, alleging her marriage to Guggenheim, she prayed for a divorce from him upon the ground of his having lived in adulterous intercourse, in the city of New York, with a woman; who, in the bill of particulars, was specified as this plaintiff. Guggenheim appeared and made answer in that action, denying the adulterous conduct charged and setting up the proceedings in the divorce action in the Illinois court and the decree granted therein; the subsequent marriages, first, of the plaintiff, (this defendant), and, then, of himself with the woman, with whom the complaint alleged he was living in adulterous relations, to wit: the plaintiff in this action, and the birth of a child, the issue of the latter marriage. The co-respondent named in that action, (this plaintiff), as she was entitled to do under our practice, also, made answer to the complaint, with denials and defenses, substantially, the same as in Guggenheim's answer. That action came to trial and resulted in a judgment for the defendant, Guggenheim, dismissing the complaint of the plaintiff therein on the merits. This judgment adjudged, in substance, that the judgment of divorce obtained in the state of Illinois was rendered by a court of competent jurisdiction over the parties and the subject-matter of the action; that the finding of that court as to the residence of the plaintiff in that action could not be disturbed in the action brought by her here; that that judgment was binding and conclusive upon the parties, and had dissolved their marriage, and that the plaintiff, (this defendant), was estopped from questioning its validity on any ground. Appeals were taken to the Appellate Division and to this court by this defendant, plaintiff in that·action; but the judgment was affirmed by both courts. (201 N. Y. 602.) Having been defeated in her action here, this defendant, under the name of Grace B. Guggenheim, subsequently, filed in the Circuit Court of Cook county, state of Illinois, an " original bill in the nature of a bill of review," making William Guggenheim sole defendant in the proceeding, wherein she prayed that the previous decree of that court, dissolving her marriage with Guggenheim, might be " revoked, declared to be a nullity and expunged from the records." The grounds, for asking this relief, were, in brief, that she was not domiciled within the state of Illinois, when she commenced her action there for a divorce, and that that action was instituted pursuant to a conspiracy between her husband and other persons to accomplish his divorce from her, of which she was ignorant, and which fact with others relating to the institution of that divorce suit and bearing upon the lack of jurisdiction in the court from the fact of non-residence, she had not been permitted to show in the divorce action brought by her in the state of New York, by reason of the conclusiveness of the Illinois judgment. The facts alleged in the complaint have now been stated, sufficiently for this review, upon which the appellant bases her right to the intervention of a court of equity. She asserts that she has no adequate remedy at law and that the conduct of the defendant is unconscionable, " in harassing and vexing her by means of suits intended to affect her status and property rights;" meaning by the latter statement the rights derived through her marriage with Guggenheim.

It will be observed that this defendant, notwithstanding the judgment of divorce granted by the Illinois court, whose jurisdiction she had invoked, and notwithstanding subsequent acts on her part, in effect, recognizing its force, now seeks to have that judgment revoked upon the ground that, as she had never been a *bona fide* resident of the state, the court was without jurisdiction to entertain the suit. The facts alleged in the complaint may show the defendant's conduct to have been harassing and vexatious to this plaintiff; but those are considerations to be addressed to the court in Illinois. We might assume that the defendant's conduct was vexatious and that it was characterized by bad faith; but then we are no nearer to a legal reason for invoking the preventive power of a court of equity to enjoin the defendant from proceeding in the foreign court to obtain a review of its judgment. There is no averment by the plaintiff that she has sought to intervene in the proceeding there pending and that leave to come in and to be heard had been denied her. She does aver that her counsel advises her that she cannot, as matter of right, intervene and be heard in the suit; but that might be true and yet not amount to an averment that justice will not be done to her by the foreign court, by granting her leave to become a party to the proceeding. Not only, therefore, does she fail in that respect; but she fails upon the other ground taken by her, that the defendant's conduct is unconscionable. It is true that this defendant involved her, as co-respondent, in the divorce action, which she instituted in this state; but the courts were open to the defendant and it is quite immaterial to the point what may have been her motives in bringing the action, when she did. However unworthy they may have been in thus attacking the validity of her foreign judgment, it is perfectly clear that she has now taken the proper course, if she has any ground for the attack. If there are any grounds, of which she is in a position to avail herself, upon which the Illinois judgment of divorce can be revoked, or annulled, for fraud, or imposition, practiced upon the court, it is for that court to hear and consider them. She was properly defeated in her attempt to attack that judgment in her proceeding in the courts of this state. The jurisdiction of the foreign court had attached and had been competently exercised, before that action was brought. It has long been the settled doctrine and practice of the courts

of this state to regard a foreign judgment as beyond
collateral attack here, when it has been rendered by a
court, duly constituted under the laws of the foreign
state, with jurisdiction over the subject-matter of the
action and having gained jurisdiction over the parties.
That the constitution and laws of the state of Illinois
vested the Circuit Court of Cook county with jurisdiction
of matrimonial actions is not disputed. It had before it
the bill of complaint, in which the complainant averred,
under oath, her residence in the state, and the appearance
and answer of the defendant. It heard testimony in
open court and rendered its judgment; which found the
residence of the plaintiff, as she had alleged, and the
commission of the adulterous act by the defendant, as
she had charged.   That was sufficient to entitle its judgment to full faith and credit in the courts of this state.
(*Kinnier* v. *Kinnier*, 45 N. Y. 535; *Hunt* v. *Hunt*, 72 ib.
217; *Lynde* v. *Lynde*, 162 ib. 405; *Starbuck* v. *Starbuck*,
173 ib. 503.) These cases, and others might be cited,
establish the principle that when, as in this case, a court
of general jurisdiction in another state has passed upon
the jurisdictional facts and has assumed to hear and to
determine the issues, the complainant, who has invoked
its jurisdiction, will not be heard here in a collateral
attack upon its judgment. It may have decided erroneously; but that does not affect the validity of the decision.
Therefore, the situation became this, that this defendant,
when denied a standing in the courts of this state to
attack the decree of the foreign court, was, in effect,
remitted to what remedies were open to her in Illinois,
under its laws and the procedure in its courts. She
should not have attempted to nullify the foreign judgment here and she has now gone to the, only forum,
where she can be heard. The Illinois court has jurisdiction to consider and to determine the pending proceeding
and by comity, as of necessity, has the exclusive right to
decide the question raised by this defendant's bill of

review. Her right to be heard there having attached, it cannot, and it should not, be arrested by proceedings in another court. (*Peck* v. *Jenness*, 48 U. S. 612, 621.) This rule, as it was observed in the case cited, "has its foundation, not merely in comity, but in necessity." If this were not so, there might be provoked the unseemly spectacle of a clash in the orders of courts, with respect to jurisdiction, (See *Mead* v. *Merritt*, 2 Paige, 402), and, especially, would it be unseemly that the right of the defendant to ask for a review by the Illinois court of its judgment, upon the grounds assigned, should be restrained by a foreign court. The matter being under investigation by that court, it is not the province of equity to interfere. The arm of equity is strong and long to prevent injustice and wrong; but it will not be put forth, unless the law affords no adequate remedy and the case presented is one appropriate to the intervention of equity, because falling under one of the acknowledged heads of its jurisdiction. I think it is clear that the plaintiff's complaint shows no cause of action. She seeks to restrain the defendant from taking the very step, in her appeal to the Illinois court, which the judgment of the courts of this state in her divorce action here made it manifest she should have taken. Having held the judgment of the Illinois court to be conclusive upon the parties in this state, to enjoin the defendant now would be to restrain her from proceeding in the only jurisdiction, where the right, if any, to review the original judgment exists. The plaintiff is not a party to the foreign suit and no proceeding is pending here between her and the defendant, in which the matters litigated in that state are involved. She seeks to restrain the prosecution of an action between other parties, in which she has no legal interest and where, though she may be affected by the result, because of her marital relations with the defendant therein, she does not show that she has applied for, and has been refused, leave to intervene for her own protection. I do not think it exceeds the mark to say that, presumably, the Illinois court, in view of the litigation in our courts over its judgment, provoked by this defendant and into which this plaintiff was brought, and because of the acts of the former upon which the latter had, not unreasonably, placed reliance in contracting her marriage, will hold her to be materially affected by the judgment to be pronounced and, therefore, will allow her to come in and be heard. However that may be, this plaintiff cannot say that such a legal remedy has been denied her and that she is without redress in the foreign court.

I think that the judgment below was right and that it should be affirmed.

Cullen, Ch. J., Haight, Vann, Werner, Chase and Collin, JJ., concur.

Judgment affirmed, with costs.

Brockport-Holley Water Company, Respondent, *v.* The Village of Brockport, Appellant.

Contract — action by water company against municipality to recover rentals claimed to be due under contract to furnish water for fire service at a certain pressure — construction of contract — liability of municipality.

1. Defendant agreed to pay plaintiff an annual rental for hydrants for fire service, plaintiff to maintain a certain pressure of water therein "except in case of unavoidable accident." The contract provided also that no rental should be paid for such time as fire protection is not furnished. The jury found that a failure to maintain the water pressure service required was owing to natural causes over which plaintiff had no control and was in the nature of an unavoidable accident. *Held*, that the plaintiff is entitled to recover the contract price for the time in which it maintained the water pressure specified in the contract; but for the time that it failed to maintain such pressure it is not entitled to recover the rental specified in the contract.

2. The defendant continued to use such water as the plaintiff was able to furnish during the entire term of the contract. *Held*, that the court correctly charged, " If you find that the defendant has had the benefit of whatever services the plaintiff was able to give and has used it, then, gentlemen, the plaintiff would be entitled to a verdict at your hands for the reasonable value of the service rendered by it and accepted by this defendant, after deducting whatever damage it has sustained and proved on account of the plaintiff being unable to furnish the contract pressure." *Held*, further, that the contract price for rental of hydrants for fire protection affords no proper basis for the determination of the value of the service of water alone.

Brockport-Holley Water Co. v. *Vil. of Brockport*, 138 App. Div. 913, reversed.

(Argued October 25, 1911; decided November 28, 1911.)

APPEAL from a judgment of the Appellate Division of the Supreme Court in the fourth judicial department, entered May 6, 1910, affirming a judgment in favor of plaintiff entered upon a verdict.

The nature of the action and the facts, so far as material, are stated in the opinion.

John D. Burns for appellant. The plaintiff failed to fulfill its contract, and was not entitled to recover. (*People* v. *N. R. W. Co.*, 38 N. Y. S. R. 92; *Bank of Montreal* v. *Recknagel*, 109 N. Y. 482; *Oakley* v. *Morton*, 11 N. Y. 25; *Roberts* v. *Opdyke*, 40 N. Y. 259; *Glacius* v. *Black*, 50 N. Y. 145; *Weeks* v. *O'Brien*, 141 N. Y. 199; *Sager* v. *Gonnermann*, 50 Misc. Rep. 500; *Belfast Water Co.* v. *City of Belfast*, 92 Me. 52.) It was error to permit the plaintiff to give in evidence excuses for the non-performance of its contract. (*Harmon* v. *Bingham*, 12 N. Y. 99; *Logan* v. *Consolidated Gas Co.*, 107 App. Div. 384; *P. P. & C. I. R. R. Co.* v. *C. I. & B. R. R. Co.*, 144 N. Y. 152; *Wheeler* v. *Conn. M. L. Ins. Co.*, 82 N. Y. 543; *Booth* v. *S. D. R. M. Co.*, 60 N. Y. 487; *Ward* v. *H. R. Building Co.*, 125 N. Y. 230; *Cobb* v. *Harmon*, 23 N. Y. 148; *Howell* v. *Coupland*, L. R. [9 Q. B.] 462;

Anderson v. *May*, 52 Minn. 280.) The damages which plaintiff claimed were not established by competent legal evidence. (*Wolfe* v. *Howes*, 20 N. Y. 197; *Gaynor* v. *Jonas*, 104 App. Div. 35; *Allen* v. *McKibben*, 5 Mich. 449; *S. W. Co.* v. *Skowhegan Village*, 66 Atl. Rep. 714, *W. W. Co.* v. *Winfield*, 51 Kans. 104; *Chamboard* v. *Cagney*, 23 J. & S. 474; *Tenpenny* v. *C. E. Ins. Co.*, 43 N. Y. 279; *Ives* v. *Quinn*, 7 Misc. Rep. 155; *Jones* v. *Morgan*, 90 N. Y. 4; *Gregory* v. *Fichtner*, 14 N. Y. Supp. 891.)

W. A. Matson for respondent. No error was committed by the court in the reception of evidence or in the submission of the case to the jury. (*S. W. Co.* v. *Skowhegan Village*, 102 Me. 323; *W. W. Co.* v. *Winfield*, 51 Kans. 104; *Kaufman* v. *Raeder*, 108 Fed. Rep. 171; *City of St. Charles* v. *Stookey*, 151 Fed. Rep. 766; *Brown* v. *Foster*, 108 N. Y. 387; *Omaha Water Co.* v. *City of Omaha*, 156 Fed. Rep. 922; *Allen* v. *McKibbin*, 5 Mich. 449; *Studer* v. *Bleistein*, 115 N. Y. 316; *Chambers* v. *Lancaster*, 160 N. Y. 342.)

HAIGHT, J. The plaintiff is a public service domestic corporation and brings this action to recover from the defendant, a municipal corporation, the contract price for the rental value of hydrants and the water supplied for fire and other services. The complaint contains two counts, one based upon contract and the other for the value of the services rendered and water supplied. The answer denies performance of the contract on the part of the plaintiff and alleges a counterclaim for money expended in procuring an engine and operating the same.

The contract under which the plaintiff seeks to recover provides as follows: "*Thirteenth.* The village hereby agrees to pay to the Company an annual rental of $2,750 for the seventy-two hydrants, now located on its existing mains, during the fulfillment of the conditions of this fire

26

service agreement by the said Company; also $37.50 per year for each additional hydrant in excess of seventy-two located hereafter on now existing mains, said annual rental to be paid in equal quarterly installments at the end of each quarter in which the Company has faithfully performed all the stipulations and promises of this agreement, the said payments to be made at the first regular meeting of the Board of Trustees in the months of December, March, June and September of each year. The first payment shall be due September 1st, 1903. The Company agrees constantly, day and night, except in case of unavoidable accident, to keep all said water mains and hydrants supplied with water, in good order and efficiency, and with such pressure of water therein as will furnish prompt and efficient fire streams therefrom when hose is properly attached and used, but at no time less than fifty-five pounds pressure at public building, to be tested by a gauge to be furnished by the company, except that in September and October the pressure shall be at least fifty pounds. In case of fire the direct pressure shall be given from pumping station. No rental shall be paid for such time as fire protection service is not furnished." This contract was entered into on the 23d day of April, 1903, and was to continue for a period of five years.

The main question of fact litigated upon the trial was as to whether the plaintiff had committed a breach of the contract. It was conceded that it had failed to maintain the water pressure required by the contract, but it sought to excuse this failure upon the ground of unavoidable accident, owing to the fact that a long drought had so dried up the wells which furnished the plaintiff's supply of water that it was impossible to maintain the pressure required. This question the trial court submitted to the jury with the instruction: "If you shall find from the evidence that when it was discovered by the plaintiff that the water supply was failing, that there was another available supply that could have been had and the plaintiff knew of it and did not exercise active vigilance to try and increase its supply, but, in effect, did not make an honest effort to increase it, and because of that, failed to furnish the contract pressure, if you find these facts from the evidence, gentlemen, the plaintiff could not recover when the pressure was below the contract pressure and your verdict would 'be for the defendant. But if you shall find that the failure in the pressure was owing to natural causes over which the plaintiff had no control, and that as soon as it was known that the supply was failing the plaintiff made an honest effort to augment its water supply and exercised active vigilance to do so from any supply that was known to it and which was available and sufficient; if you find that the defendant has had the benefit of whatever services the plaintiff was able to give and has used it, then, gentlemen, the plaintiff would be entitled to a verdict at your hands for the reasonable value of the service rendered by it and accepted by this defendant after deducting whatever damage it has sustained and proved on account of the plaintiff being unable to furnish the contract pressure."

In view of the fact that the jury found a verdict in favor of the plaintiff it must be deemed to have found the question of fact so submitted in favor of plaintiff and, inasmuch as the judgment has been unanimously affirmed, we are in our review bound by such determination. Assuming, therefore, the facts to be as found, the question arises as to the rule of damages that should be applied in this case. This involves a construction of the contract. It provides for the payment by the village to the company of an annual rental for the hydrants located on its existing mains for fire service. In consideration of such rental the company agrees constantly, day and night, except in case of unavoidable accident, to keep all its water mains and hydrants supplied with water in good order and efficiency and with such pressure of water therein as will furnish prompt and efficient fire streams therefrom when hose is properly attached and used, but at no time less than fifty-five pounds pressure except in September and October when it shall be at least fifty pounds; and then comes the provision that "no rental shall be paid for such time as fire protection service is not furnished." As we understand this agreement, its design and purpose was to furnish fire protection as well as service of water in case of fire. It is so recited in the preamble of the contract. The provision for keeping the water pressure at a specified figure, day and night, was designed to afford protection from damages resulting from fires. For, if a fire was discovered, the means would be at hand to quickly extinguish it and thus prevent the destruction of property and the damages resulting therefrom. It would, consequently, follow that, had the plaintiff kept the pressure at the point specified in the contract it would be entitled at the end of each quarter to receive the specified rental, even though in the meantime it had not been required to furnish a pail of water for the extinguishment of fires. We think it also follows that, in view of the finding of the jury, that the failure of the plaintiff to maintain the pressure required was owing to causes over which it had no control and was in the nature of "unavoidable accident," the plaintiff is entitled to recover the contract price for the time in which it maintained the water pressure specified in the contract; but for the time that it failed to maintain such pressure it is not entitled to recover the rental specified in the contract. We do not, however, think that a failure to maintain the pressure for a part of three months would justify the village in refusing to pay any portion of the quarterly rental; for, if that construction should be adopted, then an unavoidable accident which should prevent the plaintiff from maintaining the pressure for a single day would deprive it of the right to recover any rental whatever for the remaining quarter of the year. We, therefore, think that the plaintiff, under the contract, should be paid for the time it actually maintained the pressure required and that for the time that it failed to maintain the pressure it cannot recover under the provisions of the contract.   It has been suggested that fire protection was afforded, even though the company did not maintain the specified pressure.   Doubtless it did, to some extent, but the difficulty is that the contract specified the pressure which should constitute protection under its terms and specifically provided that no payment should be made for protection which did not comply with the provisions of the contract.

Under the second cause of action set forth in the complaint the plaintiff alleges the service of water to the defendant and asks to recover for its reasonable value. It appears that, notwithstanding the drought and the failure of the plaintiff to maintain the pressure of water specified in the contract, the village continued to use such water as the plaintiff was able to furnish and continued to do so during the entire term of the contract and at the end thereof renewed the same.   Upon this branch of the case the trial court charged the jury: "If you find that the defendant had the benefit of whatever services the plaintiff was able to give and has used it, then, gentlemen, the plaintiff would be entitled to a verdict at your hands for the reasonable value of the services rendered by it and accepted by the defendant, after deducting whatever damage it has sustained and proved on account of the plaintiff being unable to furnish the contract pressure."   This charge does not appear to have been excepted to by either party and it appears to us to constitute the correct rule which should be applied in determining the amount that should be awarded the plaintiff in this case.   Under the contract the plaintiff can recover nothing for fire protection for the time in which the pressure required was not maintained, but in view of the fact that the village has accepted and received water service from the plaintiff for such period it is but right that it should pay for the water so furnished its fair and reasonable value. The plaintiff claims that such value is proportionally the same as the contract price for rental service dependent upon the number of pounds pressure, and in order to prove this the plaintiff produced an expert witness upon the stand and asked him the following question: "Assume that the contract price for hydrant rental service is $37.50 for fifty-five pound service; or assume that is what fifty-five pound service is worth, $37.50 per hydrant per year, are you able to state what the variation pound service that is rendered, fifty-four pounds, fifty-three pounds, fifty-two pounds and so on down to nothing, of what value that is in the market to the Village of Brockport or others, similarly using the service?" The witness having answered that he was able to state, was then asked, "What is that value?" This was objected to as incompetent, immaterial and irrelevant, etc. The objection was overruled and an exception was taken, and the witness answered: "I should consider the service worth a *pro rata* price based upon the pressure." A motion was then made by the defendant to strike out the answer, but the court ruled that it might stand, and a further exception was taken. The witness then illustrated, stating: "If fifty-five pounds pressure was worth a certain sum of money, fifty-three pounds would be fifty-three fifty-fifths of that sum, and so on; and likewise, five pounds would be worth five fifty-fifths of that sum." We are of the opinion that these exceptions were well taken and that the plaintiff failed to prove the fair value of its services in furnishing water. As we have already shown, the contract included fire protection of a specified character, as well as service of water in case of fire; and under the contract, if the fire protection was not furnished, no payment was to be made therefor. This, therefore, limits the plaintiff to the recovery for the value of the service in furnishing water only, and, in determining that value, the contract price for rental of hydrants for fire protection affords no proper basis for the determination of the value of the service of water alone.

Complaint is made with reference to a number of other rulings made in regard to admission of evidence on behalf of the plaintiff. Some of the rulings were of doubtful propriety, but we do not deem it necessary to now consider them in detail, further than to suggest that the financial straits of the plaintiff form no legal excuse or justification for its failure to perform its contract, and the fact that the insurance companies have not as yet seen fit to raise the risks of insurance does not in any respect relieve the plaintiff from the discharge of its duty to the village. For the errors above alluded to, the judgment should be reversed and a new trial ordered, with costs to abide the event.

CULLEN, Ch. J., GRAY, VANN, WERNER, CHASE and COLLIN, JJ., concur.

Judgment reversed, etc.

GENERAL RAILWAY SIGNAL COMPANY, Respondent, *v.* THE TITLE GUARANTY AND SURETY COMPANY, Appellant.

Guaranty and surety — bond indemnifying employer against loss arising from larceny or embezzlement of a clerk — waiver of provision therein that bond shall be "of no effect unless signed by the employee."

This action was brought upon a bond issued by the defendant to the plaintiff, by which the former agreed to indemnify the latter against any pecuniary loss occurring through the larceny, or embezzlement, of one of its clerks. Defendant alleged the invalidity of the bond by reason of non-compliance with the provision that it should be "of no effect unless signed by the employé." The defendant, at the time the bond was delivered, held an agreement by the employee to repay any losses it might sustain by reason thereof. The bond was prepared by defendant's agents and forwarded with a letter stating "enclosed herewith please find bond duly executed on behalf of Ralph J. Ellis (the employee) which we trust will be satisfactory," and accepted payment of the premium thereon. *Held*, that defendant waived the signature of the employee and is liable upon the bond.

General Ry. Signal Co. v. *Title Guaranty & Surety Co.*, 139 App. Div. 925, affirmed.

(Argued October 26, 1911; decided November 28, 1911.)

APPEAL from a judgment of the Appellate Division of the Supreme Court in the fourth judicial department, entered June 6, 1910, affirming a judgment in favor of plaintiff entered upon a decision of the court at a Trial Term, a jury having been waived.

The nature of the action and the facts, so far as material, are stated in the opinion.

Charles Van Voorhis for appellant. The bond was invalid and of no effect and never became a binding obligation upon this defendant because it was not signed by the employee. (*U. C. L. Ins. Co.* v. *U. S. F. & G. Co.*, 99 Md. 423; *U. S. F. & G. Co.* v. *Ridgeley*, 97 N. W. Rep. 836; *Adelberg* v. *U. S. F. & G. Co.*, 45 Misc. Rep. 376; *Platauer* v. *American Bonding Co.*, 92 N. Y. Supp. 238; *Smith* v. *Molleson*, 148 N. Y. 246; *Union Ins. Co.* v. *Central Trust Co.*, 157 N. Y. 655.) There was no waiver of the provision of the bond that it would be invalid and of no effect unless signed by the employee; neither has the defendant by its conduct estopped itself from asserting that the bond was invalid. (*Baumgartel* v. *P. W. Ins. Co.*, 136 N. Y. 547; *N. Assur. Co.* v. *G. V. B. Assn.*, 183 N. Y. 308; *Coe* v. *Hobby*, 72 N. Y. 148; Herman on Estoppel, 954; *Wood* v. *American F. Ins. Co.*, 149 N. Y. 382; *Robbins* v. *S. F. & M. Ins. Co.*, 149 N. Y. 477; *Gray* v. *G. F. Ins. Co.*, 155 N. Y. 180; *Allen* v. *G. & A. Ins. Co.*, 123 N. Y. 6.)

Hiram R. Wood for respondent. There is ample evidence to support the findings that the signature of

Ellis to the bond in suit was waived by the appellant, and it has by its conduct estopped itself from asserting the invalidity of the bond on that account; and that the appellant issued the bond intending to be bound thereby, although the same, to its knowledge, lacked the signature of the employee. (*Williams* v. *Marshall*, 42 Barb. 524; *City of New York* v. *Kent*, 25 J. & S. 109; *Dillon* v. *Anderson*, 43 N. Y. 231; *G. V. Co.* v. *Bacon*, 148 Mass. 542; *Robin* v. *Springfield*, 149 N. Y. 484; *Wood* v. *American F. Ins. Co.*, 149 N. Y. 385; *N. A. Co.* v. *G. V. B. Assn.*, 183 U. S. 308; *Anderson* v. *Fitzgerald*, 4 H. L. Cas. 484; *American Surety Co.* v. *Pauly*, 170 U. S. 133; *Reynolds* v. *C. F. I. Co.*, 47 N. Y. 597.)

GRAY, J.   This action was brought upon a bond issued by the defendant to the plaintiff, by which the former agreed to indemnify the latter against any pecuniary loss occurring through the larceny, or embezzlement, of one of its clerks.   Among other defenses, the defendant alleged the invalidity of the bond for not having been signed by the clerk.   The plaintiff had judgment in its favor at the Trial Term and the affirmance of the judgment, at the Appellate Division, was by a divided court; the dissent being based, among other things, upon the ground of the invalidity of the bond, referred to as a defense, and that presents the only serious question for our consideration.

The plaintiff was engaged in the business of manufacturing and installing railway signaling apparatus; having its principal office at Rochester, in this state, and a branch office at Chicago, in the state of Illinois.   The manager of the Chicago office had the custody and expenditure of moneys, from time to time, remitted to it by the plaintiff and employed as cashier, one Ellis; to whom was intrusted, necessarily, the handling of some of the moneys.   It was to secure itself against any dishonesty on Ellis' part that the plaintiff applied to the local agents of the defendant, a foreign corporation, for the bond in question. They consented to the issuance of such a bond and, thereupon, sent a formal application to be filled out and executed for the plaintiff by its manager in Chicago; who duly complied and returned the paper to them in Rochester. At the same time, they, also, forwarded an application to be filled out and executed by Ellis, himself. This application, after giving certain information, by way of answers to questions, concluded with this agreement on the applicant's part: "I hereby agree for myself, my heirs and administrators in consideration of THE TITLE GUARANTY & SURETY COMPANY becoming surety for me and issuing Bond hereby applied for or any renewal thereof or any further or other bond hereby issued by the said company on my behalf in my present or any other position in this service to protect and indemnify the said Company against any loss damage or expense that it may sustain or become liable for in consequence of such guaranty on my behalf by said Company and forthwith after the said Company shall have paid the party or parties entitled to the same any money under or by reason of such guaranty to repay the said Company the amount so paid and all other losses, costs, damages and expenses if any that it shall have incurred or become liable for in consequence of such guaranty." Ellis signed and returned this instrument to the defendant's agents, as they had requested. After both these instruments had been received back by the agents, this bond was prepared and executed by the defendant and, subsequently, was mailed by its agents to the plaintiff, at its principal office, without having Ellis' signature. With it went, also, a letter stating: "enclosed herewith please find bond duly executed on behalf of Ralph J. Ellis, which we trust will be satisfactory." A bill for the premium was, thereafter, rendered to, and paid by, the plaintiff. Within three months Ellis took moneys belonging to the plaintiff, under circumstances amounting to larceny and embezzlement,

and absconded.   Upon a claim being made against the
defendant, the fact appeared, upon which the refusal to
pay is based, that the bond lacked the signature of Ellis.
Although it made reference to the plaintiff's application,
as Ellis' employer, it did not refer to any application by
Ellis; but it contained a provision that it should be " of no
effect unless signed by the employé" and an agreement
by the said employé indemnifying the defendant against
all loss and damage, which it might sustain by reason of
its having entered into the bond.   The complaint set forth
the provision, that the bond should be invalid unless
signed by the employé, and averred that the defendant
had waived that part of it.   The trial court found, among
other findings of facts, that the bond had not been signed
by the empleyé; that his signature had been waived by
the defendant and that the defendant, by its acts and
conduct, was estopped from asserting any invalidity on
that account.

This is the case, therefore, that the agents of the
defendant, to whom the application for the bond was
made and who, subsequently, caused the bond to be executed and to be delivered to the plaintiff, knew at the
time of its delivery that it had not been signed by Ellis.
They had sent to Chicago applications to be signed by
the manager and by Ellis before making out the bond
and, of course, they knew that the bond itself should be
sent there, also, if Ellis' signature was deemed essential
to the obligation.   But they did not do so and they chose
to deliver the bond without obtaining his signature to it,
with a letter, stating that it was "duly executed on
behalf of Ralph J. Ellis."   Either they were dealing
honestly with the plaintiff, intending to waive the condition of Ellis' signature, under the circumstances; or they
were scheming to deceive and to defraud.   The law will
presume the former intention.

While it might be argued that the authority of these
agents of the defendant was sufficient to waive the con-

dition of the bond, in question, in delivering it as it was and by receiving the premium, upon the same principle that insurers have been held bound by the acts of their agents in waiving conditions of a policy, (*McNally* v. *Phoenix Ins. Co.*, 137 N. Y. 389, 396), we have a broader basis of facts and circumstances in this case, upon which a waiver may securely rest. It might be said that the objection to the enforcement of this bond went a little further, in principle; in that it went to its completion as an instrument and waiver, therefore, needed fuller proof in the facts. However it may be, it is not necessary to decide the point; for a waiver by the defendant need not rest upon the fact alone of the delivery of the bond. The legal presumption of a waiver may rest upon the further fact that the defendant had in its possession, at the time of delivery, the agreement signed by Ellis, which was to the same effect as in the bond and quite as comprehensive, as an indemnification of the defendant against any loss by reason of going upon the bond. The application on behalf of the plaintiff was made a part of the bond; but that of Ellis was not. He was brought into it by supplementing the usual provisions of the bond by an agreement on his part. Acting for their principal, we must assume that the defendant's agents had its interests in view and that they considered them as well protected by the separate covenant of Ellis, as if he had subscribed to it upon the bond. To have insisted upon such subscription by him had become unnecessary; for the covenant in the bond had ceased to be of importance. All of the facts and circumstances, therefore, conclusively, support the finding of a waiver.

It might be observed that no written agreement was, in fact, essential to the defendant for the future enforcement of any claim it might have against the defaulting employé. Upon making good to the plaintiff the amount of any defalcation, the defendant would be subrogated to all of the former's rights of action against the defaulter and any action by it would be quite as well founded as though it was brought upon the express agreement of the employé to repay. While the defendant required the employé's signature to the bond as a condition of its validity as an obligation, as it had the right to do, in holding it estopped from now insisting upon the condition, it loses nothing but a technical defense; which, if suffered to prevail in the face of the facts and circumstances of the case, would mean the lending of the aid of the court to the perpetration of a fraud. Jealous as the law is of the rights of a surety, the limit of its protection is reached when the surety invokes its aid to defraud.

Other objections are raised by the appellant; but, as they are not tenable and relate to the sufficiency of the evidence, it is unnecessary to discuss them. For the reasons assigned, I think that the judgment appealed from should be affirmed.

CULLEN, Ch. J., HAIGHT, VANN, CHASE and COLLIN, JJ., concur; WERNER, J., not sitting.

Judgment affirmed, with costs.

PHILIP ROHRBACHER, Respondent, *v.* MARY A. GILLIG et al., Appellants.

Negligence — contributory negligence — when person injured by falling into elevator shaft in unlighted hall guilty of contributory negligence.

1. A person coming into an unfamiliar situation, where a condition of darkness renders the use of his eyesight ineffective to define his surroundings, is not justified in the absence of any special stress of circumstances in proceeding further, without first finding out where he is going and what may be the obstructions to his safe progress.

2. Plaintiff entered a building occupied by several tenants for the purpose of transacting business with tenants on one of the upper floors, and passing the stairway went on through the hallway

which was so dark that he could not see distinctly where he was going, and continuing "at his regular gait," stepped in a half-open door and fell to the bottom of an elevator. shaft. It was not shown that defendants, the owners of the building, had assumed any obligation to keep the hallway lighted or that any statutory provision applied to the existing condition. *Held*, that the defendants were not shown to have neglected any legal duty to plaintiff, and further that he was guilty of contributory negligence.

Rohrbacher v. *Gillig*, 140 App. Div. 883, reversed.

(Argued October 31, 1911; decided November 28, 1911.)

APPEAL from a judgment of the Appellate Division of the Supreme Court in the fourth judicial department, entered July 23, 1910, affirming a judgment in favor of plaintiff entered upon a verdict.

The nature of the action and the facts, so far as material, are stated in the opinion.

Frank Gibbons and *Henry W. Pottle* for appellants. As a general proposition and in the absence of unusual and extraordinary circumstances the owner of a building used and occupied by several tenants is not negligent simply because he fails to keep the halls and stairways of a building lighted. (*Hilsenbeck* v. *Guhring*, 131 N. Y. 674; *Brugher* v. *Buchtenkirch*, 167 N. Y. 153; *Gorman* v. *White*, 19 App. Div. 324; *Racine* v. *Morris*, 201 N. Y. 240.) The plaintiff failed to show himself free from contributory negligence. (*Brugher* v. *Buchtenkirch*, 167 N. Y. 153; *Hilsenbeck* v. *Guhring*, 131 N. Y. 674; *Dailey* v. *Distler*, 115 App. Div. 102; *Weller* v. *Consolidated Gas Co.*, 198 N. Y. 98.)

Hamilton Ward for respondent. The defendant was guilty of negligence in maintaining the premises in the condition in which they were at the time of the accident, and the questions of negligence were properly submitted by the trial court. (Thompson on Neg. § 968; *Dunn* v. *Duran*, 9 Daly, 389; *Beck* v. *Carter*, 68 N. Y. 283;

Swinarton v. *Boutillier,* 7 Misc. Rep. 639; *Flynn* v. *C. R. R. Co.,* 142 N. Y. 439; *Graham* v. *Bauland Co.,* 97 App. Div. 141; *Quirk* v. *S. C. Co.,* 43 App. Div. 464; *Hillyer* v. *L. S. S. Co.,* 133 App. Div. 125; *McRickert* v. *Flint,* 114 N. Y. 222; *Simons* v. *Peters,* 85 Hun, 93.) The question of plaintiff's contributory negligence was for the jury. (*McRickert* v. *Flint,* 114 N. Y. 222; *Simon* v. *Peters,* 85 Hun, 93; 20 App. Div. 252; *Dawson* v. *Sloan,* 17 J. & S. 304; 100 N. Y. 620; *Atkinson* v. *Abraham,* 45 Hun, 238; *Hillyer* v. *L. S. S. Co.,* 133 App. Div. 125; *Towsey* v. *Roberts,* 114 N. Y. 312; *Wilcox* v. *City of Rochester,* 190 N. Y. 137; *Totten* v. *Phillips,* 52 N. Y. 354.)

GRAY, J. This action was brought to recover damages for the personal injuries sustained by the plaintiff from falling down an elevator shaft, in a building owned by the defendants. He obtained a verdict in his favor and the judgment, upon that verdict, has been affirmed by the Appellate Division, by the divided vote of the justices.

These were the circumstances. The plaintiff, a man of fifty-six years of age, had occasion to enter the building for the purpose of transacting some business with tenants upon the fifth floor. Its five floors were leased out to several tenants; the ground, second and third floors being used as a restaurant and the fourth and fifth floors for other business purposes. The entrance to the building from the street admits to a hall, which extends some distance back into the building. Immediately, upon entering on the ground floor, appears a stairway, giving access to all of the upper stories. Passing this stairway, the hall extends back and at its end are two doorways; one on the right affording entrance into the restaurant and the other terminating the hallway and opening into the shaft of an elevator, intended and used, only, for freight purposes by the tenants of the upper floors. This latter door opened outwards into the hall and on the wall above was the sign of "Mindel's Dining Parlors." In the afternoon of the day in question, the plaintiff entered the building and, according to his testimony, saw the broad stairway leading up from the hall; but he was deterred from entering it by noticing persons walking about in the upper hall. He thought it was a part of the restaurant and that he could find another flight of stairs. So he went on. The hallway was so dark that he could not see, distinctly, where he was going; but continuing "at his regular gait" he saw, in front of him, a door half open and, stepping in to find another stairway, fell to the bottom of the elevator shaft. It was the first time he had been in the building. The defendants did not undertake to keep the hallway lighted and the lock upon the elevator door was broken. The trial court denied motions, which were made by the defendants, at the close of the plaintiff's case and at the close of the whole case, for the dismissal of the complaint and for the direction of a verdict upon the grounds of a failure to show negligence in the defendants, or that the plaintiff was free from contributory negligence. The case was sent to the jury upon the instruction, acquiesced in by the plaintiff, that the negligence charged against the defendants was that they "permitted the hallway to be in an unlighted condition, that this doorway was out of repair, the door defective."

It is very clear, I think, upon the facts, that the defendants were not shown to have neglected any legal duty to the plaintiff, with which they could properly be said to be chargeable, and it seems, equally, clear that the plaintiff contributed to the result of his ill-advised venture in the hall by a failure to exercise that caution which the situation should have suggested to him. It was not shown that the defendants had assumed any obligation to keep the hallway lighted; or that the provisions of the statute applicable to tenement houses, or tenant factories, had any application. A broad well-lighted stairway led to the floors above. There was nothing to indicate the existence of any other stairway, or of any elevators. The plaintiff had a right to be upon the premises and if, upon entering them, a plain and safe access to the upper floors was afforded him, in the usual way, the defendants owed him no other duty. They were not insurers of his safety. This hallway was no place for the public and of this persons were sufficiently advised by the absence of any light, or of any invitation to follow it up. The facts are very similar to those in the case of *Hilsenbeck* v. *Guhring*, (131 N. Y. 674). In that case, the plaintiff, going through a dimly lighted hallway of an apartment house, walked through an open door and fell down the cellar steps. The particular negligence charged against these defendants was similarly charged against the defendant there and a judgment, which the plaintiff had recovered, was reversed in this court upon reasoning quite pertinent here.

Again, the situation, as revealed by the evidence, established, conclusively, contributory negligence in the plaintiff. Being upon the premises for the first time and refusing to use the broad and safe stairway before him, without any good reason in the appearance of things, he proceeded on through the hall, "at his regular gait," although "so dark that he could not see distinctly where he was going," and plunged through a half open door into an open shaft. Had he looked to the right of the door, he would have seen an entrance to the restaurant. Had he tried to discover what there was beyond the half open door, he would have found that there was no stairway and he would have been advised of his peril in proceeding further without a light. If he was unable to perceive existing conditions, that inability imposed upon him the duty of exercising the greatest caution, or of refraining from proceeding further in the building, without first finding out where he might safely go. This observation was made in the opinion in *Brugher* v. *Buchtenkirch*, (167 N. Y. 153 at p. 157). In that case the plaintiff, also, continued past a flight of stairs, leading to the upper stories, and through a hall, which was unlighted, and fell down some steps. The judgment there recovered by the plaintiff was reversed in this court upon the authority of our decisions in *Hilsenbeck* v. *Guhring*, (*supra*), and in *Piper* v. *N. Y. C. & H. R. R. R. Co.*, (156 N. Y. 224). The principle, which these decisions have established, is that a person, coming into such an unfamiliar situation, where a condition of darkness renders the use of his eyesight ineffective to define his surroundings, is not justified, in the absence of any special stress of circumstances, in proceeding further, without first finding out where he is going and what may be the obstructions to his safe progress. That was this case. There was no good reason for the plaintiff's proceeding as he did and having elected to walk on in the darkness, without even feeling his way, he must accept the consequences of his undue precipitation. The views expressed render it unnecessary to consider certain errors in the rulings of the trial court, made upon the defendant's requests to charge. They rested upon the erroneous instructions as to defendant's negligence, stated in the main charge and to which allusion has been made, and upon the view that there was a question upon the facts as to the plaintiff's contributory negligence.

The judgment should be reversed and a new trial ordered, with costs to abide the event.

CULLEN, Ch. J., HAIGHT, WILLARD BARTLETT, HISCOCK, and COLLIN, JJ., concur; VANN, J., concurs in result on the ground that the plaintiff was guilty of contributory negligence as matter of law.

Judgment reversed, etc.

WORLD's DISPENSARY MEDICAL ASSOCIATION, Respondent,
v. ROBERT J. PIERCE, Appellant.

**Trade name — action to restrain unfair competition in the use of
a trade name — unlawful use of one's own name with prefix "Dr."**

1. While it is a general principle of law that one's name is his
property, and he has the same right to its use and enjoyment as he
has to that of any other species of property, it is also true that no
man has a right to sell his products or goods as those of another.
He may not through unfairness, artifice, misrepresentation or fraud
injure the business of another or induce the public to believe his
product is the product of the other.

2. One Ray V. Pierce, a physician, transferred to the plaintiff
upon its incorporation his business of manufacturing and selling,
under their trade names, several proprietary remedies which are
commonly known to the public as "Dr. Pierce's Remedies" and
also as "Pierce's Remedies." Ray V. Pierce has been at all times
and is now the president and a director of the plaintiff, and devised
the formula for each remedy. Defendant has advertised and sold
certain proprietary remedies in boxes under the name of "Dr.
Pierce," the words "R. J. Pierce" thereon being a facsimile signature. The defendant is not a licensed physician, nor entitled to
practice as such under the law of the state. *Held*, that the
defendant should be enjoined from using the prefix "Dr.," and
from using the words "Pierce" or "Pierce's" in advertising,
describing, designating, labeling or selling his proprietary remedies unless said word be immediately preceded on the same line
therewith by defendant's first or proper christian name, and his
middle name or the initial letter thereof in letters identical in
size, color, style of type and conspicuousness with those of said
word, so that said word shall not appear for any of the purposes
aforesaid except when thus conjoined with the words "Robert J."
or "Robert," followed by the middle name of the defendant.

World's Dispensary Medical Assn. v. *Pierce*, 138 App. Div. 401,
modified.

(Argued October 30, 1911; decided November 28, 1911.)

APPEAL from a judgment of the Appellate Division of
the Supreme Court in the fourth judicial department,
entered May 7, 1910, affirming a judgment in favor of

plaintiff entered upon a decision of the court on trial at Special Term.

The nature of the action and the facts, so far as material, are stated in the opinion.

David M. Dean for appellant. The judgment should be reversed because it protects the plaintiff, a stock corporation, in the use of the trade name "Dr. Pierce," in carrying on the unlawful business of conducting the hospital and medical practice founded by Dr. Pierce. (*People* v. *W. D. Inst.*, 192 N. Y. 454; *Falk* v. *A. W. I. T. Co.*, 180 N. Y. 445.) Defendant has the right to use his own name in his own business, even though he may thereby interfere with and injure the business of another bearing the same name, provided he does not resort to any artifice or do any act calculated to mislead the public, and produce injury to the other beyond that which results from the similarity of names. (*Meneely* v. *Meneely*, 62 N. Y. 427; *Devlin* v. *Devlin*, 69 N. Y. 212; *C. S. H. Co.* v. *H. S. Co.*, 144 N. Y. 462.)

Joseph H. Morey for respondent. This is a flagrant case of unfair competition. Defendant's business is conceded to be based upon a deliberate fraud, designed to injure the plaintiff, and the defendant is designedly and dishonestly striving to trade upon the plaintiff's reputation. (Paul on Trade Marks, 377, § 209, 414; *Ball* v. *Broadway Bazaar*, 194 N. Y. 429; *Kohler* v. *Sanders*, 122 N. Y. 65; *Meyer* v. *Bull Medicine Co.*, 18 U. S. App. 372; *Garrett* v. *T. H. Garrett Co.*, 78 Fed. Rep. 472; *Peck Bros. & Co.* v. *Peck Bros. Co.*, 113 Fed. Rep. 291; *Arnheim* v. *Arnheim*, 28 Misc. Rep. 399; *Baker* v. *Sanders*, 80 Fed. Rep. 889; *Baker Co.* v. *Baker*, 77 Fed. Rep. 181; *Allegretti Case*, 85 Fed. Rep. 643; *Stuart* v. *Stewart Co.*, 91 Fed. Rep. 243; *Duryea* v. *National Starch Co.*, 79 Fed. Rep. 651.) The defendant's claim that one part of the plaintiff's business is unlawful has no materiality whatever in this case. (*Shaver* v. *Heller*

& Merz Co., 108 Fed. Rep. 821; *General Electric Co.* v. *Wise*, 119 Fed. Rep. 922; *Trice* v. *Comstock*, 121 Fed. Rep. 620; *City of Chicago* v. *U. S. R. R. Co.*, 164 Ill. 224, 238; *Woodford* v. *Woodford*, 41 N. J. Eq. 224; *Phalen* v. *Clark*, 19 Conn. 421; *Dering* v. *Earl of Winchelsea*, 1 Cox Ch. 318; *Bateman* v. *Ferguson*, 4 Fed. Rep. 32; *Miller & Lux* v. *Enterprise Co.*, 142 Cal. 213; *Rice* v. *Rockefeller*, 134 N. Y. 174.)

COLLIN, J. The action is to restrain unfair competition in the use of trade names.

The plaintiff was incorporated in 1879 under chapter 40 of the Laws of 1848 and the acts amendatory and supplemental thereto. The amendatory act, chapter 838 of the Laws of 1866, authorized an incorporation "for the purpose of carrying on any kind of manufacturing, mining, mechanical, chemical, agricultural, horticultural, medical or curative business." The objects for which the plaintiff was incorporated were "the manufacturing, compounding and vending of medicines, consultation and operating in surgery, consultation and prescribing, furnishing and administering medicines and other curative and hygienic agents for invalids and furnishing care, attendants and home accommodations for the same." One Ray V. Pierce, a physician, transferred to the plaintiff upon its incorporation his business of manufacturing and selling under their trade names proprietary remedies and conducting a private hospital and medical practice. The proprietary remedies which the plaintiff manufactures and sells are named "Dr. Pierce's Golden Medical Discovery," "Dr. Pierce's Favorite Prescription," "Dr. Pierce's Pleasant Purgative Pellets," "Dr. Pierce's Compound Extract of Smart Weed or Water Pepper," "Dr. Pierce's Lotion Tablets," "Dr. Pierce's Cough Syrup," "Dr. Pierce's Ammonio Camphorated Liniment," and "Dr. Pierce's Medicated Soap," which are commonly known to the public as "Dr. Pierce's Remedies" and also as "Pierce's Remedies." Ray V. Pierce has been at all times and is now the president and a director of the plaintiff and devised the formula for each remedy. The lotion tablets are sold in boxes, having upon their tops the words "Dr. Pierce's Purifying and Strengthening Lotion Tablets, World's Dispensary Medical Association, Props., Buffalo, N. Y.," and elsewhere the words "Dr. Pierce's Genuine Family Medicines," together with a fac-simile signature of Ray V. Pierce, to wit: "R. V. Pierce, M. D." A part of the business of the plaintiff has been and is carrying on the hospital and medical practice founded by Ray V. Pierce. The plaintiff's remedies have become widely and favorably known and have an extensive sale throughout the United States and elsewhere.

The defendant since some time after 1899 has advertised and sold a certain proprietary remedy in the form of tablets under the name of "Dr. Pierce's Tansy, Cotton Root, Pennyroyal and Apiol Tablets," which are put up in boxes having on their tops the words "Dr. Pierce's Empress Brand Tansy, Cotton Root, Pennyroyal and Apiol Tablets," and elsewhere the words "Dr. Pierce's Empress Brand" and the words "the genuine has signature on box R. J. Pierce," the words "R. J. Pierce" being a facsimile signature. He is selling also another proprietary remedy known as "Pierce's Empress Brand Pennyroyal Tablets" in boxes having upon their tops those descriptive words and elsewhere the words "The Genuine has the signature on box R. J. Pierce," the words "R. J. Pierce" being a facsimile signature. The defendant is not a licensed physician, nor entitled to practice as such under the law of the state. The trial court found as facts that the use by defendant of the words "Dr. Pierce" is unlawful; that the names and labels used by defendant are calculated and designed to cause the public to believe that the defendant's remedies are manufactured and sold by plaintiff, and confusion between the business and remedies of the parties will be created by their continued use; and as conclusions of law that the defendant in using the names designating his remedies is unfairly competing with the plaintiff, and that by a judgment the defendant be forever restrained from using in connection with his remedies those names or the words "Dr. Pierce" or "Dr. Pierce's," or any name which includes the word "Pierce" or "Pierce's" in such manner as to be calculated or designed to cause the purchasers of his remedies to believe them to be manufactured or sold by the plaintiff, or the word "Pierce" or "Pierce's" in connection with his business in such manner as to deceive or be calculated to deceive the public or the customers of either of the parties. The judgment of the Special Term was unanimously affirmed.

The principal contention of the defendant is that the plaintiff cannot lawfully practice medicine and conduct the hospital because it is a stock corporation (See *People* v. *Woodbury Dermatological Institute*, 192 N. Y. 454), and that the judgment protects its use of the trade name "Dr. Pierce" in its illegal practice, and, therefore, violates the rule that a plaintiff who does not come into a court of equity with clean hands is refused relief. (*Prince Manfg. Co.* v. *Prince's Metallic Paint Co.*, 135 N. Y. 24; *N. Y. & N. J. Lubricant Co.* v. *Young*, 77 N. J. Eq. 321.) A majority of the court do not think it necessary, under the findings of the trial court, to consider and decide whether or no the plaintiff is violating the law of the state by practicing medicine and conducting the hospital. They are of the opinion that even if it should be held that it is violating the law in this respect, it would not thereby be debarred from protection, otherwise proper, in respect of its manufacture and sale of proprietary remedies which are entirely separate from and in no manner connected with the practice of medicine. The minority of the court, of whom the writer of this opinion is one, do not assent to the view of the majority, but refrain from an unavailing discussion. The court, therefore, leaves unconsidered and undetermined the question pressed upon us by the appellant, whether the plaintiff may lawfully practice medicine and conduct a hospital. No other contention of the appellant warrants the reversal of the judgment.

Appellant's contention that the judgment is too broad and drastic is well founded. Its restraint of the defendant from the use in any way of the designations "Dr. Pierce" or "Dr. Pierce's" is legal and just, because he is not a licensed physician nor entitled to practice under the law of the state. (Public Health Law, §§ 161, 174.) The defendant has, however, the right to use his own name in his own business. It is a general principle of law that one's name is his property, and he has the same right to its use and enjoyment as he has to that of any other species of property. (*Chas. S. Higgins Co.* v. *Higgins Soap Co.*, 144 N. Y. 462; *Brown Chemical Co.* v. *Meyer*, 139 U. S. 540.) It is, however, also a general principle of law that no man has the right to sell his products or goods as those of another. He may not through unfairness, artifice, misrepresentation or fraud injure the business of another or induce the public to believe his product is the product of that other. The law protects the honest dealer in the business which fairly is his, and the public from deception in trade. In this case, as in others which have been before the courts, these principles must, because of the identity in the surname of the defendant and the trade name used by the plaintiff, be reconciled and amalgamated. The plaintiff and its predecessor, Dr. Pierce, solely through a long period prior to 1899 associated the name Pierce with the proprietary remedies sold by it and which had acquired a high reputation and an extensive market. The name designates and causes the public to buy the remedies with which it is associated as those of the plaintiff. It when associated with the defendant's remedies is "calculated and designed to deceive and defraud the public, and the buyers and users of the plaintiff's proprietary remedies and tablets." The defendant has the right to use his name. The plantiff has the right to have the defendant use it in such a way as will not injure his business or mislead the public. When there is such a conflict of rights, it is the duty of the court so to regulate the use of his name by the defendant that, due protection to the plaintiff being afforded, there will be as little injury to him as possible. Defendant should so use his name in connection with his remedies that he will obviate deception or with an explanation which will inform or be a notice to the public that those remedies are not those of plaintiff. (*Herring-Hall-Marvin Safe Co.* v. *Hall's Safe Company,* 208 U. S. 554; *Devlin* v. *Devlin,* 69 N. Y. 212; *Meneely* v. *Meneely,* 62 N. Y. 427.)

We have already stated that the defendant cannot use his name with the prefix "Dr." We have concluded that due and adequate protection will be afforded to the plaintiff and the public if the defendant is enjoined additionally from using the words "Pierce" or "Pierce's" in advertising, describing, designating, labeling or selling his proprietary remedies unless said word be immediately preceded on the same line therewith by defendant's first or proper christian name and his middle name or the initial letter thereof in letters identical in size, color, style of type and conspicuousnesss with those of said word, so that said word shall not appear for any of the purposes aforesaid except when thus conjoined with the words "Robert J." or "Robert" followed by the middle name of the defendant.

The judgment should be modified so that the restraining part thereof will provide: "Adjudged that the defendant, his servants, agents and employees, be forever enjoined and restrained from putting up, selling, advertising or offering for sale any tablets, proprietary remedy or product, manufactured by or for the defendant, under any name having the words 'Dr. Pierce' or the words

'Dr. Pierce's' as a part thereof, or in boxes or packages having upon them or bearing labels having upon them any name having the words 'Dr. Pierce' or the words 'Dr. Pierce's' as a part thereof and from using the words 'Dr. Pierce' or the words 'Dr. Pierce's' in the business of defendant; and from using the word 'Pierce' or the word 'Pierce's' in advertising, describing, designating, labeling or selling the tablets or proprietary remedies manufactured and sold by or for the defendant unless said word be immediately preceded on the same line therewith by the defendant's first or proper christian name and his middle name or the initial letter thereof in letters identical in size, color, style of type and conspicuousness with those of said word, so that said word shall not appear for any of the purposes aforesaid except when the words 'Robert J.' or 'Robert' immediately followed by the middle name of the defendant in the form hereinbefore provided are conjoined with it;" and the judgment as thus modified should be affirmed, without costs to either party.

CULLEN, Ch. J., GRAY, HAIGHT, VANN and HISCOCK, JJ., concur; WILLARD BARTLETT, J., votes for reversal.

Judgment accordingly.

WILLIAM H. McRORIE, an Infant, by HERBERT E. McRORIE, His Guardian ad Litem, Respondent, v. WILLIAM H. MONROE, Appellant.

Negligence — evidence — admissions made by a party to an action, upon a previous trial thereof, may be proved by the testimony of a witness who heard them — erroneous exclusion of evidence tending to show that a wagon, by which plaintiff was injured, could not be used in the way alleged.

1. In a civil action the admissions by a party of any fact material to the issue are always competent evidence against him, wherever, whenever or to whomsoever made.

2. What a witness has sworn may be given in evidence either from the judge's notes or from notes that have been taken by any other person who will swear to their accuracy; or the former evidence may be proved by any person who will swear from his memory to its having been given. There is no rule which makes the stenographic reporter the only competent witness. Hence it is error to refuse to permit proof of the testimony of a party on a former trial, by a witness who had heard it given.

3. Where an accident resulted from the manner of use of a dump wagon of peculiar and exceptional construction, the question whether the wagon could be turned in the way alleged was a material inquiry, and evidence tending to show that it could not is relevant and admissible.

McRorie v. *Monroe*, 138 App. Div. 917; reversed.

(Argued October 30, 1911; decided November 28, 1911.)

APPEAL, by permission, from a judgment of the Appellate Division of the Supreme Court in the fourth judicial · department, entered May 24, 1910, affirming a judgment in favor of plaintiff entered upon a verdict.

The nature of the action and the facts, so far as material, are stated in the opinion.

Lamont Stilwell for appellant. The trial court committed reversible error in excluding proper and competent testimony offered by defendant. (*Hendrick* v. *State*, 10 Humph. [Tenn.] 479; *Donaldson* v. *Alexander*, 29 Misc. Rep. 356; *Reed* v. *McCord*, 18 App. Div. 381; *Cook* v. *Barr*, 44 N. Y. 156; *Patchin* v. *A. M. L. Ins. Co.*, 13 N. Y. 268; *E. F. C. Co.* v. *Comisky*, 40 Misc. Rep. 236; *Schofield* v. *Spaulding*, 54 Hun, 523; *Williams* v. *Sargent*, 46 N. Y. 481; *Nasanowitz* v. *Hanf*, 17 Misc. Rep. 157; *Dickman* v. *MacDonald*, 50 Misc. Rep. 531; *Weinhandler* v. *Eastern Brewing Co.*, 46 Misc. Rep. 584; *Crossman* v. *Lurman*, 33 App. Div. 422.)

Theodore E. Hancock for respondent. The exceptions to rulings on questions of evidence were frivolous in their nature and were not well taken. (*Ferguson* v. *Hubbell*, 97 N. Y. 507; *Roberts* v. *N. Y. E. R. R. Co.*, 128 N. Y. 465; *Dougherty* v. *Milliken*, 163 N. Y. 527; *Welle* v. *Celluloid Co.*, 186 N. Y. 319; *Schwander* v. *Birge*, 46 Hun, 66; *Furst* v. *Second Ave. R. R. Co.*, 72 N. Y. 542; *Plato* v. *Reynolds*, 27 N. Y. 586; *Baptist Church* v. *B. F. Ins. Co.*, 28 N. Y. 153.)

Willard Bartlett, J.   At the time of the accident which gave rise to this action, on August 8, 1907, the plaintiff was a lad six years of age, residing with his parents on Midler avenue, in East Syracuse.   Early in the afternoon he was out on that street drawing a little express wagon, such as children play with.   His brother, three years old, was with him.   The boys were walking toward James street, down the side of the road, when a team overtook them driven by a teamster in the employment of the defendant.   The horses were drawing a dump wagon.   The forward wheel next to the plaintiff passed him without touching him, as he stood at the side of the roadway; but the hind wheel ran over his left foot and injured it to such an extent that three toes had to be amputated.   By the verdict the boy has been absolved from all blame for this accident, and it has been attributed to the negligence of the defendant's teamster; this view has also been unanimously adopted by the Appellate Division, which has found no error in the record sufficient to disturb the judgment.

Our examination of the record has constrained us to reach a different conclusion.   It seems to us clear that harmful error was committed (1) in excluding oral testimony as to what the plaintiff had testified upon a previous trial; and (2) in excluding the evidence of witnesses familiar with the mechanism and operation of the defendant's dump wagon, by reason of actual personal experience in using it, as to the possibility of turning it so sharply as to bring the hind wheel in contact with the plaintiff in the manner by him described. The instructions to the jury in respect to the rule of responsibility applicable to the infant defendant (in the event of finding that he was *non sui juris*) were also so confused and contradictory as to be difficult of comprehension by even the most intelligent laymen.

(1) At the place of the accident an irregular ditch ran parallel with Midler avenue, being separated from the macadam roadway by a space or path two or three feet wide, along which the plaintiff was drawing his express wagon. The ditch was about eight feet wide, from one brow or shoulder to the other, and about $2\frac{8}{10}$ feet deep. According to the plaintiff's testimony upon the trial now under review, he had crossed this ditch by means of a bridge of planks which existed at the time of the accident. When the wagon came along, he said, he and his little brother went as close as they could to the ditch and stopped; conveying the idea that the character of the ditch at this point was such as to constitute a substantial obstacle against escape from the collision which subsequently occurred. It, therefore, became very important to the defendant to show if he could that the plaintiff had testified differently as to facts bearing upon the character of the ditch on the previous trial. He sought to do this by means of a witness who was present at that trial, heard the testimony which the plaintiff then gave as to the manner in which he crossed the ditch and remembered it. The learned trial judge refused to allow the defendant to prove by this witness what he heard the plaintiff testify on the former trial; and exceptions were duly taken to his rulings in this respect.

These rulings were plainly erroneous. The defendant was endeavoring to show that the plaintiff had admitted upon the previous trial a course of conduct on his part inconsistent with his contentions upon the present trial. "In a civil action the admissions by a party of any fact material to the issue are always competent evidence against him, wherever, whenever or to whomsoever made." (*Reed* v. *McCord*, 160 N. Y. 330, 341.)

At common law, whenever it was desired to prove the testimony given upon a former trial, it was always permissible to prove it by the recollection of any person who heard it and who would undertake to narrate it correctly. In *Mayor of Doncaster* v. *Day* (3 Taunton, 262) Lord MANSFIELD said: "What a witness, since dead, has sworn upon a trial between the same parties, may, * * * be given in evidence, either from the judge's notes, or from notes that have been taken by any other person, who will swear to their accuracy; or the former evidence may be proved by any person who will swear from his memory to its having been given."

In *Johnson* v. *Powers* (40 Vt. 611) it was said that "former evidence may be proved by any person who will swear from his memory to its having been given."

In *McGeoch* v. *Carlson* (96 Wis. 138) it was held that a justice of the peace was competent to testify as to the evidence given before him on a former trial. In *State* v. *McDonald* (65 Maine, 466) the government, to impeach one of the defendant's witnesses, offered to show that he testified differently, at a former trial, by a witness who was present and heard him testify. The testimony was objected to on the ground that it was not the best evidence and that the legally appointed stenographer who took notes of the testimony could give better evidence. The objection was overruled and the impeaching witness allowed to testify. This action on the part of the trial court was approved by the Supreme Judicial Court of Maine, which said through WALTON, J.: "A witness may be impeached by showing that he testified differently at a former trial; and his former testimony may be proved by any one who heard and recollects it. There is no rule of law which makes the stenographic reporter the only competent witness in such a case. The rule which requires the production of the best evidence is not applicable. * * * It has nothing to do with the choice of witnesses. It never excludes a witness upon the ground that another is more credible or reliable."

These authorities suffice to show the general recognition of the rule which was violated by the refusal to permit proof of the plaintiff's former testimony by a witness who had heard it given.

(2) According to the plaintiff's testimony he stood about two feet and three inches from the forward wheel of the wagon when that wheel went by him; the driver kept pulling his team in so that he brought the hind wheel around where the plaintiff's foot was. It appeared from other evidence that the distance between the center of the forward wheel and the center of the hind wheel was very nearly eight feet; between seven and eight feet. A witness named Charles Kenney called for the defendant testified that he had driven the same wagon himself with the same team and that he had had experience in turning around with it and had noticed how it acted so that he was able to say how far the driver would have to turn the horses in order to bring the hind wheel two feet and a quarter outside of where the forward wheel went. Although thus qualified to speak from his own actual experience with the vehicle the learned trial judge refused to permit him to answer either of the following questions:

"Q. Assuming that that wagon was being driven south on Midler Avenue at the point where the accident occurred in order to bring the rear wheel two feet and a quarter west of where the forward wheel went in going the distance between the two wheels how far would you have to have cramped or moved your horses to the west?"

"Q. Would it be possible without running the horses into the ditch to bring the hind wheel so that it would pass two and a quarter feet west of where the forward wheel had passed?"

It will be perceived that these interrogatories related to the capacity of the vehicle to do what the evidence for the plaintiff tended to show that it had done. This was a determining issue in the case. There was no suggestion that the team had been turned so far as to get into the ditch next to which the plaintiff stood; and the evidence sought to be elicited by these questions was designed to show that the construction and practical operation of the wagon were such that the hind wheels could not have been moved as much as the plaintiff said they were moved without a greater change of the direction in which the horses were being driven. In other words, the defendant sought to show that practical experience in the use of this very wagon demonstrated the impossibility that the accident could have occurred in the manner testified to by the plaintiff.

When such an issue arises depending for its determination upon the capacity of a machine, mechanical appliance or vehicle, the testimony of witnesses having actual experience in the use thereof may be received as an aid to the jury. While it may be true in the case at bar that if all the details of the construction of the wagon were laid before the jury the jurors themselves could draw correct inferences as to its capacity to do or not to do a particular thing, nevertheless they could hardly form as trustworthy a judgment in that respect as one who spoke from actual experience in the use of the vehicle, and witnesses having such experience have been permitted in similar cases to assist the jury by narrating it. In *O'Neil v. D. D., E. B. & B. R. R. Co.* (129 N. Y. 125) a witness who had driven trucks in New York city for years was asked within what time and space a loaded truck could be stopped, and the allowance of that question was held to be no error. It is true the court said that it belonged to a class of questions not much to be encouraged inasmuch as jurors are generally well acquainted with such common things as trucks and horses and the power,

actions and capacity of horses which are constantly
open to observation particularly in the city of New York.
Even so, the conclusion was that the expert witness probably knew more about the subject of inquiry than ordinary jurors could generally be supposed to know.   In the
present case the vehicle which caused the accident was
not one of ordinary character but a dump wagon of
peculiar and exceptional construction; and a question from
one of the jurors indicated that he and his fellow jurymen
did not clearly understand either the construction or
operation of this particular type of wagon; hence it
cannot be said here as was suggested in the *O'Neil* case
that the answers to the questions which we have quoted
could be of but little service to the jurors.   On the contrary, it was essential to an enlightened comprehension
of the case that they should understand just what the
peculiar construction of such a vehicle would permit to
be done with it, or render impossible.

In *Sprout* v. *Newton* (48 Hun, 209) the General Term of
the fifth department (BRADLEY, J., writing) sanctioned
the admission of the testimony of a witness as to the
capacity of another machine of the same kind, made at
the same place, in a case involving the capacity of a
patented machine.

When an accident alleged to be due to negligence is said
to have been caused by the operation of a machine in a
particular way, the question whether the machine *could*
operate in the way alleged must be a material inquiry;
and evidence tending to show that it *could not* thus operate must be relevant and admissible in such a case.   If
the machine be one with which laymen generally are
familiar, a description of its dimensions and weight, and
an account of the manner in which it was employed on
the occasion in question will usually suffice to enable a
jury to determine, without further aid, whether it was
capable of the action attributed to it or not; but if it be
unfamiliar, the jury may properly be assisted by the

28

experience of those who have actually used it and are thus personally acquainted with its capacity.

In the case of an alleged breach of warranty of a ditching machine, evidence as to the manner in which the machine performed at another place was held to be admissible as tending to prove the capacity of the machine to perform at the place specified in the warranty. (*Baber* v. *Rickart*, 52 Ind. 594, 597.)

Where negligence is predicated upon an accident it is a perfect defense to show that it is physically impossible that the accident could have happened in the manner alleged. This is precisely what the defendant tried to show in the present case; but he was not permitted to adduce evidence pertinent for that purpose. He endeavored to prove by the testimony of a witness who could speak from actual experience in turning the wagon which injured the plaintiff that it could not be turned as sharply as the plaintiff had stated; its physical construction precluded it.

The cases relied upon by the respondent to sustain the exclusion of this evidence have no real application. In *Ferguson* v. *Hubbell* (97 N. Y. 507) the testimony held to have been improperly admitted was the statement of a number of witnesses to the effect that the time at which the defendant set the fires upon his fallow land was a proper time to burn fallows. Such a question has no resemblance whatever to those asked in the present case. An inquiry as to what was the proper time to burn fallow land called for opinion evidence and the expression of a conclusion on the part of the witness. The questions here under consideration did not tend to elicit opinion evidence at all; they called only for a statement of fact from the witness as to his experience in the use of a particular vehicle. The purpose of the questions was to elicit answers which would show that, in actual use, the witness had found it impossible to turn the wagon which caused the accident in the way which the plaintiff said it

turned and in the way indeed in which it must have turned
in order to run over him.   There is no analogy, therefore,
between the *Ferguson* case and the case at bar; and the
others cited in the brief for the respondent are even less
helpful to him.

The judgment should be reversed and a new trial
granted, costs to abide the event.

CULLEN, Ch. J., GRAY, HAIGHT, VANN, HISCOCK and
COLLIN, JJ., concur.

Judgment reversed, etc.

HERRMANN & GRACE, Plaintiff, *v.* RICHARD W. HILLMAN
et al., Defendants.

THE CITY OF NEW YORK et al., Respondents; B. F.
STURTEVANT COMPANY et al., Appellants.

**Liens — municipal corporations — when municipality liable
only for amount due contractor at time contract was forfeited.**

1. To entitle a lienor to recover on a lien against a municipality it
is incumbent upon him to show either that the contractor performed his contract, and that by reason of such performance some
amount became due and owing thereon, or that by reason of some
special provision of the contract there was when the lien was filed
something due such contractor thereon or that something became
due him upon it thereafter applicable to the payment of such lien.
(Lien Law [Cons. Laws, ch. 33], § 60.)

2. A contract provided that on default by the contractor the
owner could cancel it and proceed to finish the work and furnish
the material required so as to fully execute it in every respect, and
further that " the cost and expense thereof at the reasonable market rates shall be a charge against the contractor, who shall pay to
the party of the first part the excess thereof, if any, over and above
the unpaid balance of the amount to be paid under this contract;
and the contractor shall have no claim or demand to such unpaid
balance, or by reason of the non-payment thereof to them." *Held*,
that after the contract was forfeited the contractor had no rights of
any kind whatever under it and hence liens filed against him attach
only to the sum actually due him at the time of the forfeiture.

Herrmann & Grace v. Hillman, 139 App. Div. 902, affirmed.

(Argued October 24, 1911; decided November 28, 1911.)

APPEAL from a judgment of the Appellate Division of the Supreme Court in the first judicial department, entered June 17, 1910, affirming a judgment in favor of defendants, respondents, entered upon a decision of the court on trial at Special Term.

The nature of the action and the facts, so far as material, are stated in the opinion.

Edward B. Bloss and *Omri F. Hibbard* for B. F. Sturtevant Company et al., appellants. The sum at least of $3,615 or $3,990 was actually earned on the original contract before the contractor's default, and became subject to the liens of the lienor appellants upon the filing of the same. (*Kane Co.* v. *Kinney*, 174 N. Y. 69; *Kelly* v. *Bloomingdale*, 139 N. Y. 343; *Miller* v. *Mead*, 127 N. Y. 544; *Van Clief* v. *Van Vechten*, 130 N. Y. 571; *Rieser* v. *Commeau*, 129 App. Div. 490.) The lienor appellants are entitled to the whole balance remaining unpaid in the hands of the city comptroller. (*Crawford* v. *Becker*, 13 Hun, 375; *Martin* v. *Flahive*, 112 App. Div. 347; *Person* v. *Stoll*, 72 App. Div. 141; 174 N. Y. 548; *People ex rel. Treat* v. *Coler*, 166 N. Y. 144; *Hutton Brothers* v. *Gordon*, 2 Misc. Rep. 267; *Bader* v. *City of New York*, 51 Misc. Rep. 358.) The board of education was not authorized by the terms of the original contract to forfeit the same, and forfeiture of the "unpaid balance" is in contravention of the Lien Law. (*Powers* v. *City of Yonkers*, 114 N. Y. 145; *Rice* v. *Culver*, 172 N. Y. 60; *Nat. W. P. Co.* v. *Sire*, 163 N. Y. 122.)

J. Power Donellan for Johnson Service Company, appellant. The city could not declare the contract abandoned under clause Q. It had only the right to complete the contract and charge the cost to the balance unpaid. (*Herrman & Grace* v. *City of New York*, N. Y. L. J., Dec. 29, 1906.) The city, having completed the contract pursuant to the right reserved therein, its right to declare a forfeiture thereof for non-performance is gone and there can be no forfeiture. (*White* v. *Livingston*, 69 App. Div. 370; *Van Clief* v. *Van Vechten*, 130 N. Y. 580; *Mack* v. *Colleran*, 136 N. Y. 617; *Ogden* v. *Alexander*, 140 N. Y. 362; *Graf* v. *Cunningham*, 109 N. Y. 369; *Wheeler* v. *Schofield*, 67 N. Y. 311; *Murphy* v. *Buckman*, 66 N. Y. 297; *Campbell* v. *Coon*, 149 N. Y. 556; *Dyer* v. *Osborne*, 28 Misc. Rep. 234; *Robinson* v. *C. C. Assn.*, 35 App. Div. 439.)

Archibald R. Watson, Corporation Counsel (*Terence Farley* and *John L. O'Brien* of counsel), for respondents. In order to entitle the lienors to enforce their liens it was incumbent upon them to show that the contractor performed his agreement and that there was something due and owing to him to which the liens could attach. (*Brainard* v. *Kings County*, 155 N. Y. 538; Code Civ. Pro. § 533; *Cochran* v. *Reich*, 91 Hun, 440; *Sager* v. *Gonnermann*, 50 Misc. Rep. 500; *Kelly* v. *Bloomingdale*, 139 N. Y. 343; *Hawkins* v. *Burrell*, 69 App. Div. 462; *Paturzo* v. *Shuldiner*, 125 App. Div. 637; *Siegel* v. *Ehrshowsky*, 46 Misc. Rep. 605; *Lemieux* v. *English*, 19 Misc. Rep. 545; *Keavy* v. *De Rago*, 29 Misc. Rep. 105; *Ball & Wood Co.* v. *Clark & Sons Co.*, 31 App. Div. 356.) When the contract in suit was declared abandoned by the board of education, pursuant to clause Q, the rights of the contractor under it ceased and determined, and he no longer had any interest in any of its terms or provisions. (*Jones* v. *City of New York*, 60 App. Div. 161; 174 N. Y. 517.) When a contractor unjustifiably abandons his contract he forfeits his right to all moneys which may subsequently accrue thereunder; and neither he nor those who claim to be subrogated to his rights are entitled to a lien on any such moneys. (30 Am. & Eng. Ency. of Law [2d ed.], 1213; *Wexler* v. *Rust*, 144 App. Div. 296; *Upson* v. *U. E. & C. Co.*, 130 N. Y. Supp.

726.) A clause authorizing the owner, in case of a contractor's default, to abrogate a contract and declare a forfeiture, is not inconsistent with a provision which empowers the owner, upon such a default, to complete the contract at the contractor's expense and charge to him the difference between .the cost of completion and the contract price. (*United States* v. *Perkins*, 143 Fed. Rep. 688.)

CHASE, J. On the 7th day of August, 1905, the board of education of the city of New York and the City of New York entered into a contract with Richard W. Hillman to erect a heating and ventilating plant in a public school building in the borough of Bronx, New York city. The contract provided among other things, as follows: "If the contractor shall well and faithfully perform and fulfill this contract, and keep every covenant on his part herein contained, the party of the first part will then, but not before, pay to the contractor the sum of $29,370.00."

It further provided that in order to enable the contractor to perform the work advantageously, the consideration should be paid in installments of eighty-five per cent of the value of the work performed upon application made in writing to the superintendent by the contractor, together with an accurate schedule in detail of the materials furnished and work done since the last preceding payment.

It also provided that the final payment of the balance due and unpaid under the contract, including fifteen per cent of the total amount of the contract price, shall be payable thirty days "after the contract is fully performed, completed, and the entire work accepted, and when the work is all complete, as herein provided, and the keys delivered to the superintendent of school buildings."

The contractor entered upon the execution of the work

and furnished materials therefor, a large part of which was purchased from others on credit. He continued in the performance of the work until June 18th, 1906, on which day a petition in involuntary bankruptcy was filed against him and he wholly abandoned the contract. At that time the contract was not completed. He had at that time been paid on account of his contract and according to the terms thereof $20,465, and there was at that time due to him and unpaid but certified for payment the sum of $2,125.

On the 27th day of June, 1906, the board of education passed a resolution that the contracts with Hillman "be and the same are hereby declared voided and forfeited for non-compliance with the terms of the contract, said action being in accordance with the provisions thereof. And be it further resolved that the superintendent of school buildings be and he hereby is authorized to proceed with the completion of the work in accordance with the original plans and specifications, and to advertise for proposals therefor. And be it further resolved that the cost and expense of completing the above-mentioned contracts be charged against the said contractor and the sureties on said contract."

A new contract was entered into by the board of education with another contractor for the completion of said contract and it was completed at an expense of $1,870.00. Prior to Hillman going into bankruptcy liens were filed by the plaintiff, the defendants Kieley and another and by the appellants. This action is brought to foreclose the plaintiff's lien.

The facts above stated are among other things found by the court or stipulated by the parties and the respondents concede that said sum of $2,125 is applicable to the payment of the liens filed as stated in the pleadings and as also conceded at the trial. The court also found as a conclusion of law "that the defendant Hillman having abandoned his work, and the defendants, the city of New

York and the board of education of the city of New York, under the provisions of said contract, having declared a forfeiture of said contract by reason of the failure of the contractor to perform, there was no amount due from the defendant, the city of New York and the board of educa-. tion of the city of New York, under said contract, except the said sum of $2,125, and the liens of the defendants, other than the defendants, Timothy J. Kieley and Frederick T. Mueller and the plaintiff are not valid as against the city."

The judgment entered upon said findings directs that the plaintiff's lien and certain costs be paid from said . $2,125 and that the balance of said amount be paid to the defendants Kieley and another on account of their lien. The appellants, subsequent lienors, appealed from said judgment to the Appellate Division, where said judgment was unanimously affirmed.

The Lien Law (Chapter 38, Laws of 1909, section 5, formerly chap. 418, Laws of 1897, section 5, as amended by chap. 37, Laws of 1902, Cons. Laws, ch. 33, section 5), provides that a person furnishing materials "to a contractor, his sub-contractor or legal representative, for the construction of a public improvement pursuant to a contract by such contractor with the state.or a municipal corporation, shall have a lien * * * upon the moneys of the state or of such corporation applicable to the construction of such improvement, to the extent of the amount due or to become due on such contract, upon filing a notice of lien as prescribed in this article."

It is also provided by the Lien Law, section 60 (formerly section 3418 of the Code of Civil Procedure), that in an action to enforce a lien on account of a public improvement if the court finds that the lien is established it shall render judgment directing the state or the municipal corporation to pay over to the lienors entitled thereto for work done or materials furnished for such public improvement — " to the extent of the sums found due the lienors

from the contractors, so much of the funds or money
which may be due from the state or municipal corporation to the contractor, as will satisfy such liens, with
interest and costs, not exceeding the amount due to the
contractor."

To entitle the appellants to recover on their liens
against the city it was incumbent upon them to show
either that Hillman performed his contract, and that by
reason of such performance some amount became due
and owing thereon, or that by reason of some special
provision of the contract there was when the lien was
filed something due Hillman thereon or that something
became due him upon it thereafter applicable to the
payment of such liens.

Where a contractor fails to perform a building contract
as provided therein and abandons the same, the owner
may insist upon his strict legal right and put an end to
the contract. This is true notwithstanding the contract
provides that in case the contractor fails in any respect in
the performance of the agreements contained therein
that the owner shall be at liberty to complete the same
and deduct the cost thereof from any amount then due
or thereafter to become due to the contractor under the
contract. (*Fraenkel* v. *Friedmann*, 199 N. Y. 351.)
Such authority in a contract to terminate the employment of the contractor is permissible to the owner. It is
for the benefit of the owner and not for the benefit of the
contractor. If the owner completes the contract under
such a provision therein, the lien attaches to the extent
of the difference between the cost of completion and the
amount unpaid on the contract when the lien was filed.
(*Fraenkel* v. *Friedmann*, *supra*.) The appellants cite a
large number of authorities in their effort to show that
the city of New York should pay the difference between
the amount of Hillman's contract and the amount paid
by the city to Hillman on account of said contract,
together with the item of $2,125 and the amount paid

to the subsequent contractor for the completion of the contract.

All of the authorities referred to by the appellants tending in any way to sustain their position are based upon contracts and upon facts that are entirely different from the contract and the facts in this case. The contract with Hillman not only expressly provides, as we have shown, that the amount thereof shall not be paid until the full completion of the same according to the terms of the contract, but it provided generally as to the rights of the parties in case of a failure to perform the contract as provided therein. Such provision of the contract is known as paragraph "Q" and is as follows:

"That in case the contractor shall at any time refuse or neglect to supply a sufficiency of workmen and materials of the proper skill and quality, or shall fail in any respect to prosecute the work required by this contract with promptness and diligence, or shall omit to fulfill any provision herein contained the Board of Education, after three days' notice, in writing by order of the Committee on Buildings or a majority thereof to the contractor, served personally, or by leaving the same at their respective places of residence or business, shall have the right and power to procure and employ, in the manner prescribed by law, by contract or otherwise, other persons to perform and finish the work and materials required by this contract, so as to fully execute the same in every respect, and the cost and expense thereof at the reasonable market rates shall be a charge against the contractor, who shall pay to the party of the first part the excess thereof, if any, over and above the unpaid balance of the amount to be paid under this contract; and the contractor shall have no claim or demand to such unpaid balance or by reason of the non-payment thereof to them and no molds, models, centers, scaffolding, planks, horses, derricks, tackle, implements, power plants or building material of any kind belonging to or used by the contractor shall be removed so long as the same may be wanted for the work. That in case the contractor shall at any time, in the opinion of the Superintendent, neglect to faithfully carry on and perform any portion of the work required by this contract, whereby safety and proper construction may be endangered or which may not be substantially rectified, or whereby damage and injury may result to life and property or either; then, and in every such case, the Superintendent shall have the right forthwith and without notice to the contractor to enter into and upon the work, and to make good any and all imperfect work and material and deficiencies arising by reason of such neglect; the expense and cost thereof shall be a charge against the contractor to be deducted from any payment or moneys which may be due or subsequently become due under this contract; and the opinion and decision of the Superintendent of School Buildings in all instances which may arise in the manner aforesaid shall be final, conclusive and binding upon the contractor. * * *"

The paragraph of the contract quoted provides for different failures on the part of the contractor to perform the contract as provided therein. The latter part of the paragraph provides for a failure to perform the work required by the contract by reason of neglect faithfully to carry on and perform the same or a portion thereof whereby safety and proper construction may be endangered or which may not be substantially rectified or whereby damage and injury may result to life and property or either; and in such case it is expressly provided that the superintendent of buildings acting in behalf of the board of education and the city of New York shall have the right forthwith to enter upon the work and to make good any and all imperfect work and material and the deficiencies arising by reason of such neglect. In such case the expense thereof is to be deducted from any payment which may be due or which shall subsequently become due under the contract, and in that case the lienors

would have a lien on any amount unpaid on the contract
notwithstanding the general provisions of the contract by
which it is provided that the final payment shall not
become due until the work is done and materials furnished in full compliance with the contract. The first
part of the paragraph covers a number of things, including the total abandonment of the contract, and in that
case the owner is given the power by express terms of the
contract that he would have had as a matter of law,
entirely independent of the terms of the contract, to cancel the same and stand upon his legal rights; but it is
therein further provided, also for the benefit of the owner,
that he can proceed to finish the work and furnish the
material required by the contract so as to fully execute
the same in every respect, and "The cost and expense
thereof at the reasonable market rates shall be a charge
against the contractor, who shall pay to the party of the
first part the excess thereof, if any, over and above the
unpaid balance of the amount to be paid under this contract; and the *contractor shall have no claim or demand
to such unpaid balance, or by reason of the non-payment
thereof to them.*" By this provision of the contract in
case it was legally declared forfeited the contractor has
no rights of any kind whatever under the contract. The
contract provides also in the interest of the owner, not
alone that it has the right to forfeit the contract, but that
it can proceed to the completion of the work and the
furnishing of materials, and if such expense exceeds the
amount unpaid on the contract it can charge the same to
the contractor.

The provisions of the resolution forfeiting the contract
relating to charging the expense thereof to the contractor,
have reference to the provisions of said paragraph allowing the excess of cost to be charged to the contractor and
was necessary for the purpose of determining whether
under such paragraph there would be an excess of costs
and expense. The appellants failed to show that at the

time of filing their liens respectively or at any time
thereafter there was anything due under the contract
applicable to the payment of their liens.

The judgment should be affirmed, with costs.

Cullen, Ch. J., Gray, Haight, Vann, Werner and
Collin, JJ., concur.

Judgment affirmed.

The People of the State of New York ex rel. John
M. Farley, Appellant, *v.* Max Winkler et al., Con-
stituting the Board of Water Commissioners of the
Town of Harrison, District No. 1, Respondents.

**Water commissioners — not quasi corporations but adminis-
trative officers — remedy for breach of contract is by mandamus
or certiorari.**

1. As a quasi corporate capacity is not essential to the proper
conduct of such an office as that of district water commissioner,
the courts should not hold that it exists where the legislature has
not spoken upon the subject.

2. As district water commissioners are not quasi corporations,
but only administrative officers with power to make contracts in
their official name and capacity, and intrusted with funds to meet
them, and as they are not agents of the town or district and are
not personally liable upon their official contracts, they cannot be
sued in actions at law.

3. For an alleged breach of a contract made by such commissioners, or for a failure to pay any debt incurred by them in their
official capacity, the writ of mandamus is, therefore, the only
appropriate remedy to compel action on their part, and the writ
of certiorari may be invoked where such action is challenged as
unlawful.

People ex rel. Farley v. *Winkler*, 146 App. Div. 314, reversed.

(Submitted November 22, 1911; decided December 5, 1911.)

Appeal from an order of the Appellate Division of the
Supreme Court in the second judicial department, entered
October 11, 1911, which reversed upon the law an order
of Special Term granting a motion for a peremptory

writ of mandamus to compel the defendants to audit a claim of the relator for services, and denied said motion. The facts, so far as material, are stated in the opinion.

Robert E. Farley and *William L. Rumsey* for appellant. The Appellate Division erred in reversing the order granting the writ of mandamus. (*Holroyd v. Town of Indian Lake,* 180 N. Y. 318; *Swift v. Mayor, etc.,* 83 N. Y. 528; *Davidson v. Vil. of White Plains,* 197 N. Y. 266; *Miller v. Bush,* 87 Hun, 507; *Gardner v. Bd. of Health,* 10 N. Y. 409; *Appleton v. Water Comrs.,* 2 Hill, 432; *People ex rel. Pennell v. Treanor,* 15 App. Div. 508.)

Henry C. Henderson for respondents. The writ of mandamus will not be granted where the relator has an adequate remedy at law. (*People ex rel. v. Crennan,* 141 N. Y. 239; *Holroyd v. Town of Indian Lake,* 180 N. Y. 318; *Todd v. Birdsall,* 1 Cow. 260; *Town of Fishkill v. Plank Road Co.,* 22 Barb. 634; *Town of Gallatin v. Loucke,* 21 Barb. 578; *Lorillard v. Town of Monroe,* 11 N. Y. 392; *People ex rel. Van Keuren v. Town Auditors,* 74 N. Y. 310.) No public officer can be compelled by mandamus to do any act which the law does not require him to do. (*People ex rel. v. Supervisors,* 65 Hun, 263; *People ex rel. v. Rice,* 129 N. Y. 391.)

WERNER, J. The relator, a supervising civil engineer, was retained in that capacity by the respondents as water commissioners of district No. 1 in the town of Harrison in the county of Westchester, to superintend and inspect the construction of a water system in the district mentioned. The relator served for a time as such engineer, and had been paid the larger part of his stipulated compensation, when a dispute arose between him and the commissioners, as the result of which he resigned, and they refused or at least neglected to pay him the balance which he claimed to be due him for such services.   Thereupon the relator instituted this proceeding to procure an order for a writ of mandamus directing the respondents either to audit or reject the claim.   Such an order was made by Mr. Justice KEOGH at Special Term.   From that order an appeal was taken to the Appellate Division of the second department, which resulted in a reversal of the order of the Special Term.   As this reversal was upon the law, and not as a matter of discretion, the appeal to this court presents a question which we must review.

At Special Term the learned justice granted the writ on the authority of *Holroyd* v. *Town of Indian Lake* (180 N. Y. 318).   In that case the contractor sought to recover unliquidated damages for an alleged breach of a contract under which he had constructed a water system in a water district established in the town of Indian Lake in the county of Hamilton.   A demurrer was there interposed to the complaint, on the ground that the latter pleading did not state facts sufficient to constitute a cause of action.   The demurrer was overruled at Special Term, but the Appellate Division reached a different conclusion, sustaining the demurrer and dismissing the complaint.   Upon appeal to this court the decision of the Appellate Division was affirmed upon the explicit ground that the plaintiff in that case had no cause of action against the town, and, in the opinion written for the court by VANN, J., it was suggested that Holroyd's appropriate remedy was by writ of mandamus against the district water commissioners, to be followed by proceedings in certiorari if a review was necessary.   It was this latter suggestion of Judge VANN in *Holroyd's* case that was followed by the Special Term in the case at bar and disregarded by the Appellate Division upon the theory that, in *Holroyd's* case, this court had actually decided nothing more than that an action could not be maintained against the town.   Proceeding upon that assumption the Appellate Division has held that an action at law may be brought against the water commissioners as a quasi corporation, which may sue and be sued upon all contracts and obligations arising out of the purposes of its creation.

Admitting for the purposes of this discussion that the Appellate Division has correctly assumed that the only question actually decided in *Holroyd's* case was that the plaintiff there was not entitled to maintain an action against the town, we are now called upon to determine whether we shall adopt the suggestions of Judge VANN in that case, to the effect that mandamus and certiorari against district water commissioners are the proper remedies in such a case as this, or whether we shall sustain the Appellate Division in holding that an action at law may be maintained against them.

The question thus 'presented is very narrow and not free from difficulty. If we should accept the premise that the respondent water commissioners constitute a quasi corporation, the conclusion would seem to follow that they can sue and be sued in their corporate capacity. But it is common knowledge that in recent times in this country there has been a constantly growing tendency to create a variety of commissions, so called, for the purpose of administering special governmental functions, whose powers and duties are sometimes very specifically enumerated in the statutes creating them, and in many other instances, as in the case before us, are left largely to implication from the character of the general purpose for which they were created. All of these products of modern legislation bear some analogies to the offices and institutions which, under the common law, were known as quasi corporations, but most of them are purely administrative departments of some local form of government, and have such widely variant relations to the state, or to some of its governmental subdivisions, that they cannot be classified with anything like scientific accuracy. There is, therefore, no uniformity of decision upon the subject, and ancient definitions and classifications of so-called quasi corporations are of little value in construing these modern statutes.

The statutes relating to the matter of procuring a water supply for the various communities in the state disclose the wide range of legislation upon this subject. In some cities the water works systems are operated as a part of the general municipal government; in others the powers and liabilities pertaining thereto are imposed upon special officers or boards either with or without distinct corporate powers. This is also true of villages, some of which obtain their water supplies under the General Village Law, while others are supplied by private water corporations or under special statutes. In a recent case arising under such a special law it was held that the water commissioners were the agents of the village and that their contract for a pumping engine rendered it liable for the purchase price. (*Davidson* v. *Village of White Plains,* 197 N. Y. 266, 269.)

The Town Law provides for several distinct and separate schemes by means of which a supply of water may be obtained.

1. Any town may acquire an existing water system, or construct one for its own use, by complying with the provisions of the statute relating exclusively to towns as distinguished from districts. (Town Law, sections 270–280.) A water system acquired or constructed under those provisions is town property which is expressly placed under the control and management of the town board. It goes without saying that all contracts made by a town board with reference to such a water system, are the contracts of the town, and the town alone is liable under them.

2. The Town Law further provides for a method by which a water district may be formed in territory which is in the town and outside of an incorporated village which owns a system of water works. (Town Law, section 281.) If a water supply district is created as directed in

29

that section, and a contract is made between the town board and a village owning a system of water works, under which the village is to furnish water to the water district, the whole town is bound by the contract; but the liability thus imposed upon the town is offset by its right to levy upon the taxable property in the water district a sum sufficient to protect or reimburse the town; and this sum, when collected from the district taxpayers, is to be turned over to the town supervisor for payment to the village water commissioners.

3. There is still another statutory plan by which the inhabitants of a rural or suburban neighborhood may secure a water supply under the Town Law, and that is the one which had given rise to the questions raised in *Holroyd's* case and in the case at bar. The sections of the Town Law applicable to this plan (sections 282–298) provide, in substance, that upon the petition of a majority of the owners of taxable real property in any proposed water district, the town board may establish such a district outside of any incorporated village or city, and wholly within such town. These provisions direct that after the necessary preliminary steps have been taken the town board shall make an order appointing three tax-payers of the district as water commissioners thereof. After the commissioners have qualified they are authorized to proceed with the construction of a water works system. For that purpose they may employ engineers and enter into contracts for construction. The money needed for these purposes must be raised by the town board by the issue and sale of town bonds, which are a charge upon the whole town, but which are to be paid out of funds raised by tax upon property within the water district. The statute is silent as to the method or the agency by and through which the money thus raised is to be disbursed, but the necessary inference seems to be that it must be paid over to the water commissioners, for they alone are authorized to employ engineers, to make con-

tracts for the construction of the plant, and manage and control the same after it is in operation. They are required to fix and promulgate a scale of water rents, adopt ordinances to enforce the collection thereof, and to file with the town clerk an annual report setting forth the financial status of the enterprise. From all of these peculiarities of the statute it is reasonably clear, as Judge VANN said in *Holroyd's* case, that "the town has no power to build the plant, which is wholly beyond its jurisdiction and control. It has no right to use it or regulate it or collect the rents. It does nothing but lend its credit to the district and in effect it is given a lien upon the taxable property of the district as security, with power to enforce it by taxation in the usual way. * * * The water district is not created for the town, but for a district in the town. * * * No action at law will lie against the town, because the contract is not made by the town and is not for its benefit." (p. 323.)

It is of course the logical corollary to the conclusion that the town is not liable for contracts made by district water commissioners, that these functionaries are themselves liable in their official capacity upon contracts made by them in that relation. It does not follow, however, that this liability must be adjudicated in an action at law. There are many administrative departments of municipal government which are by the express terms of the statutes creating them rendered liable in actions at law upon contracts made with them. In such cases no question can arise as to the fact and the form of the liability. But there are many instances in which the statutes creating such administrative boards contain no reference to their liability upon official contracts entered into by them, or to the method of enforcing such liability when it is held to exist, and in some such cases the liability of the particular board or officer seems to be predicated upon no better reason than that no one else can be found who is liable. They are neither corporations nor quasi corporations, and in such circumstances the courts should not subject purely administrative officials to the ordinary forms of litigation when there are equally effective and more expeditious remedies in the form of summary special proceedings. If we could agree with the learned justices of the Appellate Division in the conclusion that such district water commissioners, whose duties are very loosely defined and whose liabilities are not even referred to in the statutes, may be regarded collectively as quasi corporations, we should have no difficulty in deciding that they are not only liable upon their official contracts, but that the liability could be enforced against them in actions at law. We hold that they are liable, not on the theory that they are quasi corporations, but because the inference of their liability seems to be the only rational one to be drawn from the fact that no one else is liable; and in the absence of any legislative direction as to the method by which that liability may be enforced, we think that in these cases the ends of justice can be quite as fully subserved by mandamus and certiorari as in actions at law.

Even in the early development of our municipal governments there was great difficulty in determining what departments or officers thereof were, or were not, quasi corporations. That difficulty has been greatly increased by the modern tendency above mentioned to multiply and diversify offices. The result is that we have no end of learned writing upon this most troublesome subject, and, what is worse, much of it is of little use or no use in the decision of the practical questions which are presented to the courts. On that account we refrain from any attempt to analyze the many conflicting authorities and the expressions of text writers, and shall content ourselves with simply stating the conclusions which we have reached.

1. As a quasi corporate capacity is not essential to the proper conduct of such an office as that of district water

commissioner, the courts should not hold that it exists where the legislature has not spoken upon the subject. (*Walsh* v. *Trustees of N. Y. & Brooklyn Bridge,* 96 N. Y. 427.)

2. As these district water commissioners are not quasi corporations, but only administrative officers with power to make contracts in their official name and capacity, and intrusted with funds to meet them, and as they are not agents of the town or district and are not personally liable upon their official contracts, they cannot be sued in actions at law. (*Swift* v. *Mayor, etc., of N. Y.,* 83 N. Y. 528.)

3. For an alleged breach of a contract made by such commissioners, or for a failure to pay any debt incurred by them in their official capacity, the writ of mandamus is, therefore, the only appropriate remedy to compel action on their part, and the writ of certiorari may be invoked where such action is challenged as unlawful.

For these reasons the order of the Appellate Division should be reversed and the order of the Special Term affirmed, with costs in both courts.

CULLEN, Ch. J., HAIGHT, WILLARD BARTLETT, HISCOCK and COLLIN, JJ., concur; CHASE, J., concurs in result.

Order reversed, etc. .

B. T. DE WITT MILES, Respondent, *v.* CASUALTY COMPANY OF AMERICA, Appellant.

Insurance — accident — pleading and proof — clauses of policy construed.

A disability policy issued by defendant insured plaintiff under clause "G," entitled "blindness and paralysis indemnity," against paralysis, upon proof of its continuance for fifty-two successive weeks. Also under clause "H," for illness which should prevent him from performing the duties pertaining to his occupation, but for not more than twenty-six consecutive weeks. Plaintiff was stricken with paralysis and disabled thereby for more than fifty-two consecutive weeks, but this action was brought before the expiration of that period. *Held,* that plaintiff could not recover under clause "G," as no cause of action thereunder existed at that time. That he could recover, however, under the allegations of the complaint, under clause "H" of the policy. The jury found for plaintiff in the amount to which he would have been entitled for fifty-two weeks under clause "G." *Held,* that a new trial must be granted unless plaintiff stipulated to reduce the judgment to the sum to which he was entitled under clause "H," entitled "sickness indemnity."

Miles v. *Casualty Co. of America,* 136 App. Div. 908, modified.

(Argued November 23, 1911; decided December 5, 1911.)

APPEAL from a judgment of the Appellate Division of the Supreme Court in the fourth judicial department, entered December 20, 1909, affirming a judgment in favor of plaintiff entered upon a verdict.

The nature of the action and the facts, so far as material, are stated in the opinion.

John D. Teller for appellant. The complaint should have been dismissed, for the reason that from the allegations of the complaint and the evidence given upon the trial, it appears that at the time of the commencement of the action there was no liability on the part of the defendant. (Code Civ. Pro. §§ 398, 416; *Haynes* v. *Onderdonk,* 2 Hun, 619; *Matter of Griswold,* 13 Barb. 412; *Milner* v. *Milner,* 2 Edw. Ch. 114; *Tiffany* v. *Bowerman,* 2 Hun, 642; *Wisner* v. *Ocumpaugh,* 71 N. Y. 113; *Prouty* v. *L. S. & M. S. R. Co.,* 85 N. Y. 276; *Dean* v. *M. E. R. Co.,* 119 N. Y. 545; *Straus* v. *Am. Pub. Assn.,* 96 App. Div. 316; *Butler* v. *Frontier Tel. Co.,* 186 N. Y. 486; *Schell* v. *Plumb,* 55 N. Y. 594; *Bostwick* v. *Menck,* 4 Daly, 69; *Bennett* v. *Lawson,* 71 App. Div. 414.)

John L. Hunter for respondent. The assured was not compelled to wait until the expiration of fifty-two weeks of continuing paralysis before bringing action on the policy. (May on Ins. [4th ed.] 488; *N. T. Co.* v. *W. M. Ins. Co.*, 3 Blatchf. 241; *Cobb* v. *Ins. Co. of N. A.*, 11 Kans. 93; *Hagner* v. *A. P. L. Ins. Co.*, 4 J. & S. 211; *W. H. Ins. Co.* v. *Richardson*, 58 Neb. 597; *Phillips* v. *U. S. B. Society*, 79 Mich. 1; *Drilany* v. *F. & C. Co.*, 106 Md. 18; *B. Ins. Co.* v. *Loney*, 20 Md. 40; *Ins. Co.* v. *Davis*, 59 Kans. 525; *C. Ins. Co.* v. *Traub*, 80 Md. 214.) The defendant cannot avail itself of the defense that the action is prematurely brought unless it is pleaded. (Code Crim. Pro. § 413; *Eno* v. *Diefendorf*, 102 N. Y. 720; *Baumiller* v. *W. Co-Op. Assn.*, 29 N. Y. 26; *B. M. Ins. Co.* v. *Scales*, 49 Tex. App. 743; *Balliet* v. *Met. Life Ins. Co.*, 110 N. Y. 77; *McKyring* v. *Bull*, 16 N. Y. 297; *F. B. F. Ins. Assn.* v. *Kinsey*, 101 Va. 236.)

HAIGHT, J. On the 5th day of July, 1905, the defendant, in consideration of a premium of sixty dollars paid by the plaintiff, issued to him a disability policy in which the company undertook to insure the plaintiff against loss of life, limb, sight or time, in the principal sum of five thousand dollars and for a weekly indemnity of twenty-five dollars under the terms of the agreement specifically set forth, for a period of twelve months. The policy contained, among other provisions, the following:

"G. Blindness and paralysis indemnity. In case the assured shall, during the term of this insurance, contract any disease, that shall not result in death, but shall result independently of all other causes, within one year from the date of this insurance, in the irrecoverable loss of the sight of both eyes or in permanent paralysis, whereby the assured shall entirely lose the use of both hands or of both feet or of one hand and one foot, and is thereby rendered permanently unable to engage in any occupation for wages or profit, the Company will pay to him, upon the filing at the Company's home office of satisfactory proofs of the continuance of such blindness or paralysis for fifty-two consecutive weeks, one-half the principal sum." And it is also further provided:

"H. Sickness indemnity. If bodily disease or illness shall wholly prevent the assured from performing the duties pertaining to his occupation for not less than one week, the Company will pay him the weekly indemnity for the period of disability during which he shall be necessarily confined to the house, but for not more than twenty-six consecutive weeks."

On the 12th day of November, 1905, the plaintiff was stricken with paralysis and was totally disabled for more than fifty-two consecutive weeks thereafter. Notice of such illness was given to the defendant two days after the stroke. Shortly afterward the defendant canceled the policy issued to the plaintiff, as of the date of its issue and returned the premium paid to him and wrote him that the policy had no force and that the plaintiff had no claim against the defendant and that the incident was closed so far as the company was concerned, and later on refused to issue blanks for the filing of proof of loss, upon the ground that it would do no good to file any proofs and that the company would have nothing whatever to do with it. Subsequently, however, proofs of loss were made and filed with the company, in which the plaintiff claimed the right to recover six hundred and fifty dollars for twenty-six weeks of disability under clause "H" of the policy. On the 4th day of September, 1906, this action was begun by the service of the summons upon the defendant but the complaint was not served until the 21st day of April, 1908, and it set forth a cause of action under clause "G" of the policy which we have already quoted. The defendant answered admitting the issuing to the plaintiff of the policy, but denied that it had knowledge or information sufficient to form a belief as to the disability, and denied generally the other allegations of the complaint, and alleged false representations, breach of warranty and full payment.

Upon the trial the defendant's attorney asked the court to hold that no recovery could be had by the plaintiff under clause "G" of the policy and that the trial should be confined to his claim for twenty-five dollars a week for twenty-six weeks, amounting to six hundred and fifty dollars. This the court refused and the trial proceeded upon the claim for one-half of the principal sum under the paralysis clause, to wit, the sum of two thousand five hundred dollars. At the conclusion of the plaintiff's evidence the defendant again moved for a direction of a verdict as to that cause of action, and again at the conclusion of the evidence of both parties the motion was renewed on the specific ground that, at the time of the commencement of the action no liability on the part of the defendant had accrued. These motions were denied and exceptions were taken. The issues raised with reference to the alleged false representations, breach of warranty, full payment, etc., were submitted to the jury and they were all found in favor of the plaintiff and these findings have been unanimously affirmed by the Appellate Division.

In reviewing the exceptions, to which allusion has been made, it becomes necessary to construe clause "G" of the policy. It will be observed that in permanent paralysis the assured must lose the use of at least one hand and one foot, and be thereby rendered permanently unable to engage in any occupation for wages or profit, and in such case the company will pay to him, upon his filing at the company's home office satisfactory proof of the continuance of such paralysis for fifty-two consecutive weeks, one-half the principal sum. It is apparent, therefore, that the paralysis resulting in the loss of the use of a hand and foot must exist for fifty-two consecutive weeks, otherwise there could be no recovery for any amount whatever, and no claim would accrue or exist until the expiration of the fifty-two weeks. The stroke of paralysis, as we have seen, occurred on the 12th day of November, 1905. Fifty-two weeks from that date would make it November 12th, 1906. This action was commenced on the 4th day of September, 1906, more than two months before the expiration of the year. It was, therefore, not only prematurely brought, but it was brought before any claim existed under this clause of the policy upon which a cause of action could be based, and in actions at law the rights of parties must be determined as of the time of the commencement of the action. (*Wisner* v. *Ocumpaugh,* 71 N. Y. 113; *Prouty* v. *L. S. & M. S. R. R. Co.,* 85 N. Y. 272, 276, and *Dean* v. *Metr. Elevated Ry. Co.,* 119 N. Y. 540, 545.) This case is, therefore, distinguishable from those cases in which a claim exists upon a contract, promissory note, bond, or for goods sold and delivered where the action is brought after the claim existed, but before it became· due and payable. In such cases the action would be merely prematurely brought. We, therefore, are of the opinion that in this case the existence of the plaintiff's claim was put in issue by the general denial in the answer. It consequently follows that the plaintiff was not entitled to recover upon this branch of the case.

We think the court erred in refusing the defendant's motion to confine the trial of the case to the plaintiff's claim for weekly allowance under clause "H" of the policy.· It is true that the complaint demands judgment for the two thousand five hundred dollars, but the fact that the plaintiff demands more than he is entitled to does not impair the complaint. After setting forth in the third paragraph of the complaint the claim under clause "G," for which he demands two thousand five hundred dollars, he proceeds in paragraph fourth to further allege sickness and bodily diseases and total paralysis, by which he was disabled from engaging in any occupation for wages or profit, and was confined to his bed for a period of twenty weeks and to the house for an additional period of twenty-eight weeks, making forty-eight weeks in all.

This allegation was not under clause "G" of the policy, for it does not allege that the disability continued for fifty-two consecutive weeks. It was not, therefore, good as an allegation under that clause, but it is a good allegation under clause "H" of the policy. Paragraph five of the complaint follows, alleging notice of proof of the disability and compliance in all respects with the rules and regulations of the defendant company and the conditions of the policy. All of the facts bearing upon this cause of action alleged in the complaint are identical with those embraced in the other claim which was submitted to the jury and passed upon by it. It would seem, therefore, that a new trial is unnecessary unless the plaintiff so elects. It appears to be undisputed that the defendant returned to the plaintiff sixty dollars, the amount of the premium paid by him; this amount deducted from six hundred and fifty dollars would leave five hundred and ninety dollars.

The judgment should be reversed and a new trial ordered, with costs to abide the event, unless the plaintiff, within twenty days, stipulates to reduce the judgment to the sum of five hundred and ninety dollars with interest thereon from the time that it became due and payable, to wit, twenty-six weeks after the date of the stroke of paralysis occurring on the 12th day of November, 1905; if the stipulation is given, the judgment should be modified accordingly, and as so modified affirmed, without costs of this appeal to either party.

CULLEN, Ch. J., WERNER, WILLARD BARTLETT, HISCOCK, CHASE and COLLIN, JJ., concur.

Judgment accordingly.

Alice De Brauwere, Respondent, v. Louis De Brauwere, Appellant.

Husband and wife—right of wife to recover from husband for moneys expended by her for necessaries.

1. A husband is liable in equity to one who furnishes necessaries requisite for the support of his deserted wife and infant children or to one who furnishes the wife with money with which to procure such necessaries.

2. The common-law disability of the wife to sue the husband having been removed, a wife who has applied her separate estate to the purpose of an obligation resting primarily upon her husband may now recover from him the reasonable amounts which she has thus expended out of her separate estate in discharge of his obligation.

3. In an action by the wife to recover for moneys she has been obliged to expend for necessaries for herself and children, the pecuniary ability of the husband may be an element to be considered as to the character of the expenditures for which she is entitled to be reimbursed.

De Brauwere v. *De Brauwere*, 144 App. Div. 521, affirmed.

(Argued October 6, 1911; decided December 5, 1911.)

APPEAL, by permission, from an order of the Appellate Division of the Supreme Court in the first judicial department, entered May 19, 1911, which affirmed an interlocutory judgment of Special Term overruling a demurrer to the complaint.

The following question was certified: "Does the complaint state facts sufficient to constitute a cause of action?"

The nature of the action and the facts, so far as material, are stated in the opinion.

Lucius L. Gilbert and *Merle I. St. John* for appellant. No such action could have been brought at common law, and the common-law duty of support of the wife by the husband has not been changed by the statutes of New York relating to married women. A wife cannot recover from her husband moneys laid out by her for her own support, except, by alleging and proving a promise, either express or implied, of the husband to refund it to her. (*People ex rel. Kehlbeck* v. *Walsh*, 11 Hun, 292; Schouler on Dom. Rel. § 61; *Lindholm* v. *Kane*, 92 Hun, 369; *Holcomb* v. *Harris*, 166 N. Y. 257; *Ruhl* v. *Heintze*, 97 App. Div. 442; *Maron* v. *Scott*, 55 N. Y. 247; *Ellenbrogen* v. *Slocum*, 66 Misc. Rep. 611; *Byrnes* v. *Rayner*, 84 Hun, 199; *Tiemeyer* v. *Turnquist*, 85 N. Y. 516; *Ehrich* v. *Bucki*, 7 Misc. Rep. 118; *Stammers* v. *Macomb*, 2 Wend. 454; *Mitchell* v. *Treanor*, 56 Am. Dec. 421; Schouler on Husband & Wife, § 109; *Metcalf* v. *Shaw*, 3 Camp. 22; *Bentley* v. *Griffin*, 5 Taunt. 356; *Dixon* v. *Hurrell*, 8 C. & P. 717.) This is in reality an action for support by the wife, and cannot be maintained, because the wife cannot sue the husband directly for breach of the marital contract. (*Ramsden* v. *Ramsden*, 91 N. Y. 281; *Beadleston* v. *Beadleston*, 103 N. Y. 402; *Thompson* v. *Thompson*, 218 U. S. 611; 1 Bishop on Marr. Women, § 892; *Decker* v. *Kedly*, 148 Fed. Rep. 681; *Skinner* v. *Tirrell*, 159 Mass. 174.)

Albert J. Hiers and *Thomas F. Doyle* for respondent. The decision should be sustained, because the amended complaint states a cause of action in equity. (10 Abbott's N. Y. Cyc. Dig. 884; *Hemmingway* v. *Poucher*, 98 N. Y. 281; *Coppola* v. *Kraushaar*, 102 App. Div. 306; *Rogers* v. *N. Y. & T. L. Co.*, 131 N. Y. 197; *Mitchell* v. *Thorne*, 134 N. Y. 536; *Grandy* v. *Hadcock*, 85 App. Div. 173; *Hatch* v. *Leonard*, 165 N. Y. 435; *Young* v. *Valentine*, 177 N. Y. 347; *Winter* v. *Winter*, 191 N. Y. 462; Bishop on Mar., Div. & Sep. § 1190; *Dixon* v. *Chapman*, 67 N. Y. 540; 56 App. Div. 542; *Sloane* v. *Boyer*, 95 N. Y. 531.) The amended complaint states a cause of action against the defendant for a breach of contract at law. (*Young* v. *Valentine*, 177 N. Y. 347; *Winter* v. *Winter*, 191 N. Y. 462; L. 1909, ch. 19, § 51; *Manchester* v. *Tibbets*, 121 N. Y. 219.)

WILLARD BARTLETT, J. In this case the plaintiff a married woman, who has been abandoned by her husband, sues the husband to recover moneys which she has been compelled to expend out of her separate estate to provide necessaries for herself and her three infant children. Her separate estate consisted of the proceeds of her own labor as a seamstress and janitress and in part of a small sum of money received by way of inheritance from a deceased relative. Since he abandoned his family about September 1, 1904, the defendant has contributed nothing toward their support except the sum of fifty dollars; and although the plaintiff has endeavored to procure necessaries for herself and her children upon his credit she has been unable to do so. About the time when the husband left his family the wife caused him to be arrested on a charge of abandonment and he was ordered to pay her six dollars a week, but he refused to comply with this order and removed from the state of New York into the state of New Jersey where he resided at the time of the commencement of this action.

The defendant demurred to a complaint setting forth the facts substantially as they have been stated. His demurrer was overruled at the Special Term and an interlocutory judgment was rendered in favor of the plaintiff which has been affirmed by the Appellate Division. The questions presented by the demurrer were elaborately discussed in both courts, and although both arrived at the same result they reached their conclusions upon somewhat different grounds.

"A parent is under a natural obligation to furnish necessaries for his infant children; and if the parent neglect that duty, any other person who supplies such necessaries is deemed to have conferred a benefit on the delinquent parent, for which the law raises an implied promise to pay on the part of the parent." (*Van Valkinburgh* v. *Watson*, 13 Johns. 480.) This rule has long been recognized as the law both in England and this country.   A corollary of the rule is the proposition that where a person has advanced money to a wife deserted by her husband for the purchase of necessaries and the money has been so applied he can maintain a suit in equity against the husband for the money so advanced. The leading case to that effect in this country is *Kenyon* v. *Farris* (47 Conn. 510), in which the earlier English decisions are reviewed.   The doctrine of that case has found general acceptance, except in Massachusetts, where it has been expressly rejected.   (*Skinner* v. *Tirrell*, 159 Mass. 474.)   It has been followed without question by the Supreme Court in this state.   (*Wells* v. *Lachenmeyer*, 2 How. Pr. [N. S.] 252; *Kenny* v. *Meislahn*, 69 App. Div. 572.)

We may assume, then, that a husband is liable in equity to one who furnishes necessaries requisite for the support of his deserted wife and infant children or to one who furnishes the wife with money with which to procure such necessaries.   In the present case, however, the money used for procuring the necessaries was chiefly the outcome of the wife's own labors, and the question is whether she can maintain an action against the husband to recover it.   Clearly no such action was maintainable at common law.   At common law the personal property of the wife and all her earnings belonged to the husband. In this state, however, her marital disabilities have been wholly removed by statute, and the law now presumes that a married women is alone entitled to any wages, earnings or any other remuneration for services which she renders.   Such compensation constitutes a part of her separate estate and she can maintain any action in reference thereto which she could maintain if she were unmarried.

The learned judge who tried the case at Special Term was inclined to think that the plaintiff's right to recover should be sustained upon the doctrine of subrogation, the wife being subrogated to the rights of the persons who furnished the necessaries for herself and the children and whom she has paid therefor. We prefer to place his liability on a different ground. The husband was unquestionably under a legal obligation to provide his wife and children with the necessaries of life suitable to their condition. This liability would have been enforcible by the wife in her own behalf and in behalf of her infant children were it not for her disability at common law to sue her husband. That disability having been removed, a wife who has applied her separate estate to the purpose of an obligation resting primarily upon her husband may now recover from him the reasonable amounts which she has thus expended out of her separate estate in discharge of his obligation. In other words, under the common law such a claim as that in suit was not enforcible, because a married woman was incapable of owning any separate estate and likewise incapable of maintaining an action at law against her husband. These obstacles have been removed by placing a married woman on the same footing with a woman who is unmarried in respect to her property rights, and by permitting her to enforce such rights in the courts against her husband no less than against strangers. The plainest principles of justice require that a wife should have some adequate legal redress upon such a state of facts as that set forth in this complaint, and the beneficial character of our legislation removing the former disabilities of married women could not be evidenced more forcibly than it is in its application to the present case.

The obligation of the husband to provide his wife and children with the necessaries of life suitable to their condition is to be measured with reference to his pecuniary ability, honestly exercised, or his pecuniary resources; that is to say, those things might properly be deemed necessaries in the family of a man of generous income or ample fortune which would not be required in the family of a man whose earnings were small and who had saved nothing.   The husband is bound to provide for his wife and children "whatever is necessary for their suitable clothing and maintenance, according to *his* and their situation and condition in life." (*Keller* v. *Phillips*, 39 N. Y. 351, 354.)   The husband's pecuniary ability, therefore, may be an element to be considered upon the trial of the action if any question is raised as to the character of the expenditures for which the wife seeks reimbursement.

The order appealed from should be affirmed, with costs, and the question certified answered in the affirmative.

CULLEN, Ch. J., HAIGHT, VANN, WERNER, HISCOCK and CHASE, JJ., concur.

Order affirmed.

JOHN H. COLLINS, Respondent, *v.* LESLIE GIFFORD, Appellant.

Infants — liability for sale effected by fraud.

1. A matter arising *ex contractu*, though infected with fraud, cannot be changed into a tort, in order to charge an infant, by a change of the remedy. A fraudulent act, to render an infant chargeable therewith, must be wholly tortious, and if the action is substantially grounded in contract he is not liable.

2. An infant defendant warranted a horse to be "free from any and all diseases of every name and nature," etc. The trial court found that "the sale was consummated as the result of the statements of defendant, and plaintiff in paying for the said horse relied upon said statements." *Held*, that since there is no allegation or finding of any false or fraudulent representation made by the defendant with intent to induce the plaintiff to purchase the horse, this essential element of an action for deceit is wanting, and no cause of action was established against the infant.

Collins v. *Gifford*, 134 App. Div. 988, reversed.

(Argued October 20, 1911; decided December 5, 1911.)

APPEAL from a judgment of the Appellate Division of the Supreme Court in the third judicial department, entered March 15, 1910, affirming a judgment in favor of plaintiff entered upon a decision of the Rensselaer County Court on trial without a jury.

The nature of the action and the facts, so far as material, are stated in the opinion.

Benjamin E. De Groot, Edward L. Nugent and *Clarence E. Akin* for appellant. Even if fraud incident to the contract had been proved this action could not be maintained against the defendant. (*Studer* v. *Bleistein,* 115 N. Y. 324; 2 Pom. Eq. Juris. § 892; *Slaughter* v. *Gerson,* 80 U. S. 379; *Farrar* v. *Churchill,* 135 U. S. 609; *Smith* v. *Countryman,* 30 N. Y. 681.) An action to recover damages is not sustainable against an infant on a contract nor upon a tort connected with the formation of and incident to the contract. (*Nash* v. *Jewett,* 4 L. R. A. 561; 2 Kent's Comm. 242; Cooley on Torts, § 107; Addison on Torts, § 1314; *Louis* v. *Eberhardt,* 102 U. S. 300; *West* v. *Moore,* 14 Vt. 447; Bigelow on Fraud, 355.)

Henry F. Toohey for respondent. An action of deceit will lie against an infant upon the sale of a horse with the warranty of soundness where the defendant knew him to be unsound. (*Wort* v. *Vance,* 9 Am. Dec. 683.)

WILLARD BARTLETT, J. On November 10, 1905, the plaintiff purchased from the defendant, who was an infant, a sorrel mare, for the agreed price of $175. The defendant warranted the horse to be " free from any and all diseases of every name and nature, except a slight bruise on the eye, which the defendant said was caused by knocking against something in the stall." The plaintiff relied upon this statement of the defendant and believed the same to be true. The horse, at the time of the purchase, was in fact suffering from an incurable disease of the eye known as specific ophthalmia, which results in total blindness. The defendant was aware of the true condition of the horse's eye and knew that the animal was subject to recurring attacks of the malady but did not disclose his knowledge in this respect to the plaintiff. The plaintiff offered to return the horse and demanded repayment of the purchase price; but the defendant declined to receive the horse or repay the money. The trial court found that "the sale was consummated as the result of the statements of defendant, and plaintiff in paying for said horse relied upon said statements."

After finding the foregoing facts and the further fact that the plaintiff had been damaged to the amount of $175, the learned county judge proceeded to indicate, in his conclusions of law, the theory upon which he rendered judgment for that sum against the defendant notwithstanding his infancy. The defendant was liable in tort, he said, although he was an infant, because "the sale was consummated as the result of his misrepresentations, the same being relied upon by the plaintiff both in accepting and paying for the horse, defendant being at all times aware of the true condition of the horse's eye." It was further concluded, as matter of law, that a right of disaffirmance arose in favor of the plaintiff, as soon as he discovered the true condition of the horse; but, as has already been stated, his efforts in that direction met with a refusal.

The case of *Hewitt* v. *Warren* (10 Hun, 560) was an action against an infant to recover damages for false and fraudulent representations made upon the sale of a horse, in a warranty contained in the contract of sale; and it was held that the plaintiff could not recover because he he had not disaffirmed the contract or offered to return the horse. The court, however, used the following language, which the trial judge deemed declarative of the doctrine which should govern the case at bar: "If a party has been induced to purchase property from an infant, by the infant's fraud and misrepresentation, it would seem that he might, on discovering the fraud, disaffirm the contract, return, or offer to return the property, and thus put the infant in the position of a mere wrong-doer, unjustly keeping what he had fraudulently obtained. And it would seem that the infant would then be liable in damages for tort." (p. 564.)

This suggestion was obviously made to defeat the application of the general rule that "if an infant effects a sale by means of deception and fraud, his infancy protects him." (1 Cooley on Torts [3d ed.], p. 182.) For his torts generally, where they have no basis in any contract relation, an infant is liable just as any other person would be; but the doctrine is equally well settled that "a matter arising *ex contractu*, though infected with fraud, cannot be changed into a *tort*, in order to charge the *infant* by a change of the remedy." (NELSON, Ch. J., in *People* v. *Kendall*, 25 Wend. 399, 401.) A fraudulent act, to render an infant chargeable therewith, must be wholly tortious. (2 Kent Com. 241.) If the action is substantially grounded in contract he is not liable. (*Campbell* v. *Perkins*, 8 N. Y. 430, 440; *Gilson* v. *Spear*, 38 Vt. 311; *Wilt* v. *Welsh*, 6 Watts, 9; *Lowery* v. *Cate*, 108 Tenn. 54.) In the case last cited it is said: "The test of an action against an infant is whether a liability can be made out without taking notice of the contract."

If we apply the principle of the foregoing authorities to the complaint and findings in the present case, we find that no cause of action has been established against the infant defendant, even if the obiter suggestion in *Hewitt* v. *Warren* (*supra*) be accepted as correct. There is no allegation or finding of any false or fraudulent representation made by the defendant *with intent* to induce the plaintiff to purchase the horse. This essential element of an action for deceit is wanting. Neither the word *fraud* nor *fraudulent* occurs in the complaint. The breach of warranty was the gist of the cause of action which the pleader had in mind; and this would have sufficed were it not for the infancy of the defendant. Being compelled by that defense to have recourse to the theory of an action for fraud, the plaintiff finds this position equally untenable by reason of his failure to charge any fraudulent intent and the omission of the trial court to find any.

In the view which has been taken the findings of fact in this case do not sustain the conclusion of law that the plaintiff is entitled to judgment. The judgment must, therefore, be reversed and a new trial ordered, with costs to abide the event.

CULLEN, Ch. J., GRAY, WERNER, HISCOCK, CHASE and COLLIN, JJ., concur.

Judgment reversed, etc.

ROCKLAND-ROCKPORT LIME COMPANY, Respondent, *v.* MARY C. LEARY, as Administratrix of the Estate of JAMES D. LEARY, Deceased, Respondent, and DANIEL J. LEARY et al., Appellants.

Equitable conversion — definition and application of doctrine of equitable conversion — definition and effect of term "legal representative" when used in deed or contract — lease of lands giving lessee option to purchase of lessor or his legal representatives — when actual tender of purchase price need not be made to legal representatives of such lessor.

1. The doctrine of equitable conversion rests on the presumed intention of the owner of the property and on the maxim that equity regards as done what ought to be done. The conversion usually becomes effective at the date of the instrument expressing the intention, if a deed or contract, and if a will, at the date of the testator's death. This is the rule when an absolute and not a contingent conversion is intended; but where no conversion is intended, unless a contingent event happens, conversion should not be presumed as of a date earlier than when the contingent event happens.

2. The words "legal representative" ordinarily mean the executor or administrator, and that meaning will be attributed to them in any instance unless there be facts existing which show that the words were not used in their ordinary sense, but to denote some other and different idea.

3. Where one party to a contract is able and willing to perform, and has made due effort to that end, no actual tender need be made if performance has been prevented by the other party, or the situation is such that the amount to be tendered cannot be known without a judgment of the court, or some of the persons entitled to the money are infants, so that no tender can be made to them.

4. The owner of lands gave an option thereon to plaintiff, in which it was provided that the covenants therein should be binding on the parties and "their heirs, legal representatives, successors or assigns." The plaintiff, if it exercised such option, was required within a specified period to notify the owner "or his legal representative" of its intent so to do. Such notice was sought to be given to the administratrix of the owner. She had actual knowledge of plaintiff's intent to exercise the option, but sought to evade service of the notice, which was in fact given to one of the heirs who acted for all the others, such heir refusing to carry out the option. *Held*, that plaintiff had complied with the requirement of the option as to notice of its intent to purchase.

Rockland-Rockport Lime Co. v. *Leary*, 139 App. Div. 939, affirmed.

(Argued November 27, 1911; decided December 12, 1911.)

APPEAL from a judgment of the Appellate Division of the Supreme Court in the second judicial department, entered August 15, 1910, affirming a judgment in favor of plaintiff entered upon a decision of the court on trial at Special Term.

This action was brought to compel the specific performance of an alleged contract to convey land, and the following facts were found in substance by the justice who presided at the Special Term before which it was tried: On the 17th of January, 1901, the plaintiff and one James D. Leary entered into an agreement in writing and under seal whereby the latter leased to the former certain lands and riparian rights on Newtown creek in the county of Kings for the term of ten years at an annual rental of $5,000. In addition to the covenants usually made in a lease of importance there was the following: "The party of the first part, (the lessor) in consideration of this lease, hereby gives and grants unto the said party of the second part, (the lessee) the right and option to purchase the property herein demised, for the sum of $125,000 in gold coin of the United States, or its equivalent, at any time during the five years subsequent to February 1st, 1901, provided, however, and it is mutually understood and agreed, that the said party of the first part may withdraw said option and right hereby granted at any time after sixty days after he shall have given written notice to the party of the second part of his intention so to do. If the said party of the second part shall exercise said option and shall notify the said party of the first part, or his legal representative, of its intent so to do, then within thirty days thereafter, the party of the second part shall tender or cause to be tendered to the party of the first part, or his legal representative, $125,000, in the gold coin of the United States of America, or its equivalent. And the party of the first part, or his legal representatives, shall at the same time deliver or cause to be delivered to the party of the second part, a good and sufficient Warranty Deed of the premises herein described to the sole use and benefit of the said party of the second part, and its successors, forever. * * * And it is further understood and agreed, that the covenants and agreements contained in the within Lease are binding on the parties hereto, and their heirs, legal representatives, successors or assigns.''

The plaintiff entered into possession of the premises and was still in possession when this action was commenced on the 21st day of May, 1906. James D. Leary died intestate in April, 1902, leaving him surviving a widow, three adult children and two infant grandchildren, each under the age of fourteen, the children of a deceased son, all of whom are parties defendant to this action. The widow, Mary C. Leary, was soon appointed sole administratrix of his estate and she is still acting in that capacity. She was made a party defendant, both as an individual and as administratrix. Since the death of the lessor all the rent has been paid to Daniel J. Leary, one of his sons, who acted as attorney for the administratrix and as such gave receipts for all payments made. He "was the person in charge of the business connected with the land named in the indenture and the receiver of the rent derived therefrom for those interested." No effort was at any time made to withdraw the option contained in the lease.

The court found specifically that "within five years subsequent to the first day of February, 1901, the Rockland-Rockport Lime Company notified the said Daniel J. Leary of the intention of the Rockland-Rockport Lime Company to exercise the option named in said indenture, and requested him to carry out the same, which he, the said Daniel J. Leary, refused to do." This finding was not excepted to by any of the defendants.

On the 25th of January, 1906, the plaintiff caused to be delivered to the butler at No. 3 East 56th street, New York city, the residence of Mary C. Leary, a formal notice of its intention to exercise the option, and also a letter asking Mrs. Leary as the legal representative of her deceased husband to appoint an early day to close the matter up. Each of these papers was inclosed in a sealed wrapper addressed to Mary C. Leary, and when they were received by the butler he stated that she was in. He then went upstairs with the two papers, and after several minutes returned saying that Mrs. Leary was not in, and requesting the person who had delivered the papers to him to take them away. This request was declined, and the butler was instructed to give the papers to Mrs. Leary when she came in.

On the 29th of January, 1906, the plaintiff duly mailed to Mrs. Leary at her said residence a letter stating that it had served her with a notice of its intention to exercise the option, and adding that it was "the desire of the company to make the payment of the $125,000, as required by the lease, and receive the deed of the property, as in

the lease provided, at the earliest practical day and pref-
erably before the first day of February next." The letter
asked her to name a time and place where the duly authorized representative of the plaintiff could meet her to make
a tender of the money and receive the deed. This letter
was returned to the sender unopened. On the 31st of
January, 1906, two representatives of the plaintiff called
at the said residence of Mrs. Leary with $125,000 in gold
certificates of the United States, for the purpose of tendering the same to her as administratrix as the purchase
money under the lease. Upon inquiry of the butler if
she was at home, he said she was not, and, when asked
if she would return soon, replied that she was out of the
city and would be gone a week or ten days. He was told
to tell her "that George F. Harriman, attorney for the
Rockland-Rockport Lime Company, called with Orrin F.
Perry, the manager of the Rockland-Rockport Lime
Company."

The court further found that "from the testimony and
evidence in this cause, and considering in connection therewith the failure of Mary C. Leary to take the stand as a
witness in behalf of the defendants and to testify as to
the material facts necessarily within her knowledge, and
considering the failure to give any explanation of her
absence from the trial or of inability to attend, it is fairly
inferred that Mary C. Leary had actual knowledge, prior
to February 1st, 1906, of the intention and determination
of plaintiff to exercise the said option of purchase. It is
fairly inferred from the evidence herein that Mary C.
Leary sought to avoid and evade service of the notice of
intent to exercise the option and the making of tender."

The court found as conclusions of law that the plaintiff
had made sufficient efforts to comply with the provisions
of the lease relating to the exercise of the option of purchase therein contained and also the provision requiring
the tender of $125,000 to the legal representative of the
lessor; that on the 31st day of January, 1906, the plaintiff

was entitled to a good and sufficient deed of the land described in the lease, but, as said land was subject to an outstanding right of dower of Mary C. Leary, the widow, an interlocutory judgment was directed in favor of the plaintiff and a referee was appointed to compute the gross cash value of said dower right and report the amount of purchase money remaining due after deducting the same from the purchase price. The complaint was dismissed as to Mary C. Leary individually.

An interlocutory judgment was entered accordingly and in due time the referee reported that the gross cash value of said dower right on the 31st of January, 1906, was the sum of $15,631. Thereupon final judgment was entered directing conveyance to the plaintiff upon the payment of the balance amounting to $109,369.

All the defendants except Mary C. Leary, as administratrix, appealed to the Appellate Division where the judgment was affirmed. The same defendants only now appeal to this court.

Pierre M. Brown for appellants. Conversion in the case of an option occurs on the date of declaring, and does not relate back to the grant. (*Matter of Isaacs,* L. R. [3 Ch. 1899] 507; *Edwards* v. *West,* L. R. [7 Ch. Div.] 858; *Smith* v. *Lowenstein,* 50 Ohio St. 346; *Gilbert* v. *Port,* 28 Ohio St. 276; *Savage* v. *Burnham,* 17 N. Y. 561; *Clift* v. *Moses,* 116 N. Y. 144; *White* v. *Howard,* 46 N. Y. 144; *Chamberlain* v. *Taylor,* 105 N. Y. 185; *Graham* v. *De Witt,* 3 Bradf. 186; *Ogsbury* v. *Ogsbury,* 115 N. Y. 290; *Underwood* v. *Curtis,* 127 N. Y. 523.) Where the consideration should go after the transaction is closed is not controlling in fixing the identity of the person entitled to notice. (*Gall* v. *Vermuden,* 2 Freem. 199; *Taylor* v. *Sutton,* 15 Ga. 103; *Underhill* v. *Saratoga,* 20 Barb. 455; *Wilson* v. *Wilson,* 38 Me. 18; *Proprietors* v. *Grant,* 3 Gray, 142; *Ewing* v. *Jones,* 130 Ind. 251; *M. L. Ins. Co.* v. *Armstrong,* 117 U. S. 591; Redf. on

Surr. Prac. § 528; *Blakeman* v. *Sears*, 74 Conn. 516;
Johnson v. *Ames*, 28 Mass. 172; *Greenwood* v. *Holbrooke*, 11 N. Y. 467; *Baines* v. *Ottey*, 1 M. & K. 465.)
The determination of what the parties meant by the use of
the words "legal representatives" is controlling. (Pom.
on Cont. 387; *Kerr* v. *Purdy*, 51 N. Y. 629; *Babcock*
v. *Emerich*, 54 How. Pr. 435; *Fallerton* v. *McLaughlin*, 70 Hun, 568; *Bostwick* v. *Frankfield*, 74 N. Y. 207;
Blanchard v. *Archer*, 93 App. Div. 459; Story's Eq. Juris.
776.) Where there has been no fraud or concealment, and
the vendee took the contract knowing that the vendor had
a wife, and the latter refuses to take a gross sum, the
court will not decree specific performance, especially of
an option contract. (*Halsey* v. *Grant*, 13 Ves. Jr. 73;
Sternberger v. *McGovern*, 56 N. Y. 12; *Castle* v. *Wilkinson*, L. R. [5 Ch. App.] 534; *Rudd* v. *Lescelles*,
L. R. [1 Ch. Div. 1900] 815; *Balmanno* v. *Lumley*,
1 Ves. & B. 224; Fry on Spec. Perf. 1281; *Nelson* v.
Brown, 66 Hun, 311; 144 N. Y. 389; *Fern* v. *Osterhaut*, 11 App. Div. 319; *Lowry* v. *Smith*, 9 Hun,
514; *Matter of Sipperly*, 44 Barb. 370; *Lawrenson* v.
Butler, 1 S. & L. 18.) The acts done by plaintiff did not
amount to the service of a notice or the making of a
tender as a matter of law. (*Hoag* v. *Parr*, 13 Hun, 95.)

George F. Harriman and *Robert H. Ewell* for plaintiff, respondent. As to notice and tender, the plaintiff
has done all that was necessary to entitle it to a specific
performance of the contract. It is immaterial whether
the administratrix or the heirs were the "legal representative" to receive notice and tender. (*Tompkins* v.
Hyatt, 28 N. Y. 347; *Geisler* v. *Acosta*, 9 N. Y. 227;
Scholey v. *Halsey*, 72 N. Y. 578; *Lawrence* v. *Miller*, 86
N. Y. 131; *Hayner* v. *A. P. L. Ins. Co.*, 69 N. Y. 435;
Kerr v. *Purdy*, 50 Barb. 24; 4 Pom. Eq. Juris. [3d ed.]
§ 1407; *Crary* v. *Smith*, 2 N. Y. 60; *Reehil* v. *Frass*, 129
App. Div. 563; *Sugarman* v. *Brengel*, 68 App. Div. 377;

Bleecker v. *Johnston*, 69 N. Y. 309; *Schwier* v. *N. Y. C. & H. R. R. R. Co.*, 90 N. Y. 558.) The primary and ordinary meaning of the words "legal representative" is executors or administrators, they being the official representatives constituted by the proper court, and in the absence of proof requiring a different meaning to be given to these words, they must be thus construed. (*Geoffroy* v. *Gilbert*, 5 App. Div. 98; 154 N. Y. 741; *Sulz* v. *M. R. F. L. Association*, 145 N. Y. 563; *Griswold* v. *Sawyer*, 125 N. Y. 411; *Thompson* v. *United States*, 20 Ct. Cl. [U. S.] 276; *Briggs* v. *Walker*, 171 U. S. 466; *Pillow* v. *Hardeman*, 3 Humph. [Tenn.] 538; *Robinson* v. *Hurst*, 78 Md. 59; *Weaver* v. *Roth*, 105 Penn. St. 408; *Cox* v. *Curwen*, 118 Mass. 198; *Johnson* v. *Edmond*, 65 Conn. 492; *Wason* v. *Colburn*, 99 Mass. 342; 18 Am. & Eng. Ency. of Law [2d ed.], 813.) Under the principle of equitable conversion, the purchase money belonged to the testatrix of the lessor, not to his heirs. It follows that the words "legal representative," as used in the lease to designate the person to whom tender should be made, referred to the executor or administrator of the lessor. (*Potter* v. *Ellice*, 48 N. Y. 321; *McCarthy* v. *Myers*, 5 Hun, 85; *Moore* v. *Burrows*, 34 Barb. 173; *Lawes* v. *Bennett*, 1 Cox Ch. 167; *Matter of Isaacs*, L. R. [3 Ch. 1894] 506; *Kerr* v. *Day*, 14 Penn. St. 112; *McKay* v. *Carrington*, 1 McLean, 50; *Keep* v. *Miller*, 42 N. J. Eq. 100; *Newport Water Works* v. *Sisson*, 18 R. I. 411; *Williams* v. *Lilley*, 67 Conn. 50; Tiffany on Modern Law of Real Prop. 266, § 11; Pom. Eq. Juris. [3d ed.], § 1163; 1 Sugden on Vendors [8th Am. ed.], 188; Lewin on Trusts [8th ed.], 952; Waterman on Spec. Perf. § 200, and note.) Plaintiff is entitled to an abatement from the contract price equal to the cash value of the outstanding right of dower. (*Thompson* v. *Simpson*, 128 N. Y. 270; *Bostwick* v. *Beach*, 103 N. Y. 421; *Maas* v. *Morgenthaler*, 136 App. Div. 359; *Waters* v. *Travis*, 9 Johns. 450; *Harsha* v. *Reid*, 45 N. Y. 415.) **The** agreement in question was valid and enforceable, and both parties to it were capable in law of entering into such an agreement. (*Johnson* v. *Trippe*, 33 Fed. Rep. 530; Pomeroy on Spec. Perf. § 169; Waterman on Spec. Perf. § 200.)

VANN, J. Upon the death of the lessor, intestate, the real estate in question descended to his heirs at law subject to the dower right of the widow, who did not sign the lease, and subject also to the lease itself and the provision for an option contained therein. As the agreement by its terms bound "the heirs, legal representatives, successors or assigns" of the parties, the death of the lessor did not affect the right of the plaintiff to exercise the option. The contract for an option ran with the land and was still in force when the efforts to exercise it were made, and the question presented for decision is whether those efforts were sufficient to satisfy the requirements of the instrument in that respect. The appellants claim that the notice of intention should have been served upon the heirs at law. The respondents claim that notice to the administratrix and the attempt to make a tender to her as the legal representative of the deceased lessor were sufficient to call for a conveyance, and, if not, that notice to Daniel J. Leary, the heir who acted for all the others and his refusal to carry out the option, entitled the plaintiff to the relief sought.

The action was twice tried, and on the first trial the complaint was dismissed upon the ground that notice should have been given and tender made to the heirs of the lessor, mainly for the reason that they had become the owners of the property and were to make the conveyance. Upon appeal to the Appellate Division that judgment was reversed, and it was held that notice and tender to the administratrix and not to the heirs was required, because the option when exercised worked an equitable conversion of .the realty into personalty which related back to the date of the lease. (133 App. Div. 379.)

The main reliance for this conclusion is *Lawes* v. *Bennet* (1 Cox Ch. 167), decided in 1785 by Lord KENYON when master of the rolls. In that case a lease was made for a long term with an option to the lessee to purchase the demised premises within a limited period for the sum of three thousand pounds. The lessor died, and by his will, made several years before the lease, he devised all his real estate to his cousin, John Bennett, and all his personal property in equal parts to the said John and to Mary, his sister, who were appointed "joint executors." In due time the option was exercised. Bennett conveyed and the purchase price was paid to him. A bill was filed by Mary to compel him to account to her for one-half of the three thousand pounds, and, as the reporter states, the single question was "whether the premises being part of the testator's real estate at the time of his death, but sold afterwards under the circumstances aforesaid, the purchase money should be considered as part of the real or personal estate of the testator." It was argued on the one hand that there was no declared intention of the testator to convert the realty into personalty; but it was left to the lessee, a stranger, to work the conversion, with the result that a simple contract creditor might wait many years before he knew whether there were any assets or not. It was contended, on the other hand, that the absolute owner of property may give to a stranger any power over it that he thinks fit and that the testator had ample time before his death to alter his will if he had been so inclined. In a very brief opinion and without much argument, the master of the rolls held that "When the party who has the power of making the election has elected, the whole is to be referred back to the original agreement, and the only difference is, that the real estate is converted into personal at a future period." ·Accordingly he declared the

three thousand pounds to be part of the personal estate of
the testator and required Bennett to account for a moiety
thereof.

This case has been uniformly, although at times reluct-
antly, followed in England, and occasionally, but not
universally, in the United States, not, however, without
serious criticism in both countries. (*Townley* v. *Bedwell*,
14 Ves. 590; *Collingwood* v. *Rew*, 3 Jur. [N. S.] 785;
Smith v. *Loewenstein*, 50 Ohio St. 346.) The principle
has never been extended, even in England, but has been
limited whenever limitation was possible without overruling Lord KENYON. (*Emuss* v. *Smith*, 2 De G. & Sm.
722; *Edwards* v. *West*, L. R. [7 Ch. Div.] 858.) It has
been regarded as "difficult of explanation" and as creating "a very singular and inconvenient state of things."
The main reason for following it, as an eminent English
judge once intimated, is because it was "decided by so
great a man as Lord KENYON."

The Supreme Court of Ohio, in an important case,
refused to follow *Lawes* v. *Bennett* upon the ground that
it does not rest upon a firm foundation. That learned
court said: "The doctrine now most in accord with the
general course of authority and principle is, that as
between lessor and lessee, with the privilege to the latter
to purchase, the conversion will be deemed to have taken
place at the time of declaring the option and not from
the date of the contract giving the option. * * * We
see no good reason why the doctrine of relation back to
the date of the lease should be applied for the purpose of
divesting the heirs who held the freehold title when the
option was declared, and handing over the purchase
money to the personal representatives. The descent to
the heir was in the legal channel which the statute had
marked out; and after executing the lease, the lessor did
nothing to curtail the rights of the heir, upon whom the
law would cast the real estate immediately upon the death
of the ancestor. The estate having thus devolved, and the

lessee having failed or neglected to exercise the option to purchase while the lessor was alive, we do not discover upon what satisfactory ground, the real estate should be deemed converted into personalty as of the date of the lease, for the purpose of diverting the purchase money from the heir to the administrator. * * * An examination of authorities, English and American, makes manifest that the doctrine of *Lawes* v. *Bennett* does not rest upon a firm foundation." (*Smith, Administrator*, v. *Loewenstein*, 50 Ohio St. 346.) To the same effect is *Gilbert* v. *Port* (28 Ohio St. 276).

The doctrine of equitable conversion rests on the presumed intention of the owner of the property and on the maxim that equity regards as done what ought to be done. The conversion usually becomes effective at the date of the instrument expressing the intention, if a deed or contract, and if a will, at the date of the testator's death. This is the rule when an absolute and not a contingent conversion is intended. In the case before us no conversion was intended unless the option was exercised, and the conversion was contingent for it depended wholly upon a future event which might or might not happen. If it happened, there was a conversion, otherwise there was none and, hence, the date when the contingency was resolved becomes important. The lessor had the power to thus provide and in so providing, what was his intention as presumed from what he wrote, there being no other guide except the surrounding circumstances so far as they bear on his intention? As he intended no conversion unless the contingent event happened, he is presumed to have intended none until that event happened, for that would be the natural date to have it take effect in order to avoid confusion if not disaster. Upon this theory the heirs would take the land and enjoy it as land, just as the heirs in this case have done, until the contingency became a certainty by the exercise of the option when they would take the purchase money instead of the land, precisely as their ancestor would have had he survived until that time. The maxim underlying the doctrine of equitable conversion rests on a duty to do something, but in this case until the option was exercised there was no duty and it could not be known whether there ever would be a duty. Hence, conversion should not be presumed as of a date earlier than the date when the duty became certain, as that would be unreasonable and the same in effect as if the duty had existed from the outset. If the lessor had made the duty absolute instead of contingent, he could fairly be said to have intended that conversion *must* take place at some time, but as he made it contingent he could not have intended that result. In this respect the case is the same in principle as if a discretionary power of sale had been given in a will, when no conversion is effected in the absence of an actual sale, as "It must be made the duty of and obligatory upon the trustees to sell in any event" in order to work that result. (*White* v. *Howard*, 46 N. Y. 144, 162; *Chamberlain* v. *Taylor*, 105 N. Y. 185, 194; *Underwood* v. *Curtis*, 127 N. Y. 523. 533.) Hence the lessor must in reason be presumed to have intended that the discharge of the duty should take effect for all purposes only from the date when by his direction the duty became absolute through the occurrence of an uncertain event. To hold otherwise would carry a rule, unknown to the common law and created by courts of equity because founded on reason, far beyond the bounds of reason. As intention is involved, or presumed intention which must be reasonable, the manifest inconvenience of holding otherwise cannot be ignored. In the case of a lease for a long term, such as a period of twenty-one years with the privilege of renewal for twenty-one years longer, which is not unusual, with an option to purchase, which though unusual is sometimes given, it might not be known for more than a generation whether the leased property was real or personal and not until a stranger had elected to exercise the option, or the period allowed had expired. Creditors, heirs, devisees, next of kin, legatees and even the state in assessing the transfer tax, might be involved in such uncertainty and confusion as could be dispelled only after years of litigation. This would necessarily reduce the market value of the property, simply through the action of the courts in blindly following a great common-law judge, who applied a reasonable rule of equity in an unreasonable way. The courts of this state have not adopted Lord KENYON's application and we decline to adopt it. We hold that conversion was effected only from the date when conveyance became a duty and that it did not relate back to the date of the lease.

This conclusion, however, does not settle the question whether service of notice upon the administratrix was sufficient in view of the express requirement of the lease that in case the lessee should exercise the option it should notify the lessor, but not necessarily in writing, "or his *legal representative* of its intent to do so." The words "legal representative" ordinarily mean the executor or administrator, although sometimes when required by the context and surrounding circumstances they are held to mean next of kin, but only under rare and peculiar facts, heirs at law. (*Sulz* v. *Mutual Reserve Fund Life Assoc.*, 145 N. Y. 563.) The words in question are presumed to mean executors or administrators, and, as Judge PECKHAM said in the case last cited, "that meaning will be attributed to them in any instance unless there be facts existing which show that the words were not used in their ordinary sense, but to denote some other and different idea." (p. 574.)

The appellants insist that the heirs were referred to because they only could execute the good and sufficient deed called for. The legal representative was not required to execute the deed but to deliver it or cause it to be delivered. The covenant in express terms bound the heirs, and they could not take the land, hold it and accept the rent until the option was exercised without complying with the covenant either voluntarily or through compulsion of the courts. The Revised Statutes provided that the Court of Chancery should have power to compel specific performance by any infant or other person "of any bargain, contract or agreement, made by any party who may die before the performance thereof, on petition of the executors or administrators of the estate of the deceased * * *." (L. 1814, ch. 108, § 3; 2 R. S. *194, §§ 169, 175.) That power now resides in the Supreme Court. (Code Civ. Pro. § 4.) The lessor could do what he wished with his own property, and, hence, he could require notice to be given to any one he chose, even a trust company or any other stranger. If he intended that the lessor should notify his executor or administrator, he naturally expected the person would be a member of his family with whom all the other members would co-operate. If he meant his heirs, why did he not say so expressly? The lease is a long instrument, drawn with skill and is clear in every respect unless when "legal representative" was written, "heirs" were meant by implication only. I am personally of the opinion that the context does not overcome the presumption that those words were used with their ordinary meaning. I also think, as the learned trial judge found, that the efforts to notify the administratrix gave her "actual knowledge" of the fact and were sufficient to meet the requirements of the lease.

If, however, the lessor meant that notice should be given to his heirs instead of to his administratrix, still the requirement was met by notice to one of the adult heirs, the oldest and the managing heir as he may be called, and his refusal to act, which was tantamount to a refusal to convey. No "good and sufficient deed" could be given unless all the heirs united therein, and, hence, the refusal by one was the same as a refusal by all. (*Blood* v.

Goodrich, 9 Wend. 68.) After such refusal there was no necessity of making a tender, for the law does not require a vain thing to be done. Moreover, strict tender was unnecessary on account of the outstanding right of dower and because two of the heirs were infants. Where, according to allegation and evidence one party is able and willing to perform and has made due effort to that end, no actual tender need be made if performance has been prevented by the other party, or the situation is such that the amount to be tendered cannot be known without a judgment of the court, or some of the persons entitled to the money are infants, so that no tender can be made to them. (*Lawrence* v. *Miller*, 86 N. Y. 131, and cases cited on page 137.)

We find no error in the record and the judgment appealed from should, therefore, be affirmed, with costs.

CULLEN, Ch. J., GRAY, HAIGHT, HISCOCK, CHASE and COLLIN, JJ., concur.

Judgment affirmed.

THE PEOPLE OF THE STATE OF NEW YORK, Respondent, *v.* ALBERT W. WOLTER, Appellant.

Murder — when verdict of conviction under common-law indictment not against weight of evidence — when previous opinion or impression of jurors not sufficient ground for challenge for bias — exceptions to admission of evidence, charge to jury and refusal to charge examined and rulings of court sustained.

1. On review of the evidence on appeal from a judgment convicting defendant of murder in the first degree, *held*, that no plausible view of the facts can be suggested in support of the proposition that the verdict was against the weight of evidence or that justice requires a new trial so far as the facts are concerned.

2. Where jurors admitted, when examined under challenge, that they had previously formed an opinion or impression to the effect that a crime had been committed in the case, but each declared on oath that he believed such opinion or impression would not influence his verdict and that he could render an impartial verdict

according to the evidence, such previous opinion or impression is not a sufficient ground of challenge for bias. (Code Crim. Pro. § 376, subd. 2.) Furthermore the defendant was tried by a special jury drawn under chapter 602 of the Laws of 1901, which provides that the allowance or disallowance of challenges for actual bias shall be final.

3. Under an indictment for murder in the common-law form physicians were properly allowed to testify to the taking of certain matter from the vagina of the deceased which, upon a microscopic examination, was found to contain spermatozoa, as bearing not only upon the motive for the crime but also as tending to show that the killing was done while in the perpetration of another crime.

4. The court instructed the jury: "Nor is it necessary that each and every circumstance should be proved beyond a reasonable doubt. Some facts may be proved with more, some with less assurance of certainty." The court refused to charge that, "if any of the material facts of this case are at variance with the probabilities of guilt it would be the duty of the jury to give to the defendant the benefit of the doubt." *Held*, that neither such charge, nor the refusal, was harmful to the defendant when followed by the instruction that if on any branch of the case there existed in their minds a reasonable doubt, the defendant was always entitled to the benefit of that reasonable doubt.

5. Under the common-law form of indictment the court properly submitted the case to the jury upon the theory that they could convict the defendant of murder in the first degree in the absence of any premeditation or deliberation on his part provided they found that he killed the deceased while engaged in the commission of a felony.

(Argued December 4, 1911; decided December 12, 1911.)

APPEAL from a judgment of the Court of General Sessions of the Peace in the county of New York, rendered April 27, 1910, upon a verdict convicting the defendant of the crime of murder in the first degree.

The facts, so far as material, are stated in the opinion.

Wallace D. Scott, Alexander Sampson and *Lewis H. Saper* for appellant. The trial court erred in permitting witnesses to testify as to the finding of spermatozoa in

the vagina of the deceased. (*People* v. *Bennett*, 49 N. Y.
137; *State* v. *Bertoch*, 83 N. W. Rep. 967; *People* v.
Hall, 48 Mich. 482; Abb. Cr. Brief, § 619.) The court
erred in its charge to the jury on the subject of the
degree of proof that was required in a case where the
evidence is circumstantial by giving conflicting charges
thereon. (*Clair* v. *People*, 9 Col. 122; 1 Starkie on Ev.
501; *Comm.* v. *Webster*, 5 Cush. 295; *Mackey* v. *People*,
2 Col. 131; *People* v. *Campbell*, 30 Cal. 312; *Case* v.
People, 3 Neb. 369; *Green* v. *White*, 37 N. Y. 407;
Marion v. *State*, 16 Neb. 349; *Leonard* v. *Territory*, 2
Wash. Terr. 381.)

Charles S. Whitman, District Attorney (*Robert C.
Taylor* of counsel), for respondent. The evidence show-
ing rape was properly admitted. (*Buel* v. *People*, 78
N. Y. 492; *People* v. *Schermerhorn*, 203 N. Y. 57.) The
charge relating to circumstantial evidence was proper.
(*People* v. *Koenig*, 180 N. Y. 155; *People* v. *Gilbert*, 199
N. Y. 10; *People* v. *Tobin*, 176 N. Y. 278.)

WILLARD BARTLETT, J. The jurisdiction conferred by
the Constitution and the statutes upon the Court of
Appeals in cases where the judgment is of death com-
pels us to examine into the facts upon an appeal of this
character; for, irrespective of any exceptions in the
record, it is made our duty to order a new trial if satisfied that the verdict was against the weight of evidence,
or that justice requires a new trial. (Code Crim. Pro.
§ 528.) In the performance of this duty, the facts of this
shocking case as they appear in the record of the trial
have been most carefully considered and scrutinized; but
the details of the crime are so horrible as to preclude any
restatement of them here further than is absolutely necessary to a just disposition of the rights of the defendant
and the prosecution.

On the 24th day of March, 1910, at No. 224 East

Seventy-fifth street in the city of New York, Ruth Wheeler, a girl fifteen years of age, was strangled and burnt to death in an apartment on the fourth floor, occupied by the defendant. The girl was seeking employment as a stenographer, and went to the apartment of the defendant to see him in reference to procuring such employment. Portions of her dead body partly incinerated were subsequently discovered in the area, into which they had been thrown, under circumstances and in a condition indicating beyond all reasonable doubt that the girl had come to her death in the defendant's room by strangulation and burning, after having been ravished. The evidence indicated that the burning was done in the fireplace in the defendant's room, where the body was concealed until it became convenient to remove it in a bag to the fire-escape, from which it was subsequently thrown to the ground below. No witness was produced who ever saw Ruth Wheeler and the defendant together; nor was it made to appear that they had ever met one another prior to the day of her death. The proof, however, points unerringly to the defendant as the perpetrator of the crime. He admits that he wrote the postal card in response to which she set out to visit his apartment; and in a book kept by him was found in his handwriting an entry of her name and address which it is impossible he could have ascertained except from her on the occasion of her visit. In his fireplace were found a hatpin and ring which Ruth Wheeler had worn on the morning of her disappearance; and in a house to which the defendant had moved on the following day was discovered an umbrella which the girl was known to have had with her when she left home. The defendant gave no explanation to account for the presence of these articles or the traces of homicidal death upon his premises. He testified that he was absent from his apartment from half-past eight o'clock on the morning of March 24, 1910, until three o'clock in the afternoon, and that he had never seen a girl by the name of Ruth Wheeler in his life. He sought to account for the entry of her name in his handwriting in his book by saying that he wrote it there at the dictation of a man named Fred Ahner who was desirous of starting a school of shorthand and told him that he was going to engage this girl — in what capacity does not appear. Fred Ahner was not produced as a witness nor did any one else testify to the existence of such a person. A shirt belonging to the defendant upon which were stains of blood and grease was found in a package which had been thrown from the fire-escape into the area with the bag containing Ruth Wheeler's remains; but the defendant although admitting that the garment was his was unable to account for the presence of these stains upon it. That Ruth Wheeler was ravished and killed in the defendant's apartment on Thursday, March 24, 1910, is a fact which does not admit of the slightest doubt upon the proof in this case; and I think that the jury were warranted by the circumstantial evidence in reaching the conclusion that the defendant was the ravisher and murderer. No plausible view of the facts can be suggested in support of the proposition that the verdict was against the weight of evidence or that justice requires a new trial so far as the facts are concerned. It remains for us, therefore, only to consider the questions of law raised by the appeal.

The brief in behalf of the appellant consists of 167 printed pages, 152 of which are devoted to a re-statement of the evidence given by the several witnesses upon the trial. The record shows that 160 exceptions were taken by the counsel for the defendant to the rulings of the trial judge in admitting and excluding evidence. Only one group of these exceptions is argued in his brief. It is urged that the court erred in permitting Dr. Philip F. O'Hanlon and Dr. John H. Larkin to testify to the taking of certain matter from the vagina of the deceased which upon a microscopic examination was found to contain spermatozoa. This evidence was clearly relevant and material as bearing not only upon motive for the crime of murder but also as tending to show that the killing was done while in the perpetration of another crime. This was proper under the indictment, which was in the common-law form. (*People* v. *Sullivan*, 173 N. Y. 122, and cases there cited.)

The four other points in the brief for the defendant relate to the charge to the jury. As to these points it is to be noted in the first place that no exception whatever was taken to the charge or to any refusal to charge as requested. Inasmuch, however, as it is within our power to order a new trial if satisfied that substantial legal error was committed, even in the absence of any exception, it is necessary to consider these criticisms of counsel upon the instructions to the jury. The principal objection relates to the remarks of the court in reference to circumstantial evidence. Among other things the learned trial judge said: "Nor is it necessary that each and every circumstance should be proved beyond a reasonable doubt. Some facts may be proved with more, some with less assurance of certainty." It is argued that this instruction was misleading because the trial judge failed to explain that the circumstances to which he referred were merely minor and subsidiary or collateral circumstances and not those essential to a conviction.

We think the jury could not have been misled by this language in view of the explanation and qualifications by which it was accompanied. "If, however, on any branch of the case," said the trial judge to the jury, "there exists in your mind a reasonable doubt, the defendant is always entitled to the benefit of that reasonable doubt." As was said by VANN, J., in *People* v. *Tobin* (176 N. Y. 278, 288), the court did not mean "that every circumstance constituting a link in the chain of circumstances necessary to establish 'the fact of killing by the defendant' need not be proved beyond a reasonable doubt, but that every incidental circumstance, such as those bearing upon the probabilities that the main circumstances were true, * * * need not be proved beyond a reasonable doubt."

The third, fourth and fifth points of the brief for the defendant assail the propriety of the action of the trial court in submitting the case to the jury upon the theory that they could convict the defendant of murder in the first degree in the absence of any premeditation or deliberation on his part provided they found that he killed the deceased while engaged in the commission of a felony. As has already been stated, a conviction on this theory was permissible under the indictment, which was in the common law form.

In his oral argument counsel for the defendant urged upon us two propositions which are not mentioned in his printed brief. The first was that error was committed in permitting certain jurors to be sworn and try the case each of whom had admitted when examined under challenge that he had previously formed an opinion or impression to the effect that a crime had been committed in the case of Ruth Wheeler. Every one of those jurors, however, declared on oath that he believed such opinion or impression would not influence his verdict and that he could render an impartial verdict according to the evidence. Section 376, subd. 2, of the Code of Criminal Procedure provides that the previous expression or formation of an opinion or impression in reference to the guilt or innocence of the defendant, or a present opinion or impression in reference thereto, is not a sufficient ground of challenge for actual bias, to any person otherwise legally qualified, if he declare on oath that he believes that such opinion or impression will not influence his verdict and that he can render an impartial verdict according to the evidence, and the court is satisfied that he does not entertain such a present opinion or impression as will influence his verdict. The jurors in question made the

sworn declaration prescribed by this statutory provision
which was originally introduced into our law in slightly
different form in 1872, to prevent the continued disquali-
fication of intelligent citizens from serving on juries in
criminal cases.   The action of the trial judge in overruling the challenge in each instance was equivalent to a
decision in so many words that the court was satisfied
that the juror did not entertain such a present opinion or
impression as would influence his verdict.   This is ordinarily conclusive upon us except in cases where the declaration of the juror as to his ability to decide the issue
uninfluenced by his impression or opinion is so equivocal
and uncertain as to constitute cause for the rejection of
the proposed juror as matter of law.   (See *People* v.
McQuade, 110 N. Y. 284, 301.)   Here the declarations
amply satisfied the requirements of the statute.   Indeed,
the present contention of the defendant's counsel that the
court compelled the defendant to go to trial before a
prejudiced jury is difficult to reconcile with the statement
to the presiding judge at the conclusion of the case that
they considered he had given them "an absolutely fair
and impartial trial."   With this former view we quite
agree.

With reference to the qualifications of the jurors it is
furthermore to be observed that the defendant was tried
by a special jury drawn under chapter 602 of the Laws
of 1901, which provides that the allowance or disallowance of challenges for actual bias shall be final.   This
provision was pronounced constitutional by this court in
People v. *Dunn* (157 N. Y. 528).

The trial judge refused to charge the first request in
behalf of the defendant — apparently without reading it
to the jury.   That request was in these words: "If any
of the material facts of this case are at variance with the
probabilities of guilt it would be the duty of the jury to
give to the defendant the benefit of the doubt."   The
request was evidently an extract from the opinion of

GRAY, J., in the case of *People* v. *Harris* (136 N. Y. 423, 428) where that learned judge was discussing the reluctance which often exists to act upon circumstantial evidence. In the course of the discussion, contrasting the two sorts of proof, he said: "Purely circumstantial evidence may be often more satisfactory and a safer form of evidence; for it must rest upon facts, which, to prove the truth of the charge made, must collectively tend to establish the guilt of the accused. For instance, if any of the material facts of the case were at variance with the probabilities of guilt, it would be the duty of the jury to give to the defendant the benefit of the doubt raised." This remark was made *arguendo* and its meaning and scope cannot fairly be understood without reference to what preceded and followed it. It was not an attempt to state a proposition of law for the guidance of laymen sitting upon a jury; and taken alone and without the context was insufficient to be of any assistance to the jury in the present case in reaching a just and proper verdict. The refusal of the court, therefore, to instruct the jury in these precise words did not constitute an error of law and in any event cannot have been harmful to the defendant, in view of the fact already mentioned that subsequently in the course of the charge the trial judge expressly told the jury that if on any branch of the case there existed in their minds a reasonable doubt the defendant was always entitled to the benefit of that reasonable doubt.

The defendant was fairly tried and justly convicted and the judgment should be affirmed.

CULLEN, Ch. J., GRAY, HAIGHT, VANN, WERNER and CHASE, JJ., concur.

Judgment of conviction affirmed.

In the Matter of the Application of THE NIAGARA, LOCKPORT AND ONTARIO POWER COMPANY, Respondent, for an Order Directing JOHN PALLACE, JR., an Attorney, Appellant, to Deliver over Certain Papers.

Attorney and client — when relation does not exist, summary proceedings to recover papers cannot be maintained.

1. The courts will not enforce ordinary contractual obligations not springing out of the relationship of attorney and client by a summary proceeding, even though the obligor happens to be an attorney.

2. Such a proceeding to compel an attorney to deliver documents, which he claims to hold under an attorney's lien for compensation for services, cannot be maintained where the moving party denies that it ever retained the attorney in connection with the proceedings which placed in his hands the documents sought to be recovered, and expressly alleges that his retainer and employment were by another corporation, and an order in such case requiring the attorney to deliver papers, on execution by the claimant thereto of an undertaking to pay him such fees as may be determined to be due, is unauthorized.

Matter of Niagara, Lockport & Ontario Power Co., 143 App. Div. 919, reversed.

(Argued November 22, 1911; decided December 19, 1911.)

APPEAL from an order of the Appellate Division of the Supreme Court in the fourth judicial department, entered February 1, 1911, which unanimously affirmed an order of Special Term directing John Pallace, Jr., an attorney, to deliver to the petitioner certain documents, on execution by the latter of an undertaking in the sum of $20,000 conditioned to pay to the appellant "such sum as shall eventually be determined to be now justly due * * * by this petitioner on account of legal services performed or alleged by him to have been performed."

The order was made in a summary proceeding instituted by respondent to compel the appellant to deliver to it said documents which he claimed to retain by virtue of an attorney's lien for compensation for legal services. Amongst other facts, it is alleged in the petition on which the proceeding was instituted that the respondent is a corporation engaged in the transmission and sale of electrical current; that it entered into a contract with another corporation, the Iroquois Construction Company, whereby the latter, amongst other things, agreed to construct and equip certain transmission lines and to procure rights of way and franchises to operate said lines; that in performing said contract said construction company directly or indirectly retained the appellant " to perform certain legal services for it in and about making the application for and procuring said franchises," and said appellant made various applications and obtained grants of various franchises and it was his duty to file with the proper official one of the duplicate originals of the instruments conveying said franchises; that notwithstanding such duty he took from the files of the office of said company and carried away various instruments granting franchises and " now holds and retains all of said franchises, claiming a lien thereon for legal services rendered," although he has received a large amount of money from said construction company which has refused to pay him for his services until he accounts for such receipts; that appellant has commenced an action against respondent to recover a large sum of money " on account of the services so as aforesaid rendered by him to the said Iroquois Construction Company," which is being defended by respondent on the ground that it did not employ him, and is now pending undetermined; that said appellant received the said grants of franchises and each of them for the special purpose of having the same accepted by respondent and for the purpose of filing the same after acceptance with the proper officials of villages and towns.

The appellant by his answer amongst other things alleged that he was employed by respondent in the matters referred to and denies that said instruments were received by him under such circumstances as render it improper for him to retain them under a lien for his compensation.

Eugene Van Voorhis for appellant. A special proceeding can only be maintained by virtue of the provision of some statute or precedent authorizing it. (3 Am. & Eng. Ency. of Law, 447; *Rooney* v. *Second Ave. Co.*, 18 N. Y. 373; *Matter of H——, an Attorney*, 87 N. Y. 521; *Matter of an Attorney*, 63 How. Pr. 152; *Carpenter* v. *Sixth Ave. R. R. Co.*, 1 Am. L. R. 418; *St. John* v. *Diefendorf*, 12 Wend. 261; *An Attorney's Lien*, 20 Am. L. R. 736; *Howitt* v. *Merrill*, 2 Silv. 160; *Matter of Wilson*, 2 Civ. Pro. Rep. 343.) The court below had no jurisdiction to dispose of the appellant's lien by requiring the delivery of the papers in his possession, on the petitioner's giving security to pay whatever sum may ultimately be found due the attorney, without making provision for the determination of the extent and value of such services and without concluding the petitioner from ever after questioning its liability to pay the appellant for the services he rendered in its behalf, whether at the instance of the Iroquois Construction Company or otherwise. (*Schell* v. *Mayor, etc.*, 128 N. Y. 68.)

Warren Tubbs for respondent. The court at Special Term made this order upon admitted facts and in the exercise of a sound discretion. (*Matter of Hollins*, 197 N. Y. 361; *Matter of Ney Co.*, 114 App. Div. 467; *Matter of Taylor I. & S. Co.*, 49 N. Y. S. R. 645; *Greenfield* v. *Mayor*, 28 Hun, 320; *McPherson* v. *Cox*, 96 U. S. 404; *Matter of Jewett*, 34 Beav. 22; *Matter of Bevan*, 33 Beav. 439.) When it is doubtful whether an attorney is right in the assertion of a retaining lien, or there is a serious dispute as to the amount due, and his client offers security, the attorney should be ordered to deliver over papers. (*Cunningham* v. *Widing*, 5 Abb. Pr. 413; *Matter of Taylor I. & S. Co.*, 49 N. Y. S. R. 645; *West* v. *Bacon*, 164 N. Y. 425.)

HISCOCK, J. The respondent petitioner instituted this summary proceeding for the purpose of compelling the appellant, an attorney, to deliver to it certain documents to which it claims to be entitled and which he claims to hold under an attorney's lien for compensation for services. Thus far it has succeeded in its application, an order having been made requiring the appellant to deliver to it the papers in question on execution of a bond conditioned for the payment of any compensation which ultimately may be determined to be due from respondent. We think, however, that the position assumed by the respondent in denying that appellant at any time acted as its attorney is irreconcilably inconsistent with its right to maintain this proceeding, and that, therefore, the order appealed from must be reversed.

The relationship of attorney and client is the very foundation of a summary proceeding such as this. The courts will not by such a proceeding enforce ordinary contractual obligations not springing out of this relationship, even though the obligor happens to be an attorney. Thus it has been held that the courts will not on such application compel an attorney to pay money in satisfaction of an ordinary debt. (*Windsor* v. *Brown*, 15 R. I. 182; *Matter of Gray*, L. R. [2 Q. B. 1892] 440.)

Likewise it is an answer to an application to compel an attorney to deliver papers that they were received by him as a mere agent and not by reason of his professional character as an attorney. (*Matter of H——, an Attorney*, 87 N. Y. 521.)

It has been decided at the General Term, although this doctrine was somewhat questioned by the judge writing in this court on appeal, that such a proceeding is so based on the personal relationship between the attorney and the client that the right to employ it will not pass to an assignee of the client. (*Matter of Schell*, 58 Hun, 440; *Schell* v. *Mayor, etc. of N. Y.*, 128 N. Y. 67, 69.)

When, however, this relationship of attorney and client does exist the courts by virtue of their inherent power and control over their own officers, and quite independent of specific statutory provision, will under proper circumstances exercise jurisdiction and summarily compel an attorney to fulfill his obligations toward his client by paying money or delivering documents which belong to him, adequate provision being made in the latter case for satisfaction of any demands against the client for compensation and for which the attorney might have a lien on the documents. (*Matter of Knapp*, 85 N. Y. 284; *Matter of Hollins*, 197 N. Y. 361; *Matter of H——, an Attorney, supra.*)

Applying these well-established principles to the present proceedings we find that the respondent has unequivocally deprived itself of the right to maintain them by expressly and broadly contesting any relationship of attorney and client between it and the appellant. In effect it denies that it ever retained him in connection with the proceedings which placed in his hands the documents now sought and expressly alleges that his retainer and employment were by another corporation, and to emphasize this situation it sets forth the details of the litigation now pending undetermined between it and him over this very issue. The order which was made on its application fully recognizes this contest and preserves to respondent the right to continue it notwithstanding the papers in question are turned over to it. It requires the respondent as a condition of procuring the papers to execute a bond to the effect simply that it "will pay such sum as shall eventually be determined to be now justly due the said John Pallace, Jr., by this petitioner on account of legal services performed, or alleged by him to have been performed."

Thus while the courts have compelled appellant to act on the theory that he was the attorney of the respondent, it has permitted the respondent to proceed on the theory that it was not the client of the appellant. This is obviously so unreasonable and unfair that it makes it

32

easy to understand why precedents are not found for such a course or justifying such an order.

Of course what is thus said does not in any manner question the right of the court under proper circumstances to proceed in this manner against an attorney where the amount due him is controverted, the fundamental relationship not being denied, and to which situation the courts below undoubtedly assumed inadvertently the present case to be analogous.

Two minor propositions remain to be considered.

It was urged by respondent on the argument that any objections to the order appealed from might be obviated by requiring respondent's undertaking to be conditioned also for the payment of any compensation which might be determined to be due to appellant from the construction company. This suggestion is in effect condemned by what we have already said. The respondent had no part in or relation to the retainer of appellant by the construction company, and is not called on or permitted to settle the obligations or take advantage of the relationship between those parties as a basis for this application. Having denied that it entered into the relation necessary to enable it to maintain this proceeding, it cannot supply the defect by agreeing to fulfill the obligations which may exist in favor of the attorney against some other client. Such a course might protect the attorney from loss as the result of surrendering the papers and losing his lien but it would not at all give the respondent that character of client by virtue of which alone it can seek the relief which it is now asking.

It is further argued that the appellant received the documents in question under such circumstances and for such special purposes as prevent him from holding them under a lien for compensation. It is, of course, well settled that papers may come into the possession of an attorney under such conditions as are inconsistent with the enforcement of a lien for services and when such is the case he will not be allowed to hold them. (*Matter of Hollins*, 197 N. Y. 361.)

There are, however, two answers to this argument of respondent in this case. In the first place, even assuming that respondent's petition did sufficiently set forth special circumstances inconsistent with the retention of these documents under a claim of lien, these allegations were denied by the appellant in his answer. Thus an issue of fact was presented which it must be assumed from the order made by the Special Term was determined in appellant's favor.

In the second place, if we are correct in the view that respondent under the allegations of its petition is entirely without right to maintain this proceeding, it is immaterial that the appellant for the reason suggested is improperly retaining the papers. Such improper conduct might be a subject for consideration between him and his client, but it is not of consequence here and now.

The orders of the Appellate Division and the Special Term should be reversed and the application denied, with costs in all the courts.

CULLEN, Ch. J., HAIGHT, WERNER, WILLARD BARTLETT, CHASE and COLLIN, JJ., concur.

Orders reversed, etc.

CHARLES E. W. SMITH, Appellant, *v.* WESTERN PACIFIC RAILWAY COMPANY, Respondent.

Constitutional law — trial of issues — section 973 of the Code of Civil Procedure constitutional.

The legislature had the right to enact section 973 of the Code of Civil Procedure, permitting the court in its discretion to "order one or more issues to be separately tried prior to any trial of the other issues." The section applies to a case where a party is entitled to a jury trial, whether as of right or as a matter of discretion, and no constitutional right is impaired thereby.

Smith v. *Western Pacific Ry. Co.*, 144 App. Div. 180, affirmed.

(Argued November 22, 1911; decided December 19, 1911.)

APPEAL, by permission, from an order of the Appellate Division of the Supreme Court in the first judicial department, entered April 21, 1911, which affirmed an order of Special Term directing the trial of certain issues raised by the pleadings in this action prior to the trial of the remaining issues.

The appellant brought the action to recover a balance claimed to be due on a contract for services. Respondent served an answer containing a general denial, and also setting up as one amongst other affirmative defenses the Statute of Limitations both of the state of New York and of the state of California, and it was of the issues arising under this defense that the court ordered a separate and preliminary trial.

The questions certified to us by the Appellate Division are:

First. "Are the provisions of section 973 of the Code of Civil Procedure, if construed to apply to actions in which jury trial is guaranteed by section 2 of article 1 of the State Constitution, invalid so far as thus applied, because in contravention of said section of the Constitution ? "

Second. "Does section 973 of the Code of Civil Procedure authorize the court, in its discretion upon compliance with said section, to order the trial of one or more issues in advance of the remaining issues in any action in which jury trial is guaranteed by section 2 of article 1 of the State Constitution ? "

Thomas B. Hardin for appellant. Section 973 of the Code is susceptible of two constructions — by one of which it is constitutional and by the other it is unconstitutional. When applied to those cases in which the constitutional right to a trial of the cause before a jury exists, and applied, as in this case, so as to require a trial before two or more separate juries at two or more different times, it is unconstitutional. (*U. S. ex rel. Atty.-*

Gen. v. *D. & H. Co.*, 213 U. S. 407; *C. P. R. R. Co.* v. *Gallatin*, 99 U. S. 744; *Steck* v. *C. F. & I. Co.*, 142 N. Y. 250; *Malone* v. *S. P. & P. Church*, 172 N. Y. 269; *Sporza* v. *G. S. Bank*, 192 N. Y. 8; *Matter of Metz* v. *Maddox*, 189 N. Y. 469; *U. S.* v. *T. M. F. Assn.*, 166 U. S. 318.) The constitutional right of trial by jury involves or requires a trial of all the issues of fact in the case by a jury of twelve men, and no more or less. (*McClave* v. *Gibb*, 157 N. Y. 413; *People ex rel. Murray* v. *Justices*, 74 N. Y. 407; *People* v. *Dunn*, 157 N. Y. 535; *Vermilyea* v. *Palmer*, 52 N. Y. 471; *Cancemi* v. *People*, 18 N. Y. 135; *C. T. Co.* v. *Hof*, 174 U. S. 1; *Blair* v. *M. C. Co.*, 123 App. Div. 30; *People* v. *Connor*, 142 N. Y. 130.)

F. W. McCutcheon and *C. M. Travis* for respondent. Section 973 of the Code of Civil Procedure is not reasonably susceptible of a construction that would limit its application to cases where trial by jury is not a matter of right. (*Manhattan Co.* v. *Kaldenberg*, 165 N. Y. 1; *Johnson* v. *Hudson R. R. R. Co.*, 49 N. Y. 455; *T. M. L. Ry. Co.* v. *Clarke*, 27 Wkly. Rep. 677; *Weed* v. *Tucker*, 19 N. Y. 432; *Acker* v. *Leland*, 109 N. Y. 5; *Wild* v. *Hobson*, 2 V. & B. 105; *Carrick* v. *Young*, 4 Madd. 437; *Miller* v. *Priddon*, 1 McN. & G. 687; *E. S. M. Co.* v. *E. S. M. Co.*, 1 Fed. Rep. 39; *Terry* v. *Davy*, 107 Fed. Rep. 50.) The Constitution confers no right to have all of the issues in a suit at law tried by the same jury. (*People* v. *Connor*, 142 N. Y. 130; *I. Ry. Co.* v. *Massachusetts*, 207 U. S. 79; *People* v. *Dunn*, 157 N. Y. 528; *Walker* v. *N. M. & S. P. R. Co.*, 165 U. S. 593; *Hayes* v. *Missouri*, 120 U. S. 68; *Gibson* v. *Mississippi*, 162 U. S. 565; *People* v. *Meyer*, 162 N. Y. 357; *Stokes* v. *People*, 53 N. Y. 164; *Walter* v. *People*, 32 N. Y. 147.)

Hiscock, J. Section 973 of the Code provides: "The court in its discretion may order one or more issues to be separately tried prior to any trial of the other issues in the case."

This action is one in which the parties are constitutionally entitled to a trial by jury. Under the section above quoted the court ordered a separate trial of the issues raised by an affirmative defense of the Statute of Limitations before trial of the other issues involving what are ordinarily defined as the merits of the action. There is no question but that this separate and prior trial was to be before and by a common-law jury of twelve men regularly impanelled, but nevertheless the appellant objects to the order as unauthorized and improper. His objections are, *first*, that the section quoted does not relate to an· action where a party is entitled to a jury trial under the Constitution but only to those cases where trials by jury are allowed by legislative action or judicial discretion, and, *second*, that if the section does relate to a case where there is a constitutional right to a jury trial it impairs that right and is, therefore, unconstitutional.

The first objection is almost wholly based on the fact that this section is found in juxtaposition to two sections dealing with trials by jury in the discretion of the court and not as matter of right, with the argument added that if the application of the section is not so restricted it will be unconstitutional.

This contention may be very briefly dismissed. It has no basis to rest on. The section is found in an article which deals with "Issues and the mode of trial thereof;" and which contains sections relating to trials by jury where the right thereto is constitutional as well as those where it is allowed as a matter of discretion and, under the circumstances, the location of the section is a matter of no significance. Moreover, while the argument that statutory provisions are *in pari materia* may at times be of use in solving doubts concerning the application or meaning of a particular provision, it cannot be made the basis for thwarting the undoubted application and overturning the clear meaning of a statute. The language of the provision in question is so plain and comprehensive that this is what we should do if we adopted the interpretation urged by appellant.

This brings us to the second proposition, that, if given the broad application just stated, the act is unconstitutional. With this contention also I am unable to agree. The constitutional provision invoked against the act is, "The trial by jury in all cases in which it has been heretofore used shall remain inviolate forever," etc. This, of course, as asserted by appellant's counsel, secures the right of trial before a common-law jury of twelve men of certain classes of issues, which include the ones here involved.

It is well settled that the object of such a provision is to preserve the substance of the right of trial by jury rather than to prescribe the details of the methods by which it shall be exercised and enjoyed. Thus in *Walker* v. *Southern Pacific R. R. Co.* (165 U. S. 593, 596) Judge BREWER, considering whether a statute of New Mexico violated the provisions of the United States Constitution on this subject, said: "The question is whether this act of the territorial legislature in substance impairs the right of trial by jury. The Seventh Amendment, indeed, does not attempt to regulate matters of pleading or practice, or to determine in what way issues shall be framed by which questions of fact are to be submitted to a jury. Its aim is not to preserve mere matters of form and procedure, but substance of right. This requires that questions of fact in common law actions shall be settled by a jury, and that the court shall not assume directly or indirectly to take from the jury or to itself such prerogative. So long as this substance of right is preserved, the procedure by which this result shall be reached is wholly within the discretion of the legislature, and the courts may not set aside any legislative provision in this respect because the form of action — the mere manner in which questions are submitted — is different from that which obtained at the common law."

And in *People* v. *Dunn* (157 N. Y. 528, 535) Judge GRAY, expressing the same idea, also succinctly stated the fundamental elements of the trial by jury under the common law and which our Constitution preserved. He wrote: "It is to be observed that our Constitution does not secure to the defendant any particular mode of jury trial, nor any particular method of jury selection. * * * The right was conceded to the citizen (at common law) of having the judgment of an impartial committee, or body, of his fellow-citizens, upon charges involving his life, or his liberty, or his property, and two elements became essential ingredients of the right, viz.: that the jurors should be twelve in number and that they should be capable of deciding the cause fairly and impartially."

Even if we assume, as I think we should, that this section of the Code permits separates trials of separate issues at different times, before different juries, it seems very clear that it does not destroy or impair the substantial right of a litigant to have his case tried before a proper jury, but only prescribes the method in which this may be done. Every issue is submitted to the verdict of a jury. This is the substance of the right. As a matter of convenience the court may order some issues to be tried before others are taken up. This is a matter of procedure and detail. The Constitution does not provide, and there should not be interpolated into it a provision, that all of the issues, even though completely separate and distinct, must be tried at one and the same time. No amount of analysis will disclose any such protection or benefit to a litigant in having all of the issues submitted to a single jury as will render such a right one of the essential ones secured by the Constitution. On the contrary, it is at once apparent that the convenience of litigants may be much promoted by a prior trial of various jurisdictional and preliminary issues, and it is to be presumed that courts will so administer the provision in question as to make it remedial and beneficial rather than burdensome.

There are many decisions which in my opinion sustain the view that the legislature had power to enact the section as a regulation of mere procedure and without impairing any constitutional rights and reference will be made to some of them.

In *People* v. *Connor* (142 N. Y. 130) it appeared that the court had ordered the trial first and separately of issues raised by defendant's special plea of a former trial and conviction, and when this had been passed on by the jury adversely to the defendant, the court had directed the trial to proceed before the same jury on the other issues raised by the general plea of not guilty. The defendant objected to the latter step, asking that the trial be suspended after disposition of the first issue, and that he be permitted to examine the jurors before proceeding to the trial of the general issue, thus exactly reversing the position assumed by the present appellant. There was no statutory provision for separate trials of different issues at this time, and this court held that there was no basis for appellant's claim to such a method of procedure, and that the trial must be one continuous proceeding. It did say, however, even under these conditions: "The order in which the issues should be disposed of was a matter in the discretion of the court, which had power to direct them to be tried separately or together." (p. 134.)

In *Stokes* v. *People* (53 N. Y. 164) the court considered the constitutionality of an act which overturned what was claimed to be the rule of the common law that the prior formation or expression of an opinion by a proposed juror conclusively proved want of impartiality, and disqualified him from serving. Said act, however, amply provided that at the time of the trial it must appear that the proposed juror, notwithstanding such opinion so formed or expressed, was able to render an impartial verdict according to the evidence, and would not be biased or influenced by his prior views. The court, overruling the defendant's plea, said: "While the Constitution secures the right of trial by an impartial jury, the mode of procuring and impanelling such jury is regulated by law, either common or statutory, principally the latter, and it is within the power of the legislature to make, from time to time, such changes in the law as it may deem expedient, taking care to preserve the right of trial by an impartial jury." (p. 173.)

To similar effect is *Hayes* v. *Missouri* (120 U. S. 68, 70).

In the following cases it was held directly, or by necessary inference, that separate trials may be had of preliminary or jurisdictional issues: *Fisher* v. *Fraprie* (125 Mass. 472); *Central of Georgia Ry. Co.* v. *Brown* (38 S. E. Rep. 989); *Jones & Co.* v. *O'Donnell* (9 Ala. 695, 698); *Tyler* v. *Murray* (57 Md. 418, 441).

In *Lavelle* v. *Corriguio* (86 Hun, 135), while that question was not actually decided, it was discussed, and the view expressed that on appeal in a partition action where several distinct and independent issues had been submitted to the jury, one of them incorrectly and the others correctly, a new trial might be granted as to the one without retrial of the others.

The legality of such a course of procedure has, however, fairly been affirmed in *Boyd* v. *Brown* (17 Pick. [Mass.] 453, 461); *Kent* v. *Whitney* (9 Allen [Mass.], 62); *Pratt* v. *Boston H. & L. Co.* (134 Mass. 300); *Leiter* v. *Lyons* (52 Atl. Rep. [R. I.] 78, 81, 82); *McKay* v. *New England, etc., Co.* (44 Atl. Rep. [Me.] 614); *Oberbeck* v. *Mayor* (59 Mo. App. 289, 298).

In the state of Missouri there is a provision in its Practice Act providing for the separate trial of different issues at the same or different terms of court, and so far as appears there has been no judicial opinion that this provision was a violation of the Missouri Constitution securing the right of trial by jury.

In *People* v. *Trimble* (60 Hun, 364; affirmed, 131 N. Y. 118) the court upheld a conviction for a felony where the issue under plea of former conviction was first tried before one jury and the issues raised by a general plea of not guilty before another jury.

None of the authorities cited by the appellant impair the reasoning or authority of these decisions, and I feel no doubt that the order appealed from should be affirmed, with costs, and the first question certified should be answered in the negative, and the second one in the affirmative.

CULLEN, Ch. J., HAIGHT, WERNER, WILLARD BARTLETT, CHASE and COLLIN, JJ., concur.

Order affirmed.

MARY A. GLEASON, Appellant, *v*. THE NORTHWESTERN MUTUAL LIFE INSURANCE COMPANY, Respondent.

Judgment — insurance (life) — when judgment obtained by administrator of insured in another state not a bar to an action on the same policy in this state by the assignee thereof.

1. A life insurance policy issued to a resident of Vermont provided that it was a contract made and to be performed in the state of Wisconsin. The insured assigned the policy to plaintiff and gave notice to the defendant as required by its terms. The assignee was not a relative or creditor of the insured and the policy was assigned without consideration therefor. Immediately after the death of the insured the assignee became a resident of this state. Letters of administration upon the estate of the insured having been issued in Vermont, and the defendant having refused to pay, the administrator brought a suit in that state to recover the amount of the policy. That litigation resulted in a judgment against defendant in favor of the administrator, who was permitted to prove that the assignment was made in consideration of the promise of the present plaintiff to continue meretricious relations with the

assured. Thereupon defendant paid the judgment and pleaded such recovery and payment as a bar to this action which had, in the meantime, been brought in this state. When this action was brought to trial no proof was offered to show any illegal or immoral consideration for the assignment, but on the contrary it was stipulated that the assignment was a gift. The facts hereinbefore recited, including the judgments and próceedings in the Vermont action, were placed in evidence. *Held,* that the decision on demurrer herein (189 N. Y. 100) did not dispose of the issue now presented; that, while it is true that, in the Vermont suit, it was found that the assignment was invalid, the present plaintiff was not a party to that action, and that, upon the facts as they appear in this case, the Vermont judgment is not a bar to this suit.

2. The common-law rule as to the right of an assignee to sue for the enforcement of a chose in action considered, and *held,* that by the terms of the policy it was made a Wisconsin contract to be performed there; that by the law of Wisconsin the assignment of a chose in action transfers the legal title and the courts of Vermont, therefore, had no jurisdiction of the person of the plaintiff, nor was the subject-matter of the litigation in that State, and hence no adjudication there had could conclude this plaintiff's rights.

Gleason v. *Northwestern Mutual Life Ins. Co.,* 139 App. Div. 64, reversed.

(Argued November 28, 1911; decided December 19, 1911.)

APPEAL from a judgment, entered July 20, 1910, upon an order of the Appellate Division of the Supreme Court in the first judicial department reversing a judgment in favor of plaintiff entered upon a verdict directed by the court and directing a dismissal of the complaint.

The nature of the action and the facts, so far as material, are stated in the opinion.

Eugene Frayer and *Harry W. Alden* for appellant. The plaintiff's assignment was, on the admitted facts, valid and effectual to transfer to her the policy and the right to recover and receive the proceeds thereof. (*St. John* v. *A. M. L. Ins. Co.,* 13 N. Y. 31; *Valton* v. *N. F. L. Assur. Co.,* 20 N. Y. 32; *Olmstead* v. *Keyes,* 85 N. Y. 593; *Carraher* v. *M. L. Ins. Co.,* 11 N. Y. S. R. 665; *Classey*

v. *M. Life Ins. Co.*, 84 Hun, 350; *Breeze* v. *M. Life Ins. Co.*, 37 App. Div. 152; *Steinbach* v. *Diepenbrock*, 158 N. Y. 24; *Harrison* v. *N. W. M. L. Ins. Co.*, 78 Vt. 473; *Fairchild* v. *N. E. M. L. Ins. Co.*, 51 Vt. 613; *Watson* v. *Watson*, 69 Vt. 243.) The plaintiff was not in fact or in law a party or privy to the suit in Vermont nor in any manner represented therein. (*Harrison* v. *N. W. M. L. Ins. Co.*, 78 Vt. 473.) The Vermont court never obtained or had jurisdiction of either the plaintiff's person or her property in this policy, and had no power to adjudicate in respect to the policy or the assignment so as to bind her by its adjudication. (*Pennoyer* v. *Neff*, 95 N. Y. 714; *Haddock* v. *Haddock*, 201 U. S. 562; *Goldey* v. *Morning News*, 156 U. S. 518; *Morgan* v. *M. B. L. Ins. Co.*, 119 App. Div. 645; *Huntley* v. *Baker*, 33 Hun, 578.) The plaintiff was under no obligation to go into the state of Vermont and defend the suit brought by the administrator against the defendant there; and the notice of suit and tender to her of the defense thereto by the defendant did not create any such obligation. (*Morgan* v. *M. B. L. Ins. Co.*, 119 App. Div. 645; 189 N. Y. 447.) The plaintiff did not take the assignment and policy subject to the right of Harrison's administrator thereafter to do anything affecting her or her property, except in some court having jurisdiction of her or the property. (*Davenport* v. *N. E. M. L. Ins. Co.*, 47 Vt. 528.) Comity does not require the courts of this state to deny to a citizen and resident of the state the right to recover therein from a defendant domiciled here the amount of a debt admitted to be due to her, merely because some third person in another state, in a suit there to which she was not a party nor represented therein, sets up a claim that the defendant owes the same money to him and not to .her, and, without making, or attempting to make, her a party to his suit, succeeds in procuring in her absence a judgment of a court of that state to that effect. (*Platt* v. *Elias*, 186 N. Y. 374.)

Alfred Opdyke and *William W. Ladd* for respondent. The defendant has been without fault or negligence in the entire transaction. It gave notice to the plaintiff of the administrator's action and tendered her the defense thereof. (*Konitzky* v. *Meyer*, 49 N. Y. 571; *Minn. Bank* v. *Holyoke Bank*, 182 Mass. 130.) It ought to be and it is the object of courts to prevent the payment of any debt twice over. (*Harris* v. *Balk*, 198 U. S. 215; *Embree* v. *Hanna*, 5 Johns. 101; *Green* v. *Clark*, 12 N. Y. 343; *Marsden* v. *Cornell*, 62 N. Y. 215; *Thomas* v. *Coe*, 51 Hun, 481; *Sulz* v. *M. R. Assn.*, 145 N. Y. 563; *Traflet* v. *E. L. Ins. Co.*, 64 N. J. L. 387.) To permit this plaintiff to recover a second judgment upon this policy would be particularly inequitable, because (1) she was a mere donee of the policy; (2) her rights were acquired in, and while a resident of, Vermont, by the laws of which state she never had a right of action against the defendant independent of the insured's personal representative; and (3) she has a complete remedy in Vermont against the administrator. (*Harrison* v. *N. W. M. L. Ins. Co.*, 78 Vt. 473; 80 Vt. 148.)

CULLEN, Ch. J. On August 31, 1891, Oliff F. Harrison and the plaintiff resided in Rutland, Vermont. On that date the defendant, a life insurance corporation organized under the laws of Wisconsin but doing business in Vermont, issued to said Harrison a policy on his life for $2,000, payable to his "executors, administrators or assigns." The policy recited that it was delivered at its office in Milwaukee, Wisconsin. It further provided that the policy was "a contract made and to be performed in the state of Wisconsin, and shall be construed only according to the Charter of the Company and the laws of said State," and also that if it should be assigned, a duplicate of the assignment should, within thirty days, be given to the company.

On September 12th, 1891, Harrison assigned the policy

to the plaintiff by an instrument in writing executed in duplicate and delivered the policy and one of the duplicates to the plaintiff, in whose possession they have remained ever since. The other duplicate was sent to the defendant, received by it, and it thereafter carried the policy on its books as assigned to the plaintiff. Harrison paid the annual premiums up to the time of his decease on October 11th, 1903. On the following day the plaintiff removed from Vermont to the city of New York, and has ever since resided in said city. The policy and assignment have been in her possession there during this time, except that they were in the hands of her Vermont attorney for about a year, but just when this year was does not appear. Satisfactory proofs of death were delivered to and received by the defendant.

It was stipulated by the parties on the trial of this action that the plaintiff was not a relative, connected in blood with, or a creditor of said Harrison, and that the policy was assigned to her by him without consideration as a gift. Thereafter letters of administration upon the estate of Harrison having been issued in Vermont, and the defendant having refused to pay, the administrator brought a suit in that state to recover the amount of the policy. The defendant pleaded the general issue with notice of special matter. On the trial the defendant offered to prove the assignment to the plaintiff; that she was in no way related to the deceased; that the plaintiff here held the policy and the assignment, and had brought suit on the policy in the state of New York, which suit was still pending, and that the Vermont action was not brought by the administrator at her request or for her benefit, but for the next of kin of the deceased. The evidence was excluded and the plaintiff administrator had judgment. On appeal the judgment was reversed, the Supreme Court of Vermont holding (*Harrison* v. *Northwestern M. L. Ins. Co.*, 78 Vt. 473) that the insurance having been procured by the assured

on his own life was not a wager and could be made the subject of a gift although the donee had no interest in the life
of the assured, citing an earlier decision of the court to
that effect. (*Fairchild* v. *Northeastern M. L. Assn.*, 51
Vt. 613.) As to the right of the plaintiff in that action to
recover, the court further held that while as a general rule a
plaintiff who in a suit at common law has the legal interest
in the subject-matter of the litigation cannot be defeated
by showing an equitable ownership in a third person, the
rule does not apply when the recovery in such suit will
not protect the defendant against the claim of the equitable owner, and for that reason the defendant should have
been allowed to prove that the action was not brought
with the consent of nor for the benefit of the assignee,
but in hostility to her for the benefit of the next of kin.

After the commencement of the Vermont action, the
plaintiff brought this suit in the county of New York, of
which she was a resident. When the administrator
recovered judgment in Vermont the defendant, by a
supplemental answer in this action, pleaded that judgment as a bar. The plaintiff demurred to this defense,
but its sufficiency was upheld by this court. (189 N. Y.
100.) After that decision and the reversal of the Vermont judgment by the Supreme Court of that state, the
plaintiff withdrew her demurrer and replied to the
defense that the judgment pleaded had been reversed.
Subsequently the Vermont suit was again brought to
trial. The defendant there made proof of the assignment and other facts which had been excluded on the
first trial. In answer thereto the Vermont plaintiff was
permitted to prove that the assignment was made in
consideration of the promise of the present plaintiff to
continue meretricious relations with the assured. That
issue was found in favor of the administrator, who again
recovered a judgment which on appeal was affirmed by
the Supreme Court. (80 Vt. 148.) Thereupon the
defendant paid the judgment and by another supple-

mental answer pleaded such recovery and payment as a
bar to this action.

Thereafter this action was brought to trial. The
assignment to the plaintiff was conceded. No proof was
offered to show any illegal or immoral consideration for
such assignment, but on the contrary it was stipulated
that the assignment was a gift. The facts hereinbefore
recited, including the judgments and proceedings in the
Vermont action, were placed in evidence. Thereupon
the court, over defendant's objection and exception,
directed a verdict for the plaintiff for the amount due on
the policy. The Appellate Division, by a divided court,
reversed that judgment and directed judgment dismissing the complaint on the merits, it being conceded that
the facts could not be varied on another trial.

The sole question before us is whether the recovery in
Vermont is a bar to this suit. Counsel for the respondent contends that the question has been determined in
the affirmative by our previous decision, and one at least
of the learned justices who concurred in the decision of
the Appellate Division placed his concurrence solely upon
that ground, his personal opinion being that the Vermont
judgment was not a bar. We are of opinion that our
previous decision does not dispose of the issue now presented to us. A reference to the report of that decision
shows that the only opinion written was that of the late
Judge O'BRIEN, but that opinion did not obtain the concurrence of any other member of the court, the determination of which was not unanimous. We must, therefore, look, not to the opinion, but to what the defendant
had pleaded in the supplemental answer to see what our
previous determination necessarily decided. It was there
alleged that by the laws of Vermont the assignment of a
life insurance policy is no bar or defense to a claim of the
personal representatives of the assured after his death,
but that the personal representatives hold the policy or

33

its proceeds for the benefit of the said assignee. If it now appears that these allegations are not the law of Vermont, our former decision does not control the case now before us. It was the rule at common law that an assignment of a chose in action, with certain exceptions, such as negotiable instruments, vested in the assignee only an equitable ownership, not a legal title, and that an action on the assigned claim must be brought in the name of the assignor.

In this state over sixty years ago the common-law rule was abolished, and it was required that every action should be prosecuted in the name of the real party in interest. This change was made so long ago that none of us is familiar with the practice from personal experience, but must derive his knowledge solely from a study of the text books and decided cases. From this examination it appears that while the law courts adhered in form strictly to the theory that a chose in action was unassignable, at an early date they recognized the fact that the assignee was the real owner, and protected him against hostile action by the assignor after assignment and notice thereof given to the debtor. It seems to have been the rule everywhere, so far as we can discover, that the assignment of a chose in action gave the right to the assignee to sue for its enforcement free from any control or interference of the assignor, except that in some jurisdictions the latter was entitled to intervene to the extent of obtaining indemnity for costs in case the suit was unsuccessful. Also, the defendant could not defeat an assigned claim of which assignment he had notice by subsequent payment to or set-off against the assignor, or release from him. But the practice to effect this result seems to have differed in different jurisdictions. In England relief against such a plea could be secured only by motion to strike it out made to the court in advance of the trial. When the case was brought to trial the court would consider only the nominal parties to the record.

(*Gibson* v. *Winter*, 5 B. & Ad. 96; Chitty on Contracts [ed. of 1842], pp. 779, 780.) In this state, while the common-law rule prevailed, the practice was to file a reply to the defendant's plea of payment, set-off or release that before the matter set up in such plea the plaintiff had assigned the claim, and that the action was prosecuted for the assignee's benefit. Thus, the assignment was passed upon by the jury as one of the issues in the case, though it was unnecessary to allege it in the declaration, and the assignee was not in name a party to the suit. (*Timan* v. *Leland*, 6 Hill, 237; *Littlefield* v. *Storey*, 3 Johns. 425; *Raymond* v. *Squire*, 11 id. 47; *Andrews* v. *Beecker*, 1 Johns. Cas. 411.) This seems to have been the practice also in the Federal courts. (*Welch* v. *Mandeville*, 1 Wheat. 233.) I have not, however, been able to find any authority, nor have we been referred to any, which clearly points out the practice adopted, where the dispute was between the assignor and assignee as to the alleged existence or validity of an assignment. Such an inquiry, however, is material only to enable us to ascertain how far a defendant would be justified in satisfying an action brought against him by an assignor in his own right insisting upon the invalidity of an assignment. But the law of the state of Vermont, with which alone we are concerned, is settled by the decision made by the Supreme Court on the first appeal in the action brought in that state. It was held error to exclude the evidence offered by the defendant to show the assignment of the claim, and that the action was not prosecuted in the assignee's interest, on the very ground that the recovery in the action would not bar the assignee's claim. The provision of the Federal Constitution cannot require us to give greater effect to the Vermont judgment than would be accorded to it in the state in which it was recovered. It is true that in the Vermont suit it was found that the assignment was invalid, but to that action the present plaintiff was not a party, and upon the facts as they appear in this case her title cannot be impeached.

Further, though the policy was taken out in the state of Vermont, it was made by the express agreement of the parties a Wisconsin contract to be performed there. While the assignment was made in Vermont, under the law as held by the Supreme Court of that state, it might be the subject of a valid gift, and under the acts appearing in this case it was a valid gift. The law of Wisconsin is the same as our own. The assignment of a chose in action transfers the legal title. The common-law rule in Vermont that suit must be brought in the name of the assignor is one of practice and not of property; of remedy, not of right. (*Lodge* v. *Phelps*, 1 Johns. Cas. 139.) When the administrator of the assured was appointed, and when the action was brought in Vermont, plaintiff was a resident of this state, and the policy evidencing the contract was in her possession here. The courts of Vermont, therefore, had no jurisdiction of the person of the plaintiff, nor was the subject-matter of the litigation in that state, and hence no adjudication there had could conclude this plaintiff's rights. But if the claim on the insurance policy was property within the state of Vermont, which we think it was not, the defendant's remedy was by bill of interpleader, in which suit jurisdiction might have been obtained over a non-resident so far as to determine title to property within the state. (*Morgan* v. *Mut. Benefit Life Ins. Co.*, 189 N. Y. 447.) If the action at law by the administrator for the benefit of the estate of his intestate would not have barred an action by the assignee in the name of the administrator, but on his own behalf, had that assignee been a resident of the state of Vermont, we do not see how its efficacy can be enhanced by the fact that the assignee was a non-resident and without the jurisdiction of the court.

The respondent relies on two cases as authorities in its behalf. In our view neither is in point. The first is in this court. (*Sulz* v. *Mut. Reserve Fund Life Assn.*, 145 N. Y. 563.) There an insurance policy was issued to a man payable on his death to his legal representatives. He removed from the state of New York to the state of Washington and died a resident of that state with the policy there in his possession. The administrator appointed in Washington brought suit on the policy. Subsequently an administrator was appointed in this state who also sued the defendant. The judgment recovered here was reversed by this court, the court holding that under the circumstances the action ought not to be entertained, the deceased being a resident of Washington, the policy being in that state and the first action being there instituted. It will be seen that both of these actions were instituted in the same right, that of the deceased for the benefit of his estate, and the question involved was simply in which state the claim was to be reduced to possession and be administered. But in the action in this state the administratrix, who was the widow of the deceased, sought to sustain her recovery on the ground that under the terms of the policy she individually was entitled to the insurance money. This court examined that claim and held that it was unfounded, thus conceding that if such had been the case the Washington action could be no bar. The other is *Traflet* v. *Empire Life Ins. Co.* (64 N. J. L. 387). The question there involved was substantially the same as that in the *Sulz* case. A New Jersey administrator sued in that state on an insurance policy. A New York administrator of the same estate sued on the same policy in New York. The principal office of the defendant corporation was in New York and the New York suit was first instituted. It was held that while both courts had jurisdiction, comity required that precedence should be given to that which first acquired jurisdiction. Neither of these cases has any application to the case of hostile claims to the same right of action.

The judgment of the Appellate Division should be reversed and that of the Trial Term affirmed, with costs in both courts.

GRAY, VANN, HISCOCK, CHASE and COLLIN, JJ., concur; HAIGHT, J., dissents.

Judgment reversed, etc.

GEORGE T. JIMERSON, Respondent, *v.* ERIE RAILROAD COMPANY, Appellant.

Railroads — construction and application of section 52 of Railroad Law (Cons. Laws, ch. 49) requiring railroad companies to maintain fences along their rights of way — railroad company not liable for animals injured by falling through railroad bridge.

Section 52 of the Railroad Law (Cons. Laws, ch. 49) requiring railroad companies to erect and maintain fences along their rights of way limits their liability for failure to do so to "damages done by their agents or engines or cars to any domestic animals thereon;" hence, there is no liability for injuries sustained by animals which by reason of such failure have escaped from a pasture and are injured by falling through a bridge on the roadway of a railroad company.

Jimerson v. *Erie R. R. Co.*, 138 App. Div. 914, reversed.

(Submitted December 6, 1911; decided December 19, 1911.)

APPEAL from a judgment of the Appellate Division of the Supreme Court in the fourth judicial department, entered May 31, 1910, which affirmed a final judgment in favor of plaintiff entered upon an interlocutory judgment of Special Term overruling a demurrer to the complaint.

The nature of the action and the facts, so far as material, are stated in the opinion.

J. P. Quigley for appellant. The statute under which this action is brought, being in derogation of a rule of the common law, should be construed strictly. The act itself specifically provides the penalty for a violation of its provisions. The injuries received by plaintiff's horses, as set forth in the complaint, do not come within the penalty prescribed by the statute. (*Beck* v. *Carter*, 68 N. Y. 289; *Stafford* v. *Ingersoll*, 3 Hill, 38; *Knight* v. *R. R. Co.*, 99 N. Y. 25; *Lent* v. *R. R. Co.*, 130 N. Y. 504; *Donnegan* v. *Erhardt*, 119 N. Y. 174.)

M. B. Jewell for respondent.   Section 32 of the Railroad Law enjoins upon railroad corporations the duty of building and thereafter maintaining fences along the sides of their railroads.   This provision is for the benefit of passengers upon trains and the owners and occupants of lands through which the road passes.   Negligence of the defendant to perform this duty renders it liable for all damages which are the direct result of the injury. (*Corwin* v. *N. Y. & E. R. R. Co.*, 13 N. Y. 42; *Shepard* v. *B., N. Y. & P. Ry. Co.*, 35 N. Y. 640; *Purdy* v. *N. Y. & N. H. Ry. Co.*, 61 N. Y. 353; *Tracy* v. *T. & B. Ry. Co.*, 38 N. Y. 433; *Graham* v. *President, etc., of D. & H. C. Co.*, 46 Hun, 386; *French* v. *W. N. Y. & P. Ry. Co.*, 72 Hun, 469; *Grannan* v. *Westchester Racing Assn.*, 16 App. Div. 8; *Donnegan* v. *Erhardt*, 119 N. Y. 468; *Mendizabel* v. *N. Y. C. & H. R. R. R. Co.*, 89 App. Div. 386; *Crandall* v. *Eldridge*, 46 Hun, 411.)

CULLEN, Ch. J.   The complaint, which the defendant contends states no cause of action, alleges that the defendant failed to erect and maintain fences on the line of its road where it passed through the reservation of the Seneca Indians, as a result of which two colts belonging to the plaintiff, which were rightfully pastured on said reservation (plaintiff himself being an Indian) escaped from the pasture to the defendant's road and following along it fell through a railroad bridge whereby one colt received injuries from which he died and the other was seriously damaged and its value impaired. The point of the demurrer is that the liability of the defendant is solely the creation of the statute and that the statute does not impose liability for injuries to stock received in the manner stated in the complaint. Section 52 of the present Railroad Law (Cons. Laws, ch. 49) reads: "Every railroad corporation, and any lessee or other person in possession of its road, shall, before the lines or its road are open for use, and so soon as it has acquired the right of way for its roadway, erect and thereafter maintain fences on the sides of its road of height and strength sufficient to prevent cattle, horses, sheep and hogs from going upon its road from the adjacent lands, * * *. So long as such fences are not made, or are not in good repair, the corporation, its lessee or other person in possession of its road, shall be liable for all damages done by their agents or engines or cars to any domestic animals thereon." We think the question not an open one in this court. In *Knight* v. *N. Y., Lake Erie & Western Railroad Company* (99 N. Y. 25) the action was brought for injury to a colt which escaped from a barnyard to the highway and ran thence along the highway through a gap in the fence to defendant's railway, which it followed till it came to a bridge through which it fell. The plaintiff having recovered a verdict at Circuit the court set it aside, which action was reversed by the General Term, but reinstated by this court, which held the defendant not liable. It was there said by Judge RAPALLO: "The statute referred to requires railroad companies to erect and maintain fences on the sides of their roads, but it does not impose upon them a general liability for any consequences which may result from an omission to do so, nor does it leave the question open what liability to third parties they shall be subjected to for such omission, for it defines in express terms the consequences for which they shall be liable to owners of cattle and horses getting on the track * * * for damages which shall be done by

the *engines* or *agents* of any such corporation." (p. 28.)
It was held that the bridge was not an agent and that the
defendant was not liable. Since that decision two cases
have been decided in the Supreme Court (*Graham* v.
Delaware & Hudson Canal Co., 46 Hun, 386; *French* v.
Western N. Y. & Penn. R. R. Co., 72 Hun, 469), in
which recoveries for injuries to animals escaping from
fields adjacent to the track encountered in the same
manner as that which occurred in the *Knight* case have
been upheld. In the opinions rendered in those cases the
Knight decision is distinguished on the theory that it
did not apply where the animals escaped from an adjacent field. In other words, that the liability for failure
to maintain the fence was greater to adjacent owners
than to other parties. If we assume that the *Knight* case
might have been decided on the theory that the plaintiff
was not an adjacent landholder it is sufficient to say that
it was decided on no such ground, but solely on the
ground that the liability of failing to comply with the
mandates of the statute was expressly limited by it. It
is also to be observed that in *Corwin* v. *New York &
Erie Railroad Company* (13 N. Y. 42) this court had
already held that the statute applied equally to the tres-
passing cattle of strangers and those of adjacent owners.
But if it were an open question we think it would be difficult to avoid the conclusion reached by the court in the
Knight case. The correctness of that decision is empha-
sized by the subsequent act of the legislature. As the
statute stood at the time of the *Knight* case the liability
was for damage occasioned by their "engines or agents."
In 1900, when the present Railroad Law (now Cons.
Laws, ch. 49) was enacted, the old statute was amended
by adding to "engines or agents" the word "cars." It
may be, as argued by the learned judges of the Supreme
Court, that there is little reason for making the railroad
companies liable for damages to cattle run down by cars
or engines but not for injuries caused by falling through

bridges, when the original source of the injury is the same in both cases, the failure to comply with the statutory requirement. If this, however, had been the view of the legislature it would have, in amending the statute, made the liability general, instead of which it simply added liability for injuries by cars.

The judgments of the Appellate Division and of the Special Term must be reversed and judgment rendered for the defendant on demurrer, with costs in all courts, with leave to plaintiff to serve amended complaint within twenty days on payment of costs.

GRAY, VANN, WERNER, WILLARD BARTLETT and CHASE, JJ., concur; HAIGHT, J., not voting.

Judgment accordingly.

In the Matter of the Application of ROBERT TOWNSEND, as Administrator of the Estate of MARIA F. TOWNSEND, Deceased, Appellant, for Authority to Sell Real Property.

In the Matter of the Petition of ERNEST K. HUTCHINSON, Respondent, to Be Relieved of His Purchase.

Decedent's estate — proceedings to sell decedent's real estate for the payment of his debts — judgment creditors of an heir or devisee of decedent necessary parties thereto.

Under the provisions of the Code of Civil Procedure (§§ 2752-2756), regulating the sale of a decedent's real estate for the payment of his debts, judgment creditors of an heir or devisee of such decedent have a substantial interest to protect in the proceeding, and must be made parties thereto.

Matter of Townsend, 144 App. Div. 912, affirmed.

(Argued November 21, 1911; decided December 22, 1911.)

APPEAL from an order of the Appellate Division of the Supreme Court in the second judicial department, entered April 21, 1911, which affirmed a decree of the Nassau

County Surrogate's Court relieving the respondent herein of his purchase of real property.

The facts, so far as material, are stated in the opinion.

Calvin D. Van Name for appellant.   It was not necessary to name the judgment creditors of the heirs in the petition, or to serve them with citations on the application of the administrator to sell for the payment of debts of the decedent.   (Code Civ. Pro. § 2752.)   The petition to the surrogate for authority to sell for the payment of debts of decedent contained facts sufficient to confer jurisdiction upon the Surrogate's Court to make the decree, so far as the judgment creditors of the heirs were concerned.   (*Matter of Ibert*, 48 App. Div. 510; *Richmond* v. *F. Nat. Bank*, 86 App. Div. 158; *Matter of Dolan*, 88 N. Y. 309.)

A. G. De Riesthal for respondent.   The grantees and the judgment creditors of the heirs of the decedent should have been mentioned in the petition for the sale of decedent's real estate to pay debts, and should have been cited in order to give the Surrogate's Court jurisdiction. (Code Civ. Pro. § 2752; *Raynor* v. *Gordon*, 23 Hun, 264.) The statements required to be set forth in the petition are jurisdictional and an omission to set them forth does not give the court jurisdiction and invalidates the whole proceedings and the sale.   (*Kammerer* v. *Ziegler*, 1 Dem. 177; *Matter of John.* 21 Civ. Pro. Rep. 326; *Jenkins* v. *Young*, 35 Hun, 569; *Matter of Slater*, 17 Misc. Rep. 474; *Dennis* v. *Jones*, 1 Dem. 80; *Mead* v. *Sherwood*, 4 Redf. 352; *Ackley* v. *Dygert*, 33 Barb. 176; *Kelly's Estate*, 1 Abb. [N. C.] 102; *Stillwell* v. *Swarthout*, 81 N. Y. 109.)

CULLEN, Ch. J.   This was a proceeding for the sale of the real estate of a decedent for the payment of her debts, and the appeal is from the affirmance of an order of the surrogate which relieved the purchaser, upon a sale made under a decree in the proceeding, from his purchase on the ground that the proceedings were so irregular that the title acquired by the purchaser would be doubtful. We think the proceedings were so irregular that the respondent was properly granted the relief he asked. Without referring to other objections, we are of opinion that the proceeding was defective for failing to make parties to it the judgment creditors of the heirs at law of the deceased. Doubtless, as claimed by the learned counsel for the appellant and as held by this court in *Matter of Dolan* (88 N. Y. 309), it is necessary in a proceeding of this character only to comply with the requirements of the statute and make such persons parties thereto as the statute prescribes. When the *Dolan* case arose the proceeding was governed by the provisions of the Revised Statutes (2 R. S. ch. 6, title 4, §§ 5 and 6) which required service of the notice of the application upon the widow, heirs and devisees of the deceased. It was held that service on no other person was requisite. The present case, however, is governed by the Code of Civil Procedure, sections 2752 to 2756. These sections require that the citation shall be issued to "husband or wife, and of all the heirs and devisees of the decedent, and also every other person claiming under them, or either of them." The question before us is whether judgment creditors of an heir or devisee should be deemed as persons claiming under him within the meaning of the statute. We think they should. Though the lien of a judgment creditor on the real estate of his debtor is general and not specific, he has a substantial interest to protect in the proceeding. The effect of granting the application is to destroy his lien on the real estate. In *Brainard* v. *Cooper* (10 N. Y. 356) it was held that a judgment creditor having a lien had a subsisting interest under the mortgagor such as entitled him to redeem from a defective mortgage sale. In *Raynor* v. *Gordon* (23 Hun, 264) it was held that a judgment creditor of a devisee was a person claiming under him and entitled under the language of another section of the Revised Statutes (2 R. S. 101, § 10) to intervene and set up the Statute of Limitations in bar of the application, though at that time, as already said, it was not necessary to make him a party to the proceeding. That decision has never been overruled or questioned. Now that the statute has been changed, the same construction should be given to the term "persons claiming under them or either of them," as was given to it in the case cited. In actions to foreclose mortgages or for the sale of property in partition judgment creditors are necessary parties. The same rule should apply in proceedings of this kind if the language of the statute permits it. In our judgment it not only permits the rule, but requires its adoption.

The order appealed from should be affirmed, with costs.

HAIGHT, WERNER, WILLARD BARTLETT, HISCOCK, CHASE and COLLIN, JJ., concur.

Order affirmed.

MEMORANDA

DECISIONS RENDERED DURING THE PERIOD EMBRACED IN THIS VOLUME.

THE PEOPLE OF THE STATE OF NEW YORK, Respondent,
v. WILLIAM DARRAGH, Appellant.

People v. *Darragh*, 141 App. Div. 408, affirmed.
(Submitted June 8, 1911; decided October 3, 1911.)

APPEAL from an order of the Appellate Division of the Supreme Court in the first judicial department, entered December 30, 1910, which affirmed a judgment of the Court of General Sessions of the Peace in the county of New York rendered upon a verdict convicting the defendant of the crime of manslaughter in the first degree.

Charles A. Flammer, Ralph M. Frink and *Edward F. Flammer* for appellant.

Charles S. Whitman, District Attorney (Robert C. Taylor of counsel), for respondent.

Judgment of conviction affirmed; no opinion.
Concur: CULLEN, Ch. J., GRAY, HAIGHT, VANN, WERNER, HISCOCK and COLLIN, JJ.

HARRISON LAPIER, Appellant, *v.* FRANK GONYO, Respondent.

Lapier v. *Gonyo*, 136 App. Div. 903, affirmed.
(Argued June 8, 1911; decided October 3, 1911.)

APPEAL from a judgment of the Appellate Division of the Supreme Court in the third judicial department, entered January 8, 1910, affirming a judgment in favor of defendant entered upon a decision of the court at a Trial Term without a jury in an action to recover for an alleged trespass and to obtain an injunction.

C. J. Vert for appellant.

John H. Booth for respondent.

Judgment affirmed, with costs; no opinion.
Concur: CULLEN, Ch. J., GRAY, HAIGHT, WERNER, HISCOCK and COLLIN, JJ.

WARNER-QUINLAN ASPHALT COMPANY, Appellant, *v.* CENTRAL NEW YORK TELEPHONE AND TELEGRAPH COMPANY, Respondent.

Warner-Quinlan Asphalt Co. v. *Central N. Y. Telephone & Telegraph Co.*, 136 App. Div. 912, affirmed.
(Argued June 8, 1911; decided October 3, 1911.)

APPEAL from a judgment of the Appellate Division of the Supreme Court in the fourth judicial department, entered January 28, 1910, affirming a judgment in favor of defendant entered upon a dismissal of the complaint by the court on trial at Special Term in an action to restrain defendant from having work, alleged to have been let by contract to plaintiff, done by other parties.

A. H. Cowie for appellant.

Edward Nottingham and *George A. Smith* for respondent.

Judgment affirmed, with costs; no opinion.
Concur: CULLEN, Ch. J., GRAY, HAIGHT, VANN, WERNER, HISCOCK and COLLIN, JJ.

CHARLESTON ILLUMINATING COMPANY, Respondent, *v.*
KNICKERBOCKER TRUST COMPANY, as Trustee,
Appellant.

Charleston Illuminating Co. v. *Knickerbocker Trust Co.*, 188
App. Div. 107, affirmed.
(Argued June 8, 1911; decided October 3, 1911.)

APPEAL from a judgment of the Appellate Division of
the Supreme Court in the first judicial department,
entered May 12, 1910, in favor of plaintiff, upon the submission of a controversy, pursuant to section 1279 of the
Code of Civil Procedure, as to the correct interpretation
of a provision of a mortgage executed by the plaintiff to
the defendant as trustee and known as the refunding
and improvement mortgage of the plaintiff.

Charles H. Tuttle for appellant.

William M. Wherry, Jr., for respondent.

Judgment affirmed, without costs, on opinion of MIL-
LER, J., below.

Concur: CULLEN, Ch. J., GRAY, HAIGHT, VANN,
WERNER, HISCOCK and COLLIN, JJ.

———————

MEYER SERLING, Respondent, *v.* HARRY SERLING et al.,
Appellants.

Serling v. *Serling*, 137 App. Div. 930, affirmed.
(Argued June 8, 1911; decided October 3, 1911.)

APPEAL from a judgment of the Appellate Division of
the Supreme Court in the fourth judicial department,
entered March 31, 1910, affirming a judgment in favor of
plaintiff entered upon a verdict in an action to recover
for personal injuries alleged to have been sustained by
plaintiff through the negligence of defendants, his
employers.

34

Frederick T. Pierson for appellants.

T. Aaron Levy for respondent.

Judgment affirmed, with costs; no opinion.
Concur: CULLEN, Ch. J., GRAY, HAIGHT, VANN, WERNER, HISCOCK and COLLIN, JJ.

AUGUSTUS LINDEN, Appellant, *v.* HAROLD H. FRIES, Respondent.

Linden v. *Fries*, 136 App. Div. 980, affirmed.
(Argued June 9, 1911; decided October 3, 1911.)

APPEAL from a judgment of the Appellate Division of the Supreme Court in the first judicial department, entered January 26, 1910, affirming a judgment in favor of defendant entered upon a dismissal of the complaint by the court at a Trial Term in an action to recover damages alleged to have been sustained by plaintiff through the false representations of defendant.

L. Laflin Kellogg and *William K. Hartpence* for appellant.

Alexander S. Andrews and *John Larkin* for respondent.

Judgment affirmed, with costs; no opinion.
Concur: CULLEN, Ch. J., GRAY, HAIGHT, VANN, WERNER, HISCOCK and COLLIN, JJ.

THE PEOPLE OF THE STATE OF NEW YORK, Respondent, *v.* CHARLES TEELING, Appellant.

People v. *Teeling*, 140 App. Div. 945, affirmed.
(Argued June 9, 1911; decided October 3, 1911.)

APPEAL from an order of the Appellate Division of the Supreme Court in the third judicial department, entered December 7, 1910, which affirmed a judgment of the

Albany County Court rendered upon a verdict convicting the defendant of the crime of violating section 986 of the Penal Law, in recording and registering bets and wagers.

Thomas F. Powers for appellant.

Rollin B. Sanford, District Attorney, for respondent.

Judgment of conviction affirmed; no opinion.
Concur: CULLEN, Ch. J., GRAY, HAIGHT, VANN, WERNER, HISCOCK and COLLIN, JJ.

FERGUSON CONTRACTING COMPANY, Appellant, *v.* THE HELDERBERG CEMENT COMPANY, Respondent.

Ferguson Contracting Co. v. *Helderberg Cement Co.*, 189 App. Div. 901, affirmed.
(Argued June 9, 1911; decided October 3, 1911.)

APPEAL from a judgment of the Appellate Division of the Supreme Court in the first judicial department, entered June 3, 1910, affirming a judgment in favor of defendant entered upon a dismissal of the complaint by the court at a Trial Term in an action to recover on contract.

Brainard Tolles and *Julien T. Davies* for appellant.

Murray Downs for respondent.

Judgment affirmed, with costs; no opinion.
Concur: CULLEN, Ch. J., GRAY, HAIGHT, VANN, WERNER, HISCOCK and COLLIN, JJ.

THE JOHN J. HART COMPANY, Appellant, *v.* THE CITY OF NEW YORK, Respondent.

Hart Company v. *City of New York*, 129 App. Div. 903, affirmed.
(Argued June 12, 1911; decided October 3, 1911.)

APPEAL from a judgment of the Appellate Division of the Supreme Court in the first judicial department,

entered January 25, 1909, affirming a judgment in favor of defendant entered upon a dismissal of the complaint by the court at a Trial Term without a jury in an action to recover for excess work alleged to have been performed in connection with a contract for paving.

George B. Hayes for appellant.

Archibald R. Watson, Corporation Counsel (*Terence Farley* and *Francis Martin* of counsel), for respondent.

Judgment affirmed, with costs; no opinion.
Concur: CULLEN, Ch. J., GRAY, VANN, WERNER, WILLARD BARTLETT, HISCOCK and CHASE, JJ.

JOSEPHINE A. BEACH, Respondent, *v.* ELIZABETH G. LARGE, Appellant, and PHŒBE E. SMITH, Respondent.

Beach v. *Large*, 134 App. Div. 968, affirmed.
(Argued June 12, 1911; decided October 3, 1911.)

APPEAL from a judgment, entered May 11, 1911, upon an order of the Appellate Division of the Supreme Court in the third judicial department, which affirmed an interlocutory judgment in favor of plaintiff entered upon a decision of the court on trial at Special Term in an action of partition.

Edgar T. Brackett and *A. J. Dillingham* for appellant.

William W. Morrill and *William H. Hollister, Jr.,* for respondent.

Judgment affirmed, with costs; no opinion.
Concur: CULLEN, Ch. J., GRAY, VANN, WERNER, WILLARD BARTLETT, HISCOCK and CHASE, JJ.

MEYER BROTHERS DRUG COMPANY, Respondent, *v.*
EDWARD P. MCKINNEY et al., Appellants.

Meyer Brothers Drug Co. v. *McKinney*, 137 App. Div. 541,
affirmed.
(Argued June 12, 1911; decided October 3, 1911.)

APPEAL from a judgment of the Appellate Division of
the Supreme Court in the third judicial department,
entered March 17, 1910, affirming a judgment in favor
of plaintiff entered upon a decision of the court at a Trial
Term without a jury in an action to recover for an
alleged breach of contract.

William Nottingham and *Theodore R. Tuthill* for
appellants.

Israel T. Deyo for respondent.

Judgment affirmed, with costs; no opinion.
Concur: CULLEN, Ch. J., GRAY, VANN, WERNER,
WILLARD BARTLETT, HISCOCK and CHASE, JJ.

LE COMPTE MANUFACTURING COMPANY, Appellant, *v.*
WILLIAM J. ASCHENBACH'S SONS HARNESS COMPANY,
Respondent.

Le Compte Manfg. Co. v. *Aschenbach's Sons Harness Co.*, 138 App.
Div. 908, affirmed.
(Argued June 13, 1911; decided October 3, 1911.)

APPEAL from a judgment of the Appellate Division of the Supreme Court in the first judicial department, entered May 25, 1910, affirming a judgment in
favor of defendant entered upon a dismissal of the complaint by the court at a Trial Term in an action to
recover brokerage commissions alleged to have been

earned by plaintiff's assignee in negotiating the sale of defendant's capital stock.

Walter Carroll Low for appellant.

Theodore B. Richter for respondent.

Judgment affirmed, with costs; no opinion.
Concur: CULLEN, Ch. J., GRAY, VANN, WERNER, WILLARD BARTLETT, HISCOCK and CHASE, JJ.

SOLOMON L. PAKAS, Respondent, *v.* WALTER J. CLARKE, Appellant.

Pakas v. *Clarke*, 136 App. Div. 492, affirmed,
(Submitted June 13, 1911; decided October 3, 1911.)

APPEAL from so much of a judgment of the Appellate Division of the Supreme Court in the first judicial department, entered March 12, 1910, affirming a judgment in favor of plaintiff entered upon a decision of the court on trial at Special Term, as awards costs to the plaintiff.

William L. Stone and *Albert I. Sire* for appellant.

John Frankenheimer for respondent.

Judgment affirmed, with costs; no opinion.
Concur: CULLEN, Ch. J., GRAY, VANN, WERNER, WILLARD BARTLETT, HISCOCK and CHASE, JJ.

WILSON R. HUNTER, Appellant, *v.* ALEXANDER S. BACON, Respondent.

Hunter v. *Bacon*, 135 App. Div. 920, affirmed.
(Argued June 13, 1911; decided October 3, 1911.)

APPEAL from a judgment of the Appellate Division of the Supreme Court in the first judicial department,

entered December 28, 1909, affirming a judgment in favor of defendant entered upon a verdict in an action to recover upon promissory notes.

Louis Sturcke for appellant.

Alexander S. Bacon respondent in person.

Judgment affirmed, with costs; no opinion.
Concur: CULLEN, Ch. J., GRAY, VANN, WERNER, WILLARD BARTLETT, HISCOCK and CHASE, JJ.

WALTER B. MANNY, Appellant, *v.* DANIEL T. WILSON, Respondent.

Manny v. *Wilson*, 137 App. Div. 140, affirmed.
(Argued June 14, 1911; decided October 3, 1911.)

APPEAL from an order of the Appellate Division of the Supreme Court in the first judicial department, entered March 17, 1910, reversing a judgment in favor of plaintiff entered upon a verdict directed by the court and granting a new trial in an action to recover for an alleged conversion.

Edward H. Tatum for appellant.

John H. Corwin for respondent.

Order affirmed and judgment absolute ordered against appellant on the stipulation, with costs in all courts, on opinion of MILLER, J., below.
Concur: CULLEN, Ch. J., GRAY, VANN, WERNER, WILLARD BARTLETT, HISCOCK and CHASE, JJ.

In the Matter of the Accounting of MOSES F. DENNIS, as Executor of VAN WYCK HORTON, Deceased, Appellant. GEORGE P. MCCOY et al., Respondents.

Matter of Dennis, 137 App. Div. 917, affirmed.
. (Argued June 15, 1911; decided October 3, 1911.)

APPEAL from an order of the Appellate Division of the Supreme Court in the first judicial department, entered March 11, 1910, which affirmed a decree of the New York County Surrogate's Court judicially settling and surcharging the accounts of Moses F. Dennis, as executor of Van Wyck Horton, deceased.

William H. Hamilton, Norman C. Conklin and *Warren E. Sammis* for appellant.

Henry B. Corey for respondents.

Order affirmed, with costs; no opinion.
Concur: CULLEN, Ch. J., GRAY, VANN, WERNER, WILLARD BARTLETT, HISCOCK and CHASE, JJ.

JULIA F. ARNOLD, Respondent, *v.* VILLAGE OF NORTH TARRYTOWN, Appellant.

Arnold v. *Village of North Tarrytown*, 137 App. Div 68, affirmed.
(Submitted June 15, 1911; decided October 3, 1911.)

APPEAL from a judgment of the Appellate Division of the Supreme Court in the second judicial department, entered April 13, 1910, affirming a judgment in favor of plaintiff entered upon a verdict in an action to recover for personal injuries alleged to have been sustained through the defendant's negligence.

Smith Lent, Clarence S. Davison and *William G. Given* for appellant.

George A. Blauvelt for respondent.

Judgment affirmed, with costs, on opinion of CARR, J., below.

Concur: CULLEN, Ch. J., GRAY, VANN, WERNER, WILLARD BARTLETT, HISCOCK and CHASE, JJ.

THE NEW YORK STEAM COMPANY, Respondent, *v.* PATRICK RYAN et al., Composing the Firm of RYAN & PARKER, Appellants.

New York Steam Co. v. *Ryan*, 137 App. Div. 941, affirmed.
(Argued June 15, 1911; decided October 3, 1911.)

APPEAL from a judgment of the Appellate Division of the Supreme Court in the first judicial department, entered April 13, 1910, affirming a judgment in favor of plaintiff entered upon a verdict in an action to recover for labor and materials alleged to have been furnished.

William L. Bowman for appellants.

Frederick E. Fishel for respondent.

Judgment affirmed, with costs; no opinion.

Concur: CULLEN, Ch. J., GRAY, VANN, WERNER, WILLARD BARTLETT, HISCOCK and CHASE, JJ.

In the Matter of the Application of WILFRED E. YOUKER, Appellant, for a Peremptory Writ of Mandamus against EDWARD LAZANSKY, as Secretary of State, et al., Respondents.

Matter of Youker, 146 App. Div. 894, appeal dismissed.
(Argued October 2, 1911; decided October 3, 1911.)

APPEAL from an order of the Appellate Division of the Supreme Court in the second judicial department,

entered September 25, 1911, which affirmed an order of
Special Term denying a motion for a peremptory writ of
mandamus to compel the secretary of state to make and
transmit to the custodian of primary records a notice
under his hand and seal specifying the office of the
Municipal Court justice for the sixth district Municipal
Court within the borough of Brooklyn, city of New
York, as one of the officers to be voted for at the coming
election in November, 1911.

Charles B. Law for appellant.

*Thomas Carmody, Attorney-General (Wilber W.
Chambers* and *Robert P. Beyer* of counsel), for secretary
of state, respondent.

*Archibald R. Watson, Corporation Counsel (James
D. Bell* of counsel), for board of elections of the city of
New York, respondent.

Appeal dismissed, with costs; no opinion.
Concur: CULLEN, Ch. J., HAIGHT, VANN, WERNER,
WILLARD BARTLETT, HISCOCK and CHASE, JJ.

HARLOW C. CURTISS, Respondent, *v.* WILLIAM T. JEBB,
Appellant.

Practice — form of judgment.

Under no rule of practice is there any justification for inserting
in a judgment a provision for the issuance of an execution against
the person or for quoting extracts from the judge's charge to the
jury.

Curtiss v. *Jebb*, 137 App. Div. 928, modified.

(Argued June 12, 1911; decided October 3, 1911.)

APPEAL from a judgment of the Appellate Division of
the Supreme Court in the fourth judicial department,
entered March 16, 1910, unanimously affirming a judgment in favor of plaintiff entered upon a verdict in

an action to recover money alleged to have been paid under fraudulent representations.

Charles B. Sears and *Louis L. Babcock* for appellant.

James McCormick Mitchell for respondent.

Per Curiam. Upon this appeal there are only two questions that survive the unanimous affirmance by the Appellate Division. One relates to the exclusion of certain testimony offered by the defendant, and the other arises upon the form of the judgment entered in favor of the plaintiff. As to the first of these questions we have only to say that since the trial court, upon defendant's objection, had previously excluded similar evidence offered by the plaintiff, the ruling excepted to by the defendant was clearly right.

As to the form of the judgment we hold that under no rule of practice is there any justification for inserting in a judgment a provision for the issuance of an execution against the person, and much less for quoting extracts from the judge's charge to the jury. These parts of the judgment are, therefore, to be stricken out, and the judgment, as thus modified, should be affirmed, without costs of this appeal to either party.

CULLEN, Ch. J., GRAY, VANN, WERNER, WILLARD BARTLETT, HISCOCK and CHASE, JJ., concur.

Judgment accordingly.

ANTHONY FISHER, Respondent, *v.* WAKEFIELD PARK REALTY COMPANY, Appellant.

Fisher v. *Wakefield Park Realty Co.*, 135 App. Div. 808, modified.

(Argued June 12, 1911, decided October 3, 1911.)

APPEAL from a judgment of the Appellate Division, of the Supreme Court in the second judicial department, entered January 15, 1910, affirming a judgment in favor of plaintiff entered upon a verdict.

Francis B. Wood, Alfred G. Reeves and *Ambrose G. Todd* for appellant.

Adrian M. Potter for respondent.

HISCOCK, J. Respondent has recovered on two causes of action. The first one was based on a contract made with the appellant for filling and grading certain streets on a tract of land in which it was interested; the second one was for work performed in grading and preparing for use a certain public street which appellant itself had undertaken to grade and prepare under a contract with the city of Yonkers.

Without going too much into details I find no reason for reversing the judgment which has been entered so far as it rests on the first cause of action. Appellant's counsel advances various reasons why the judgment should be reversed as to that cause of action, as, that the work was to be paid for on measurements of an engineer and that the surface of the street was to be left in a certain condition and that the evidence did not show compliance with these provisions. It is sufficient to say that if there were any such defects in the plaintiff's evidence they were not made the basis for any motion to dismiss this cause of action. Apparently the motion for a nonsuit was only directed at the second cause of action, but even if this is otherwise no break in plaintiff's evidence such as is now complained of was pointed out. If it had been, it is quite possible that it might have been remedied.

On the other hand, I think that the judgment, so far as it is based on the second cause of action, must be reversed, and the verdict so distinguished the amount awarded on each cause of action, that it is entirely feasible to affirm the judgment as to one cause of action and to reverse it as to the other.

As has been indicated, the appellant itself made a contract for grading and filling Sterling avenue, which is the street involved in the second cause of action. After it had done this it became anxious for some reason to sublet the contract to respondent at a less price than that for which it had engaged to do the work. The contract between the parties to this action contemplated an assignment of the original contract with the municipality upon its consent and upon the consent of the bonding company, which had given an undertaking conditioned for the faithful performance by appellant of its contract. Neither the municipality nor the bonding company, however, was willing to consent to this arrangement, and it fell through. The respondent then appears to have entered into a contract with the appellant by which he was to do the work which it had agreed to do, and in accordance with the provisions and requirements of its contract with the municipality, and also he was to give to the appellant a bond for the faithful performance by him of his contract. In view of what is to be said later it is especially to be noted that the respondent was to receive his pay in accordance with certificates of performance made by the commissioner of public works of the city of Yonkers, under the original contract with the appellant. I should judge that such payments as were made by appellant to respondent under their contract were made by simply turning over certificates which the appellant had received from the city. But however this may be, the respondent testified: "I was to get my pay as the Commissioner of Public Works found it to be due under the contract."

The main defense to this cause of action is that the respondent stopped work before he had completed his contract, and, therefore, is not entitled to recover any balance for work which he had completed before stopping and which had not been paid for. In avoidance of this defense the learned trial judge permitted the jury to find that the respondent discontinued work for either one of two sufficient reasons. One was that the appellant stopped him because he had not given a bond, and in connection with that I suppose the trial judge intended to allow the jury to determine whether the respondent was guilty of any fault in not giving a bond, so that the appellant could rightfully stop him. The second reason was that the appellant did not make payments to respondent as he was entitled to them under his contract, and that, therefore, he was justified in refusing to proceed further. This is the ground explicitly stated by respondent in his testimony as the one upon which he rests his refusal to proceed with the work, and this complaint against appellant is limited to its alleged failure to make payment to him as justified and required by a certificate issued by the commissioner of public works for one month, December. It is conceded by respondent that he had received pay in accordance with all of the certificates issued by said commissioner down to said month, but it is insisted that for said month said commissioner issued to appellant a certificate for further work completed under the contract which entitled him to pay and which the appellant refused to give. In my opinion there is no evidence which justified the jury in finding any such default on the part of the appellant. The respondent originally attempted to testify in a very general way that such a certificate for said month was issued, but, on cross-examination, his assertions on that point substantially faded away. Later the appellant called a witness who, although not asked by counsel to state his position, was apparently the commissioner of public works. In his evidence he absolutely and positively denied that any certificate had been issued for the month in question, and whereby respondent would have become entitled to further payments from appellant. Subsequently the respondent himself took the stand, and made no attempt to contradict or qualify the testimony of this witness. Therefore, I think that the conclusion is quite justified that there was no evidence to sustain this feature of respondent's case.

In accordance with these views the judgment should be affirmed as to the first cause of action, without costs, and reversed and a new trial granted as to the second cause of action, with costs to abide event.

CULLEN, Ch. J., GRAY, VANN, WERNER, WILLARD BARTLETT and CHASE, JJ., concur.

Judgment accordingly.

In the Matter of the Application of CARROLL F. SMITH, as Treasurer of the Manhattan State Hospital, Respondent, to Compel the Support and Maintenance at Said Hospital of RACHEL WELLER, an Inmate.

JOSEPH L. WELLER, Appellant.

Matter of Smith (In re Weller), 143 App. Div. 907, appeal dismissed.
(Argued October 2, 1911; decided October 10, 1911.)

MOTION to dismiss an appeal from an order of the Appellate Division of the Supreme Court in the first judicial department, entered February 17, 1911, which affirmed an order of the Court of General Sessions of the Peace in the county of New York requiring the appellant herein to pay a certain sum weekly for the maintenance of his wife at the Manhattan State Hospital.

The motion was made upon the ground that the order of affirmance was not appealable of right to the Court of Appeals, and that permission to appeal had not been obtained.

Selden Bacon for motion.

K. Henry Rosenberg opposed.

Motion granted and appeal dismissed.

LUIGI FRANCO, Respondent, *v.* MAX RADT, Appellant.

Franco v. Radt, 145 App. Div. 918, appeal dismissed.
(Submitted October 2, 1911; decided October 10, 1911.)

MOTION to dismiss an appeal from a judgment of the Appellate Division of the Supreme Court in the first judicial department, entered June 24, 1911, affirming a judgment in favor of plaintiff entered upon a verdict in an action to recover the purchase price of a bond and mortgage.

The motion was made upon the grounds that the Appellate Division had unanimously decided that the judgment was supported by the evidence; that the exceptions were frivolous and presented no questions of law for review and that the appeal was taken for purposes of delay.

Maxwell Slade for motion.

Emanuel Eschwege opposed.

Motion granted and appeal dismissed, with costs and ten dollars costs of motion.

LITTLEFIELD STOVE COMPANY, Appellant, *v.* THE CITY OF ALBANY, Respondent.

Reported below, 145 App. Div. 951.
(Submitted October 2, 1911; decided October 10, 1911.)

MOTION to dismiss an appeal from a judgment of the Appellate Division of the Supreme Court in the third judicial department, entered June 28, 1911, affirming a judgment in favor of defendant entered upon the report of a referee in an action to recover damages alleged to have been caused by the overflow of a sewer.

The motion was made upon the grounds that the Appellate Division had unanimously decided that the findings of fact were supported by the evidence; that the exceptions were frivolous and presented no question for review and that the appeal was taken merely for purposes of delay.

Arthur L. Andrews, Corporation Counsel, for motion.

John A. Delehanty opposed.

Motion denied, with ten dollars costs.

MIDWOOD PARK COMPANY, Respondent, *v.* KOUWENHOVEN
REALTY AND IMPROVEMENT COMPANY, Appellant.

Reported below, 144 App. Div. 939.
(Argued October 2, 1911; decided October 10, 1911.)

MOTION to dismiss an appeal from a judgment of the
Appellate Division of the Supreme Court in the second
judicial department, entered May 22, 1911, affirming a
judgment in favor of plaintiff entered upon a decision of
the court on trial at Special Term in an action to foreclose a mortgage.

The motion was made upon the ground that the
appeal was unauthorized and the Court of Appeals had
no jurisdiction to entertain the same.

Augustus Van Wyck for motion.

George C. Lay opposed.

Motion denied, with ten dollars costs.

WILSON F. WAKEFIELD, Respondent, *v.* PHILIP B.
GAYNOR et al., Defendants, and EDWARD V. BROPHY
et al., Appellants.

Reported below, 144 App. Div. 905.
(Argued October 2, 1911; decided October 10, 1911.)

MOTION to dismiss an appeal from a judgment of the
Appellate Division of the Supreme Court in the second
judicial department, entered May 8, 1911, affirming a
judgment in favor of plaintiff entered upon a decision of
the court on trial at Special Term in a taxpayer's action
to restrain the officials of the village of Portchester from
paying certain moneys.

The motion was made upon the grounds that the
35

parties appealing were not parties to the action nor interested in the subject-matter thereof.

Frederick W. Sherman for motion.

Clinton T. Taylor opposed.

Motion denied, with ten dollars costs.

SILVERIUS KOELLHOFFER, Respondent, *v.* HENRY HILLE-BRAND, Appellant, and CHARLES H. SCHNEIDER et al., Respondents, Impleaded with Others.

Reported below, 144 App. Div. 915.
(Argued October 2, 1911; decided October 10, 1911.)

MOTION to dismiss an appeal from a judgment of the Appellate Division of the Supreme Court in the second judicial department, entered May 19, 1911, affirming a judgment in favor of plaintiff entered upon the report of a referee in an action to recover damages alleged to have been occasioned plaintiff by fraudulent representations of defendants.

The motion was made upon the grounds that the Appellate Division had unanimously affirmed the judgment appealed from; that no question of law was involved and that the exceptions were frivolous.

Fred L. Gross for motion.

Joab H. Banton opposed.

Motion denied, with ten dollars costs.

JEFFREY SMITH, Appellant, *v.* WILLIAM GEIGER, Respondent.

(Submitted October 2, 1911; decided October 10, 1911.)

Motion for re-argument denied, with ten dollars costs. (See 202 N. Y. 306.)

LORENZ REICH, Appellant, *v.* EVA S. COCHRAN et al., as Executors and Trustees under the Will of WILLIAM F. COCHRAN, Deceased, Respondents.

(Submitted October 2, 1911 ; decided October 10, 1911.)

Motion for re-argument denied, with ten dollars costs. (See 201 N. Y. 450.)

SAMUEL J. STIEBEL et al., Respondents, *v.* JOHN GROSBERG, Appellant.

(Submitted October 2, 1911; decided October 10, 1911.)

Motion for re-argument denied, with ten dollars costs. (See 202 N. Y. 266.)

JANE DARCY, Appellant, *v.* THE PRESBYTERIAN HOSPITAL IN THE CITY OF NEW YORK, Respondent.

(Submitted June 13, 1911; decided October 10, 1911.)

Motion for re-argument denied, with ten dollars costs. (See 202 N. Y. 259.)

EMMA E. NESTELL, Appellant, *v.* CHARLES H. HART et al., Respondents.

(Submitted June 12, 1911; decided October 10, 1911.)

Motion for re-argument denied, with ten dollars costs. (See 202 N. Y. 280.)

RUSSELL DIXON, Respondent, *v.* JAMES J. COZINE, Appellant.

(Submitted October 2, 1911; decided October 10, 1911.)

Motion for re-argument denied, with ten dollars costs. (See 202 N. Y. 554.)

In the Matter of the Application of ENGREY F. NORMAN, Appellant, *v.* THE BOARD OF EDUCATION OF THE CITY OF NEW YORK, Respondent.

Matter of Norman v. *Bd. of Education*, *N. Y.*, 142 App. Div. 939, affirmed.

(Argued October 8, 1911; decided October 10, 1911.)

APPEAL from an order of the Appellate Division of the Supreme Court in the first judicial department, entered January 27, 1911, which affirmed an order of Special Term denying a motion for a peremptory writ of mandamus to compel the appointment of the petitioner to the position of assistant to the principal or head of department in the public schools of the city of New York upon the nomination of the board of superintendents.

Ira Leo Bamberger and *Frederick Cyrus Leubuscher* for appellant.

Archibald R. Watson, Corporation Counsel (*Terence Farley* and *Charles McIntyre* of counsel), for respondent.

Per Curiam.   Order affirmed for the reason that even if subdivision 12 of section 67 of the by-laws of the board of education of the city of New York should be held unreasonable, and said board should have passed upon the relator's nomination by the board of superintendents in disregard of such by-law, the application to the court for a writ of mandamus was not made within forty days from the filing of such recommendation in the office of the secretary of said board of education and while a vacancy existed to which said board could have appointed the relator. The other questions presented upon this appeal are not passed upon. No costs are allowed on this appeal.

CULLEN, Ch. J., HAIGHT, VANN, WERNER, WILLARD BARTLETT, HISCOCK and CHASE, JJ., concur.

Order affirmed.

In the Matter of the Application of SAMUEL S. KOENIG, Appellant, *v.* J. GABRIEL BRITT et al., Constituting the Board of Elections of the City of New York, Respondents.

Matter of Koenig v. *Britt*, 146 App. Div. 871, reversed.
(Argued October 3, 1911; decided October 10, 1911.)

APPEAL from an order of the Appellate Division of the Supreme Court in the first judicial department, entered September 28, 1911, which reversed an order of Special Term granting a motion for a peremptory writ of mandamus to compel the board of elections of the city of New York to print ballots to be used at the coming general election in accordance with the provisions of section 331 of the Election Law as it stood prior to its amendment by chapter 649 of the Laws of 1911.

Herbert R. Limburg, A. S. Gilbert and *Albert S. Bard* for appellant.

Archibald R. Watson, Corporation Counsel (*Abram I. Elkus, Terence Farley* and *George P. Nicholson* of counsel), for respondents.

D-Cady Herrick for Democratic State Committee, intervening.

The order of the Appellate Division should be reversed and that of the Special Term in substance affirmed, without costs. There are some errors, however, in the form of the Special Term order, for which reason it must be modified, and the order for this may be settled on two days' notice before the chief judge of this court.

Concur: CULLEN, Ch. J., HAIGHT, VANN, WERNER, WILLARD BARTLETT, HISCOCK and CHASE, JJ.

In the Matter of the Application of THEODORE B. BAR-
RINGER, Appellant, *v.* THE BOARD OF EDUCATION OF
THE CITY OF NEW YORK, Respondent.

Matter of Barringer v. *Bd. of Education, N. Y.,* 140 App. Div. 903,
affirmed.
(Argued October 2, 1911; decided October 17, 1911.)

APPEAL from an order of the Appellate Division of the
Supreme Court in the first judicial department, entered
June 17, 1911, which affirmed an order of Special Term
denying a motion for a peremptory writ of mandamus to
compel the defendant to reinstate the relator as principal
of Public School No. 39 in the borough of Manhattan.

Arnon L. Squiers and *Warren I. Lee* for appellant.

Archibald R. Watson, Corporation Counsel (*Terence
Farley* and *Charles McIntyre* of counsel), for respondent.

Order affirmed, with costs; no opinion.
Concur: VANN, WERNER, WILLARD BARTLETT, HIS-
COCK and CHASE, JJ. Dissenting: CULLEN, Ch. J., and
HAIGHT, J.

THE PEOPLE OF THE STATE OF NEW YORK ex rel. JOHN
B. FOREST, Appellant, *v.* FRANK M. WILLIAMS, as
State Engineer and Surveyor of the State of New York,
Respondent.

People ex rel. Forest v. *Williams,* 140 App. Div. 728, affirmed.
(Argued October 2, 1911; decided October 17, 1911.)

APPEAL from an order of the Appellate Division of the
Supreme Court in the fourth judicial department, entered
November 16, 1910, which affirmed an order of Special
Term denying a motion for a peremptory writ of man-
damus to compel defendant to reinstate the relator in the

position of axeman in the office of the division engineer at Rochester

Albert C. Olp for appellant.

Thomas Carmody, Attorney-General (Wilber W. Chambers of counsel), for respondent.

Order affirmed, without costs; no opinion.
Concur: CULLEN, Ch. J., HAIGHT, VANN, WERNER, WILLARD BARTLETT, HISCOCK and CHASE, JJ.

THE PEOPLE OF THE STATE OF NEW YORK ex rel. EMANUEL BARNET, Appellant, *v.* RAYMOND B. FOSDICK, as Commissioner of Accounts of the City of New York, Respondent.

People ex rel. Barnet v. *Fosdick*, 142 App. Div. 935, affirmed.
(Submitted October 3, 1911; decided October 17, 1911.)

APPEAL from an order of the Appellate Division of the Supreme Court in the first judicial department, entered January 13, 1911, which affirmed an order of Special Term denying a motion for a peremptory writ of mandamus to compel the defendant to reinstate the relator in the position of accountant in the office of the commissioner of accounts of the city of New York.

Ira E. Miller, Leon Levy and *Harry Greenberg* for appellant.

Archibald R. Watson, Corporation Counsel (Theodore Connoly and *Clarence L. Barber* of counsel), for respondent.

Order affirmed, with costs; no opinion.
Concur: CULLEN, Ch. J., HAIGHT, VANN, WERNER, WILLARD BARTLETT, HISCOCK and CHASE, JJ.

THE PEOPLE OF THE STATE OF NEW YORK ex rel. PAT-
RICK J. REID, Appellant, *v.* THEODORE A. BINGHAM,
as Police Commissioner of the City of New York,
Respondent.

People ex rel. Reid v. *Bingham*, 143 App. Div. 928, affirmed.
(Submitted October 3, 1911; decided October 17, 1911.)

APPEAL from an order of the Appellate Division of the
Supreme Court in the first judicial department, entered
March 10, 1911, which dismissed a writ of certiorari and
affirmed the proceedings of the defendant in dismissing
the relator from the police force of the city of New York.

Gilbert D. Lamb for appellant.

*Archibald R. Watson, Corporation Counsel (Terence
Farley* and *Harry Crone* of counsel), for respondent.

Order affirmed, with costs; no opinion.
Concur: CULLEN, Ch. J., HAIGHT, VANN, WERNER,
WILLARD BARTLETT, HISCOCK and CHASE, JJ..

In the Matter of the Application of HERMAN HUEG,
Respondent, for a Peremptory Writ of Mandamus
against ARCHIBALD R. WATSON, as Corporation Counsel of the City of New York, Appellant.

Matter of Hueg v. *Watson*, 144 App. Div. 939, affirmed.
(Argued October 3, 1911; decided October 17, 1911.)

APPEAL from an order of the Appellate Division of the
Supreme Court in the second judicial department, entered
May 12, 1911, which affirmed an order of Special Term
granting a motion for a peremptory writ of mandamus
to compel the defendant to institute proceedings to ascertain the compensation due the petitioner under chapter
1006 of the Laws of 1905 by reason of the closing and

discontinuing of Thomson avenue, in the borough of Queens, city of New York.

Archibald R. Watson, Corporation Counsel (Joel J. Squier and *James Regan Fitz Gerald* of counsel), for appellant.

Benjamin Trapnell and *Joseph A. Flannery* for respondent.

Order affirmed, with costs; no opinion.
Concur: CULLEN, Ch. J., HAIGHT, VANN, WERNER, WILLARD BARTLETT, HISCOCK and CHASE, JJ.

FLORA CARSON, Respondent, *v.* VILLAGE OF DRESDEN, Appellant.

(Submitted October 2, 1911; decided October 17, 1911.)

Motion for re-argument denied, with ten dollars costs. (See 202 N. Y. 414.)

ANNIE STENSON, as Administratrix of the Estate of THOMAS STENSON, Deceased, Appellant, *v.* J. H. FLICK CONSTRUCTION COMPANY, Respondent.

Stenson v. *Flick Construction Co.,* 146 App. Div. 66, appeal dismissed.

(Submitted October 9, 1911; decided October 17, 1911.)

MOTION to dismiss an appeal from a judgment of the Appellate Division of the Supreme Court in the first judicial department, entered July 14, 1911, affirming a judgment in favor of defendant entered upon a dismissal of the complaint by the court at a Trial Term.

The motion was made upon the ground that the undertaking required to perfect the appeal had not been filed.

Louis Cohn for motion.

No one opposed.

Motion granted and appeal dismissed, with costs and ten dollars costs of motion.

In the Matter of the Application of FRANCIS MACHOLDT, Respondent, for a Peremptory Writ of Mandamus against WILLIAM A. PRENDERGAST, as Comptroller of the City of New York, Appellant.

Matter of Macholdt v. *Prendergast*, 144 App. Div. 252, affirmed.
(Submitted October 4, 1911; decided October 24, 1911.)

APPEAL from an order of the Appellate Division of the Supreme Court in the second judicial department, entered April 21, 1911, which affirmed an order of Special Term granting a motion for a peremptory writ of mandamus to compel defendant to pay a certain award theretofore made in condemnation proceedings to the petitioner.

Archibald R. Watson, Corporation Counsel (*Joel J. Squier* and *G. E. Draper* of counsel), for appellant.

Benjamin Trapnell and *Joseph A. Flannery* for respondent.

Order affirmed, with costs; no opinion.
Concur: CULLEN, Ch. J., HAIGHT, VANN, WERNER, WILLARD BARTLETT, HISCOCK and CHASE, JJ.

MARX OTTINGER et al., Appellants, *v.* JOHN R. BENNETT, Respondent, Impleaded with Others.

Ottinger v. *Bennett*, 144 App. Div. 525, reversed.
(Argued October 4, 1911; decided October 24, 1911.)

APPEAL, by permission, from an order of the Appellate Division of the Supreme Court in the first judicial department, entered May 19, 1911, which reversed an interlocutory judgment of Special Term sustaining a demurrer to the complaint and overruled such demurrer in an action for deceit.

The following questions were certified:
" *First.* Does the complaint state facts sufficient to constitute a cause of action ?

" *Second.* Is the partial defense contained in the answer of the defendant John R. Bennett insufficient in law upon the face thereof ? "

Nathan Ottinger for appellants,

Thomas D. Adams for respondent.

Order of Appellate Division reversed and interlocutory judgment affirmed, with costs in both courts, on dissenting opinion of MILLER, J., below, and both questions certified answered in the affirmative.

Concur: CULLEN, Ch. J., HAIGHT, VANN, WERNER, WILLARD BARTLETT, HISCOCK and CHASE, JJ.

THE PEOPLE OF THE STATE OF NEW YORK ex rel. CHARLES H. STEBBINS, as Executor of MARY L. VAIL, Deceased, Appellant, *v.* LAWSON PURDY et al., as Commissioners of Taxes and Assessments of the City of New York, Respondents.

People ex rel. Stebbins v. Purdy, 144 App. Div. 361, affirmed.
(Argued October 4, 1911; decided October 24, 1911.)

APPEAL from an order of the Appellate Division of the Supreme Court in the first judicial department, entered May 5, 1911, which reversed an order of Special Term vacating an assessment against personal property of relator and dismissed the proceeding.

Theodore L. Bailey for appellant.

Archibald R. Watson, Corporation Counsel (Curtis A. Peters and *Eugene Fay* of counsel), for respondents.

Order affirmed, with costs; no opinion.
Concur: CULLEN, Ch. J., HAIGHT, VANN, WERNER, WILLARD BARTLETT, HISCOCK and CHASE, JJ.

THE NATIONAL PARK BANK OF NEW YORK, Respondent,
v. HENRY BILLINGS et al., Appellants.

National Park Bank v. *Billings,* 144 App. Div. 536, affirmed.
(Argued October 4, 1911; decided October 24, 1911.)

APPEAL, by permission, from an order of the Appellate
Division of the Supreme Court in the first judicial department, entered May 19, 1911, which modified and affirmed
as modified an order of Special Term granting a motion
for judgment upon the pleadings in a judgment creditor's action to secure the sale of an alleged interest of
the defendant Billings in his father's estate to satisfy a
judgment.

The following questions were certified:

"*First.* May the court upon motion, after issue joined
in an action by demurrer to the complaint, give judgment upon the pleadings?

"*Second.* Does the complaint state facts sufficient to
constitute a cause of action?"

J. Culbert Palmer for appellants.

C. H. Payne and *Louis F. Doyle* for respondent.

Order affirmed, with costs, on opinion of MILLER,
J., below, and questions certified answered in the
affirmative.

Concur: CULLEN, Ch. J., VANN, WERNER, WILLARD
BARTLETT, HISCOCK and CHASE, JJ.; HAIGHT, J., concurs with MILLER, J., below, so far as the merits are
concerned, but dissents as to the practice upon opinion
of McLAUGHLIN, J., below.

WILLIAM H. KOUWENHOVEN, Respondent, v. ELECTA
GIFFORD et al., Appellants.

Kouwenhoven v. *Gifford,* 143 App. Div. 913, appeal dismissed.
(Submitted October 4, 1911; decided October 24, 1911.)

APPEAL, by permission, from an order of the Appellate
Division of the Supreme Court in the second judicial

department, entered February 17, 1911, which affirmed an order of Special Term granting a motion for judgment upon the pleadings in an action to foreclose a mortgage.

The following questions were certified:

"*First.* In this action for the foreclosure of a purchase-money mortgage, in which no allegation of the complaint is denied, does the counterclaim for breach of covenant against incumbrances so put in issue the amount due plaintiff under the mortgage as to prevent the making of an order at Special Term directing judgment on the pleadings?

"*Second.* Is the appellant, mortgagor, entitled as a matter of right to a jury trial of the issues raised on her counterclaim for breach of covenant against incumbrances in this action to foreclose a purchase-money mortgage?

"*Third.* Does the failure of the plaintiff in this action to reply to the mortgagor's counterclaim for breach of a covenant against incumbrances so diminish the plaintiff's recovery as to prevent the court at Special Term from making an order directing judgment of foreclosure on the pleadings?"

Charles J. Katzenstein and *Gates Hamburger* for appellants.

James C. Van Siclen and *Edwin G. Wright* for respondent.

Appeal dismissed, with costs, on the authority of *Porter* v. *Int. Bridge Co.* (163 N. Y. 79) and *Guarantee Trust & S. D. Co.* v. *P., R. & N. E. R. R. Co.* (160 N. Y. 1); no opinion.

Concur: CULLEN, Ch. J., HAIGHT, VANN, WERNER. WILLARD BARTLETT, HISCOCK and CHASE, JJ.

In the Matter of the Application of the CITY OF NEW
YORK, Respondent, Relative to Acquiring Property
Required for an Extension to the Manhattan Terminal
of the New York and Brooklyn Bridge.

DAVID KEANE et al., as Executors of ANNA C. KEANE,
Deceased, Appellants.

Matter of City of New York (Manh. Terminal N. Y. & B. Bridge),
143 App. Div. 929, affirmed.

(Argued October 4, 1911; decided October 24, 1911.)

APPEAL from an order of the Appellate Division of
the Supreme Court in the first judicial department,
entered March 16, 1911, which affirmed an order of Special
Term confirming a report of commissioners of estimate
and appraisal in condemnation proceedings.

David Keane and *Morgan J. O'Brien* for appellants.

*Archibald R. Watson, Corporation Counsel (Terence
Farley* and *Charles D. Olendorf* of counsel), for respondent.

Order affirmed, with costs; no opinion.
Concur: CULLEN, Ch. J., HAIGHT, VANN, WERNER,
WILLARD BARTLETT, HISCOCK and CHASE, JJ.

THE PEOPLE OF THE STATE OF NEW YORK ex rel. MAN-
HATTAN-HUDSON REALTY COMPANY, Appellant, *v.*
CLARK WILLIAMS, as Comptroller of the State of New
York, Respondent.

People ex rel. Manhattan-Hudson Realty Co. v. Williams, 143 App.
Div. 972, affirmed.

(Submitted October 5, 1911; decided October 24, 1911.)

APPEAL from an order of the Appellate Division of
the Supreme Court in the third judicial department,
entered May 5, 1911, which confirmed, on certiorari, the

proceedings of defendant in assessing a franchise tax against the relator.

Alfred B. Thacher for appellant.

Thomas Carmody, Attorney-General (Irving D. Vann of counsel), for respondent.

Order affirmed, with costs; no opinion.
Concur: CULLEN, Ch. J., HAIGHT, VANN, WERNER, WILLARD BARTLETT, HISCOCK and CHASE, JJ.

DAVID J. KING et al., as Surviving Executors of and Trustees under the Will of EDWARD J. KING, Deceased, Plaintiffs, *v.* HERMAN M. BEERS, Appellant, and FISS, DOERR AND CARROLL HORSE COMPANY, Respondent, Impleaded with Others.

King v. *Beers*, 145 App. Div. 177, affirmed.
(Argued October 5, 1911; decided October 24, 1911.)

APPEAL from an order of the Appellate Division of the Supreme Court in the first judicial department, entered June 8, 1911, which reversed an order of Special Term confirming the report of a referee in surplus-money proceedings subsequent to the foreclosure of a mortgage upon real property.

Edward S. Seidman, Henry Wollman, Benjamin F. Wollman and *Robert G. Starr* for appellant.

Martin Conboy and *Frank A. Clary* for respondent.

Order affirmed, with costs; no opinion.
Concur: CULLEN, Ch. J., HAIGHT, VANN, WERNER, WILLARD BARTLETT, HISCOCK and CHASE, JJ.

MANUFACTURERS' COMMERCIAL COMPANY, Suing in Its Own Behalf and in Behalf of Other Creditors of NEW-FOUNDLAND SYNDICATE, Appellant, *v.* AUGUST HECK-SCHER et al., as Copartners, Constituting the Firm of J. M. CEBALLOS & COMPANY et al., Respondents.

Manufacturers' Commercial Co. v. *Heckscher*, **144 App. Div. 601,** affirmed.

(Argued October 5, 1911; decided October 24, 1911.)

APPEAL, by permission, from an order of the Appellate Division of the Supreme Court in the first judicial department, entered July 14, 1911, which reversed an interlocutory judgment of Special Term overruling demurrers to the complaint and sustained such demurrers in a creditor's action against stockholders of the Newfoundland Syndicate who, it was alleged, had procured their stock for less than par.

The following questions were certified:

"*First.* Does the complaint herein state facts sufficient to constitute a cause of action in favor of the plaintiff against any of the defendants?

"*Second.* Does it appear upon the face of the complaint herein that the plaintiff has not legal capacity to sue, in that suit can be brought only in the right of the trustee in bankruptcy of Newfoundland Syndicate, for the benefit of said syndicate's creditors and for the benefit of the estate in bankruptcy?"

Elbridge L. Adams and *Nelson S. Spencer* for appellant.

Francis D. Pollak and *Justus P. Sheffield* for respondents.

Order affirmed, with costs, on opinion of DOWLING, J., below. First question certified answered in the negative; second question not answered.

Concur: CULLEN, Ch. J., HAIGHT, VANN, WERNER, WILLARD BARTLETT, HISCOCK and CHASE, JJ.

In the Matter of the Petition of the SOUTHFIELD BEACH
RAILROAD COMPANY, Appellant, for the Condemnation
of Certain Property.

ROBERT W. BARNES et al., Respondents.

Matter of Southfield Beach R. R. Co., 145 App. Div. 988, affirmed.
(Argued October 6, 1911; decided October 24, 1911.)

APPEAL from an order of the Appellate Division of
the Supreme Court in the second judicial department,
entered June 16, 1911, which modified and affirmed as
modified an order of Special Term confirming the report
of commissioners in condemnation proceedings.

Harold Russell Griffith, Adrian H. Larkin and *Lewis
H. Freedman* for appellant.

John Brooks Leavitt and *Stuart G. Gibboney* for
respondents.

Order affirmed, with costs, on authority of *Philadelphia,
R. & N. E. R. R. Co.* v. *Bowman* (23 App. Div. 170); no
opinion.

Concur: CULLEN, Ch. J., HAIGHT, WERNER, WILLARD
BARTLETT, HISCOCK and CHASE, JJ. Absent: VANN, J.

THE PEOPLE OF THE STATE OF NEW YORK ex rel. JOHN
W. LISK, Appellant, *v.* THE BOARD OF EDUCATION OF
THE CITY OF NEW YORK, Respondent.

People ex rel. Lisk v. *Bd. of Education, New York City*, 143 App.
Div. 932, affirmed.
(Submitted October 6, 1911; decided October 24, 1911.)

APPEAL from an order of the Appellate Division of the
Supreme Court in the first judicial department, entered
March 24, 1911, which dismissed a writ of certiorari

36

and affirmed the proceedings of defendant in dismissing the relator from the position of inspector of fuel in the bureau of supplies of the department of education of the city of New York.

William Armstrong for appellant.

Archibald R. Watson, Corporation Counsel (Terence Farley and *Charles McIntyre* of counsel), for respondent.

Order affirmed, without costs; no opinion.
Concur: CULLEN, Ch. J., HAIGHT, WERNER, WILLARD BARTLETT, HISCOCK and CHASE, JJ. Absent: VANN, J.

In the Matter of Proving the Will of CHARLES A. COUTANT, Deceased.

MARGARET B. COUTANT, Appellant; JENNIE C. MASON, Respondent.

Matter of Coutant (Will), 145 App. Div. 918, affirmed.
(Argued October 3, 1911; decided October 24, 1911.)

APPEAL from an order of the Appellate Division of the Supreme Court in the first judicial department, entered June 23, 1911, which affirmed a decree of the New York County Surrogate's Court admitting to probate the will of Charles A. Coutant, deceased.

Henry A. Foster for appellant.

Charles E. Travis, Benjamin L. Blauvelt, Adolph Bloch and *Henry Bloch* for respondent.

Order affirmed, with costs; no opinion.
Concur: CULLEN, Ch. J., HAIGHT, WERNER, WILLARD BARTLETT, HISCOCK and CHASE, JJ. Absent: VANN, J.

THE PEOPLE OF THE STATE OF NEW YORK ex rel.
GEORGE A. MENCKE, Appellant, *v.* WILLIAM F. BAKER,
as Police Commissioner of the City of New York,
Respondent.

People ex rel. Mencke v. *Baker,* 143 App. Div. 940, affirmed.
(Argued October 6, 1911; decided October 24, 1911.)

APPEAL from an order of the Appellate Division of
the Supreme Court in the second judicial department,
entered March 10, 1911, which affirmed the determination of the police commissioner of the city of New York
in dismissing the relator from the position of patrolman
in the police department of said city.

Jacob Rouss and *Louis J. Grant* for appellant.

*Archibald R. Watson, Corporation Counsel (James
D. Bell* of counsel), for respondent.

Order affirmed, with costs, on authority of *People ex
rel. McCormack* v. *McClave* (29 N. Y. S. R. 368; affd.,
121 N. Y. 710); no opinion.

Concur: CULLEN, Ch. J., HAIGHT, WERNER, WILLARD
BARTLETT, HISCOCK and CHASE, JJ. Absent: VANN, J.

In the Matter of the Application of ADA M. MORSE,
Respondent, to Alter a Highway in the Towns of
Monroe and Chester.

THE TOWN OF CHESTER, Appellant.

Matter of Morse, 145 App. Div. 936, affirmed.
(Argued October 6, 1911; decided October 24, 1911.)

APPEAL from an order of the Appellate Division of the
Supreme Court in the second judicial department, entered
June 12, 1911, which affirmed an order of the Orange
County Court confirming the report of commissioners of
appraisal appointed in a proceeding to alter a highway.

Henry Bacon for appellant.

M. N. Kane for respondent.

Order affirmed, with costs; no opinion.
Concur: CULLEN, Ch. J., HAIGHT, VANN, WERNER, WILLARD BARTLETT, HISCOCK and CHASE, JJ.

THE PEOPLE OF THE STATE OF NEW YORK ex rel. THE NEWBURGH NEWS PRINTING AND PUBLISHING COMPANY, Appellant, *v.* THE BOARD OF SUPERVISORS OF ORANGE COUNTY, Respondent.

People ex rel. Newburgh News P. & P. Co. v. Bd. Supervisors, 140 App. Div. 227, affirmed.
(Argued October 6, 1911; decided October 24, 1911.)

APPEAL from an order of the Appellate Division of the Supreme Court in the second judicial department, entered November 25, 1910, which quashed a writ of certiorari and affirmed the proceedings of the defendant in auditing a claim of the relator.

Henry Bacon for appellant.

M. N. Kane and *J. F. Halstead* for respondent.

Order affirmed, with costs; no opinion.
Concur: CULLEN, Ch. J., HAIGHT, WERNER, WILLARD BARTLETT, HISCOCK and CHASE, JJ. Absent: VANN, J.

In the Matter of the Application of the CITY OF NEW YORK, Respondent, Relative to Acquiring Title to Land Required for the Opening of Jerome Avenue, Extending from Woodlawn Road to Mosholu Avenue, in the Borough of the Bronx.

WOODLAWN CEMETERY, Appellant.

Matter of City of New York (Jerome Avenue), 145 App. Div. 865, affirmed.
(Argued October 9, 1911; decided October 24, 1911.)

APPEAL from an order of the Appellate Division of the Supreme Court in the first judicial department, entered

July 7, 1911, which affirmed an order of Special Term confirming the report of commissioners of estimate and assessment in a street opening proceeding.

Benjamin Trapnell and *Joseph A. Flannery* for appellant.

Archibald R. Watson, Corporation Counsel (Joel J. Squier and *James Regan Fitz Gerald* of counsel), for respondent.

Order affirmed, with costs; no opinion.

Concur: CULLEN, Ch. J., VANN, WERNER, WILLARD BARTLETT, HISCOCK, CHASE and COLLIN, JJ.

THE PEOPLE OF THE STATE OF NEW YORK ex rel. BUF-FALO AND LAKE ERIE TRACTION COMPANY, Respondent, *v.* EGBURT E. WOODBURY et al., Composing the State Board of Tax Commissioners, Appellants.

People ex rel. Buffalo & L. E. Traction Co. v. *Woodbury,* 144 App. Div. 812, affirmed.

(Argued October 9, 1911; decided October 24, 1911.)

APPEAL from an order of the Appellate Division of the Supreme Court in the third judicial department, entered June 15, 1911, which annulled, on certiorari, a determination of the state board of tax commissioners as to the relative portion of a mortgage covering property both within and without the state, taxable under the Mortgage Tax Law.

Thomas Carmody, Attorney-General (Irving D. Vann of counsel), for appellants.

Daniel J. Kenefick and *Howard S. Jones* for respondent.

Order affirmed, with costs, on opinion of HOUGHTON, J., below.

Concur: CULLEN, Ch. J., VANN, WERNER, WILLARD

WILHELM ALBRECHT, Respondent, *v.* ROCHESTER, SYRA-
CUSE AND EASTERN RAILROAD COMPANY, Appellant.

Albrecht v. *Rochester, Syr. & E. R. R. Co.*, 136 App. Div. 914,
affirmed.
(Argued October 9, 1911; decided October 24, 1911.)

APPEAL from a judgment of the Appellate Division of
the Supreme Court in the fourth judicial department,
entered January 29, 1910, affirming a judgment in favor
of plaintiff entered upon a verdict in an action to recover
for personal injuries alleged to have been sustained
through the negligence of defendant.

Ernest I. Edgcomb for appellant.

Percival De Witt Oviatt for respondent.

Judgment affirmed, with costs; no opinion.
Concur: CULLEN, Ch. J., VANN, WERNER, WILLARD
BARTLETT and CHASE, JJ. Not voting: HISCOCK and
COLLIN, JJ.

CHARLES E. BULKLEY, Respondent, *v.* WHITING MANU-
FACTURING COMPANY, Appellant.

Bulkley v. *Whiting Manfg. Co.*, 132 App. Div. 929, affirmed.
(Argued October 10, 1911; decided October 24, 1911.)

APPEAL from a judgment of the Appellate Division of
the Supreme Court in the first judicial department, entered
July 16, 1909, affirming a judgment in favor of plaintiff
entered upon a verdict dismissing defendant's counterclaim for funds alleged to have been unlawfully appropriated by plaintiff while acting as president of the
defendant company.

J. Noble Hayes for appellant.

Ralph S. Rounds for respondent.

Judgment affirmed, with costs, on the ground that the plaintiff's motion for the direction of a verdict in his favor should have been granted; no opinion.

Concur: VANN, WERNER, WILLARD BARTLETT and CHASE, JJ.

CULLEN, Ch. J., HISCOCK and COLLIN, JJ. (dissenting). We are all of the opinion that there is but one question in this case, whether the unpaid salary of the treasurer, Salisbury, had been relinquished by him, or whether it remained a valid claim against the company. A majority of the court think that, as a matter of law, on the evidence it was not relinquished; that, therefore, the plaintiff was entitled to the direction of a verdict, and that the errors in the submission of the case to the jury were immaterial. We are of opinion that the relinquishment by Salisbury of the salary was a question of fact to be determined by the jury.

GUILLAUME REUSENS, Appellant and Respondent, *v.* OLIVER M. ARKENBURGH, Respondent and Appellant.

Reusens v. *Arkenburgh*, 138 App. Div. 908, affirmed.
(Argued October 10, 1911; decided October 24, 1911.)

CROSS-APPEALS from a judgment of the Appellate Division of the Supreme Court in the first judicial department, entered May 24, 1910, affirming a judgment in favor of plaintiff entered upon a verdict directed by the court in an action to recover upon an account stated.

Edgar J. Nathan for plaintiff, appellant and respondent.

Herman B. Goodstein and *Harry A. Gordon* for defendant, respondent and appellant.

Judgment affirmed, without costs; no opinion.
Concur: CULLEN, Ch. J., WERNER, WILLARD BARTLETT, HISCOCK, CHASE and COLLIN, JJ. Absent: VANN, J.

HARGRAVES MILLS, Respondent, *v.* WILLIAM S. GORDON, Appellant.

Hargraves Mills v. *Gordon*, 137 App. Div. 695, affirmed.
(Argued October 10, 1911; decided October 24, 1911.)

APPEAL from an order of the Appellate Division of the Supreme Court in the first judicial department, entered April 8, 1910, reversing a judgment in favor of plaintiff entered upon a verdict and granting a new trial in an action on contract.

Charles E. Rushmore and *Walter D. Clark* for appellant.

Wallace Macfarlane, Charles O. Brewster and *S. J. Rosensohn* for respondent.

Order affirmed and judgment absolute ordered against appellant on the stipulation, with costs in all courts; no opinion.

Concur: CULLEN, Ch. J., VANN, WERNER, WILLARD BARTLETT, HISCOCK, CHASE and COLLIN, JJ.

EDWARD P. FLOYD-JONES, Respondent, *v.* ESTHER SCHAAN, Appellant.

Floyd-Jones v. *Schaan*, 129 App. Div. 82, appeal dismissed.
(Submitted October 16, 1911; decided October 24, 1911.)

APPEAL, by permission, from an order of the Appellate Division of the Supreme Court in the first judicial department, entered December 11, 1908, which affirmed a determination of the Appellate Term reversing a judgment of the Municipal Court of the city of New York entered upon a verdict in favor of defendant and granting a new trial.

Arleigh Pelham for appellant.

Louis W. Stotesbury for respondent.

Per Curiam. This action was brought in the Municipal Court of the city of New York to recover for rent and in that court the defendant succeeded, procuring a judgment in her favor on the issues there tried, with costs against the plaintiff. An appeal was taken to the Appellate Term from the judgment, no motion for a new trial being made. The Appellate Term reversed the judgment so appealed from and ordered a new trial, with costs to the appellant to abide the event. From this order and judgment a further appeal was taken by permission to the Appellate Division, a stipulation being given by the appellant that if the order so appealed from should be affirmed or the appeal dismissed judgment absolute should be rendered against her. While there may be some question whether under such provisions as we have been able to find on that subject appellant could be required to give this stipulation for judgment absolute, that question is immaterial on this appeal. The appellant gave the stipulation without question and the respondent did not take advantage of it. The only order or judgment entered on the decision of the Appellate Division which affirmed that of the Appellate Term was one "that said determination so appealed from be and the same is hereby affirmed, with * * * costs to the said plaintiff as against the said defendant." This was not a judgment absolute against the defendant, but simply an affirmance of the order of the Appellate Term reversing the judgment of the Municipal Court and granting a new trial. Permission was granted by the Appellate Division to appeal to this court, but no stipulation was given by the appellant as required by section 190, subdivision 1, requiring that on an appeal from an order granting a new trial the appellant must stipulate that on affirmance judgment absolute shall be rendered against him.

Under these circumstances, although the respondent has not considered this question, we think that our only course is to dismiss the appeal, with costs.

CULLEN, Ch. J., GRAY, WERNER, WILLARD BARTLETT, HISCOCK, CHASE and COLLIN, JJ., concur.

A al dismissed.

In the Matter of the Application of the CITY OF NEW YORK,
Relative to Acquiring Title to Lands Required for the
Opening of Van Alst Avenue, in the Borough of Queens.

JOHN CARTLEDGE et al., Co-partners under the Firm
Name of JOSEPH WILD & COMPANY, Appellants ; THE
CITY OF NEW YORK et al., Respondents.

Matter of City of New York (*Van Alst Ave.*), 143 App. Div. 564,
affirmed.
(Argued October 4, 1911; decided October 31, 1911.)

APPEAL from an order of the Appellate Division of the
Supreme Court in the second judicial department, entered
March 24, 1911, which affirmed an order of Special Term
confirming the report of commissioners in street opening
proceedings.

Hartwell P. Heath, Arthur C. Bostwick and *R. A.
Mansfield Hobbs* for appellants.

Archibald R. Watson, Corporation Counsel (*Joel J.
Squier* and *William B. R. Faber* of counsel), and *Clarence
Edwards* for respondents.

Order affirmed, with costs; no opinion.
Concur: HAIGHT, VANN, WERNER, WILLARD BARTLETT,
HISCOCK and CHASE, JJ. Not voting: CULLEN, Ch. J.

In the Matter of the Application of the CITY OF NEW
YORK, Relative to Acquiring Title to Lands Required
for the Opening of West One Hundred and Seventy-
seventh Street, from Amsterdam Avenue to St. Nicholas
Avenue, in the Borough of Manhattan.

MEYER A. BERNHEIMER, Appellant; THE CITY OF NEW
YORK et al., Respondents.

Matter of City of New York (*West 177th Street*), 145 App. Div. 913,
affirmed.
(Submitted October 5, 1911; decided October 31, 1911.)

APPEAL from an order of the Appellate Division of the
Supreme Court in the first judicial department, entered

June 23, 1911, which affirmed an order of Special Term confirming the report of commissioners in street opening proceedings.

Harry G. Smith for appellant.

Archibald R. Watson, Corporation Counsel (Joel J. Squier, Samuel J. Benson and *Frederick W. Gahrmann* of counsel), and *L. C. Dessar,* for respondents.

Order affirmed, with costs; no opinion.

Concur: HAIGHT, VANN, WERNER, HISCOCK and CHASE, JJ. Not voting: CULLEN, Ch. J., and WILLARD BARTLETT, J.

GEORGE DEIS, SON AND COMPANY, Respondent, *v.* HENRY HART, Appellant.

Deis, Son & Co. v. *Hart,* 134 App. Div. 994, affirmed.
(Argued October 11, 1911; decided October 31, 1911.)

APPEAL from a judgment of the Appellate Division of the Supreme Court in the fourth judicial department, entered November 17, 1909, affirming a judgment in favor of plaintiff entered upon the report of a referee in an action to recover for goods alleged to have been sold and delivered.

Walter Welch for appellant.

A. B. Steele and *William Witherstine* for respondent.

Judgment affirmed, with costs; no opinion.

Concur: CULLEN, Ch. J., VANN, WERNER, WILLARD BARTLETT, HISCOCK, CHASE and COLLIN, JJ.

NATHANIEL L. CARPENTER et al., Appellants, *v.* GEORGE W. HOADLEY, Respondent, Impleaded with Another.

Carpenter v. *Maloney,* 138 App. Div. 190, affirmed.
(Argued October 11, 1911; decided October 31, 1911.)

APPEAL from a judgment of the Appellate Division of the Supreme Court in the first judicial department, entered

May 18, 1910, upon an order reversing a judgment in favor of plaintiffs entered upon a verdict directed by the court and directing judgment in favor of defendant in an action to recover on two promissory notes.

Edmund L. Mooney, Frederick A. Card and *Lawrence A. Sullivan* for appellants.

John H. McCrahon and *Ralph Polk Buell* for respondent.

Judgment affirmed, with costs; no opinion.
Concur: CULLEN, Ch. J., VANN, WERNER, WILLARD BARTLETT, HISCOCK, CHASE and COLLIN, JJ.

JENNIE E. SMITH, Respondent, *v.* THE ULSTER AND DELAWARE RAILROAD COMPANY, Appellant.

Smith v. *Ulster & Delaware R. R. Co.,* 137 App. Div. 935, affirmed. (Argued October 11, 1911; decided October 31, 1911.)

APPEAL from a judgment of the Appellate Division of the Supreme Court in the third judicial department, entered March 29, 1910, modifying and affirming as modified a judgment in favor of plaintiff entered upon a verdict in an action to recover for personal injuries alleged to have been sustained through the negligence of defendant.

H. H. Fleming and *Amos Van Etten* for appellant.

A. L. Kellogg for respondent.

Judgment affirmed, with costs; no opinion.
Concur: CULLEN, Ch. J., VANN, WERNER, WILLARD BARTLETT, HISCOCK, CHASE and COLLIN, JJ.

WILLIAM E. PEASE, Respondent, *v.* PENNSYLVANIA RAILROAD COMPANY, Appellant.

Pease v. *Pennsylvania R. R. Co.*, 137 App. Div. 458, 929, affirmed.
(Argued October 12, 1911; decided October 31, 1911.)

APPEAL from a judgment of the Appellate Division of the Supreme Court in the fourth judicial department, entered March 16, 1910, affirming a judgment in favor of plaintiff entered upon a verdict in an action to recover for personal injuries alleged to have been sustained through the negligence of defendant.

Ernest C. Whitbeck and *Frank Rumsey* for appellant.

George D. Forsyth for respondent.

Judgment affirmed, with costs; no opinion.
Concur; CULLEN, Ch. J., VANN, WERNER, WILLARD BARTLETT, HISCOCK, CHASE and COLLIN, JJ.

REBECCA I. GOLDSMITH, Appellant, *v.* MORITZ TOLK, Respondent.

Goldsmith v. *Tolk*, 138 App. Div. 287, affirmed.
(Argued October 13, 1911; decided October 31, 1911.)

APPEAL from a judgment entered June 4, 1910, upon an order of the Appellate Division of the Supreme Court in the first judicial department, which affirmed an interlocutory judgment of Special Term sustaining a demurrer to the complaint in an action to compel specific performance of an alleged contract.

Henry C. Burnstine for appellant.

Nathan Tolk for respondent.

Judgment affirmed, with costs; no opinion.
Concur: CULLEN, Ch. J., VANN, WERNER, WILLARD BARTLETT, HISCOCK, CHASE and COLLIN, JJ.

VOGEL & BINDER COMPANY, Appellant, *v.* WILLIAM J. MONTGOMERY et al., Respondents, and CHARLES P. EVANS COMPANY et al., Appellants.

Vogel & Binder Co. v. *Montgomery*, 139 App. Div. 926, affirmed.
(Argued October 13, 1911; decided October 31, 1911.)

APPEAL from a judgment of the Appellate Division of the Supreme Court in the fourth judicial department, entered June 11, 1910, affirming a judgment in favor of defendant respondents entered upon a decision of the court on trial at Special Term in an action to foreclose a mechanic's lien.

C. C. Werner, Frederick M. Whitney and *Albert H. Stearns* for appellants.

W. C. Carroll, George Y. Webster and *Hiram R. Wood* for respondents.

Judgment affirmed, with one bill of costs against appellants; no opinion.

Concur: CULLEN, Ch. J., VANN, WILLARD BARTLETT, HISCOCK, CHASE and COLLIN, JJ. Not sitting: WERNER, J.

KATHRYN O'REILLY, Doing Business under the Name of T. P. GALLIGAN'S SONS, Appellant, *v.* PATRICK GALLAGHER, Respondent, Impleaded with Others.

O'Reilly v. *Gallagher*, 138 App. Div. 907, affirmed.
(Submitted October 13, 1911; decided October 31, 1911.)

APPEAL from a judgment of the Appellate Division of the Supreme Court in the first judicial department, entered May 25, 1910, affirming a judgment in favor of defendant entered upon a decision of the court on trial at Special Term in an action to foreclose a mechanic's lien.

Adrian T. Kiernan for appellant.

Louis B. Hasbrouck and *Frederick J. Moses* for respondent.

Judgment affirmed, with costs; no opinion.
Concur: CULLEN, Ch. J., VANN, WERNER, WILLARD BARTLETT, HISCOCK, CHASE and COLLIN, JJ.

JAMES THEDFORD, Appellant, *v.* HENRY L. HERBERT, Respondent.

Thedford v. *Herbert*, 139 App. Div. 903, reversed.
(Argued October 16, 1911; decided October 31, 1911.)

APPEAL from a judgment of the Appellate Division of the Supreme Court in the first judicial department, entered June 16, 1910, affirming a judgment in favor of defendant entered upon a dismissal of the complaint by the court at a Trial Term in an action to recover for an alleged breach of contract.

George H. Fletcher and *James H. Richards* for appellant.

Lyman E. Warren for respondent.

Judgment reversed and new trial granted, costs to abide event, on opinion rendered on previous appeal. (195 N. Y. 63.)
Concur: CULLEN, Ch. J., GRAY, WERNER, WILLARD BARTLETT, HISCOCK, CHASE and COLLIN, JJ.

ELLIS P. EARLE, Respondent, *v.* LLOYD G. McCRUM, Appellant.

Earle v. *McCrum*, 138 App. Div. 909, affirmed.
(Argued October 16, 1911; decided October 31, 1911.)

APPEAL from a judgment of the Appellate Division of the Supreme Court in the first judicial department,

entered May 31. 1910, affirming a judgment in favor of plaintiff entered upon a verdict directed by the court in an action to recover upon a promissory note.

William P. Maloney for appellant.

Richard T. Greene and *George F. Hurd* for respondent.

Judgment affirmed, with costs; no opinion.
Concur: CULLEN, Ch. J., GRAY, WERNER, WILLARD BARTLETT, HISCOCK, CHASE and COLLIN, JJ.

HENRY WALDER, Respondent, *v.* BRIDGET ENGLISH, Appellant.

Walder v. *English*, 137 App. Div. 43, affirmed.
(Argued October 17, 1911; decided October 31, 1911.)

APPEAL from a judgment of the Appellate Division of the Supreme Court in the second judicial department, entered April 6, 1910, affirming a judgment in favor of plaintiff entered upon a verdict in an action to recover damages arising from an alleged breach of a lease.

Joseph W. Middlebrook and *Ellery E. Albee* for appellant.

Walter G. C. Otto and *Michael J. Tierney* for respondent.

Judgment affirmed, with costs; no opinion.
Concur: CULLEN, Ch. J., GRAY, WERNER, WILLARD BARTLETT, HISCOCK, CHASE and COLLIN, JJ.

JULIAN PRZECZEWSKI, Respondent, *v.* JOSEPH BARDSLEY et al., Composing the Firm of BARDSLEY BROTHERS, Appellants.

Przeczewski v. *Bardsley*, 138 App. Div. 907, affirmed.
(Argued October 17, 1911; decided October 31, 1911.)

APPEAL, by permission, from a judgment of the Appellate Division of the Supreme Court in the first judicial department, entered May 21, 1910, affirming a judgment in favor of plaintiff entered upon a verdict in an action to recover for personal injuries alleged to have been sustained by plaintiff through the negligence of defendants, his employers.

Orlando P. Metcalf and *Herbert Noble* for appellants.

Julius Hilbern Cohn for respondent.

Judgment affirmed, with costs; no opinion.

Concur: CULLEN, Ch. J., GRAY, WERNER, WILLARD BARTLETT, HISCOCK, CHASE and COLLIN, JJ.

WILLIAM S. ANDERSON et al., Appellants, *v.* NEW YORK AND HARLEM RAILROAD COMPANY et al., Respondents.

Anderson v. *N. Y. & Harlem R. R. Co.*, 136 App. Div. 939, affirmed.

(Argued October 17, 1911; decided October 31, 1911.)

APPEAL from a judgment of the Appellate Division of the Supreme Court in the first judicial department, entered April 25, 1910, affirming a judgment in favor of defendants entered upon a dismissal of the complaint by the court on trial at Special Term in an action to obtain a judicial determination that the defendant Wheeler is a trustee for the benefit of the plaintiffs of all damages, fee and rental, sustained through the maintenance and use of the viaduct on Park avenue in front of certain property by the defendant railroad companies; for an injunction restraining the defendant Wheeler and the defendant railroad companies from settling as between themselves the claims for said damages, and for an injunction restraining the defendant railroad companies from maintaining and using said viaduct until they pay the plaintiffs the fee damages to be fixed by the court.

L. M. Berkeley for appellants.

Horace E. Deming for Everett P. Wheeler, respondent.

Alexander S. Lyman, Ira A. Place and *William Greenough* for New York and Harlem Railroad Company et al., respondents.

Judgment affirmed, with costs; no opinion.

Concur: CULLEN, Ch. J., WERNER, WILLARD BARTLETT, HISCOCK, CHASE and COLLIN, JJ. Not sitting: GRAY, J.

JOHN HATTEN, Respondent, *v.* HYDE-MCFARLIN COMPANY, Appellant.

Hatten v. *Hyde-McFarlin Co.*, 137 App. Div. 932, affirmed.
(Argued October 17, 1911; decided October 31, 1911.)

APPEAL from a judgment of the Appellate Division of the Supreme Court in the fourth judicial department, entered April 12, 1910, affirming a judgment in favor of plaintiff entered upon a verdict in an action to recover for personal injuries alleged to have been sustained by plaintiff through the negligence of defendant, his employer.

Clinton B. Gibbs for appellant.

Hamilton Ward for respondent.

Judgment affirmed, with costs; no opinion.

Concur: CULLEN, Ch. J., GRAY, WERNER, WILLARD BARTLETT, HISCOCK, CHASE and COLLIN, JJ.

WILLIAM HECHT, Respondent. *v.* A. G. HYDE & SONS, Appellant.

Hecht v. *Hyde & Sons*, 139 App. Div. 902, affirmed.
(Argued October 17, 1911; decided October 31, 1911.)

APPEAL from a judgment of the Appellate Division of the Supreme Court in the first judicial department,

entered June 21, 1910, affirming a judgment in favor of plaintiff entered upon a verdict in an action to recover for an alleged breach of contract.

James J. Allen for appellant.

Morgan J. O'Brien, Samson Lachman and *Morton Stein* for respondent.

Judgment affirmed, with costs; no opinion.
Concur: CULLEN, Ch. J., GRAY, WERNER, WILLARD BARTLETT, HISCOCK, CHASE and COLLIN, JJ.

GARDINER'S BAY COMPANY, Appellant, *v.* ATLANTIC FERTILIZER AND OIL COMPANY, Respondent.

Gardiner's Bay Co. v. *Atlantic Fertilizer & Oil Co.*, 139 App. Div. 913, modified.
(Argued October 17, 1911; decided October 31, 1911.)

. APPEAL from a judgment of the Appellate Division of the Supreme Court in the second judicial department, entered June 27, 1910, affirming a judgment in favor of defendant entered upon a dismissal of the complaint by the court on trial at Special Term in an action to restrain the defendant from so operating a fish factory as to constitute an alleged nuisance.

Percy L. Housel for appellant.

Nathan D. Stern for respondent.

Judgment modified by striking therefrom award of extra allowance, and as modified affirmed, without costs to either party; no opinion.
Concur: CULLEN, Ch. J., GRAY, WERNER, WILLARD BARTLETT, HISCOCK, CHASE and COLLIN, JJ.

FLORENZ ZIEGFELD, JR., Respondent, *v.* NORA B.
NORWORTH et al., Appellants.

(Submitted October 23, 1911; decided October 31, 1911.)

Motion for re-argument of motion to dismiss appeal
denied, with ten dollars costs. (See 202 N. Y. 580.)

ABRAHAM LEAVITT, Appellant, *v.* HENRY DE VRIES,
Respondent.

Leavitt v. *De Vries*, 133 App. Div. 893, affirmed.
(Argued October 18, 1911; decided November 3, 1911.)

APPEAL from a judgment of the Appellate Division of
the Supreme Court in the first judicial department,
entered November 15, 1909, affirming a judgment in
favor of defendant entered upon a dismissal of the complaint by the court at a Trial Term in an action on contract.

I. M. Dittenhoefer for appellant.

S. Livingston Samuels and *Isaac Fromme* for
respondent.

Judgment affirmed, with costs; no opinion.
Concur: CULLEN, Ch. J., GRAY, WERNER, WILLARD
BARTLETT, HISCOCK, CHASE and COLLIN, JJ.

THE NATIONAL CONDUIT AND CABLE COMPANY, Respondent, *v.* THE COMMERCIAL UNION ASSURANCE COMPANY,
LIMITED, Appellant.

National Conduit & Cable Co. v. *Commercial Union Assur. Co.*,
135 App. Div. 136, affirmed.
(Argued October 18, 1911; decided November 3, 1911.)

APPEAL from a judgment, entered January 25, 1910,
upon an order of the Appellate Division of the Supreme

Court in the first judicial department, which reversed a judgment in favor of defendant entered upon the report of a referee and directed judgment in favor of the plaintiff in an action to recover upon a policy of fire insurance.

Frederick B. Campbell, John F. Devlin and *Paul C. Whipp* for appellant.

Clarence G. Galston and *Arthur Watson* for respondent.

Judgment affirmed, with costs, on opinion of CLARK, J., below; no opinion.

Concur: CULLEN, Ch. J., GRAY, WERNER and WILLARD BARTLETT, JJ. Dissenting: HISCOCK, CHASE and COLLIN, JJ.

CHARLES McMICHAEL, Respondent, *v.* FEDERAL PRINTING COMPANY, Appellant.

McMichael v. *Federal Printing Co.*, 139 App. Div. 225, affirmed. (Argued October 18, 1911; decided November 3, 1911.)

APPEAL from a judgment of the Appellate Division of the Supreme Court in the second judicial department, entered June 27, 1910, affirming a judgment in favor of plaintiff entered upon a verdict in an action to recover for personal injuries alleged to have been sustained by plaintiff through the negligence of defendant, his employer.

William N. Cohen, C. H. Duell, R. W. France and *F. P. Warfield* for appellant.

D-Cady Herrick for respondent.

Judgment affirmed, with costs; no opinion.

Concur: CULLEN, Ch. J., GRAY, WERNER, WILLARD BARTLETT, HISCOCK, CHASE and COLLIN, JJ.

CHARLES SCHMEISER, Appellant, *v.* MONTAGUE LESSLER,
Respondent.

Schmeiser v. *Lessler*, 139 App. Div. 914, affirmed.
(Argued October 19, 1911; decided November 3, 1911.)

APPEAL from a judgment of the Appellate Division of
the Supreme Court in the second judicial department,
entered June 23, 1910, affirming a judgment in favor of
defendant entered upon a dismissal of the complaint by
the court at a Trial Term in an action for libel.

Harry K. Jacobs and *Reno R. Billington* for appellant.

Leonard J. Obermeier for respondent.

Judgment affirmed, with costs; no opinion.
Concur: CULLEN, Ch. J., GRAY, WERNER, WILLARD
BARTLETT, HISCOCK, CHASE and COLLIN, JJ.

MICHAEL BARTHOLOMA, Respondent, *v.* THE TOWN OF
FLORENCE, Appellant.

Bartholoma v. *Town of Florence*, 136 App. Div. 906, affirmed.
(Argued October 19, 1911; decided November 3, 1911.)

APPEAL from a judgment of the Appellate Division of
the Supreme Court in the fourth judicial department,
entered December 3, 1909, affirming a judgment in favor
of plaintiff entered upon a verdict in an action to recover
for personal injuries alleged to have been sustained by
plaintiff through the negligence of defendant in failing
to keep its highways in repair.

William S. Mackie for appellant.

Albert T. Wilkinson for respondent.

Judgment affirmed, with costs, on the ground that the
evidence presented a question of fact for the jury; no
opinion.
Concur: CULLEN, Ch. J., GRAY, WERNER, WILLARD
BARTLETT, HISCOCK, CHASE and COLLIN, JJ.

WILLIAM B. BIRD et al., Constituting the Firm of J. A. & W. BIRD & COMPANY, Respondents, *v.* THE CASEIN COMPANY OF AMERICA, Appellant.

THE ALDEN SPEARE'S SONS COMPANY, Respondent, *v.* THE CASEIN COMPANY OF AMERICA, Appellant.

Bird v. *Casein Co. of America*, 187 App. Div. 918, affirmed.
Speare's Sons Co. v. *Casein Co. of America*, 137 App. Div. 918, affirmed.
(Argued October 19, 1911; decided November 3, 1911.)

APPEAL, in each of the above-entitled actions, from a judgment of the Appellate Division of the Supreme Court in the first judicial department, entered March 16, 1910, affirming a judgment in favor of plaintiffs entered upon a verdict in an action on contract.

Charles J. Hardy, George J. Gillespie, William F. Delaney and *Frederick P. Whitaker* for appellant.

William S. Haskell for respondents.

Judgment in each case affirmed, with costs; no opinion.
Concur: CULLEN, Ch. J., GRAY, WERNER, WILLARD BARTLETT, HISCOCK, CHASE and COLLIN, JJ.

CHARLES J. VOGT et al., as Surviving Partners of the Firm of BUFFALO GALVANIZING AND TINNING WORKS, Respondents, *v.* EDGAR M. HAYMAN et al., as Surviving Partners of the Firm of MICHAEL HAYMAN AND COMPANY, Appellants.

Vogt v. *Hayman*, 136 App. Div. 912, affirmed.
(Submitted October 20, 1911; decided November 3, 1911.)

APPEAL from a judgment of the Appellate Division of the Supreme Court in the fourth judicial department, entered January 14, 1910, affirming a judgment in favor of plaintiffs entered upon a verdict directed by the court in an action to recover for an alleged breach of contract of sale.

George E. Pierce for appellants.

George A. Lewis for respondents.

Judgment affirmed, with costs; no opinion.
Concui: CULLEN, Ch. J., GRAY, WERNER, WILLARD BARTLETT, HISCOCK, CHASE and COLLIN, JJ.

LOUIS SMYTH et al., as Administrators with the Will Annexed of HUGH SMITH, Deceased, Appellants, *v.* THE CITY OF NEW YORK et al., Respondents.

(Submitted October 30, 1911; decided November 3, 1911.)

MOTION to amend remittitur by respondent City of New York. (See 203 N. Y. 106.)

Motion denied, without costs. Where an award of costs on appeal is made to several respondents, each respondent is entitled to tax his disbursements as part of the bill of costs, and on its payment each party is entitled to the amount of his disbursements as taxed and the allowance should be divided equally between all the parties.

ATLANTIC DREDGING COMPANY, Respondent, *v.* WILLIAM BEARD et al., as Directors of THE W. H. BEARD DREDGING COMPANY et al., Defendants, and WILLIAM BEARD, Appellant.

Atlantic Dredging Co. v. Beard, 145 App. Div. 342, affirmed.
(Argued October 5, 1911; decided November 3, 1911.)

APPEAL, by permission, from an order of the Appellate Division of the Supreme Court in the first judicial department, entered June 23, 1911, which affirmed an order of

Special Term granting a motion for judgment on the pleadings in favor of plaintiff.

Ralph James M. Bullowa and *Sutherland D. Smith* for appellant.

Walter L. McCorkle for respondent.

HAIGHT, J. The defendant had demurred to the complaint, and the granting of a motion for judgment, in effect, overruled the demurrer. The questions certified for our determination are as follows:

1st. Does the complaint state facts sufficient to constitute causes of action.

2d. Upon the facts alleged in the complaint and before obtaining judgment against the corporation is the corporation a necessary party defendant.

3d. Upon the facts alleged in the complaint are the stockholders of the W. H. Beard Dredging Company necessary parties defendant in this action without obtaining judgment against the corporation.

4th. Have the causes of action been improperly united in the complaint.

The complaint alleges four different causes of action, arising out of the rent of a scow, for work, labor and services in dredging at different times, at the instance and request of the W. H. Beard Dredging Company, in and about the harbor of the city of New York, and for dumping the material dredged.

The plaintiff is a domestic corporation, having its principal office and place of business in the borough of Manhattan. The William H. Beard Dredging Company is a foreign corporation, created under the laws of the state of West Virginia, but having an office for the transaction of its business in the borough of Manhattan in the city of New York. The defendants William Beard, Lavinia Beard and John B. Summerfield were the directors of the William H. Beard Dredging Company, and the defendants William Beard and Lavinia Beard were copartners composing the firm of William Beard &

Company.   After the performance by the plaintiff of the
work, labor and services for the William H. Beard
Dredging Company, alleged in the complaint, the William
H. Beard Dredging Company dissolved and discontinued
business as a corporation and surrendered to the state of
West Virginia its charter and corporate franchise, and
duly authorized its existing board of directors, who were
the defendants William Beard, Lavinia Beard and John
B. Summerfield, to proceed to pay off and discharge its
debts, liabilities and obligations, and to transfer and set
over to William Beard and Lavinia Beard, composing the
firm of William Beard & Company, the whole of the
property belonging to the corporation.   This was done
under the laws of West Virginia, which is set forth in
the plaintiff's complaint, with the provision that "When
a corporation shall expire or be dissolved, its property
and assets shall, under the order and direction of the
board of directors then in office, or the receiver or receivers
appointed for the purpose by such circuit court as is mentioned in the fifty-seventh section of this chapter, be subject to the payment of the liabilities of the corporation,
and the expenses of winding up its affairs; and the surplus, if any, then remaining, to the distribution among
the stockholders according to their respective interests.
And suits may be brought, continued or defended, the
property, real or personal of the corporation, be conveyed
or transferred under the common seal or otherwise, and
all lawful acts be done, in the corporate name, in like
manner and with like effect as before such dissolution or
expiration; but so far only as shall be necessary or proper
for collecting the debts and claims due to the corporation,
converting its property and assets into money, prosecuting and protecting its rights, enforcing its liabilities, and
paying over and distributing its property and assets, or
the proceeds thereof to those entitled thereto."

We think that, under this statute, the directors in
office at the time of the dissolution of the corporation are
empowered to collect the assets, pay the liabilities and
distribute the surplus; that in discharging that duty they

represent both the corporation and its stockholders and that, consequently, in an action brought to compel them to discharge their duty neither the corporation nor the stockholders are necessary parties. Upon the other questions involved in the case we concur in the opinion of INGRAHAM, P. J., below.

The order of the Appellate Division should be affirmed, with costs, and the questions certified answered, the first in the affirmative, and the rest in the negative.

CULLEN, Ch. J., VANN, WERNER, WILLARD BARTLETT, HISCOCK and CHASE, JJ., concur.

Order affirmed.

ELIZABETH HALL, Respondent, *v.* THE COOPER LAND COMPANY, Appellant.

Hall v. *Cooper Land Company*, 139 App. Div. 922, affirmed.
(Argued October 19, 1911; decided November 21, 1911.)

˙APPEAL from a judgment of the Appellate Division of the Supreme Court in the third judicial department, entered July 5, 1910, affirming a judgment in favor of plaintiff entered upon a verdict in an action to recover for personal injuries alleged to have been sustained by plaintiff through the maintenance by the defendant of an alleged nuisance in permitting a stop cock connected with a water service pipe, laid down by defendant's predecessor in title for the purpose of supplying his premises with water, to protrude above the sidewalk.

Martin T. Nachtmann for appellant.

Richard O. Bassett and *Smith O'Brien* for respondent.

Judgment affirmed, with costs; no opinion.

Concur: CULLEN, Ch. J., WERNER, WILLARD BARTLETT, HISCOCK, CHASE and COLLIN, JJ. Not voting: GRAY, J.

THE PEOPLE OF THE STATE OF NEW YORK, Respondent, *v.* PHILIP MANGANO, Appellant.

(Argued October 23, 1911; decided November 21, 1911.)

APPEAL from a judgment of the Supreme Court, rendered November 23, 1909, at a Trial Term for the county of New York, upon a verdict convicting the defendant of the crime of murder in the first degree.

George H. Taylor, Jr., Francis S. McAvoy and *Samuel Feldman* for appellant.

Charles S. Whitman, District Attorney (Robert C. Taylor of counsel), for respondent.

Judgment of conviction affirmed; no opinion.

Concur: CULLEN, Ch. J., GRAY, HAIGHT, VANN, WERNER, CHASE and COLLIN, JJ.

———————

MAGDALENA E. HOSKIN et al., Respondents, *v.* THE LONG ISLAND LOAN AND TRUST COMPANY, Appellant.

Hoskin v. *Long Island Loan & Trust Co.*, 139 App. Div. 258, affirmed.

(Argued October 23, 1911; decided November 21, 1911.)

APPEAL from a judgment of the Appellate Division of the Supreme Court in the second judicial department, entered June 28, 1910, in favor of plaintiffs upon the submission of a controversy under section 1279 of the Code of Civil Procedure as to the proper interpretation of an instrument establishing a trust fund.

George S. Ingraham for appellant.

Charles J. Ryan and *John R. Kuhn* for respondents.

Judgment affirmed, with costs, on opinion of BURR, J., below.

Concur: CULLEN, Ch. J., GRAY, HAIGHT, VANN, WERNER, CHASE and COLLIN, JJ.

CITY OF BUFFALO, Respondent, *v.* THE FRONTIER TELE-
PHONE COMPANY et al., Appellants.

City of Buffalo v. *Frontier Telephone Co.,* 139 App. Div. 926,
affirmed.
(Argued October 24, 1911; decided November 21, 1911.)

APPEAL from a judgment of the Appellate Division of
the Supreme Court in the fourth judicial department,
entered June 10, 1910, affirming a judgment in favor of
plaintiff entered upon a decision of the court at a Trial
Term without a jury in an action to recover under an
alleged agreement whereby the defendants were to pay
to plaintiff a certain percentage of their gross receipts in
consideration of permission to string their wires along the
streets and avenues of the city of Buffalo.

Daniel J. Kenefick and *Guy Wellman* for appellants.

Clark H. Hammond, Corporation Counsel (*George E.
Pierce* of counsel), for respondent.

Judgment affirmed, with costs.   The defendant having
applied for and voluntarily entered into the agreement
with the city, it is not in a position to challenge its
validity; no opinion.
Concur: CULLEN, Ch. J., GRAY, HAIGHT, VANN,
WERNER, CHASE and COLLIN, JJ.

PATRICK NEYLAN, Respondent, *v.* JAMES REILLY'S SONS
COMPANY, Appellant.

Neylan v. *Reilly's Sons Co.,* 136 App. Div. 938, affirmed.
(Argued October 24, 1911; decided November 21, 1911.)

APPEAL from a judgment of the Appellate Division of
the Supreme Court in the first judicial department,
entered February 14, 1910, modifying and affirming as
modified a judgment in favor of plaintiff entered upon a
verdict in an action to recover for personal injuries

alleged to have been sustained by plaintiff through the negligence of defendant.

H. Schieffelin Sayers and *Guernsey Price* for appellant.

Nelson L. Keach and *Louis Steckler* for respondent.

Judgment affirmed, with costs; no opinion.

Concur: CULLEN, Ch. J., GRAY, HAIGHT, VANN, WERNER, CHASE and COLLIN, JJ.

CATHERINE CLOSE, Respondent, *v.* WILLIAM M. CALDER COMPANY, Appellant.

Close v. *Calder Company*, 139 App. Div. 175, affirmed.
(Argued October 24, 1911; decided November 21, 1911.)

APPEAL from a judgment of the Appellate Division of the Supreme Court in the second judicial department, entered July 8, 1910, in favor of plaintiff upon the submission of a controversy, under section 1279 of the Code of Civil Procedure, as to the marketabilty of the title to certain real property.

Harry Percy David for appellant.

James A. Sheehan for respondent.

Judgment affirmed, with costs, on the authority of *Loring* v. *Binney* (38 Hun, 152; affd., 101 N. Y. 623); no opinion.

Concur: CULLEN, Ch. J., GRAY, HAIGHT, VANN, WERNER, CHASE and COLLIN, JJ.

THE NEW HARTFORD COTTON MANUFACTURING COMPANY, Respondent, *v.* MORRIS LOWENSTEIN et al., Appellants.

New Hartford Cotton Manfg. Co. v. *Lowenstein*, 136 App. Div. 907, affirmed.
(Argued October 25, 1911; decided November 21, 1911.)

APPEAL from a judgment of the Appellate Division of the Supreme Court in the fourth judicial department,

entered December 17, 1909, affirming a judgment in favor of plaintiff entered upon a verdict in an action to recover for an alleged breach of contract of sale.

William Rubin and *Jacob Klein* for appellants.

Henry J. Cookinham for respondent.

Judgment affirmed, with costs; no opinion.
Concur: CULLEN, Ch. J., GRAY, HAIGHT, VANN, WERNER, CHASE and COLLIN, JJ.

LETITIA ROY, Respondent, *v.* LOUIS FLAXMAN et al., Appellants.

Roy v. *Flaxman*, 138 App. Div. 926, affirmed.
(Argued October 25, 1911; decided November 21, 1911.)

APPEAL from a judgment of the Appellate Division of the Supreme Court in the second judicial department, entered May 31, 1910, affirming a judgment in favor of plaintiff entered upon a decision of the court on trial at Special Term in an action to rescind a contract to sell real property and cancel a deed delivered pursuant thereto upon the ground of fraud.

Eli J. Blair for appellants.

L. Harding Rogers, Jr., for respondent.

Judgment affirmed, with costs; no opinion.
Concur: CULLEN, Ch. J., GRAY, HAIGHT, VANN, WERNER, CHASE and COLLIN, JJ.

RICHARD J. CULLEN, Respondent, *v.* BATTLE ISLAND PAPER COMPANY, Appellant.

Cullen v. *Battle Island Paper Co.*, 138 App. Div. 915, affirmed.
(Argued October 25, 1911; decided November 21, 1911.)

APPEAL from a judgment of the Appellate Division of the Supreme Court in the fourth judicial department,

entered May 20, 1910, affirming a judgment in favor of plaintiff entered upon a verdict in an action to recover on an alleged contract.

Irving G. Hubbs for appellant.

John N. Carlisle and *Frederick G. Spencer* for respondent.

Judgment affirmed, with costs; no opinion.
Concur: CULLEN, Ch. J., GRAY, HAIGHT, VANN, WERNER, CHASE and COLLIN, JJ.

LOUIS F. MASSA, Respondent, *v.* WATERTOWN ENGINE COMPANY, Appellant.

Massa v. *Watertown Engine Co.*, 138 App. Div. 913, affirmed.
(Argued October 25, 1911; decided November 21, 1911.)

APPEAL from a judgment of the Appellate Division of the Supreme Court in the fourth judicial department, entered May 9, 1910, affirming a judgment in favor of plaintiff entered upon a verdict in an action to recover for an alleged breach of contract.

Edward N. Smith for appellant.

Elon R. Brown and *Henry H. Babcock* for respondent.

Judgment affirmed, with costs; no opinion.
Concur: CULLEN, Ch. J., GRAY, HAIGHT, VANN, WERNER, CHASE and COLLIN, JJ.

JAMES B. DIXON, as Administrator of the Estate of SUSAN DIXON, Deceased, Appellant, *v.* FRANK BARKELY, Respondent.

Dixon v. *Barkley*, 131 App. Div. 918, affirmed.
(Argued October 25, 1911; decided November 21, 1911.)

APPEAL from a judgment of the Appellate Division of the Supreme Court in the third judicial department, entered January 28, 1910, affirming a judgment in favor of defendant entered upon the report of a referee in an action to set aside an alleged satisfaction of a mortgage on the ground of fraud.

Fred. A. Bratt for appellant.

Edgar T. Brackett and *Wyman S. Bascom* for respondent.

Judgment affirmed, with costs; no opinion.

Concur: CULLEN, Ch. J., GRAY, HAIGHT, VANN, WERNER, CHASE and COLLIN, JJ.

THE CITY OF NEW YORK, Appellant, *v.* NEW YORK CITY RAILWAY COMPANY, Respondent. (Actions Nos. 1, 2.)

City of New York v. *New York City Ry. Co.* (*No. 1*), 138 App. Div. 131, affirmed.

City of New York v. *New York City Ry. Co.* (*No. 2*), 138 App. Div. 138, affirmed.

(Argued October 26, 1911; decided November 21, 1911.)

APPEAL in each of the above-entitled actions, by permission, from a judgment of the Appellate Division of the Supreme Court in the first judicial department, entered June 24, 1910, upon an order which reversed a determination of the Appellate Term affirming a judgment of the Muncipal Court of the city of New York in favor of plaintiff, and dismissed the complaint in an action to recover penalties for the operation of surface cars without the display in such cars of certificates of payment of license fees, as required by a city ordinance.

Archibald R. Watson, Corporation Counsel (Terence Farley and *Frank B. Pierce* of counsel), for appellant.

George Rublee, Joseph P. Cotton, Jr., George S. Franklin and *James L. Quackenbush* for respondent.

Judgment in each action affirmed, with costs; no opinion.

Concur: CULLEN, Ch. J., HAIGHT, WERNER and COLLIN, JJ. VANN and CHASE, JJ., concur on the ground that the ordinance is unreasonable. Not sitting: GRAY, J.

WILLIAM E. HANNA, Respondent, *v.* S. JENNIE SORG, Appellant.

Hanna v. *Sorg*, 187 App. Div. 889, affirmed.
(Argued October 26, 1911; decided November 21, 1911.)

APPEAL from a judgment of the Appellate Division of the Supreme Court in the second judicial department, entered March 11, 1910, affirming a judgment in favor of plaintiff entered upon a verdict in an action on contract.

Charles A. Boston and *James Allison Kelly* for appellant.

Norman B. Beecher for respondent.

Judgment affirmed, with costs; no opinion.
Concur: CULLEN, Ch. J., GRAY, HAIGHT, VANN, WERNER, CHASE and COLLIN, JJ.

JOHN B. SMITH, Respondent, *v.* EDWARD F. HUTTON et al., as Copartners under the Firm Name of E. F. HUTTON & COMPANY, Appellants.

Smith v. *Hutton*, 138 App. Div. 859, affirmed.
(Argued October 26, 1911; decided November 21, 1911.)

APPEAL from a judgment of the Appellate Division of the Supreme Court in the first judicial department, entered June 14, 1910, affirming a judgment in favor of plaintiff entered upon a verdict in an action to recover damages alleged to have been sustained by plaintiff through the failure of defendant stockbrokers to execute his order to sell certain stock.

William F. S. Hart and *Millard F. Tompkins* for appellants.

Lewis H. Freedman and *Albert Stickney* for respondent.

Judgment affirmed, with costs, on opinion of MILLER, J., below.

Concur: CULLEN, Ch. J., HAIGHT, VANN, WERNER, CHASE and COLLIN, JJ. Dissenting on opinion of INGRAHAM, P. J., below: GRAY, J.

BLANCHE A. MAGILL, Respondent, *v.* SUSAN A. MAGILL et al., Appellants.

Magill v. *Magill*, 138 App. Div. 920, affirmed.

(Argued October 27, 1911; decided November 21, 1911.)

APPEAL from a judgment of the Appellate Division of the Supreme Court in the second judicial department, entered May 10, 1910, affirming a judgment in favor of plaintiff entered upon a decision of the court on trial at Special Term in an action to determine the legal beneficiary of the proceeds of a certain certificate of life insurance.

Walter E. Warner for appellants.

Frank W. Holmes for respondent.

Judgment affirmed, with costs; no opinion.

Concur: CULLEN, Ch. J., GRAY, HAIGHT, VANN, WERNER, CHASE and COLLIN, JJ.

DUNELLE VAN SCHAICK, Respondent, *v.* OSCAR HEYMAN et al., Doing Business under the Firm Name of OSCAR HEYMAN & Co., Appellants.

Van Schaick v. *Heyman*, 138 App. Div. 905, affirmed.

(Argued October 27, 1911; decided November 21, 1911.)

APPEAL from a judgment of the Appellate Division of the Supreme Court in the first judicial department, entered May 9, 1910, affirming a judgment in favor of plaintiff entered upon a verdict directed by the court in an action to recover for goods alleged to have been sold and delivered.

Arthur B. Hyman, Martin Paskus and *William S. Gordon* for appellants.

William H. Hamilton and *Thomas Gregory* for respondent.

Judgment affirmed, with costs; no opinion.

Concur: CULLEN, Ch. J., GRAY, HAIGHT, VANN, WERNER, CHASE and COLLIN, JJ.

HENRY S. STRAUSS, Appellant, *v.* EASTERN BREWING COMPANY, Respondent.

Strauss v. *Eastern Brewing Co.*, 134 App. Div. 174, 930, affirmed. (Submitted October 27, 1911; decided November 21, 1911.)

APPEAL from an order of the Appellate Division of the Supreme Court in the second judicial department, entered October 8, 1909, sustaining defendant's exceptions, ordered to be heard in the first instance by the Appellate Division, and granting a motion for a new trial in an action to recover broker's commissions.

Samuel H. Guggenheimer for appellant.

Jay C. Guggenheimer for respondent.

Order affirmed and judgment absolute ordered against appellant on the stipulation, with costs in all courts; no opinion.

Concur: CULLEN, Ch. J., GRAY, HAIGHT, VANN, WERNER, CHASE and COLLIN, JJ.

FRANK KOEWING, Appellant, *v.* ERNST THALMANN et al.,
Doing Business under the Firm Name of LADENBURG,
THALMANN & Co., Respondents.

Koewing v. *Thalmann*, 139 App. Div. 893, affirmed.
(Argued October 30, 1911; decided November 21, 1911.)

APPEAL from a judgment of the Appellate Division of
the Supreme Court in the first judicial department, entered
June 23, 1910, affirming a judgment in favor of defendants entered upon a dismissal of the complaint by the
court at a Trial Term in an action to recover damages
alleged to have been occasioned plaintiff through the negligence of defendants as stockbrokers in handling his
account.

E. C. Crowley for appellant.

J. Markham Marshall for respondents.

Judgment affirmed, with costs; no opinion.
Concur: CULLEN, Ch. J., GRAY, HAIGHT, VANN WIL-
LARD BARTLETT, HISCOCK and COLLIN, JJ.

ROBERT M. WHITING, Respondent, *v.* THE FIDELITY
MUTUAL LIFE ASSOCIATION OF PHILADELPHIA, PENN-
SYLVANIA, Appellant.

Whiting v. *Fidelity Mutual Life Assn.*, 137 App. Div. 758,
affirmed.
(Argued October 31, 1911; decided November 21, 1911.)

APPEAL from an order of the Appellate Division of the
Supreme Court in the first judicial department, entered
April 22, 1910, reversing a judgment in favor of defendant entered upon a dismissal of the complaint by the
court on trial at Special Term and granting a new trial
in an action to obtain a construction of certain policies of
life insurance.

William B. Ellison and *F. H. Calkins* for appellant.

Alexander S. Bacon for respondent.

Order affirmed and judgment absolute ordered against appellant on the stipulation, with costs in all courts, on opinion of SCOTT, J., below.

Concur: CULLEN, Ch. J., GRAY, HAIGHT, VANN and WILLARD BARTLETT, JJ. Dissenting: HISCOCK and COLLIN, JJ.

FISS, DOERR AND CARROLL HORSE COMPANY, Respondent, *v.* LOUIS GOLDE et al., Appellants.

Fiss, Doerr & Carroll Horse Co. v. *Golde*, 188 App. Div. 907, modified.

(Argued October 31, 1911; decided November 21, 1911.)

APPEAL from a judgment of the Appellate Division of the Supreme Court in the first judicial department, entered May 25, 1910, affirming a judgment in favor of plaintiff entered upon a verdict in an action to recover a balance alleged to be due for work done under a contract.

Benjamin N. Cardozo and *Harry A. Gordon* for appellants.

Franklin Pierce for respondent.

Judgment reversed and new trial granted, costs to abide event, unless within twenty days plaintiff stipulates to reduce its judgment by the sum of $1,521, with interest from the date of the assessment to the date of the judgment, in which case judgment as reduced is affirmed, without costs of this appeal to either party; no opinion.

Concur: CULLEN, Ch. J., GRAY, HAIGHT, VANN, WILLARD BARTLETT, HISCOCK and COLLIN, JJ.

THIRD NATIONAL BANK OF PHILADELPHIA, Appellant, *v.* THE R. G. CHASE COMPANY, Respondent.

Third Nat. Bank of Philadelphia v. *Chase Company*, 140 App. Div. 881, affirmed.

(Argued October 31, 1911; decided November 21, 1911.)

APPEAL from a judgment of the Appellate Division of the Supreme Court in the fourth judicial department,

entered July 15, 1910, affirming a judgment in favor of defendant entered upon a dismissal of the complaint by the court at a Trial Term without a jury in an action to recover upon a promissory note.

George L. Bachman and *W. S. Bachman* for appellant.

Charles A. Hawley for respondent.

Judgment affirmed, with costs; no opinion.

Concur: CULLEN, Ch. J., GRAY, HAIGHT, VANN, WILLARD BARTLETT, HISCOCK and COLLIN, JJ.

ALBERT R. BRANDLY, Respondent, *v.* THE UNITED STATES FIDELITY AND GUARANTY COMPANY, Appellant.

Brandly v. *U. S. Fidelity & Guaranty Co.*, 189 App. Div. 932, affirmed.

(Submitted October 31, 1911; decided November 21, 1911.)

APPEAL from a judgment of the Appellate Division of the Supreme Court in the first judicial department, entered July 13, 1910, affirming a judgment in favor of plaintiff entered upon a decision of the court on trial at Special Term in an action upon an undertaking given to discharge an attachment.

Schuyler C. Carlton and *George F. Allison* for appellant.

Benjamin N. Cardozo and *Nathan Ottinger* for respondent.

Judgment affirmed, with costs and ten per cent damages for delay under subdivision 5 of section 3251 of the Code of Civil Procedure; no opinion.

Concur: CULLEN, Ch. J., GRAY, HAIGHT, VANN, WILLARD BARTLETT, HISCOCK and COLLIN, JJ.

McEwan Brothers, Respondent, *v*. Ledrue Billings, Appellant, Impleaded with Others.

McEwen Brothers v. *Kervin*, 138 App. Div. 915, reversed.
(Argued November 1, 1911; decided November 21, 1911.)

Appeal from a judgment of the Appellate Division of the Supreme Court in the fourth judicial department, entered May 24, 1910, affirming a judgment in favor of plaintiff entered upon a verdict in an action to recover upon an account for goods alleged to have been sold and delivered.

M. B. Jewell for appellant.

James T. Ward for respondent.

Judgment reversed and new trial granted, costs to abide event, because of error in admission of declarations of Whitney as to the interest of appellant Billings in oil leases and his membership in the Billings Oil Company; no opinion.

Concur: Cullen, Ch. J., Gray, Haight, Vann, Willard Bartlett, Hiscock and Collin, JJ.

Herman D. Walters, Respondent, *v*. David Grinberg et al., Appellants.

Walters v. *Grinberg*, 138 App. Div. 933, affirmed.
(Submitted November 1, 1911; decided November 21, 1911.)

Appeal from a judgment of the Appellate Division of the Supreme Court in the third judicial department, entered May 20, 1910, affirming a judgment in favor of plaintiff entered upon a verdict in an action to recover for an alleged conversion.

T. B. Merchant and *L. M. Merchant* for appellants.

Archibald Howard for respondent.

Judgment affirmed, with costs; no opinion.
Concur: Cullen, Ch. J., Gray, Haight, Vann, Willard Bartlett, Hiscock and Collin, JJ.

FRANK LYNCH, Respondent, *v.* LACKAWANNA STEEL COMPANY, Appellant.

Lynch v. *Lackawanna Steel Co.*, 140 App. Div. 882, affirmed.
(Argued November 1, 1911; decided November 21, 1911.)

APPEAL from a judgment of the Appellate Division of the Supreme Court in the fourth judicial department, entered July 25, 1910, affirming a judgment in favor of plaintiff entered upon a verdict in an action to recover for personal injuries alleged to have been sustained by plaintiff through the negligence of defendant, his employer.

Evan Hollister for appellant.

Frederick S. Jackson and *Edmund L. Ryan* for respondent.

Judgment affirmed, with costs; no opinion.
Concur: CULLEN, Ch. J., GRAY, HAIGHT, VANN, WILLARD BARTLETT and COLLIN, JJ. Not voting: HISCOCK, J.

———————

ROLLAND M. BICKERSTAFF, Respondent, *v.* FRANK L. PERLEY, Appellant.

Bickerstaff v. *Perley*, 137 App. Div. 919, affirmed.
(Argued November 2, 1911; decided November 21, 1911.)

APPEAL from a judgment of the Appellate Division of the Supreme Court in the first judicial department, entered March 25, 1910, affirming a judgment in favor of plaintiff entered upon a verdict directed by the court in an action to recover money alleged to be due for labor performed and materials furnished.

Franklin Bien for appellant.

George Edwin Joseph and *Leon Laski* for respondent.

Judgment affirmed, with costs; no opinion.
Concur: GRAY, HAIGHT, VANN, WILLARD BARTLETT, HISCOCK and COLLIN, JJ. Not voting: CULLEN, Ch. J.

MARY J. SHIRLEY, Appellant, *v.* THE NEW YORK CENTRAL AND HUDSON RIVER RAILROAD COMPANY, Respondent.

Shirley v. N. Y. C. & H. R. R. R. Co., 133 App. Div. 939, affirmed. (Argued November 2, 1911; decided November 21, 1911.)

APPEAL from a judgment of the Appellate Division of the Supreme Court in the fourth judicial department, entered June 18, 1909, upon an order overruling plaintiff's exceptions, ordered to be heard in the first instance by the Appellate Division, denying a motion for a new trial and directing judgment for defendant on the nonsuit granted by the trial court in an action to recover for personal injuries alleged to have been sustained through defendant's negligence.

Walter H. Knapp and *James A. Rolfe* for appellant.

Edward Harris, Jr., for respondent.

Judgment affirmed, with costs; no opinion.

Concur: CULLEN, Ch. J., GRAY, HAIGHT, VANN, WILLARD BARTLETT, HISCOCK and COLLIN, JJ.

WILLIAM BURFEIND, Respondent, *v.* PEOPLE'S SURETY COMPANY OF NEW YORK, Appellant.

Burfeind v. People's Surety Co. of N. Y., 139 App. Div. 762, affirmed. (Argued November 2, 1911; decided November 21, 1911.)

APPEAL from a judgment of the Appellate Division of the Supreme Court in the second judicial department, entered July 29, 1910, affirming a judgment in favor of plaintiff entered upon a verdict in an action to recover on a guaranty bond.

F. Sidney Williams, Edward M. Grout and *Paul Grout* for appellant.

Ernest G. Stevens and *William O. Gantz* for respondent.

Judgment affirmed, with costs; no opinion.

Concur: CULLEN, Ch. J., GRAY, HAIGHT, VANN, WIL-

MILTON SCHNAIER, Respondent, *v.* THE ONWARD CON-
STRUCTION COMPANY et al., Appellants, Impleaded with
Others.

Schnaier v. *Onward Construction Co.*, 138 App. Div. 909, affirmed.
(Argued November 2, 1911; decided November 21, 1911.)

APPEAL from a judgment of the Appellate Division of
the Supreme Court in the first judicial department,
entered June 22, 1910, affirming a judgment in favor of
plaintiff entered upon the report of a referee in an action
to foreclose a mechanic's lien.

L. Laflin Kellogg and *Hiram R. Fisher* for appellants.

Milton Mayer for respondent.

Judgment affirmed, with costs; no opinion.
Concur: CULLEN, Ch. J., GRAY; HAIGHT, VANN, WIL-
LARD BARTLETT,. HISCOCK and COLLIN, JJ.

JOHN C. ROBBINS, Respondent, *v.* ELLEN D. CLOCK,
Appellant.

Robbins v. *Clock*, 131 App. Div. 917, affirmed.
(Argued November 2, 1911; decided November 21, 1911.)

APPEAL from a judgment of the Appellate Division of
the Supreme Court in the second judicial department,
entered April 10, 1909, affirming a judgment in favor of
plaintiff entered upon a decision of the court on trial at
Special Term in an action to compel specific performance
of a contract to convey real property.

Alfred W. Varian for appellant.

Le Roy M. Young for respondent.

Judgment affirmed, without costs; no opinion.
Concur: CULLEN, Ch. J., GRAY, HAIGHT, VANN, WIL-
LARD BARTLETT, HISCOCK and COLLIN, JJ.

AUGUSTUS D. JUILLIARD et al., Appellants, *v.* NATHAN TROKIE et al., Respondents.

Juilliard v. *Trokie*, 139 App. Div. 530, affirmed.
(Argued November 2, 1911; decided November 21, 1911.)

APPEAL from a judgment of the Appellate Division of the Supreme Court in the first judicial department, entered July 13, 1910, affirming a judgment in favor of defendants entered upon a dismissal of the complaint by the court at a Trial Term in an action to recover for an alleged breach of contract.

Eliphalet W. Tyler for appellants.

J. Solon Einsohn for respondents.

Judgment affirmed, with costs; no opinion.
Concur: CULLEN, Ch. J., GRAY, HAIGHT, VANN, WILLARD BARTLETT, HISCOCK and COLLIN, JJ.

JAMES WILSON, Appellant, *v.* THE CENTRAL INSURANCE COMPANY, LIMITED, Respondent.

Wilson v. *Central Ins. Co., Limited*, 135 App. Div. 649, appeal dismissed.
(Argued October 2, 1911; decided November 28, 1911.)

MOTION to dismiss an appeal from an order of the Appellate Division of the Supreme Court in the first judicial department, entered December 10, 1909, reversing a judgment in favor of plaintiff entered upon a verdict and granting a new trial in an action to recover on a policy of accident insurance.

The motion was made upon the ground that the order of the Appellate Division was not appealable to the Court of Appeals.

John S. Sheppard, Jr., and *Russel R. Vaughn* for motion.

Franklin M. Danaher opposed.

Motion granted and appeal dismissed, with costs and ten dollars costs of motion.

In the Matter of the Application of the GRADE CROSSING COMMISSIONERS OF THE CITY OF BUFFALO, Appellants.

ERIE RAILROAD COMPANY, Respondent.

Matter of Grade Crossing Comrs., City of Buffalo, 146 App. Div. 883, appeal dismissed.

(Submitted November 22, 1911; decided November 28, 1911.)

APPEAL from an order of the Appellate Division of the Supreme Court in the fourth judicial department, entered July 11, 1911, which reversed an order of Special Term confirming the report of commissioners appointed to ascertain the compensation to be paid to owners of land taken for street purposes and remitted the proceedings to said commissioners.

Ralph K. Robertson and *Spencer Clinton* for appellants.

William L. Marcy and *Helen Z. M. Rodgers* for respondent.

Appeal dismissed, with costs; no opinion.

Concur: CULLEN, Ch. J., HAIGHT, WERNER, WILLARD BARTLETT, HISCOCK, CHASE and COLLIN, JJ.

In the Matter of Proving the Will of JOHN C. LATHAM, Deceased.

ELSIE G. LATHAM, Individually and as Guardian of ALICE LATHAM, an Infant, Appellant; HARRY ALLEN, Respondent.

Reported below, 145 App. Div. 849.

(Argued November 20, 1911; decided November 28, 1911.)

MOTION to dismiss an appeal from an order of the Appellate Division of the Supreme Court in the first judicial department, entered July 7, 1911, which reversed an order of the New York County Surrogate's Court sustaining objections to the granting of letters testamentary to the respondent herein, one of the executors named in the will of John C. Latham, deceased.

The motion was made upon the grounds that the Court of Appeals had no jurisdiction to review the order of reversal for the reason that it was not an order finally determining a special proceeding but was discretionary and that no question of law was involved. .

H. B. Walmsley for motion.

John Thomas Smith opposed.

Motion denied, with ten dollars costs.

In the Matter of Acquiring Title by the CITY OF NEW YORK to Land for Bridge Purposes.

In the Matter of the Application of JOHN T. MURPHY, Respondent, for an Order Directing the Comptroller of the City of New York to Pay over the Balance of an Award.

REALTY PROTECTIVE COMPANY, Appellant.

Reported below, 146 App. Div. 125.
(Argued November 20, 1911; decided November 28, 1911.)

MOTION to dismiss an appeal from an order of the Appellate Division of the Supreme Court in the first judicial department, entered July 7, 1911, which reversed an order of Special Term denying a motion for an order directing the payment of the balance of an award theretofore made in condemnation proceedings against which a lien had been filed.

The motion was made upon the ground that the order appealed from was an intermediate one and that permission to appeal had not been obtained.

Joseph W. Murphy for motion.

Isidor Wels opposed.

Motion denied, with ten dollars costs.

MOE PARIS et al., Respondents, *v.* LAWYERS' TITLE INSURANCE AND TRUST COMPANY, Appellant, and DAVID KRATENSTEIN et al., Respondents, Impleaded with Others.

Reported below, 141 App. Div. 866.
(Submitted November 20, 1911; decided November 28, 1911.)

MOTION to dismiss an appeal from a judgment of the Appellate Division of the Supreme Court in the second judicial department, entered December 30, 1910, affirming a judgment in favor of respondents herein, entered upon a decision of the court on trial at Special Term in an action to foreclose a mortgage wherein it was decided that a certain mechanic's lien had priority over a mortgage held by the appellant.

The motion was made upon the ground that the appeal was frivolous, no question of law being involved and said appeal being taken for purposes of delay only.

Abraham H. Spigelgass for motion.

Philip S. Dean opposed.

Motion denied, with ten dollars costs.

JAMES C. TABOR, Respondent, *v.* THE CITY OF BUFFALO, Appellant.

Tabor v. *City of Buffalo*, 136 App. Div. 258, appeal withdrawn.
(Argued November 20, 1911; decided November 28, 1911.)

MOTION for leave to withdraw an appeal from an order of the Appellate Division of the Supreme Court in the fourth judicial department, entered January 12, 1910, reversing a judgment in favor of defendant entered upon a verdict and granting a new trial in an action to recover for personal injuries alleged to have been sustained through the negligence of defendant.

The motion was made upon the ground that the order of reversal was not appealable to the Court of Appeals.

H. A. Hickman for motion.

H. J. Westwood opposed.

Motion granted on payment, within twenty days, of ten dollars costs and taxable costs that have accrued on appeal.

EDWARD P. FLOYD-JONES, Respondent, *v.* ESTHER SCHAAN, Appellant.

(Submitted October 24, 1911; decided November 28, 1911.)

MOTION to amend remittitur. (See 203 N. Y. 568.)

Motion denied, with ten dollars costs.

THE PEOPLE OF THE STATE OF NEW YORK ex rel. THE NEW YORK CENTRAL AND HUDSON RIVER RAILROAD COMPANY, Appellant, *v.* EGBURT E. WOODBURY et al., Constituting the State Board of Tax Commissioners, et al., Respondents.

(Submitted November 20, 1911; decided November 28, 1911.)

Motion for re-argument denied, with ten dollars costs. (See 203 N. Y. 167.)

THE PEOPLE OF THE STATE OF NEW YORK ex rel. JOHN W. LISK, Appellant, *v.* THE BOARD OF EDUCATION OF THE CITY OF NEW YORK, Respondent.

(Submitted November 20, 1911; decided November 28, 1911.)

Motion for re-argument denied, with ten dollars costs. (See 203 N. Y. 561.)

HARLOW C. CURTISS, Respondent, *v.* WILLIAM T. JEBB, Appellant.

(Submitted October 30, 1911; decided November 28, 1911.)

Motion for re-argument denied, with ten dollars costs. (See 203 N. Y. 538.)

THE PEOPLE OF THE STATE OF NEW YORK, Respondent, *v.* MILLIE J. NEWCOMB, as Administratrix of SARAH A. WIGGINS, Deceased, Appellant.

(Argued November 20, 1911; decided November 28, 1911.)

MOTION to amend remittitur.   (See 201 N. Y. 151.)

Motion denied, without costs.

In the Matter of the Application of the CITY OF NEW YORK, Appellant, for a Writ of Certiorari against RICHARD MITCHELL et al., as Assessors of the Town of Southeast, Respondents.

Matter of City of New York v. *Mitchell,* 145 App. Div. 931, affirmed.

(Argued November 20, 1911; decided December 5, 1911.)

APPEAL from an order of the Appellate Division of the Supreme Court in the second judicial department, entered June 2, 1911, which affirmed an order of Special Term sustaining an assessment of the petitioner's property in the town of Southeast for purposes of taxation.

Archibald R. Watson, Corporation Counsel (I. J. Beaudrias of counsel), for appellant.

Charles H. Young for respondents.

Order affirmed, with costs; no opinion.

Concur: CULLEN, Ch. J., HAIGHT, WERNER, WILLARD BARTLETT, HISCOCK, CHASE and COLLIN, JJ.

In the Matter of the Application of the CITY OF NEW YORK, Appellant, Relative to Acquiring Title to Lands Required for Approaches to the Bridge over the Spuyten Duyvil and Port Morris Railroad.

EDWIN B. SHELDON, as Administrator with the Will Annexed and Trustee of an Unexecuted Trust under the Will of WILLIAM B. OGDEN, Deceased, Respondent.

Matter of City of New York (Spuyten Duyvil Bridge), **144 App.** Div. 447, affirmed.
(Argued November 20, 1911; decided December 5, 1911.)

APPEAL from an order of the Appellate Division of the Supreme Court in the first judicial department, entered May 16, 1911, which modified and affirmed as modified an order of Special Term confirming the report of commissioners of estimate and assessment in condemnation proceedings.

Archibald R. Watson, Corporation Counsel (Joel J. Squier and *Edward F. Reynolds* of counsel), for appellant.

John C. Shaw for respondent.

Order affirmed, with costs; no opinion.
Concur: CULLEN, Ch. J., HAIGHT, WERNER, WILLARD BARTLETT, HISCOCK, CHASE and COLLIN, JJ.

In the Matter of the Application of PATRICK K. ROCHE, Appellant, for a Peremptory Writ of Mandamus against RHINELANDER WALDO, as Fire Commissioner of the City of New York, Respondent.

Matter of Roche, 141 App. Div. 872, affirmed.
(Argued November 20, 1911; decided December 5, 1911.)

APPEAL from an order of the Appellate Division of the Supreme Court in the second judicial department, entered December 30, 1910, which affirmed an order of Special

Term denying an application for a peremptory writ of mandamus to compel the fire commissioner of the city of New York to place the petitioner on the pension roll of the fire department of that city.

Francis A. McCloskey for appellant. .

Archibald R. Watson, Corporation Counsel (*James D. Bell* of counsel), for respondent.

Order affirmed, with costs, on opinion of WOODWARD, J., below.

Concur: CULLEN, Ch. J., HAIGHT, WERNER, WILLARD BARTLETT, HISCOCK, CHASE and COLLIN, JJ.

WILLIAM J. LOGAN, Respondent, *v.* THE GREENWICH TRUST COMPANY of GREENWICH, CONNECTICUT, as Administrator of the Estate of GEORGE P. SHELDON, Deceased, Appellant.

Logan v. Greenwich Trust Co., 144 App. Div. 872, affirmed.
(Argued November 26, 1911; decided December 5, 1911.)

APPEAL, by permission, from an order of the Appellate Division of the Supreme Court in the first judicial department, entered May 9, 1911, which reversed an order of Special Term granting a motion to vacate a warrant of attachment, an order purporting to revive and continue an action against defendant, and a judgment entered against defendant.

The following questions were certified:

"1. Did the Supreme Court have power to make the order herein dated the 15th day of January, 1910, purporting to continue the action against the Greenwich Trust Company of Greenwich, Connecticut, as administrator of the goods, chattels and credits of George P. Sheldon, deceased, and amending the summons and pleadings accordingly?

" 2. Did the Supreme Court have power to make the order herein dated the 15th day of January, 1910, directing service of the summons herein upon the Greenwich Trust Company of Greenwich, Connecticut, as administrator of the goods, chattels and credits of George P. Sheldon, deceased, by publication or without the state?

" 3. Did the Supreme Court have power to make the order herein dated the 26th day of April, 1910, directing the entry of judgment herein in favor of the plaintiff and against the Greenwich Trust Company of Greenwich, Connecticut, as administrator of the goods, chattels and credits of George P. Sheldon, deceased?

" 4. A valid attachment having been granted in this action on the ground that the defendant was a non-resident of the state of New York, and a valid levy having been made under such attachment by the sheriff of the county of New York, did the attachment fall by reason of the death of the defendant before service of the summons or the commencement of the publication thereof, where, within thirty days after the granting of the warrant of attachment, service of the summons by publication, under an order duly granted, was commenced against the defendant who had been substituted in the action in the place and stead of the deceased defendant, said substituted defendant being the personal representative of the deceased defendant?"

Graham Sumner and *Reeve Schley* for appellant.

John D. Fearhake and *James M. Gifford* for respondent.

Order affirmed, with costs, on opinion of INGRAHAM, P. J., below; first, second and third questions certified answered in the affirmative; fourth question answered in the negative.

Concur: CULLEN, Ch. J., HAIGHT, WERNER, WILLARD BARTLETT and CHASE, JJ. Dissenting: HISCOCK and COLLIN, JJ.

THE PEOPLE OF THE STATE OF NEW YORK ex rel. BROWN-ING, KING AND COMPANY, Respondent, *v.* CHARLES B. STOVER et al., as Commissioners of Parks of the City of New York, Respondents.

ENGLISH-AMERICAN REALTY COMPANY et al., Appellants.

People ex rel. Browning, King & Co. v. Stover, 145 App. Div. 259, affirmed.

(Argued November 21, 1911; decided December 5, 1911.)

APPEAL from an order of the Appellate Division of the Supreme Court in the first judicial department, entered July 1, 1911, which reversed an order of Special Term denying a motion for a peremptory writ of mandamus to compel defendants to proceed with the removal of incumbrances on certain streets of the city of New York, consisting of show windows, cornices and stoops attached to a certain building in said city, and granted said motion.

Eugene D. Boyer, Charles Strauss and *Peter Zucker* for appellants.

Charles P. Northrop for relator, respondent.

Order affirmed, with costs; no opinion.

Concur: CULLEN, Ch. J., HAIGHT, WERNER, WILLARD BARTLETT, HISCOCK, CHASE and COLLIN, JJ.

In the Matter of ARMAND SPENSER, an Attorney, Appellant.

ASSOCIATION OF THE BAR OF THE CITY OF NEW YORK, Respondent.

Matter of Spenser, 143 App. Div. 229, affirmed.
(Argued November 21, 1911; decided December 5, 1911.)

APPEAL from an order of the Appellate Division of the Supreme Court in the first judicial department, entered April 6, 1911, disbarring the appellant Armand Spenser from practicing as an attorney and counselor at law in the state of New York.

Louis S. Posner, Walter S. Dryfoos and *Cyril F. Dos Passos* for appellant.

Paul Fuller, Jr., for respondent.

Order affirmed; no opinion.

Concur: CULLEN, Ch. J., HAIGHT, WERNER, HISCOCK, CHASE and COLLIN, JJ.

WILLARD BARTLETT, J. (dissenting). I dissent on the ground that the order of the Appellate Division is defective in omitting to state the specific misconduct of the attorney. The opinion of the Appellate Division indicates that the judges of that tribunal have found the appellant guilty of the most serious charges upon which he was acquitted by the official referee; but however this may be, I think that a definite and specific adjudication of misconduct should be required to be made by the Appellate Division, as the basis of an order disbarring or suspending an attorney. As was pointed out by Judge WERNER in *Matter of Droege* (197 N. Y. 44), this court from an early day has exercised jurisdiction to review the action of the Supreme Court in cases of this character; but, in the absence of some adjudication analogous to findings of fact, no effective review is practicable. I think the case should be sent back to the Appellate Division in order that the defect which I have pointed out may be remedied.

ARNOLD TANZER, Appellant, *v.* GEORGE W. MORGAN, Respondent, Impleaded with Others.

Tanzer v. *Breen,* 139 App. Div. 10, appeal dismissed.

(Argued November 24, 1911; decided December 5, 1911.)

APPEAL from a judgment of the Appellate Division of the Supreme Court in the first judicial department, entered June 17, 1910, which modified and affirmed as modified a judgment in favor of defendant entered upon a dismissal of the complaint by the court at a Trial Term in an action for false imprisonment.

Laurence Arnold Tanzer for appellant.

Martin S. Lynch for respondent.

Appeal dismissed, with costs; no opinion.
Concur: CULLEN, Ch. J., GRAY, HAIGHT, VANN, HIS-COCK, CHASE and COLLIN, JJ.

JAMES PAUL, Appellant, *v.* ALLIE D. SWEARS, Respondent.

Paul v. *Swears*, 138 App. Div. 638, appeal withdrawn.
(Submitted November 27, 1911; decided December 5, 1911.)

MOTION for leave to withdraw stipulation and appeal from an order of the Appellate Division of the Supreme Court in the third judicial department, entered May 11, 1910, reversing a judgment in favor of plaintiff entered upon a decision of the Warren County Court after trial without a jury and granting a new trial in an action to compel specific performance of a contract to purchase real property.

The motion was made upon the ground that the Court of Appeals had no jurisdiction to entertain the appeal.

Robert Imrie for motion.

H. A. Howard opposed.

Motion granted on payment, within twenty days, of costs of appeal and ten dollars costs of motion.

NEW YORK CENTRAL AND HUDSON RIVER RAILROAD COMPANY, Respondent, *v.* FRANK J. MOORE, Appellant.

N. Y. C. & H. R. R. R. Co. v. *Moore*, 137 App. Div. 461, affirmed.
(Argued November 29, 1911; decided December 12, 1911.)

APPEAL from a judgment entered April 11, 1910, upon an order of the Appellate Division of the Supreme Court in the fourth judicial department, overruling defendant's exceptions, ordered to be heard in the first instance by the Appellate Division, denying a motion for a new trial and directing judgment for plaintiff upon the verdict.

Eugene Van Voorhis for appellant.

Daniel M. Beach for respondent.

HAIGHT, J. This action was brought to recover the possession of a parcel of land situate in the town of Irondequoit, county of Monroe, state of New York, adjoining the plaintiff's right of way, fifty feet in breadth and about two hundred and sixty feet in length. The plaintiff's title is traced back to a deed executed by the Duke of Cumberland and others to one John Hornby, dated September 1st, 1815, conveying two parcels of land; the first was located in the north part of township No. 14, 7th range, now Irondequoit, bounded on the east by Irondequoit bay, on the north by Lake Ontario and on the west by lot 22, in that township, containing 494.56 acres. The other parcel conveyed was called the sand bar adjoining, lying between the bay and the lake, containing 15.17 acres. In 1819, Hornby conveyed to Sylvester Woodman a portion of the premises adjoining the sand bar, bounded as follows: "Beginning at the northeast corner of said lot; running thence westerly along north line of lot, being the Lake Shore 100 rods; then south parallel with the west line of lot so far that a line drawn from thence easterly parallel with the south line to the east line of lot, being the shore of Gerundegut (now Irondequoit) Bay, and thence northerly along said east line of lot to the place of beginning, will contain one hundred acres and no more." The plaintiff claims that the premises thus conveyed to Woodman cover the land in question, and traces its title thereto through mesne conveyances from Woodman.

In 1825 John Hornby conveyed to Roger Bronson a parcel of land described as lying in township No. 14, 7th range, and described as follows: "Being three undivided fourth parts of the Sand Bar, so called, lying at the mouth of Irondequoit Bay and in the west side thereof, containing about fifteen acres more or less, bounded on the west by the east line of a tract of one hundred acres sold to Sylvester Woodman." By a subsequent deed the remaining one-fourth interest was conveyed to Bronson, and the defendant claims the premises in question through mesne conveyances from Bronson. It is thus apparent that, in view of the fact that the defendant's title is bounded upon the west by the east line of Woodman's title, the question to be determined is as to whether Woodman's deed covered the lands in question.

It appears that at about the time of the conveyance by Hornby to Woodman in 1819, E. Johnson made a survey of these lands. Whether he made a map at that time of the land embraced in the conveyance does not clearly appear from the evidence. We have, however, a copy of a map introduced in evidence as Exhibit 20, the original of which is on file in the Guarantee Company's office, bearing the name of Elisha Johnson, purporting to describe the 494.56 acre lot conveyed to Hornby, as well as the 100 acre lot conveyed by him to Woodman. Upon that map there appears at the mouth of Irondequoit bay on the western shore thereof the letter "A" upon a body of land extending some distance into the bay, and on the north side of which there is a narrow strip of water extending north around the mainland, forming a cove, separating the mainland from the sand bar extending out into the lake and bay, which is the land sold by Hornby to Bronson through whom the defendant claims title. We then have introduced in evidence Johnson's field notes of a survey made by him of the tract conveyed to Woodman. It is as follows: "Undivided lot lying in township No. 14, 7th Range, and at the intersection of the Irondequoit Bay with Lake Ontario. 1st. Lay off one hundred acres agreeable to I. Woodman's deed. Beginning at the intersection of Bay and Lake Ontario and at the neck of the bar at A on map; thence north 67° west nine chains and seventy five links; thence north 82° west

fifteen chains and twenty-five links along the lake."
Referring to map, Exhibit 20, and commencing at the
point marked by the letter "A" thereon, thence running
as specified in his field notes, the line would pass along
the northern shore of the land as indicated in that map
to the end of the cove; thence through the neck of the
sand bar as there indicated out to the edge of the lake
and thence by the second course along the lake shore;
the two courses making one hundred rods from the starting point.   It would thus appear that he treated this portion of land marked as the intersection of the bay with
the lake, or as the mouth of the bay, the cove and the
sand bar then being north and westerly of the starting
point.   The field notes further proceed to give the course
and distances surrounding the hundred acre lot conveyed
to Woodman, reaching a point on the south line of the
lot line, being the eastern shore of Irondequoit bay;
thence north along that shore to the place of beginning.
But instead of its being in fact the western line of Irondequoit bay at the water's edge it was a zigzag line on the
top of the high bank, starting at a point south 290.4 feet
distant from the water line.   As this line approaches the
lake it turns eastward, running north 32° east five chains
twenty links and thence north 50° east five chains fifty-
three links to the place of beginning.

On behalf of the defendant the contention is that the
line disclosed by these field notes became the eastern
boundary of the Woodman property and that, consequently, his land was bounded upon the west by that
line.   Neither the trial judge nor the Appellate Division
has adopted this claim.   Instead, they have approved the
contention of the plaintiff that the express language of
the deed carried the title "to the line of the lot, being
the shore of Irondequoit Bay," and, therefore, the shore
line instead of the surveyed line became the boundary
line of its property.   This contention, we think, is unan-
swerable.   It must be borne in mind that, at the time
the survey was made, the bank upon the shore in many
places was nearly perpendicular and accessible with diffi-

culty. And it is quite possible that the surveyor, in running the line as he did upon the brink of the bank, intended it as a set off or base line and made the measurements for the purpose of obtaining the quantity of land required to be conveyed by the deed. If we are correct in this conclusion it would necessarily follow that the title to the lands lying east of the surveyed line and west of the bay line, which were described as uplands covered with timber, vested in Woodman under his deed and excludes the defendant's lands from being any part thereof. This, we think, is made clear by the original map that was introduced in evidence by the defendant as Exhibit 27. It was made by F. J. M. Cornell, surveyor, in March, 1860, following the field notes of Johnson made in 1819. This map shows that the Johnson survey began at a point upon the mainland south of the cove and south of the old sand bar, running thence along the line of land south of the cove and across the sand bar to the lake front, as already indicated in the Johnson field notes. The map also shows the lake line, the sand bar and cove as they existed in 1819; also the lake front as it existed in 1860, with the remains of the bridge which was constructed in 1855. At that time the cove and sand bar on the north had disappeared and the shore line of the lake then commenced at the bridge.

It appears from the testimony of the defendant's witnesses that formerly the Woodman road ran out upon the old sand bar, but that in 1853 or 1854 the neck of the sand bar was washed away during a heavy storm, and that in 1855 a bridge about three hundred feet in length was constructed by the towns of Irondequoit and Webster, whose line it crossed, for the purpose of affording a passage over on to the remaining part of the sand bar, but that in a year or so later the bridge itself was washed away; the sand bar also was washed farther into the bay and a new bar formed at the place where the bridge was constructed, and that the lake had encroached upon the highlands for a considerable distance. It is thus apparent from the defendant's own showing that the old sand bar as it existed in 1819 has disappeared, and that the mainland abutting thereon has been washed away for a distance more than sufficient to cover any claim that the plaintiff has made to the beach as it now exists.

As to the other questions involved in this appeal, we concur in the opinion of ROBSON, J., below.

The judgment should be affirmed, with costs.

CULLEN, Ch. J., GRAY, VANN, HISCOCK, CHASE and COLLIN, JJ., concur.

Judgment affirmed.

THE PEOPLE OF THE STATE OF NEW YORK ex rel. WARNER L. CONLEY, Appellant, *v.* SAMUEL H. BEACH et al., Constituting the Board of Fire and Police Commissioners of the City of Rome, Respondents.

Civil service — improper dismissal of veteran fireman.

Upon review of the statutes relative to the fire department of the village and city of Rome, *held*, that the board of fire and police commissioners should not be allowed to so construe the Civil Service Law (Cons. Laws, ch. 7, § 22) as to permit it to summarily discharge the relator, without a hearing, from his office in the police department, while he has in his possession an honorable discharge from the fire department of the city signed by said board and recommended by the chief engineer of the fire department.

People ex rel. Conley v. *Beach*, 143 App. Div. 712, reversed.

(Argued November 22, 1911; decided December 12, 1911.)

APPEAL from an order of the Appellate Division of the Supreme Court in the fourth judicial department, entered March 8, 1911, which affirmed an order of Special Term denying a motion for a peremptory writ of mandamus to compel defendants to reinstate the relator in the office of patrolman in the police department of the city of Rome.

An alternative writ of mandamus was issued April 2, 1910, commanding the respondents to reinstate the relator to the office of policeman in the city of Rome, from which office he had been removed, or show cause why the writ should not be obeyed and make return thereto as required by statute. A return was duly filed to the writ and upon the trial an order was made denying the writ of peremptory mandamus. An appeal was taken therefrom to the Appellate Division where the order appealed from was affirmed by a divided court. (*People ex rel. Conley* v. *Beach*, 143 App. Div. 712.) From the order and the judgment entered thereon an appeal is taken to this court.

The facts, so far as material, are stated in the opinion.

M. H. Powers and *W. J. Powers* for appellant.

M. J. Larkin for respondents.

CHASE, J. It is provided by section 22 of the Civil Service Law (Consolidated Laws, chap. 7) that " No person holding a position by appointment or employment in the state of New York or in the several cities, counties, towns or villages thereof * * * who shall have served the term required by law in the volunteer fire department of any city, town or village in the state * * * shall be removed from such position except for incompetency or misconduct shown after a hearing upon due notice upon stated charges. * * *"

The relator, after a competitive examination, was, on the 9th day of July, 1896, duly appointed a police officer in the city of Rome by the board of fire and police commissioners of said city and he served as such officer until the 5th day of February, 1910, when he was summarily removed from such office without a hearing upon due notice upon stated charges.

In the month of November, 1883, the relator became a member of Fort Stanwix Hose Company No. 2, an unincorporated volunteer fire company in said city, and continued as an active volunteer fireman and member of such company until May, 1892, a period of more than eight years.

On or about the 5th day of November, 1897, the relator was given a certificate by such volunteer fire company, which was signed by the foreman and secretary thereof and confirmed by the chief engineer of the fire department of the city as follows: "We, the undersigned, hereby certify that Mr. Warner L. Conley has served five years as an active member of Fort Stanwix Hose Company No. 2 of the Rome Fire Department.

   "C. J. FARR, *Foreman.*
   "H. C. ANDERSON, JR., *Secretary.*
"Confirmed.
  "L. BRIGGS,
   "*Chief Engineer.*"

On that day, at a meeting of said board of fire and police commissioners, a resolution was adopted which appears in the minutes of the commissioners as follows: "Com. Bingham moved that Warner L. Conley be granted a discharge from the fire department. Carried."

He was thereupon given a written certificate of honorable discharge from the fire department of the city signed by the chairman and clerk of said board of fire and police commissioners, of which the following is a copy:

   "FIRE DEPARTMENT, CITY OF ROME.

"This is to certify that Warner L. Conley has served five years as a member of the Rome Fire Department, and at his own request is hereby honorably discharged by order of the Board of Fire and Police Commissioners.

   "W. L. KINGSLEY, *Chairman.*
"Dated ROME, N. Y., *Nov. 5th,* 1897.
 "W. O. JENKS, *Clerk.*"

If the relator's service in said hose company entitles him to the protection afforded by said section 22 of the Civil Service Law, the order appealed from should be reversed.

Fort Stanwix Hose Company No. 2 was and is a volunteer fireman's association, which has existed as such for more than fifty years, having a president, secretary, foreman and an assistant foreman, and during all of the years of its history its members have responded to every alarm of fire within the territory of the city and of the village that existed prior to the incorporation of the city, and it has been furnished by the city and by the village with a suitable place for its meetings and also with uniforms, belts and appliances for fighting fire. A horse was also furnished to them by the city to aid in hauling the apparatus used by them in fighting fire.

The city of Rome was first incorporated in 1870. (Laws of 1870, chap. 25.) Prior to the incorporation of the city a large part of the territory now constituting the city of Rome was incorporated as a village. It was first so incorporated as a village in 1819. (Laws of 1819, chap. 77.) Before the village of Rome was so incorporated the inhabitants included within such territory had made provision for fighting fire, and by chapter 79 of the Laws of 1818 Joel Hayes and such other persons associated or that might associate with him, not exceeding twenty in number, were constituted the "Rome Fire Company" as a body corporate, and such persons were, among other things, by the act exempt from serving as jurors. Five of their number to be chosen by themselves as trustees had power to remove any firemen so appointed and appoint others in their stead as often as they should think proper. When the village was incorporated in 1819 the trustees thereof were given power "to appoint twenty firemen * * * in addition to the number now (then) in said village and they are authorized to displace all or any of them as often as they shall think fit and others to appoint in their place." The charter of the village was amended from time to time as was the act for the incorporation of the Rome Fire Company until 1855, when a fire department of the village of Rome was incorporated by chapter 388 of the laws of that year. That act provided (Section 1) that "all persons who now are or hereafter shall become members of the fire engine, hook and ladder and hose companies, not exceeding forty in number to each company of the village of Rome, * * * by appointment of the trustees of the village of Rome, as hereinafter provided, shall be and are hereby ordained and constituted a body politic and corporate in fact and in name, by the name and style of the ' Fire Department of the Village of Rome.'"

It was provided by the act that the members of such

fire department should be appointed and could be removed by resolution of the board of trustees of the village. That act with some amendments continued in existence not only until the incorporation of the city of Rome but to and including the year 1881, and it was in substance provided in that act and in the charter of 1870 that the engineers of the fire department, fire wardens and all firemen, hook and ladder, hose and axemen of the city shall be exempt from serving on juries in all cases.

It is also provided in said charter of 1870 (Title VIII. §§ 8, 9) that "the present firemen of the village of Rome shall be firemen of the said city, subject to be removed by the common council, in like manner as other firemen of said city," and also that "every fireman who shall have faithfully served as such in said city, including as well any period before as after the passage of this act, five consecutive years, shall be thereafter exempt from serving on juries in all courts or in the militia. * * *."

In 1881 an act was passed (Laws of 1881, chapter 517) establishing a board of fire commissioners for the city of Rome to fulfill the duties connected with and incident to the control, government and discipline of the fire department of said city.

It was therein provided (Section 6): "The board thus constituted shall organize *fire companies* and appoint a sufficient number of able-bodied and reputable inhabitants of the city of Rome firemen to belong to such companies, and shall pay them a reasonable compensation for their services as such firemen. They shall appoint one of said firemen chief engineer of the fire department, who shall, under the direction of the board, have full control of the department. * * * The number of firemen to be appointed and so paid shall not exceed in the aggregate twenty-five in number."

The provisions of the act clearly refer to paid firemen, and the number was limited to twenty-five men, except that by direction of the fire commissioners the chief engineer, "in case of emergency," was given authority to appoint additional special firemen. No provision was included therein in recognition of the volunteer firemen then lawfully existing in companies in said village, aggregating about one hundred and seventy-five men.

By chapter 428 of the Laws of 1890 the board was changed so as to become the board of fire and police commissioners for the city of Rome, and to their powers as fire commissioners were added powers as police commissioners, and such board of fire and police commissioners are continued by the new city charter (Laws of 1904, chap. 650) to the present time. In the city charter of 1904 it is provided: "The said board shall, subject to the limitations of this act, maintain fire companies and appoint a sufficient number of able-bodied and reputable inhabitants of the city of Rome firemen to belong to such companies, and pay them a reasonable compensation for their services as such firemen. Said board shall appoint one of said firemen chief engineer of the fire department who shall under its direction have full control of the fire department." (Section 115.)

The Fort Stanwix Hose Company No. 2 was undoubtedly a part of a duly incorporated fire department of the city prior to 1881, and although the act of 1855 and the amendments thereto were repealed by the act of 1881, the several volunteer fire companies continued to exist as volunteer associations and to act as a subsidiary volunteer fire department in conjunction with the limited number of men constituting the paid fire department of the city. The board of fire and police commissioners assumed to have authority and control over them, and such firemen submitted to such authority and control.

The charter of 1904 expressly provides that the board of fire and police commissioners shall "maintain fire companies," and the city has continuously since 1881 maintained the Fort Stanwix Hose Company No. 2 as such volunteer association, and has accepted the service of such volunteer firemen and they have been recognized as part of the fire department of the city. It clearly appears from the record that the recognition of such volunteer fire companies has been shown in every possible way by the municipal corporation and by its officers, including the board of fire and police commissioners and the chief engineer of the fire department. Since 1881 they have been continued as they existed prior to that time and maintained as theretofore by the city. Appointments have been made to said company and discharges given from time to time to its members as from the fire department of the city, including the honorable discharge to the relator which we have quoted herein.

The board of fire and police commissioners should not now be allowed to so construe the Civil Service Law as to permit them to discharge the relator from his office in the police department while he has in his possession an honorable discharge from the fire department of the city signed by said board and recommended by the chief engineer of the fire department.

The order should be reversed, with costs in all courts, and the peremptory mandamus should be granted.

CULLEN, Ch. J., HAIGHT, WERNER, WILLARD BARTLETT, HISCOCK and COLLIN, JJ., concur.

Order reversed, etc.

WILLIAM E. BURKE, Respondent, *v.* THE CONTINENTAL INSURANCE COMPANY OF THE CITY OF NEW YORK, Appellant.

Burke v. Continental Ins. Co. of N. Y., 139 App. Div. 927, affirmed. (Argued November 3, 1911; decided December 12, 1911.)

APPEAL from a judgment of the Appellate Division of the Supreme Court in the fourth judicial department, entered June 6, 1910, affirming a judgment in favor of plaintiff entered upon a decision of the court at a Trial Term without a jury in an action to recover on a policy of fire insurance.

Ralph S. Kent and *Clarence M. Bushnell* for appellant.

Moses Shire and *Vernon Cole* for respondent.

Judgment affirmed, with costs; no opinion.

In the Matter of the Transfer Tax upon the Estate of MATTHIAS H. ARNOT, Deceased.

THE COMPTROLLER OF THE STATE OF NEW YORK, Appellant; JAMES B. RATHBONE et al., as Executors, Respondents.

Matter of Arnot, 145 App. Div. 708, affirmed.
(Argued November 21, 1911; decided December 12, 1911.)

APPEAL from an order of the Appellate Division of the the Supreme Court in the third judicial department, entered June 27, 1911, which affirmed an order of the Chemung County Surrogate's Court exempting certain portions of the estate of Matthias H. Arnot, deceased, from the imposition of a transfer tax.

William Law Stout for appellant.

Alexander D. Falck for respondents.

Order affirmed, with costs; no opinion.
Concur: CULLEN, Ch. J., HAIGHT, WERNER, WILLARD BARTLETT, HISCOCK and CHASE, JJ. Not sitting: COLLIN, J.

MONCURE ROBINSON, Respondent, *v.* THE NEW YORK CENTRAL AND HUDSON RIVER RAILROAD COMPANY, Appellant.

Robinson v. *N. Y. C. & H. R. R. R. Co.*, 145 App. Div. 891, affirmed.
(Argued November 22, 1911; decided December 12, 1911.)

APPEAL, by permission, from an order of the Appellate Division of the Supreme Court in the first judicial department, entered June 2, 1911, which affirmed an order of Special Term sustaining a demurrer to a partial defense in the answer in an action to recover for the alleged negligent loss of a trunk and its contents delivered by the plaintiff to defendant for transportation as baggage.

The following question was certified: "Is the second and partial defense set up in the amended answer herein insufficient in law upon the face thereof as a partial defense to the cause of action set forth in the complaint?"

William Mann and *Alexander S. Lyman* for appellant.

Clifton P. Williamson and *Phœnix Ingraham* for respondent.

Order affirmed, with costs, on opinion of MILLER, J., below. Question certified answered in the affirmative.

Concur: CULLEN, Ch. J., HAIGHT, WERNER, WILLARD BARTLETT, HISCOCK, CHASE and COLLIN, JJ.

In the Matter of the Application of THE GRADE CROSSING COMMISSIONERS OF THE CITY OF BUFFALO for the Appointment of Commissioners to Ascertain the Compensation to Be Paid to Owners of Lands Injured by the Change of Grade of Delaware Avenue and Claimed to Be Owned by HENRY D. KIRKOVER et al., Respondents.

THE NEW YORK CENTRAL AND HUDSON RIVER RAILROAD COMPANY, Appellant.

Matter of Grade Crossing Comrs., Buffalo, 146 App. Div. 885 affirmed.

(Argued November 22, 1911; decided December 12, 1911.)

APPEAL from an order of the Appellate Division of the Supreme Court in the fourth judicial department, entered July 14, 1911, which affirmed an order of Special Term confirming the report of commissioners in the above-entitled proceeding.

Alfred L. Becker and *Daniel E. Meegan* for appellant.

Clark H. Hammond, Corporation Counsel (*Harry D. Sanders* of counsel), for city of Buffalo, intervening.

Moses Shire, Vernon Cole and *Louis L. Babcock* for respondents.

Order affirmed, with costs; no opinion.
Concur: CULLEN, Ch. J., HAIGHT, WERNER, WILLARD BARTLETT, HISCOCK, CHASE and COLLIN, JJ.

HERMAN GOTTLIEB, Appellant, *v.* SIMON J. ALTSCHULER et al., Respondents.

Gottlieb v. *Altschuler*, 148 App. Div. 935, affirmed.
(Submitted November 22, 1911; decided December 12, 1911.)

APPEAL from an order of the Appellate Division of the Supreme Court in the first judicial department, entered March 31, 1911, which affirmed an order of Special Term directing plaintiff to release defendant Altschuler from a judgment heretofore directed against him.

Herman Gottlieb appellant in person.

A. Rosenstein for respondents.

Order affirmed, with costs; no opinion.
Concur: CULLEN, Ch. J., HAIGHT, WERNER, WILLARD BARTLETT, HISCOCK, CHASE and COLLIN, JJ.

THE PEOPLE OF THE STATE OF NEW YORK ex rel. THE TRUSTEES AND ASSOCIATES OF THE BROOKLYN BENEVOLENT SOCIETY, Appellant, *v.* LAWSON PURDY et al., as Commissioners of Taxes and Assessments of the City of New York, Respondents.

People ex rel. Trustees Brooklyn Benevolent Society v. *Purdy*, 148 App. Div. 935, affirmed.
(Argued November 22, 1911; decided December 12, 1911.)

APPEAL from an order of the Appellate Division of the Supreme Court in the first judicial department, entered

March 31, 1911, which affirmed an order of Special Term dismissing a writ of certiorari and confirming certain assessments against relator for purposes of taxation.

Austen G. Fox and *Thomas G. Barry* for appellant.

Archibald R. Watson, Corporation Counsel (Curtis A. Peters and *George H. Folwell* of counsel), for respondents.

Order affirmed, with costs; no opinion.
Concur: CULLEN, Ch. J., HAIGHT, WERNER, WILLARD BARTLETT, HISCOCK, CHASE and COLLIN, JJ.

In the Matter of the Application of JOHN J. O'BRIEN, Appellant, for a Peremptory Writ of Mandamus against RHINELANDER WALDO, as Police Commissioner of the City of New York, Respondent.

Matter of O'Brien v. *Waldo*, 146 App. Div. 983, appeal dismissed. (Submitted November 22, 1911; decided December 12, 1911.)

APPEAL from an order of the Appellate Division of the Supreme Court in the first judicial department, entered October 17, 1911, which affirmed an order of Special Term denying a motion for a peremptory writ of mandamus to compel defendant to restore the relator to the office of police captain of the police force of the city of New York.

George W. Morgan for appellant.

Archibald R. Watson, Corporation Counsel (Terence Farley and *Josiah Stover* of counsel), for respondent.

Appeal dismissed, with costs; no opinion.
Concur: CULLEN, Ch. J., HAIGHT, WERNER, WILLARD BARTLETT, HISCOCK, CHASE and COLLIN, JJ.

The New York Central and Hudson River Railroad Company, Appellant, *v.* The Federal Sugar Refining Company et al., Respondents.

N. Y. C. & H. R. R. R. Co. v. *Federal Sugar Refining Co.*, 145 App. Div. 936, affirmed.
(Argued November 23, 1911; decided December 12, 1911.)

APPEAL from an order of the Appellate Division of the Supreme Court in the second judicial department, entered June 9, 1911, which affirmed an order of Special Term confirming the report of commissioners in condemnation proceedings.

John F. Brennan and *Albert H. Harris* for appellant.

Charles Philip Easton for respondents.

Order affirmed, with costs; no opinion.
Concur: CULLEN, Ch. J., HAIGHT, WERNER, WILLARD BARTLETT, HISCOCK, CHASE and COLLIN, JJ.

The People of the State of New York ex rel. HARRY F. DWYER, Appellant, *v.* THEODORE A. BINGHAM, as Police Commissioner of the City of New York, Respondent.

People ex rel. Dwyer v. *Bingham*, 144 App. Div. 905, affirmed.
(Argued November 23, 1911; decided December 12, 1911.)

APPEAL from an order of the Appellate Division of the Supreme Court in the second judicial department, entered April 7, 1911, which confirmed the proceedings of defendant in dismissing the relator from the police force of the city of New York.

Louis J. Grant and *Jacob Rouss* for appellant.

Archibald R. Watson, Corporation Counsel (*James D. Bell* and *Frank Julian Price* of counsel), for respondent.

Order affirmed, with costs; no opinion.
Concur: CULLEN, Ch. J., HAIGHT, WERNER, WILLARD BARTLETT, HISCOCK, CHASE and COLLIN, JJ.

THE PEOPLE OF THE STATE OF NEW YORK ex rel.
WILLIAM A. LEAVY, Appellant, *v.* WILLIAM F. BAKER,
as Police Commissioner of the City of New York,
Respondent.

People ex rel. Leavy v. *Baker*, 143 App. Div. 917, affirmed.
(Argued November 23, 1911; decided December 12, 1911.)

APPEAL from an order of the Appellate Division of the
Supreme Court in the second judicial department, entered
February 24, 1911, which confirmed the determination of
defendant in dismissing the relator from the police force
of the city of New York.

Jacob Rouss and *Louis J. Grant* for appellant.

*Archibald R. Watson, Corporation Counsel (James
D. Bell* and *John B. Shanahan* of counsel), for respondent.

Order affirmed, with costs; no opinion.
Concur: CULLEN, Ch. J., HAIGHT, WERNER, WILLARD
BARTLETT, HISCOCK, CHASE and COLLIN, JJ.

ROBERT E. DEYO et al., Respondents, *v.* THE CITY OF
NEWBURGH, Appellant.

Deyo v. *City of Newburgh*, 138 App. Div. 465, affirmed.
(Argued November 23, 1911; decided December 12, 1911.)

APPEAL from an order of the Appellate Division of
the Supreme Court in the second judicial department,
entered May 11, 1910, affirming a judgment in favor of
plaintiffs entered upon a decision of the court on trial at
Special Term in an action to secure the cancellation of
certain certificates of sale of lands for non-payment of
certain assessments levied thereon and to set aside said
assessments.

Henry Kohl for appellant.

Charles F. Brown and *George R. Brewster* for
respondents.

Judgment affirmed, with costs. The eleventh conclusion of law, that the assessment was unconstitutional, does not import that the statute itself is unconstitutional, and we are of the opinion that the statute is valid; no opinion.

Concur: CULLEN, Ch. J., HAIGHT, WERNER, WILLARD BARTLETT, HISCOCK, CHASE and COLLIN, JJ.

WALTER C. ANTHONY, Respondent, *v.* THE CITY OF NEWBURGH, Appellant.

Anthony v. *City of Newburgh*, 145 App. Div. 932, affirmed.
(Argued November 23, 1911; decided December 12, 1911.)

APPEAL from a judgment of the Appellate Division of the Supreme Court in the second judicial department, entered June 8, 1911, affirming a judgment in favor of plaintiff entered upon a decision of the court on trial at Special Term in an action to secure the cancellation of certain certificates of sale of lands for non-payment of certain assessments levied thereon and to set aside said assessments.

Henry Kohl for appellant.

Graham Witschief for respondent.

Judgment affirmed, with costs; no opinion.

Concur: CULLEN, Ch. J., HAIGHT, WERNER, WILLARD BARTLETT, HISCOCK, CHASE and COLLIN, JJ.

FRED BAUER, Respondent, *v.* INTER-OCEAN TELEPHONE AND TELEGRAPH COMPANY, Appellant.

Bauer v. *Inter-Ocean Tel. & Tel. Co.*, 139 App. Div. 927, affirmed.
(Argued November 24, 1911; decided December 12, 1911.)

APPEAL from a judgment of the Appellate Division of the Supreme Court in the fourth judicial department, entered June 3, 1910, affirming a judgment in favor of plaintiff entered upon a verdict in an action to recover

for personal injuries alleged to have been sustained by plaintiff through the negligence of defendant, his employer.

Theodore H. Lord and *Harold S. Rankine* for appellant.

Hamilton Ward for respondent.

Judgment affirmed, with costs; no opinion.
Concur: CULLEN, Ch. J., HAIGHT, WERNER, WILLARD BARTLETT, HISCOCK, CHASE and COLLIN, JJ.

JOSEPH LYONS, Appellant, *v.* THE NEW YORK CENTRAL AND HUDSON RIVER RAILROAD COMPANY, Respondent.

Lyons v. *N. Y. C. & H. R. R. R. Co.*, 136 App. Div. 903, affirmed.
(Argued November 24, 1911; decided December 12, 1911.)

APPEAL from a judgment of the Appellate Division of the Supreme Court in the third judicial department, entered January 6, 1910, affirming a judgment in favor of defendant entered upon a dismissal of the complaint by the court at a Trial Term in an action to recover for personal injuries alleged to have been sustained by plaintiff through the negligence of defendant, his employer.

Andrew J. Nellis for appellant.

William L. Visscher for respondent.

Judgment affirmed, with costs; no opinion.
Concur: CULLEN, Ch. J., HAIGHT, WERNER, WILLARD BARTLETT, HISCOCK, CHASE and COLLIN, JJ.

THE PEOPLE OF THE STATE OF NEW YORK, Respondent, *v.* JOHN WULFORST, Appellant.

People v. *Wulforst*, 146 App. Div. 938, affirmed.
(Argued November 27, 1911; decided December 12, 1911.)

APPEAL from an order of the Appellate Division of the Supreme Court in the first judicial department, entered

October 27, 1911, which affirmed a judgment of the Court of Special Sessions of the city of New York convicting the defendant of a violation of section 2412 of the Penal Law in having in his possession a false measure.

James C. Van Siclen for appellant.

Charles S. Whitman, District Attorney (*Robert S. Johnstone* of counsel), for respondent.

Judgment of conviction affirmed; no opinion.
Concur: GRAY, VANN, CHASE and COLLIN, JJ. Dissenting: CULLEN, Ch. J., HAIGHT and HISCOCK, JJ.

ABRAHAM LEVY, Appellant, *v.* ADRIAN H. JOLINE et al., as Receivers of the METROPOLITAN STREET RAILWAY COMPANY, Respondents.

Levy v. *Joline*, 139 App. Div. 932, affirmed.
(Argued November 27, 1911; decided December 12, 1911.)

APPEAL from a judgment of the Appellate Division of the Supreme Court in the first judicial department, entered July 28, 1910, affirming a judgment in favor of defendants entered upon a dismissal of the complaint by the court at a Trial Term in an action to recover for personal injuries alleged to have been sustained by plaintiff through the negligence of defendants.

Clifford C. Roberts for appellant.

Bayard H. Ames and *Walter Henry Wood* for respondents.

Judgment affirmed, with costs; no opinion.
Concur: CULLEN, Ch. J., HAIGHT, VANN, HISCOCK, CHASE and COLLIN, JJ. Not sitting: GRAY, J.

ALBERT H. FLINT, Respondent, *v.* BOWERS H. LEONARD, Appellant, Impleaded with Others.

Flint v. *Leonard,* 140 App. Div. 882, affirmed.
(Argued November 27, 1911; decided December 12, 1911.)

APPEAL from a judgment of the Appellate Division of the Supreme Court in the fourth judicial department, entered July 15, 1910, affirming a judgment in favor of plaintiff entered upon a decision of the court on trial at Special Term in an action to compel specific performance of a contract.

John M. Brainard for appellant.

E. C. Aiken for respondent.

Judgment affirmed, with costs; no opinion.
Concur: CULLEN, Ch. J., GRAY, HAIGHT, VANN, HISCOCK, CHASE and COLLIN, JJ.

LEE SHUBERT, Respondent, *v.* LEOPOLD SONDHEIM, as Executor of MEYER R. BIMBERG, Deceased, Appellant.

Shubert v. *Sondheim,* 138 App. Div. 800, affirmed.
(Argued November 28, 1911; decided December 12, 1911.)

APPEAL from a judgment of the Appellate Division of the Supreme Court in the first judicial department, entered June 18, 1910, affirming a judgment in favor of plaintiff entered upon a verdict in an action to recover liquidated damages for an alleged breach of an agreement to lease or secure a lease to the plaintiff of certain premises.

George W. Schurman, Eugene Sondheim and *Harley L. Stowell* for appellant.

Max D. Steuer, Gerald B. Rosenheim and *William Klein* for respondent.

Judgment affirmed, with costs; no opinion.
Concur: CULLEN, Ch. J., GRAY, HAIGHT, VANN, HISCOCK, CHASE and COLLIN, JJ.

WILLIAM F. EASLEY, Respondent, *v.* MAX LOEWENSTEIN, Appellant.

Reported below, 141 App. Div. 931.
(Submitted December 4, 1911; decided December 12, 1911.)

MOTION to dismiss an appeal from a judgment of the Appellate Division of the Supreme Court in the first judicial department, entered December 30, 1910, affirming a judgment in favor of plaintiff entered upon the report of a referee in an action to recover for an alleged breach of certain contracts.

The motion was made upon the ground that the Court of Appeals had no jurisdiction to entertain the appeal.

Robert W. Hardie for motion.

Robert B. Killgore opposed.

Motion denied, with ten dollars costs.

——— ——— ———

DEXTER AND NORTHERN RAILROAD COMPANY, Appellant, *v.* LUTHER I. FOSTER et al., Respondents.

Dexter & Northern R. R. Co. v. *Foster*, 142 App. Div. 240, affirmed.
(Argued November 21, 1911; decided December 19, 1911.)

APPEAL, by permission, from an order of the Appellate Division of the Supreme Court in the fourth judicial department, entered January 14, 1911, which affirmed an order of Special Term awarding separate bills of costs and extra allowances to various defendants in a condemnation proceeding.

The following question was certified: "Are the several defendants to whom costs have been awarded in this proceeding severally entitled to a bill of costs under section

3372 of the Code of Civil Procedure as a matter of right?"

Elon R. Brown and *Henry H. Babcock* for appellant.

Charles A. Phelps for respondents.

Order affirmed, with costs, and question certified answered in the affirmative; no opinion.

Concur: CULLEN, Ch. J., HAIGHT, WERNER, WILLARD BARTLETT, HISCOCK, CHASE and COLLIN, JJ.

WILLIAM SMITH, Respondent, *v.* NATIONAL STARCH COMPANY, Appellant.

Smith v. *National Starch Company*, 134 App. Div. 994, affirmed.
(Argued December 4, 1911; decided December 19, 1911.)

APPEAL from a judgment of the Appellate Division of the Supreme Court in the fourth judicial department, entered December 15, 1909, affirming a judgment in favor of plaintiff entered upon a verdict in an action to recover for personal injuries alleged to have been sustained through the defendant's negligence.

Elisha B. Powell and *Herrick C. Allen* for appellant.

D. P. Morehouse and *Charles N. Bulger* for respondent.

Judgment affirmed, with costs, no opinion.
Concur: CULLEN, Ch. J., GRAY, HAIGHT, VANN, HISCOCK, CHASE and COLLIN, JJ.

FREDERICK SCHERR, Suing for Himself and Other Stockholders of THE PIONEER IRON WORKS, Appellant, *v.* THE PIONEER IRON WORKS et al., Respondents.

Scherr v. *Pioneer Iron Works*, 134 App. Div. 989, affirmed.
(Argued December 4, 1911; decided December 19, 1911.)

APPEAL from a judgment of the Appellate Division of the Supreme Court in the second judicial department, entered October 23, 1909, affirming a judgment in favor of defendants entered upon a decision of the court on trial at Special Term in an action by a minority stockholder of a corporation to recover for alleged waste and mismanagement.

John C. Wait, Charles A. Winter and *William L. Bowman* for appellant.

Gustav Lange, Jr., for respondents.

Judgment affirmed, with costs; no opinion.
Concur: CULLEN, Ch. J., GRAY, HAIGHT, VANN, HISCOCK, CHASE and COLLIN, JJ.

JOHN P. KRAEMER, Appellant, *v.* RICHARD H. WILLIAMS, Respondent, Impleaded with Another.

Kraemer v. *Williams,* 131 App. Div. 236, affirmed.
(Argued December 5, 1911; decided December 19, 1911.)

APPEAL, by permission, from a judgment of the Appellate Division of the Supreme Court in the second judicial department, entered March 26, 1909, affirming a judgment in favor of defendant entered upon a dismissal of the complaint by the court on trial at Special Term in an action to recover for goods alleged to have been sold and delivered; to have certain deeds declared fraudulent and void; to establish a lien on certain property, for an injunction and for an accounting.

Emil Schneeloch for appellant.

Harrison S. Moore for respondent.

Judgment affirmed, with costs; no opinion.
Concur: CULLEN, Ch. J., GRAY, HAIGHT, VANN, WERNER, WILLARD BARTLETT and CHASE, JJ.

THE TOWN OF IRONDEQUOIT, Respondent, *v.* SEPHARINE COSTICH, Appellant.

Town of Irondequoit v. *Costich*, 138 App. Div. 916, affirmed.
(Argued December 5, 1911; decided December 19, 1911.)

APPEAL, by permission, from a judgment of the Appellate Division of the Supreme Court in the fourth judicial department, entered May 20, 1910, affirming a judgment in favor of plaintiff entered upon a verdict in an action to recover a penalty for violation of an ordinance of the board of health of the town of Irondequoit.

Frank J. Hone for appellant.

Herbert Leary and *W. H. Sullivan* for respondent.

Judgment affirmed, with costs; no opinion.
Concur: CULLEN, Ch. J., GRAY, HAIGHT, VANN, WERNER, WILLARD BARTLETT and CHASE, JJ.

JAMES F. LOFTUS, Respondent, *v.* CONTINENTAL CASUALTY COMPANY, Appellant.

Loftus v. *Continental Casualty Co.*, 134 App. Div. 994, affirmed.
(Argued December 5, 1911; decided December 19, 1911.)

APPEAL from a judgment of the Appellate Division of the Supreme Court in the fourth judicial department, entered November 29, 1909, affirming a judgment in favor of plaintiff entered upon a verdict directed by the court in an action to recover on a policy of accident insurance.

Walter S. Jenkins and *Manton Maverick* for appellant.

Thomas C. Burke for respondent.

Judgment affirmed, with costs; no opinion.
Concur: CULLEN, Ch. J., GRAY, HAIGHT, VANN, WERNER, WILLARD BARTLETT and CHASE, JJ.

THE PEOPLE OF THE STATE OF NEW YORK, Respondent,
v. CHARLES SWENTON, Appellant.

(Argued December 11, 1911; decided December 19, 1911.)

APPEAL from a judgment of the Court of General Sessions of the Peace in the county of New York, rendered January 5, 1911, upon a verdict convicting defendant of the crime of murder in the first degree.

Charles J. Campbell and *William A. Sweetser* for appellant.

Charles S. Whitman, District Attorney (*Robert C. Taylor* of counsel), for respondent.

Judgment of conviction affirmed; no opinion.
Concur: CULLEN, Ch. J., GRAY, HAIGHT, VANN, WILLARD BARTLETT, HISCOCK and COLLIN, JJ.

CHARLES E. BULKLEY, Respondent, v. WHITING MANUFACTURING COMPANY, Appellant.

(Submitted December 11, 1911; decided December 19, 1911.)

Motion for re-argument denied, with ten dollars costs. (See 203 N. Y. 566.)

PATRICK NOLAN, Respondent, v. THE FERRIS PAVING BRICK COMPANY, Appellant.

Nolan v. *Ferris Paving Brick Co.*, 138 App. Div. 931, **affirmed.**
(Argued November 29, 1911; decided December 22, 1911.)

APPEAL from a judgment of the Appellate Division of the Supreme Court in the third judicial department, entered May 10, 1910, affirming a judgment in favor of plaintiff entered upon a verdict in an action to recover for personal injuries alleged to have been sustained by plaintiff through the negligence of defendant, his employer.

41

Edward M. Angell, George R. Salisbury and *Franklin A. Rowe* for appellant.

Timothy I. Dillon for respondent.

Judgment affirmed, with costs; no opinion.
Concur: CULLEN, Ch. J., GRAY, HAIGHT, VANN, HISCOCK, CHASE and COLLIN, JJ.

HERBERT T. FOOTE, Respondent, *v.* HENRY H. TODD, Appellant.

Foote v. *Todd,* 137 App. Div. 918, affirmed.
(Argued December 6, 1911; decided December 22, 1911.)

APPEAL from a judgment of the Appellate Division of the Supreme Court in the first judicial department, entered March 23, 1910, affirming a judgment in favor of plaintiff entered upon a verdict directed by the court in an action to recover upon a promissory note.

William L. Snyder for appellant.

Philip W. Russell for respondent.

Judgment affirmed, with costs; no opinion.
Concur: CULLEN, Ch. J., GRAY, HAIGHT, VANN, WERNER, WILLARD BARTLETT and CHASE, JJ.

FRANK RICH, Respondent, *v.* PENNSYLVANIA RAILROAD COMPANY, Appellant.

Rich v. *Pennsylvania R. R. Co.,* 134 App. Div. 993, affirmed.
(Argued December 6, 1911; decided December 22, 1911.)

APPEAL from a judgment of the Appellate Division of the Supreme Court in the fourth judicial department, entered November 29, 1909, affirming a judgment in favor of plaintiff entered upon a verdict in an action to recover for personal injuries alleged to have been sustained through the negligence of defendant, his employer.

George A. Larkin and *A. J. Hastings* for appellant.

George H. Harris for respondent.

Judgment affirmed, with costs; no opinion.

Concur: CULLEN, Ch. J., GRAY, HAIGHT, WERNER, WILLARD BARTLETT and CHASE, JJ. Not sitting: VANN, J.

GEORGE W. ROBERTS et al., Appellants, *v.* ALONZO L. ROBERTS et al., Respondents.

Roberts v. *Roberts*, 134 App. Div. 816, reversed.
(Submitted December 6, 1911; decided December 22, 1911.)

APPEAL from an order of the Appellate Division of the Supreme Court in the fourth judicial department, entered November 17, 1909, reversing a judgment in favor of plaintiffs entered upon a decision of the court at a Trial Term without a jury, and granting a new trial in an action to recover rent alleged to be due under a lease.

John B. Rogers for appellants.

Thomas Burns for respondents.

Order of Appellate Division reversed and judgment of Trial Term affirmed, with costs in both courts, on dissenting opinion of McLENNAN, P. J., below.

Concur: CULLEN, Ch. J., GRAY, HAIGHT, VANN, WERNER, WILLARD BARTLETT and CHASE, JJ.

THE PEOPLE OF THE STATE OF NEW YORK, Respondent, *v.* ABRAHAM LEWIS, Appellant.

People v. *Lewis*, 143 App. Div. 941, affirmed.
(Argued December 6, 1911; decided December 22, 1911.)

APPEAL from an order of the Appellate Division of the Supreme Court in the second judicial department, entered March 3, 1911, which affirmed a judgment of the Kings County Court rendered upon a verdict convicting defendant of the crime of robbery in the first degree.

Thomas Kelby for appellant.

John F. Clarke, District Attorney (*Peter P. Smith* of counsel), for respondent.

Judgment of conviction affirmed; no opinion.
Concur: CULLEN, Ch. J., GRAY, HAIGHT, VANN, WERNER, WILLARD BARTLETT and CHASE, JJ.

PERCY S. HILDRETH, Appellant, *v.* THE CITY OF NEW YORK, Respondent.

Hildreth v. *City of New York*, 138 App. Div. 108, affirmed.
(Argued December 6, 1911; decided December 22, 1911.)

APPEAL from a judgment of the Appellate Division of the Supreme Court in the first judicial department, entered June 8, 1910, affirming a judgment in favor of defendant entered upon a dismissal of the complaint by the court at a Trial Term without a jury in an action to recover for an alleged breach of contract.

William D. Leonard for appellant.

Archibald R. Watson, Corporation Counsel (*Clarence L. Barber* and *Theodore Connoly* of counsel), for respondent.

Judgment affirmed, with costs; no opinion.
Concur: CULLEN, Ch. J., GRAY, HAIGHT, VANN, WERNER, WILLARD BARTLETT and CHASE, JJ.

ISBELL-PORTER COMPANY, Respondent, *v.* ISAAC HEINEMAN, Appellant.

Isbell-Porter Company v. *Heineman*, 137 App. Div. 946, affirmed.
(Argued December 7, 1911; decided December 22, 1911.)

APPEAL from a judgment of the Appellate Division of the Supreme Court in the first judicial department, entered June 6, 1910, affirming a judgment in favor of plaintiff entered upon a verdict in an action to recover on contract.

Jesse S. Epstein for appellant.

Jay E. Whiting for respondent.

Judgment affirmed, with costs; no opinion.

Concur: CULLEN, Ch. J., GRAY, HAIGHT, VANN, WERNER, WILLARD BARTLETT and CHASE, JJ.

JOHN G. PENDORF, Respondent, *v.* THE CITY OF ROME, Appellant.

Pendorf v. *City of Rome*, 138 App. Div. 913, affirmed.
(Argued December 7, 1911; decided December 22, 1911.)

APPEAL from a judgment of the Appellate Division of the Supreme Court in the fourth judicial department, entered May 10, 1910, affirming a judgment in favor of plaintiff entered upon a decision of the court on trial at Special Term in an action to restrain the defendant from continuing to empty its sewers into a creek bordering plaintiff's lands and for damages.

M. J. Larkin for appellant.

Albert T. Wilkinson for respondent.

Judgment affirmed, with costs, on authority of *Sammons* v. *City of Gloversville* (175 N. Y. 346); no opinion.

Concur: CULLEN, Ch. J., GRAY, HAIGHT, VANN, WERNER, WILLARD BARTLETT and CHASE, JJ.

HARRY SUTPHIN, Respondent, *v.* THE NEW YORK TIMES COMPANY, Appellant.

Sutphin v. *New York Times Co.* 138 App. Div. 487, affirmed.
(Submitted December 7, 1911; decided December 22, 1911.)

APPEAL from a judgment of the Appellate Division of the Supreme Court in the second judicial department, entered May 26, 1910, affirming a judgment in favor of plaintiff entered upon a verdict in an action for libel.

Alfred A. Cook for appellant.

William Willett for respondent.

Judgment affirmed, with costs; no opinion.
· Concur: CULLEN, Ch. J., GRAY, HAIGHT, VANN, WERNER, WILLARD BARTLETT and CHASE, JJ.

———————————

CHARLOTTE L. MILLER et al., as Administrators of the Estate of FRED W. MILLER, Deceased, et al., Appellants, *v.* EMMA L. HILL et al., Individually and as Executrices of ROSETTA G. MILLER, Deceased, et al., Respondents.

Miller v. *Hill*, 137 App. Div. 378, affirmed.
(Argued December 7, 1911; decided December 22, 1911.)

APPEAL from a judgment of the Appellate Division of the Supreme Court in the fourth judicial department, entered March 25, 1910, affirming a judgment in favor of defendants entered upon a dismissal of the complaint in an action to establish a trust.

Fletcher C. Peck for appellants.

Sanford T. Church for respondents.

Judgment affirmed, with costs; no opinion.
Concur: CULLEN, Ch. J., GRAY, HAIGHT, VANN, WERNER, WILLARD BARTLETT and CHASE, JJ.

———————————

PINCUS LOWENFELD et al., Respondents, *v.* MARIA WIMPIE et al., Defendants, and EMPIRE CITY WOOD WORKING COMPANY, Appellant.

Lowenfeld v. *Wimpie*, 139 App. Div. 617, affirmed.
(Argued December 7, 1911; decided December 22, 1911.)

APPEAL from a judgment of the Appellate Division of the Supreme Court in the first judicial department, entered

July 29, 1910, modifying and affirming as modified a judgment of Special Term directing that the claim of defendant appellant be paid prior to the payment of an amount due plaintiffs under a mortgage in an action to foreclose said mortgage.

J. Charles Weschler for appellant.

Alexander Pfeiffer for respondents.

Judgment affirmed, with costs, on opinion of SCOTT, J., below.

Concur: CULLEN, Ch. J., GRAY, HAIGHT, VANN, WERNER and WILLARD BARTLETT, JJ. Dissenting: CHASE, J.

WEEKS-THORNE PAPER COMPANY, Appellant, *v.* THE CITY OF SYRACUSE et al., Respondents.

Weeks-Thorne Paper Co. v. *City of Syracuse*, 139 App. Div. 853, affirmed.

(Argued December 8, 1911; decided December 22, 1911.)

APPEAL from a judgment of the Appellate Division of the Supreme Court in the fourth judicial department, entered July 19, 1910, affirming a judgment in favor of defendants entered upon a dismissal of the complaint by the court on trial at Special Term in an action by a riparian owner to restrain defendants from diverting water from Skaneateles lake.

George Barrow for appellant.

Walter W. Magee for respondents.

Judgment affirmed, with costs; no opinion.

Concur: CULLEN, Ch. J., GRAY, HAIGHT, WERNER, WILLARD BARTLETT and CHASE, JJ. Not sitting: VANN, J.

THE PEOPLE OF THE STATE OF NEW YORK, Respondent, *v.* EDWARD CONWAY, Appellant.

People v. *Conway,* 147 App. Div. —, affirmed.
(Argued December 14, 1911; decided December 22, 1911.)

APPEAL from an order of the Appellate Division of the Supreme Court in the fourth judicial department, entered November 15, 1911, which affirmed a judgment of a Trial Term rendered upon a verdict convicting the defendant of a violation of the Liquor Tax Law.

William L. Barnum for appellant.

George H. Bond for respondent.

Judgment of conviction affirmed; no opinion.
Concur: CULLEN, Ch. J., GRAY, HAIGHT, VANN, HISCOCK and COLLIN, JJ. Dissenting: WILLARD BARTLETT, J.

THE PEOPLE OF THE STATE OF NEW YORK, Respondent, *v.* SALVATORE CARUSO, Appellant.

(Submitted December 18, 1911; decided December 22, 1911.)

MOTION to dismiss an appeal from a judgment of the Supreme Court, rendered May 31, 1911, at a Trial Term for Columbia county, upon a verdict convicting the defendant of the crime of murder in the first degree.

The motion was made upon the ground of failure to prosecute the appeal.

William B. Daley for motion.

Daniel V. McNamee opposed.

Motion denied and cause set down for argument on the 22d of January, 1912. If the counsel for the appellant fails to be ready to proceed with the argument of the case at that time the court will substitute counsel in his place.

INDEX.

ACCIDENT INSURANCE.
Clauses of policy construed.

See INSURANCE, 2.

ACCOMPLICE.
When person playing poker is not an accomplice of dealer or gamekeeper with whom he plays.

See CRIMES, 10.

ACCOUNTING.
See Matter of Dennis (Mem.), 536.

ACCOUNT STATED.
See Reusens v. Arkenburgh (Mem.), 567.

AMBULANCE.
Ordinance giving right of way does not authorize driving at dangerous speed.

See NEGLIGENCE, 4.

APPEAL.
1. *Exception to refusal to dismiss complaint waived by introduction of evidence on defense.* A defendant, by introducing evidence on the defense, waives an exception to the refusal of the court to dismiss the complaint at the close of plaintiff's evidence in chief. *Porges* v. *U. S. M. & Trust Co.*   181

2. *When appellate courts limited to review of questions raised by exceptions taken at trial.* Where the defendant did not move for a new trial, but appealed from the judgment rendered upon a verdict, both the Appellate Division and the Court of Appeals are limited to an examination of errors of law raised and pointed out by exceptions taken by the defendant during the trial.   *Id.*

3. *Questions raised by exception to denial of motion to dismiss complaint made at close of entire evidence.* A motion by defendant to dismiss the complaint at the close of the entire evidence upon the grounds "that no cause of action has been proven" may be treated as a motion for a nonsuit, and exception taken by defendant to a denial of the motion raises the question whether, admitting all the facts presented and giving to the plaintiff the advantage of every inference that could properly be drawn from them, there is any evidence to support the plaintiff's cause of action.   *Id.*

4. *Condemnation of property for water supply for city of New York — Special Term order, vacating an award by commissioners of appraisal, appealable to Appellate Division.* An appeal lies to the Appellate Division from an order of the Special Term which vacated an award made by the commissioners of appraisal to ascertain the compensation to be made for land taken for water supply for the city of New York, by virtue of chapter 724 of the Laws of 1905, and the acts amendatory thereof. *Matter of Simmons.*   241

See *Matter of Smith* (Mem.), 543; *Franco* v. *Radt* (Mem.), 543; *Littlefield Store Co.* v. *City of Albany* (Mem.), 544; *Midwood Park Co.* v. *Kouwenhoven R. & I. Co.* (Mem.), 545; *Wakefield* v. *Gaynor* (Mem.), 545; *Koellhoffer* v. *Hillebrand* (Mem.), 546; *Stenson* v. *Flick Construction Co.* (Mem.), 553; *Wilson* v. *Central Ins. Co.* (Mem.), 604; *Matter of Latham* (Mem.), 605; *Matter of City of New York* (Mem.), 606; *Paris* v. *Lawyers' T. Ins. & Trust Co.* (Mem.), 607; *Tabor* v. *City of Buffalo* (Mem.), 607; *Paul* v. *Swears* (Mem.), 615; *Easley* v. *Loewenstein* (Mem.), 637; *People* v. *Caruso* (Mem.), 648.

APPEAL— *Continued.*

Application by bankrupt for cancellation of judgment a special proceeding, and appealable to Court of Appeals.

See BANKRUPTCY, 1.

APPELLATE DIVISION.

When limited to review of questions raised by exceptions taken at the trial.

See APPEAL, 2.

Special Term order vacating award in condemnation proceedings appealable to Appellate Division.

See APPEAL, 4.

ASSESSMENT.

See Deyo v. *City of Newburgh* (Mem.), 632; *Anthony* v. *City of Newburgh* (Mem.) 633.

Subway railroads — assessment of special franchises — assessment of railroad under construction — equalization of assessment.

See TAX, 1-6.

Assessment upon special franchises — rule for ascertaining value of tangible property — method of ascertaining net earnings.

See TAX, 9-11.

Valuation and assessment of special franchises — when city assessors may apportion special franchise assessment between different parts of a tax district.

See TAX, 12, 13.

ATTORNEY AND CLIENT.

When relation does not exist, summary proceedings to recover papers cannot be maintained. The courts will not enforce ordinary contractual obligations not springing out of the relationship of attorney and client by a summary proceeding, even though the obligor happens to be an attorney. Such a proceeding to compel an attorney to deliver documents, which he claims to hold under an attorney's lien for compensation for services, cannot be maintained where the moving party denies that it ever retained the attorney in connection with the proceedings which placed in his hands the documents sought to be recovered, and expressly alleges · that his retainer and employment were by another corporation, and an order in such case requiring the attorney to deliver papers, on execution by the claimant thereto of an undertaking to pay him such fees as may be determined to be due, is unauthorized. *Matter of Niagara, L. & O. P. Co.*   **493**

ATTORNEYS.

Matter of Spenser (Mem.), 613.

BAGGAGE.

Meaning of term "baggage," as used in section 38 of Public Service Commissions Law — liability of express company for baggage lost in transit not limited by provisions of that section.

See CARRIERS, 1.

Manager of tourist party who engaged to look after baggage not liable for baggage lost while in custody of steamship company.

See CONTRACT, 1.

BAILMENT.

Contract — Person in possession of property of another, as bailee, cannot appropriate it under, and for the purpose of carrying out, another contract between the same parties. A party having in his possession property of another as bailee has no right to appropriate

BAILMENT — *Continued.*

it contrary to the direction of the owner for the purpose of carrying out the terms of another and independent contract between them, by which the owner was to sell and deliver to such bailee property of like character. Such action on the part of the bailee justifies the owner in canceling the contract of bailment. *Atlantic B. S. Co.* v. *V. P. Cement Co.* 133

BALLOTS.

Unconstitutionality of statute providing that name of a person nominated by more than one party shall be printed but once upon the ballot.

See CONSTITUTIONAL LAW, 3.

BANKING.

When indorsement of check by holder of power of attorney constitutes forgery — collecting bank liable.

See PRINCIPAL AND AGENT, 2.

BANKRUPTCY.

1. *Application by bankrupt for cancellation of judgment a special proceeding.* An application by a bankrupt for an order canceling a judgment under section 1268 of the Code of Civil Procedure, now section 150 of the Debtor and Creditor Law (Cons. Laws, ch. 12) is a special proceeding and an order made therein is appealable to the Court of Appeals. *Guasti* v. *Miller.* 259

2. *Cancellation of judgment denied when claim was improperly scheduled.* On examination of defendant's schedules in bankruptcy, it sufficiently appears that the claim from which he seeks to be discharged was not scheduled in accordance with the requirement of section 7 of the Bankruptcy Act, in that it stated that the residence of the claimant was "unknown," when defendant had actual notice thereof, and hence his application to have the judgment canceled was properly denied. *Id.*

BETTING AND GAMING.

See People v. *Teeling* (Mem.), 530.

BILLS, NOTES AND CHECKS.

1. *Foreign bills of exchange — What damages recoverable by payee upon foreign bill of exchange protested for non-payment.* The damages recoverable by the payee of a negotiable foreign bill of exchange protested for non-payment against the drawer may be deemed to be made up as follows: (1) The face of the bill; (2) interest thereon; (3) protest fees; (4) re-exchange, *i. e.*, the additional expense of procuring a new bill for the same amount payable in the same place on the day of dishonor; or a percentage in lieu of such re-exchange in jurisdictions where it is prescribed by statute. *Pavenstedt* v. *N. Y. Life Ins. Co.* 91

2. *Measure of damages.* Where a bill of exchange was drawn in South America by a New York corporation directed to itself in New York, and requiring itself to pay a certain sum in New York in our currency, the measure of damages to the payee upon its refusal to pay is the amount of the draft, with interest and protest fees. This is true although the currency of the country in which the bill was drawn depreciated after the date of the bill and its dishonor, so that the holder was required to pay a larger number of dollars in such depreciated currency for the amount of American money for which the bill was drawn than he was able to realize upon the draft in the country where it was drawn in the first instance. *Id.*

See Hunter v. *Bacon* (Mem.), 534; *Carpenter* v. *Hoadley* (Mem.), 571; *Earle* v. *McCrum* (Mem.), 575; *Third Nat. Bank* v. *R. G. Chase Co.* (Mem.), 598; *Foote* v. *Todd* (Mem.), 642.

BILLS, NOTES AND CHECKS — *Continued.*

When indorsement of check by holder of power of attorney constitutes forgery — collecting bank liable.

See PRINCIPAL AND AGENT, 2.

BONDS.

Bond indemnifying employer against loss arising from larceny or embezzlement of clerk — waiver of provision therein that bond shall be "of no effect unless signed by the employee."

See PRINCIPAL AND SURETY.

CARRIERS.

1. *Meaning of term "baggage," as used in section 38 of Public Service Commissions Law — Liability of express company for baggage lost in transit not limited by provisions of that section.* The term "baggage," used in section 38 of the Public Service Commissions Law (Consol. Laws, ch. 48), does not include property which is being moved by express or otherwise apart from and disconnected with the transportation of the owner; hence, a company, which enters into a contract with a passenger on a railroad train to deliver a trunk at his home or other designated point, cannot avail itself of the limitation in that section upon the amount of the recovery against a common carrier, where the value of the baggage is not stated. *Morgan v. Woolverton.* 52

2. *Evidence — Contract to transport goods signed by carrier and shipper, but silent as to route, cannot be varied by evidence of previous parol instructions to ship by a particular route.* A written contract to transport goods from one place to another, duly signed by both carrier and shipper, but silent as to the route, cannot be varied by evidence of previous parol instructions to ship by a particular route. No effect can be given to such evidence, even when received without objection, provided the court is asked in due form to instruct the jury that it was merged in the written agreement if they found there was one. Certain blank spaces in the printed form of a railroad shipping order were left unfilled, such as "Route ......, Charges advanced $ ...." Such a writing when signed by both parties, is a contract complete upon its face; the unfilled blanks, although material, were not necessary to make the contract complete upon its face and the blanks cannot be filled by parol evidence and effect given thereto in an action at law. *Loomis v. N. Y. C. & H. R. R. R. Co.* 359

See Robinson v. N. Y. C. & H. R. R. R. Co. (Mem.), 627.

CHARGE.

Improper charge on trial for murder — when failure to charge fully as to degrees of manslaughter not erroneous.

See CRIMES, 3, 4.

On trial for murder — refusal to charge.

See CRIMES, 15, 16.

CHARITABLE INSTITUTIONS.

Not exempt from liability for tort — when not liable for negligence of ambulance driver furnished by livery stable.

See NEGLIGENCE, 2, 3.

CIVIL SERVICE.

Improper dismissal of veteran fireman. Upon review of the statutes relative to the fire department of the village and city of Rome, *held*, that the board of fire and police commissioners should not be allowed to so construe the Civil Service Law (Cons. Laws, ch, 7, § 22)

CIVIL SERVICE — *Continued.*
as to permit it to summarily discharge the relator, without a hearing, from his office in the police department, while he has in his possession an honorable discharge from the fire department of the city signed by said board and recommended by the chief engineer of the fire department. *People ex rel. Conley* v. *Beach* (Mem.), 620.

> *See People ex rel. Forest* v. *Williams* (Mem.), 550; *People ex rel. Barnet* v. *Fosdick* (Mem.), 551; *People ex rel. Lisk* v. *Bd. of Education* (Mem.), 561.

CODE OF CIVIL PROCEDURE.

1. § 973 — *Constitutional law — Trial of issues.* The Legislature had the right to enact section 973 of the Code of Civil Procedure, permitting the court in its discretion to "order one or more issues to be separately tried prior to any trial of the other issues." The section applies to a case where a party is entitled to a jury trial whether as of right or as a matter of discretion and no constitutional right is impaired thereby. *Smith* v. *Western Pacific Ry. Co.* 499

2. § 1268 — *Application by bankrupt for cancellation of judgment.* An application by a bankrupt for an order canceling a judgment under section 1268 of the Code of Civil Procedure, now section 150 of the Debtor and Creditor Law (Cons. Laws, ch. 12) is a special proceeding and an order made therein is appealable to the Court of Appeals. *Guasti* v. *Miller.* 259

3. §§ 2752–2756 — *Proceedings to sell decedent's real estate for the payment of his debts — Judgment creditors of an heir or devisee of decedent necessary parties thereto.* Under the provisions of the Code of Civil Procedure (§§ 2752–2756), regulating the sale of a decedent's real estate for the payment of his debts, judgment creditors of an heir or devisee of such decedent have a substantial interest to protect in the proceeding, and must be made parties thereto. *Matter of Townsend.* 522

CODE OF CRIMINAL PROCEDURE.

1. § 376 — *Jurors — Challenge for bias.* Where jurors admitted, when examined under challenge, that they had previously formed an opinion or impression to the effect that a crime had been committed in the case, but each declared on oath that he believed such opinion or impression would not influence his verdict and that he could render an impartial verdict according to the evidence, such previous opinion or impression is not a sufficient ground of challenge for bias. (Code Crim. Pro. § 376, subd. 2.) Furthermore the defendant was tried by a special jury drawn under chapter 602 of the Laws of 1901, which provides that the allowance or disallowance of challenges for actual bias shall be final. *People* v. *Wolter.* 484

2. § 399 — *Gambling — When witness not an accomplice.* Defendant was indicted for and convicted of being a common gambler. He was convicted on the testimony of a single witness who participated with him in a game of draw poker. The defendant was indicted not for engaging as a player in a game of poker but for engaging therein as a dealer and gamekeeper. *Held,* that the witness was not an accomplice in the sense of being a gamekeeper within the meaning of the statute requiring the testimony of an accomplice to be corroborated (Code Crim. Pro. § 399); hence, the evidence was sufficient to warrant the conviction and the court was not called upon to charge that "if the jury find that the People's witness was an accomplice their verdict must be a verdict of acquittal." *People* v. *Bright.* 78

COMITY.
When judgment obtained by administrator of insured in another state not a bar to an action on the same policy in this state by the assignee thereof.

See FORMER ADJUDICATION, 1, 2.

COMMISSIONS.
See Le Compte Mfg. Co. v. *Aschenbach's Sons Harness Co.* (Mem.), 533; *Strauss* v. *Eastern Brewing Co.* (Mem.), 596.

COMMITMENT.
Invalidity of commitment issued by a justice of the peace of a municipal corporation which is not a county, city, town or village.

See CONSTITUTIONAL LAW, 7.

CONDEMNATION PROCEEDINGS.
See Matter of Macholdt (Mem.), 554; *Matter of City of New York* (Mem.), 558; *Matter of Southfield Beach R. R. Co.* (Mem.), 561; *Matter of Grade Crossing Comrs.* (Mem.), 605; *Matter of City of New York* (Mem.), 610; *Matter of Grade Crossing Comrs.* (Mem.), 628; *N. Y. C. & H. R. R. R. Co.* v. *Federal Sugar Refining Co.* (Mem.), 631.

Special Term order vacating an award appeable to Appellate Division.

See APPEAL, 4.

CONFESSIONS.
Propriety of their admission in evidence.

See CRIMES, 7.

CONSOLIDATED LAWS.

Ch. 7. *See* SESSION LAWS, 7.

Ch. 12. *See* SESSION LAWS, 8.

Ch. 17. *See* SESSION LAWS, 16.

Ch. 33. *See* SESSION LAWS, 9.

Ch. 48. *See* SESSION LAWS, 10, 11, 12.

Ch. 49. *See* SESSION LAWS, 13.

Ch. 59. *See* SESSION LAWS, 12.

Ch. 60. *See* SESSION LAWS, 2.

CONSTITUTIONAL LAW.
1. *Election Law — Registration of electors — Unconstitutionality of the statute* (L. 1911, *ch.* 649, § 6) *requiring personal registration of electors residing outside of cities or villages with a population of five thousand or more.* Whatever is necessary to render effective any provision of a Constitution, whether it is a grant, restriction or prohibition, must be deemed implied and intended in the provision itself. Hence, when the Constitution provides that certain voters "shall not be required to apply in person for registration at the first meeting of the" inspectors, it is implied that the legislature is prohibited from passing any statute to the contrary, because that implication is necessary to render the provision effective. The legislature exceeded its power in providing that all voters residing outside of cities or villages with a population of five thousand or more whose names do not appear on the poll book of the last general election shall apply in person in order to be registered, and the attempt to impose this requirement, as made by section 6 of chapter 649 of the Laws of 1911, is unconstitutional and void. *Matter of Fraser* v. *Brown.* **136**

CONSTITUTIONAL LAW — *Continued.*

2. *Power of legislature to prescribe method of conducting elections.* Not only is legislation contravening the express commands of the Constitution void, but legislation contravening what the Constitution necessarily implies is also void. The power granted to the legislature to prescribe the method of conducting elections cannot be so exercised as to disfranchise constitutionally qualified electors, and any system that unnecessarily prevents the elector from voting or from voting for the candidate of his choice violates the Constitution. *Matter of Hopper* v. *Britt.* 144

3. *Unconstitutionality of statute providing that name of a person, nominated by more than one party, shall be printed but once upon the ballot.* The provision of section 12 of chapter 649 of the Laws of 1911, that the name of a person nominated by more than one political party shall be printed but once upon the ballot, and regulating in detail the method of carrying out such provision, is unconstitutional as unjustly discriminating between electors in the facility afforded them for casting their votes for the candidates of their choice. *Id.*

4. *New York (city of) — Justices of the Municipal Court — Unconstitutionality of statute (L. 1907, ch. 603, § 3) amending section 1357 of New York city charter relative to vacancies in office of justices.* The statute of 1907 (Ch. 603, § 3), amending section 1357 of the charter of the city of New York, relating to vacancies in office of justices of the Municipal Court, violates the Constitution. *First*, in prohibiting an election unless the vacancy occurs three months before the general election. *Second*, in requiring the mayor to appoint a person to fill the vacancy in the interim, which in this case would be for two years and about five months. *Third*, in requiring the election to fill vacancies to be for a full term, which might occur in an even numbered year. Hence the section of the charter as it existed before the amendment must be deemed to remain in force. *Matter of Markland* v. *Scully.* 158

5. *When election must be had to fill vacancy.* Where a justice of the Municipal Court of the city of New York died on the eighth day of August, and the annual election occurs on the seventh day of November thereafter, an election to fill the vacancy should be had at such annual election, and no appointment to fill a vacancy can continue longer than to the first day of January after such annual election. *Id.*

6. *Notice of election.* The city clerk of the city of New York being required by the statute to give notices of an election and of the offices to be filled, it is his duty to do so upon the happening of a vacancy which is required to be filled at the ensuing election, notwithstanding that such vacancy occurred after said clerk had issued notices of election in accordance with conditions then existing, and such duty may be enforced by mandamus. *Id.*

7. *Unconstitutionality of statutes (L. 1896, ch. 812 and L. 1901, ch. 861) creating a municipal corporation which is not a county, city, town or village — Invalidity of commitment issued by a justice of the peace of the "area or territory known as Sylvan Beach."* The Constitution constitutes the counties, cities, towns and villages of the state the civil divisions for political purposes and indispensable to the continuation of the government organized by it, and this is equivalent to a direct prohibition against the creation of any other civil divisions vested with similar powers. The legislative acts, chapter 812 of the Laws of 1896 and chapter 361 of the Laws of 1901, purporting to revise and consolidate previous acts creating the

CONSTITUTIONAL LAW — *Continued.*
"area or territory known as Sylvan Beach," are without constitutional warrant, and a commitment issued by a police justice claiming to hold his office under such acts is void. *People ex rel. Hon Yost v. Becker.* 201

8. *Election Law — Section* 128 (*as amended by* L. 1911, *ch.* 649), *relating to the signing and filing of certificates of independent nominations, construed and held to be constitutional.* The Election Law (Cons. Laws, ch. 17, as amended by L. 1911, ch. 649) permits an independent certificate of nomination to be made up of several different sheets. Section 123 provides that "The signatures to the certificate of nomination need not all be appended to one paper," and further that "No separate sheet comprising an independent certificate of nomination, where such certificate consists of more than one sheet, shall be received and filed with the custodian of primary records if five per centum of the names appearing on such sheet are fraudulent or forged." *Held*, that the latter provision may be upheld because independent nominators are not constrained to subject themselves to its operation. They may all sign a single sheet or each may sign a sheet by himself. This liberty of action relieves the provision from any constitutional objection. *Matter of Burke* v. *Terry.* 293

9. *Trial of issues — Section* 973 *of the Code of Civil Procedure constitutional.* The legislature had the right to enact section 973 of the Code of Civil Procedure, permitting the court in its discretion to "order one or more issues to be separately tried prior to any trial of the other issues." The section applies to a case where a party is entitled to a jury trial whether as of right or as a matter of discretion and no constitutional right is impaired thereby. *Smith* v. *Western Pacific Railway.* 499

CONTRACT.
1. "*Tourist parties*" — *When person engaged in managing* "*tourist parties,*" *who engaged to look after baggage of tourist, not liable for baggage lost while in custody of steamship company upon whose ship the tourist was a passenger.* Plaintiff was a passenger on board a steamship under a contract with defendant who was engaged in managing tourist parties, by which "every detail, baggage, carriages, hotel rates, fees, everything pertaining to the tour from New York back to New York would be attended to." On arrival at plaintiff's destination a steamer steward took plaintiff's trunk from her stateroom and thereafter it could not be found. In this action, brought to recover damages for its loss, the court charged: "I leave to the jury the question of whether a substantial compliance with that contract required the service of a representative of the defendant upon the steamer." *Held*, error. *Coleman* v. *Clark.* 86

2. *Agreements under seal — Contract under seal, by which one brother agrees to support his mother, cannot be enforced by another brother not a party to it, although the latter joined in the consideration for the contract.* As a general rule an instrument under seal cannot be enforced by or against one who is not a party to it, although a different rule exists as to simple contracts on which an action may be brought by or against the real principal, although he is not named in the instrument. This action is brought by the plaintiff against his brother, upon a contract under seal, made by the latter with his mother for her support and maintenance. The contract recites that it was entered into by the defendant upon the consideration that the mother, who is the other party thereto, had

CONTRACT — *Continued.*

united with the plaintiff in a deed of a farm to the defendant, and that by the contract, based upon that consideration, the defendant bound himself to support the mother during her life. The complaint alleges that the defendant failed to keep this covenant, and that by reason of such failure the plaintiff has been compelled to support and maintain the mother, for the expense of which he asks judgment. *Held,* that the action cannot be maintained as the mother alone has the right to enforce the contract. *Case* v. *Case.* 268

8. *Sale — Construction of contract for purchase and sale of foreign goods — When buyer may not repudiate contract and refuse to accept goods, because invoices were mutilated and because goods were not imported expressly for buyer.* Defendant contracted to purchase from plaintiff certain bales of silk as specified. The defendant refused to receive the silk when tendered upon the ground that the documents attached to the invoice had been mutilated and that the silk was not imported by plaintiff but bought by it on the market expressly for the defendant. *Held,* that as the alleged mutilation consisted only of cutting out the name of the person to whom certain certificates were issued as to qualities of the silk, and as it was no part of the contract that the silk should be imported by plaintiff, defendant had no right to reject it on either ground. *Jardine, Matheson & Co.* v. *Huguet Silk Co.* 273

4. *When offer of evidence properly rejected.* As to some of the silk offered by plaintiff to meet the requirements of the contract, defendant offered evidence tending to show that it did not comply with its terms. Objection was taken that the silk was not rejected upon the question of quality, and upon inquiry by the court as to the object of the evidence, which was not disclosed, the objection was sustained. *Held,* that it is apparent from the record that the evidence was offered as matter of defense rather than in reduction of damages, and if the plaintiff wished to introduce the evidence in order to reduce damages it should under the circumstances have so stated so that the court could have understood its position. *Id.*

5. *Action for breach of contract — Expulsion from bathhouse of person holding ticket entitling her to admission — Price of ticket not measure of damages.* The plaintiff purchased a ticket and took her position in a line of the defendant's patrons leading to a window at which the ticket entitled her to receive, upon its surrender, a key admitting her to a bathhouse. When she approached the window a dispute arose between her and the defendant's employees as to the right of another person not in the line to have a key given to him in advance of the plaintiff. As a result of this dispute plaintiff was ejected from the defendant's premises, the agents of the latter refusing to furnish her with the accommodations for which she had contracted. The plaintiff was awarded substantial damages, defendant contending that she was not entitled to any recovery in excess of the sum paid for the ticket. *Held,* that the jury had a right to award damages for the indignity thus inflicted upon her. *Aaron* v. *Ward.* 851

6. *Action by water company against municipality to recover rentals claimed to be due under contract to furnish water for fire service at a certain pressure.* Defendant agreed to pay plaintiff an annual rental for hydrants for fire service, plaintiff to maintain a certain pressure of water therein "except in case of unavoidable

CONTRACT — *Continued.*

accident." The contract provided also that no rental should be paid for such time as fire protection is not furnished. The jury found that a failure to maintain the water pressure service required was owing to natural causes over which plaintiff had no control and was in the nature of an unavoidable accident. *Held*, that the plaintiff is entitled to recover the contract price for the time in which it maintained the water pressure specified in the contract; but for the time that it failed to maintain such pressure it is not entitled to recover the rental specified in the contract. *Brockport H. W. Co. v. Village of Brockport.*   399

7. *Measure of damages.* The defendant continued to use such water as the plaintiff was able to furnish during the entire term of the contract. *Held*, that the court correctly charged, "If you find that the defendant has had the benefit of whatever services the plaintiff was able to give and has used it, then, gentlemen, the plaintiff would be entitled to a verdict at your hands for the reasonable value of the service rendered by it and accepted by this defendant, after deducting whatever damage it has sustained and proved on account of the plaintiff being unable to furnish the contract pressure." *Held*, further, that the contract price for rental of hydrants for fire protection affords no proper basis for the determination of the value of the service of water alone.   *Id.*

8. *Equitable conversion — Definition and application of doctrine of equitable conversion.* The doctrine of equitable conversion rests on the presumed intention of the owner of the property and on the maxim that equity regards as done what ought to be done. The conversion usually becomes effective at the date of the instrument expressing the intention, if a deed or contract, and if a will, at the date of the testator's death. This is the rule when an absolute and not a contingent conversion is intended; but where no conversion is intended, unless a contingent event happens, conversion should not be presumed as of a date earlier than when the contingent event happens. *Rockland-R. Lime Co. v. Leary.*   459

9. *Definition and effect of term "legal representative."* The words "legal representative" ordinarily mean the executor or administrator, and that meaning will be attributed to them in any instance unless there be facts existing which show that the words were not used in their ordinary sense, but to denote some other and different idea.   *Id.*

10. *When actual tender need not be made.* Where one party to a contract is able and willing to perform, and has made due effort to that end, no actual tender need be made if performance has been prevented by the other party, or the situation is such that the amount to be tendered cannot be known without a judgment of the court, or some of the persons entitled to the money are infants, so that no tender can be made to them.   *Id.*

11. *Sufficiency of notice of intent to exercise option to purchase lands.* The owner of lands gave an option thereon to plaintiff, in which it was provided that the covenants therein should be binding on the parties and "their heirs, legal representatives, successors or assigns." The plaintiff, if it exercised such option, was required within a specified period to notify the owner "or his legal representative" of its intent so to do. Such notice was sought to be given to the administratrix of the owner. She had actual knowledge of plaintiff's intent to exercise the option, but sought to evade service of the notice, which was in fact given to one of the heirs who acted

CONTRACT— *Continued.*
for all the others, such heir refusing to carry out the option. *Held,* that plaintiff had complied with the requirement of the option as to notice of its intent to purchase. *Id.*

> *See Warner-Quinlan Asphalt Co.* v. *C. N. Y. Tel. & Tel. Co.* (Mem.), 528; *Ferguson Contracting Co.* v. *Helderberg Cement Co.* (Mem.), 531; *Hart Co.* v. *City of New York* (Mem.), 531; *Meyer Bros. Drug Co.* v. *McKinney* (Mem.), 533; *N. Y. Steam Co.* v. *Ryan* (Mem.), 537; *Fisher* v. *Wakefield Park Realty Co.* (Mem.), 539; *Hargraves Mills* v. *Gordon* (Mem.), 568; *Thedford* v. *Herbert* (Mem.), 575; *Hecht* v. *Hyde & Sons* (Mem.), 578; *Leavitt* v. *De Vries* (Mem.), 580; *Bird* v. *Casein Co.* (Mem.), 583; *Vogt* v. *Hayman* (Mem.), 583; *City of Buffalo* v. *Frontier Telephone Co.* (Mem.), 589; *New Hartford C. M. Co.* v. *Lowenstein* (Mem.), 590; *Cullen* v. *Battle Island Paper Co.* (Mem.), 591; *Massa* v. *Watertown Engine Co.* (Mem.), 592; *Hanna* v. *Sorg* (Mem.), 594; *Fiss, Doerr & Carroll Horse Co.* v. *Golde* (Mem.), 598; *Bickerstaff* v. *Perley* (Mem.), 601; *Juilliard* v. *Trokie* (Mem.), 604; *Shubert* v. *Sondheim* (Mem.), 636; *Hildreth* v. *City of New York* (Mem.) 644; *Isbell-Porter Co.* v. *Heineman* (Mem.), 644.

Person in possession of property of another, as bailee, cannot appropriate it under, and for the purpose of carrying out, another contract between the same parties.

> *See* BAILMENT.

Contract to transport goods signed by carrier and shipper, but silent as to route, cannot be varied by evidence of previous parol instructions to ship by a particular route.

> *See* CARRIERS, 2.

Of life insurance — When judgment obtained by administrator of insured in another state not a bar to an action on the same policy in this state by the assignee thereof.

> *See* FORMER ADJUDICATION, 1, 2.

Accident insurance — clauses of policy construed.

> *See* INSURANCE, 2.

When municipality liable only for amount due contractor at time contract was forfeited.

> *See* LIENS.

Contractors' liability to abutting owner for damages caused by explosion of dynamite due to sub-contractor's negligence.

> *See* NEGLIGENCE, 1.

Remedy for breach of contract by water commissioners.

> *See* OFFICERS 1, 2.

Syndicate contract by which subscribers agreed to take stock in corporation to be organized may be rescinded for fraud — when tender of stock sufficient to entitle subscriber to return of money paid.

> *See* PRINCIPAL AND AGENT, 3, 5.

Waiver of provision in indemnity bond.

> *See* PRINCIPAL AND SURETY.

CONTRACT — *Continued.*

Of sale — acceptance — when execution by vendee of chattel mortgage on machine before test not a waiver of right of inspection.

See SALE, 1.

Liability of infant for sale effected by fraud.

See SALE, 2.

CONVERSION.

See Manny v. *Wilson* (Mem.), 535; *Walters* v. *Grinberg* (Mem.), 600.

Definition and application of doctrine of equitable conversion.

See CONTRACT, 8.

CORPORATIONS.

1. *Public service commissions — When discretion of commission cannot override the discretion of the officers of a corporation — Duty and powers of commission to determine under section* 69 *of the Public Service Commissions Law whether a proposed bond issue is necessary for purposes of corporation and authorized by law.* One of the paramount purposes of the legislature in establishing the public service commissions was to protect and enforce the rights of the public, and the statute should be construed with that in view. The discretion of a public service commission cannot override the discretion of the officers of a corporation in the management of its affairs, or the provisions of the statute which prescribes the cases in which securities are permitted to be issued. Its duty upon an application under section 69 of the Public Service Commissions Law (Cons. Laws, ch. 48) is to determine whether a proposed issue of bonds is necessary for the proper purposes of the company, is authorized by law and is to by used in a proper manner. If such are the facts it cannot withhold its certificate; otherwise it cannot grant it. *People ex rel. Binghamton L., H. & P. Co.* v. *Stevens.*　　7

2. *Beyond power of commission to permit issue of improper securities.* It is beyond the power of the commission to permit the issue of improper securities upon condition that the company reduce its capital stock and such a condition is wholly unauthorized.　*Id.*

3. *Machines and tools paid for and charged to capital account should be replaced when worn out.* A reasonable consideration of the interests of a corporation and the ultimate good of its stock and bondholders, and a regard for the investing public and that fair dealing which should be observed in all business transactions, require that machines and tools paid for and charged to capital account but which necessarily become obsolete or wholly worn out within a period of years after the same are purchased or installed, should be renewed or replaced by setting aside from time to time an adequate amount in the nature of a sinking fund or that by some other system of financing the corporation put upon the purchaser from the corporation the expense not alone of the daily maintenance of the plant but a just proportion of the expense of renewing and replacing that part of the plant which although not daily consumed must necessarily be practically consumed within a given time.　*Id.*

4. *Duty of public service commission to determine as to what expenditures are a proper basis for permanent capitalization.* The question as to what expenditures are a proper basis for permanent capitalization is always a proper and necessary object for consideration, not alone by the directors of a corporation, but by any commission that has authority to grant or withhold its consent to the issue of new stock or bonds which are to become a part

CORPORATIONS — *Continued.*

of the corporation's permanent capitalization, and it is the duty of the public service commission to determine whether the stock and bonds proposed by a corporation are to secure money to pay floating indebtedness incurred in the ordinary running expenses of the corporation. Such determination by the commission would not be substituting the judgment of the commission for the judgment of the directors of the company in the management of its affairs. *Id.*

5. *Statement of financial transactions.* A statement of a petitioner's financial transactions in proceedings of this kind should be made in sufficient detail and with sufficient classification to show with reasonable certainty the exact question to be determined. *Id.*

6. *Procedure before public service commission — Evidence.* While the commission may not be bound by technical rules of evidence, still it is plainly intended that the whole proceeding for leave to issue bonds should assume a quasi-judicial aspect. *Id.*

7. *Inspectors and agents of commission may be compelled to attend and be examined by either party.* The commission being empowered to subpoena witnesses and take testimony, its inspectors or agents can be required to appear and verify any reports made by them, or if such reports could be received in the first instance without verification, the inspectors or agents can be compelled to attend at the instance of either party and be examined as to the truth of the statements in their reports and their knowledge of the facts therein contained. *Id.*

8. *Public Service Commissions Law — Provisions not in conflict with sections 9–12 of Stock Corporation Law — Reorganization of railroad corporation.* The enactment of the Public Service Commissions Law (Cons. Laws, ch. 48) did not repeal the provisions in the Stock Corporation Law (Cons. Laws, ch. 59) for the reorganization of the property and franchises of corporations sold under foreclosure, and, on the other hand, the provisions of the Stock Corporation Law do not withdraw corporations formed on reorganizations from compliance with section 55 of the Public Service Commissions Law. The two statutes must be construed together. Sections 53 and 54 of the Public Service Commissions Law, requiring the approval by a public service commission of the exercise or transfer of franchises by a railroad corporation, do not apply to a corporation formed on the reorganization of a railroad corporation after foreclosure. *People ex rel. Third Ave. Ry. Co.* v. *Public Service Comm.* 299

9. *Authority of commission as to issue of securities.* Under the provisions of section 55 of the Public Service Commissions Law, a public service commission is not justified in refusing to consent to the issue of securities by a railroad corporation under a plan of reorganization after foreclosure because the value of the mortgaged property and the amount of new capital to be invested is less than the amount of securities sought to be issued. *Id.*

10. *Trust companies — Duties and powers.* Trust companies should be confined not only within the words, but also within the spirit, of the statutory provision which declares that a corporation shall not possess or exercise any corporate powers not given by law or not necessary to the exercise of the powers so given. Such authority does not permit a trust company to enter into speculative and uncertain schemes, or, unless under peculiar circumstances, become the guarantor of the indebtedness or business of others. *Davidge* v. *Guardian Trust Co.* 331

CORPORATIONS — *Continued.*

11. *When trust company not liable for erroneous statements of an officer thereof as to value and validity of bonds for which it was trustee.* The plaintiff, a real estate improvement company, executed to the defendant, a domestic trust company, a mortgage covering a tract of land to secure bonds to be issued by the improvement company. There were five prior mortgages on the property and a sale under prior mortgages left a deficiency. This action is brought to recover plaintiff's loss on bonds purchased by him. Evidence was given that a vice-president of the defendant stated, in answer to an inquiry made by plaintiff at the time of his purchase from a third party, that these were first mortgage bonds. It is not shown that defendant was in any way interested in the improvement company or the bonds to secure which the trust mortgage was given, or that it was to receive a commission or pecuniary advantage by the sale of the bonds. *Held, first,* defendant was not required by the trust mortgage, nor, so far as appears, was it authorized by statute or otherwise to make representations to prospective purchasers as to the value of the bonds or to insure the title to the mortgaged property or the relative priority of the trust mortgage upon the improvement company's real property. *Second,* there is no presumption of law that the vice-president of defendant had authority to make representations on its behalf in regard to the priority of the trust mortgage as a lien upon the property. *Id.*

Definition of special franchise — taxation — equalization of assessments.

See TAX, 1–6.

Special franchise tax upon steam railroad crossings over public streets and highways.

See TAX, 7, 8.

Assessments upon special franchises — rule for ascertaining value of tangible property — method of ascertaining net earnings in assessment of special franchise — rate of capitalization.

See TAX, 9–11.

Valuation and assessment of special franchises.

See TAX, 12, 13.

COSTS.

Partition — Extra allowances — Total amount allowed to all parties cannot exceed five per cent of value of property — Allowance to plaintiff based on value of the whole property — Allowance to any defendant based on value of that defendant's interest in the property — Construction of provision limiting allowance to $2,000 to each side of action. In no event can the total allowance in actions for partition exceed five per centum upon the value of the subject-matter involved. For the purpose of fixing the allowance which may be made to the plaintiff, the value of the subject-matter involved is the value of the whole property, and for the purpose of fixing the allowance to any defendant, the value of that particular defendant's interest is the value of the subject-matter involved. The limitation that in no event shall the allowances to a plaintiff, or to a party or two or more parties on the same side exceed $2,000, means that the allowance to a plaintiff cannot exceed $2,000, and the allowance to all the defendants, considered as a class or "side," shall not exceed another $2,000. *Warren* v. *Warren.* 250

See Pakas v. *Clarke* (Mem.), 534; *D. & N. R. R. Co.* v. *Foster* (Mem.), 637.

COUNTIES.
See *People ex rel. Newburgh News P. & P. Co.* v. *Board of Supervisors* (Mem.), 564.

COURT OF APPEALS.
When Court of Appeals limited to review of questions raised by exceptions taken at trial.

See APPEAL, 2.

Application by bankrupt for cancellation of judgment a special proceeding and appealable to Court of Appeals.

See BANKRUPTCY, 1.

CREDITOR'S SUIT.
See *Nat. Park Bank* v. *Billings* (Mem.), 556; *Manufacturers' Commercial Co.* v. *Heckscher* (Mem.), 560.

CRIMES.
1. *Murder — Sufficiency of evidence to warrant conviction.* The defendant was convicted of murder in the first degree. The conviction was clearly warranted by the evidence, and none of the exceptions are of sufficient importance to justify a reversal of the judgment. *People* v. *Brown.* 44

2. *Defendant, by becoming a voluntary witness, subjects himself to cross-examination as to truth of his statements.* The defendant, in exercising his right to become a voluntary witness on this trial, subjected himself to all the rules under which the testimony of witnesses may be probed by cross-examination. The People had the right to test the truth and accuracy of his statements, made as a witness upon the trial, by eliciting any other statements previously made either as a witness in some prior proceeding or otherwise. *Id.*

3. *Improper charge.* The trial justice charged "that William Brown, the deceased, bullied and beat the defendant prior to May 21st, and that they (the jury) may take that into consideration on the question as to whether or not it furnished a motive for the crime." *Held*, that although this charge is technically open to criticism, the evidence as to the homicide was so unequivocal that the question of motive was not one of controlling importance. *Id.*

4. *When failure to charge fully as to degrees of manslaughter not erroneous.* When a jury excludes from the case the alternative of murder in the second degree by a finding of murder in the first degree, all lower degrees are necessarily eliminated. In such case failure to charge fully as to the degrees of manslaughter is not error. *Id.*

5. *Murder — Sufficiency of indictment in common-law form.* An indictment in the common-law form is sufficient to sustain a conviction of murder in the first degree, even though there is no evidence of premeditation and deliberation, where the proof clearly brings the case within the statutory definition that a homicide committed by a person while engaged in the commission of a felony constitutes the crime of murder in the first degree. *People* v. *Schermerhorn.* 57

6. *Properly left to jury to say whether murder was committed in connection with perpetration of other felonies.* On examination of the evidence against defendant who was convicted of murder in the first degree, *held*, that the case was properly submitted to the jury to find whether it was committed while the perpetrator was engaged in the commission of the two distinct felonies of rape and burglary, since the evidence connects him with both, and discloses

CRIMES — *Continued.*

facts which tend to unite the two felonies as parts of one general scheme and to identify the defendant as its author and perpetrator. *Id.*

7. *Confessions — Propriety of their admission in evidence.* Several separate statements in the nature of confessions were made by defendant. The question whether the last of these confessions was made under the influence of fear and hope of leniency was submitted to the jury on conflicting evidence; and the verdict necessarily implies that the confessions were fairly obtained. *Held*, that the facts disclosed by the record show that the confessions were properly admitted in evidence. *Id.*

8. *Trial — Propriety of argument of prosecuting attorney.* The district attorney was clearly within his rights in arguing to the jury that the defendant's unexplained possession of the stolen property was evidence which should be considered upon the question whether the defendant committed the burglary, and in the commission thereof perpetrated the murder. *Id.*

9. *Gambling — A person who takes part in a game, or games, of poker for amusement is not a "common gambler" within the meaning of the statute (Penal Law, § 970).* A person who merely takes part in a game or series of games of poker on precisely the same terms as the other participants in the game, for mere amusement or recreation and not as a professional gamester, does not thereby become a common gambler under our statute. *People* v. *Bright.* 78

10. *When person playing poker is not an accomplice of dealer or gamekeeper with whom he plays.* Defendant was indicted for and convicted of being a common gambler under section 970 of the Penal Law. He was convicted on the testimony of a single witness who participated with him in a game of draw poker. The defendant was indicted not for engaging as a player in a game of poker but for engaging therein as a dealer and gamekeeper. *Held*, that the witness was not an accomplice in the sense of being a gamekeeper within the meaning of the statute requiring the testimony of an accomplice to be corroborated (Code Crim. Pro. § 399); hence, the evidence was sufficient to warrant the conviction and the court was not called upon to charge that "if the jury find that the People's witness was an accomplice their verdict must be a verdict of acquittal." *Id.*

11. *Evidence — District attorney may not attempt to create false impressions by questions concerning matters foreign to the issues.* A district attorney may not, by questions actually containing no element of misconduct and by calling witnesses as a challenge to the defendant to go into the details of transactions foreign to the issues, create false impressions that defendant has been guilty of misdeeds similar to those charged against him, when the evidence does not sustain such a conclusion. *People* v. *Freeman.* 267

12. *Murder — When verdict of conviction under common-law indictment not against weight of evidence.* On review of the evidence on appeal from a judgment convicting defendant of murder in the first degree, *held*, that no plausible view of the facts can be suggested in support of the proposition that the verdict was against the weight of evidence or that justice requires a new trial so far as the facts are concerned. *People* v. *Wolter.* 484

13. *When previous opinion or impression of jurors not sufficient ground for challenge for bias.* Where jurors admitted, when examined under challenge, that they had previously formed an opinion

CRIMES — *Continued.*

or impression to the effect that a crime had been committed in the case, but each declared on oath that he believed such opinion or impression would not influence his verdict and that he could render an impartial verdict according to the evidence, such previous opinion or impression is not a sufficient ground of challenge for bias. (Code Crim. Pro. § 376, subd. 2.) Furthermore the defendant was tried by a special jury drawn under chapter 602 of the Laws of 1901, which provides that the allowance or disallowance of challenges for actual bias shall be final. *Id.*

14. *Evidence tending to show motive and that killing was committed while in perpetration of another crime admissible.* Under an indictment for murder in the common-law form physicians were properly allowed to testify to the taking of certain matter from the vagina of the deceased which, upon a microscopic examination, was found to contain spermatozoa, as bearing not only upon the motive for the crime but also as tending to show that the killing was done while in the perpetration of another crime. *Id.*

15. *Charge and refusal to charge.* The court instructed the jury: "Nor is it necessary that each and every circumstance should be proved beyond a reasonable doubt. Some facts may be proved with more, some with less assurance of certainty." The court refused to charge that, "if any of the material facts of this case are at variance with the probabilities of guilt it would be the duty of the jury to give to the defendant the benefit of the doubt." *Held,* that neither such charge, nor the refusal, was harmful to the defendant when followed by the instruction that if on any branch of the case there existed in their minds a reasonable doubt, the defendant was always entitled to the benefit of that reasonable doubt. *Id.*

16. *When premeditation and deliberation not necessary to sustain conviction for murder in first degree.* Under the common-law form of indictment the court properly submitted the case to the jury upon the theory that they could convict the defendant of murder in the first degree in the absence of any premeditation or deliberation on his part provided they found that he killed the deceased while engaged in the commission of a felony. *Id.*

DAMAGES.

What damages recoverable by payee upon foreign bill of exchange protested for non-payment.

See BILLS, NOTES AND CHECKS, 1, 2.

Measure of damages in action for breach of contract arising from expulsion from bathhouse of person holding ticket entitling her to admission.

See CONTRACT, 5.

Measure of damages in action by water company against municipality to recover rentals claimed to be due under contract to furnish water for fire service at a certain pressure.

See CONTRACT, 6, 7.

DEBTOR AND CREDITOR.

Cancellation of judgment against bankrupt denied where it was improperly scheduled.

See BANKRUPTCY, 2.

Judgment creditors of an heir or devisee of a decedent necessary parties to a proceeding to sell decedent's real property for payment of his debts.

See DECEDENT'S ESTATE.

DECEDENT'S ESTATE.

Proceedings to sell decedent's real estate for the payment of his debts — Judgment creditors of an heir or devisee of decedent necessary parties thereto. Under the provisions of the Code of Civil Procedure (§§ 2752–2756), regulating the sale of a decedent's real estate for the payment of his debts, judgment creditors of an heir or devisee of such decedent have a substantial interest to protect in the proceeding, and must be made parties thereto. *Matter of Townsend.* 522

Construction of provision of will devising real estate.

See WILL, 1.

Rules for construction of testamentary provisions creating trusts for benefit of "religious, educational, charitable or benevolent uses" — validity of testamentary provisions.

See WILL, 2, 3.

DEFENSE.

Insufficiency of defense in action for libel.

See LIBEL, 3.

DISTRICT ATTORNEYS.

Propriety of argument of prosecuting attorney.

See CRIMES, 8.

District attorney may not attempt to create false impressions by questions concerning matters foreign to the issues.

See CRIMES, 11.

DIVORCE.

1. *When entry or memorandum from which witness has refreshed his memory not admissible in evidence.* Where a witness has refreshed his recollection by reference to an entry or memorandum and testified to the fact therein set forth, such entry is not thereafter properly received in evidence. *Mattison v. Mattison.* 79

2. *When entries on hotel register and testimony of conversations inadmissible.* Entries on a hotel register made by an alleged paramour and conversations between him and a hotel clerk not made or had in defendant's presence are not proper evidence against her. *Id.*

3. *Judgment of divorce against alleged paramour not admissible in evidence.* A judgment for divorce against a paramour not a defendant in the action is erroneously received in evidence, although the court states that it was not admitted as against the actual defendant. *Id.*

4. *Entries in hotel register alleged to be in handwriting of alleged paramour inadmissible.* Entries claimed to be in the handwriting of the alleged paramour upon the register of a hotel other than that where the adultery is claimed to have been committed, were admitted upon the statement of counsel that they were offered as standards of handwriting and as bearing on the question whether the writer may have registered elsewhere under an assumed name. *Held,* error.. *Id.*

Courts of this state will not restrain prosecution of action in another state to annul a judgment of divorce previously rendered in that state by a court of competent jurisdiction.

See JUDGMENT.

DOMESTIC RELATIONS.
Action for divorce — evidence.

See DIVORCE, 1–4.

Right of wife to recover from husband for moneys expended by her for necessaries.

See HUSBAND AND WIFE.

ELECTIONS.
See Matter of Youker (Mem.), 537; *Matter of Koenig* (Mem.), 549.

Registration of electors — unconstitutionality of statute requiring personal registration of electors residing outside of cities or villages with a population of five thousand or more.

See CONSTITUTIONAL LAW, 1.

Power of legislature to prescribe method of conducting elections — unconstitutionality of statute providing that name of a person, nominated by more than one party, shall be printed but once upon the ballot.

See CONSTITUTIONAL LAW, 2, 3.

Unconstitutionality of statute amending section 1357 of New York city charter relative to filling vacancies in office of justice of Municipal Court — when election must be had to fill vacancy — notice of election.

See CONSTITUTIONAL LAW, 4–6.

Section 123 of Election Law as amended by chapter 649 of Laws of 1911, reating to the signing and filing of certificates of independent nominations, constitutional.

See CONSTITUTIONAL LAW, 8.

ELEVATORS.
When person injured by falling into elevator shaft in unlighted hall guilty of contributory negligence.

See NEGLIGENCE, 5.

ENCROACHMENTS.
See People ex rel. Browning, King & Co. v. Stover (Mem.), 613.

EQUITABLE CONVERSION.
Definition and application of doctrine of equitable conversion.

See CONTRACT, 8.

EQUITY.
Wife may recover from husband for moneys expended by her for necessaries.

See HUSBAND AND WIFE.

ESTATES.
Proceedings to sell decedent's real estate for payment of his debts — judgment creditors of an heir or devisee of decedent necessary parties thereto.

See DECEDENT'S ESTATE.

Construction of a provision of will devising real estate.

See WILL, 1.

Rules for construction of testamentary provisions creating trusts for benefit of "religious, educational, charitable or benevolent uses" — validity of testamentary provisions.

See WILL, 2, 3.

EVIDENCE.

1. *Negligence — Evidence of discharge of motorman — When inadmissible.* On trial of an action to recover damages for injuries alleged to have resulted from negligence of a motorman employed by defendant, rulings that the motorman should state whether or not he was discharged subsequent to the accident, and that he should state the cause of his discharge are erroneous. *Engel* v. *United Traction Co.* 321

2. *Admission of any material fact competent evidence.* In a civil action the admissions by a party of any fact material to the issue are always competent evidence against him, wherever, whenever or to whomsoever made. *McRorie* v. *Monroe.* 426

3. *Testimony given on a previous trial may be proved by any person who will swear to its having been given.* What a witness has sworn may be given in evidence either from the judge's notes or from notes that have been taken by any other person who will swear to their accuracy; or the former evidence may be proved by any person who will swear from his memory to its having been given. There is no rule which makes the stenographic reporter the only competent witness. Hence it is error to refuse to permit proof of the testimony of a party on a former trial, by a witness who had heard it given. *Id.*

4. *Negligence — Evidence that accident could not occur in manner alleged relevant.* Where an accident resulted from the manner of use of a dump wagon of peculiar and exceptional construction, the question whether the wagon could be turned in the way alleged was a material inquiry, and evidence tending to show that it could not is relevant and admissible. *Id.*

Contract to transport goods signed by carrier and shipper, but silent as to route, cannot be varied by evidence of previous parol instructions to ship by a particular route.

See CARRIERS, 2.

When offer of evidence properly rejected.

See CONTRACT, 4.

Sufficiency of evidence to warrant conviction for murder — defendant by becoming voluntary witness subjects himself to cross-examination as to truth of his statements.

See CRIMES, 1, 2.

Confessions — propriety of their admission in evidence.

See CRIMES, 7.

District attorney may not attempt to create false impressions by questions concerning matters foreign to the issues.

See CRIMES, 11.

When verdict of conviction under common-law indictment for murder not against weight of evidence — evidence tending to show motive and that killing was committed while in perpetration of another crime admissible.

See CRIMES, 12, 14.

Action for divorce — when entry or memorandum from which witness has refreshed his memory inadmissible — when entries on hotel register and testimony of conversations inadmissible — judgment of divorce against alleged paramour not admissible.

See DIVORCE, 1–4.

EXPLOSION.
Liability of insurer for loss resulting from explosion preceded and caused by fire.

See INSURANCE, 1.

EXPRESS COMPANIES.
Liability of, for baggage lost in transit not limited by provisions of section 38 of Public Service Commissions Law.

See CARRIERS.

FALSE IMPRISONMENT.
See Tanzer v. *Morgan* (Mem.), 614.

FALSE MEASURES.
See People v. *Wulforst* (Mem.), 634.

FALSE REPRESENTATIONS.
See Linden v. *Fries* (Mem.), 530.

FIRE INSURANCE.
Liability of insurer for loss resulting from explosion preceded and caused by fire.

See INSURANCE.

FIREMEN.
See Matter of Roche v. *Waldo* (Mem.), 610.

See CIVIL SERVICE.

FORECLOSURE.
See Kouwenhoven v. *Gifford* (Mem.), 556; *Lowenfeld* v. *Wimpie* (Mem.), 646.

FORGERY.
When indorsement of check by holder of power of attorney constitutes forgery.

See PRINCIPAL AND AGENT, 2.

FORMER ADJUDICATION.
1. *Insurance (life) — When judgment obtained by administrator of insured in another state not a bar to an action on the same policy in this state by the assignee thereof.* A life insurance policy issued to a resident of Vermont provided that it was a contract made and to be performed in the state of Wisconsin. The insured assigned the policy to plaintiff and gave notice to the defendant as required by its terms. The assignee was not a relative or creditor of the insured and the policy was assigned without consideration therefor. Immediately after the death of the insured the assignee became a resident of this state. Letters of administration upon the estate of the insured having been issued in Vermont, and the defendant having refused to pay, the administrator brought a suit in that state to recover the amount of the policy. That litigation resulted in a judgment against defendant in favor of the administrator, who was permitted to prove that the assignment was made in consideration of the promise of the present plaintiff to continue meretricious relations with the assured. Thereupon defendant paid the judgment and pleaded such recovery and payment as a bar to this action which had, in the meantime, been brought in this state. When this action was brought to trial no proof was offered to show any illegal or immoral consideration for the assignment, but on the contrary it was stipulated that the assignment was a gift. The facts hereinbefore recited, including the judgments and proceedings in the Vermont action, were placed in evidence. *Held*, that the decision on demurrer herein (189 N. Y. 100) did not dispose of the issue now presented; that, while it is true that, in the Vermont suit, it was found

FORMER ADJUDICATION — *Continued.*

that the assignment was invalid, the present plaintiff was not a party to that action, and that, upon the facts as they appear in this case, the Vermont judgment is not a bar to this suit. *Gleason v. Northwestern Mut. L. Ins. Co.* 507

2. *Jurisdiction.* The common-law rule as to the right of an assignee to sue for the enforcement of a chose in an action considered, and *held,* that by the terms of the policy it was made a Wisconsin contract to be performed there; that by the law of Wisconsin the assignment of a chose in action transfers the legal title and the courts of Vermont therefore had no jurisdiction of the person of the plaintiff, nor was the subject-matter of the litigation in that State, and hence no adjudication there had could conclude this plaintiff's rights. *Id.*

FRANCHISE TAX.

See *People ex rel. M. H. Realty Co.* v. *Williams* (Mem.), 558.

Definition of special franchise — when tunnels and railroads under Hudson river not an exercise of a special franchise — tunnels constructed entirely under grant of rapid transit commission taxable as special franchise — right to enter streets of city of New York a special franchise and taxable as such — equalization of assessments.

See TAX, 1–6.

Special franchise tax upon steam railroad crossings over public streets and highways — when highway is opened across right of way of railroad, such crossing is not subject to the tax.

See TAX, 7, 8.

Assessments upon special franchises — rule for ascertaining value of tangible property — method of ascertaining net earnings in assessment of special franchise — rate of capitalization.

See TAX, 9–11.

Valuation and assessment of special franchises — when city assessors may apportion special franchise assessment between different parts of a tax district.

See TAX, 12, 13.

FRAUD.

See *Dixon* v. *Barkeley* (Mem.), 592.

Syndicate contract by which subscribers agree to take stock in corporation to be organized may be rescinded for fraud.

See PRINCIPAL AND AGENT, 4.

Liability of infant for sale effected by fraud.

See SALE, 2.

GAMBLING.

Person who merely takes part in a game, or games, of poker for amusement is not a " common gambler " within meaning of statute — when person playing poker is not an accomplice of dealer or gamekeeper with whom he plays.

See CRIMES, 9, 10.

GUARANTY.

See *Burfeind* v. *People's Surety Co.* (Mem.), 602.

Waiver of provision in indemnity bond.

See PRINCIPAL AND SURETY.

HIGHWAYS.
See Matter of Morse (Mem.), 563.

Navigable streams not within ordinary nomenclature of highways.
See TAX, 1.

Special franchise tax upon steam railroad crossings over public streets and highways — when highway is opened across right of way of railroad, such crossing is not subject to the tax.
See TAX, 7, 8.

HUSBAND AND WIFE.
Right of wife to recover from husband for moneys expended by her for necessaries. A husband is liable in equity to one who furnishes necessaries requisite for the support of his deserted wife and infant children or to one who furnishes the wife with money with which to procure such necessaries. The common-law disability of the wife to sue the husband having been removed, a wife who has applied her separate estate to the purpose of an obligation resting primarily upon her husband may now recover from him the reasonable amounts which she has thus expended out of her separate estate in discharge of his obligation. In an action by the wife to recover for moneys she has been obliged to expend for necessaries for herself and children, the pecuniary ability of the husband may be an element to be considered as to the character of the expenditures for which she is entitled to be reimbursed. *De Brauwere* v. *De Brauwere.* 460

Action for divorce — evidence.
See DIVORCE, 1–4.

INDICTMENT.
For murder in common-law form — sufficiency.
See CRIMES, 5.

INFANTS.
Liability for sale effected by fraud.
See SALE, 2.

INJUNCTION.
Courts of this state will not restrain prosecution of action in another state to annul a judgment of divorce previously rendered in that state by a court of competent jurisdiction.
See JUDGMENT.

Action to restrain unfair competition in the use of a trade name.
See TRADE NAMES, 1, 2.

INSURANCE.
1. *Liability of insurer for loss resulting from explosion preceded and caused by fire.* When a policy of insurance against fire upon a grain elevator provides that the company should not be liable for loss by explosion of any kind unless fire ensues, and in that event for the damage by fire only, a fire preceding and causing the explosion is not embraced in the exception from the provision which insures against all direct loss or damage by fire, and if a negligent or hostile fire exists within the insured premises and an explosion results therefrom under such circumstances as to constitute the fire the proximate cause of the loss and the explosion merely incidental, the company becomes liable upon its policy for the loss resulting therefrom. *Wheeler* v. *Phenix Ins. Co.* 283

2. *Accident — Clauses of policy construed.* As disability policy issued by defendant insured plaintiff under clause "G," entitled

INSURANCE — *Continued.*

"blindness and paralysis indemnity," against paralysis, upon proof of its continuance for fifty-two successive weeks. Also under clause "H," for illness which should prevent him from performing the duties pertaining to his occcupation, but for not more than twenty-six consecutive weeks. Plaintiff was stricken with paralysis and disabled thereby for more than fifty-two consecutive weeks, but this action was brought before the expiration of that period. *Held,* that plaintiff could not recover under clause "G," as no cause of action thereunder existed at that time. That he could recover, however, under the allegations of the complaint, under clause "H" of the policy. The jury found for plaintiff in the amount to which he would have been entitled for fifty-two weeks under clause "G." *Held,* that a new trial must be granted unless plaintiff stipulated to reduce the judgment to the sum to which he was entitled under clause "H," entitled "sickness indemnity." *Miles* v. *Casualty Co.*   453

Life — when judgment obtained by administrator of insured in another state not a bar to an action on the same policy in this state by the assignee thereof.

See FORMER ADJUDICATION, 1, 2.

JUDGMENT.

Foreign judgment — Divorce — Courts of this state will not restrain prosecution of action in another state to annul a judgment of divorce previously rendered in that state by a court of competent jurisdiction. The courts of this state will not restrain a party from prosecuting an action in another state, the object of which is to annul a judgment of divorce obtained by her in that state when such judgment was rendered by a court of competent jurisdiction over the parties and the subject-matter of that action, and it has been held in a previous action in the courts of this state to which this plaintiff was a party that such judgment was binding and conclusive. *Guggenheim* v. *Wahl.*   390

Application by bankrupt for cancellation of judgment a special proceeding — cancellation denied when claim was improperly scheduled.

See BANKRUPTCY, 1, 2.

When judgment obtained by administrator of insured in another state not a bar to an action on the same policy in this state by the assignee thereof.

See FORMER ADJUDICATION, 1, 2.

Form of.

See PRACTICE.

JURORS.

When previous opinion or impression of jurors not sufficient ground for challenge for bias.

See CRIMES, 13.

LANDLORD AND TENANT.

LEASE.
See *Walder* v. *English* (Mem.), 576.

LEGAL REPRESENTATIVES.
Definition and effect of term "legal representatives."
See CONTRACT, 9.

LEGISLATURE.
Power of legislature to prescribe method of conducting elections.
See CONSTITUTIONAL LAW, 2.

LIBEL.
1. *Privileged communications — Qualified privilege.* On an occasion that rebuts any presumption of express malice one may publish statements, although defamatory of the person referred to, if he does so in the performance of a legal or moral duty and in good faith believing that such statements so made by him are true, without being liable for damages arising from such publication. Such privilege is known as a qualified privilege. A person having an interest as a citizen or otherwise in a public official may, in good faith, make a statement to the superior of the person to whom the communication refers. In a communication so privileged it is not necessary in defense of an action for an alleged libel by reason thereof to show that the statements contained therein are true, except, perhaps, as the truth of the allegations bear upon the question of express malice. This qualified privilege does not extend to communications to newspapers and to the public generally. The publication of a letter containing libelous matter in a newspaper in advance of its delivery to the officer to whom it is addressed destroys the qualified privilege in the writer to send such communication solely for the purpose of presenting facts to such officer in order that he may determine whether the plaintiff should be continued in such office or removed therefrom. A well-established rule of law, also commonly called a qualified privilege, protects a person in making any fair and honest criticism of the conduct of a public officer. In such a communication the writer makes statements of fact at his peril, and if the statements made therein are libelous and untrue the fact that they are about a public officer does not exempt the writer on the ground of privilege. *Bingham* v. *Gaynor.* 27

2. *Pleading — General allegation charging libel per se not successfully answered by general allegation that charge is true.* A general allegation charging a person with something that is libelous *per se* cannot be successfully answered by a general allegation in the answer that the charge is true. The answer in such a case should set forth the *facts* upon which it is alleged that the allegations of the complaint are true. *Id.*

3. *Insufficiency of defenses.* Upon examination of the allegations of plaintiff's complaint, of two separate defenses interposed thereto and of a demurrer to the defenses and on application thereto of the principles stated, *held*, that such defenses are insufficient either as pleas of privilege or in justification. *Id.*

See *Schmeieser* v. *Lessler* (Mem.), 582; *Sutphin* v. *N. Y. Times Co.* (Mem.), 645.

LIENS.
When municipality liable only for amount due contractor at time contract was forfeited. To entitle a lienor to recover on a lien against a municipality it is incumbent upon him to show either that the contractor performed his contract, and that by reason of such performance some amount became due and owing thereon, or that by reason of some special provision of the contract there was

LIENS — *Continued.*

when the lien was filed something due such contractor thereon or that something became due him upon it thereafter applicable to the payment of such lien. A contract provided that on default by the contractor the owner could cancel it and proceed to finish the work and furnish the material required so as to fully execute it in every respect, and further that "the cost and expense thereof at the reasonable market rates shall be a charge against the contractor, who shall pay to the party of the first part the excess thereof, if any, over and above the unpaid balance of the amount to be paid under this contract; and the contractor shall have no claim or demand to such unpaid balance, or by reason of the non-payment thereof to them." *Held*, that after the contract was forfeited the contractor had no rights of any kind whatever under it and hence liens filed against him attach only to the sum actually due him at the time of the forfeiture. *Herrmann & Grace v. Hillman.* 435

LIFE INSURANCE.

When judgment obtained by administrator of insured in another State not a bar to an action on the same policy in this State by the assignee thereof.

See FORMER ADJUDICATION, 1, 2.

LIMITATION OF ACTIONS.

When Statute of Limitations begins to run against right to enforce voluntary trust of interest in real property.

See TRUST.

LIQUOR TAX.

See People v. *Conway* (Mem.), 648.

MAGISTRATES.

Invalidity of commitment issued by justice of peace of municipal corporation which is not a county, city, town or village.

See CONSTITUTIONAL LAW, 7.

MANDAMUS.

When will issue directing comptroller of New York city to examine claim, illegal in form, and certify his opinion whether it should be paid.

See NEW YORK (CITY OF).

MANSLAUGHTER.

See People v. *Darragh* (Mem.), 527.

MECHANIC'S LIEN.

See Vogel & Binder Co. v. *Montgomery* (Mem.), 574; *O'Reilly* v. *Gallagher* (Mem.), 574; *Schnaier* v. *Onward Construction Co.* (Mem.), 603.

MORTGAGE.

See Charlestown Ill. Co. v. *Knickerbocker Trust Co.* (Mem.), 529.

MORTGAGE TAX.

See People ex rel. B. & L. E. Traction Co. v. *Woodbury* (Mem.), 565.

MUNICIPAL CORPORATIONS.

Unconstitutionality of statutes creating a municipal corporation which is not a county, city, town or village.

See CONSTITUTIONAL LAW, 7.

MUNICIPAL CORPORATIONS — *Continued.*

Action by water company against municipality to recover rentals claimed to be due under contract to furnish water for fire service at a certain pressure — measure of damages.

See CONTRACT, 6, 7.

Liens — when municipality liable only for amount due contractor at time contract was forfeited.

See LIENS.

When city not liable for negligence of contractor in construction of subway.

See NEGLIGENCE, 1.

Ordinance giving ambulance right of way does not authorize driving at dangerous speed.

See NEGLIGENCE, 4.

When mandamus will issue directing comptroller of New York city to examine claim, illegal in form, and certify his opinion whether it should be paid.

See NEW YORK (CITY OF).

Water commissioners not quasi corporations but administrative officers — remedy for breach of contract.

See OFFICERS, 1, 2.

MUNICIPAL COURT.

Unconstitutionality of statute amending section 1357 of New York city charter relative to filling vacancies in office of justice — when election must be had to fill vacancy.

See CONSTITUTIONAL LAW, 4, 5.

MURDER.

See People v. *Mangano* (Mem.) 588; *People* v. *Swenton* (Mem.), 641.

Sufficiency of evidence to warrant conviction — defendant by becoming voluntary witness subjects himself to cross-examination as to truth of his statement — improper charge — when failure to charge fully as to degrees of manslaughter not erroneous.

See CRIMES, 1–4.

Sufficiency of indictment in common-law form — properly left to jury to say whether murder was committed in connection with perpetration of other felonies — confessions — propriety of their admission in evidence — propriety of argument by district attorney.

See CRIMES, 5–8.

When verdict of conviction under common-law indictment not against weight of evidence — when previous opinion or impression of jurors not sufficient ground for challenge for bias — evidence tending to show motive and that killing was committed while in perpetration of another crime admissible — charge and refusal to charge — when premeditation and deliberation not necessary to sustain conviction for murder in the first degree.

See CRIMES, 12–16.

NAMES.

Action to restrain unfair competition in the use of a trade name — unlawful use of one's own name.

See TRADE NAMES, 1, 2.

NEGLIGENCE.

1. *Construction of subway by contractors — When city not liable for negligence of contractor — Contractor's liability to abutting owner for damages caused by explosion of dynamite due to sub-contractor's negligence.* Through the negligence of a sub-contractor engaged in the construction of the rapid transit subway in New York city, plaintiff's abutting property was injured by an explosion of dynamite. The contract between the contractor and the city provided: "The contractor shall be responsible for all damage which may be done to abutting property or buildings or structures thereon by the method in which the construction hereunder shall be done, but not including in such damage any damage necessarily arising from proper construction pursuant to this contract or the reasonable use, occupation or obstruction of the streets thereby." *Held, First,* that the city is not liable for the negligence of the contractor to whom the work had been let, nor is it liable on the ground that it suffered a nuisance to be maintained in the street. *Second,* the contractor is liable for the damages sustained by reason of the negligence of the sub-contractor. *Third,* as this was not an agreement of indemnity to the city, but an agreement to be responsible to abutting owners for damages arising from improper construction or unreasonable use and occupation of the streets, an abutting owner can maintain an action under this provision of the contract, although he was not a party thereto. *Smyth* v. *City of New York.* 106

2. *Charitable corporations not exempt from liability for tort.* A charitable corporation is not exempt from liability for a tort against a stranger because of the fact that it holds its property in trust to be applied to purposes of charity. *Kellogg* v. *Church Charity Foundation.* 191

3. *When not liable for negligence of ambulance driver furnished by livery stable.* Where an ambulance owned by the defendant and bearing the name of its hospital was kept at a livery stable, the proprietor of which furnished a horse to draw the ambulance and a man to drive it on such occasions as the defendant might indicate, the driver having been hired and paid by the livery stable keeper, who alone had the power to discharge him, the relation of master and servant is not established between the defendant and such ambulance driver as might be furnished from the livery stable. Such a contract does not make the driver the servant of the hirer or render his negligence imputable to the latter. *Id.*

4. *Ambulance not a dangerous instrumentality as matter of law.* The fact that a city ordinance gives the right of way to ambulances in the public streets in no manner authorizes the driving of such vehicles at a dangerous rate of speed. There is no foundation, therefore, for the doctrine that an ambulance is necessarily a dangerous instrumentality. *Id.*

5. *Contributory negligence — When person injured by falling into elevator shaft in unlighted hall guilty of contributory negligence.* A person coming into an unfamiliar situation, where a condition of darkness renders the use of his eyesight ineffective to define his surroundings, is not justified in the absence of any special stress of circumstances in proceeding further, without first finding out where he is going and what may be the obstructions to his safe progress. Plaintiff entered a building occupied by several tenants for the purpose of transacting business with tenants on one of the upper floors, and passing the stairway went on through the hallway which was so dark that he could not see distinctly where he was going, and continuing "at his regular gait," stepped in a half-open

NEGLIGENCE — *Continued.*

door and fell to the bottom of an elevator shaft. It was not shown that defendants, the owners of the building, had assumed any obligation to keep the hallway lighted or that any statutory provision applied to the existing condition. *Held*, that the defendants were not shown to have neglected any legal duty to plaintiff, and further that he was guilty of contributory negligence. *Rohrbacher* v. *Gillig.* 413

> *See Serling* v. *Serling* (Mem.), 529; *Arnold* v. *Vil. of North Tarrytown* (Mem.), 536; *Albrecht* v. *R. S. & E. R. R. Co.* (Mem.), 566; *Smith* v. *U. & D. R. R. Co.* (Mem.), 572; *Pease* v. *Penn. R. R. Co.* (Mem.), 573; *Przeczewski* v. *Bardsley* (Mem.), 576; *Hatten* v. *Hyde-McFarlin Co.* (Mem.), 578; *McMichael* v. *Federal Printing Co.* (Mem.), 581; *Bartholoma* v. *Town of Florence* (Mem.), 582; *Neylan* v. *Reilly's Sons Co.* (Mem.), 589; *Lynch* v. *Lackawanna Steel Co.* (Mem.), 601; *Shirley* v. *N. Y. C. & H. R. R. R. Co.* (Mem.), 602; *Bauer* v. *Inter-Ocean Tel. & Tel. Co.* (Mem.), 633; *Lyons* v. *N. Y. C. & H. R. R. R. Co.* (Mem.), 634; *Levy* v. *Joline* (Mem.), 635; *Smith* v. *Nat. Starch Co.* (Mem.), 638; *Nolan* v. *Ferris Paving Brick Co.* (Mem.), 641; *Rich* v. *Pennsylvania R. R. Co.* (Mem.), 642.

When evidence of discharge of motorman inadmissible in action to recover for injuries alleged to have been occasioned by his negligence.

> *See* EVIDENCE, 1.

Evidence that accident could not occur in manner alleged, elevant.

> *See* EVIDENCE, 4.

When railroad company not liable for animals injured by falling through railroad bridge.

> *See* RAILROADS.

NEGOTIABLE INSTRUMENTS.

What damages recoverable by payee upon foreign bill of exchange protested for non-payment.

> *See* BILLS, NOTES AND CHECKS, 1, 2.

When indorsement of check by holder of power of attorney constitutes forgery — collecting bank liable.

> *See* PRINCIPAL AND AGENT, 2.

NEW YORK (CITY OF).

Mandamus — *When writ will be issued directing comptroller to examine claim, illegal in form, against city and certify his opinion whether it should be paid.* Where the board of estimate and apportionment of the city of New York refers an application made by a person having an illegal or invalid claim against the city to the comptroller for investigation and opinion as to whether it should be paid or compromised under section 246 of the charter (L. 1907, ch. 601), it is his duty to consider the claim, and if in his judgment it is equitable and proper for the city to pay the same in whole or in part to so certify to the board, and this duty may be enforced by mandamus. *People ex rel. Dady* v. *Prendergast.* 1

Special Term order vacating an award in condemnation proceedings appealable to Appellate Division.

> *See* APPEAL, 4.

PARTITION.
See Beach v. *Large* (Mem.) 532.

Amount of extra allowances of costs.
See COSTS.

Extra allowances — total amount allowed to all parties cannot exceed five per cent of value of property — allowance to plaintiff based on value of the whole property — allowance to any defendant based on value of that defendant's interest in the property — construction of provision limiting allowance to $2,000 to each side of action.
See COSTS.

PENAL LAW.
Gambling — A person who takes part in a game, or games, of poker for amusement is not a "common gambler" within the meaning of the statute. A person who merely takes part in a game or series of games of poker on precisely the same terms as the other participants in the game, for mere amusement or recreation and not as a professional gamester. does not thereby become a common gambler under section 970 of the Penal Law. *People* v. *Bright.* 78

PENALTIES.
See Town of Irondequoit v. *Costich* (Mem.), 640.

PLEADING.
See Ottinger v. *Bennett* (Mem.), 554; *Atlantic Dredging Co.* v. *Beard* (Mem.), 584.

General allegation charging libel *per se* not successfully answered by general allegation that charge is true — insufficiency of defense.
See LIBEL, 2, 3.

POLICE.
See People ex rel. Reid v. *Bingham* (Mem.), 552; *People ex rel. Mencke* v. *Baker* (Mem.), 563; *People ex rel. Conley* v. *Beach* (Mem.), 620; *Matter of O'Brien* v. *Waldo* (Mem.), 630; *People ex rel. Dwyer* v. *Bingham* (Mem.), 631; *People ex rel. Leavy* v. *Baker* (Mem.), 632.

POWERS.
Construction of power of attorney — when indorsement of check by holder of power of attorney constitutes forgery.
See PRINCIPAL AND AGENT, 1, 2.

PRACTICE.
Form of judgment. Under no rule of practice is there any justification for inserting in a judgment a provision for the issuance of an execution against the person or for quoting extracts from the judge's charge to the jury. *Curtiss* v. *Jebb* (Mem.) 538
See Logan v. *Greenwich Trust Co.* (Mem.), 611.

When relation of attorney and client does not exist, summary proceedings to recover papers cannot be maintained.
See ATTORNEY AND CLIENT.

Trial of issues — section 973 of the Code of Civil Procedure constitutional.
See CONSTITUTIONAL LAW, 9.

Amount of extra allowances of costs in action of partition.
See COSTS.

PRINCIPAL AND AGENT.

1. *Construction of power of attorney.* The extent to which a principal shall authorize his agent is completely within his determination, and a party dealing with the agent must ascertain the scope and reach of the powers delegated to him and must abide by the consequences if he transcends them. A power of attorney, like any other contract, is to be construed according to the natural meaning of the words in view of the purpose of the agency and the needs to its fulfillment. The authority within it under such construction is not to be broadened or extended. *Porges* v. *U. S. M. & Trust Co.* 181

2. *When indorsement of check by holder of power of attorney constitutes forgery.* The holder of a power of attorney from plaintiff indorsed a check payable to her order and converted the proceeds to his own use by depositing it with the defendant which collected the check and placed the amount thereof to his credit. *Held*, upon examination of the power of attorney, that it did not authorize the holder to indorse the check for his own benefit and that plaintiff is entitled to recover from defendant the amount of the check and interest, less a sum found by the jury as damages to defendant by reason of the failure of plaintiff to exercise due diligence in notifying defendant of the alleged forgery. *Id.*

3. *When agent may not sell his own property to principal — When executed contract may be rescinded.* A person occupying a position of agent to purchase may not sell his own property to his principal. If one by misrepresentation or suppression of facts, when he ought to speak, induces another ignorantly to make a contract appointing the first his agent to buy and conferring upon him discretionary power to purchase his own property, the contract is voidable; and even if executed may be rescinded and the money recovered back upon restoration of what has been received. *Hecksher* v. *Edenborn.* 210

4. *Syndicate contract by which subscribers agree to take stock in corporation to be organized, may be rescinded for fraud.* In this action, brought to recover amounts subscribed and paid by plaintiff and his assignors to defendant under a syndicate agreement on the ground that they were induced so to do by fraud of defendant, the jury was entitled to find that the defendant was the chief promoter and organizer of an enterprise which contemplated as its basis the purchase of a million dollars par value of the stock of a corporation of which he was the majority owner; that the syndicate agreement made defendant and his two associate managers agents of the various subscribers and gave them discretionary power to purchase this stock; that defendant in effect invited or solicited plaintiff's assignors to become subscribers to the agreement; that at the time they were ignorant of his interest in the property to be acquired, and that he did not inform them of such interest, but on the contrary his apparent subscription on the paper showed to them, and various statements which he made, tended to exclude the idea that defendant was the owner of a large amount of property to be acquired, and which would in effect offset or pay his large subscription, when, as a matter of fact, he always intended to transfer his stock to the syndicate as he did. *Held*, that if these facts should be found a court would be entitled to find fraud as a matter of fact, for which the agreement could be rescinded and moneys paid thereunder recovered back. *Id.*

5. *When tender of stock sufficient to entitle subscriber to return of money paid.* Defendant and his associates acquired not only his stock in the corporation but also other property, and all of this was transferred to a reorganized corporation and represented by new

PRINCIPAL AND AGENT — *Continued.*
stock issued to the syndicate subscribers. Plaintiff and his assignors tendered to defendant the stock so issued to them and demanded the return of the money subscribed. *Held*, that such tender was a sufficient offer to restore defendant to his original position, so as to entitle plaintiff and his assignors to recover the moneys which had been paid to him; that the agreement cannot be subdivided and a rescission allowed as to part and not as to the rest; that on a rescission of the agreement and on restoration of what they received plaintiff and his assignors would be entitled to recover the entire amounts paid to defendant, even though part of such moneys were applied to the purchase of other property than that owned by defendant. *Id.*

PRINCIPAL AND SURETY.
Bond indemnifying employer against loss arising from larceny or embezzlement of a clerk — Waiver of provision therein that bond shall be "of no effect unless signed by the employee." This action was brought upon a bond issued by the defendant to the plaintiff, by which the former agreed to indemnify the latter against any pecuniary loss occurring through the larceny, or embezzlement, of one of its clerks. Defendant alleged the invalidity of the bond by reason of non-compliance with the provision that it should be "of no effect unless signed by the employé." The defendant, at the time the bond was delivered, held an agreement by the employee to repay any losses it might sustain by reason thereof. The bond was prepared by defendant's agents and forwarded with a letter stating "enclosed herewith please find bond duly executed on behalf of Ralph J. Ellis (the employee) which we trust will be satisfactory," and accepted payment of the premium thereon. *Held*, that defendant waived the signature of the employee and is liable upon the bond. *General Ry. Signal Co. v. Title G. & S. Co.* 407

PRIVILEGE.
Privileged communications — qualified privilege.
See LIBEL, 1.

PUBLIC SERVICE COMMISSIONS.
When discretion of commission cannot override discretion of officers of corporation — duty and powers of commission to determine under section 69 of Public Service Commissions Law whether a proposed bond issue is necessary for purposes of corporation and authorized by law.
See CORPORATIONS, 1-7.

Provisions of Public Service Commissions Law not in conflict with sections 9-12 of Stock Corporation Law — reorganization of railroad corporation — authority of commission as to issue of securities.
See CORPORATIONS, 8, 9.

PUBLIC SERVICE COMMISSIONS LAW.
Meaning of term "baggage" as used in section 38.
See CARRIERS, 1.

RAILROADS.
Construction and application of section 52 of Railroad Law (Cons. Laws, ch. 49) requiring railroad companies to maintain fences along their rights of way — Railroad company not liable for animals injured by falling through railroad bridge. Section 52 of the Railroad Law (Cons. Laws, ch. 49) requiring railroad companies to erect and maintain fences along their rights of way limits their liability for failure to do so to "damages done by their agents or engines or cars to any domestic animals thereon;" hence, there

ROBBERY.
See *People* v. *Lewis* (Mem.), 643.

SALE.

1. *When acceptance of machine by vendee question for a jury— When execution by vendee of chattel mortgage on machine before test not a waiver of right of inspection.* Defendant's testator sold a machine to plaintiff's assignor under a contract which provided that the price should be $8,000, and that settlement should be "made for same as follows: On the acceptance of this proposition you (the vendee) to pay us the sum of $3,000 cash, which amount will be returned to you if the machine does not prove satisfactory." Thereafter to secure his indorsement of certain notes and before the testing of the machine had been completed, the vendee executed a chattel mortgage on this and other property to plaintiff, who was the president of the vendee and who testified, among other things, that he was acquainted with the terms under which the company held the machine, and was present at a meeting of its board of directors and voted for a resolution authorizing the vice-president to execute the mortgage, that he knew that no test had been made, and subsequently requested the vendor to remove the machine on the ground that it was not satisfactory. At the sale under this mortgage the interest sold was "the interest that the Arto-Litho Company (the vendee) has in this machine to the extent of $3,000. * * * The right, title and interest that was in there," the vendor at that time giving notice of its claim of title. At such sale a claim was made in its behalf that the title remained in the vendor. The machine was subsequently retaken by the vendor because of alleged default by the vendee in the performance of its contract. *Held*, that a jury would have had the right to determine that the mortgage was executed and accepted subject to the terms of the contract of sale and subject to the right of the mortgagor to complete its test and return the machine if it proved unsatisfactory, leaving the mortgagee in that case to recover under his mortgage, as the interest covered thereby, the payment which had been made, and that there was no intention on the part of the vendee to waive its right of inspection and accept the machine irrespective thereof. *Harrison* v. *Scott.* 869

2. *Infants — Liability for sale effected by fraud.* A matter arising *ex contractu*, though infected with fraud, cannot be changed into a tort, in order to charge an infant, by a change of the remedy. A fraudulent act, to render an infant chargeable therewith, must be wholly tortious, and if the action is substantially grounded in contract he is not liable. An infant defendant warranted a horse to be "free from any and all diseases of every name and nature," etc. The trial court found that "the sale was consummated as the result of the statements of defendant, and plaintiff in paying for the said horse relied upon said statements." *Held*, that since there is no allegation or finding of any false or fraudulent representation made by the defendant with intent to induce the plaintiff to purchase the horse, this essential element of an action for deceit is wanting, and no cause of action was established against the infant. *Collins* v. *Gifford.* 465

See *Deis, Son & Co.* v. *Hart* (Mem.), 571; *Van Schaick* v. *Heyman* (Mem.), 595; *McEwan Bros.* v. *Billings* (Mem.), 600; *Kraemer* v. *Williams* (Mem.), 639.

Construction of contract for purchase and sale of foreign goods — when buyer may not repudiate contract and refuse to accept goods, because invoices were mutilated and because goods were not imported expressly for buyer.

See CONTRACT, 3.

SEALED INSTRUMENTS.

Contract under seal, by which one brother agrees to support his mother, cannot be enforced by another brother not a party to it, although the latter joined in the consideration for the contract.

See CONTRACT, 2.

SESSION LAWS.

1. 1896, *Ch.* 812. The legislative acts, chapter 812 of Laws of 1896 and chapter 361 of the Laws of 1901, purporting to revise and consolidate previous acts creating the "area or territory known as Sylvan Beach," are without constitutional warrant, and a commitment issued by a police justice claiming to hold his office under such acts is void. *People ex rel. Hon Yost v. Becker.* 201

2. 1899, *Ch.* 712 — *Special franchise tax upon steam railroad crossings over public streets and highways — When highway is opened across right of way owned and occupied by railroad, such crossing is not subject to the tax.* On review and examination of the statutory provisions on the subject, *held,* that the term "surface" as applied to railroads in the statute (Laws of 1899, ch. 712, § 1; Tax Law, Cons. Laws, ch. 60, § 2, subd. 3) defining special franchises for the purpose of taxation, does not refer exclusively to street railroads, and hence a special franchise includes railroads operated by steam, running across the state from one terminal point to another, and the crossings made by constructing such railroads across streets already in existence. The object of the Special Franchise Tax Act is to tax railroad corporations for privileges granted them in the streets which they occupy on their lines of railway, and if, after they have their rights of way secured over private land, a public highway is laid across the tracks, while there is a crossing, it is not a crossing made by the railroad, or through public favor so far as the railroad is concerned, and hence is not liable to taxation as a special franchise. *People ex rel. N. Y. C. & H. R. R. R. Co. v. Woodbury.* 167

1901, *Ch.* 361. See par. 1, this title.

3. 1901, *Ch.* 602 — *Jurors — Challenge for bias.* Where jurors admitted, when examined under challenge, that they had previously formed an opinion or impression to the effect that a crime had been committed in the case, but each declared on oath that he believed such opinion or impression would not influence his verdict, and that he could render an impartial verdict according to the evidence, such previous opinion or impression is not a sufficient ground of challenge for bias. (Code Crim. Pro. § 376, subd. 2.) Furthermore the defendant was tried by a special jury drawn under chapter 602 of the Laws of 1901, which provides that the allowance or disallowance of challenges for actual bias shall be final. *People v. Wolter.* 484

4. 1905, *Ch.* 724 — *Appeal — Practice — Condemnation of property for water supply for city of New York — Special Term order, vacating an award by commissioners of appraisal, appealable to Court of Appeals.* An appeal lies to the Appellate Division from an order of the Special Term which vacated an award made by the commissioners of appraisal to ascertain the compensation to be made for land taken for water supply for the city of New York, by virtue of chapter 724 of the Laws of 1905, and the acts amendatory thereof. *Matter of Simmons.* 241

5. 1907, *Ch.* 601 — *New York city charter — Mandamus — When writ will be issued directing comptroller of New York city to examine claim, illegal in form, against city and certify his opinion whether it should be paid.* Where the board of estimate and apportionment of the city of New York refers an application made

SESSION LAWS — *Continued.*

by a person having an illegal or invalid claim against the city to the comptroller for investigation and opinion as to whether it should be paid or compromised under section 246 of the charter (L. 1907, ch. 601), it is his duty to consider the claim, and if in his judgment it is equitable and proper for the city to pay the same in whole or in part to so certify to the board, and this duty may be enforced by mandamus. *People ex rel. Dady* v. *Prendergast.* · 1

6. 1907, *Ch.* 603 — *New York city charter — Unconstitutionality of statute amending section 1357 of New York city charter, relative to vacancies in office of Municipal Court justices.* The statute of 1907 (Ch. 603, § 3), amending section 1357 of the charter of the city of New York, relating to vacancies in office of justices of the Municipal Court, violates the Constitution. *First,* in prohibiting an election unless the vacancy occurs three months before the general election. *Second,* in requiring the mayor to appoint a person to fill the vacancy in the interim, which in this case would be for two years and about five months. *Third,* in requiring the election to fill vacancies to be for a full term, which might occur in an even numbered year. Hence the section of the charter as it existed before the amendment must be deemed to remain in force. *Matter of Markland* v. *Scully.* 158

7. 1909, *Ch.* 15 — *Civil service — Improper dismissal of veteran fireman.* Upon review of the statutes relative to the fire department of the village and city of Rome, *held,* that the board of fire and police commissioners should not be allowed to so construe the Civil Service Law (Cons. Laws, ch. 7, § 22) as to permit it to summarily discharge the relator, without a hearing, from his office in the police department, while he has in his possession an honorable discharge from the fire department of the city signed by said board and recommended by the chief engineer of the fire department. *People ex rel. Conley* v. *Beach* (Mem.), 620.

8. 1909, *Ch.* 17 — *Debtor and Creditor Law — Application by bankrupt for cancellation of judgment.* An application by a bankrupt for an order canceling a judgment under section 1268 of the Code of Civil Procedure, now section 150 of the Debtor and Creditor Law (Cons. Laws, ch. 12) is a special proceeding and an order made therein is appealable to the Court of Appeals. *Guasti* v. *Miller.* 259

9. 1909, *Ch.* 38 — *Lien Law — When municipality liable only for amount due contractor at time contract was forfeited.* To entitle a lienor to recover on a lien against a municipality it is incumbent upon him to show either that the contractor performed his contract, and that by reason of such performance some amount became due and owing thereon, or that by reason of some special provision of the contract there was when the lien was filed something due such contractor thereon or that something became due him upon it thereafter applicable to the payment of such lien. (Lien Law [Cons. Laws, ch. 33], § 60.) *Herrmann & Grace* v. *Hillman.* 435

1909, *Ch.* 61. See par. 11, this title.

1909, *Ch.* 62. See par. 2, this title.

10. 1910, *Ch.* 480 — *Public Service Commissions Law — Duty and powers of commission to determine under section 69 whether a proposed bond issue is necessary for purposes of corporation and authorized by law.* The discretion of a public service commission cannot override the discretion of the officers of a corporation in the management of its affairs, or the provisions of the statute which prescribes the cases in which securities are permitted to be issued

SESSION LAWS— *Continued.*
Its duty upon an application under section 69 of the Public Service Commissions Law (Cons. Laws, ch. 48) is to determine whether a proposed issue of bonds is necessary for the proper purposes of the company, is authorized by law and is to be used in a proper manner. If such are the facts it cannot withhold its certificate; otherwise it cannot grant it. *People ex rel. Binghamton L., H. & P. Co. v. Stevens.*   7

11. *Idem — Public Service Commissions Law — Liability of express company for baggage lost in transit not limited by provisions of section 38.* The term "baggage," used in section 38 of the Public Service Commissions Law (Consol. Laws, ch. 48), does not include property which is being moved by express or otherwise apart from and disconnected with the transportation of the owner; hence, a company, which enters into a contract with a passenger on a railroad train to deliver a trunk at his home or other designated point, cannot avail itself of the limitation in that section upon the amount of the recovery against a common carrier, where the value of the baggage is not stated. *Morgan v. Woolverton.* 52

12. *Idem — Public Service Commissions Law — Provisions not in conflict with sections 9–12 of Stock Corporation Law — Reorganization of railroad corporation — Authority of commission as to issue of securities.* The enactment of the Public Service Commissions Law (Cons. Laws, ch. 48) did not repeal the provisions in the Stock Corporation Law (Cons. Laws, ch. 59) for the reorganization of the property and franchises of corporations sold under foreclosure, and, on the other hand, the provisions of the Stock Corporation Law do not withdraw corporations formed on reorganizations from compliance with section 55 of the Public Service Commissions Law. The two statutes must be construed together. Sections 53 and 54 of the Public Service Commissions Law, requiring the approval by a public service commission of the exercise or transfer of franchises by a railroad corporation, do not apply to a corporation formed on the reorganization of a railroad corporation after foreclosure. Under the provisions of section 55 of the Public Service Commissions Law, a public service commission is not justified in refusing to consent to the issue of securities by a railroad corporation under a plan of reorganization after foreclosure because the value of the mortgaged property and the amount of new capital to be invested is less than the amount of securities sought to be issued. *People ex rel. Third Ave. Ry. Co. v. Public Service Commission.* 299

13. *1910, Ch. 481 — Railroad Law — Construction and application of section 52 requiring railroad companies to maintain fences along their rights of way — Railroad company not liable for animals injured by falling through railroad bridge.* Section 52 of the Railroad Law (Cons. Laws, ch. 49) requiring railroad companies to erect and maintain fences along their rights of way limits their liability for failure to do so to "damages done by their agents or engines or cars to any domestic animals thereon;" hence, there is no liability for injuries sustained by animals which by reason of such failure have escaped from a pasture and are injured by falling through a bridge on the roadway of a railroad company. *Jimerson v. Erie R. R. Co.* 518

14. *1911, Ch. 649 — Election Law — Unconstitutionality of section 6.* The legislature exceeded its power in providing that all voters residing outside of cities or villages with a population of five thousand or more whose names do not appear on the poll book of the last general election shall apply in person in order to be registered, and the attempt to impose this requirement, as made by section 6

SESSION LAWS — *Continued.*
of chapter 649 of the Laws of 1911, is unconstitutional and void.
Matter of Fraser v. *Brown.* 136

15. *Idem — Unconstitutionality of section* 12, *relating to printing of names on ballots.* The provision of section 12 of chapter 649 of the Laws of 1911, that the name of a person nominated by more than one political party shall be printed but once upon the ballot, and regulating in detail the method of carrying out such provision, is unconstitutional as unjustly discriminating between electors in the facility afforded them for casting their votes for the candidates of their choice. *Matter of Hopper* v. *Britt.* 144

16. *Idem — Election Law — Amendment to section* 123, *relating to the signing and filing of certificates of independent nominations, construed and held to be constitutional.* The Election Law (Cons. Laws, ch. 17, as amended by·L. 1911, ch. 649) permits an independent certificate of nomination to be made up of several different sheets. Section 123 provides that " The signatures to the certificate of nomination need not all be appended to one paper," and further that " No separate sheet comprising an independent certificate of nomination, where such certificate consists of more than one sheet, shall be received and filed with the custodian of primary records if five per centum of the names appearing on such sheet are fraudulent or forged." *Held,* that the latter provision may be upheld because independent nominators are not constrained to subject themselves to its operation. They may all sign a single sheet or each may sign a sheet by himself. This liberty of action relieves the provision from any constitutional objection. *Matter of Burke* v. *Terry.* 293

SPECIFIC PERFORMANCE.
See Goldsmith v. *Tolk* (Mem.), 573; *Robbins* v. *Clock* (Mem.), 603; *Flint* v. *Leonard* (Mem.), 636.

STATUTE OF LIMITATIONS.
When begins to run against right to enforce voluntary trust in real property.
See TRUST.

STOCKBROKERS.
See Smith v. *Hutton* (Mem.), 594; *Koewing* v. *Thalmann* (Mem.), 597.

STOCKHOLDERS.
Syndicate contract by which subscribers agree to take stock in corporation to be organized, may be rescinded for fraud — when tender of stock sufficient to entitle subscriber to return of money paid.
See PRINCIPAL AND AGENT, 3–5.

STOCKHOLDER'S ACTION.
See Scherr v. *Pioneer Iron Works* (Mem.), 638.

STREET CLOSING.
See Matter of Hueg (Mem.), 552.

STREET OPENING.
See Matter of City of New York (Jerome Ave.) (Mem.), 564;
Matter of City of New York (Van Alst. Ave.) (Mem.), 570;
Matter of City of New York (W. 177th St.) (Mem.), 570.

STREETS.
Ordinance giving ambulance right of way does not authorize driving at dangerous speed.
See NEGLIGENCE, 4.

STREETS — *Continued.*

Right of railroad to enter streets a special franchise and taxable as such.

See TAX, 4.

Special franchise tax upon steam railroad crossings over public streets and highways — when street is opened across right of way of railroad, such crossing is not subject to tax.

See TAX, 7, 8.

SUMMARY PROCEEDINGS.

To recover papers cannot be maintained when relation of attorney and client does not exist.

See ATTORNEY AND CLIENT.

SURETIES.

Waiver of provision in bond indemnifying employer against loss arising from larceny or embezzlement of a clerk.

See PRINCIPAL AND SURETY.

SURPLUS MONEY.

See King v. *Beers* (Mem.), 559.

TAX.

1. *Definition of special franchise — Navigable streams not within ordinary nomenclature of highways.* A special franchise, so far as railroads are concerned, is the right or permission to construct, maintain and operate the same in, under, above, on or through streets, highways or public places. The Hudson river is a highway in the broad sense of that term, and its waters being subject to the ebb and flow of the tide, the title to the bed of the river is in the state, but navigable streams do not fall within the ordinary nomenclature of highways, unless the intent to include them is apparent. *People ex rel. Hudson & Manhattan R. R.* v. *State Bd. Tax Comrs.*   119

2. *When tunnels and railroads under Hudson river not an exercise of a special franchise.* Where relator's predecessor in title acquired land from the state by grant for the purpose of building a railroad under the Hudson river, its tunnels and railroads constructed in this part of its route are constructed on its own right of way and are not to be deemed the exercise of a special franchise.   *Id.*

3. *Tunnels constructed entirely under grant of rapid transit commission taxable as special franchise.* This principle does not apply to tunnels, the relator's right to construct and maintain which proceeds entirely from the grant of the rapid transit commission as a part of a continuous subway road under the streets of the city of New York and the waters of the Hudson to the state line, and hence such property is taxable as a special franchise. *Id.*

4. *Right to enter streets of city of New York a special franchise and taxable as such.* No one has a right to use the streets of the city of New York for the purpose of a railroad except by virtue of a franchise proceeding from the state. The right to enter the streets is unquestionably a special franchise and the state board is expressly directed to include as part of the special franchise the value of the tangible property. Relator may be taxed on such property the same as any other property situated within the state.   *Id.*

5. *Assessment of railroad under construction.* Where a railroad under construction under the Hudson was uncompleted and it was uncertain whether it would be a profitable venture or otherwise,

TAX— *Continued.*
the structure was properly assessable under the Special Franchise Act at the cost of reproduction, but under the circumstances no assessment should have been placed upon the franchise. *Id.*

6. *Equalization of assessments.* There is no authority in the state board to assess special franchises at less than their full value, or to consider the general rate of taxation in any particular taxing district. In the absence of a finding to the contrary, it must be assumed that the state board assessed the relator's property at its full value, and the court should equalize such assessment with that of other property when such other property is not assessed at full value. *Id.*

7. *Special franchise tax upon steam railroad crossings over public streets and highways.* On review and examination of the statutory provisions on the subject, *held*, that the term "surface" as applied to railroads in the statute (Laws of 1899, ch. 712, § 1; Tax Law, Cons. Laws, ch. 60, § 2, subd. 3) defining special franchises for the purpose of taxation, does not refer exclusively to street railroads, and hence a special franchise includes railroads operated by steam, running across the state from one terminal point to another, and the crossings made by constructing such railroads across streets already in existence. *People ex rel. N. Y. C. & H. R. R. R. Co. v. Woodbury.* 167

8. *When highway is opened across right of way of railroad, such crossing is not subject to the tax.* The object of the Special Franchise Tax Act is to tax railroad corporations for privileges granted them in the streets which they occupy on their lines of railway, and if, after they have their rights of way secured over private land, a public highway is laid across the tracks, while there is a crossing, it is not a crossing made by the railroad, or through public favor so far as the railroad is concerned, and hence is not liable to taxation as a special franchise. *Id.*

9. *Tax — Assessments upon special franchises — Rule for ascertaining value of tangible property.* In fixing the value of the relator's special franchises the court applied the net earnings rule to the evidence. *Held*, that in ascertaining the value of the relator's tangible property, upon which a return should be allowed, there should have been included the value of the relator's interest in the subway, or subservice conduits, through which its power and light cables pass, the cash and cash items on hand, and the cost of relator's easements. *People ex rel. Manhattan Ry. Co. v. Woodbury.* 231

10. *Method of ascertaining net earnings in assessment of special franchises.* The rule as to net earnings is to ascertain the gross earnings of the corporation and then deduct the operating expenses, together with the annual taxes paid. From the remainder there should also be deducted a fair and reasonable return on that portion of the capital of the corporation which is invested in tangible property, the result becoming the net earnings contributable to the special franchise; which, when capitalized at a certain fixed rate, becomes the value of the tangible property of the special franchise. The question of the fair and reasonable return is one of fact under the control of the courts below and one which this court should nor review. *Id.*

11. *Rate of capitalization.* To provide against unforeseen contingencies that may arise in the prosecution of the business of a corporation, which may result in the impairment of the net earnings, a gross sum should be deducted annually for the purposes of

TAX—*Continued.*

reconstruction, and the rate of capitalization to meet depreciation should be at least one per cent higher than the rate of income allowed. *Id.*

12. *Valuation and assessment of special franchises.* The intention of the Tax Law is to give the state board of tax commissioners exclusive power and authority to fix and determine the valuation of each special franchise subject to assessment in each city, town and tax district, and to lodge in local boards and officers the power and authority to apportion the valuation of a single special franchise for the purposes of assessment among school districts and where for other special reason it is required. The state board of tax commissioners performs its full duty when it fixes and determines in one amount the value of a special franchise to occupy the streets and public places in a single tax district, with a continuous and unbroken line of pipes and wires. *People ex rel. Troy Gas Co.* v. *Hall.* 312

13. *When city assessors may apportion special franchise assessment between different parts of a tax district.* Where certain territory in a city constitutes a separate school district which is not subject to taxation for general school purposes, the city assessors are authorized to apportion a special franchise, the full value of which has been determined by the state board of tax commissioners, between such school district and the territory under the control of the board of education of such city. *Id.*

See *People ex rel. Stebbins* v. *Purdy* (Mem.), 555; *Matter of City of New York* v. *Mitchell* (Mem.), 609; *People ex rel. Brooklyn Benevolent Society* v. *Purdy* (Mem.), 629.

TEACHERS.

See *Matter of Norman* (Mem.), 548; *Matter of Barringer* (Mem.), 550.

TENDER.

When actual tender need not be made.

See CONTRACT, 10.

Sufficiency of tender.

See PRINCIPAL AND AGENT, 5.

TITLE.

See *Close Co.* v. *Calder* (Mem.), 590.

TOURIST PARTIES.

Manager of tourist party who engaged to look after baggage not liable for baggage lost while in custody of steamship company.

See CONTRACT, 1.

TRADE NAMES.

1. *Action to restrain unfair competition in the use of a trade name.* While it is a general principle of law that one's name is his property, and he has the same right to its use and enjoyment as he has to that of any other species of property, it is also true that no man has a right to sell his products or goods as those of another. He may not through unfairness, artifice, misrepresentation or fraud injure the business of another or induce the public to believe his product is the product of the other. *World's D. M. Assn.* v. *Pierce.* 419

2. *Unlawful use of one's own name.* One Ray V. Pierce, a physician, transferred to the plaintiff upon its incorporation his business of manufacturing and selling, under their trade names,

TRADE NAMES — *Continued.*

several proprietary remedies which are commonly known to the public as "Dr. Pierce's Remedies" and also as "Pierce's Remedies." Ray V. Pierce has been at all times and is now the president and a director of the plaintiff, and devised the formula for each remedy. Defendant has advertised and sold certain proprietary remedies in boxes under the name of "Dr. Pierce," the words "R. J. Pierce" thereon being a facsimile signature. The defendant is not a licensed physician, nor entitled to practice as such under the law of the state. *Held*, that the defendant should be enjoined from using the prefix "Dr.," and from using the words "Pierce" or "Pierce's" in advertising, describing, designating, labeling or selling his proprietary remedies unless said word be immediately preceded on the same line therewith by defendant's first or proper christian name, and his middle name or the initial letter thereof in letters identical in size, color, style of type and conspicuousness with those of said word, so that said word shall not appear for any of the purposes aforesaid except when thus conjoined with the words "Robert J." or "Robert," followed by the middle name of the defendant.   *Id.*

TRANSFER TAX.
See Matter of Arnot (Mem.), 627.

TRESPASS.
See Lapier v. *Gonyo* (Mem.), 527.

TRIAL.
Exception to refusal to dismiss complaint waived by introduction of evidence on defense — questions raised by exception to denial of motion to dismiss complaint made at close of entire evidence.

See APPEAL, 1-3.

Section 973 of Code of Civil Procedure relating to separate trial of issues, constitutional.

See CONSTITUTIONAL LAW, 9.

When offer of evidence properly rejected.

See CONTRACT, 4.

Sufficiency of evidence to warrant conviction for murder — defendant by becoming voluntary witness subjects himself to cross-examination as to truth of his statements — improper charge — when failure to charge fully as to degrees of manslaughter not erroneous.

See CRIMES, 1-4.

Sufficiency of indictment for murder in common-law form — properly left to jury to say whether murder was committed in connection with perpetration of other felonies — propriety of admission of alleged confessions in evidence — propriety of argument of district attorney.

See CRIMES, 5-8.

District attorney may not attempt to create false impressions by questions concerning matters foreign to the issues.

See CRIMES, 11.

Murder — when verdict of conviction under common-law indictment not against weight of evidence — when previous opinion or impression of jurors not sufficient ground for challenge for bias — evidence tending to show motive, and that killing was committed while in perpetration of another crime, admissible — charge and

TRIAL — *Continued.*

refusal to charge — when premeditation and deliberation not necessary to sustain conviction for murder in first degree.

See CRIMES, 12–16.

When entry or memorandum from which witness has refreshed his memory not admissible in evidence — when entries on hotel register and testimony of conversations inadmissible in action for divorce — judgment of divorce against alleged paramour not admissible in evidence.

See DIVORCE, 1–4.

When evidence of discharge of motorman inadmissible.

See EVIDENCE, 1.

Admission of any material fact competent evidence — testimony given on previous trial may be proved by any person who will swear to its having been given — negligence — evidence that accident could not occur in manner alleged, relevant.

See EVIDENCE, 2–4.

TRUST.

Action to impress a trust — Construction of voluntary trust of leasehold interest in real property for benefit of children of a deceased brother of trustee — Statute of Limitations. Defendant's husband held a leasehold interest with right of renewal for two terms. He filed an instrument in the office of the register of the county of New York declaring a trust under which the children of his deceased brother became entitled to the transfer of his interest therein on the youngest survivor attaining the age of twenty-one years on compliance with certain conditions therein contained. Neither plaintiff, who represents the interest of such children, nor the defendant had actual notice of the existence of the paper. Defendant after the death of her husband took renewal leases of the property. *Held, first,* that in the absence of any fraudulent concealment the trust terminated and the Statute of Limitations began to run when the youngest child arrived at the age of twenty-one. *Second,* that when defendant took the lease in her own name and entered into possession of the premises she held the same in her own right and the statute began to run from that date. *Finnegan v. McGuffog.* 342

See *Hoskin* v. *L. I. Loan & Trust Co.* (Mem.), 588; *Miller* v. *Hill* (Mem.), 646.

Rules for construction of testamentary provisions creating trusts for benefit of "religious, educational, charitable or benevolent uses" — validity of provisions of will creating such trusts.

See WILL, 2, 3.

TRUST COMPANIES.

Duties and powers — when trust company not liable for erroneous statements of an officer thereof as to value and validity of bonds for which it was trustee.

See CORPORATIONS, 10, 11.

UNDERTAKING.

See *Brandly* v. *U. S. Fidelity & Guaranty Co.* (Mem.), 599.

VENDOR AND PURCHASER.

See *Roy* v. *Flaxman* (Mem.), 591.

VENDOR AND PURCHASER — *Continued.*
Option to purchase lands — when actual tender need not be made — sufficiency of notice of intent to exercise option.

See CONTRACT, 10, 11.

VENDOR AND VENDEE.
When acceptance of machine by vendee question for jury — when execution by vendee of chattel mortgage on machine before test not a waiver of right of inspection.

See SALE, 1.

Liability of infant for sale effected by fraud.

See SALE, 2.

VETERANS.
See CIVIL SERVICE.

WAIVER.
Exception to refusal to dismiss complaint waived by introduction of evidence on defense.

See APPEAL, 1.

Of provision in indemnity bond.

See PRINCIPAL AND SURETY.

WATER COMMISSIONERS.
Not quasi corporations but administrative officers — remedy for breach of contract.

See OFFICERS, 1, 2.

WATERS AND WATERCOURSES.
Navigable streams not within ordinary nomenclature of highways.

See TAX, 1.

WATER WORKS.
Action against municipality to recover rentals claimed to be due under contract to furnish water for fire service at a certain pressure — measure of damages.

See CONTRACT, 6, 7.

WILL.
1. *Rule of construction applied.* It is an established rule that the courts should give effect to every word and provision of a will, in so far as they may, without violating the intent of the testator or well-established rules of law. A provision in a will, "I leave to my wife the house and all the furnishings at No. 326 E. 43 St. for the rest of her natural life the interest in the real estate held by me and my brother John C. Eidt to be held together for Two years or less in case of death of my wife within two years or date of settlement one third Interest to go to Mrs. Anna Deibel," is to be construed as a devise to the wife of the one-half interest in the real estate owned by the testator in common with his brother. *Eidt* v. *Eidt*, 325.

2. *Testamentary trusts — Trust for benefit of "religious, educational, charitable or benevolent uses" — Rules for construction of testamentary provisions creating such trusts.* A will must sufficiently define the beneficiaries and the purpose of the testator so that a trust can be enforced by the courts, otherwise the will does not come within the provisions of the statutes which permit gifts for religious, educational, charitable or benevolent uses, to indefinite or uncertain beneficiaries. The gifts must also be for a public

WILL — *Continued.*

and not for a private purpose. Where certain things are enumerated and such enumeration is followed or coupled with a more general description, such general description is commonly understood to cover only things *ejusdem generis* with the particular things mentioned. In such case it is presumed that the testator had only things of that class in mind. A construction which is fairly within the rules of law and that sustains a trust and devotes the fund included therein to purposes permitted by law and to the good of humanity should be preferred. *Matter of Robinson.* 380

3. *Validity of provision of will creating trust for charitable and benevolent purposes.* Testatrix directed her trustees to disburse the principal or interest of her residuary estate, or both, in their discretion "To provide shelter, necessaries of life, education, general or specific, and such other financial aid as may seem to them fitting and proper to such persons as they shall select as being in need of the same," and authorized her trustees to carry out such provisions or to cause to be created a corporation therefor. *Held*, that the purpose of the testatrix was within the language of the statute which authorizes gifts "to religious, educational, charitable, or benevolent uses," and that the courts can and will, at the suit of the attorney-general of the state, compel the trustees to carry out the will according to such purpose and for such uses. *Id.*

See *Matter of Coutant* (Mem.), 562.

TABULAR LIST OF OPINIONS.

CULLEN, Ch. J.

BILLS, NOTES AND CHECKS.
Foreign bills of exchange; What damages recoverable by payee upon foreign bill of exchange protested for non-payment. (Con. op.)
Pavenstedt v. N. Y. Life Insurance Co., 91, 103.

MUNICIPAL CORPORATIONS.
Construction of subway by contractors; When city not liable for negligence of contractor; Contractor's liability to abutting owner for damages caused by explosion of dynamite due to sub-contractor's negligence.
Smyth v. City of New York, 106, 109.

TAX.
Special franchise tax upon railroad corporation's right to construct, maintain and operate its railroad in, under, above or through streets, highways or public places; When right of way for tunnel under Hudson river not subject to franchise tax; When subject thereto; Duty and powers of state board of tax commissioners in making assessments on special franchises.
People ex rel. H. & M. R. R. Co. v. Tax Comrs., 119, 123.

BAILMENT.
Contracts; Person in possession of property of another, as bailee, cannot appropriate it under, and for the purpose of carrying out, another contract between the same parties.
A. B. Supply Co. v. V. P. Cement Co., 133, 134.

CONSTITUTIONAL LAW.
Legislation contravening the spirit of the Constitution is void as well as legislation which violates its express commands; Election Law; Unconstitutionality of the statute (L. 1911, ch. 649, § 12) providing that the name of a person nominated by more than one party shall be printed but once upon the ballot.
Matter of Hopper v. Britt, 144, 146.

CONSTITUTIONAL LAW.
New York (city of); Justices of the Municipal Court; Constitutionality of statute (L. 1907, ch. 603, § 3) amending section 1357 of New York city charter relative to vacancies in office of justices. (Dis. op.)
Matter of Markland v. Scully, 158, 166.

PUBLIC SERVICE COMMISSIONS LAW.

Provisions not in conflict with sections 9-12 of Stock Corporation Law; Reorganization of railroad corporation; Authority of commission as to issue of securities.

People ex rel. T. A. Ry. Co. v. P. S. Comm., 299, 302.

CONTRACT.

Action for breach of contract; Expulsion from bathhouse of person holding ticket entitling her to admission; Price of ticket not measure of damages.

Aaron v. Ward, 351, 353.

JUDGMENT.

Insurance (life); When judgment obtained by administrator of insured in another state not a bar to an action on the same policy in this state by the assignee thereof.

Gleason v. Northwestern M. L. Ins. Co., 507, 510.

RAILROADS.

Construction and application of section 52 of Railroad Law (Cons. Laws, ch. 49) requiring railroad companies to maintain fences along their rights of way; Railroad company not liable for animals injured by falling through railroad bridge.

Jimerson v. Erie R. R. Co., 518, 519.

DECEDENT'S ESTATE.

Proceedings to sell decedent's real estate for the payment of his debts; Judgment creditors of an heir or devisee of decedent necessary parties thereto.

Matter of Townsend, 522, 523.

GRAY, J.

CONTRACT.

"Tourist parties;" When person engaged to look after baggage of tourist not liable for baggage lost while in custody of steamship company upon whose ship the tourist was a passenger. (Con. op.)

Coleman v. Clark, 36, 40.

TAX.

Special franchise tax upon railroad corporation's right to construct, maintain and operate its railroad in, under, above or through streets, highways or public places; When right of way for tunnel under Hudson river not subject to franchise tax; When subject thereto. (Con. op.)

People ex rel. H. & M. R. R. Co. v. Tax Comrs., 119, 132.

Assessments upon special franchises; Rule for ascertaining value of tangible property; Method of ascertaining net earnings in assessment of special franchises; Rate by which capitalization should be fixed.

People ex rel. Manhattan Ry. Co. v. Woodbury, 231, 233.

CRIMES.

Evidence; When judgment of conviction should not be reversed because district attorney attempts to create false impressions by questions concerning matters foreign to the issues. (Dis. op.)
People v. Freeman, 267, 272.

FOREIGN JUDGMENT.

Divorce; Courts of this state will not restrain prosecution of action in another state to annul a judgment of divorce previously rendered in that state by a court of competent jurisdiction.
Guggenheim v. Wahl, 390, 392.

GUARANTY AND SURETY.

Bond indemnifying employer against loss arising from larceny or embezzlement of a clerk; Waiver of provision therein that bond shall be "of no effect unless signed by the employee."
General Ry. Signal Co. v. Title G. & S. Co., 407, 409.

NEGLIGENCE.

Contributory negligence; When person injured by falling into elevator shaft in unlighted hall guilty of contributory negligence.
Rohrbacher v. Gillig, 413, 415.

HAIGHT, J.

MUNICIPAL CORPORATIONS.

Construction of subway by contractors; When city liable for negligence of contractor; Contractor's liability to abutting owner for damages caused by explosion of dynamite due to sub-contractor's negligence. (Dis. op.)
Smyth v. City of New York, 106, 116.

CONSTITUTIONAL LAW.

New York (city of); Justices of the Municipal Court; Unconstitutionality of statute (L. 1907, ch. 603, § 3) amending section 1357 of New York city charter relative to vacancies in office of justices.
Matter of Markland v. Scully, 158, 161.

TAX.

Special franchise tax upon steam railroad crossings over public streets and highways; When highway is opened across right of way owned and occupied by railroad, such crossing is subject to the tax. (Dis. op.)
People ex rel. N. Y. C. & H. R. R. R. Co. v. Woodbury, 167, 180.

TAX.

Assessments upon special franchises; Rule for ascertaining value of tangible property; Method of ascertaining net earnings in assessment of special franchises; Rate by which capitalization should be fixed. (Con. op.)

People ex rel. Manhattan Ry. Co. v. Woodbury, 231, 236.

APPEAL.

. Practice; Condemnation of property for water supply for city of New York; Special Term order vacating an award by commissioners of appraisal, appealable to Appellate Division.

Matter of Simmons, 241, 242.

SPECIAL PROCEEDINGS.

Judgment against bankrupt will not be canceled under statute (Debtor and Creditor Law, Cons. Laws, ch. 12, § 150) when schedule states residence of creditor was "unknown," although bankrupt had notice thereof.

Guasti v. Miller, 259, 260.

INSURANCE (FIRE).

Liability of insurer for loss resulting from explosion preceded and caused by fire.

Wheeler v. Phenix Ins. Co., 283, 284.

EQUITY.

Action to impress a trust; Construction of voluntary trust of leasehold interest in real property for benefit of children of a deceased brother of trustee; Statute of Limitations.

Finnegan v. McGuffog, 342, 344.

CONTRACT.

Action by water company against municipality to recover rentals claimed to be due under contract to furnish water for fire service at a certain pressure; Construction of contract; Liability of municipality.

B.-H. Water Co. v. Vil. of Brockport, 399, 401.

INSURANCE.

Accident; Pleading and proof; Clauses of policy construed.

Miles v. Casualty Co. of America, 453, 455.

STOCK CORPORATIONS.

Action to recover for services rendered to dissolved corporation; Parties defendant; When directors only, and neither the corporation nor its stockholders are necessary parties.

Atlantic Dredging Co. v. Beard, 584, 585.

DEED.

Construction of description therein.

N. Y. C. & H. R. R. R. Co. v. Moore, 615, 616.

VANN, J.

ELECTION LAW.

Registration of electors; Unconstitutionality of the statute (L. 1911, ch. 649, § 6) requiring personal registration of electors residing outside of cities or villages with a population of five thousand or more.

Matter of Fraser v. Brown, 136, 138.

TAX.

Special franchise tax upon steam railroad crossings over public streets and highways; When highway is opened across right of way owned and occupied by railroad, such crossing is not subject to the tax.

People ex rel. N. Y. C. & H. R R. R. Co. v. Woodbury, 167, 170.

SALE.

Construction of contract for purchase and sale of foreign goods; When buyer may not repudiate contract and refuse to accept goods because invoices were mutilated and because goods were not imported expressly for buyer; Rejection of evidence.

Jardine, Matheson & Co. v. Huguet Silk Co., 278, 278.

CARRIERS.

Evidence; Contract to transport goods signed by carrier and shipper, but silent as to route, cannot be varied by evidence of previous parol instructions to ship by a particular route.

Loomis v. N. Y. C. & H. R. R. R. Co., 359, 360.

EQUITABLE CONVERSION.

Definition and application of doctrine of equitable conversion; Definition and effect of term "legal representative" when used in deed or contract; Lease of lands giving lessee option to purchase of lessor or his legal representatives; When actual tender of purchase price need not be made to legal representatives of such lessor.

Rockland-Rockport Lime Co. v. Leary, 469, 477.

WERNER, J.

MURDER.

Evidence examined and held sufficient to sustain judgment of conviction; When verdict of murder in the first degree eliminates any question arising from failure of court to charge as to the various degrees of manslaughter.

People v. Brown, 44, 46.

MURDER.

Sufficiency of indictment in common-law form; Evidence examined, and held that case was properly submitted to the jury to determine if murder was committed while defendant was engaged in commission of felonies of rape and burglary; Confessions; Possession of stolen property as evidence that defendant committed burglary.

People v. Schermerhorn, 57, 59.

PARTITION.

Costs; Practice; Extra allowances of costs; Total amount allowed to all parties cannot exceed five per cent of value of property; Allowance to plaintiff based on value of the whole property; Allowance to any defendant based on value of that defendant's interest in the property; Construction of provision limiting allowance to $2,000 to each side of action.

Warren v. Warren, 250, 252.

CONTRACT.

Agreements under seal; Contract under seal, by which one brother agrees to support his mother, cannot be enforced by another brother not a party to it, although the latter joined in the consideration for the contract.

Case v. Case, 263, 264.

WATER COMMISSIONERS.

Not quasi corporations but administrative officers; Remedy for breach of contract is by mandamus or certiorari.

People ex rel. Farley v. Winkler, 445, 446.

WILLARD BARTLETT, J.

GAMBLING.

A person who takes part in a game, or games, of poker for amusement is not a "common gambler" within the meaning of the statute (Penal Law, § 970); When person playing poker is not an accomplice of dealer or gamekeeper with whom he was playing.

People v. Bright, 73, 74.

BILLS, NOTES AND CHECKS.

Foreign bills of exchange; What damages recoverable by payee upon foreign bill of exchange protested for non-payment.

Pavenstedt v. N. Y. Life Insurance Co., 91, 93.

NEGLIGENCE.

Charitable corporations not exempt from liability for tort; When not liable for injuries due to negligence of ambulance driver furnished by livery stable; Ambulance not a dangerous instrumentality as a matter of law.

Kellogg v. Church Charity Foundation, 191, 193.

ELECTION LAW.

Section 123 (as amended by L. 1911, ch. 649) relating to the signing and filing of certificates of independent nominations construed and held to be constitutional.

Matter of Burke v. Terry, 293, 294.

NEGLIGENCE.

Evidence; Admissions made by a party to an action, upon a previous trial thereof, may be proved by the testimony of a witness who heard them; Erroneous exclusion of evidence tending to show that a wagon, by which plaintiff was injured, could not be used in the way alleged.

McRorie v. Monroe, 426, 428.

HUSBAND AND WIFE.

Right of wife to recover from husband for moneys expended by her for necessaries.

De Brauwere v. De Brauwere, 460, 462.

INFANTS.

Liability for sale effected by fraud.

Collins v. Gifford, 465, 466.

MURDER.

When verdict of conviction under common-law indictment not against weight of evidence; When previous opinion or impression of jurors not sufficient ground for challenge for bias; Exceptions to admission of evidence, charge to jury and refusal to charge examined and rulings of court sustained.

People v. Wolter, 484, 486.

ATTORNEYS.

Proceeding for disbarment of attorney; When order of disbarment is defective for omitting to state specific misconduct of attorney. (Dis. op.)

Matter of Spenser, 613, 614.

HISCOCK, J.

MANDAMUS.

When writ will be issued directing comptroller of New York city to examine claim, illegal in form, against city and certify his opinion whether it should be paid.

People ex rel. Dady v. Prendergast, 1, 3.

CONTRACT.

"Tourist parties;" When person engaged to look after baggage of tourist, not liable for baggage lost while in custody of steamship company upon whose ship the tourist was a passenger.

Coleman v. Clark, 36, 37.

BAGGAGE.

Meaning of term "baggage" as used in section 38 of Public Service Commissions Law; Liability of express company for baggage lost in transit not limited by provisions of that section.

Morgan v. Woolverton, 52.

PRINCIPAL AND AGENT.

Syndicate contract by which subscribers agree to take stock in corporation organized to take business and property of existing corporations; When person acting as agent and organizer for subscribers sells property of his own to new corporation without knowledge of his principals, the syndicate agreement is voidable.

Heckscher v. Edenborn, 210, 218.

CRIMES.

Evidence; District attorney may not attempt to create false impressions by questions concerning matters foreign to the issues.

People v. Freeman, 267, 269.

SALE.

When acceptance of machine by vendee question for a jury; When execution by vendee of chattel mortgage on machine before test not a waiver of right of inspection.

Harrison v. Scott, 369, 371.

ATTORNEY AND CLIENT.

When relation does not exist, summary proceedings to recover papers cannot be maintained.

Matter of Niagara, L. & O. Power Co., 493, 495.

CONSTITUTIONAL LAW.

Trial of issues; Section 973 of the Code of Civil Procedure constitutional.

Smith v. Western Pacific Ry. Co., 499, 501.

CONTRACT.

Action by sub-contractor to recover for work done in grading streets for municipality.

Fisher v. Wakefield Park Realty Co., 539, 540.

Chase, J.

PUBLIC SERVICE COMMISSIONS.

When discretion of commission cannot override the discretion of the officers of a corporation; Duty and powers of commission to determine under section 69 of the Public Service Commissions Law whether a proposed bond issue is necessary for purposes of corporation and authorized by law; Evidence; Procedure.

People ex rel. B. L., H. & P. Co. v. Stevens, 7, 10.

LIBEL.

Privileged communications; Qualified privilege; Pleading; General allegation charging a person with something libelous per se cannot be defended under general allegation that charge is true; Facts must be stated.

Bingham v. Gaynor, 27, 30.

EVIDENCE.

Action for divorce; Erroneous admissions of entries in hotel register as evidence against defendant in divorce action; Judgment of divorce against alleged paramour not admissible evidence against defendant in action for divorce.

Mattison v. Mattison, 79, 81.

TAX.

Special franchises; When city assessors may apportion special franchise assessment between different parts of a tax district.

People ex rel. Troy Gas Co. v. Hall, 312, 314.

TRUST COMPANIES.

Duties and powers; When trust company not liable for erroneous statements of an officer thereof as to value and validity of bonds for which it was trustee.

Davidge v. Guardian Trust Co., 331, 337.

TESTAMENTARY TRUSTS.

Trusts for benefit of "religious, educational, charitable or benevolent uses;" Rules for construction of testamentary provisions creating such trusts; Will examined and held to create a valid trust within the meaning of the statute.

Matter of Robinson, 380, 384.

LIENS.

Municipal corporations; When municipality liable only for amount due contractor at time contract was forfeited.

Herrmann & Grace v. Hillman, 435, 438.

CIVIL SERVICE.

Improper dismissal of veteran fireman.

People ex rel. Conley v. Beach, 620, 621.

COLLIN, J.

PRACTICE.

Appeal; When defendant, by introducing evidence, waives exception to refusal of trial court to dismiss complaint; On appeal from judgment, without motion for new trial, appellate courts are limited to review of questions of law raised by exceptions taken at the trial; Principal and agent; Construction of power of attorney; When indorsement of check by agent constitutes forgery.

Porges v. U. S. Mortgage & Trust Co., 181, 184.

CONSTITUTIONAL LAW.

Unconstitutionality of statutes (L. 1896, ch. 812, and L. 1901, chap. 361) creating a municipal corporation which is not a county, city, town or village; Invalidity of commitment issued by a justice of the peace of the "area or territory known as Sylvan Beach."

People ex rel. Hon Yost v. Becker, 201, 202.

NEGLIGENCE.

Evidence of discharge of motorman; When inadmissible.

Engel v. United Traction Co., 321, 322.

WILL.

Rule of construction applied.

Eidt v. Eidt, 325, 327.

TRADE NAME.

Action to restrain unfair competition in the use of a trade name; Unlawful use of one's own name with prefix "Dr."

World's D. M. Assn. v. Pierce, 419, 421.

PER CURIAM.

PRACTICE.

Form of judgment.

Curtiss v. Jebb, 538, 539.

NEW YORK (CITY OF).

Mandamus to compel board of education to appoint relator to position in department of public instruction of New York city; When writ properly denied.

Matter of Norman v. Bd. of Education of N. Y. City, 548.

APPEAL.

Appeal by permission of Appellate Division upon condition that judgment absolute should be rendered if appellant failed; When stipulation is effective.

Floyd-Jones v. Schaan, 568.

Lightning Source UK Ltd.
Milton Keynes UK
UKHW020630120219

337137UK00005B/472/P